6-8pm Theers
2pm Fire
6-8pm Fri

gold g

W9-DEJ-291

@
VofCalgary

ALBERTA
AND THE NORTHWEST TERRITORIES
HANDBOOK
INCLUDING BANFF, JASPER, AND THE CANADIAN ROCKIES

Lynn Grindley
249-2865

#63 Anatapi Lane

<u>SW</u>

#1 to Sarcee Trail south
west on 17th Ave SW

After 85th St NW
After school on Rt
turn left on
Anatapi lane

Stay left go over
2 speed

ALBERTA
AND THE NORTHWEST TERRITORIES
HANDBOOK

INCLUDING BANFF, JASPER, AND THE CANADIAN ROCKIES

**ANDREW HEMPSTEAD
AND NADINA PURDON**

MOON
PUBLICATIONS INC.

ALBERTA AND THE NORTHWEST TERRITORIES HANDBOOK

Published by
Moon Publications, Inc.
P.O. Box 3040
Chico, California 95927-3040, USA

Printed by
Webcom Limited

Please send all comments,
corrections, additions,
amendments, and critiques to:

**ALBERTA/NWT HANDBOOK
MOON PUBLICATIONS, INC.
P.O. BOX 3040
CHICO, CA 95927-3040, USA**
e-mail: **travel@moon.com**

ISBN: 1-56691-067-6
ISSN: 1079-9338

Printing History
First edition—June 1995

Editor: Don Root
Copy Editor: Nicole Revere
Production & Design: David Hurst
Cartographers: Robert Race, Brian Bardwell, and Jason Sadler
Index: Nicole Revere

Front cover photo: Banff National Park, Alberta. Photo by Michael J. Howell/Leo deWys Inc.
All photos by Andrew Hempstead unless otherwise noted.

Distributed in the United States by Publishers Group West

Printed in Canada

CONTENTS

MAPS

CHARTS AND SPECIAL TOPICS

ABBREVIATIONS

B&B—bed-and-breakfast inn
B.C.—British Columbia
C.P.R.—Canadian Pacific Railway
d—double occupancy
GST—Goods and Services Tax
km—kilometer
kph—kilometers per hour
NHL—National Hockey League

NWMP—North West Mounted Police
NWT—Northwest Territories
P.P.—Provincial Park
RCMP—Royal Canadian Mounted Police
s—single occupancy
T.P.—Territorial Park
UNESCO—United Nations Educational,
   Scientific, and Cultural Organization

MAP SYMBOLS

INTERNATIONAL BORDER
PROVINCIAL/STATE BORDER
OTHER BOUNDARY
FOUR LANE DIVIDED HWY.
MAJOR ROAD
SECONDARY ROAD
UNPAVED HWY.
UNPAVED ROAD
PATH/TRAIL

BRIDGE
PASS
TRANSCANADA HWY.
PRIMARY HWY.
SECONDARY HWY.
POINT OF INTEREST
HOTEL/ ACCOMMODATION
CAMPGROUND

MOUNTAIN
GOLF COURSE
WATER
ICEFIELDS
SKI AREA
T.P. = TERRITORIAL PARK
P.P. = PROVINCIAL PARK

ACKNOWLEDGMENTS

The herculean task of researching and writing this handbook took two years. Along the road many people contributed in a variety of ways. In the book's earliest stages, thanks to Angie Timpson of the Salisbury Arms Hotel, Hertford, England for typing the proposal and to Phil X who gave us a good deal on a computer in a dark corner of the above pub.

This book wouldn't have come about if it wasn't for fellow Moon author Deke Castleman whose encouragement caused us to abandon careers as globe-trotting ski bums and jump headlong into the travel-writing business; goodonya mate and thanks for your belief in us and continued support.

In Alberta, thanks to all the staff of Tourist Information Centres whose knowledge and enthusiasm went toward producing a more complete guide. At Alberta Tourism, a hearty thanks to Lorena Tyschuk and Sharon Cruthers who helped in the latter stages of the project. Ditto to Lorraine Browne and Barb Dillon of NWT Economic Development and Tourism. A big Ya-HOO must go to Dan Sullivan, of the Calgary Exhibition and Stampede, for his help.

As far as a home-base for road-weary travel writers, they don't come much better than Banff. Thanks to Wendy Lash for encouraging us to stay, staying with the project till the end, and being a great friend. Thanks also to Nancy DaDalt, perfect roommate and supplier of Ben and Jerry's ice cream. Still in Banff, thanks to the staff of Banff/Lake Louise Tourism, Jeannette Fish and her staff at the library, and Shirley of the "other" post office.

On the 40,000 kilometers covered while writing this handbook we were accompanied by our four-wheeled, gas-guzzling friend Biff who lasted the distance and is currently cruising around Alaska; hey Rick and Phil, I hope you checked the oil.

IS THIS BOOK OUT OF DATE?

Probably. Although we have strived to produce the most up-to-date guidebook humanly possible things change—restaurants and accommodations open and close, attractions come and go, and prices go up. If you come across a great out-of-the-way place, a new restaurant or lodging, or you think a particular hike warrants a mention please write to us. Letters from tour operators and Albertan and NWT people in the tourism and hospitality industries are also appreciated. When writing, be as accurate as possible; write notes on the road or even send brochures.

Write to:

Alberta-NWT Handbook
c/o Moon Publications Inc.
P.O. Box 3040
Chico, CA 95927-3040
USA

e-mail: travel@moon.com

KAREN MCKINLEY

INTRODUCTION

The prosperous province of Alberta is the heart of western Canada, sandwiched between the mountains of British Columbia to the west and the prairies of Saskatchewan to the east. Edmonton, Alberta's capital, and Calgary, to the south, are, respectively, Canada's fifth- and sixth-largest cities, between them holding over half the province's population. These boomtowns have been Canada's fastest-growing cities since WW II, centers for the staggering oil and gas reserves that have propelled Alberta to the forefront of world energy markets and technology. Edmonton is a modern, livable city boasting some of Canada's finest cultural facilities, as well as the world's largest shopping and amusement mall. Calgary, meanwhile, is home to the world-famous Calgary Exhibition and Stampede—a Western wingding of epic proportions—and the city received international attention as the host of the 1988 Winter Olympic Games. Its futuristic skyline rises from the prairie like the oil derricks that put the city on the map, and cattlemen in Caddies drive past gleaming skyscrapers on their way out to the ranch.

But for most visitors to Alberta, it's not the big cities or the fast bucks that are the draw, it's the great outdoors. The stunning mountain playgrounds of Banff, Jasper, and Waterton national parks show off the Canadian Rockies at their best, with pristine glaciers, rushing rivers, and snowcapped peaks reflected in hundreds of high-country lakes. The parks, and much of the rest of the province, are home to an abundance of wildlife such as moose, elk, bighorn sheep, wolves, bears, and an amazing array of birds; some 340 species of birds migrate through or nest in Alberta. And ancient wildlife thrived here, too; one of the world's greatest concentrations of dinosaur bones continues to be unearthed in the Red Deer River Valley outside Drumheller. The "Dinosaur Valley," as it's called, attracts tourist tyros and professional palaeontologists alike to learn more about earth's once-dominant former tenants.

Throughout the province, wide-open spaces, endless blue skies, and accessible wilderness beckon, and big-city culture awaits when you come down from the hills. So whether your interests lean toward high peaks, or high tea, you're sure to find plenty to suit you in Alberta.

THE LAND

Alberta is the fourth-largest province in Canada. With an area of 661,185 square km, it's larger than all U.S. states except Alaska and Texas. The province lies between the 49th and 60th parallels, bordered on the south by Montana, U.S.A., and on the north by Canada's Northwest Territories. To the west is British Columbia and to the east is Saskatchewan. Along its roughly rectangular outline, the only natural border is the Continental Divide in the southwest. Here, from the International Boundary to Jasper, the lofty peaks of the **Rocky Mountains** rise to heights of over 3,000 meters. Alberta's Rockies are only one small but exquisitely beautiful link in this mountain chain that forms the backbone of

North America, extending from the jungles of central Mexico to the Arctic. Running parallel to the mountains along their eastern edge is a series of long, rolling ridges known as the **foothills.** This region was once a coal-mining center, and today holds abundant recreational opportunities. Finally, east of the foothills and across the rest of Alberta are **plains,** which cover almost three-quarters of the province. The plains provide practically all of Alberta's arable soil and natural resources. The term "plains" is very broad. Alberta's plains encompass three distinct vegetation zones: prairies, parklands, and boreal forests (see "Flora," below).

ALBERTA LOCATION

GREENLAND

U.S.A. (ALASKA)

NORTHWEST TERRITORIES

CANADA

ALBERTA

U. S. A.

0   400 mi

0   400 km

© MOON PUBLICATIONS, INC.

GEOLOGY

The rocks of Alberta range in age from ancient to almost "brand new," in geologic time. The 70-million-year-old Rocky Mountains, Alberta's most distinctive natural feature, are relatively young compared to the world's other major mountain ranges. By contrast, the Precambrian rock of the Canadian Shield, exposed in the province's northeast corner and underlying parts of the rest, was the progenitor of North America. It was the first land on the continent to remain permanently above sea level, and is among the oldest rock on earth, formed over 2.5 billion years ago.

Around 700 million years ago, in the Precambrian era, forces beneath the earth caused uplift, pushing the coastline of the Pacific Ocean—which then covered most of the province—westward. The ocean advanced, then receded, several times over the next half billion years. Each time the ocean flooded eastward it deposited layers of sediment on its bed, layers that built up with each successive inundation. This sediment is now a layer of sedimentary rock covering most of Alberta, up to seven km deep in the southwest.

Alberta's Oil

Oil pools are created when oil globules—converted from decayed organic matter by the forces of heat and pressure beneath the earth's surface—are trapped in porous rock capped by nonporous rock. During the Middle Devonian period, 375 million years ago, with the Pacific Ocean once again covering Alberta, coral reefs formed. Over time, this coral would be transformed into the porous rock that would hold the pools of oil. Also during this period, as well as in later years of the Palaeozoic era, trillions of microscopic organisms in the sea died and sank to the bottom of the ocean, creating mass quantities of decaying organic matter in and around the coral. This organic matter would be transformed over time into the oil itself. Finally, around 300 million years ago, in the Carboniferous period, the Pacific Ocean extended as far as the foothills and many rivers flowed into it from the east, carrying with them sediment that covered the porous reefs in nonporous layers. All the ele-

ALBERTA AND CALIFORNIA

© MOON PUBLICATIONS, INC.

ments necessary to eventually create and contain reserves of oil were then in place. A few hundred million years of "cooking" later, the primordial goo that fuels our modern, internal-combustion society is pumped nonstop from beneath Alberta. And one other huge source of oil in Alberta isn't pumped but *mined*. In the early Cretaceous period, 130 million years ago, the Arctic Ocean flooded Alberta from the north, laying down the **Athabasca Oil Sands** along the Arctic seaway. These sands hold more than one trillion barrels of heavy oil—more than all the known reserves of conventional crude oil on the planet.

Birth Of The Rockies

Also during the Cretaceous period, the Mackenzie Mountains began to rise, cutting off the Arctic seaway and forming an inland sea where marinelife such as ammonites, fish, and large marine reptiles flourished. Dinosaurs roamed the coastal areas, feeding on the lush vegetation as well as on each other.

Then, some 70 million years ago, two plates of the earth's crust collided. According to plate tectonics theory, the Pacific Plate butted into the North American Plate and was forced

The face of Banff's Temple Mountain reveals horizontal layers of sedimentary rock.

beneath it. The land at this subduction zone was crumpled and thrust upward, creating the Rocky Mountains. Layers of sediment laid down on the ocean floor over the course of hundreds of millions of years were folded, twisted, and squeezed; great slabs of rock broke away, and in places older strata were pushed on top of younger. By the beginning of the Tertiary period, around 65 million years ago, the present form of mountain contours was established and the geological framework of Alberta was in place. Then the forces of erosion went to work. The plains of the Late Tertiary period were at a higher altitude than those of today. The flat-topped Caribou Mountains, Buffalo Head Hills, Cypress Hills, Clear Hills, and Porcupine Hills are remnants of those higher plains.

The Ice Ages

No one knows why, but around one million years ago the world's climate cooled and ice caps formed in Arctic regions, slowly moving south over North America and Eurasia. These advances, followed by retreats, occurred four times.

The final major glaciation began moving southward 35,000 years ago. A sheet of ice up to 2,000 meters deep covered all but the highest peaks of the Rocky Mountains and Cypress Hills. The ice scoured the terrain, destroying all vegetation as it crept slowly forward. In the mountains, these rivers of ice carved hollows, known as **cirques,** into the slopes of the higher

peaks. They rounded off lower peaks and reamed out valleys from their preglacier V shape to a trademark, postglacial U shape. The retreat of this ice sheet, beginning around 12,000 years ago, was just as destructive. Rock and debris that had been picked up by the ice on its march forward melted out during the retreat, creating high ridges known as **moraines.** Many of these moraines blocked natural drainages, resulting in thousands of lakes across the north. And meltwater drained into rivers and streams, incising deep channels into the sedimentary rock of the plains.

The only remnants of this ice age are the scattered icefields along the Continental Divide —including the 325-square-km **Columbia Icefield.** But wind and water erosion continues, uncovering dinosaur bones hidden among layers of sediment and carving an eerie landscape of badlands along the sides of many prairie river valleys.

Waterways

Alberta has three major watersheds draining 245 named rivers and 315 named creeks. Over half the province drains into the **Mackenzie River System,** which flows north into the Arctic Ocean. The **Peace River**—which originates in the interior of British Columbia and flows northeast through Alberta—and the **Athabasca River** —whose initial source is the Columbia Icefield— are the province's two major tributaries in this system. They eventually meet to form the Slave

River, which flows into the Mackenzie at Great Slave Lake in the Northwest Territories.

Central Alberta is drained mainly by the **Saskatchewan River System,** the major source of water for Alberta's farmers. This river system, which eventually flows into Hudson Bay, has three main tributaries: the **North Saskatchewan River,** originating from the Columbia Icefield; the **Red Deer River,** originating in the heart of Banff National Park and flowing through "Dinosaur Valley" on its way east; and the **South Saskatchewan River.** The latter is fed in large part by the **Bow River,** flowing down from Banff, and the **Oldman River,** which cascades out of the Rockies south of Kananaskis Country.

A small area in the south of the province is drained by the **Milk River,** which flows southeast into the Mississippi River System, ending up in the Gulf of Mexico.

The amount of water flowing in any one of Alberta's rivers is dependent on that particular river's source. Rivers originating from melt-out of the winter snowpack reach peak flow in mid-summer and often run dry by late summer. Those that originate from glaciers run light in spring and also reach a peak in midsummer, but continue a light flow until winter. Those that rise in the foothills and higher areas of the plains have highly variable flows, dependent entirely on precipitation.

CLIMATE

Alberta spans 11 degrees of latitude, and its varied topography includes elevations ranging from 170 to over 3,700 meters. As a result, the climate of the province varies widely from place to place. In addition, the Rocky Mountains create some of Alberta's unique climatic characteristics. As prevailing, moisture-laden westerlies blow in from British Columbia, the cold heights of the Rockies wring them dry. This makes for clear, sunny skies in southern Alberta; Calgary gets up to 350 hours of sunshine in June alone—good news, unless you're a farmer. In winter, the dry winds blasting down the eastern slopes of the Rockies can raise temperatures on the prairies by up to 40° C in 24 hours. Called **chinooks,** these desiccating blows are a phenomenon unique to Alberta.

Another interesting phenomenon occurring in southern Alberta's Rocky Mountain regions is the **temperature inversion,** in which a layer of warm air sits on top of a cold air mass. During these inversions, high- and low-country roles are reversed; prairie residents can be shivering and bundling up, while their mountain fellows are sunning themselves in shirtsleeves.

The Seasons

On the whole, Alberta features cold winters and short, hot summers. May to mid-September is ideal for touring, camping out, and seeing the sights; a month either side and the weather is cooler, but still pleasant; and the rest of the year the skiing is fantastic.

January is usually the coldest month, when Calgary's mean average temperature is -13° C and Fort McMurray's is -20° C. In winter, extended spells of -30° C are not uncommon anywhere in the province and occasionally temperatures drop below -40° C. Severe cold weather is often accompanied by sunshine; the cold is a dry cold, unlike the damp cold experienced in coastal regions. Cold temperatures and snow can continue until mid-March.

Although March, April, and May are officially the months of spring, snow often falls in April, many lakes may remain frozen until May, and snow cover on higher mountain hiking trails remains until June. Late snowfalls, though not welcomed by golfers in Calgary, provide important moisture for crops.

The official months of summer are June, July, and August, with July being the hottest month and providing the most uniform temperatures throughout the province. On hot days, the temperature will hit 30° C (usually every second summer day in the south) and very occasionally climb above 40° C. Again, because of the dryness of the air, these high temperatures are more bearable here than in coastal regions experiencing the same temperatures.

The frost-free growing season is over by late September, when the air begins to have a distinctive chill. October brings the highest temperature variations of the year, with the thermometer hitting 30° C but also dipping as low as -20° C. Mild weather can continue until early December, but generally the first snow falls in October and by mid-November winter has set in.

FLORA

Alberta can be divided into two major geographical areas: the mountain-and-foothill region along its southwestern border, and the plains covering the rest of the province. Within each of these two main areas are a number of distinct vegetation zones, the boundaries of which are determined by factors such as precipitation, latitude, and altitude.

THE MOUNTAINS AND FOOTHILLS

In southwest Alberta, west of Hwy. 2 between the U.S. border and Edmonton, the land climbs through foothills to the high peaks of the Rockies. Along the way it gains over 2,000 meters of elevation and passes through the montane, subalpine, and alpine vegetation zones. Although Banff and Jasper national parks are the obvious places to view these mountain biomes, the changes in vegetation are more abrupt and just as spectacular in less-visited Waterton Lakes National Park.

Montane
The foothills, along with most major valleys below an elevation of about 1,500 meters, are primarily cloaked in montane forest. **Aspen, balsam poplar,** and **white spruce** thrive here, and **lodgepole pine** dominates areas affected by fire. On dry, south-facing slopes, **Douglas fir** is the climax species. Where sunlight penetrates the forest, such as along riverbanks, flowers like **lady's slipper, Indian paintbrush,** and **saxifrage** are common. Large tracts of **fescue grassland** are common at lower elevations.

The montane forest holds the greatest diversity of life of any vegetation zone in the province, and is prime winter habitat for larger mammals. But much of this habitat has been given over to agriculture and development.

Subalpine
Subalpine forests occur where temperatures are lower and precipitation higher than the montane. Generally, this is 1,500-2,200 meters above sea level. The climax species in this zone are **Engelmann spruce** and **subalpine fir,** although extensive forests of **lodgepole pine** occur in areas that have been scorched by fire in the last 100 years. At higher elevations, stands of **larch** are seen. Larches are conifers, but unlike other evergreens, their needles turn a burnt-orange color each fall, producing a magnificent display for photographers.

Alpine
The alpine zone extends from the treeline to mountain summits. Vegetation at these high al-

VEGETATION ZONES

BOREAL FOREST

FOOTHILLS

EDMONTON
ASPEN PARKLAND

MOUNTAINS

CALGARY

PRAIRIE

0   100 mi
0   100 km

© MOON PUBLICATIONS, INC.

titudes occurs only where soil has been deposited. Large areas of alpine meadows burst with color for a short period each summer as **lupines, mountain avens, alpine forget-me-nots, moss campion,** and a variety of **heathers** bloom.

THE PLAINS

Like the mountain-and-foothill region, Alberta's plains also are made up of three different vegetation zones. Across Hwy. 2, east of the mountains and foothills, southeast Alberta is dominated by the prairie—a vast, dry region of grasslands. Just north of the prairie is the aspen parkland, a belt of forest that runs across central Alberta to the foothills and covers approximately 10% of the province. Finally, Alberta's largest ecological zone by far, covering over half of the province, is the boreal forest. It is located north of the aspen parkland and extends into the Northwest Territories to the treeline, where the tundra begins.

Prairie

Prairie is the warmest and driest ecological zone, with an annual precipitation under 75 cm. This harsh climate can support trees only where water flows, so for the most part, the prairie is open grassland—flat or lightly undulating. Irrigation has made agriculture possible across much of the south, and the patches of native grasses such as **rough fescue** and **grama** are rapidly disappearing. Among the cultivated pastureland and seemingly desolate plains, flowers punctuate the otherwise ochre-colored landscape. Alberta's floral emblem, the **prickly wild rose,** grows here, as does **pincushion cactus, buckbrush** (or yellow rose), and **sagebrush.** In river valleys, **aspen, willow,** and **cottonwood** grow along the banks.

The stands of large cottonwoods in Dinosaur Provincial Park were part of the reason this park was designated a UNESCO World Heritage Site. (The park is a good example of prairie habitat.) The Cypress Hills, which rise above the driest part of the province, contain vegetation not generally associated with the prairies, including **spruce, aspen,** a variety of **berries,** and the **calypso orchid.**

Aspen Parkland

This is a transition zone between the prairie grassland to the south and the boreal forest to the north. As the name suggests, **aspen** is the climax species, but much of this zone has been given over to agriculture—its forests burned and its soil tilled. Scattered stands of aspen, interspersed with **willow, balsam poplar,** and **white spruce,** still occur, while areas cleared by early settlers now contain **fescue grass.** Flowering plants such as **prairie crocus, snowberry, prickly wild rose,** and **lily-of-the-valley** decorate the shores of the many lakes and marshy areas found in this biome. Elk Island National Park, best known for its mammal populations, is an ideal example of this unique habitat.

Boreal Forest

Only a few species of trees are able to adapt to the harsh northern climate characteristic of this zone. The area is almost totally covered in forest, with only scattered areas of prairielike vegetation occurring in the very driest areas. In the southern part of the boreal forest the predominate species are **aspen** and **balsam poplar.** Farther north, conifers such as **white spruce, lodgepole pine,** and **balsam fir** are more common, with **jack pine** growing on dry ridges, and **tamarack** also present. The entire forest is interspersed with lakes, bogs, and sloughs where **black spruce** and **larch** are the dominant species. Like the trees, the ground cover also varies with latitude. To the south, and in the upland areas where aspen is the climax species, the undergrowth is lush with a variety of shrubs including **raspberries, saskatoons,** and **buffalo berries.** To the north, where drainage is generally poor, the ground cover is made up of dense mats of **peat.**

Most areas of boreal forest accessible by road have been affected by fire or development. But some areas of old growth can be found. Highway 63, which ends in Fort McMurray, runs through pristine northern boreal forest, while Sir Winston Churchill Provincial Park, on an island in Lac La Biche, hasn't been burned for over 300 years and supports stands of balsam fir up to 150 years old.

FAUNA

For 10,000 years, hundreds of thousands of bison roamed Alberta's plains, and wolves and grizzly bears inhabited all parts of the province. But this all changed with the coming of white men. Trappers and traders first decimated beaver and mink populations, then killed off all the bison, wolves, and grizzlies on the prairies.

Today, due to the foresight of early conservationists, mammal populations have stabilized and Alberta's wilderness once again provides some of North America's best opportunities for viewing wildlife.

THE DEER FAMILY

Deer

Alberta's **mule deer** and **white-tailed deer** are similar in size and appearance. Their color varies with the season but is generally light brown in summer, turning dirty-gray in winter. Both species are considerably smaller than elk. The mule deer has a white rump, a white tail with a dark tip, and large mule-like ears. It inhabits open forests bordering prairie. The white-tailed deer's tail is dark—on top. But when the animal runs, it holds its tail erect, revealing an all-white underside. Whitetails frequent thickets along the rivers and lakes of the foothills and aspen parkland.

Elk

The elk, or **wapiti,** is common throughout the Rockies and foothills. It has a tan body with a dark-brown neck and legs and a white rump. This second-largest member of the deer family weighs 250-450 kilograms and stands 1.5 meters at the shoulder. Stags grow an impressive set of antlers which they shed each spring. Rutting season takes place between August and October; listen for the shrill bugles of the stags serenading the females. During the rut, randy males will challenge anything with their antlers and can be dangerous. In spring, females protecting their young can be equally dangerous.

Moose

The giant of the deer family is the moose, an awkward-looking mammal that appears to have been designed by a cartoonist. It has the largest antlers of any animal in the world, stands 1.8 meters at the shoulder, and weighs in excess of 450 kilograms. Its body is dark brown, and it has a prominent nose, long spindly legs, small eyes, big ears, and an odd flap of skin called a "bell" dangling beneath its chin. Apart from all that, it's good-looking. Each spring the bull begins to grow palm-shaped antlers which by August will be fully grown. Moose are solitary animals preferring marshy areas and weedy lakes. They forage in and around ponds on willows, aspen, birch, grasses, and all aquatic vegetation. Although they may appear docile, moose will attack humans if they feel threatened.

Caribou

Small populations of caribou inhabit the forest and alpine regions of northern and west-central Alberta. Diminishing habitat and declining numbers have led to their placement on Alberta's Threatened Wildlife List. These woodland caribou are smaller than elk and have a dark-brown coat with creamy patches on the neck and rump. Both sexes grow antlers—those of the females are shorter and have fewer points. On average males weigh 180 kilograms, females 115 kilograms.

BEARS

Alberta's two species of bears—black bears and grizzlies—can be differentiated by size and shape. Grizzlies are larger than black bears and have a flatter, dish-shaped face and a distinctive hump of muscle behind their neck. Color is not a reliable way to tell them apart. Black bears are not always black. They can be brown or cinnamon, causing them to be confused with the brown-colored grizzly.

Black Bears

If you spot a bear feeding beside the road, chances are it's a black bear. These mammals are widespread throughout all forested areas of the province (except Cypress Hills Provincial Park). Their weight varies considerably, but males average 150 kilograms and females 100 kilograms. Their diet is omnivorous, consisting primarily of grasses and berries but supplemented by small mammals. In winter, they can sleep for up to a month at a time before changing position.

Grizzly Bears

Most of Alberta's grizzlies are spread through the Rockies—in Banff and Jasper national parks, Kananaskis Country, and Alberta's four designated wilderness areas. A small population inhabiting the Swan Hills is distinct from those found in the mountains and is probably related more closely to the grizzlies that once roamed the prairies.

Grizzlies are widespread, but not abundant in the province. Most sightings occur in alpine and subalpine zones, although sightings at lower elevations are not unusual, especially when snow falls early or late. The bears' color ranges from light brown to almost black, with dark tan being the most common. On average, males weigh 200-250 kilograms. The bears eat small and medium-sized mammals, and berries in fall. Like black bears, they sleep through most of the winter. When they emerge in early spring, the bears scavenge carcasses of animals that succumbed to the winter, until the new spring vegetation becomes sufficiently plentiful.

WILD DOGS AND CATS

Foxes

Smallest of North American wild canids is the **swift fox.** It has a gray body with a long, black-tipped bushy tail, large ears, and smoky-gray

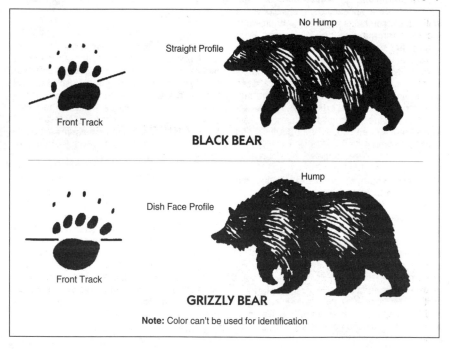

No Hump

Straight Profile

Front Track

BLACK BEAR

Hump

Dish Face Profile

Front Track

GRIZZLY BEAR

Note: Color can't be used for identification

facial spots. The species was eradicated from the prairies by 1928, but Alberta is currently considering a program to reintroduce the animals to their former habitat. The **red fox** is slightly larger than the swift fox and is common throughout Alberta.

Coyotes

The resilient coyote has successfully survived human attempts to eradicate him from the prairies; today his eerie concerts of yips and howls can be heard across much of Alberta. A mottled mix of brown and gray, with lighter-colored legs and belly, the coyote is a skillful and crafty hunter preying mainly on rodents. Both foxes and coyotes have the remarkable ability to hear the movement of small mammals under the snow, allowing them to hunt these animals without actually seeing them.

Wolves

Now inhabiting only the mountains and boreal forests, the wolf was once the target of a relentless campaign to exterminate the species. Wolves are larger than coyotes, resembling a large husky or German shepherd in size and stature. Their color ranges from snow-white to brown or black. They are complex and intriguing animals that adhere to a hierarchical social order and are capable of expressing happiness, humor, and loneliness.

Wild Cats

The elusive **lynx** is identifiable by its pointy black ear tufts and an oversized "tabby cat" appearance. The animal has broad, padded paws which distribute its weight, allowing it to "float" on the surface of snow. It is uncommon but widespread through remote, forested regions of the province. **Bobcats** live in the coulees and caves of badlands such as in Writing-On-Stone and Dinosaur provincial parks.

BOB RACE

WILDLIFE AND YOU

Alberta's abundance of wildlife is one of its biggest drawcards. To help preserve this unique resource, obey fishing and hunting regulations and use common sense.

- **Do not feed the animals.** Many animals may seem tame, but feeding them endangers yourself, the animal, and other visitors, as animals become aggressive when looking for handouts.

- **Store food safely.** When camping keep food in your vehicle or out of reach of animals. Just leaving it in a cooler isn't good enough.

- **Keep your distance.** Although it's tempting to get close to animals for a better look or photograph, it disturbs the animal and, in many cases, can be dangerous.

- **Drive carefully.** The most common cause of premature death for larger mammals is being hit by cars.

Solitary and secretive, **cougars** (also called mountain lions) can grow to a length of 1.5 meters and can weigh 75 kilograms. These versatile hunters inhabit the mountain and foothill regions.

OTHER LARGE MAMMALS

Mountain Goats

The remarkable rock-climbing ability of these nimble-footed creatures allows them to live on rocky ledges or near-vertical slopes, safe from predators. They also frequent the alpine meadows and open forests of the Rockies, where they congregate around natural licks of salt. The goats stand one meter at the shoulder and weigh 80-130 kilograms. Both sexes possess black horns and a peculiar beard, or rather, goatee.

Wolves were once hunted to near extinction.

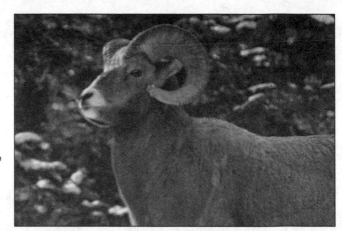

bighorn sheep

Bighorn Sheep

Bighorn sheep are found on grassy mountain slopes throughout the mountains. The males have impressive horns that curve backwards up to 360 degrees. The color of their coat varies with the season; in summer it is brownish-gray (with a cream-colored belly and rump), turning grayer in winter.

Pronghorn

Found roaming the prairie grasslands of southeastern Alberta, the pronghorn, often called pronghorn antelope, is one of the fastest animals in the New World, capable of sustained speeds up to 80 kph. Other remarkable attributes also ensure its survival, including incredible hearing and eyesight, and the ability to go without water for long periods.

Bison

Bison are found in Elk Island and Wood Buffalo national parks and in a number of privately owned herds throughout the province. Two subspecies of bison inhabit Alberta, but for the most part they have interbred. **Wood bison** are darker in color, larger (an average bull weighs 840 kilograms), and have long, straight hair covering the forehead. **Plains bison** are smaller, have shorter legs, a larger head, and frizzy hair. In summer they grow a distinctive cape of woolly hair that covers their front legs, head, and shoulders.

Recreational Vehicles

These migratory creatures, which have unique herding instincts, are widespread through Alberta June-August. Generally, those less than 10 meters long are met with derision by other members of the species. They are most often seen lumbering along the highway, feeding at gas stations, or, like elk, causing traffic jams in the resort towns of Banff and Jasper. Come nightfall, they congregate in designated areas where strange appendages known as "satellite dishes" appear, apparently vital to their survival in wilderness areas. When resting, a "generator," located deep inside their bodies, emits a deep rumble for most of the night, presumably to keep campers at a safe distance. In many ways these creatures are still developing; wing mirrors used to detect the long line of traffic behind them are seldom used. Although they pose no real danger to other species, recreational vehicles have a tendency to kidnap toy poodles in the belief that these small dogs actually enjoy bouncing around on the dashboard for thousands of kilometers.

RODENTS AND OTHER SMALL MAMMALS

Squirrels

Several species of squirrels are common in Alberta. The **golden-mantled ground squirrel,** found in rocky outcrops of subalpine and alpine regions, has black stripes along its sides and looks like an oversized chipmunk. The **Columbian ground squirrel** has reddish legs, face, and underside, and a flecked, grayish back. The bushy-tailed **red squirrel,** bold chatterbox of the forest, leaves telltale shelled cones at the base of conifers. The lightly colored **Richardson's ground squirrel,** which chirps and flicks its thin tail when it senses danger, is found across much of Alberta; on the prairie, it is often misidentified as a "gopher." Another species, the nocturnal **northern flying fox,** glides through the montane forests of mountain valleys but is rarely seen.

Other Rodents

One of the animal kingdom's most industrious mammals is the **beaver.** Tipping the scales at around 20 kilograms, it has a flat, rudderlike tail and webbed back feet that enable it to swim at speeds up to 10 kph. Beavers build their dam walls and lodges of twigs, branches, sticks of felled trees, and mud. They eat the bark and smaller twigs of deciduous plants and store branches underwater, near the lodge, as a winter food supply. **Muskrats** also inhabit Alberta's waterways and wetlands. They are agile swimmers, able to stay submerged for up to 12 minutes.

Closely related to muskrats are **voles,** often mistaken for mice. They inhabit the prairies and lower elevations of forested areas. **Kangaroo rats** live on the shortgrass prairie within the Palliser Triangle. They propel themselves with leaps of up to two meters. The furry **shrew** has a sharp-pointed snout and is closely related to the mole. It must eat almost constantly as it is susceptible to starvation within only a few hours of its last meal. One variety, the **pygmy shrew,** is North America's smallest mammal.

High in the mountains, **hoary marmots** are often seen sunning themselves in rocky areas at or above the treeline. When danger approaches, these large rodents emit a shrill whistle to warn their colony. **Porcupines** are common and widespread throughout all forested areas of the province.

Hares And Pikas

Hares and pikas are technically lagomorphs, distinguished from rodents by a double set of incisors in the upper jaw. Alberta's **varying hares** are commonly referred to as snowshoe hares because their thickly furred, wide-set hind feet mimic snowshoes. Unlike rabbits, which maintain a brown coat year-round, snowshoe hares turn white in winter, providing camouflage in the snowy climes they inhabit. One of their Albertan cousins, the **white-tailed prairie hare,** has been clocked at speeds of 60 kph. Finally, the small, gray **pika,** or rock rabbit, lives among the rubble and boulders of scree slopes above the treeline.

Weasels

The weasel family is comprised of several species of small, carnivorous mammals, many of which can be found in Alberta. The **badger,** a large member of the weasel family, inhabits the grasslands. It is endowed with large claws and strong forelegs, making it an impressive digger. The **wolverine** is the largest of the weasels, inhabiting northern forests and subalpine and lower alpine regions. It is powerful, cunning, and cautious. Males weigh around 15 kilograms. **Fishers,** carnivores weighing up to five kilograms, also frequent subalpine and lower alpine regions; **marten** prey on birds, squirrels, mice, and voles.

Two other related species can be found around Alberta's waterways. **River otters** have round heads, short, thick necks, webbed feet, and long facial whiskers. These playful characters are active both day and night, and prey on both beaver and muskrat. **Mink,** at home in or out of water, are smaller than otters and feed on muskrats, mice, voles, and fish.

REPTILES AND AMPHIBIANS

Two species of snakes, the **wandering garter snake** and the **red-sided garter snake** (North America's northernmost reptile), are found as far north as the boreal forest. The other six species of snakes in the province, of which the plains garter snake is the most common, are restricted to the southern grasslands. Rattlesnakes are rarely encountered; their range is restricted to the badlands.

Three species of frogs and one species of salamander are present in Alberta.

FISH

Alberta's waters hold eight species of trout; rainbow, cutthroat, and brook trout are the predominate species in southern Alberta and the mountain regions, while lake trout, which grow to 20 kilograms, are common in the north. The bull trout, often confused with the brook trout but lacking black markings on the dorsal fin, is a unique species whose slow growth makes it prone to overfishing. Other fish inhabiting Alberta's waters include arctic grayling, two species of whitefish, sturgeon (largest of the freshwater fish), burbot, northern pike, and walleye.

BIRDS

Birdwatching is popular in Alberta, thanks to the 340 species of birds recorded in the province and the millions of migratory birds that pass through each year. All it takes is a pair of binoculars, a good book detailing species, and patience.

bald eagle

Shorebirds And Waterfowl

Alberta is home to 40 species of shorebirds, among them plovers, sandpipers, dowitch-

ers, turnstones, gulls, terns, and herons. Widespread waterfowl species include loons, grebes, ducks, geese, and the threatened trumpeter swan.

Raptors

Bald eagles soar over the northern half of the province, the foothills, and mountains. Golden eagles inhabit open and sparsely vegetated areas of grasslands and mountains. Both species are migratory. Ospreys are uncommon; look for them around mountain and parkland lakes. The territory of the prairie falcon extends from the prairies to the foothills. The threatened ferruginous hawk, largest hawk in North America, also inhabits the prairies. The rare peregrine falcon has been clocked at speeds of up to 290 kph when diving for prey.

Alberta's provincial bird, the great horned owl, is identified by its prominent "horns," which are actually tufts of feathers. Owls have acute hearing, and binocular vision gives them excellent depth perception.

Others

Birdwatchers will be enthralled with the diversity of eastern and western bird species in Alberta. Widespread are magpies, sparrows, starlings, grouse, ravens, and crows. Blackbirds, finches, thrushes, hummingbirds, woodpeckers, flycatchers, and 28 species of warblers are common in forested areas. The popular campground visitor, the cheeky gray jay, is similar in appearance to that of the curious Clark's nutcracker.

BOB RACE

HISTORY

THE EARLIEST INHABITANTS

The first *Homo sapiens* probably arrived in North America some 15,000 years ago—migrating from northeastern Asia across a land bridge spanning Bering Strait. At the time, most of what is now western Canada was covered by an ice cap, so these first immigrants headed south along the coast and into the lower, ice-free latitudes of North America (to what is now the United States). Other waves of similar migrations followed, and eventually these ancestors of today's American Indians fanned out across North and South America.

Thousands of years later, the receding polar ice cap began to uncover the land north of the 49th Parallel. Indian hunters probably first ventured into the area around 11,000 years ago, in pursuit of large mammals at the edge of the melting ice mass. The population gradually spread north, and the people who ended up in what would become Alberta formed several different tribes, each with a unique language and lifestyle. The Assiniboine, a break-away of the more southerly Sioux, lived on the prairies; Cree territory extended into Alberta from Hudson Bay; Chipewyan, Beaver, and Slavey lived in the north; Stoney lived in the southwest; Sarcee migrated across southern Alberta; and the Blackfoot tribe, made up of Blackfoot, Piegan, and Blood bands, lived on the prairies and was the most powerful and feared of all.

The Indians of the prairies relied on buffalo (*Bison bison*) for almost all their needs. They ate buffalo meat, both fresh and dried into pemmican; made clothing, blankets, and tepee covers from the hides; and fashioned the bones into knives and other tools. One of their most successful ways of killing buffalo was by stampeding a whole herd over a cliff, at places known today as "buffalo jumps." The best example of such a site is Head-Smashed-In Buffalo Jump, northwest of Fort Macleod.

EXPLORATION AND THE FUR TRADE

In 1670 the British government granted the Hudson's Bay Company the right to govern Rupert's Land, a vast area of western Canada that included all of present day Manitoba, Saskatchewan, Alberta, and Northwest Territories. The land was rich in fur-bearing mammals, which both the British and the French sought to exploit for profit. The Hudson's Bay Company first built forts around Hudson Bay and encouraged Indians to bring furs to the posts. But soon, French fur traders based in Montreal began traveling west to secure furs, forcing their British rivals to do the same.

In June 1754, Anthony Henday embarked on a journey up the North Saskatchewan River from York Factory on Hudson Bay, becoming the first white man to enter what is now Alberta on 11 September 1754. He returned to the east the following spring, bringing canoes loaded with furs and providing reports of snowcapped peaks.

In 1787 traders from Montreal formed the North West Company, whose men were known as Norwesters. A year later, Norwester Peter Pond built Fort Chipewyan on Lake Athabasca. It was the first fur-trading post in what is now Alberta. The Hudson's Bay Company built *its* first post in present-day Alberta—Buckingham House—right beside the North West Company's Fort George on the North Saskatchewan River. This practice of moving in right next to the competition—engaged in by both companies—produced a rivalry between the two that continued unabated until they merged in 1821.

Trading posts were scattered over the entire west. Most were of solid log construction and were located beside rivers, the main routes for transportation. Furs were the only reason white man came west for over a century. Traders lived by their own rules and were opposed to settlement, which would have changed their lifestyle. But change was in the wind. In 1857 the British government sent Capt. John Palliser west to Rupert's Land to determine whether the land was fit for agriculture. The Palliser Report, which he prepared upon his return to England, was unfavorable to an area in what is now southern Alberta (an area known as "Palliser Triangle"; see the Special Topic in the Southern Alberta chapter), but it encouraged settlement to the north.

The Dominion Of Canada

By 1867, some of the eastern provinces were tiring of British rule, and a movement was abuzz to push for Canadian independence. The British government, wary of losing Canada as it had lost the U.S., passed legislation establishing the Dominion of Canada. It created a central government with certain powers and delegated other powers to the provinces.

At that time, the North-West Territories, as Rupert's Land had become known, was a foreign land to those in eastern Canada: life was primitive with no laws, and no post had more than a couple of dozen residents. But in an effort to solidify the Dominion, the government bought the North-West Territories back from the Hudson's Bay Company in 1869, even as beaver stock was being depleted and the whiskey trade was having disastrous effects on the native population.

Native animals, such as this moose, were used for more than meat and clothing.

End Of An Era

For centuries the buffalo population of the prairies had remained relatively constant. The Indians slaughtered many, but not enough to make a significant impact on total numbers. As beaver populations dwindled, however, traders turned to buffalo hides. Within 10 years, the once-prolific herds had been practically eradicated. Without their traditional food source, the Indians of the plains were weakened and left susceptible to European-borne diseases such as smallpox and scarlet fever. The whiskey trade also took its toll on native populations. Living conditions among the Indians were pitiful and frequent uprisings were taking place.

On 6 June 1874, a band of North West Mounted Police left Toronto under the command of James F. Macleod. Their task was to curb the whiskey trade and restore peace on the western prairies. They built a post on the Oldman River, and within a year, three other posts had been established in what is now southern Alberta.

Facing starvation, many Indian chiefs had no choice but to sign treaties, relegating the tribes to reservations. Chief of all chiefs, Crowfoot, of the powerful Blackfoot Confederacy, signed the first major treaty on 22 September 1877, followed by the chiefs of the Piegans, Stoneys, Sarcees, and Bloods. Their self-sufficiency taken away, the tribes were forced to accept what they were given.

HISTORICAL BOUNDARIES OF ALBERTA

SETTLEMENT

An essential ingredient to the success of settling the west was the construction of a rail line across the continent, replacing canoe and cart routes. This idea was met with scorn by those in the east, who saw it as unnecessary and uneconomical. In 1879 a line reached Winnipeg. After much debate over a route through the Rocky Mountains, the Canadian Pacific Railway line reached Fort Calgary and what is now Banff in 1883. Workers pushed on across the mountains, and on 7 November 1885, the final spike was laid, linking the fledgling province of British Columbia to the rest of the country. A northern route, through Edmonton and Jasper, was completed by the Grand Trunk Railway in 1914.

With two expensive rail lines in place, the government set about putting them to use by settling the land and encouraging tourists to visit the thriving resort towns of Banff and Jasper. The prairies were surveyed and homesteads were offered at $10 per quarter section (200 acres). People from diverse ethnic backgrounds flooded the western prairies, tending to settle in communities of their own people. Life was hard for the early settlers; those in the south found the land dry, while those in the north had to clear land.

The first to take advantage of the extensive grasslands that had once supported millions of bison was Senator Matthew Cochrane, who in 1881 secured a grazing lease on 100,000 acres west of Calgary. This was the first of many ranches in the foothills, and many herds of cattle were driven to their new homes by American cowboys.

Entering The Confederation

British Columbia had gained provincial status in 1871, four years after the Dominion of Canada was established. But the North-West Territories remained under federal control. It had been divided into districts, of which Alberta—named after Princess Louise Caroline Alberta, the fourth daughter of Queen Victoria—was one. On 1 September 1905, Alberta and Saskatchewan were admitted as provinces of the Canadian Confederation, and Edmonton was named Alberta's capital.

For the years preceding WW I, the new province of Alberta led the way in Canadian agricultural export. But strict controls on wheat prices left many farmers in debt. After the war, the Canadian Wheat Board, later to become the Alberta Wheat Pool, was established to give farmers a fairer price and an incentive to stay on the land. The early 1930s were a time of terrible drought and worldwide depression, both of which hit especially hard in a province dependent almost entirely on agriculture. But again, for the second time in 30 years, war bolstered the economy and agricultural production increased. For 50 years agriculture was Alberta's primary industry and the main attraction for settlers, but this was to change dramatically.

OIL

Arguably the most important date in the country's industrial history was 13 February 1947. Until that date, small discoveries of oil and gas beneath Alberta had been made, and the modest reserves under Turner Valley constituted the British Empire's largest oil field. But when Leduc Oil Well No. 1 belched black rings of smoke on that cold February morning, Alberta had hit the jackpot. A new economy for Alberta and all of Canada had begun.

American capitalists poured billions of dollars into Alberta as every valley, hill, and flat was surveyed. Seismic cut lines (lines cut through the forests by seismologists charting new oil fields) across northern Alberta are testimony to this frantic period. Early in 1948 a major field at Redwater was tapped and farmers' fields throughout the province were soon littered with beam pumps bobbing up and down. Calgary became the financial and administrative headquarters of the industry, while Edmonton—in the center of a large proportion of the fields—became the technological, service, and supply center.

By 1954 the eight major fields had been proven to contain eight billion barrels of recoverable crude oil; the Leduc-Woodbend field alone had 1,278 wells, and Pembina had 1,700. But nothing came close to the staggering resources of the Athabasca Oil Sands in northern Alberta, where one trillion barrels of oil lay—more than all the proven reserves of conven-

Turner Valley became a hive of activity when oil was discovered there in 1914.

tional oil on earth. By 1967 Alberta was producing 67% of Canada's crude oil and 87% of its natural gas.

Each of the major fields needed services, and towns such as Drayton Valley, Swan Hills, High Level, and Rainbow Lake sprang up in otherwise unsettled areas. In less than a decade, the province's population doubled to over one million.

The 1970s

In the early '70s, despite abundant resources and frenzied activity in Alberta, the eastern Canadian provinces were importing oil from overseas—taking advantage of low prices obtained, most notably, from the oil-exporting countries of the Middle East. But then the Arab oil ministers got smart, banding together to form the Organization of Petroleum Exporting Countries (OPEC). OPEC began demanding $6 a barrel—up from under $2—and the price of oil quadrupled within three months. Suddenly, cheap, foreign oil was a thing of the past, and Alberta—after decades of feeling snubbed by the eastern provinces—held a trump card. With enormous reserves of oil, and constitutional control over all of it, Alberta braced itself for the coming boom. The value of the province's petroleum resources tripled almost overnight; within another four years it quadrupled again.

A change in government roughly coinciding with the oil boom also contributed to Alberta's success. For 36 years the agricultural-based Social Credit party had controlled Alberta. But in 1971, the Conservative Party—led by Peter Lougheed—came to power. Lougheed was an uncompromising leader who cared little what the powers in eastern provinces thought of his policies. Described by many as an Albertan sheik, he tripled oil-royalty rates for the province, requiring Alberta's producers to pay the province 65 cents out of every dollar earned from the oil. The federal government refused to allow the oil companies to deduct those royalties on their federal income-tax returns, and many major oil companies pulled out of Alberta. But not for long. Alberta had the goods, and with a number of incentives from the government, the companies returned. It was only a slight hiccup in Lougheed's vision of a new and powerful west. Revenues were flowing into the provincial coffers at $6000 per minute, more millionaires were created than at any other time in Canadian history, and Calgary and Edmonton became two of North America's greatest boomtowns and the center of world oil technology. Calgary became the fastest-growing city in the country—a city of dreams, where no expense was spared and to where the power and wealth of eastern provinces moved.

After The Boom

Things have slowed down in Alberta today. The late 1970s to the mid-'90s have been a quiet time. World oil prices steadied in the late '70s and international oil companies spent money elsewhere. But the boom's impact on the province has been positive and the feeling of a western frontier made good still prevails. The Heritage Savings and Trust Fund—a legacy of Lougheed's days—amassed fortunes in oil royalties to be spent on facilities for the people of Alberta. Kananaskis Country was the most grandiose creation of the fund, while other facilities—interpretive centers, urban park systems, and museums—preserve the province's natural and human history.

Self-made millionaires, who often came from humble beginnings, poured their enormous wealth back into the province that had made them rich. The philanthropies of oilman Eric Harvie—including the Glenbow Foundation, Banff Centre for the Arts, and Calgary Zoo—totaled at least $100 million.

The 1978 Commonwealth Games and 1988 Winter Olympic Games provided boosts to Alberta's economy, but petroleum has remained the province's number-one money earner. With staggering resources still in the ground and a relatively young and well-educated population, the future remains bright.

ECONOMY AND GOVERNMENT

ECONOMY

Alberta's economy has always been closely tied to the land—based first on the fur trade, then agriculture, now on abundant reserves of oil and gas. The province's location away from main trade routes has hindered economic diversity and fostered a boom-or-bust dependence on the land's resources. Without these resources, Alberta's industrial and commercial sectors would collapse. The Alberta Department of Energy promotes effective management of the province's mineral resources and collects royalties for the government. The Energy Resources Conservation Board administers the Conservation Act and regulates the production rate of wells.

Oil

Alberta lies above a vast basin of porous

Beam pumps, also called donkey pumps, dot the Albertan landscape.

BRIAN BARDWELL

rock containing abundant deposits of oil, natural gas, and coal. The oil in Alberta occurs in three forms: crude oil, heavy oil, and oil sands. Conventional crude oil is recovered through normal drilling methods. More than 5,000 pools have been discovered, but half the oil production comes from just 25 of them. Most of this oil is refined for use as gasoline in cars, diesel for trucks, and heating fuel for homes. Heavy oil is more difficult to extract and its uses limited. But in the future, as technology improves, recovering Alberta's estimated 300 million barrels of this oil will become viable. Oil sands consist of a tarlike mixture of sand and bitumen that is mined, then refined into synthetic crude for use in fuel products. The Athabasca Oil Sands, near Fort McMurray, are the world's largest such deposit and Alberta is the world's largest producer of synthetic crude. As conventional crude diminishes, Alberta's heavy oil and oil sands will play an increasingly important role in meeting world energy demands.

Natural Gas

Natural gas was first discovered near Medicine Hat in 1883, but it wasn't until 1900 that it was seen as a viable source of energy. The province has always had more gas than it can use (currently proven reserves stand at two trillion cubic feet), and 70% of it is exported, via pipelines to other provinces and the United States. Gas is mostly used for home heating but is also a source material for the petrochemical industry.

Coal

Large deposits of coal were mined early on in Crowsnest Pass, Drumheller, and the foothills, and by the 1920s coal mining had developed into a major industry. Coal was first used to heat homes and provide fuel for steam locomotives, but oil took over those duties in the early 1950s. The industry was revived in 1962 when a coal-fired electric power plant opened at Wabamun, west of Edmonton. This market has since broadened and today Alberta supplies 44% of Canada's coal, of which 70% is used for power production.

Minerals

Industrial, nonmetallic minerals such as limestone, shale, and salt are mined for consumption within Alberta. Sulphur, extracted as a co-product of natural gas, is exported to the large agricultural markets of the United States, Europe, and Africa, for use in fertilizer. Metallic minerals such as copper, silver, and gold have all been mined at some stage, but compared to other areas of Canada, the province has been poorly explored.

Agriculture

Although oil and gas form the backbone of Alberta's economy, farms and ranches still dominate the landscape. Over 20 million hectares are used for agriculture, over half of them cultivated—a back-breaking job that was started when the first homesteaders moved west. Alberta produces about 20% of Canada's total agricultural output, directly employing 50,000 people in the process. The largest portion of

the province's $4 billion annual farm income comes from cattle ($1.2 billion). Alberta has four million head of beef cattle—just under half of Canada's total—as well as 140,000 dairy cows. The largest crop is wheat, used mainly for bread and pasta. Barley, used for livestock feed and making beer, accounts for over $500 million. The other major crops are canola (recognizable by the bright yellow fields), oats, rye, and flax. The largest areas of vegetable production are east of Lethbridge, where the corn and sugar beet industries thrive.

Forestry

Although 60% of Alberta is forested, the forestry industry makes up only one-tenth of one percent of the province's gross domestic product; current annual harvest is five million cubic meters. The main reason for such a small yield is the slow regrowth rate of the northern forests. The province has 300 sawmills, primarily producing dressed lumber.

Tourism

Tourism is the second-most important industry to the economy, lagging only slightly behind the petroleum industry in revenues but employing twice as many people. The government's Alberta Tourism agency markets the province worldwide as a tourist destination. The government has helped in other ways too, investing millions of dollars of royalties from the oil-and-gas industry into improved facilities, interpretive centers, and the development of Kananaskis Country.

GOVERNMENT

Canada is part of the British Commonwealth, but the monarchy and the elected government of Great Britain have no control over Canada's political affairs. The British monarchy is represented in Canada by a governor general. The country's constitution is based on five important acts of British Parliament, the most recent being the Canada Act of 1982. That act gave Canada the power to amend its constitution, provided for recognition of the nation's multicultural heritage, and most importantly for Alberta, strengthened provincial ownership of natural resources.

The Canadian government operates through three main agencies: the Parliament (made up of the Senate and House of Commons), which makes the laws; the Executive (Cabinet), which applies the laws; and the Judiciary, which interprets the laws. Elections are held every five years, and the leader of whichever political party is voted into power by Canadian citizens becomes the head of government, known as the prime minister. The prime minister then chooses a cabinet of ministers from members of his or her party. Each of the ministers is responsible for the administration of a department.

In Alberta, like the other nine provinces, the monarchy is represented by a lieutenant governor. Like the governor general, the position is mainly ceremonial. The members of the Alberta Legislature are elected on a party system for a maximum of five years. Alberta's three main political parties are the Progressive Conservative, New Democratic, and Liberal parties. The leader of the party in power is known as a premier. With so much control over the province's natural resources and, in turn, Alberta's future, many premiers have enjoyed a particularly high profile. One, Peter Lougheed, initiated the Heritage Savings and Trust Fund, which collected billions of dollars in oil royalties for the people of Alberta.

THE PEOPLE

For thousands of years before the arrival of Europeans to Alberta, several distinct indigenous peoples had lived off the land's abundant natural resources. But with the coming of the white man, the native groups were overrun and reduced in numbers, today making up only about two and a half percent of Alberta's population. The Europeans came in droves—first drawn by game and arable land, later by the oil-and-gas boom. People of many diverse cultures moved west, forming a melting pot of traditions. A census as early as 1921 noted 30 different languages in the province, above and beyond the many distinct languages of the natives. Today Alberta's population is 2,621,000—fourth-largest among the Canadian provinces and slightly less than 10% of the country's total.

Natives
As natives signed treaties, giving up traditional lands, their lifestyles changed forever. They were no longer free, they no longer hunted or fought, their medicine men could do nothing to stop the spread of the white man's diseases, and slowly they lost their pride. Today, 63,200 "status" Indians live in Alberta, approximately 60% of them on reservations. Alberta has 93 Indian reserves covering 6,598 square km. The largest is a Blood reserve near Fort Macleod covering 136,760 hectares. Other major reserves include the Stoney reserve at Morley, Sarcee reserve near Calgary, Blackfoot reserve at Gleichen, and the Piegan reserve at Brocket. The reservations are administered by the Department of Indian Affairs and Northern Development. Most of the 41 bands are governed by a chief, elected for two years. Only three, all in the northern half of the province, are governed by a chief elected for life.

Many reserves generate revenue from natural resources, and some bands have become wealthy owning factories, housing developments, and, in the case of the Sarcee near Bragg Creek, a golf course. A biweekly magazine focuses on native issues in the province. For subscription information, write to *Windspeaker,* 15001 112th Ave., Edmonton, Alberta T5M 2V6; or call (403) 455-2700.

Nonnatives
In the last 100 years, Alberta has seen a great influx of people from around the world. The Dominion census of 1881 recorded only 18,072 nonnatives in the province; Calgary had a population of only 75. The French, predominantly fur traders and missionaries, were the first permanent settlers and today make up the fourth-largest ethnic group in the province. The first Asians to settle in the province were Chinese who came seeking gold in the 1860s, and later settled, took up trades, and opened businesses.

Today, with the 1997 transfer of Hong Kong to the People's Republic of China looming on the horizon, Canada is seeing a significant influx

WHYTE MUSEUM OF THE CANADIAN ROCKIES

a Stoney family, photographed by Mary Schäffer in 1907

of immigrants from Hong Kong. Although Vancouver and Toronto have the largest Chinese communities in the country, those of both Edmonton and Calgary are growing. Calgary has a thriving pan-Asian population of about 50,000-60,000, while the pride of Edmonton's Chinese community is well-evidenced by such facilities as the Chinese Cultural Centre (see "Sights" in the Edmonton chapter).

One of the largest influxes occurred between 1901 and 1906, when the Canadian government was selling tracts of land to homesteaders for $10. During this time the population increased from 73,000 to 185,400; in another five years it doubled again. A large percentage of settlers during this period were British and it is this group that today makes up Alberta's largest ethnic group. Germans also migrated to Alberta for a variety of reasons and today make up the province's second-largest ethnic group. Many

were lured by cheap land. Others, such as Hutterites, were persecuted in their homeland for refusing to do military service. Hutterites have become the most successful of all ethnic groups at working the land. They live a self-sufficient lifestyle in tight-knit communities throughout southern and central Alberta. Ukrainians make up the third-largest ethnic group. They were also attracted by the province's agricultural potential and today over 130,000 residents of Ukrainian descent live mostly in Edmonton and to the east.

The oil-and-gas boom brought a population explosion similar to that of 1901-06, but this time, with one exception, the immigrants came from eastern provinces rather than from other countries. The exception was a wave of Americans, whose oil business acumen and technological know-how were vital to the burgeoning industry.

KAREN MCKINLEY

ON THE ROAD
RECREATION

PARKS

Alberta has five national parks, 62 provincial parks, four wilderness areas, a forest reserve covering much of the foothills, over 200 ecological reserves and natural areas, and one historic park. Combined, they encompass all the province's most spectacular natural features, are home to a large proportion of Alberta's mammals, provide safe nesting areas for millions of birds, and protect areas that would otherwise be given over to agriculture or other resource-based industry.

Banff National Park is the jewel of the Canadian national parks system, although **Waterton Lakes,** to the south, and **Jasper,** to the north, are equally beautiful mountain parks. The others are **Elk Island National Park,** where mammal densities are similar to the Serengeti Plains, and **Wood Buffalo National Park,** second-largest national park in the world, accessible by road only through the Northwest Territories.

Provincial parks, widespread throughout Alberta, provide ample opportunities to explore the province's varied natural habitat. All the parks provide day-use facilities or campgrounds. Those not to miss are: **Writing-On-Stone Provincial Park,** so named for the abundant native rock art; **Dinosaur Provincial Park,** a UNESCO World Heritage Site with one of the world's highest concentrations of dinosaur bones; and **Cypress Hills Provincial Park,** a forested oasis on the prairies.

Wilderness areas are located high in Alberta's Rockies. None has road access and all are in remote locations, perfect for wilderness trips for those with backcountry experience. From south to north they are **Ghost River, Siffleur, White Goat,** and **Willmore.**

OUTDOOR ACTIVITIES

The great outdoors is one of Alberta's prime attractions, and a diverse array of activities is available to those who seek them out. The mountains are center of most activity. Raft and canoe tours operate on many mountain rivers, and the vast wilderness provides virtually limitless opportunities for camping, photography, and wildlife viewing. The national parks are a mecca for hikers and climbers in summer, downhill and cross-country skiers in winter. Fishing is good in almost all lakes and rivers in the province, while golfers can enjoy over 220 courses. A comprehensive listing of all outfitters and tour operators is available from Alberta Tourism, P.O. Box 2500, Edmonton, Alberta T5J 2Z4; tel. (800) 661-8888.

Hiking
It's no wonder that hiking is the most popular outdoor activity in Alberta—it's free, anyone can participate, and the mountains offer some of the world's most spectacular scenery. **Banff National Park** holds the greatest variety of trails in the province. Here you can find anything from short interpretive trails with little elevation gain to strenuous slogs up high alpine passes. Trailheads for most of the best hikes are accessible by public transportion or on foot from the town of Banff. Those farther north begin at higher elevations, from which access to the high country is less painful. The trails in **Jasper National Park** are oriented more toward the experienced backpacker, offering plentiful routes for long, backcountry trips. Other areas popular for hiking are **Kananaskis Country,** where crowds are minimal; **Waterton Lakes National Park,** where many trails lead to beautiful subalpine lakes; and the province's four wilderness areas, remote mountain regions accessible only on foot.

Some out-of-the-ordinary companies based at the helipad in Canmore offer **heli-hiking** packages. The day starts with a helicopter ride into the alpine, where short, guided hikes are offered and a picnic lunch is served. Another option is hiking into backcountry lodges. The Alpine Club of Canada, P.O. Box 2040, Canmore, Alberta T0L 0M0, tel. (403) 678-3200, maintains a series of huts, each generally a full-day hike from the nearest road. And Banff National Park has a number of privately owned backcountry lodges—great bases for day-hiking—where onsite hosts provide hot meals; rates start at $95

per person per day including meals. Hikers must register at park information centers for all overnight hikes in national parks.

Topographic maps aren't required for the hikes detailed in this book, but they provide an interesting way to identify natural features. For extended hiking in the backcountry they are vital. Several series of maps, in different scales, cover the entire province. You can purchase them from park information centers, some bookstores, or Maps Alberta, 2nd Floor, 9945 108th St., Edmonton, Alberta T5K 2G6; tel. (403) 427-3520.

Cycling
Alberta is perfect for both road biking and mountain biking. On-road cyclists will appreciate the wide shoulders on all main highways, while those on mountain bikes will enjoy the many designated trails in the mountain national parks. One of the most challenging and scenic on-road routes is the **Icefields Parkway** between Lake Louise and Jasper, which has a number of well-placed hostels along its length.

Most large bookstores stock copies of cycling publications. The *Alberta Cycling Information Map* is available from Alberta Transportation and Utilities, Public Communications Branch, 1st Floor, 4999 98th Ave., Edmonton, Alberta T6B 2X3; tel. (403) 427-7674. The **Alberta Bicycle Association** represents all touring clubs in the province and can provide further information. Write to 11759 Groat Rd., Edmonton, Alberta T5M 3K6, or call (403) 453-8518.

Tour operators include **Rocky Mountain Cycle Tours,** P.O. Box 1978, Canmore, Alberta T0L 0M0, tel. (403) 678-6770, which offers guided trips through the Rockies; **Castle River Mountain Biking,** P.O. Box 723, Pincher Creek, Alberta T0K 1W0, tel. (403) 627-5283, which offers trips in the southwest corner of the province; and **Canusa Cycle Tours,** P.O. Box 45, Okotoks, Alberta T0L 1T0, tel. (403) 560-8959, whose three-day tour along the Icefields Parkway costs $250, including campground fees, all meals, and use of a back-up van.

Horseback Riding
Horses are a traditional means of transportation in the Canadian West; many of the main hiking trails began as horse trails. Within na-

tional parks, horse travel is restricted to certain areas. And horse-packing guide companies are also limited; many of them have been operating since before the parks were established. Outside the parks, riding is available at many ranches and outfitting operations in the foothills and at **Grande Cache.** For a full list, see the back of *Alberta Accommodation Guide,* available at all Alberta Tourist Information Centres.

Rafting, Kayaking, And Canoeing

Canoeing, like horseback riding, has long been a form of transportation in the province, going back to the days of the voyageurs. Qualified guides operate on major whitewater rivers such as the **Maligne River,** in Jasper National Park, offering the biggest thrills, and the **Kickinghorse River,** on the British Columbia side of the Rockies. Guides also operate on larger, quieter rivers such as **Milk River,** through Writing-On-Stone Provincial Park; **Red Deer River,** through the foothills or badlands; **Athabasca River,** in Jasper National Park; and **Bow River,** in Banff National Park. Extended trips are possible along the Peace and Athabasca rivers in the northern part of the province, but any wilderness trips should be attempted only by those with experience.

Canoeing provides an unparalleled opportunity for viewing wildlife around lakes that would otherwise be inaccessible. Most provincial parks with lake systems offer canoe rentals. The book *Canoeing Alberta,* by Lone Pine Publishing (cur-

rently out of print but most libraries have a copy), is the best source of information on all canoe routes.

Rocky Mountain Paddling Centre, P.O. Box 34140, Calgary, Alberta T3C 2W2, tel. (403) 651-4849, offers more than a dozen different courses in all aspects of canoeing and kayaking year-round. In Calgary, their office is in Totem Outdoor Outfitters at 341 10th Ave. SW.

Fishing

Fishing is productive in almost all Alberta's lakes, rivers, and streams, and the fly-fishing on the Bow and Crowsnest rivers is world renowned. Many lakes are stocked annually with a variety of trout. Although fishing is good throughout the province, northern Alberta is the destination of most dedicated anglers.

Fishing licenses are required for all fishing in the province. Licenses are available at Fish and Wildlife offices (Mon.-Fri. only) and many sporting and hardware stores. An annual license for Alberta residents ages 16-64 is $15; for non-residents it is $30, or $20 for a five-day license. A sturgeon license is an extra $5. Pick up a booklet outlining all the open seasons, bag limits, and a handy identification chart from outlets selling licenses, or write to Alberta Fish and Wildlife Services, Main Floor, North Tower, Petroleum Plaza, 9945 108th St., Edmonton, Alberta T5K 2G6.

Fishing in national parks requires a separate license, available from park offices and some

Whitewater rafting is an exciting way to enjoy mountain scenery.

WILD WATER ADVENTURES

sport shops; $6 for a seven-day license, $13 for an annual license.

Climbing And Mountaineering

The Canadian Rockies are a mecca for those experienced in mountain sports. The main centers of activity are Kananaskis Country and Banff and Jasper national parks. Canmore is the self-proclaimed capital, with many skilled mountaineers in town offering instruction and guiding services. Experienced climbers should gather as much information as possible before attempting any unfamiliar routes; quiz locals, hang out at climbing stores, and contact park information centers. For further information contact Parks Canada, Information Services, P.O. Box 2989, Station M, Calgary, Alberta T2P 3H8, tel. (403) 292-4401; or Kananaskis Country, Suite 100, 1011 Glenmore Trail SW, Calgary, Alberta T2V 4R6, tel. (403) 297-3362.

For the inexperienced, the Rockies are the perfect place to learn to climb. Climbing schools are located in Canmore, Banff, and Jasper. Each offers personalized instruction, courses, and mountain guiding for all levels of ability. **Canadian School of Mountaineering,** P.O. Box 723, Canmore, Alberta T0L 0M0, tel. (403) 678-4134, offers mountaineering, rock-climbing, and ice-climbing courses as well as guided summit attempts on nearby peaks. **Yamnuska,** P.O. Box 1920, Canmore, Alberta T0L 0M0, tel. (403) 678-4164, has summer and winter programs throughout the Rockies.

Golfing

With beautiful scenery, long sunny days, over 220 courses, and a golfing season that extends from April to October, Alberta is a golfer's hole-in-one. Getting a game can be difficult on city courses, especially on weekends. Rates range from $5 a round on the smaller municipal courses to $70 in the national parks. Outside of Edmonton and Calgary most courses are public or semiprivate, and getting a game, with advance reservations, isn't a problem.

The best courses are: **Banff Springs Golf Course,** tel. (403) 762-6801, a 27-hole championship course strung out along the Bow River and rated one of the world's most scenic; **Jasper Park Lodge Golf Course,** tel. (403) 852-6090, a challenging par-73 course surrounded by spectacular mountain scenery; **Kananaskis**

Country Golf Course, tel. (403) 591-7272, a 36-hole, Robert Trent Jones–designed course built in the 1980s at a cost of $1,000,000 per hole; and **Wolf Creek Golf Resort,** tel. (403) 783-6050, an oasis on the prairies between Calgary and Edmonton. For a complete listing, check the back of the *Alberta Accommodation Guide* or *Alberta Campground Guide* (available from all Alberta Tourist Information Centres).

Scuba Diving

Being landlocked, Alberta is not renowned for scuba diving. A few interesting opportunities do exist, however, and rentals are available in Lethbridge, Calgary, and Edmonton. The old townsite of **Minnewanka Landing,** in Banff National Park, has been flooded, and although a relatively deep dive, the site is interesting. **Patricia Lake,** in Jasper National Park, has a sunken WW II barge, and due to the high altitude and clear water, visibility is exceptional. Another sunken boat is located at the bottom of Emerald Bay in Waterton National Park. Nearby are a number of wagons which fell through ice many winters ago. For a list of dive shops and sites contact Alberta Scuba Divers' Council, Percy Page Centre, 11759 Groat Rd., Edmonton; tel. (403) 453-8566.

Downhill Skiing

Six world-class ski areas are perched among the high peaks of Alberta's Rockies. The largest, and also Canada's largest, is **Lake Louise,** overlooking the lake of the same name in Banff National Park. The area boasts 1,500 hectares of skiing on four distinct faces, with wide-open bowls and runs for all abilities. Banff's other two resorts are **Sunshine Village,** sitting on the Continental Divide and accessible only by gondola, and **Mystic Ridge & Norquay,** a resort with heart-pounding runs overlooking the town of Banff. Just outside Banff in Kananaskis Country is **Nakiska,** a resort developed especially for the downhill events of the 1988 Winter Olympic Games. Nearby **Fortress Mountain** is in a spectacular location and has runs for all abilities. **Marmot Basin,** in Jasper National Park, has minimal crowds with a maximum variety of terrain.

Nearly 50 other ski hills are scattered through the province, most with less than a 200-meter vertical drop. One area unique for its proximity to

The skiing is legendary in the Canadian Rockies.

ALBERTA TOURISM

the city center is the **Edmonton Ski Club** hill in the North Saskatchewan River Valley, overlooking downtown Edmonton. **Canada Olympic Park,** within Calgary city limits, was built for the 1988 Winter Olympic Games and maintains some of the world's finest ski-jumping facilities. Most major resorts begin opening in early December and close in May or, in the case of Sunshine Village, early June.

Other Winter Activities

All hiking trails provide ideal routes for **cross-country skiing,** and many are groomed for that purpose. The largest concentration of groomed trails is in Kananaskis Country. Other areas are Banff, Jasper, and Waterton national parks, the urban parks of Calgary and Edmonton, and the many provincial parks scattered through the province. Anywhere you can cross-country ski you can **snowshoe,** a traditional from of winter transportation that is making a comeback. **Ice fishing** for whitefish and burbot is good in all major rivers and those lakes large enough not to freeze to the bottom. **Sleigh rides** are offered in Banff, Lake Louise, and Jasper.

Winter travel brings its own set of potential hazards such as hypothermia, avalanches, frostbite, and sunburn. Necessary precautions should be taken. All park information centers can provide information on hazards and advise on current weather conditions. For avalanche information call (800) 667-1105.

ENTERTAINMENT

Museums

The best way to gain insight into Alberta's natural and human history is to visit one of its many museums. Not all are the crowded, stuffy kind, and many of the best are outside the cities. The **Royal Tyrrell Museum of Palaeontology,** located in the dinosaur-rich badlands of the Red Deer River Valley, is the largest palaeontological museum in the world. Inside you'll find over 50 full-size dinosaurs on display. If you only visit one museum in Alberta, make it this one. Other major museums include the extensive **Provincial Museum of Alberta** in Edmonton; **Glenbow Museum** in Calgary; **Remington-Alberta Carriage Centre** at Cardston, which houses over 200 carriages, buggies, and wagons; and the **Reynolds-Alberta Museum** on the outskirts of Wetaskiwin, which catalogues the history of machinery.

Performing Arts

For a province that prides itself on a Western heritage, Alberta has a surprising number of cultural diversions. Edmonton alone has 13 professional theater companies, equal to any North American city of comparable size. Both Edmonton and Calgary have ballet troupes, an orchestra, and opera.

Country Music

For most of this century, singers and songwriters have found inspiration in the ranching lifestyle and mountain scenery of Alberta. In the 1930s, **Wilf Carter,** a cowboy by trade, began singing on Calgary radio. Within three years he had become a star in the United States as "Montana Slim," the yodeling cowboy. More recently **K.D. Lang,** of Consort, has become a country superstar with Grammy-winning albums pushing the boundaries of country music toward pop. **George Fox** and **Ian Tyson,** who both have ranches west of Calgary, also have made their mark on Canadian country music.

Nightlife

Although most cities have dance clubs and rock 'n' roll discos, it is the Western bars where Alberta's heritage lives on. Bars like **Ranchman's** (which has a chuckwagon hanging from the roof), **Longhorn Dance Hall,** and **Rockin' Horse Saloon** in Calgary, and **Cook Country Saloon** and **Denim and Diamonds** in Edmonton, keep the Western image alive.

Spectator Sports

The **ice hockey** season may be only seven months long, but to fans of the Edmonton Oilers and Calgary Flames—Alberta's National Hock-

ey League teams—it's a year-round obsession. The best seats are taken by die-hard season-ticket holders, but for $12.50-15 you can usually score tickets through Ticketmaster a few days in advance. Both cities also have professional Canadian Football League teams and AAA Pacific Coast League baseball teams.

SHOPPING

Arts And Crafts

The arts and crafts of Canada's indigenous people are available throughout the province. Jewelry, beaded moccasins, baskets, and leatherwork such as headdresses are favorite souvenirs. The stylistic art of the native people is also popular, but prints of the most recognizable works run into thousands of dollars. Two of the best outlets are the **Indian Trading Post** in Banff and the **Alberta Indian Arts and Crafts Society** at 10105 109th St., Edmonton.

Western Wear

You don't have to be able to ride a horse to dress like a cowboy—just ask the thousands of city folk who dress the part for the Calgary Exhibition and Stampede. Major department stores are the best places to find the basic Western

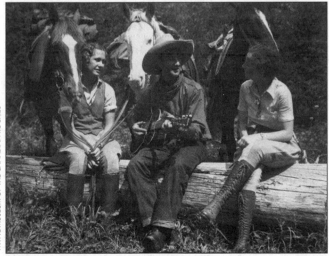

Calgarian Wilf Carter, better known as "Montana Slim," was a country music superstar in the 1930s.

accessories, while specialty shops are the places to go for gear that the real cowboys wear. Most of the latter sell handmade jewelry, authentic Stetsons, belt buckles big enough to fry an egg on, and hundreds of pairs of boots in every style imaginable.

FESTIVALS AND EVENTS

Spring
The year's first major event for cowboys is the **Rodeo Royal,** held at Calgary's Saddledome in March, followed by the **Silver Buckle Rodeo,** held in April in Red Deer. Both Calgary and Edmonton host an **International Children's Festival** in May, with a wide variety of events for the younger generation. Alberta's ski resorts usually have snow on the ground until late spring, and many ski resorts hold major events at season's end. Sunshine Village hosts its **Slush Cup** and a **Dummy Downhill** in May.

Summer
Summer is the biggest event season in Alberta. Edmonton hosts a major festival just about every weekend, and there's almost always something going on in much of the rest of the province.

The **Alberta Cowboy Poetry Gathering** comes to Pincher Creek each June . . . hear cowpokes read poems by the light of the, uh, stars? Stars of another type come to perform at the **Jazz City International Festival,** in late June. The festival draws famous jazz musicians from around the world.

Canada Day, 1 July, is a national holiday celebrated in many towns with various events, often including a rodeo. The most famous is the **Calgary Exhibition and Stampede,** the world's richest rodeo with 10 days of action and a winner-take-all format. This western extravaganza is a not-to-be-missed event. The same week as the Calgary Exhibition and Stampede, a very different equestrian event is taking place just outside the city. The **National**—at **Spruce Meadows,** one of the world's finest international riding centers—is a showjumping competition attracting thousands of enthusiasts. Also in early July, the **Edmonton International Street Performers' Festival** offers over 1,000 free performances at outdoor venues throughout the city, while Lethbridge's **Whoop-up Days**

celebrates that city's past.

Late July brings **Edmonton's Klondike Days,** a celebration centered around the city's tenuous connection to the Yukon goldfields; the **Edmonton Heritage Festival,** a celebration of days gone by; and the big **Medicine Hat Rodeo,** held annually since 1887. Calgary hosts an **International Jazz Festival** and **Folk Music Festival** in July, and the month ends on a high note with the **Red Deer International Air Show** on the last weekend of July, featuring performances by some of the world's best stunt pilots. Meanwhile, the air over Grande Prairie is also alive with color when one of many **hot air balloon championships** takes place.

The **Edmonton Folk Music Festival** picks and strums its way into town in early August; the city's **Fringe Theatre Festival** in mid-August is centered around Old Strathcona, with performances of alternative theater from throughout North America. Calgary's cultural festivals are low-profile affairs compared to those in Edmonton, but the city does offer the **International Native Arts Festival** in August.

Fall
Just when all the summer festivals are winding down, the action at Spruce Meadows equestrian center, outside Calgary, is heating up. **Spruce Meadows Masters** is the world's richest showjumping event and the finale to a packed season. Also in Calgary is a large **antique show** in September. In late fall, the mountain ski resorts begin opening and Banff hosts **Winterstart,** a six-week period of cheap deals and events held throughout the town. The first weekend of November is the **Banff Festival of Mountain Films,** a gathering of the world's greatest adventure-film makers.

Winter
Most Albertan towns and cities have **winter carnivals** featuring weird and wonderful events that only people affected by the long winter could dream up. The largest ones, each lasting two weeks, are in Calgary, Banff, Jasper, and Edmonton; all are in January. The one in Canmore, in late January, is held in conjunction with the **Alberta Sled Dog Championships. First Night** is an alcohol-free celebration of the New Year that takes place in downtown Calgary, Edmonton, and Banff.

ACCOMMODATIONS AND FOOD

Hotels And Motels

Hotels and motels of some sort exist in just about every Albertan town. They range from substandard road motels advertising "Color TV" to sublime resorts high in the Rocky Mountains. The only time you'll have a problem finding a room is in Calgary during Stampede Week and in the national parks in July and August. In both cases plan ahead or be prepared to camp. Accommodation prices in Banff and Jasper national parks are slashed by as much as 70% outside summer. In cities always ask for the best rate available and check local tourist literature for discount coupons. Rates are usually lower on weekends. All rates quoted in this handbook are for the cheapest category of rooms during the most expensive time period (summer). To all rates quoted you must add the seven percent Goods and Services Tax (GST) and five percent provincial room tax. The former is refundable to nonresidents of the province.

In many towns, you'll find older-style hotels where bathrooms are shared, the phone is in the lobby, and check-in is at the bar. Rooms are generally sparsely furnished, and what furniture there is dates to the 1960s. Expect to pay from $15 s, $20 d for shared bathroom, and a few bucks more for a private bathroom.

Park-at-your-door, single-story road motels are located in all towns and on the outskirts of all major cities. In most cases rooms are fine, but check before paying, just to make sure. Most have a few rooms with kitchenettes, but these fill fast. In the smaller towns expect to pay $25-40 s, $30-50 d.

Most major towns and all cities have larger hotels, each of which typically has a restaurant, cafe, lounge, and pool. At these establishments expect to pay from $45 s, $50 d for a basic room. Downtown hotels in Calgary and Edmonton begin at $70. A good deal can be suites or executive suites, with kitchenettes and one or two bedrooms for little more money than a regular room.

Finding inexpensive lodging in the mountain national parks is difficult in summer. By late afternoon the only rooms left will be the more expensive categories and by nightfall all of these will go. Hotel rooms in Banff begin around $100, those in Jasper and Waterton are a little less. For a list of all hotels and motels in the province, pick up a copy of *Alberta Accommodation Guide,* available from tourist information centers or by calling (800) 661-8888.

Bed And Breakfasts

The bed and breakfast phenomenon is well-entrenched in Alberta. Hosts are generally well-informed local people and rooms are cozy. The establishments are often moneymaking ventures so don't expect the bargains of European bed and breakfasts. The best way to find out about individual lodging is from local tourist information centers or listings in the back of the *Alberta Accommodation Guide.* Major bed and breakfast associations are: **Alberta's Gem B&B and Reservation Agency,** 11216 48th Ave.,

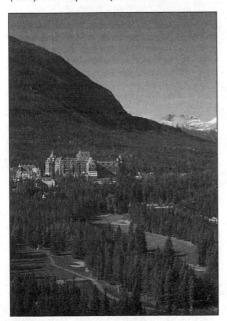

Banff Springs Hotel

Edmonton T6H 0C7, tel. (403) 434-6098, which has listings throughout the province; **A.H.H.A.,** 10808 54th Ave., Edmonton T6H 0T9, tel. (403) 436-0649, a Canada-wide booking agency; **High Country B&B Association,** P.O. Box 61, Millarville, T0L 1K0, which books B&Bs and ranch accommodations in southern Alberta; **B&B Association of Calgary,** 6016 Thornburn Dr. NW, Calgary T2K 3P7, tel. (403) 531-0065, listing homes in Calgary; and **Edmonton B&B,** 13824 110A Ave., Edmonton T5M 2M9, tel. (403) 455-2297, which books homes in that city.

Backcountry Huts And Lodges

Scattered through the backcountry of Banff and Jasper national parks are a number of huts maintained by the Alpine Club of Canada. The huts are rustic—typically bunk beds, a wood-stove, wooden dining table, and an outhouse. Reservations should be made in advance by contacting the Alpine Club of Canada, P.O. Box 2040, Canmore, Alberta T0L 0M0; tel. (403) 678-3200. Banff National Park has two privately operated backcountry lodges, **Shadow Lake Lodge and Cabins,** northwest of Banff, and **Skoki Lodge**, east of Lake Louise (see that chapter for more information). Both require some degree of effort to reach—either by hiking or on horseback in summer, or by cross-country skiing in winter. The lodges are typically 8-15 km from the nearest road. Rates begin at $95 per person including three meals. Neither has television, but both have running water and a congenial atmosphere.

Hostels

Hostelling International–Alberta operates 16 hostels in the province. They are located in Calgary, Edmonton, the town of Banff, at Lake Louise, all along the Icefields Parkway (which runs through Banff and Jasper national parks), in the town of Jasper, in Kananaskis Country, and in the towns of Coleman, Drumheller, and Nordegg. All are accessible by road, and all but the Nordegg hostel are accessible by public transportation. During busy periods males and females have separate dormitories. A sheet or sleeping bag is required although these can usually be rented. All are equipped with a kitchen and lounge room, and some have laundries. Those in Banff and Lake Louise are world-class, with hundreds of beds, libraries, and cafes. The

five rustic hostels along the Icefields Parkway are evenly spaced, perfect for a bike trip along one of the world's great mountain highways. Rates for members are $9-17 per night, non-members $14-21. Whenever you can, make reservations in advance, especially in summer. The easiest way to do this is through Hostelling International's **International Booking Network** (I.B.N.), contacting the individual hostel, or, calling (800) 363-0096 within Alberta.

If you plan to travel extensively using hostels, join Hostelling International before you leave home. In the U.S. write to American International Hostels, Inc., 133 1st St. NW, Suite 800, Washington, D.C. 20005, USA. In Canada contact Hostelling International–Canada, 333 River Rd., Vanier City, Ontario K1L 8B9, Canada; tel. (800) 668-4487. Membership in Canada is $26.75 for one year or $37.45 for two years.

Hostel Shops sell memberships and reasonably priced camping gear. They also provide general travel information, and can book air, bus, and train trips for you. You'll find the shops in Edmonton at 10926 88th Ave., tel. (403) 432-7798, and in Calgary at 1414 Kensington Rd. NW, tel. (403) 283-8311.

The **YMCA** and **YWCA** are another inexpensive lodging alternative, often with prime locations. Calgary has a YWCA for women only; Banff has a YWCA open to both sexes, with some family rooms; Edmonton has one of each. Rates begin at $12 per night with reasonable weekly rates available.

Campgrounds

Spending some money on a reliable tent and sleeping bag quickly pays off wherever you are traveling, but especially so in many parts of Alberta. Calgary has a half dozen campgrounds spread around its outskirts, Edmonton has one near downtown, and most towns have a **municipal campground**. These range in price from free to $13-16 depending on facilities and location. Often those in smaller towns are a bargain—it's not uncommon to pay less than $10 for a site with hookups and hot showers. Except in major cities, reservations aren't necessary—just roll up and pay the campground host or use the honor box. Most **provincial parks** have a campground; prices are $5.50-15 depending on facilities available. Some have hookups, showers, boat rentals, and occasionally laundry facilities. Throughout the foothills are **Forest Service campgrounds,** which have pit toilets, picnic tables, and a supply of firewood. Most are accessed along the Forestry Trunk Rd.; for a complete listing contact the Recreation Section, Alberta Forest Service, Alberta Forestry, Lands and Wildlife, 6th Floor, 9920 108th St., Edmonton, Alberta T5K 2M4; tel. (403) 427-3582. Each of Alberta's **national parks** has excellent campgrounds. At least one campground in each park has hot showers and full hookups. Prices are $5.50-17. All national park campgrounds operate on a first-come, first-served basis and often fill by midday in July and August. Banff, Jasper, and Waterton have winter camping but with limited facilities. Backcountry camping in all parks is free, but before heading out you must register at the respective park information center. Most campgrounds in the backcountry have pit toilets, and some have bear bins for secure food storage. Fires are discouraged so bring a stove.

FOOD AND DRINK

The best way to eat cheap is with a campstove. Those made by Coleman are the most reliable. Most urban campgrounds discourage open fires and many provincial and national parks are beginning to charge $2-5 for firewood. The two largest supermarkets, Safeway and I.G.A., generally have the least expensive groceries, but prices are still higher than in the United States. In most I.G.A. stores you'll find an excellent bakery.

Although Alberta isn't renowned for its culinary delights, the staple of the province—Alberta beef—is delicious and is served in most restaurants. For a three-course meal in a family-style restaurant, including a steak dish, expect to pay $20-25 per person—double that in the better eateries. Edmonton, Calgary, and Banff have an astonishing array of ethnic restaurants with the latter, a town of 7,000, having over 100 restaurants. Inexpensive options are Husky restaurants, located in gas stations of the same name along all major routes. Their portions are generous, prices are good, and they're open 24 hours. Calgary and Edmonton also have a number of excellent buffets where an all-you-can eat Chinese or western meal is $5-7 for lunch and $8-11 for dinner.

Drink
Calgary and Edmonton each have specialty brewers who brew boutique beers for sale in the immediate area. Alberta's largest homegrown brewery is **Big Rock** in Calgary. The Banff Springs Hotel has a beer bottled for itself, available only in Banff. The province's only winery is west of Edmonton.

The minimum age for alcohol consumption in Alberta is 18. From the United States, visitors may bring 1.1 liters of liquor or wine or 24 cans or bottles of beer into Canada free of duty.

TRANSPORTATION

GETTING THERE

Air
Calgary and Edmonton have international airports served by major airlines from throughout the world. Many flights from the south are routed through Calgary before continuing to Edmonton, giving you a choice of final destinations for little or no price difference. **Canadian,** based at Calgary International Airport, is one of the world's largest airlines, serving five continents. They offer direct flights to Calgary from all major Canadian cities, as well as from Los Angeles, San Francisco, London, Manchester, and Frankfurt. Flights from Paris, Munich, Rome, and Milan are routed through Toronto. From Australia and the South Pacific, Canadian operates in alliance with Qantas and Air New Zealand, which fly passengers to Honolulu where they change to Canadian. Asian cities served include Bangkok, Hong Kong, Taipei, Nagoya, and Tokyo. Canadian's flights from South America are routed through Toronto. For further information on Canadian's routes and schedules call (800) 665-1177 in Canada, (800) 426-7000 in the U.S., and (071) 930-3501 in Great Britain.

Air Canada also offers flights from all major Canadian cities as well as nonstop service from

Los Angeles and San Francisco. The only Air Canada nonstop international flights to Alberta originate in London. All other European flights are routed through Toronto and those from Asia and the South Pacific through Vancouver. For information on Air Canada flights, call (800) 332-1080, (800) 776-3000 in the U.S., or (081) 759-2331 in London.

U.S. carriers offering service to Calgary are: **American Airlines,** tel. (800) 443-7300; **Delta Air Lines,** tel. (800) 221-1212; and **United Airlines,** tel. (800) 241-6522. Edmonton is served by American, Delta, and **Northwest Airlines,** tel. (800) 225-2525. Other international carriers serving the province include **Qantas, Air New Zealand, Japan Airlines,** and **KLM.**

Cutting Flight Costs

Ticket structuring for international air travel is so complex that often even travel agents have problems coming to grips with it. The first step when planning your trip to Alberta is to contact the airlines that fly there and ask for the best price they have for the time of year you wish to travel. Then shop around the travel agencies—you should be able to save 30-50% of the price you were quoted by the airline. Check the Sunday travel section of most newspapers for an idea of current discount prices. Many cheaper tickets have strict restrictions regarding changes of flight dates, lengths of stay, and cancellations. A general rule is: the cheaper the ticket, the more restrictions in place. Apart from airline promotional fares, consolidators—bucket shops as they are commonly called—consistently offer the lowest airfares. Once only prevalent in Asian cities such as Singapore and Bangkok and in the popular European travel hubs, this form of travel agent is now common throughout the world. They buy blocks of seats on scheduled flights that airlines decide they wouldn't normally be able to sell, then either sell them directly to the public or to other travel agents. Within Canada, **Travel Cuts,** with offices in all major cities, consistently offers the lowest airfares available. Within the U.S., one of the largest consolidators is **Unitravel,** tel. (800) 325-2222. In London, **Trailfinders,** 194 Kensington High St., London W8 7RG, tel. (071) 938-3232, always has good deals to Canada and other North American destinations.

Rail

VIA Rail provides transcontinental rail service from coast to coast. This form of transportation, which opened up the West to settlers and the Rocky Mountains to tourists, began to fade with the advent of efficient air services. Scheduled services to Calgary ended in 1991; the remaining transcontinental route passes through Edmonton and Jasper. The **Canadian,** as this train is known, operates three days a week in either direction and provides three classes of travel: **Coach, Sleeping-car,** and **Silver and Blue.** Silver and Blue class is the most luxurious, providing extra amenities and use of a dome car reserved exclusively for passengers in the class. Discounts of 25-40% apply to travel Oct.-June (applicable to all classes). Those over 60 and under 25 receive a 10% discount which can be combined with other seasonal fares. Students receive a 50% discount year-round. Check for advance purchase restrictions on all discount tickets.

The **Canrail Pass** allows unlimited travel anywhere on the VIA Rail system for 13 days within any given 30-day period. Until recently these passes were only available to foreign visitors, but now anyone can purchase them, with certain advance-purchase restrictions. During high season (June-Sept.) the pass is $545, $373 the rest of the year. Even if you plan limited train travel the pass is an excellent deal; the regular Toronto-Edmonton one-way fare alone is $354.17. For VIA Rail information and reservations in western Canada call (800) 561-8630; for other Canadian locations contact your local VIA Rail Station. In the U.S. call (800) 561-3949 or contact any travel agent. Other general sales agents are Walshes World, 92 Pitt St., Sydney, tel. (02) 232-7499 or (008) 22-7122; Walshes World, 2nd Floor, Dingwall Building, 87 Queen St., Auckland, tel. (09) 379-3708; Canada Reise Dienst, Rathausplatz 2, 2070 Ahrensburg/Hamburg, tel. 4904102-51167; Long-Haul Leisurail, Box 113, Peterborough PE1 1LE, England, tel. (8862) 503-3302.

Rocky Mountaineer Railtours operates a luxurious rail trip through the spectacular interior mountain ranges of British Columbia. Travel is during daylight hours only so you don't miss anything. Options from Vancouver are to Banff ($499 per person one way), Calgary ($548), or a more northerly route from Vancouver through the spectacular Monashee Mountains to Jasper ($499). Rates include overnight accommodations in Kamloops, B.C., two breakfasts, two lunches, and light snacks. During value season (late May and late September) fares are reduced $100. And all fares will cost $50 more if you travel alone. For further information and reservations call (800) 665-7245.

Bus

Greyhound serves areas throughout Canada and the United States. From Vancouver, the main routes are along the TransCanada Hwy. to Banff and Calgary and a more northern route through to Jasper and Edmonton. From the east, buses depart Toronto daily for Calgary and Edmonton along two different routes. If you're traveling to Alberta from the U.S., get yourself to Great Falls, Montana, from where regular services continue north to the Coutts/Sweetgrass port of entry. There you change to a Canadian Greyhound bus. Calgary buses depart from the port of entry daily at 12:10 p.m.

Travel by Greyhound is simple—just roll up at the depot and buy a ticket. No reservations are necessary. Greyhound bus depots in all major Albertan cities are near inexpensive accommodations and other public transportation. Always check for any promotional fares that might be available at the time of your travel. Regular-fare tickets are valid for one year and allow unlimited stopovers between paid destinations.

The **Greyhound Canada Pass** is valid on all Greyhound routes in Canada. It is sold in periods of seven days ($191.53), 15 days ($255.73), 30 days ($352.08), and 60 days ($459.03). It must be purchased seven days in advance and is nonrefundable. You can buy the pass at any bus depot. For more information call (403) 265-9111 or, in Canada only (800) 661-8747. In the U.S. the pass can be bought from most travel agents. Outside of North America it is sold as the **International Canada Pass** with a similar pricing structure except that there is a low season with a 25% discount which runs mid-September to mid-June. In England purchase the pass at Greyhound World Travel, Sussex House, London Rd., East Grinstead, West Sussex RH19 1LD; tel. (0342) 31-7317.

GETTING AROUND

Air

Canadian Regional, tel. (800) 665-1177, and **Air B.C.,** tel. (800) 332-1080, are air carriers with scheduled flights to all cities and many larger towns within the province. From Calgary, Canadian Regional serves Lethbridge, Medicine Hat, Edmonton, Grande Prairie, and many B.C. towns. From Edmonton it serves Grande Prairie, Peace River, High Level, Rainbow Lake, Fort McMurray, and northern B.C. towns. These flights out of Edmonton depart from the municipal airport, so allow time for a trip across the city if you're coming in from the U.S. or other international destinations. Domestic flights are generally expensive but discounts apply if tickets are purchased in advance or in conjunction with a long-haul flight.

Airlines in Alberta rarely offer promotional fares, but by buying a roundtrip ticket 7-14 days in advance and staying over a Saturday night, discounts of up to 50% apply.

Departure tax on all domestic flights is seven percent of the ticket price plus $10 to a maximum of $40. Add to this the GST and you have the actual price you'll be paying. For example, after adding taxes to the one-way Calgary-Edmonton fare of $131, you'll pay $160.68.

Rail

The only scheduled rail service within the province is between Jasper and Edmonton. This thrice-weekly service is part of the transcontinental route. The 8.5-hour run is $81 one way. For further information on VIA Rail services, see "Getting There," above, or call (800) 561-8630 in Canada only.

Bus

Greyhound bus routes radiate from Calgary and Edmonton to points throughout the province. Service is regular, fast, and efficient. The only downside is that in larger centers, bus depots are often in seedy parts of town. Many depots have cafeterias, some have lockers, but none of them remain open all night. For schedules and fares call (403) 265-9111 or, in Canada only (800) 661-8747.

Brewster Transportation and Tours provides coach service between Calgary and Banff and Jasper national parks. Brewster's advantage over Greyhound is that its service departs from Calgary International Airport and major Calgary hotels. One-way fare to Banff is $28. You can book a trip at their booking desk on the arrivals level of Calgary International Airport, or call (403) 762-6700.

Pika is a shuttle service for hostelers linking Calgary International Hostel to all hostels in Banff and Jasper national parks. The fare from Calgary to Banff is $15; Banff to Jasper $34. The only condition of travel is that you *must* have a reservation at your destination hostel. For information call (800) 363-0096.

Car And RV Rental

All major car-rental agencies have outlets at Calgary and Edmonton international airports; to ensure a vehicle is available for you, book in advance. Generally vehicles can be booked through parent companies in the United States. Rates start at $55 a day for a small economy car, $65 for a midsize car, and $75 for a full-size car. Most major agencies now offer unlimited mileage, but check to make sure. Cheaper cars are available from agencies such as **Rent-A-Wreck,** but each kilometer driven over 100 km each day will cost 15-30 cents. In all cases insurance is from $12 per day and is compulsory. Rates are often lower outside summer. Charges apply if you need to drop off the car at an agency other than the rental location. All agencies provide free pick-up and drop-off at major city hotels. Major rental agencies include: **Avis,** tel. (800) 879-2847; **Budget,** tel. (800) 268-8900; **Discount Car Rentals,** tel. (403) 299-1222; **Dollar,** tel. (800) 263-6552; **Economy,** tel. (403) 291-1640; **Hertz,** tel. (800) 263-0600; **Thrifty,** (800) 367-2277; and **Tilden,** (800) 387-4747.

Camper-vans, recreational vehicles, and travel trailers are a great way to get around the province without having to worry about accommodations each night. The downside is cost. The smallest vans, capable of sleeping two people, start at $80 per day with 100 free kilometers. The major agencies, based near Calgary and Edmonton international airports, are: **Canada Campers,** tel. (403) 250-3209; **Cruise Cana-**da, tel. (403) 291-4963 or (800) 327-7799 or, in the U.S., (800) 327-7778; **Everett's,** tel. (403) 291-0077; and **Go Vacations,** tel. (403) 291-6450 or (800) 387-3998.

Driving In Alberta

Driving is the most practical and popular way to travel to and around Alberta. Driver's licenses from all countries are valid in the province for up to three months. An **International Driving Permit,** available in your home country, is valid in Alberta for one year. You should also carry car-registration papers or rental contracts. Proof of insurance must be carried and you must wear seat belts. If coming from the U.S., check that your American insurance covers travel in Canada. All highway signs in Alberta give distances in **kilometers** and speeds in **kilometers per hour** (kph). The speed limit on major highways is 100 kph (62 mph). U.S. motorists are advised to obtain a Canadian Non-resident Inter-provincial Motor Vehicle Liability Insurance Card, available through U.S. insurance companies, which is accepted as evidence of financial responsibility in Canada. Members of the American Automobile Association are entitled to services provided by the Canadian Automobile Association, including travel information.

Buying a car is relatively straightforward in Alberta. Proof of insurance in your home country will lower the standard liability insurance of $1200 per year. Automobiles are cheaper in the U.S. but insurance is higher, and unless you can convince customs that you won't be selling the car in Canada, you'll be up for hefty import charges.

Tours

For those with limited time, an organized tour is the best way of seeing the province. **Brewster Transportation And Tours,** P.O. Box 1140, Banff, Alberta T0L 0C0, tel. (403) 762-6700 or (800) 661-1152, offers a variety of tours to various parts of the province, as well as car-rental and accommodation packages, overnight packages in Calgary and Edmonton, Calgary Exhibition and Stampede packages, golfing adventures, and round trips to Alberta from Vancouver, British Columbia.

OTHER PRACTICALITIES

VISAS AND OFFICIALDOM

Entry For U.S. Citizens
Citizens and permanent residents of the United States do not require a passport for entry to Canada. Although photo driver's licenses are acceptable forms of identification for entry, it is advisable to carry extra identification such as a birth certificate, passport, or alien card (the latter essential for U.S. resident aliens to re-enter the United States).

Other Foreign Visitors
Visitors from countries other than the U.S. require a valid passport and, in some cases, a visa for entry to Canada. Presently, citizens of the British Commonwealth and Western Europe do not require a visa, but check with the Canadian embassy in your home country. The standard entry permit is valid for six months; proof of onward tickets and/or sufficient funds is required in order to obtain the permit. Extensions are possible from the Employment and Immigration Canada offices in Calgary and Edmonton ($60 per person).

Employment And Study
Anyone wishing to work or study in Canada must obtain authorization *before* entering Canada. Authorization to work will only be granted if there are no qualified Canadians available for the work in question. Applications for work and study are available from all Canadian embassies and must be submitted with a nonrefundable processing fee.

The Canadian government has a reciprocal agreement with Australia for a limited number of **holiday work visas** to be issued each year. Australian citizens under the age of 26 are eligible; contact your nearest Canadian embassy or consulate for more information.

Entry By Private Aircraft
For a list of Canadian airports with customs clearance facilities, request the *Canada Flight Supplement* from Canada Map Office, 615 Booth St., Ottawa, Ontario K1A 0E9, tel. (613) 952-7000. This office also has aeronautical charts; $14 each. The publication *Air Tourist Information–Canada* (TP771E) lists all Alberta's airports and has other necessary information for visiting pilots; it's available from Transport Canada, AAN DHD, Ottawa, Ontario K1A 0N8, tel. (613) 991-9970.

Taxes
Canada levies a seven percent **Goods and Services Tax** (GST) on most goods and services sold in Canada. Visitors to Canada can obtain a refund of the tax they pay on their accommodations (except campgrounds) and on most goods that they take out of Canada within 60 days of purchase. To make a claim, keep all receipts, grab a **GST Rebate Form** (available

where the rules are made—the legislature building in Edmonton at most gift shops and airports), and mail it to Revenue Canada, Customs and Excise, Visitor's Rebate Program, Ottawa, Ontario K1A 1JF, Canada. For more information call (800) 668-4748 or, outside Canada, call (613) 991-3346. Rebates cannot be claimed on groceries, restaurant meals, gas, alcohol, tobacco, or antiques.

Provincial Sales Tax applies in all provinces except Alberta and ranges 5-12% on most goods purchased in shops or restaurants. Although Alberta doesn't have this tax, it does have a five-percent **Provincial Room Tax.**

Note: All accommodations prices quoted in this guide do not include tax.

Firearms
Handguns, automatic guns, and sawed-off rifles and shotguns are not allowed entry into Canada. Visitors must declare all firearms at the border, and those that are restricted will be held by customs for the duration of your stay. Those not declared will be seized and charges may be laid. It is also illegal to be in possession of a firearm in a national park unless it is dismantled or carried in an enclosed case. Up to 5,000 rounds of ammunition may be imported but should be declared on entry. For further information on firearm regulations write to Revenue Canada, Customs and Excise, Commercial Verification and Enforcement, Connaught Building, Mackenzie Ave., Ottawa, Ontario K1A 0L5, Canada; tel. (613) 954-7129.

MONEY

As in the United States, Canadian currency is based on dollars and cents. Coins come in denominations of one, five, 10, and 25 cents, and one dollar. The one-dollar coin is the 11-sided gold-colored "loonie," named for the bird featured on it. The most common notes are $2, $5, $10, $20, and $50. A $100 bill does exist but is uncommon. Each note features a different bird. Until recently they depicted various Canadian scenes, including the town of Bluesky, north of Grande Prairie (on the $2 note), and Moraine Lake, in Banff National Park (on the $20 note).

All prices quoted in this book are in **Canadian dollars.** The exchange rate varies. For most of the '80s and early '90s it was around C$1.20: US$1, but in 1994 the Canadian dollar lost value against its American counterpart. The rate is currently in the neighborhood of C$1.40: US$1. American dollars are accepted at many tourist areas but the exchange rate will be more favorable at banks. Traveler's checks are the safest way to carry money but often a fee is charged to cash them if they're in a currency other than Canadian dollars. All major credit cards are honored at Canadian banks, gas stations, and most commercial establishments.

Tips are not usually added to a bill, and in general 15% of the total amount is given. Tips are most often given to waiters, waitresses, taxi drivers, doormen, bellhops, and bar staff.

Costs
The cost of living is lower in Alberta than in other provinces, but higher than in the United States. By planning ahead, having a tent or joining Hostelling International, and being prepared to cook your own meals, it is possible to get by on well under $50 per person per day. Gasoline is sold in liters (3.78 liters equals one U.S. gallon) and is generally 45-55 cents a liter for regular unleaded. North of Edmonton the price is higher, up to 70 cents a liter.

HEALTH

Compared to other parts of the world, Canada is a relatively safe place to visit. Vaccinations are required only if coming from a endemic area. That said, wherever you are traveling, carry a medical kit that includes bandages, insect repellent, sunscreen, antiseptic, antibiotics, and water-purification tablets. Good first-aid kits are available through most camping shops.

Taking out a travel-insurance policy is a sensible precaution, as hospital and medical charges start at around $1000 a day. Copies of prescriptions should be brought to Canada for any medicines already prescribed.

Giardia
Giardiasis, also known as beaver fever, is a real concern for those heading into the backcountry. It's caused by an intestinal parasite, *Giardia lamblia,* that lives in lakes, rivers, and streams. Once ingested, its effects, although not instan-

taneous, can be dramatic; severe diarrhea, cramps, and nausea are the most common. Preventive measures should always be taken, and include boiling all water for at least 10 minutes, treating all water with iodine, or filtering all water using a filter with a small enough pore size to block the *Giardia* cysts.

Winter Travel
Travel through the province during winter months should not be undertaken lightly. Before setting out in a vehicle, check antifreeze levels, and always carry a spare tire and blankets or sleeping bags. **Frostbite** is a potential hazard, especially when cold temperatures are combined with high winds (a combination known as **wind-chill**). Most often it leaves a numbing, bruised sensation and the skin turns white. Exposed areas of skin, especially the nose and ears, are most susceptible.

Hypothermia occurs when the body fails to produce heat as fast as it loses it. It can strike at any time of the year, but is more common during cooler months. Cold weather, combined with hunger, fatigue, and dampness, creates a recipe for disaster. Symptoms are not always apparent to the victim. The early signs are numbness, shivering, slurring of words, dizzy spells, and, in extreme cases, violent behavior, unconsciousness, and even death. The best way to dress for the cold is in layers, including a waterproof outer layer. Most importantly, wear headgear. The best treatment is to get the patient out of the cold, replace wet clothing with dry, slowly give hot liquids and sugary foods, and place the victim in a sleeping bag. Warming too quickly can lead to heart attacks.

SERVICES AND COMMUNICATIONS

All mail posted in Canada must have Canadian postage stamps attached. First-class letters and postcards are 43 cents to destinations within Canada, 47 cents to the U.S., and 88 cents to all other destinations. If you would like mail sent to you while traveling, have it addressed to yourself, c/o General Delivery, Main Post Office, in the city or town you request, Alberta, Canada. The post office will hold all general delivery mail for 15 days before returning it to the sender.

The telephone area code for Alberta and most of the Northwest Territories is **403.** All phone numbers in this book (except in the Keewatin and Baffin regions of the NWT which are **819**), unless otherwise noted, must be dialed with this prefix, including long-distance calls made within the province. The country code for Canada is 1, the same as the United States. Public phones accept 5-, 10-, and 25-cent coins. Local calls are 25 cents, and most long-distance calls cost at least $2.50 for the first minute from public phones.

Electrical voltage is 120 volts, the same as the United States. Alberta is on the **metric system** (see the "Metric Sysytem" chart at the back of this book), although many people talk in miles and supermarket prices are advertised in ounces and pounds. Visitors from outside North America will be confused with all electrical switches — they are upside-down. Visitors from the Southern Hemisphere will marvel at the washing-up water—when drained it flows clockwise. Visitors from England will be surprised at the color of the sky—it's always blue.

Shops are generally open Mon.-Fri. 9 a.m.-5 p.m., Saturday 9 a.m.-noon, and are closed on Sunday. Major shopping centers and those in resort towns are often open till 9 p.m. and all weekend. **Banks** are open Mon.-Fri. 9:30 a.m.-3:30 p.m., and till 4:30 or 5 p.m. on Friday.

MAPS AND INFORMATION

Maps
The province's major distributor of maps is **Maps Alberta,** 2nd Floor, 9945 108th St., Edmonton, Alberta T5K 2G6. By written request they can send out a catalogue of maps designed specifically for hiking (topographical maps), camping (road/access maps), fishing (hydrographic charts of over 100 lakes), and canoeing (river details such as gradients). They can also supply **Alberta Wall Maps, Canada Wall Maps, Thematic Maps, Historic Maps,** and **Aerial Photography.** These maps are also available over the counter at some sport and camping stores. **Map Town** at 640 6th Ave. SW in Calgary, tel. (403) 266-2241, and at 10815 100th Ave. in Edmonton, tel. (403) 429-2600, are the best city retail outlets for all of the above maps; some may have to be ordered.

Information

The best source of tourist information—up-to-date information on all accommodations, attractions, and events—is **Alberta Tourism,** P.O. Box 2500, Edmonton, Alberta T5J 2Z4, tel. (403) 427-4321 or, from within North America, (800) 661-8888. They also produce two excellent publications, *Alberta Accommodation Guide* and *Alberta Campground Guide* and a road map. All major routes into the province have a **Travel Alberta Information Centre,** generally open in summer only with all the same information (except you must pay for the road maps). Each town has a **tourist information center,** each with its own hours, and usually open June-August. When these are closed head to the chamber of commerce (year-round, Mon.-Fri. only) for information.

Within the United States, offices for Alberta Economic Development and Tourism are located in San Diego, Washington, New York, and Chicago. But the best source of information is Alberta Tourism's 800-number, listed above.

Canada House, Trafalgar Square, London SWI 5BJ, has a large tourism section with current information and well-informed staff. **Alberta House,** 1 Mount St., London, tel. (071) 491-3430, has limited tourism information, but a small library and business section is open to the public. In Germany, the same office is at Taunusstrasse 52-60, 6000 Frankfurt. In Australia, **Integra Travel,** at Level 4, 3 Northcliff St., Milsons Point, tel. (02) 959-4277 is the agent for Alberta Tourism.

BOB RACE

KAREN McKINLEY

SOUTHERN ALBERTA

Southern Alberta is bordered to the east by Saskatchewan, to the south by Montana, U.S.A., and to the west by British Columbia. The Alberta/British Columbia border is along the Continental Divide, where the Rocky Mountains rise dramatically from the prairies and are visible from up to 200 km away. From high in these mountains the Oldman, Crowsnest, Waterton, St. Mary, and Belly rivers flow east through the rolling foothills and across the shortgrass prairies into the South Saskatchewan River, which eventually drains into Hudson Bay. Among southern Alberta's rivers, only the Milk River is not part of this system; from its headwaters in northern Montana, the river flows north and east across southern Alberta before re-entering the U.S. west of Wild Horse. From there it joins the Missouri/Mississippi River system, eventually draining into the Gulf of Mexico. All these rivers have carved deep gorges into the prairies, providing a haven for many species of wildlife including pronghorn, deer, foxes, coyotes, and bobcats.

For many people, a trip to southern Alberta starts in Alberta's third-largest city, **Lethbridge,** a farming and ranching center 216 km southeast of Calgary. Lethbridge offers a host of interesting things to see including Fort Whoop-Up, a reconstruction of a notorious post where whiskey was traded with the Indians for buffalo hides, guns, and horses.

East of Lethbridge, in an area declared "unsuitable for agriculture" by early explorer John Palliser, the city of **Medicine Hat** has grown up on top of vast reserves of natural gas. Traveling south from Medicine Hat, the **Cypress Hills** soon come into view, rising 500 meters above the prairies. The tree-covered plateau provides a refuge for many species of mammals, and mountain plants flourish here, far from the Rockies.

Southern Alberta reveals plentiful evidence of its history and prehistory. Thousands of years of wind and water erosion have uncovered the world's best-preserved dinosaur eggs near **Milk River,** and have carved mysterious-looking sandstone hoodoos farther downstream at **Writing-On-Stone Provincial Park**—named for the abundant rock carvings and paintings created there by ancient artists. And **Head-Smashed-In Buffalo Jump,** west of Fort Macleod, was used for at least 5,700 years by native peoples to drive massive herds of buffalo to their deaths.

The breathtaking mountainscapes of **Waterton Lakes National Park** are comparable to those of Banff and Jasper national parks, Waterton's two northern neighbors. The route to the park is scenic as the transition from prairie to mountain peaks is abrupt. Most activities in the park center around a series of deep lakes, but the park also offers some of the best wildlife-viewing opportunities in the province. One of the highlights of a visit to Waterton is an international cruise across the border to Goat Haunt, Montana.

The **Municipality of Crowsnest Pass** is comprised of a number of small communities that extend from the ranching center of **Pincher Creek** west to the British Columbia border. They were established to serve the pass's coal-mining industry, but after a series of disasters—some mining related, some not—the mines closed. Today the towns are only a shadow of their former selves, and the entire corridor has been declared an ecomuseum. Here you can walk through the foundations of once-thriving communities, tour an underground mine, or climb infamous Turtle Mountain.

For more information on southwestern Alberta, write to Chinook Country Tourist Association, 2805 Scenic Dr., Lethbridge, Alberta T1K 5B7; tel. (403) 329-6777 or (800) 661-1222. For information on the Medicine Hat region including Cypress Hills write to Southeastern Travel Association, P.O. Box 605, Medicine Hat, Alberta T1A 7G5; tel. (403) 527-6422.

LETHBRIDGE

An urban oasis on the prairies, this city of rich ethnic origins has come a long way since the 1860s when **Fort Whoop-Up,** the most notorious whiskey-trading fort in the West, was the main reason folks came to town. Today, Lethbridge is an important commercial center serving the surrounding ranch and farm country. With a population of 60,000, it is Alberta's third-largest city, and on any given day the downtown streets are busy with a colorful array of ranchers, cowboys, Hutterites, Indians, and suited professionals. The city is also a transportation hub, with Highways 3, 4, and 5 converging here.

Calgary is 215 km to the north, Medicine Hat 168 km to the east, Waterton Lakes National Park 130 km to the west, and the International Boundary 105 km to the south.

In the last 20 years, Lethbridge has blossomed in a controlled way. Many of the city's sites of historical importance have been preserved, or in the case of Fort Whoop-Up, reconstructed. The Sir Alexander Galt Museum is one of the best museums in the province and the Nikka Yuko Japanese Garden is symbolic of the culture from which many of the city's residents descended.

© MOON PUBLICATIONS, INC.

History

Lethbridge has always been a transportation and trade crossroads. Until the first half of the 19th century it was the territory of various tribes of the powerful Blackfoot Indians. The tribes sheltered from the extreme winters at a site in the Oldman River Valley known to them as Sikooh-kotoks or "black rocks" because of an exposed coal seam on the east bank of the river at that spot. The first white traders to the area arrived in the 1850s. Soon after came the whiskey traders who had been forced north by the U.S. Army. Fort Whoop-Up, built on the east bank of the Oldman River, became the most notorious of some 50 whiskey posts in southern Alberta.

The arrival of whiskey on the plains coincided with a smallpox epidemic and the dislocation of Cree, who had been forced by the arrival of European settlers into the territory of the Blackfoot, their traditional enemies. These factors all combined to create a setting for the last great intertribal Indian battle to be fought in North America.

At dawn on 25 October 1870, a party of around 800 Cree warriors attacked a band of Blood Blackfoot camping on the west bank of the Oldman River. Unknown to the Cree, a large party of Piegan Blackfoot were camped nearby. Alerted by scouts, they crossed the river and joined the fray, forcing the Cree back into what is now known as Indian Battle Park. Over 300 Cree and around 50 Blackfoot were killed.

By 1880, the whiskey forts had been closed down by the North West Mounted Police and the last of the plains Indians had been resettled in reservations.

Nicholas Sheran, an Irish-American adventurer, was the first to realize the potential of the coal-bearing seams along the Oldman River. He established the first mine on the river, named Coalbanks. It was only a small operation, but it was large enough to attract the attention of English entrepreneur Elliot Galt. With the help of his father—Sir Alexander Galt—Elliot financed a large-scale drift mine in the east bank of the river, where the Coalbanks Interpretive Site now sits. By 1884, the hamlet of Coalbanks had sprung up around the mine entrance and a sawmill was established. At first the Galts used sternwheel river steamers to transport the coal to Medicine Hat. But on many occasions, the current was so strong that the steamers required as much coal for the return trip as they were capable of hauling on the way out. So after two years, a narrow-gauge railway was constructed to haul the coal. This shifted the community's focus away from the river's edge and up onto the prairie, where the town that took root came to be named Lethbridge. William Lethbridge was an Englishman who never set foot in Alberta, but being a friend of Galt, and a major financier in the Galt's coal mine, the town was named for him.

In 1909 the High Level Bridge—at that time the highest and longest structure of its type in the world—was constructed over the river valley, completing a more permanent link to Fort Macleod and Calgary. The last of the mines closed in 1942 and by 1960 the first of what is now a string of urban parks along the valley was established.

We have passed through a country, dry, desolate, and barren, a very Sahara. It was the northern portion of the Great American Desert: but now we have fortunately come into a country that shows even in this late season, evidence of great fertility. We are just near the base of the Rocky Mountains; their snow-capped summits rise up to our left in jagged, rough peaks; the sun sinks behind them every night in one blaze of glory, making the most gorgeous sunsets that I have ever seen.

—R.B. Nevitt, 11 October 1874

SIGHTS

Downtown

With Lethbridge continuing to sprawl, particularly on the west side of the river, downtown businesses are trying their hardest to convince shoppers and visitors that "Downtown L.A." really does have something to offer. Almost all sites downtown are within walking distance of each other. **Lethbridge Centre** is a modern shopping mall; **Galt Gardens** is a pleasant spot for people-watching; a small **Chinatown** is located along 2nd Ave. S; and many historic buildings

© MOON PUBLICATIONS, INC.

still stand. On market days, the many Hutterites who come to town are easy to recognize—the men wear black pants and have beards, the women wear colorful purple and red dresses and bonnets. Arty types will enjoy hanging out in **Crafter's Mall,** 435 5th St. S, which has shops selling woodcrafts, painting supplies, and do-it-yourself kits. The **Southern Alberta Art Gallery,** 601 3rd Ave. S in Galt Gardens, tel. (403) 327-8770, has contemporary and historical exhibitions that change throughout the year. It's open Tues.-Sat. 10 a.m.-5 p.m., Sunday 1-5 p.m.; admission by donation.

Sir Alexander Galt Museum

This excellent history-and-art museum is in a former hospital, named for Sir Alexander Galt who helped finance the coal-mining operation that was fundamental in the establishment of the city. It was renovated in 1985 at a cost of $2.85 million and is now considered one of the best small-city museums in the country. The first gallery provides a view across the valley—in effect a panorama of the city's past. From this vantage point you can see the site of the last major intertribal battle in North America, as well as old coal mines, Fort Whoop-Up, and the High Level Bridge. Other galleries contain exhibits explaining the history of the coal mines, the introduction of irrigation, the area's immigrants, and the city since WW II. Two additional galleries have rotating art exhibits of local interest. The museum is located at the west end of 5th Ave. S off Scenic Drive. It's open July-Aug., Mon.-Thurs. 9 a.m.-8 p.m., Friday 9 a.m.-4 p.m., Sat.-Sun. 1-8 p.m.; the rest of the year, Mon.-Fri. 10 a.m.-4 p.m., Sat.-Sun. 1-4 p.m. Admission is free. For more information call (403) 320-3898.

DOWNTOWN LETHBRIDGE

Fort Whoop-Up

This impressively palisaded structure in Indian Battle Park is a replica of the most notorious whiskey-trading post in the West. After the U.S. Army put a stop to the illicit trade in Montana, these traders of sorts simply began moving north into what is now Alberta. In December 1869, John J. Healy and Alfred B. Hamilton came north from Fort Benton, Montana and established a fort on the Oldman River which soon became the whiskey-trading headquarters for southern Alberta. The story goes that its name was coined by someone who had returned to Fort Benton and when asked how things were going at Hamilton's Fort replied, "oh, they're still whoopin' it up." Trading was simple. Indians pushed buffalo hides through a small opening in the fort wall. In return they were handed a tin cup of whiskey. The success of the trade led to the formation of the North West Mounted Police, who rode west with orders to close down all whiskey-trading forts and end the lawless industry. The Mounties were preceded by word of their approach and the fort was empty by the time they arrived. A cairn marks the fort's original location.

A reconstruction of the fort, complete with costumed staff, relives the days when firewater was traded for hides and horses. The fort looks much as it would have in 1869. A cannon used to defend the fort is on display, an audiovisual presentation is shown, and the Whoop-Up flag—now the official flag of Lethbridge—flies high above. To get there from the city center turn west onto 3rd Ave. S and follow it down into the coulee. It's open mid-May to early September, Mon.-Sat. 10 a.m.-6 p.m., Sunday noon-8 p.m.; admission by donation. For more information call (403) 329-0444.

Lethbridge Nature Reserve And Helen Schuler Coulee Centre

Lethbridge is unique in that it's built on the prairie benchlands and not beside the river that flows so close to town. The largely undisturbed Oldman River Valley has been developed into a series of reserves and parks. One of these, the Lethbridge Nature Reserve, is a 78-hectare area of floodplain and coulees. It's home to Alberta's provincial bird—the great horned owl—as well as porcupines, white-tailed deer, and prairie rattlesnakes. It's also home to the Helen Schuler Coulee Centre, which offers interpretive displays focusing on the entire urban park system. The center is the best place to start exploration of the valley. From here three short trails lead through the reserve. To get there from downtown, head west on 3rd Ave. S, take a right just before Fort Whoop-Up, and pass under the High Level Bridge. It's open June-Aug., Sun.-Thurs. 10 a.m.-8 p.m., Fri.-Sat. 10 a.m.-6 p.m.; the rest of the year, Tues.-Sun. 1-4 p.m. For more information call (403) 320-3064.

Other Valley Parks

The most historically important urban park in Lethbridge is **Indian Battle Park.** It is named after the last great battle fought between Cree and Blackfoot which took place on the west side of the river in 1870. Within the park, near Fort Whoop-Up, is a "medicine stone" that the Blackfoot believed had sacred significance—for many years they left offerings around it. Also in the park, the **Coalbanks Interpretive Site** is located at the site of the original mine entrance towards the Helen Schuler Coulee Centre. Coalbanks, founded in 1874, was the original settlement in the valley. Indian Battle Park extends from the Oldman River to behind the buildings up on Scenic Drive. Many viewpoints can be found along the top of the coulee, accessible by timber steps leading up from the floodplain below.

Botterill Bottom Park, adjacent to Indian Battle Park, houses underground utility lines and cannot be developed. Across the Oldman River is **Bull Trail Park,** an undeveloped area that extends south to the university. To the north is **Elizabeth Hall Wetlands,** a 15-hectare reserve of floodplain habitat that encompasses an oxbow pond. North of the Lethbridge Nature Reserve is **Peenaquim Park,** 97 hectares of floodplain that was formerly a stockyard. Access to **Alexander Wilderness Park** is from Stafford Dr. North. This road descends into a coulee and three short trails radiate out along the floodplain to viewpoints of the Oldman River. The northernmost river-valley park is **Pavan Park.** The entrance road winds down a narrow coulee to a day-use area by the Oldman River. Here a reclaimed gravel pit is stocked with trout; short walks lead along the floodplain; and a picnic area has firewood and fire rings.

High Level Bridge

High Level Bridge

High Level Bridge spans 1.6 km and towers 100 meters above the Oldman River Valley—the longest and highest trestle-construction bridge in the world. It was built by the C.P.R. for $1.3 million in 1909, replacing 22 wooden bridges and drastically reducing the length of line between Lethbridge and Fort Macleod. Over 12,000 tons of steel were used in its construction, as well as 17,000 cubic yards of concrete, and 7,600 gallons of paint. Of the many views of the bridge available along the valley, none is better than standing directly underneath (walk down from the tourist information center on Brewery Hill).

Nikka Yuko Japanese Garden

This garden was established in 1967 by the City of Lethbridge and its Japanese residents as a monument "to the contribution made to Canadian culture by Canadians of Japanese origin." It has been designed as a place to relax and contemplate, with no bright flowers, only green shrubs and gardens of rock and sand. The buildings and bridges were built in Japan under the supervision of a renowned Japanese architect. The main pavilion is of traditional design housing a *tokonoma* or tea ceremony room. Japanese women in traditional dress lead visitors through the gardens and explain the philosophy behind different aspects of the design. The best view of the garden is from the bell tower whose gentle "gong" signifies good things happening in both countries simultaneously. Open mid-May to early October, daily 9 a.m.-5 p.m., till 8 p.m. during summer; admission $2.50. The gardens are located in Henderson Lake Park on Mayor Magrath Dr., tel. (403) 328-3511.

RECREATION

Activities in **Henderson Lake Park** on Mayor Magrath Dr. center around a 20-hectare man-made lake that attracts residents year-round. The park features an outdoor swimming pool, tennis courts, demonstration gardens, boat rentals on the lake, and an 18-hole golf course. A paved trail for hikers and cyclists encircles the lake. Another popular recreation spot is **Park Lake Provincial Park,** 17 km north of Lethbridge on Hwy. 25. This once-arid prairie region has been transformed by irrigation. In summer, the lake is a good spot for swimming, windsurfing, fishing, and boating (boat rentals available). Camping is $11 per night; a concession sells fast food.

Lethbridge linksters can choose among five area golf courses. **Henderson Lake Golf Club,** tel. (403) 329-6767, is within walking distance of the lake's campground ($24); **Bridge Valley Golf Club,** tel. 381-6363, is a par-three course on the west side of the High Level Bridge ($9); and **Paradise Canyon,** tel. 381-7500, near the University, is Alberta's newest championship course and was constructed on a reclaimed floodplain along the Oldman River ($28). The other two courses are private.

Across from the library is the **YMCA,** 515

Stafford Dr. S, tel. 327-9622, which has a pool, weight room, and health club available for $2.80 per session. Ask about the "first visit is free" program. The $5.3-million **Max Bell Regional Aquatic Centre** in the University of Lethbridge, tel. 329-2583, is also open to the public; $2.80 for a swim. **Grand Slam Canada Recreation Centre,** on the corner of Mayor Magrath and Scenic drives, tel. 320-5800, has automated batting cages, as well as go-carts and mini-golf. It's open in summer daily 10 a.m.-6 p.m., shorter hours the rest of the year.

Anderson Aquatics, 314 11th St. S., tel. 328-5040, is one of Alberta's few scuba-diving shops. Diving trips and lessons run throughout summer. The shop also rents equipment and fills tanks for those heading to Waterton Lakes National Park.

ENTERTAINMENT

A Little Bit Of Culture
The Sterndale Bennett Theatre in the Yates Memorial Centre at 110 4th Ave. S is home to **New West Theatre,** an amateur company whose popular summer performances sell out most nights. Productions are generally a combination of comedy, song, and dance appealing to everybody. For ticket information call (403) 320-3844. The **Lethbridge Symphony Orchestra** has its office in Yates Centre but performs at various locations throughout the city; call 328-6808 for dates and prices. The **Performing Arts Centre** at the University of Lethbridge attracts national and international acts to its three theaters. For upcoming events call 329-2656. The four **movie theaters** in town charge $6-7 and Tuesday is half-price night. One is in the Lethbridge Centre downtown, another on the corner of 8th St. and 4th Ave. South.

A Little Less Culture
The **Cactus Club** in the Parkside Inn at 1009 Mayor Magrath Dr. S whoops it up with live country music on Friday and Saturday nights; cover charge $2. Rhinestone cowboys head to **Rattlesnake Saloon** in Billy MacIntyre's Cattle Company at 1621 3rd Ave. S, for country atmosphere with authentic furnishings, piped-in music, and a pool table. It's open till 2 a.m. nightly except Sunday. If country music isn't your style, head to **Hollywood** at 202 5th St. S for Top 40, or have a beer with the boys next door in the **Lethbridge Hotel.**

Festivals And Events
For a city of its size, Lethbridge offers surprisingly few festivals. The year's biggest event, **Whoop-Up Days,** is held at Fort Whoop-Up and at other locations in the city throughout the first week of July. The celebration features pancake breakfasts, a parade, midway, casino, trade show, and grandstand events such as a rodeo. Nightly concerts and cabarets end each day's excitement. For more information call (403) 328-4491. Also at Fort Whoop-Up, on the second Sunday in July, fiddlers and other country musicians gather for pickin' and grinnin'. For more information call 329-0444.

ACCOMMODATIONS

Downtown
Of the four downtown accommodations, **Motel Magic,** 100 3rd Ave. S, tel. (403) 327-6000 or (800) 661-8085, has the best-value rooms. Rates include a continental breakfast, coffee, and use of an exercise room; $46 s, $50 d. Across the road is the **Travelodge,** 207 4th Ave. S, tel. 327-2104 or (800) 578-7878, which has large rooms; $52 s, $56 d. **Lethbridge Lodge Hotel,** 320 Scenic Dr. S, tel. 328-1123 or (800) 661-1232, has the most modern facilities. Many rooms have views of the Oldman River Valley, the others of an enclosed tropical atrium. Amenities include a cafe, restaurant, cocktail lounge, and an indoor pool with a whirlpool; $76 s, $81 d. At the other end of the scale is the **Lethbridge Hotel,** 202 5th St. S, tel. 327-3151, where rooms with shared bathrooms are $26-31 s or d.

Mayor Magrath Drive
About a dozen motels of varying standards but similar prices line Mayor Magrath Dr. S (Hwy. 5). Many have restaurants, those that don't are within walking distance of others that do. Also nearby is Nikka Yuko Japanese Garden and Henderson Lake Park. From north to south the best are: **Sandman Inn,** 421 Mayor Magrath Dr. S, tel. (403) 328-1111 or (800) 663-6900,

with an indoor pool and a 24-hour restaurant, $66 s, $71 d; **El Rancho,** 526 Mayor Magrath Dr. S, tel. 327-5701, with rooms much nicer than the exterior suggests, $42 s or d; **Bridge Town House,** 1026 Mayor Magrath Dr. S, tel. 327-4576, which has large rooms, $42 s, $46 d. **Sundance Inn,** 1030 Mayor Magrath Dr. S, tel. 328-6636 or (800) 561-9815, with rooms as good as anywhere along the strip but only $45 s or d; **Heidelberg Inn,** 1303 Mayor Magrath Dr. S, tel. 329-0555 or (800) 528-1234, a Best Western with a pool and restaurant, $58 s, $62 d; and **Chinook Motel,** next door to the Heidelburg Inn, $37 s or d; check in at the Heidelberg.

Heritage House B&B
Heritage House B&B, 1115 8th Ave. S, tel. (403) 328-9011, is an excellent alternative to the motels. The 1937 home is considered one of the finest examples of International–Art Deco design in the province. Its rooms are spacious and tastefully decorated, a hearty breakfast is served downstairs in the dining room, and town is only a short walk along the tree-lined streets of Lethbridge's most sought-after suburb. The bathroom is shared, but for $35 s, $45 d, that is of little consequence.

Campgrounds
Henderson Lake Campground is located on 7th Ave. S. in Henderson Lake Park, tel. (403) 328-5452. It has full hookups, showers, a laundry, groceries, firewood, and fire rings. The serviced section is little more than a paved parking lot, but tenters and those with small vans will enjoy the privacy afforded by trees at the back of the campground. Unserviced sites cost $11, those with hookups are $13.50-17.50. **Bridgeview Campground,** on the west bank of the Oldman River at 910 4th Ave. S, tel. 381-2357, has similar facilities to Henderson Lake Campground, but the nearby highway can be noisy. Unserviced sites here go for $11, while hookups are $13.50-17.50. Two other alternatives are **Park Lake Provincial Park,** 17 km

Fort Whoop-Up's flag is now the official flag of Lethbridge.

northwest of town on Hwy. 25, which offers camping (no showers or hookups) for $11 per night; and **St. Mary Reservoir,** 40 km south on Hwy. 5, where sites in a primitive campground cost $7.50 a night.

FOOD

Downtown
It's the nostalgic 1890s at **Showdowns Eatin' Adventures,** 329 5th St. S, tel. (403) 329-8830, with gunfights down the aisles and can-can girls giving you glimpses of things you shouldn't be looking at—and that's before you've even ordered! Eating here really is an experience not to be missed. The best action is in the evening but the act goes on all day. Most of the dishes are under $10, steaks are $11-15. Digging into a generous portion of Texas ribs ($13.95) without a knife and fork is a good way to get into the swing of things and it'll keep the can-can dancers off your lap to boot. It's open Mon.-Thurs. 11 a.m.-11 p.m., Fri.-Sat. 11 a.m.-midnight, Sunday noon-10 p.m.

Anton's, in the Lethbridge Lodge, tel. 328-1123, is the only true fine-dining restaurant in town, serving dinner daily from 5 p.m. The menu is extensive and the dishes well prepared. Appetizers start at $2, entrees from $13. Also in the lodge is the **Garden Cafe,** open daily 6:30 a.m.-11:30 p.m. and always busy with guests and locals alike. Meals are moderately priced and are served amid much greenery. The dessert cabinet is strategically placed so that even the most health-conscious diner can't help but be tempted by it.

Good, inexpensive Vietnamese food is dished up at **Kim Long Restaurant,** 328 5th St. S, tel. 380-3866, open daily 10 a.m.-10 p.m., till midnight on Friday and Saturday. Most dishes are under $8. If the menu looks Greek to you, ask to see the family photo album which has color photographs of each dish. Leave a tip; the service is good and the place needs a coat of paint. Lethbridge has some fine coffee shops—pick of the bunch is **The Penny Coffee House,** 331 5th St. S, tel. 320-5282, where coffee is a buck, refills are free, and a nice, thick, healthy, sandwich with soup is $5.25. It's open Mon.-Fri. 8:30 a.m.-10 p.m., Saturday 8:30 a.m.-5:30 p.m., Sunday noon-5 p.m.

Third Avenue South
Billy MacIntyre's Cattle Company, 1621 3rd Ave. S, tel. (403) 327-2727, has a real Western atmosphere and is always busy (expect a wait on Saturday nights). Though chicken and seafood are on the menu, the steaks are the reason locals keep coming back. Unless you're a vegetarian, it would be a shame to order anything else. Dinner entrees start at $11; the lunch menu is much the same but slightly less expensive. Open Mon.-Thurs. 11:30 a.m.-9 p.m., Friday 11:30 a.m.-11 p.m., Saturday 4-11 p.m., and Sunday 4-9 p.m. The Chinese buffet at **Enjoy Gardens,** 1903 3rd Ave. S, tel. 328-8770, is also popular. Lunch (daily 11 a.m.-2:30 p.m.) is $4.95, and dinner (5-8:30 p.m.) is $7.95. Nearby, **Treasure Chest Restaurant,** 311 4th St. S, tel. 327-6133, has a menu offering over 200 Chinese dishes, which is both unique and a little worrying at the same time. **O-Sho Japanese Restaurant,** 1219 3rd Ave. S, tel. 327-8382, serves authentic Japanese cuisine; you can sit at standard tables or dine in traditional style on mats in partitioned lounges. Lunch is $4-6, dinner $6.70-10. It's open for lunch Mon.-Fri. 11:30 a.m.-2:30 p.m., and for dinner Mon.-Fri. 4:30-10 p.m., Saturday 4-10:30 p.m.

Mayor Magrath Drive
As well as having the bulk of Lethbridge's accommodations, this road has many fast-food and family restaurants. **Treats Eatery,** 1104 Mayor Magrath Dr. S, tel. (403) 380-4880, is another Western-style family-dining restaurant. It has an enormous gold-rimmed wagon wheel hanging from the ceiling—ask to sit away from it if you like. The menu is straightforward, basically burgers and beef, but is well-priced. Hours are Mon.-Sat. 11 a.m.-10 p.m., Sunday 4-10 p.m. The **Beefeater Steakhouse,** 1917 Mayor Magrath Dr. S, tel. 320-6211, is a traditional English restaurant offering traditional Albertan dishes; the prime rib of beef is especially good. Lunch is $7-12, and dinner specials start at $12. It's open Mon.-Sat. 11 a.m.-midnight, Sunday 11 a.m.-9 p.m. Farther up the road is the impressive **Sven Ericksen's Family Restaurant,** 1715 Mayor Magrath Dr. S, tel. (403) 328-7756. The menu here is heavy on the seafood—odd for a place so far from the ocean. But enough beef and chicken dishes are offered for fishophobes to get by. It's open Mon.-Fri. 11 a.m.-10 p.m., Sat.-Sun. 11 a.m.-11 p.m.

TRANSPORTATION

Lethbridge Airport is eight km south of town on Hwy. 5. It is served by **Canadian Regional,** tel. (403) 327-3000 or (800) 665-1177, and **Air B.C.,** tel. (800) 332-1080, an Air Canada connector. Both fly to Calgary four to seven times daily ($76 one way, $98 roundtrip if bought 14 days in advance) with connections to Edmonton and other national and international destinations. Some motels and car-rental companies have courtesy phones at the airport. A cab to downtown is around $16.

The **Greyhound** bus depot is at 411 5th St. S, tel. 327-1551 or (800) 661-8747. Buses leave twice daily for Fort Macleod ($5.78), four times daily for Calgary ($24.82) with connections to Edmonton ($54.78), twice daily to Medicine Hat ($19.10) and to the United States border at Coutts ($12.04), where connections to Great Falls and Helena (Montana) can be made. The depot is open daily 7:30 a.m.-7:30 p.m. and has a small cafe and lockers that are large enough for backpacks ($1).

L.A. Transit city buses run daily with limited service on Sunday. The main routes radiate from Lethbridge Centre on 4th Ave. S, out to the university, Henderson Lake Park, and along Mayor Magrath Drive. The adult fare is $1.10. Call 320-3885 for schedules and information. The various car-rental agency numbers are: **Rent-A-Wreck,** tel. 328-9484 ($28.95 per day with 100 free km); **Avis,** tel. 382-4880; **Budget,** tel. 328-6555; and **Tilden,** tel. 329-3521. For a taxi call **Fifth Avenue Cabs,** tel. 381-1111; **Lethbridge Cabs,** tel. 327-4005; or **Royal Taxi,** tel. 328-5333.

SERVICES AND INFORMATION

The **post office** is in a historic stone building at 704 4th Ave. South. Make a day of it at **Family Coin Laundry,** 128 Mayor Magrath Dr. N, one block north of the highway, where there's a lounge, TV, and free coffee; open daily 8 a.m.-9 p.m. **Lethbridge Regional Hospital** is at 9th Ave. and 18th St. S, tel. (403) 382-6111. For the **RCMP** call 329-5010.

Lethbridge Public Library, 810 5th Ave. S, tel. 380-7310, is an excellent facility with a wide range of literature; open Mon.-Fri. 9:30 a.m.-9 p.m., Saturday 9:30 a.m.-5:30 p.m., and Sunday 1:30-5:30 p.m. The best bookstore in town is **B. Macabee's Booksellers** at 333 5th St. S, tel. 329-0771. They have a large selection of local history and Canadiana books. After brows-ing, why don't you let the smell from The Penny Coffee House lure you next door. The **Lethbridge Herald** is a daily (except Sunday) newspaper available throughout town.

Lethbridge's main **tourist information center** is at 2805 Scenic Dr. (at the corner of Highways 4 and 5). It's open in summer daily 8 a.m.-9 p.m., the rest of the year Mon.-Sat. 9 a.m.-5 p.m., tel. 320-1222 or (800) 661-1212 from western Canada and the northwestern United States. A second office near downtown is on Hwy. 3 W (1st Ave. S from the east) at Brewery Hill, beside the former site of the Lethbridge Brewery (a site known as **Brewery Gardens** for the thousands of vividly colored flowers that bloom there each summer). This small center is open in summer daily 8 a.m.-9 p.m., the rest of the year Tues.-Sun. 9 a.m.-5 p.m.; tel. 320-1223.

EAST OF LETHBRIDGE

THE MILK RIVER

The town of Milk River (population 920) sits on the northern bank of its namesake, 90 km southeast of Lethbridge and 40 km north of the Montana border. The Milk River is unique among western Canada's river systems. All the others eventually drain east into Hudson's Bay, but the Milk River flows south to the Missouri River, eventually draining into the Gulf of Mexico. The area itself is historically unique for western Canada in that it has come under the jurisdiction of eight different governments and countries. During the 1700s, France claimed all the lands of the Mississippi, so a small part of Alberta was under French rule. Later, the same area was part of the Spanish empire, and it's also at one time or another fallen under the rule of the Hudson's Bay Company, the British, and the Americans. It finally became part of the province of Alberta in 1905. A flag display and a historical cairn on the north bank of the river explain this complicated piece of Albertan history.

On 14 May 1987, an amateur palaeontologist was exploring the coulees near her family's ranch outside of Milk River when she discovered some fossilized egg shells. The find sent waves of excitement around the scientific world and become known as **Devil's Coulee Dinosaur Egg Site,** one of the most exciting fossil discoveries ever made. What she had discovered were clutches of eggs that had been laid by hadrosaurs around 75 million years ago. Each prehistoric egg was about 20 centimeters long and contained the perfectly formed embryonic bones of unborn dinosaurs. No find in the world has taught scientists more about this part of the dinosaur's life cycle. The site is closed to the public. It is managed by the Royal Tyrrell Museum of Palaeontology in Drumheller; for more information call (403) 823-7707.

The **Southgate Inn,** at the north end of town, tel. 647-3733, has basic rooms, $40 s, $44 d, as does **Milk River Inn** downtown, tel. 647-2257. **Milk River Campground** in town is nothing more than a dusty parking lot with firewood and power; $5 per night. South toward Montana, 20 km along Hwy. 4, **Gold Spring Park** is much nicer and the same price. A cafe/restaurant in the Milk River Inn is open till 10 p.m., and across the road is the **Delicia Bakery** which lives up to its name. Highway 4 is the main route into Alberta from the United States. The Coutts/Sweetgrass border crossing is open 24 hours a day year-round. An **Alberta Tourism Information Centre** south of Milk River greets travelers crossing the border. It provides copious information and an interpretive center highlighting aspects of tourism within the province. The center, tel. 647-3938, is open May-Sept., daily 8 a.m.-7:30 p.m.; the rest of the year, Thurs.-Mon. 10 a.m.-5 p.m.

Water Sports On The Milk River

The Milk River is popular with canoeists of all levels of expertise, although no rapids exceed class I. What the river lacks in rapids it more than makes up for in scenic beauty and rich history. The first section from Del Bonita to Milk River passes through shortgrass prairie, and the shallow river valley allows panoramic views of the landscape. This long section (103 km) passes through mainly private property and has a few fence wires that cross the river. Past the town of Milk River, the river valley becomes deeper and enters the badlands of Writing-On-Stone Provincial Park (69 km from Milk River).

Milk River Raft Tours, P.O. Box 396, Milk River, Alberta TOK 1MO, tel. (403) 647-3586, offers a selection of trips down the river in inflatable rafts. The trips last from two to four hours and can be enjoyed by everyone. Tours run throughout summer, leaving from various staging areas downstream of the town of Milk River. Costs range $10-25. Call ahead for more information and reservations. **Roger's Outdoor Adventures,** 922 9th St. S, Lethbridge, Alberta T1J 2M2, tel. (403) 329-1374, offers longer canoe trips lasting one to four days. Each trip has a different theme such as wildlife (two days, $130), history and geology (two days, $130), and painting and drawing (four days, $250).

WRITING-ON-STONE PROVINCIAL PARK

This park 43 km east of the town of Milk River on Hwy. 501 has everything: a warm river for swimming, great canoeing, intriguing rock formations, abundant wildlife, and the largest concentrations of petroglyphs (rock carvings) and pictographs (rock paintings) found in North America. The native rock art lies hidden on sandstone cliffs along the banks of the **Milk River,** which has cut a deep valley into the rolling shortgrass prairie. The soft sandstone and shale cliffs here are capped with harder, iron-rich sediments. Years of wind and water erosion have carved out the softer, lower rock, leaving mushroom-shaped pinnacles and columns called **hoodoos.** A number of plant and animal species here are found nowhere else in Alberta. Look for pronghorn on the grassland, bobcats and mule deer in the coulees, yellow-bellied marmots sunning themselves on sandstone outcrops. Don't look *too* hard for rattlesnakes, usually found in shady spots among the cliffs.

The Meaning Of It All

Writing-On-Stone was a place of great spiritual importance to generations of plains Indian tribes, a place for contact with the supernatural. They attempted to interpret previous carvings and paintings, added their own artwork to the rock, and left gifts of tobacco and beads as a way of communicating with the spirits of the dead. Much

hoodoos above the campground

of the cliff art remains visible today, providing clues to the region's early inhabitants.

Artifacts excavated from below the cliffs suggest the area had been inhabited for at least 3,000 years, but any rock art of that age would have been destroyed by erosion long ago. Dating the remaining petroglyphs and pictographs is difficult. They aren't covered in the layers of sediment usually used to date sites, nor can radiocarbon dating be applied—it requires wood or bone to test. The only way of dating the rock art is to estimate its age based on recognizable artistic styles or the depiction of certain historic events (such as the arrival of the white man). Of the carvings visible today, the earliest are thought to be the work of the Shoshones, done around 700 years ago. Their work is characterized by warriors on foot carrying ornately decorated shields, while isolated images of elk, bears, and rattlesnakes appear as simple stylized outlines. During the 1730s, the Shoshones were driven into the mountains by Blackfoot Indians, who had acquired horses and guns before other plains Indians. The valley's strange rock formations led the Blackfoot to believe that the area was a magical place—a place to be respected and feared—and that existing carvings were created by the spirits. The Blackfoot added their own artistry to the rocks, and many of the Blackfoot carvings are panels that tell a story. A striking change of lifestyle was documented on the rock faces, corresponding to the arrival of guns and horses to the plains Indian tribes. Mounted warriors armed with rifles dominate later artworks, the most famous being a battle scene containing over 250 characters.

Into The Twentieth Century

A North West Mounted Police post was established at Writing-On-Stone in 1889 to stop the whiskey trade and curb fighting among Indian tribes. The Mounties passed time by using the petroglyphs for target practice and carving their names into a cliff that has become known as Signature Rock. The original NWMP post buildings were washed away by floodwaters, replaced, then destroyed by fire in 1918. In 1957 the area was officially designated a provincial park. Access to much of the park is restricted to prevent further damage to the carvings. A reconstructed NWMP post sits within this area at the mouth of **Police Coulee**. The best way to

get a feel for the park and its history is by participating in the interpretive program; details are posted on notice boards throughout the park. The **Hoodoo Interpretive Trail** is a two km (one-way) hike along the cliffs, with numbered posts that correspond to a trail brochure available from the information center. Along the way are some examples of petroglyphs and pictographs (including the famous battle scene) that have been ravaged by time and vandals.

Accommodations And Information

The nearest motel rooms are in Milk River, but the park has an excellent campground nestled below the hoodoos in a stand of cottonwood trees; $10.75 per night. For more information on the park write to Writing-On-Stone Provincial Park, P.O. Box 297, Milk River, Alberta T0K 1M0; tel. (403) 647-2364.

THE DRY BELT

Not a tree in sight—just rolling shortgrass prairie, occasionally dissected by dried-up streams and eroded gullies. This is the sight that first greeted settlers to the area, and even with the help of complex irrigation systems the land looks similar today. The far southeastern corner of Alberta has never been heavily populated, but not for a lack of trying. Before it was linked to the outside world by rail, settlers entered the area. Small villages emerged, but as was often the case, the Canadian Pacific Railway decided to bypass many of these and create its own towns. Population bases moved and towns slipped into oblivion. Highway 61 passes through this dry, unforgiving part of the province, past the towns of Wrentham and Skiff with their boarded-up buildings and grim futures to the town of **Foremost,** and on through other small communities whose future hangs in the balance. The highway finally peters out at Manyberries. A gravel road (Hwy. 889) heads northeast from Manyberries to Hwy. 41 just south of Cypress Hills Provincial Park.

Foremost

In 1915, the Canadian Pacific Railway built a line east from Stirling through to Saskatchewan with great hopes of the area becoming heavily settled. But they hadn't counted on years of heavy drought, dust storms, and outbreaks of influenza that severely affected the populations of towns in the area. One of the few surviving towns was Foremost, whose population of 500 has remained relatively stable through trying times. Irrigation has played a major role in Foremost's longevity. The interpretive center at **Forty Mile Coulee Reservoir,** 23 km north of town, explains the importance of irrigation to these farming communities. Nearby is a viewpoint and day-use area. On the west side of town is a small campground with tent sites for $5.50 and hookups $8-11.

Etzikom

The C.P.R. built towns approximately every 16 km along its lines, its strategy being that farmers would have access to a grain elevator within a day's haul of their farm, yet the towns would be far enough apart to survive independently. Between Foremost and Etzikom, the town of Nemiskam hasn't survived. The once busy streets are quiet. The residents that remain head to the larger centers of Foremost and Medicine Hat to go shopping and do their business. The fate of Etzikom is similar. Once a thriving center with many businesses and two hotels, the streets are now quiet, and fewer than 100 people live in town. Travel 16 km east or west of Etzikom to see what the town's future holds. **Etzikom Museum,** tel. (403) 666-3737, relives the past—the railway, influenza, droughts, and the tenacity of its people. An outdoor display includes a large collection of windmills. The museum is open during summer, Tues.-Sat. 10 a.m.-6 p.m., Sunday 1-6 p.m.

Continuing East

The farmland east of Etzikom is particularly poor. The railway town of **Pakowki** slipped into oblivion long ago, its early residents preferring to do business in **Orion,** the next town to the east. Orion was once a thriving prairie town, but a terrible drought throughout much of the 1920s forced most farmers into bankruptcy. Those that survived were moved by the government to other parts of the province. A few residents still hang on, forever optimistic. And why not? The elevators still take in grain. To the south of Orion on Hwy. 887 are the **Manyberries Sandhills,** a prairie phenomena well worth the detour—especially in the berry-picking season. Highway

PALLISER TRIANGLE

On July 4, 1857, Capt. John Palliser set out west from Winnipeg on an assignment from the British government to make a comprehensive assessment of the agricultural potential, mineral reserves, soil quality, and timber resources of the prairies. Under his command were 20 men, two wagons, six Red River carts and 29 horses. For three long years the expedition traveled the length and breadth of the prairies, before eventually submitting their findings in 1862. Palliser's report favored a band of territory stretching from Manitoba to the Peace River in northern Alberta. On the other hand, to the south he reported a vast land of shortgrass prairie that he called "an extension of the Great American Desert." He considered it unfit for agriculture: "[The land] is desert or semi-desert in character . . . [and] can never be expected to become occupied by settlers." This region—extending along the U.S. border and as far north as Red Deer—soon became known as the Palliser Triangle. Although the report wasn't favorable to the southern part of the province, it changed people's perception of the west. His report led to the settlement of southern Alberta, although it didn't happen overnight. Eventually the C.P.R. rail line was built across the prairies, and irrigation opened up arid parts of the land previously thought unsuitable for settlement.

887 heads north to Seven Persons and Medicine Hat. Highway 61 jogs south and east from Orion to the small town of **Manyberries,** from where Hwy. 889 heads northeast to **Cypress Hills Provincial Park** or south then east to Saskatchewan; either way it's gravel.

HIGHWAY 3 EAST

Coaldale

The first town east of Lethbridge on Hwy. 3 is Coaldale. The area was first settled in 1889 by Mennonites, and when the C.P.R. built a rail line between Lethbridge and Medicine Hat in 1926, they encouraged more Mennonite families to farm in the region. With their long agricultural traditions and doctrines of simple living, Mennonites were always welcome additions to prairie communities such as Coaldale. Today this rural community and its Mennonite population continue to prosper, mostly due to their proximity to Lethbridge.

The main reason to leave the highway here is to visit the **Birds of Prey Centre,** north of Hwy. 3 at 20th St., then left on 16th Ave., tel. (403) 345-4262. The aim of the center is to ensure the survival of birds of prey such as hawks, falcons, eagles, and the great horned owl, Alberta's provincial bird. Many of the birds are brought to the center injured or as young chicks. They are nurtured at the center until they are strong enough to be released back into the wild. The interpretive building features the works of various wildlife artists and has displays cataloguing human fascination with birds of prey through thousands of years. The center is open April-Oct., daily 10 a.m.-5 p.m. Admission is $4.

Taber

Taber, 51 km east of Lethbridge, is most famous for its deliciously sweet corn. It's also a base for the food-processing industry and a service center for the oil-and-gas industry. The original settlement began around Water Tank No. 77 (the site was 77 miles from Medicine Hat) along the C.P.R. rail line. In 1901, the area was opened up to homesteaders, attracting settlers from eastern Canada and the United States, many of whom were Mormons. The name Taber was taken from Tabernacle, reflecting the religious influence of the Mormons. Local Blackfoot called the settlement "itah soyop," which translates to "where we eat from." Apparently they mistook the name Taber for table.

Taber corn, as it is called, can be bought throughout western Canada and is the cornerstone of the town's economy. August is the best time to look for corn vendors along the road. Or find corn along with other fresh, local produce each Thursday at the farmer's market in the Taber Agriplex. On the last weekend of August, when the corn has ripened, the town's **Cornfest** celebration takes place, with a pancake breakfast, a midway, hot-air-balloon flights, a classic-car show, and of course, plenty of corn to taste.

On the eastern outskirts of town is the **Taber Sugar Beet Factory,** which processes in excess of 500,000 tons of sugar beets annually. During peak periods, enormous piles of beets sit beside the highway waiting to be processed into icing sugar, granulated sugar, and various powdered sugars. The factory does not offer tours, and judging by the smell *outside* the factory this is a good thing. One plant that does offer tours is **Lucerne Foods,** 5115 57th St., tel. (403) 223-3566, which bottles fruit juices and cans vegetables at its Taber plant. Tours are available weekdays 9 a.m.-3 p.m.

Taber Motel, tel. 223-4411, has the least expensive rooms in town. They are clean, but don't expect much; $35 s or d. The much nicer and larger **Heritage Inn,** tel. 223-4424, offers a restaurant, cafe, and lounge; rooms start at $49 s or d. **Taber Provincial Park,** on a floodplain above the Oldman River two km west and three km north of town, is a welcome relief from the surrounding prairie. Campsites are near a stand of large cottonwood trees. The unserviced sites are $11, and some can be reserved; tel. 223-7929.

Bow Island

Vast reserves of natural gas in the area around Bow Island were first tapped in 1909 by a discovery well named "Old Glory," which soon developed into Alberta's first commercial gas field. The reserve of gas declined by the '20s and Bow Island's role in the industry changed—it became the first major gas-storage field in Canada. Today its storage reservoirs help meet southern Alberta's peak winter demand. Agriculture now plays an important role in the town's economy, as evidenced by large grain elevators and an **Alfalfa Dehydrating and Cubing Plant** two km west of town (for tours call 403-545-2293). On the east side of town are two inexpensive motels and an information booth which is open in summer daily 9 a.m.-6 p.m. On the west side of town is a campground.

Petroglyphs record early human history in the region.

Seven Persons

Seven Persons is the last community on Hwy. 3 before Medicine Hat. South of the town is a small area of badlands on a gentle rise in the surrounding plains. The bedrock here is relatively close to the surface, and wind and water erosion have cut through the topsoil to expose it. In some places, the erosion has extended into the bedrock itself, revealing varicolored strata laid down millions of years ago. This strange landscape is dotted with small hoodoos and red boulder-shaped concretions measuring up to 2.5 meters across. These concretions formed under the surface of a prehistoric sea, when sand, calcite, and iron oxide collected on a nucleus of shells, bones, and corals. They became part of the bedrock as layers of sediment were laid down. But as erosion took its course, the surrounding bedrock disappeared and the concretions emerged. The formations here are believed to be the largest of their type in the world. To get there follow Hwy. 887 south from Seven Persons for 24.6 km. Where the road curves to the east (left) continue straight ahead one km farther. You can't miss it.

MEDICINE HAT AND VICINITY

The prosperous industrial city of Medicine Hat (pop. 43,000) is in the southeastern corner of the province, 168 km east of Lethbridge and 40 km west of the Saskatchewan border. The city straddles the South Saskatchewan River and is above some of western Canada's most extensive natural-gas fields. The gas was discovered by accident in 1883, by a C.P.R. crew drilling for water. At first nobody was particularly excited, except for the workers who got to heat their isolated homes. But eventually the word got out about the size of the reserves beneath the town, leading English writer Rudyard Kipling to describe Medicine Hat as "a city with all hell for a basement."

It wasn't long before industries developed around the gas fields; oil-and-gas extraction operations, petrochemical plants, mills, farms, and fertilizer factories today generate $1.5 billion annually. New housing estates, shopping centers, and an award-winning city hall are testimony to the success of these local industries. As an added bonus, a river that flows beneath the the city gives Medicine Hat an unlimited supply of water for its industries.

One other area resource is no longer exploited today, but has left its mark on the face of the city. Nearby clay deposits led to a large pottery and brick industry that thrived from late last century until WW II. Many turn-of-the-century brick buildings have been restored and can be seen in the downtown core (where gas lamps still burn 24 hours a day).

Also of note is the **Saamis Archeological Site,** within city limits, regarded as one of the most extensive and richest finds from the late prehistoric time period of native history. And an hour south of the city is **Cypress Hills Provincial Park,** an upland plateau that survived the last ice age. This densely forested plateau that rises abruptly from the surrounding prairie is home to many species of mammals and provides a variety of recreational opportunities. (See "Cypress Hills Provincial Park," below.)

The Name Medicine Hat

For centuries before white settlers had come to the area, the Cree and Blackfoot had battled each other over their right to claim this land as their own. Many tales recording these battles describe how the name Medicine Hat evolved. One of the most popular tells the story of the Cree chief who led his people to the cliffs above the South Saskatchewan River. Here, the Great Serpent told him that he must sacrifice his wife to the river in exchange for a *saamis* or *medicine hat.* This would give him magical powers and allow him to defeat the Blackfoot when they attacked later that night. Another story tells of how the Blackfoot were forced into the waters of the South Saskatchewan River by the Cree, who then fired an arrow into the heart of the Blackfoot medicine man. As he slowly sank below the water's surface, his hat was swept away into the hands of the Cree. The Blackfoot saw this as a terrible omen and retreated.

MEDICINE HAT

SEE "DOWNTOWN MEDICINE HAT" MAP

PARKVIEW DR

TO REDCLIFF AND CALGARY

EL BRONCO MOTEL

3rd ST. NW

2nd ST. NW

SOUTH SASKATCHEWAN RIVER

CITY HALL

LIBRARY

C.P.R. STATION

YMCA

GREYHOUND BUS DEPOT

POST OFFICE

LIONS PARK

POLICE POINT PARK

GAS CITY CAMPGROUND

11th AVE. SW

1st ST. SW

STRATHCONA ISLAND PARK

HOSPITAL

5th ST. SE

BRIDGE ST.

STRATHCONA CENTRE

CLAY PRODUCT INTERPRETIVE CENTRE

7th ST. SW

SEE INSET BELOW

GERSHAW DR.

DIVISION AVE.

4th AVE. SE

KINGSWAY AVE.

INDUSTRIAL AVE.

CYPRESS CYCLE

SOUTH RAILWAY ST.

TO ECHO DALE PARK

TRANS-CANADA HWY

SEVEN

HUTCHINSON AVE.

PERSONS

CREEK

SATELLITE MOTEL

SAAMIS ARCHEOLOGICAL SITE

10th AVE. SW

EXHIBITION AND STAMPEDE GROUNDS

MUNICIPAL AIRPORT

SAAMIS TEEPEE

COLLEGE AVE.

13th AVE. SE

DUNMORE RD.

SOUTHVIEW DR.

30th ST. SW

SOUTH RIDGE DR.

TOURIST INFORMATION CENTRE

IMPERIAL MOTOR INN

6th ST. SW

MEDICINE HAT LODGE

7th ST. SW

7th ST. SW

QUALITY INN

SEARRA MOTEL

8th ST. SW

8th ST. SW

BEST WESTERN

CLOVERLEAF MOTEL

ROSE ST.

RUSTLER'S

CROCUS ST.

GERSHAW DR.

8th ST. SW

TO CYPRESS HILLS P.P. AND SASKATCHEWAN

CACTUS ST.

BULIVANT CIR

11th ST. SW

TRAVELODGE MOTOR INN

12th ST. SW

WILD ROSE TRAILER PARK

10th AVE. SW

TO LETHBRIDGE

0   0.1 mi
0   0.1 km

MEDICINE HAT MUSEUM AND ART GALLERY

14th ST. SW

10th AVE. SW

15th ST. SW

9th AVE. SW

8th AVE. SW

BEL-AIRE MOTEL

0   0.5 mi
0   0.5 km

MOON

© MOON PUBLICATIONS, INC.

SIGHTS

Downtown

Many turn-of-the-century buildings located in the downtown area are still in active use, including private homes, churches, and businesses. The availability of local clay led to thriving brick-manufacturing plants here during the late 1800s; many original buildings still stand in mute testimony to the quality of the bricks. Near City Hall on 1st St. are three fine examples of this brickwork. The 1919 **Provincial Courthouse** has been restored. It features an elaborately carved entrance, an interior marble-walled stairway, and a leaded-glass archway. Across the road is the 1887 **Ewart-Duggan Home.** This is the oldest brick residence still standing in Alberta and is topped by its original cedar shingles. On the corner of 4th Ave. is the **Kerr-Wallace Home,** the first of many early prestigious homes along 1st St. toward the Trans-Canada Hwy. (Hwy. 1).

Among other historical landmarks are the 1913 **St. Patrick's Church** (across the river from downtown on 2nd St.), said to be one of the finest examples of Gothic Revival architecture in North America; the **C.P.R. Station** (east of downtown), built shortly after the railway came to town in 1883; and the 1905 **Canadian Bank of Commerce** (corner 6th Ave. and 2nd St.), a classic example of early bank architecture. These buildings and others are listed in the *Historic Walking Tour* brochure available from the tourist information center.

Another notable piece of architecture from a much later era is the **Medicine Hat City Hall,** which won the Canadian Architectural Award in 1986. Located on the banks of the South Saskatchewan River, it's open to the public on weekdays and contains many fine pieces of art.

Because of the abundance of natural gas in the area, city officials in the early days found it cheaper to leave the city's gas lamps on 24 hours a day rather than pay someone to turn them on and off. Over 200 copper replicas of the early gaslight fixtures were imported from England and now line the streets, burning 24 hours a day in the historical section of downtown.

Saamis Teepee

Standing over 20 stories high beside the Trans-Canada Hwy., with a base diameter of 50 meters and made entirely of steel, this is one sight that you don't need directions to find. The Saamis Teepee was originally erected at the 1988 Calgary Winter Olympics to commemorate the cultural roles played by natives in the history of North America and has since been moved to its present site. It overlooks Seven Persons Creek Coulee, an archaeological site which was used in late prehistoric times as a native camp where buffalo were dried and processed. Paths behind the monument lead to a bluff and into the valley where the camp was located. Native American ceremonial events are sometimes held here. The site is open year-round but during the summer months tours are offered and a small store sells native arts and crafts. For more information call (403) 527-6773.

Medicine Hat Museum And Art Gallery

This large museum at 1302 Bomford Crescent SW, tel. (403) 527-6626 or 526-0486, has a permanent collection of exhibits explaining the history of the plains Indians, the growth of the city, the important role played by ranching and farming in southeastern Alberta, the North West Mounted Police, and the arrival of the railway. A military display catalogues the development of biological warfare through the ages from its earliest form—throwing snake-filled jars onto enemy ships! A large collection of photographs and manuscripts pertaining to the area's history is open by appointment only. The art gallery is a National Exhibition Centre hosting more than 20 national and international exhibitions annually. The complex is open Mon.-Fri. 9 a.m.-5 p.m., Sat.-Sun. 1-5 p.m.; admission $3.

Clay Products Interpretive Centre

Medicine Hat's early pottery industry relied on the same nearby clay deposits as the brick industry. The Interpretive Centre, at the corner of Medalta and Industrial avenues, tel. (403) 529-1070, is on the old Medalta Potteries site, where for many years the local Saskatchewan clay was mass-produced into high-quality china. For most of the middle period of this century Medalta was a household name in Canada. The china was popular in homes and was used exclusively by

C.P.R.-owned hotels. During WW II, German prisoners of war worked in the factory making plates that were sent to allied soldiers fighting in Europe. Since closing in 1954, fire, wind, and rain have taken their toll on the building which has been declared a National Historical Site. The center displays the history of the clay and pottery industries in Medicine Hat, has some fine examples of the now highly prized Medalta pieces, and is the start of a walking tour of the area. It's open June-Aug., daily 10 a.m.-6 p.m.

Redcliff

This small suburb of Medicine Hat bills itself as "Greenhouse Capital of the Prairies"; over 10 hectares of greenhouses here are filled with brilliantly colored flowers and various vegetables such as cucumbers (12 million grown annually) and tomatoes (eight million grown annually). The greenhouses are open to the public year-round at 404 4th St. SW. To arrange a tour call (403) 548-3931. **Redcliff Museum,** 2 3rd St. NE, tel. 548-6260, depicts the area's history and has some interesting photos and manuscripts. It's open in summer Tues.-Sat. 2-4 p.m., Sunday only the rest of the year. To get to Redcliff follow the TransCanada Hwy. west of Medicine Hat and take the first exit to the north after the industrial estate.

City Parks

Medicine Hat's urban park system covers over 400 hectares of open space and natural environment linked by 50 km of multiuse trails developed for walking, biking, and cross-country skiing. **Strathcona Island Park,** on the banks of the South Saskatchewan River, is a heavily wooded area linked to the city center by a riverside trail that leads through **Lions Park.** From Lions Park there's a viewpoint of the steep cliffs formed by the undercutting power of the river at a shallow point. Within Strathcona Island Park is the **Strathcona Centre,** which has a pool, paddleboat and canoe rentals, and is the start of a short hiking trail. The park is at the end of 5th St. Southeast.

On the north side of the river, opposite Strathcona Island Park is **Police Point Park** (turn off Parkview Dr. just past the golf club), which has many kilometers of trails that wind through stands of giant cottonwood trees and provide plentiful wildlife-spotting opportunities. White-tailed deer, foxes, and beavers are commonly seen. The **interpretive center,** tel. (403) 529-6225, outlines the area's natural and human history through exhibits and films; open in summer daily 1-9 p.m., the rest of the year weekends only 9 a.m.-5 p.m.

West of the airport on Holsam Rd. is **Echo Dale Park,** where the locals head on hot weekends to sunbake on the sandy beach, and swim, fish, and boat in the man-made lake. Within the park is **Echo Dale Farm,** where you'll find farm animals, a two-story log house currently being restored, and an interpretive center that's open in summer daily 9 a.m.-9 p.m.

FESTIVALS AND EVENTS

The first weekend of June is the **Spectrum Festival,** a celebration of Medicine Hat's claim as the sunniest city in Canada. Kids' activities and street performers are plentiful, and tons of sand are dumped in a parking lot, transforming it into a beach for a volleyball tournament and beer garden. A free pancake breakfast in Lions Park kicks off **Canada Day** (1 July) celebrations, which end with a spectacular fireworks display in the evening—watch it from Athletic Park or the Golf and Country Club off Parkview Drive. The **Medicine Hat Exhibition and Stampede,** held on the last weekend of July, has been an annual event since 1887. It has grown to become Alberta's second-richest rodeo (behind the Calgary Stampede), guaranteeing three days of knuckle-clenching, bronc-riding, foot-stompin' fun. Various events are held throughout the city the preceding week, culminating Thurs.-Sat. with the rodeo and chuck wagon races. The stampede also features many exhibitors displaying their wares, as well as a midway, free entertainment, and pig and duck races. Each night, top U.S. country-music stars strut their stuff. For more information, call the stampede office at (403) 527-1234. Throughout summer various other events are held at the Exhibition and Stampede Grounds, including tractor pulls, sporting events, concerts, horse races, and smash-up derbies. For dates and prices, call the tourist information center at (403) 527-6422.

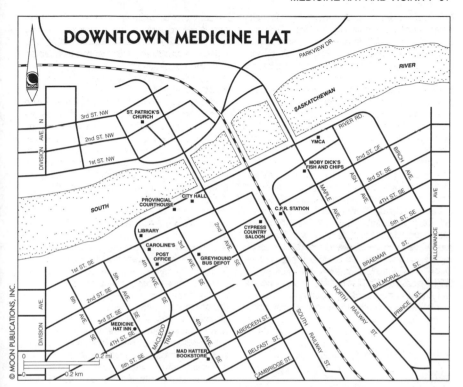

DOWNTOWN MEDICINE HAT

ACCOMMODATIONS

Hotels And Motels

With only two exceptions, all motels are clumped along the TransCanada Hwy. around Gershaw Dr., separated only by fast-food restaurants and gas stations. Many of the cheaper ones are continuously full with work crews. Also, check the rooms before handing over any cash and lock your car at night.

The **Medicine Hat Inn,** 530 4th St. SE, tel. (403) 526-1313, is the only accommodation downtown. Although small, it is relatively modern, has a restaurant, and is within walking distance of most sights. Rooms are $65 s or d. East of the strip of motels on Dunmore Rd. is the **Travelodge Motor Inn,** 1100 Redcliff Dr. SE, tel. 527-2275 or (800) 578-7878. It has a large indoor water slide complex, indoor pool, restau-

rant, and lounge. Standard rate for rooms is $75-85, but ask about off-season and weekend rates.

Along the TransCanada Hwy. are 16 other choices ranging from poor to excellent (as far as road motels go). Following are the best value from northwest to southeast: **El Bronco Motel,** 1177 1st St. SW, tel. 526-5800, $30-35 s or d; **Quality Inn,** 954 7th St. SW, tel. 527-8844, with an indoor pool and restaurant, $46 s, $54 d; **Best Western Inn,** 722 Redcliff Dr. SW, tel. 527-3700, with a pool and exercise room, $53 s, $59 d; **Searra Motel,** 767 7th St. SW, tel. 526-3355, with divey rooms for $28 s, $32 d, but free coffee; **Cloverleaf Motel,** 773 8th St. SW, tel. 526-5955, with a laundry, $35 s, $40 d; **Bel-Aire Motel,** 633 14th St. SW, tel. 527-4421, the best value at the bottom end, $26 s, $30 d; **Satellite Motel,** 1705 Bomford Crescent SW, tel. 526-5951, $25 s, $30 d; and **Imperial Motor**

Inn, 3282 13th Ave. SE, tel. 527-8811, with large, clean rooms for $42 s, $45 d.

Medicine Hat Lodge, 1051 Ross Glen Dr. SE, tel. 529-2222, is away from all those listed above and is overpriced.

Campgrounds
Gas City Campground, tel. (403) 526-0644, is on the edge of town, has nearly 100 sites, and is far enough away from the highway to be relatively quiet. From the back of the park a trail heads to the river and into town. At night this is a good spot to view the illumination of Medicine Hat's industrial core. It's open early May-late Sept.; tent sites are $10, hookups $14-18. Good hot showers, laundry facilites, groceries, and full hookups make this the place to try first. Turn off the highway at 7th St. SW and follow the signs down 11th Avenue. Another option, **Wild Rose Trailer Park,** 28 Camp Dr., tel. 526-2248, is in the same general area and has a large population of trailers. Unserviced sites go for $10, hookups $12-15. It's open year-round. Finally, west of town in Redcliff, a municipal campground offers showers and electrical hookups for $5 per night.

FOOD AND DRINK

Downtown
Lunchtime at bright and airy **Caroline's,** 101 4th Ave. SE, tel. (403) 529-5300, is always busy; soups, salads, sandwiches, and daily specials begin at $4. The service is fast and efficient for those who don't want to dawdle. Thursday at Caroline's is Beer and Bones night when Brontosaurus Ribs are 25 cents each. **Moby Dick's Fish and Chips,** 140 Maple Ave. SE, tel. 526-1807, has a delightful variety of English dishes. Fish in batter is $2.10 per piece, fries $1.25. Also on the menu are other seafood specialties (from $9), traditional pub grub (from $2.50), and nine different meat pies (from $6). English draught beers are around $6 a pint. You can eat in the restaurant, the pub next door, or get it to go. Hours are Mon.-Sat. 11 a.m.-9 p.m., Sunday 3-8 p.m. **Cafe Mundo,** 579 3rd St., tel. 528-2808, is one of many downtown coffee shops. It's located in Gaslight Plaza, and the only food it serves is bagels, $2.50 each. **Season's Restaurant** in the Medicine Hat Inn, 530 4th

St. SE, tel. 526-1313, is a typical hotel restaurant and is always busy. Dinner specials are $13, menu items $9-18, and all dishes include a helping from a small salad bar. It's open daily 6 a.m.-10 p.m.

Rustler's
Rustler's, 901 8th St. SW, tel. (403) 526-8004, within walking distance of the strip motels along the TransCanada Hwy., is one of the town's oldest eating establishments. Located in a historic house (see the menu for its amusing history), a real Wild West atmosphere prevails. Set out under the glass top of one table is a poker game complete with gun and bloodstained playing cards. The place is popular all day but breakfast is especially crowded. Large portions of eggs, bacon, and hash browns begin at $4, omelettes at $4.95. For the rest of the day, it's southwestern-style cooking from $4.25, salads from $4, and pasta, steak, and chicken dishes from $8. It's open daily 6 a.m.-10 p.m. Coffee is 50 cents and refills are free.

Other Restaurants
Close to Rustler's are two excellent, inexpensive restaurants. **O'Rileys Restaurant and Bar** in the Quality Inn on 7th St. SW, tel. (403) 527-8844, is a dimly lit, nostalgic place with gold-rimmed furniture and old posters on the walls. Monday is Mexican night (dishes from $6.50), Wednesday is pasta night (dishes from $5.50), and Friday and Saturday are rib nights (dishes from $12). Expect a wait on weekends. It's open daily 6 a.m.-11 p.m. Across the motel parking lot and beside the Best Western is **Black Angus Restaurant,** 925 7th St. SW, tel. 529-0777, a family-style steakhouse specializing in Alberta beef. To the east along Dunmore Rd. are a smattering of chain restaurants including A&W, Bonanza (ask for the all-you-can-eat ice cream for $1.50), and Earl's.

Drinking And Dancing
Captain's Cabin Pub, 140 Maple Ave. SE, tel. (403) 529-6629, has a variety of English and Scottish draught beers on tap and is decked out in the style of a traditional British pub. On S. Railway St., **Cypress Country Saloon** often has local bands playing. Just around the corner is **Gas Light Pub,** which has pool tables. **O'Rileys** in the Quality Inn on 7th St. SW, tel. 527-

8844, is popular with the local population of British soldiers. On Mug Mondays all glass mugs, vases, and jars will be filled with beer for $1. And Tuesday night is Yuk Yuk's Komedy Kabaret, admission $5. **Concerts** are often held at the Exhibition and Stampede Grounds—look for big-name country-music stars during Stampede Week at the end of July; call 527-1234 for details.

TRANSPORTATION

Medicine Hat Municipal Airport is five km west of downtown on Hwy. 3 toward Lethbridge. Within the airport is a small cafe and courtesy phones for Avis, Budget, and Tilden rental cars. **Canadian Regional,** tel. (403) 526-6633 or (800) 665-1177, flies five times daily between here and Calgary, $90 one way or $94 round trip if purchased 14 days in advance. No city bus serves the airport. Cabs meet all flights; expect to pay around $6 to get downtown.

The **Greyhound** bus depot is at 557 2nd St. SE, tel. 527-4418, in a convenient downtown location. The ticket office is open 5 a.m.-11 p.m. Inside the terminal are coin lockers and a popular cafe. Buses run twice daily to and from Calgary with a change in Fort Macleod. The fare to Lethbridge is $19.10, to Calgary $33.17. Buses also go east to Regina and Winnepeg four times daily. **Medicine Hat Transit** buses run from the terminal downtown throughout the suburbs. One-way fare anywhere on the route is $1.30; a day pass is $4.50. The following car-rental agencies have outlets in town: **Avis,** tel. 527-3310; **Budget,** tel. 527-7368; **Rent-A-Wreck,** tel. 526-5400; and **Tilden,** tel. 527-5665. **Cypress Cycle** at 951 S. Railway St. SE, tel. 529-5525, rents bikes from $5 per hour and $20 per day.

SERVICES AND INFORMATION

The **post office** is at 406 2nd St. Southeast. The spotless **One Stop Laundry** at 3215 Dunmore Rd. is open Mon.-Sat. 9 a.m.-9 p.m., Sunday 10 a.m.-9 p.m., and has a TV and free coffee. The **YMCA,** 150 Ash Ave. SE, tel. (403) 527-4426, has a pool, weight room, and squash courts; $2.35 for a swim, $4.90 for use of all facilities, first visit free. The large **Medicine Hat Public Library,** 414 1st St. SE, tel. 527-5551, overlooks the river and has a free paperback exchange. It's open Mon.-Thurs. 10 a.m.-9 p.m., Fri.-Sat. 10 a.m.-5:30 p.m., Sunday 1-5:30 p.m. **Mad Hatter Bookstore,** 399 Aberdeen St. SE, tel. 526-8563, has thousands of secondhand books. **Medicine Hat Regional Hospital** is at 666 5th St. SW, tel. 529-8000. For the **RCMP** call 527-8181.

The **tourist information center** is at 8 Gehring Rd. SE, tel. 527-6422. To get there take the Southridge Dr. exit from the Trans-Canada Hwy. just east of the big tepee. It's open in summer daily 8 a.m.-9 p.m., the rest of the year daily 9 a.m.-5 p.m. The Medicine Hat Museum also has a small information booth.

CYPRESS HILLS PROVINCIAL PARK

Covering an area of 200 square km, Cypress Hills is the second-largest provincial park in the province. It occupies only a small section of an upland plateau that extends well into Saskatchewan. The hills rise as much as 500 meters above the surrounding grasslands, and at their highest elevation (1,466 meters, the same as Banff townsite) they are the highest point between the Canadian Rockies and Labrador. A forested oasis in the middle of the prairies, the park is thickly covered in lodgepole pine with stands of white spruce, poplar and aspen. The French word for lodgepole pine is *cyprès,* which led to the hills being named *Les Montagnes de Cyprès* and in turn Cypress Hills, when in fact cypress trees have never grown in the park. Fall and spring are particularly pleasant times of year to visit the park—crowds are nonexistent and wildlife is more visible—but bring a jacket.

The park is 70 km southeast of Medicine Hat along Hwy. 41. It offers good hiking, fishing, or just plain relaxing, and is very popular as a place to escape the high summer temperatures of the prairies. The only commercial facilities within the park are in the townsite of **Elkwater,** which sits in a natural amphitheater overlooking **Elkwater Lake.** The facilities are limited (no bank, one restaurant, one motel, one gas station) so come prepared.

The Land

The hills are capped with a conglomerate composed of rounded pebbles carried east from the Rockies by a broad stream around 40 million years ago. When the massive sheets of ice moved slowly southward druring the ice age, they thinned and split at the 1,400-meter level of the plateau. The top 100 meters remained unglaciated, forming a nunatak (an island of land surrounded by ice) of approximately 150 square km. When the climate warmed and the sheet of ice slowly receded, its meltwaters rushed around and through the hills, slashing into the plateau and forming the narrow canyons and coulees that are visible today.

Flora

The park supports over 400 recorded plant species in four ecological zones: prairie, parkland, foothills, and boreal forest. The best way to view the flora of the park is on foot; many trails pass through two or three zones in the space of a couple of kilometers. Sixteen species of orchids are found in the park—some are very common, while others such as the sparrow's egg lady's slipper are exceedingly rare. The book *A Guide To The Orchids Of Cypress Hills* by Robert M. Fisher will tell you all you want to know. The visitor center has a copy of the book you can look at.

Fauna

The unique environment of the hills provides a favorable habitat for 37 species of mammals, 400 species of birds, and a few turtles. Big game was at one time common throughout the hills, but in 1926 the last remaining large mammal—a wolf —was shot. Soon thereafter, elk were reintroduced to the park and now number over 200. Moose, never before present in the park, were introduced in the 1950s and now number about 60. Other large mammals present in the park are mule deer, white-tailed deer, coyotes, and beavers.

orchid

BOB RACE

Many bird species here are more typically found in the Rocky Mountain foothills, 250 km to the west. About 90 species are transient, coming to the hills only to nest. Other species spend the entire year in the park. This is the only spot in the province with recordings of the common poorwill, which is rarely seen but occasionally heard. Wild turkeys were introduced in the '30s and their descendants can be heard warbling in certain parts of the park. Elkwater Lake and Spruce Coulee Reservoir are good spots for water-bird watching. Cormorants and trumpeter swans are common. A bird checklist is available at the visitor center.

Cultural History

To the native bands of Cree, Blackfoot, and Assiniboine, the area was known as "Thunder Breeding Hills," a mysterious place that was home to plains grizzly bears, cougars, wolves, and kit foxes—all long since extinct in the area. These people followed the wandering herds of bison and had little need to visit the hills except to pick berries and collect various plants for medicinal and ceremonial uses. Little evidence of this early culture remains, although one archaeological site dating from 5000 B.C. has been studied. After the Cypress Hills Massacre, when 20 innocent Assiniboine were killed, the North West Mounted Police sent nearly 300 men to Fort Walsh (on the Saskatchewan side of the hills). The fort is now a National Historical Site.

Exploring The Park

Various roads link the townsite of Elkwater to lakes and viewpoints within the park. Due to glacial sediment called loess, the paved roads at higher elevations are terribly potholed. Unpaved roads are even worse and can become impassable after heavy rain. To access the center of the park, take Reesor Lake Rd. east from Hwy. 41, passing a herd of cattle and a viewpoint with spectacular views of the transition from grass-

CYPRESS HILLS PROVINCIAL PARK

© MOON PUBLICATIONS, INC.

land to boreal forest. The road then descends steeply to **Reesor Lake,** which has a campground, picnic area, a short hiking trail to a viewpoint, and excellent fishing for rainbow trout. Bull Trail Rd. off Reesor Lake Rd. leads to **Spruce Coulee** and a reservoir stocked with eastern brook and rainbow trout. Unmarked gravel roads crisscross the park and head into Saskatchewan. Hiking within the park is limited. Most of the trails are easy to moderate, following the shores of Elkwater Lake (wheelchair accessible) and climbing out of the townsite into open fields and mixed forests. **Spruce Coulee Trail** (eight km) is the longest hike. It starts behind the rodeo grounds and leads through woodland and past a number of beaver ponds before ending at Spruce Coulee.

At the marina, **Elkwater Boat & Bike,** tel. 893-3877, rents mountain bikes ($5 per hour, $20 a day), canoes ($8 per hour), motorboats

($12 per hour), and Jet Skis ($45 per hour). The **Elkwater Complex** opposite the marina holds a restaurant to avoid, a grocery store, a post office, and a laundromat. The town has a gas station but no bank. **Elkwater Park Golf Club,** tel. 893-2167, offers a nine-hole course at $10 per round.

Wintertime

Although summer is the park's busiest time of year, many people are attracted by the range of winter activities possible. **Hidden Valley** is a large ski hill (by prairie standards) with a vertical drop of 176 meters and three lifts that access a limited number of beginner and intermediate runs. Lift tickets are $20. Rentals are available at the hill or from **Lauder Cycles and Ski,** 702 Kingsway Ave. SE, tel. (403) 526-2328, in Medicine Hat. The hill is located three km south of Elkwater, and is closed on Tuesday. For more information call 893-3961. The park also offers

25 km of cross-country ski trails for all levels of expertise, ice fishing in the lakes, toboggan hills, and winter camping for the brave.

Campgrounds And Lodging
Within the park are 550 campsites in 13 campgrounds. Closest to town are **Beaver Creek Campground** ($15-17) with full hookups, and **Elkwater Campground** ($13) with unserviced sites. Both have showers. **Firerock Campground** ($13) on Elkwater Lake is particularly nice. It is linked to town by the Shoreline Trail. **Reesor Lake Campground** ($11) at the eastern end of the park is much quieter—listen for bugling elk in the fall. An eight-km hike from the rodeo grounds follows an abandoned road to **Spruce Coulee,** where you'll find 10 sites ($7.50) and good fishing in the reservoir. Reservations for campsites are taken; phone (403) 893-3777.

Green Tree Motel, P.O. Box 19, Elkwater, Alberta T0J 1C0, tel. 893-3811, is the only motel in the park; $40 s or d, kitchenettes an extra $5, and log cabins $55. During winter, ski packages are offered.

Services And Information
The large **visitor center** overlooks Elkwater Lake, a short walk from the townsite campgrounds, and offers lots of information on the park and its history. Audiovisual programs explain the natural history and archaeological and historical resources of the park. It's open mid-May through Labor Day, daily 9 a.m.-5 p.m. (until 9 p.m. Thurs.-Sat. in July and August). An interpretive program operates nightly during July and August; ask at the visitor center for a program. For information in the off-season, try the park office along the first road to the left as you enter town from the east. It's open weekdays 8:15 a.m.-4:30 p.m. For more information, write to the office at P.O. Box 12, Elkwater, Alberta T0J 1C0; or call (403) 893-3777.

WEST OF LETHBRIDGE

FORT MACLEOD

Southern Alberta's oldest permanent settlement is Fort Macleod, 44 km west of Lethbridge and just east of the junction of Highways 2 and 3. In 1873, the West was in turmoil. Relations between American whiskey traders and natives had reached an all-time low, and intertribal Indian wars were resulting in murder and massacre. That's when politicians in eastern Canada decided to do something about it. A paramilitary mounted police force was sent west with orders to close down Fort Whoop-Up, a notorious whiskey-trading post located where the city of Lethbridge now stands. After finding it empty they decided to push on farther west and build their own fort. The site chosen was an island in the **Oldman River,** one km east of the present town of Fort Macleod. These first troops of the North West Mounted Police eventually put an end to the illicit whiskey trade. And with the help of scout Jerry Potts—who ironically didn't mind a drop of the hard stuff himself—they managed to restore peace between the warring tribes. The original fort had continual flooding problems. It was relocated to higher ground in the 1880s and the town of Fort Macleod gradually grew up around it.

Historic Downtown
In 1906, a fire destroyed most of the wooden buildings on Main Street so a bylaw was passed requiring any new structures to be built of brick or stone. The legacy of this bylaw remains in the 30 buildings of historical significance forming the downtown core (which has been declared a historic district). Many of the buildings function as they did during the town's boom years; the **Queens Hotel** has rooms, the **Empress Theatre** is the oldest operating theater in the province, and Main Street comes alive with parades and dances during the summer months. Throughout summer, guided walking tours of town leave regularly from the Fort Museum. Or you can get the walking-tour brochure and do it at your own pace.

Beside the museum is **Macleod Livery,** tel. (403) 553-4868, a reconstruction of pioneer buildings, with farm animals running around and a shaded picnic area. A small admission fee is charged. Horse-drawn carriage rides through

FORT MACLEOD

SEE INSET

25th ST.
MAIN ST. (24th ST.)
23rd ST.
22nd ST.
21st ST.

SCARLET AND
GOLD INN

TOURIST
INFORMATION
CENTRE

DAISY MAY
CAMPGROUND

LYNDON RD.

2nd AVE. 3rd AVE. 4th AVE. 5th AVE. 6th AVE.

3

TO OLDMAN RIVER P.R.A.,
HEAD - SMASHED - IN BUFFALO JUMP,
AND HWY. 2 NORTH

3

TO
LETHBRIDGE

INSET

FORT MUSEUM
MACLEOD
LIVERY
QUEENS
HOTEL

EMPRESS
THEATRE

25th ST.

RED
COAT
INN

KOSY
MOTEL

NEW HONG KONG
RESTAURANT

DIANA'S
DRIVE IN

2

MAIN ST.

(24th ST.)

WESTERNER
RESTAURANT

GREYHOUND
BUS DEPOT

23rd ST.

SUNSET MOTEL

1st AVE.

2nd AVE.

POST OFFICE

3rd AVE.

4th AVE.

5th AVE.

22nd ST.

6th AVE.

TO
CARDSTON

MOON

NOT TO SCALE

© MOON PUBLICATIONS, INC.

town are $5.50 per person, and rides down to the old fort site are $6.25 per person. The carriages used are beautifully restored and worth a look even if you don't plan on a tour.

Fort Macleod Museum

The original fort on the Oldman River would have looked much like the Fort Museum does today. The museum details the history of the North West Mounted Police and the early days of settlement in southern Alberta. Inside are various buildings reflecting aspects of frontier life including a chapel, blacksmith shop, NWMP building, law office, tepee, and the Centennial Building, which is devoted to the history of the plains Indian tribes. Two corner blockhouses with panoramic views of the Oldman River were used as lookouts. In the arena during summer, riders dress in period costume and perform the **Mounted Police Musical Ride**—a spectacular display of precision riding—four times daily at 10 a.m., 11:30 a.m., 2 p.m., and 3:30 p.m. The museum is located at 219 25th St. (westbound); tel. (403) 553-4703. It's open July-Aug., daily 9 a.m.-8:30 p.m.; May, June, September, daily 9 a.m.-5 p.m.; the rest of the year, weekdays 9:30 a.m.-4 p.m. Admission is $3.50, which includes the Musical Ride.

Entertainment

The stage of the venerable 1912 **Empress Theatre** at 235 24th St., has been graced by acts from as far away as New York and Australia. Through its long history, it has hosted vaudeville shows, opera and theater performances, political rallies, and film screenings—changing uses with the changing times. The theater has been renovated and returned to its former glory, and once again provides a venue for live shows and musical theater. For schedule and ticket information call (403) 553-4404 or 553-2199. Most shows are under $10. If nothing's happening at the Empress, check out the loud and boisterous **Midnight Lounge** in the Westerner Restaurant. It's open till 2 a.m. nightly, with a DJ on Saturday nights.

Accommodations

Motel rooms fill up fast every afternoon in summer, so book ahead or check in early. Rates fluctuate with the season; expect to pay 20-30% less outside of summer. The least expensive rooms in town (with good reason) are at the **Queens Hotel,** 207 24th St., tel. (403) 553-4343, $20 s, $25 d. The strip of motels along the east end of 24th St. is the best place to start looking. At **Kosy Motel,** 433 24th St., tel. 553-3115, rates include a hot breakfast at the restaurant next door; $40 s or d. One step up is the **Red Coat Inn,** 359 24th St., tel. 553-4434, offering an indoor pool; $46 s or d. At the west entrance to town is the **Sunset Motel,** 104 Hwy. 3 W, tel. 553-4448, where each room has a fridge, and coffee and toast are available at reception in the morning; $46 s, $52 d.

Daisy May Campground is beside Alberta's oldest golf course and within walking distance of the museum and downtown. It provides showers, a heated pool, laundry, and game room. Tent sites cost $11, sites with hookups $14-16; tel. 553-2455. North of the junction of Highways 2 and 3 towards Calgary is **Oldman River Provincial Recreation Area** with primitive campsites going for $5.50 a night.

Food

The restaurant scene in Fort Macleod is not particularly exciting. The **Silver Grill** and **Rex Cafe** on 24th St. have been restored and offer some nostalgic value. The **Westerner Restaurant,** 404 Main St., tel. 553-4066, has big break-

fasts for $4-6; the omelettes are excellent. Lunch and dinner items range $5.50-10 and all include soup or salad. It's open Mon.-Sat. 6 a.m.-2 a.m., Sunday 6 a.m.-10 p.m. The **Scarlet and Gold Inn** at the east end of town, 2323 7th Ave., tel. 553-3337, has a busy coffee shop and a dining room. Breakfast starts at 6 a.m., then it's salads, sandwiches, and hamburgers the rest of the day. The dining room opens at 4:30 p.m. for dinner and the choices are many: steaks (from $10.50), seafood (from $10), prime rib (from $12), and house specials (from $10). **New Hong Kong Restaurant,** 510 25th St., tel. 553-3838, lays out a small smorgasbord Fri.-Sun. 5-8 p.m. For low-priced fast food try **Diana's Drive In,** at the corner of 24th St. and 6th Ave., tel. 553-4227, where you can get a burger, fries, and a shake for under $5.

Services And Information

Greyhound, 2302 2nd Ave., tel. (403) 553-3383, leaves five times daily for Calgary ($19.05) and twice daily for Lethbridge ($5.78). The **Kome Kleen Laundry** is behind the Sunset Motel and open daily 8 a.m.-10 p.m. The **library,** 264 34th St., tel. 553-3880, is open Mon.-Sat. 1-5 p.m. The museum gift shop has a large selection of local history and Canadiana books. The **tourist information center** is at the east end of town on 24th St., tel. 553-4955; open mid-May to August, daily 9 a.m.-8 p.m.

HEAD-SMASHED-IN BUFFALO JUMP

Archaeologists have discovered dozens of buffalo jumps across the North American plains. The largest, oldest, and best preserved is Head-Smashed-In, located along a weathered sandstone cliff in the Porcupine Hills 19 km northwest of Fort Macleod. At the base is a vast graveyard with thousands of years worth of bones from butchered bison piled 10 meters high. The jump represents an exceptionally sophisticated and ingenious hunting technique used by plains Indians at least 5,700 years ago—possibly up to 10,000 years ago—to cunningly outwit thousands of bison, once the largest mammal on the plains.

At the time white settlers arrived on the prairies, over 60 million American bison (also known as buffalo) roamed the plains. The Indians of the plains depended almost entirely on these prehistoric-looking beasts for their survival. They ate the meat fresh or dried it for pemmican; made tepees, clothing, and moccasins from the hides; and fashioned tools and decorations from the horns. The Indians used several means to kill the bison, but by far the most successful method was to drive entire herds over a cliff face. The topography of this region was ideal for such a jump. To the west is a large basin of approximately 40 square km where bison grazed. They were herded from the basin east along carefully constructed stone cairns (known as drive lines) that led to a precipice where the stampeding bison, with no chance of stopping, plunged to their death below. Nearby was a campsite where they butchered and processed the meat.

The site has been well preserved. Although a small section of the hill has been excavated, most of it appears today the same as it has for thousands of years. The relative height of the cliff, however, drastically decreased with the build-up of bones. Along with the bones are countless numbers of artifacts such as stone points, knives, and scrapers used to skin the fallen beasts. Metal arrowheads found in the top layer of bones indicate that the jump was used up until the coming of whites in the late 1700s. In recognizing the site's cultural and historical importance, UNESCO declared the jump a World Heritage Site in 1981.

How The Jump Got Its Name

The name Head-Smashed-In has no connection to the condition of the bisons' heads after tumbling over the cliff. It came from a Blackfoot legend: About 150 years ago a young hunter wanted to watch the buffalo as they were driven over the steep cliff. He stood under a ledge watching as the stampeding beasts fell in front of him, but the hunt was better than usual and as the animals piled up he became wedged between the animals and the cliff. Later his people found him, his skull crushed under the weight of the buffalo—hence the name, Head-Smashed-In.

Interpretive Centre

As you approach the jump site along Spring Point Rd., the Head-Smashed-In Interpretive Centre doesn't become visible until you've

Allow at least two hours in the interpretive center.

parked your car and actually arrived at the entrance. The center—disguised in the natural topography of the landscape—is set into a cliff, part of which had to be blasted away to build it. A series of ramps and elevators marks the beginning of your tour as you rise to the roof from where a trail leads along the cliff-top to the jump site. It isn't hard to imagine the sounds and spectacle of thousands of bison stampeding over the rise to the north and tumbling to their deaths below. To the east is the **Calderwood Buffalo Jump,** which can be seen farther along the cliff face.

Back inside you walk down floor by floor passing displays and films explaining in an interesting and informative way the traditional way of life that existed on the prairies for nearly 10,000 years, as well as the sudden changes that took place when the first white men arrived. The lowest level describes the archaeological methods used to excavate the site and how the ancient cultures of the various plains Indians are unraveled from the evidence found. A 10-minute movie, *In Search Of The Buffalo,* cataloguing the hunt, is shown every half hour on Level Four.

Outside the center is another trail that leads along the base of the cliff for a different perspective. Here a large aluminum building covers a recent dig site; the ground is littered with shattered bones. The center also has a gift shop and cafe selling, of all things, buffalo burgers. The year's largest event is the **Annual Pow Wow** in mid-July, when a large tepee village is constructed on the grounds, and native dance competitions, food tastings, and activities for all ages are presented. Each Saturday afternoon in July and August, a noted authority on a subject relevant to the jump presents a short show on his or her field of expertise.

The center is open in summer daily 9 a.m.-8 p.m., the rest of the year Tues.-Sun. 9 a.m.-5 p.m. Admission is $5; half-price on Tuesday from October through April. For more information, contact the center at P.O. Box 1977, Fort Macleod, Alberta T0L 0Z0; tel. (403) 553-2731.

CARDSTON

Cardston is a town of 3,500 at the base of the foothills 76 km southwest of Lethbridge and 35 km north of the United States border. Its rich heritage and many museums make it an inter-

Cardston's Mormon Temple

esting stop in itself, as well as a good base for exploring Waterton Lakes National Park (a half-hour drive to the west). The town was founded in 1887 by Charles Ora Card of the Church of Jesus Christ of Latter-day Saints (better known as the Mormon Church) after leading 11 families north from Utah in covered wagons. Card chose a spot to settle on Lee Creek and soon established a townsite, including a main street over 30 meters wide, resembling those in Salt Lake City. These settlers developed Alberta's first irrigation system, which has grown to become the lifeblood of southern Alberta's economic base.

Cardston was the birthplace of Fay Wray, a leading lady during the golden years of Hollywood. She appeared in 80 movies, but is best known for her role as the leading-ape's love object in the 1933 classic *King Kong.*

Remington-Alberta Carriage Centre
This world-class museum focusing on the era of horse-drawn transportation opened in 1993. It is one of North America's largest collections of carriages, buggies, and wagons—over 200 at last count. The main exhibit galleries tell the story of the horse-and-buggy era through a life-sized turn-of-the-century townscape. You can transport yourself through time by watching blacksmiths at work in the carriage factory, listening to deals being made at the carriage dealer, or wandering over to the racetrack, where the rich liked to be seen on their elegant carriages. A program of equestrian events featuring Clydesdales and quarter horses takes place

daily in the demonstration arena, and rides are offered on restored and replica carriages. The center also has a theater, cafeteria, gift shop, and information booth. It's located at 623 Main St., tel. (403) 653-5139; open 15 May to Labour Day 9 a.m.-8 p.m., the rest of the year 9 a.m.-5 p.m. Admission is $5, half-price on Tuesday from October through April.

Mormon Temple
While living in simple log cabins, the early Mormon pioneers started planning the construction of the first Mormon temple built outside of the United States. The grand marble and granite structure was completed in 1923 and has become the town's centerpiece. Only members of the Mormon faith in good standing may enter the temple itself. To be in good standing, a Mormon must neither smoke, nor drink coffee or tea, and must pay 10% of his or her net annual income to the church. A visitor center open to the public shows films and pictures depicting the interior of the temple and its history. The landscaped gardens make for a pleasant stroll. The center is open May-June, daily 10 a.m.-6 p.m. and July-Aug. 9 a.m.-8 p.m. You can see the temple from almost anywhere in town. It's located at 348 3rd St. W; tel. (403) 653-3552.

Other Sights
On Cardston's main drag is the **Card Pioneer Home,** 337 Main St., tel. (403) 653-4322, built by the town's founder when he first arrived in 1887. This small log cabin, still in its original location,

was the center of the community for many years. Town meetings were held inside, and the building served as a rest stop for travelers until a hotel was built in 1894. The building is now a Provincial Historic Site, open daily April-Aug. 10 a.m.-5 p.m.; admission by donation.

The **Courthouse Museum,** on 3rd Ave. just off Main St., tel. 653-4322, was built in 1907 from locally quarried sandstone, and was used longer than any other courthouse in the province before being refurnished as a museum. Exhibits include a pioneer home, artifacts from early settlers, and a geology display. In the basement are the original jail cells with graffiti-covered walls. The museum is open April-Aug. 10 a.m.-5 p.m.; admission by donation.

Woolford Provincial Park

Original surveys of the area show the park as an island in the St. Mary River. A stand of large cottonwood trees here provides a pleasant shaded area surrounded by prairie. A North West Mounted Police post was established in 1883 one km northwest of the park to patrol the Canada/U.S. border but was short-lived, closing in 1908. Annual flooding after spring break-up is a continuing problem; the main river channel changes and chunks of the island break off. The campground is small and facilities are limited to cook shelters, firewood, and pit toilets. Sites are $5.50 a night. To get to the park from Cardston head northeast on Hwy. 5 for three km, then southeast along a gravel road for 13 km.

Entertainment And Events

The **Carriage House Theatre,** 353 Main St., tel. (403) 653-1000, has a summer program of live theater productions including musicals, comedy, and special events with a local theme. The performances are held July-Aug., Tues.-Sat. nights at 7:30.

On the third weekend of September is the **Combined Driving Event** held in conjunction with the Remington-Alberta Carriage Centre. The meet consists of three events: carriage dressage, an obstacle course, and a marathon. With the exception of the marathon, all the excitement takes place at the Carriage Centre.

Accommodations

Plenty of choices here—four motels, many bed and breakfasts, and camping downtown or in one of the nearby provincial parks. The **Evergreen Motel,** 40 1st Ave. W, tel. (403) 653-4904, is at the north end of town. The rooms are basic, but clean; $42 s, $47 d. Two blocks up the hill from the Remington-Alberta Carriage Centre are two motels at the corner of Main St. and 8th Avenue: **Trail's End Motel,** tel. 653-4481, $40 s, $45 d; and **Flamingo Motel,** tel. 653-3952, which has a coin laundry and pool, $45 s, $50 d.

In the last few years a number of private residences have converted spare rooms to accommodate paying guests. One of the best is the **Historic Granite Inn,** 140 2nd Ave. W, tel. 653-3157, which was built in 1918 and has been kept in the family ever since. The small single room is $35, a larger room runs $45 s or d, and the rose room, which has a small private sitting area, is $50 s or d. The bathroom is shared, and a hot breakfast is served in the communal dining room. **The Crab Tree,** 171 2nd St. W, tel. 653-1414, has shared bath, theme rooms, and great breakfasts, from $40 s, $45 d. South of town in a rural setting are **Country Manor,** 901 Homeseeker's Ave., tel. 653-4608, and **Lamb's Gate B&B,** 1010 Homeseekers Ave., tel. 653-3647. Both have rooms with shared or private bath starting at $35 s, $45 d including a hot breakfast.

Within walking distance of the Remington-Alberta Carriage Centre is **Lee Creek Campground,** an excellent facility open May-Oct. with full hookups and showers. Tent sites are $8, hookups $12. It's at the end of 7th Ave. W, off Main Street. Another option is **Buffalo View Campground,** at the Agridome along 9th Ave., which has no services except pit toilets; $5 per night. Farther out you'll find camping at **Woolford Provincial Park,** 16 km to the east ($5.50); **Police Outpost Provincial Park,** 33 km south of town ($11); and at **Paine Lake,** 24 km southwest toward Waterton ($5.50).

Food

The **Cobblestone Manor Restaurant,** 173 7th Ave. W, tel. (403) 653-1519, is a unique place to indulge in some fine food. The original log structure was built in 1889, two years after the first Mormons arrived. In 1913 the house was bought by a Belgian immigrant who added more rooms, using cobblestones as building blocks. The interior wall panels and ceilings are inlaid with thousands of pieces of hardwood, and the stained glass bookshelves, Tiffany lights, and antique furniture give you the feeling of dining in an English manor. And the food isn't too bad either. Light lunches start at $7, dinner entrees of steak, seafood, and chicken, all served with baked potato, fresh vegetables, and delicious homemade bread start at $10. The restaurant is open daily for lunch 11 a.m.-2 p.m. and for dinner 5-9 p.m. It's located on a quiet residential street, across the road from Lee Creek Campground.

The only other dining choices in Cardston are along Main St., among them two Chinese restaurants, a few pizza places, and **Humpty's Family Restaurant,** which is the place to go for breakfast.

Services And Information

The **post office** is on 2nd Avenue. Laundromats are located at 165 Main St. and 77 3rd Ave. West. **Cardston Municipal Hospital** is at 124 2nd St. W, tel. (403) 653-4411. For the **RCMP** call 653-4931. The **tourist information center** is beside Lee Creek at 490 Main St., tel. 653-3787. It's open mid-May to August, daily 9 a.m.-5 p.m., or try the information booth at the Remington-Alberta Carriage Centre, which is open year-round.

Which Way Now?

From Cardston, highways lead in five directions. South of Cardston is the Old Mormon Trail that settlers from Utah used on their way north. The town of **Aetna,** just off Hwy. 2, was once a thriving Mormon community with a cheese factory, school, and store. A worthwhile stop in Aetna is **Jenson's Trading Post,** a general store with an interesting collection of antiques. This is the beginning of the true prairie, and if you're heading east from here, it's hard not to keep glancing

in the rear-view mirror for glimpses of the Rocky Mountains you're leaving behind. From Aetna, Hwy. 501 skirts the International Boundary passing the ruins of a community once known as Whiskey Gap. It crosses Hwy. 62 north of the Del Bonita port of entry (open June 1-Sept. 15, 9 a.m.-9 p.m., the rest of the year 9 a.m.-6 p.m.) and continues east to Milk River through arid grassland not suitable for cultivation (see "Milk River" earlier in this chapter). Along much of the way the **Sweetgrass Hills** in Montana are visible rising high above the prairies south of Writing-On-Stone Provincial Park.

Highway 2 passes through Cardston on its way north to Calgary and south to the International Boundary. **Police Outpost Provincial Park,** on a small lake beside the International Boundary, is accessible along a 23-km gravel road 10 km south of Cardston. The police outpost that gave the park its name was set up in 1891 to control smuggling, but the remote location led to its closure before the turn of the century. From the park, spectacular **Chief Mountain** can be seen to the southwest. Most of the park is grassland interspersed with isolated stands of aspen and marshy areas. The park's campground has pit toilets and cook shelters; sites are $11. The highway crosses into Montana at the Carway/Piegan port of entry (open 16 May-31 Oct., 7 a.m.-11 p.m., the rest of the year 9 a.m.-6 p.m.).

Highway 5 goes northeast to Magrath and Lethbridge. **Magrath** has a "Buffalo Slope" grain elevator, the latest concept adopted by the Alberta Wheat Pool; open for tours Mon.-Fri. 8 a.m.-5 p.m., tel. (403) 758-3231. In the opposite direction, Hwy. 5 leaves Cardston heading southwest to Mountain View, a small community from where the abrupt rise of the mountains from the prairies is at its most spectacular. From here, it is a further 20 km to Waterton Lakes National Park.

WATERTON LAKES NATIONAL PARK

Everybody traveling to this rugged 526-square-km park does so by choice. It's not on the way to anywhere else or on a major highway but is tucked away in the extreme southwestern corner of Alberta. The park is bounded to the north and east by the rolling prairies which cover southern Alberta; to the south by the U.S. border and Glacier National Park in Montana; and to the west by the Continental Divide which forms the Alberta/British Columbia border. The natural mountain splendor, a chain of deep glacial lakes, large and diverse populations of wildlife, an unbelievable variety of day-hikes, and a changing face each season make this park a gem that shouldn't be missed.

The route to Waterton is almost as scenic as the park itself. From whichever direction you arrive, the transition from prairie to mountains is abrupt, almost devoid of the foothills which characterize other areas along the eastern slopes of the Canadian Rockies. From the park gate, two roads penetrate the mountains to the west. One ends at a large glaciated lake and the other at a spectacular canyon. All visitors to the park are required to stop at the gate and buy a permit. Four types of permit are available; a one-day permit is $5, a four-day permit is $10, an annual permit for Waterton is $20, and an annual pass valid in all Canadian national parks is $30.

THE LAND

Geology

Major upheavals under the earth's surface around 85 million years ago forced huge plates of rock upward and began folding them over each other. One major sheet known as the Lewis Overthrust forms the backbone of Waterton's topography as we see it today. It slid up and over much younger bedrock along a 300-km length extending north to the Bow Valley. Around 45 million years ago this powerful uplift ceased and the forces of erosion took over. About 1.9 million years ago, glaciers from the sheet of ice that once covered most of Alberta crept through the mountains. As these thick sheets of ice advanced and retreated with climatic changes, they gouged out valleys such as the classically U-shaped **Waterton Valley.** The three Waterton Lakes are depressions left at the base of the steep-sided mountains after the ice had completely retreated 11,000 years ago. The deepest is 150 meters. **Cameron Lake,** at the end of the Akamina Parkway, was formed when a moraine —the pile of rock that accumulates at the foot of a retreating glacier—dammed Cameron Creek. From the lake, Cameron Creek flows through a glaciated valley before dropping into the much deeper Waterton Valley at **Cameron Falls,** behind the town of Waterton. The town itself sits on an alluvial fan composed of silt and gravel picked up by mountain streams and deposited in Upper Waterton Lake.

Climate plays an active role in the park's natural landscape. This corner of the province tends to receive more rain, snow, and wind—much more wind—than other parts of Alberta. These factors, combined with the park's varied topography, create an environment where some 900 species of plants have been recorded, more than half the known species in Alberta. Wind is the most powerful presence in the park. Prevailing winds from the south and west bring Pacific weather over the divide, creating a climate similar to that experienced farther west. These warm fronts endow the region with **chinooks,** dry winds that can raise temperatures in the park by up to 40° C in 24 hours. One of the nicest aspects of the park is that it can be enjoyed in all seasons. Summer for the sunny windless days, fall for the wildlife viewing, winter for the solitude, and spring for the long days of sunlight as the park seems to be waking up from its winter slumber.

Flora

Botanists have recorded 1,200 species of plants growing within the park's several different vegetation zones. In the park's northeastern corner, near the park gate, a region of **prairies** is covered in semiarid vegetation such as fescue grass. As Hwy. 5 enters the park it passes **Maskinonge Lake,** a **wetlands** area of marshy ponds where aquatic plants flourish. **Parkland** habitat dominated by aspen is found along the north side of Blakiston Valley and near Belly River Campground, while **montane forest** covers most mountain valleys and lower slopes. This latter zone is dominated by a high canopy of lodgepole pine and Douglas fir shading a forest floor covered with wildflowers and berries. An easily accessible section of this habitat is along the lower half of Bertha Lake Trail; an interpretive brochure is available at the park information center.

Above the montane forest is the **subalpine** zone, which rises as far as the timberline. These distinct forests of larch, fir, Engelmann spruce, and whitebark pine can be seen along the Carthew Lakes Trail. On the west-facing slopes of Cameron Lakes are mature groves of subalpine trees up to 400 years old—this oldest growth in the park has managed to escape fire over the centuries. Blanketing the open mountain slopes in this zone is bear grass, which grows up to a meter in height and is topped by a bright blossom often likened to a lighted torch. Above the treeline is the **alpine** zone where harsh winds and short summer seasons make trees a rarity. Only lichens and alpine wildflowers flourish at these high altitudes. Crypt Lake is a good place for viewing this zone.

Fauna

Two major flyways pass the park and from September to November many thousands of waterfowl stop on Maskinonge and Lower Waterton lakes. On a powerline pole beside the entrance to the park is an active osprey nest—ask staff to point it out for you.

Wildlife viewing in the park requires patience and a little know-how, but the rewards are ample, as good as anywhere in Canada. Elk inhabit the park year-round. A large herd gathers by Entrance Road in late fall, wintering on the lowlands. By early fall many mule deer are wandering around town. Bighorn sheep are often seen on the north side of Blakiston Valley or on the slopes above the park information center; occasionally they will end up in town. White-tailed deer are best viewed along Red Rock Canyon Parkway. The park has a small population of moose occasionally seen in low-lying wetlands. Mountain goats rarely leave the high peaks of the backcountry, but from Goat, Crypt, or Bertha lakes, you might catch a glimpse of one high above you.

The most common predators in the park are the coyotes that spend their summer days chasing ground squirrels around the prairie and parkland areas. For its size, Waterton has a healthy population of cougars. But these shy, solitary animals are rarely seen. Around 50 black bears live in the park. They spend most of the summer in the heavily forested montane regions. During August and September, scan the slopes of Blakiston Valley where they can often be seen feasting on saskatoon berries before going into winter hibernation. Much larger than black bears are the grizzlies which roam the entire backcountry but are rarely encountered.

Golden-mantled ground squirrels live on the Bear's Hump and around Cameron Falls. Columbian ground squirrels are just about everywhere. Chipmunks scamper about on Bertha Lake Trail. The best time for viewing beavers is dawn and dusk along the Belly River. Muskrats can be seen on the edges of Maskinonge Lake eating bulrushes. Mink also live in the lake but are seen only by those with patience.

HISTORY

Evidence found within the park suggests that the Kootenai people who lived west of the park made trips across the Continental Divide around 8,400 years ago to hunt bison on the plains and fish in the lakes. They camped in the valleys during winter, sheltering from the harsh weather. But by around 1,500 years ago, they were spending more time in the west and only crossing the mountains a few times a year to hunt bison. By the 1700s, the Blackfoot—with the help of horses—had expanded their territory from the Battle River throughout southwestern Alberta. They patrolled the mountains on horseback, making it difficult for the Kootenai hunting parties to cross. But their dominance was short-lived. With the arrival of guns and the encroaching homesteads of early settlers, Blackfoot tribes retreated to the east, leaving the Waterton Lakes Valley uninhabited.

"Kootenai" Brown

John George Brown was born in England in the 1840s and reputedly educated at Oxford University. He joined the army and went to India, later continuing to San Francisco. Then,

NEWMAN PEAK (2515 m)

MT. GLENDOWAN (2635 m)

AVION RIDGE

PARK BOUNDARY

CONTINENTAL DIVIDE

GOAT LAKE

LOST LAKE

BAUERMAN CREEK

MT. DUNGARVAN (2566 m)

RED ROCK CANYON

TWIN LAKES

ANDERSON PEAK (2698 m)

BLAKISTON FALLS

MT. GALWEY (2348 m)

RED ROCK CANYON PKWY.

SOUTH KOOTENAY PASS

LONE MOUNTAIN (2420 m)

CRANDELL MOUNTAIN

LONE LAKE

MT. HAWKINS (2685 m)

MT. BLAKISTON (2920 m)

CRANDELL LAKE

MT. CRANDELL (2378 m)

LINEHAM LAKES

RUBY RIDGE

BRITISH COLUMBIA

MT. LINEHAM (2728 m)

DISCOVERY WELL

OIL CITY

CAMERON CREEK

ROWE LAKES

CONTINENTAL DIVIDE

MT. ROWE (2446 m)

AKAMINA PKWY.

BERTHA'S PEAK (2440 m)

MT. CARTHEW (2630 m)

ALDERSON LAKE

CARTHEW LAKES

BERTHA LAKE

MT. ALDERSON (2692 m)

MT. RICHARDS (2416 m)

SUMMIT LAKE

FORUM PEAK (2225 m)

CAMERON LAKE

GLACIER NATIONAL PARK/UNITED STATES

like thousands of others, he headed for the Cariboo goldfields of British Columbia, quickly spending any of the gold he found. After a while he moved on, heading east into Waterton Valley, where his party was attacked by Blackfoot Indians. He was shot in the back with an arrow and pulled it out himself. For a time he worked with the U.S. Army as a Pony Express rider. One day he was captured by Chief Sitting Bull, stripped, and tied to a stake until his fate could be decided, but he managed to escape during the night with his scalp intact. Brown acquired his nickname through his close association with the Kootenai people, hunting buffalo and wolves with them until they had all but disappeared. Even though Brown had been toughened by the times he was a conservationist at heart. After marrying in 1869 he built a cabin by the Waterton Lakes, and became the valley's first permanent resident. Soon he started promoting the beauty of the area to the people of Fort Macleod. One of his friends, local rancher F.W. Godsal, began lobbying the Federal government to establish a reserve. In 1895 an area was set aside as a Forest Reserve, with Brown as its first warden. In 1911 the area was declared a National Park and Brown, aged 71, was appointed its superintendent. He continued to push for an expansion of park boundaries until his final retirement at age 75. He died a few years later. His grave along the main access road to the townsite is a fitting resting place for one of Alberta's most celebrated mountain men.

buffalo effigy

BOB RACE

Oil City

It was Kootenai Brown who first noticed beads of oil floating on Cameron Creek. He and a business partner siphoned it from the water's surface, bottled it, and sold it in Fort Macleod and Cardston. This created much interest among the oil starved entrepreneurs of Alberta, who formed the Rocky Mountain Development Co. to do some exploratory drilling. At this stage the park was still a Forest Reserve; the trees were protected, but prospecting and mining were still allowed. A rough road was constructed through the Cameron Creek Valley, and in September 1901 the company struck oil at a depth of 311 meters. It was the first producing oil well in western Canada and only the second in the country. In the resulting euphoria, a townsite named Oil City was cleared and surveyed, a bunkhouse and dining hall were constructed, and the foundations for a hotel were laid. The boom was short-lived. Drilling rigs kept breaking down and the flow of oil soon slowed to a trickle. A monument along the Akamina Parkway stands at the site of the well, and a little further up the road at a roadside marker a trail leads through thick undergrowth to the townsite. All that remains are the ill-fated hotel foundations and some depressions in the ground.

Waterton-Glacier International Peace Park

Shortly after Montana's Glacier National Park was created in 1910, the Canadian government set aside an area of land in the Waterton Valley as Waterton Lakes Dominion Park (later to be renamed a national park). Many people followed the footsteps of Kootenai Brown and a small town named Waterton Lakes grew up on the Cameron Creek delta. The town had no rail link, so unlike Banff and Jasper—its famous mountain neighbors to the north—it didn't draw large crowds of tourists. Nevertheless, it soon became a popular summer retreat with a hotel, restaurant, and dance hall. The Great Northern Railway decided to operate a bus service from its Montana rail line to Jasper, with a stop at Waterton Lakes. This led to the construction of the **Prince of Wales Hotel.** Boat cruises from the hotel across the International Boundary were soon the park's most popular activity. This brought the two parks closer together, and in 1932, after much lobbying from Rotary International members on both sides of the border, the Canadian and U.S. governments agreed to establish Waterton-Glacier International Peace Park, the first of its kind in the world. The parks are administered separately, but cooperate in preserving this pristine mountain wilderness. Peace Park celebrations take place each year, and the **Peace Park Pavilion** by the lake is dedicated to this unique bond. In 1979, UNESCO declared the park an **International Biosphere Reserve,** only the second such reserve in Canada.

HIKING

Although the park is relatively small, its trail system is extensive; 183 km of well-maintained trails lead to alpine lakes and lofty summits affording spectacular views. One of the most appealing aspects of hiking in Waterton is that with higher trailheads than other parks in the Canadian Rockies, the treeline is reached quickly. Most of the lakes can be reached in a few hours. Once you've finished hiking the trails in Waterton, you can cross the border and start on the 1,200 kilometers of trails in Glacier National Park.

The eight hikes detailed below comprise only a small cross-section of Waterton's extensive trail system. As most of the hikes climb to alpine lakes or viewpoints, the ratings that are given reflect the elevation gain. Anyone of reasonable fitness could complete them in the time allotted. Strong hikers will need less time, and if you stop for lunch it will take you a little longer. Remember, all distances and times are one-way—allow yourself time at the objective, and time to return to the trailhead. Topographical maps (one map covers the entire park) are available at various outlets in town. If you are planning to stay overnight in the backcountry you must obtain a permit (free) from the park information center or administration office.

Don't underestimate the forces of nature. Weather can change dramatically anywhere in the park and at any time. That clear sunny sky that looked so inviting during breakfast can turn into a driving snowstorm within hours. Ill-prepared hikers get lost in the park each year. Read the updated weather reports that are posted at all information centers before setting out, go prepared for all climatic conditions (always carry food, a sweater, and matches), and take plenty of water—open slopes can get very hot on sunny days.

Bear's Hump
- Length: 1.2 km (40 minutes) one way
- Elevation gain: 215 meters
- Rating: moderate

This is one of the most popular short hikes in the park, and although steep, it affords panoramic views of the Waterton Valley. The trailhead is at the park information center, opposite the Prince of Wales Hotel. The trail consists of a number of switchbacks up the northern flanks of the Bear's Hump, finishing at a rocky ledge high above town. From this vantage point the sweeping view extends across the prairies and down Upper Waterton Lake to the northern reaches of Glacier National Park.

Bertha Lake Trail
- Length: 5.8 km (2 hours) one way
- Elevation gain: 460 meters
- Rating: moderate

Bertha Lake is a popular destination with day-hikers and campers alike. The trail begins at the end of Evergreen Ave. near the far corner of Townsite Campground. For the first 1.5 km little elevation gain is made as the trail coincides with the Lakeshore Trail. Then the trail branches right and climbs steadily through a forest of lodgepole pine and Douglas fir along a well-maintained section to **Lower Bertha Falls.** Signs along this first, easier section correspond with the *Bertha Falls Self-Guiding Nature Trail* brochure available from the Information Centre. From here the trail passes **Upper Bertha Falls** and begins switchbacking steeply through a subalpine forest to its maximum elevation on a ridge above the hanging valley in which Bertha Lake lies. A trail encircles the lake. The backcountry campground on the lake's edge is one of the park's busiest.

Waterton Lakeshore Trail
- Length: 13 km (4 hours) one way
- Elevation gain: minimal
- Rating: easy/moderate

This trail follows the heavily forested western shores of Upper Waterton Lake across the International Boundary to **Goat Haunt, Montana,** linking up with over 1,200 km of trails in Glacier

National Park. Many hikers take the **Inter-Nation Shoreline Cruise Co.** boat one-way ($9; tel. 403-859-2362) and hike the other. The boat dock at Boundary Bay, six km from town, is a good place for lunch. Hikers heading south and planning to camp in Glacier National Park must register at the Goat Haunt ranger station.

Crypt Lake Trail
• Length: 8.7 km (3-4 hours) one way
• Elevation gain: 680 meters
• Rating: moderate/difficult

This is one of the most spectacular day-hikes in Canada. Access to the trailhead on the eastern side of Upper Waterton Lake is by boat. The trail switchbacks for 2.5 km past a series of waterfalls and continues steeply up to a small green lake before reaching a campground. The final ascent to Crypt Lake from the campground causes the most problems, especially for those who suffer from claustrophobia. A ladder on the cliff face leads into a natural tunnel that you must crawl through on your hands and knees. The next part of the trail is along a narrow precipice with a cable for support. The lake at the end of the trail, nestled in a hanging valley, is no disappointment. Its dark green waters are rarely free of floating ice, and the steep walls of the cirque rise over 500 meters above the lake on three sides. The International Boundary is at the southern end of the lake. A good way to avoid the crowds on this trail is by camping at the dock and setting out before the first boat arrives in the morning. The **Crypt Lake Shuttle** leaves the Marina regularly for Crypt landing; $9 round trip. Reservations are necessary in summer; call (403) 859-2362.

Crandell Lake
• Length: 2.4 km (40 minutes) one way
• Elevation gain: 120 meters
• Rating: easy

This easy hike to a subalpine lake from the Red Rock Canyon Parkway is popular with campers staying at Crandell Mountain Campground. The trailhead can be reached from within the campground, or by noncampers along the Canyon Church Camp access road. The lake can also be accessed from a trailhead seven km west of town along the Akamina Parkway. This trail is shorter (0.8 km) and follows a wagon road that was cut through the valley to Oil City.

Goat Lake Trail
• Length: 6.7 km (2 hours) one way
• Elevation gain: 500 meters
• Rating: moderate

The first hour of walking from the trailhead at Red Rock Canyon follows the Snowshoe Trail along **Bauerman Creek** before branching to the right and climbing a series of switchbacks through a mixed forest. The steep gradient evens out as the trail enters the Goat Lake Cirque. The lake is a welcome sight after the uphill slog, its emerald green waters reflecting the towering headwalls that surround it. Look for the lake's namesake on the open scree slopes to the west of the lake.

Carthew-Alderson Trail
• Length: 20 km (6-7 hours) one way
• Elevation gain: 650 meters
• Rating: moderate/difficult

This hike linking Cameron Lake to Waterton townsite can be completed in one long strenuous day or done with an overnight stop at Alderson Lake, 13 km from Cameron Lake. It leads through most of the climatic zones of the park and offers some of the best scenery to be had on any one hike. Most hikers begin at Cameron Lake. Transportation to the trailhead can be arranged through the **Park Transport Company** in the Tamarack Mall ($6 one way; tel. 403-859-2378), which operates a hiker shuttle service to this and other trailheads in the park. From Cameron Lake the trail climbs four km to **Summit Lake,** a worthy destination in itself. The trail then forks to the left and climbs steeply to Carthew Ridge. After rising above the treeline and crossing a scree slope the trail reaches its highest elevation of 2,310 meters at **Carthew Summit.** The views from here are spectacular, even more so if you scramble up to one of Mt. Carthew's lower peaks. To the north is a hint of prairie, to the southeast the magnificent bowl-shaped cirque around Cameron Lake, to the south, directly below are the Carthew Lakes, and on the horizon are glaciated peaks in Montana. From this summit, the trail descends steeply to the Carthew Lakes, reenters the subalpine forest, and emerges at **Alderson Lake,** nestled under the headwalls of Mt. Alderson. The trail then descends through the Carthew Creek Valley and finishes at Cameron Falls in the townsite.

Vimy Peak

- Length: 12 km (5 hours) one way
- Elevation gain: 825 meters
- Rating: moderate

Vimy Peak overlooks the townsite from across Upper Waterton Lake. It was once part of a ridge that extended across the Waterton Valley and was worn down by the relentless forces of glacial action. The trailhead is along the Chief Mountain International Hwy., a half km from the Hwy. 5 junction. The first six km is along the eastern bank of Lower Waterton Lake through forest and grassland. The trail then continues along the lake to Bosporus Landing opposite the town or climbs steeply to Vimy Peak (2,379 meters). The Vimy Peak trail actually ends at a basin short of the summit, which is still a painfully steep 40-minute scramble away.

SCENIC DRIVES

Akamina Parkway

This 16-km drive starts in the townsite and switchbacks up into the Cameron Creek Valley, ending at Cameron Lake. The viewpoint one km from the junction of the park road is on a tight curve so park off the road. It looks out over the townsite and the **Bear's Hump,** which was originally part of a high ridge that extended across the lake to Vimy Peak until glacial action wore it down. This section of the road is also a good place to view bighorn sheep. From here to Cameron Lake are a number of picnic areas and stops of interest including the site of Alberta's first producing oil well, and a little farther along the road, the site of **Oil City,** the town that never was. **Cameron Lake,** at the end of the road, is a subalpine lake in a large cirque carved around 11,000 years ago by a receding glacier. Mount Custer at the southern end of the lake is in Montana. Waterton has no glaciers, but Herbst Glacier on Mt. Custer can be seen from here. To the west (right) of Custer is **Forum Peak** (2,225 meters), whose summit has a cairn marking the boundaries of Alberta, Montana, and British Columbia. Canoes ($8-10 per hour), row boats ($8 per hour), and paddle boats ($8-10 per hour) can be rented at the lake or you can hike one of the many nearby trails. See "Hiking," above, for details. Grizzlies frequent the avalanche slope at the southwestern end of the lake so hike with someone you can outrun.

Red Rock Canyon Parkway

The best roadside wildlife viewing within the park is along this 13-km road which starts near the golf course and finishes at **Red Rock Canyon.** The transition between rolling prairies and mountains takes place abruptly as you travel up the Blakiston Valley. Black bears and very occasionally grizzly bears can be seen feeding on saskatoon berries along the open slopes to the north. **Mount Blakiston** (2,920 meters), the park's highest summit, is visible from a viewpoint three km along the road. The road passes

prairies to peaks along the Red Rock Canyon Parkway

a number of interpretive signs, picnic areas, and Crandell Mountain Campground. Red Rock Canyon, at the end of the road, is a water-carved gorge. The bedrock, known as argillite, has a high concentration of iron that oxidizes and turns red when exposed to air—it is literally going rusty. A short interpretive trail leads along the canyon.

Chief Mountain International Highway

This 25-km highway borders the eastern boundaries of the park and joins it to Glacier National Park in Montana. It starts east of the park gate at **Maskinonge Lake** and climbs for seven km to a viewpoint where many jagged peaks and the entire Waterton Valley can be seen. The next stop, three km farther south, has views of Chief Mountain, which has been separated from the main mountain range by erosion. The road then passes more spectacular viewpoints, Belly River Campground, and Chief Mountain. Hours of operation at the port of entry are 15-31 May, daily 9 a.m.-6 p.m.; June to mid-September, 7 a.m.-10 p.m.; closed the rest of the year. When the post is closed you must use the Carway/Piegan port of entry. It's on Alberta Hwy. 2 south of Cardston or Montana Hwy. 89 north of St. Mary (depending on your direction of travel). From the border it's 50 km to St. Mary and the spectacular Going-To-The-Sun highway through Glacier National Park. For more information on Glacier Park write to Park Superintendent, Glacier National Park, West Glacier, MT 59936, U.S.A.

OTHER RECREATION

On The Water

Winds of up to 70 kph attract hard-core windsurfers throughout summer and into fall. The winds are predominately south to north, providing fast runs across Upper Waterton Lake from the beach at Cameron Bay. The lake is deep, keeping the water temperature low and making a wetsuit necessary. Read the warning signs at the beach before heading out. Fishing in the lakes is above average with most anglers chasing brook and rainbow trout, pike, and whitefish. A National Park fishing license is required and can be obtained from the park information center or any of the administration offices. The li-

cense costs $6 for seven days, or $13 for an annual permit.

On any given summer day, scuba divers can be seen slipping into the frigid waters of Emerald Bay. A steamer was scuttled in the bay in 1918. It had been used to haul logs and as a tearoom but now sits on the lake's floor, attracting divers who find it a novelty to explore a sunken ship so far from the ocean. No equipment rental is available in the park. The closest is at **Anderson Aquatics** in Lethbridge at 314 11th St. S, tel. (403) 328-5040, where you can also get your tanks filled. Full gear rental from Anderson is $50 per day, $75 for the weekend, including air fills. Their National Association of Underwater Instructors (NAUI) run certification courses and field trips to Waterton Lakes throughout the summer. Stop in on your way through for a rundown on all the dives, or ask at the park information center.

On Dry Land

The rolling fairways and spectacular mountain backdrop of **Waterton Lakes Golf Club** can distract even the keenest golfer's attention. The 18-hole course, designed by Stanley Thompson, is located four km north of the townsite on the main access road and is open June to early October. Its facilities include a rental shop, clubhouse, and restaurant serving sandwiches and snacks. A round of golf costs $22 during the day, dropping to $12 after 6 p.m. (which may have something to do with the healthy local bear population). For tee times call (403) 859-2383.

Along the same road is **Alpine Stables,** tel. 859-2462, which offers hour-long trail rides (starting on the hour) for $12.50. Two-hour wildlife rides leave at 10 a.m. and 5 p.m. and cost $22.50. If you find Emerald Bay a little cold for swimming, try the outdoor heated swimming pool on Cameron Falls Dr. ($2.50 per day). Across the road are four tennis courts. The courts are free, but you'll need your own racket.

When The Sun Goes Down

Interpretive programs are held nightly during the summer in Crandell Campground and at the **Interpretive Theatre** opposite Cameron Falls. Programs begin at at 8:30 p.m. Ask at the park information center or call (403) 859-2445 for details. Being the biggest bar in town,

the **Thirsty Bear Saloon** in the Bayshore Inn gets crowded. It pours happy hour daily 3-6 p.m., and a band plays three or four nights a week. It's open 11 a.m.-2 a.m. Much smaller and much quieter is **Levi's Place** on Windflower Ave., tel. 859-2020; open 11 a.m.-2 a.m. In the Prince of Wales Hotel, the **Windsor Lounge** has live entertainment most nights, and the **Rams Head Lounge** in the Kilmorey Lodge has a fireplace and an outside deck with views of the lake. **Waterton Lakes Opera House,** 309 Windflower Ave., tel. 859-2466, shows movies daily at 7:30 and 9:30 p.m. In July and August, live shows featuring songs from the movies are performed at the Bayshore Inn Convention Centre; tickets are $5-10, available from the inn.

Wintertime

Winter is a quiet time in the park. Traffic on the roads is light, a few trails are maintained for cross-country skiing, and the snowcapped peaks and abundant big game provide plenty of photographic opportunities. The main access road is plowed regularly and the Akamina Parkway is cleared to allow access to ski trails. Skiing in the park is usually possible from December to March, but conditions can change dramatically. Arctic fronts scream down from the north, and chinook winds from the west can raise temperatures by up to 25° C in a matter of hours. Ski trails are set on weekends and the ski-touring opportunities are endless. Trails in the backcountry are not marked. Groups should carry avalanche beacons, be capable of self rescue, and register with the warden before setting out. Ice climbing, snowshoeing, and backcountry winter camping are also popular. Winter camping is possible at Pass Creek where there is a kitchen shelter, woodstove, and pit toilets. The **Kilmorey Lodge** stays open year-round and offers all-inclusive winter packages. Gas may or may not be available in winter. Obtain trail information and weather forecasts at the park administration office on Mount View Rd., open weekdays 8 a.m.-4 p.m., tel. (403) 859-2262, or call the Warden's Office at 859-2275. For information regarding backcountry skiing conditions and avalanche danger contact the **Canadian Avalanche Association,** tel. (800) 667-1105.

ACCOMMODATIONS

Hotels And Motels

Waterton has a limited number of seasonal accommodations. They start opening in May and will be full every night during July and August. By mid-October many are closed. They are all within the townsite so walking to the marina and shops isn't a problem.

The **Kilmorey Lodge,** P.O. Box 100, Waterton Park, Alberta T0K 2M0, tel. (403) 859-2334, is a historic inn on the shores of Emerald Bay. From the lobby a narrow stairway leads up to rooms tucked under the eaves, many of which have spectacular lake views. Each is furnished with antiques and the beds have down comforters to ensure a good night's sleep. Downstairs is one of the town's finest restaurants, along with a lounge and gazebo for enjoying a quiet drink on those warm summer nights. The lodge is the only accommodation that stays open year-round. Rooms start at $70 s or d in summer. Inexpensive packages are offered during the off-season. Across the road is **Crandell Mountain Lodge,** P.O. Box 114, Waterton Park, Alberta T0K 2M0, tel. 859-2288, a country-style inn with beautifully furnished rooms of the same high standard as the Kilmorey Lodge; $69 s, $74 d.

Waterton's most well-known landmark is the **Prince of Wales Hotel,** General Delivery, Waterton Park, Alberta T0K 2M0, tel. 859-2231, a seven-story gabled structure built in 1927 on a hill overlooking Upper Waterton Lake. It was another grand mountain resort financed by the railway, except unlike those in Banff and Jasper, it had no rail link. It was built as part of a chain of first-class hotels in Glacier National Park. Early guests were transported to the hotel by bus from the Great Northern Railway in Montana. After extensive restoration inside and out, the hotel has been returned to its former splendor. Guests from the U.S. travel to the park in vintage touring buses. Rooms, some of which are small, start at $110 s or d. The hotel is open June to early September. Its off-season mailing address is Station 0928, Phoenix, AZ 85077, U.S.A.; tel. (602) 207-6000.

Other accommodations in the park are: **Northland Lodge,** General Delivery, Waterton

Prince of Wales Hotel

Park, Alberta T0K 2M0, tel. (403) 859-2353, a converted house with guest lounge, $46-62 s or d; **Stanley Hotel,** Waterton Ave., Waterton Park, Alberta T0K 2M0, tel. 859-2345, usually full and with shared bathrooms, $45 s or d; **El Cortez Motel,** P.O. Box 67, Waterton Park, Alberta T0K 2M0, tel. 859-2366, with some kitchenettes, $55-85 s or d; **Aspen Village Inn,** P.O. Box 100, Waterton Park, Alberta T0K 2M0, tel. 859-2255, $80 s or d; **Bayshore Inn,** P.O. Box 38, Waterton Park, Alberta T0K 2M0, tel. 859-2211, lacking in atmosphere but with a waterfront location, hot tub, and restaurant to make up for it, $85 s or d for a basic room, $95 lake view.

Campgrounds

Townsite Campground, tel. (403) 859-2224, is in a prime location on the lake within walking distance of many trailheads, restaurants, and shops. Many of its over 200 sites have power, water, and sewer hookups. The campground also has showers and kitchen shelters. Sites are available on a first-come, first-served basis, and fill up by mid-afternoon most summer days. Open mid-May to mid-October; unserviced sites $13, full hookups $17.50. **Crandell Mountain Campground** is located 10 km from the townsite on Red Rock Canyon Parkway. It has 129 unserviced sites, flush toilets, firewood, and kitchen shelters. It's open mid-May to August, sites $10.50. **Belly River Campground** is 29 km from the townsite on Chief Mountain International Hwy. and is the smallest and most primitive of the park's three developed campgrounds. It has pit toilets, firewood, and kitchen shelters; sites are $7.25 per night. Waterton also has 13 backcountry campgrounds. Each has pit toilets, a cook shelter, and a water supply. Open fires are discouraged, and prohibited during periods of high fire danger; check with a warden. If you are planning to camp in the backcountry you must obtain a permit (free) from the park information center or administration office. If your planned itinerary takes you over the border, ask at the information center about border-crossing regulations.

Outside of the park, two private campgrounds take up the nightly overflow. **Waterton Homestead Campground,** tel. 859-2247, has full hookups, showers, laundry, and a heated pool. It is three km north of the park gate on Hwy 6. Tent sites are $9, trailers and RVs $12-17. On Hwy. 5, five km east of the park gate, **Waterton Riverside Campground,** tel. 653-2888, has powered sites, showers, and a barbecue on Saturday nights. Tent sites are $10, powered sites $13. Both these campgrounds close by the middle of September.

FOOD

Within town are a variety of restaurants ranging from pizza and fast food to elegant dining. If you plan on cooking your own food, stock up before you get to the park. Groceries are available at the **Rocky Mountain Food Mart** on Windflower Ave. (open 8 a.m.-10 p.m.) and in the Tamarack Mall on Mount View Road. For great pizza try **Pizza of Waterton,** 103 Fountain Ave., tel. (403) 859-2660, where they pile the dough with all kinds of meats, fresh vegetables, and a special savory sauce. It's open 4:30-10 p.m. For inexpensive breakfasts, homemade soups, delicious salads, and breads covered in homemade preserves head to **Pearl's Patio Cafe and Deli,** 305 Windflower Ave., tel. 859-2284, where the indoor/outdoor tables are always busy. **New Frank's Restaurant,** 106 Waterton Ave., tel. 859-2240, serves inexpensive Chinese food (from $7) and western food (from $9.50), and lays out a simple six-course buffet every night in summer ($10). **Gazebo Cafe on the Bay** in the Kilmorey Lodge serves light snacks and simple meals; seating is on an outdoor deck on the waterfront. It's open daily 10 a.m.-10 p.m. **Waterton Park Cafe,** on Waterton Ave., tel. 859-2393, serves basic hamburgers starting at $4. It has a liquor license and fills up with the seasonal worker crowd after 10 p.m. Its hours are noon-2 a.m.

One Step Up
The **Kootenai Brown Dining Room** in the Bayshore Inn, tel. (403) 859-2211, overlooks Upper Waterton Lake and the mountains. Mule deer often feed within sight of diners. The food is excellent, especially the trout and beef dishes which start at $12. The view is free. It's also open for breakfast and lunch. Hours are daily 7 a.m.-10 p.m. One of the most popular restaurants in town is in the Kilmorey Lodge. The **Lamp Post Dining Room,** tel. 859-2334, has all the charm of the Prince of Wales Hotel but with a more casual atmosphere and prices to match. The mouthwatering menu has appetizers starting at $3, entrees ranging $10-18, and you should leave room to finish with a delicious piece of homemade pie. It's open 7:30 a.m.-10 p.m. The **Garden Court Dining Room** is a formal restaurant in the Prince of Wales Hotel with views of the lake through large windows. Its high ceiling and Old World elegance create a first-class ambience that is overshadowed only by the quality of the food. Prices are similar to any big-city restaurant of the same standard—expect to pay around $90 for two with a bottle of wine. If you are going to splurge, do it here. A

large breakfast buffet every morning (6:30-9:30 a.m.) is worth trying if you won't be coming for dinner. It's open for lunch noon-2 p.m., dinner 5:30-9:30 p.m. Reservations are required; tel. 859-2231.

TRANSPORTATION

Getting There And Around
The nearest commercial airport is at Lethbridge, 140 km away. Cars can be rented at the airport. **Greyhound** terminated its summer service to the park a couple of years ago. The closest they come to the park is Pincher Creek, 50 km away. From the depot there, at 2025 Hewetson St., a cab to Waterton will cost around $40. Call **Crystal Taxi** at (403) 627-4262.

The **Park Transport Company** operates hiker shuttle services to various trailheads within the park. Cameron Lake, the starting point for the Carthew-Alderson Trail, which ends back in town is a popular drop-off point; $6 one way. You could take one of these shuttles, and return on the bus later in the day if driving the steep mountain roads doesn't appeal to you. They also run a taxi service around town. Their office is in Tamarack Mall on Mount View Rd., tel. 859-2378. **Pat's Rentals** is also on Mount View Rd., tel. 859-2266. Pat rents mountain bikes ($5.50 per hour, $27 per day) and motorized scooters ($13 per hour, $60 per day). Pat's also operates the only car-rental agency in the park; **Budget** compact cars are $59.95 per day with unlimited mileage.

To Goat Haunt, Montana
Waterton Inter-Nation Shoreline Cruise Co. runs scheduled cruises across the International Boundary to Goat Haunt, Montana at the southern end of Upper Waterton Lake. The 45-minute trip along the lakeshore passes spectacular mountain scenery, and wildlife is usually seen. A half-hour stopover is made at Goat Haunt, which is located in a remote part of Glacier National Park and consists of little more than a dock, a peace-park pavilion, and a ranger station. You can return on the same boat or go hiking and return later in the day. If you are planning an overnight hike from here you are required to register at the ranger station. Another popular option is to take an early boat trip and

walk back to town on the **Waterton Lakeshore Trail,** which takes about four hours. Boats leave the Waterton marina five times daily during summer. Fewer trips are made during May and September. The cruises operate until the end of September, but after the U.S. ranger station closes for the season in midmonth, the boats pass by Goat Haunt without stopping. Tickets cost $14 round trip, $8 one way, and you'll need to book ahead in summer; tel. (403) 859-2362. The same company operates a regular shuttle service to the Crypt Lake Trailhead for $9 round trip.

SERVICES AND INFORMATION

Shopping And Services

The proliferation of tourist-oriented gift shops along Waterton Ave. is worth browsing through when the weather isn't cooperating. In the **Tamarack Mall** on Mount View Rd. you'll find a sports store selling camping gear and fishing tackle, a good bookshop, an outdoor-clothing store, and a Royal Bank cash machine. The **post office** is beside the fire station on Fountain Avenue. The **Itussiststukiopi Coin-Op Launderette** at 301 Windflower Ave. is open daily 8 a.m.-10 p.m. The closest **hospitals** are in Cardston, tel. (403) 653-4411, and Pincher Creek, tel. 627-3333. The park's 24-hour emergency number is 859-2636. For the **RCMP** call 859-2244.

Maps And Information

Topographical maps of the park (one map covers the entire area) are available from the park information center, administration office, and Heritage Centre for $9.50. For an in-depth look at the natural and human history of the park, pick up a copy of *A Guide to Waterton Lakes National Park* by Heather Pringle at bookshops in town. A free brochure entitled *Catalogue of Publications* lists every book ever written about the park as well as many titles pertaining to Western Canada in general. It's available from the Waterton Natural History Association in the Heritage Centre, P.O. Box 145, Waterton Park, Alberta T0K 2M0.

On the main access road opposite the Prince of Wales Hotel is the **park information center,** tel. (403) 859-2445, which provides general information on the park, sells fishing licenses, and issues backcountry permits. Open June-Aug. 8 a.m.-9 p.m., May and early September 9 a.m.-5 p.m., closed the rest of the year. The park's **administration office** on Mount View Rd. offers the same services as the park information center and is open year-round, weekdays 8 a.m.-4 p.m.; tel. 859-2224. The **Heritage Centre,** 117 Waterton Ave., tel. 859-2267, is another good source of information and has a good selection of books and an art gallery. It's open May-Oct. 9 a.m.-5 p.m., longer hours in summer. For more information on the park write to Superintendent, Waterton Lakes National Park, Waterton Park, Alberta T0K 2M0.

BOB RACE

CROWSNEST PASS AND VICINITY

The Municipality of Crowsnest Pass is located along Hwy. 3 between Pincher Creek and the Continental Divide in the southwestern corner of the province. The municipality encompasses a handful of once-bustling coal-mining communities, including Bellevue, Hillcrest, Frank, Blairmore, and Coleman. Many topographic features in the area are named "Crowsnest," including a river, a mountain, and the actual pass (1,396 meters) on the Continental Divide. From Pincher Creek it is 62 km to the pass. Continuing west from there, the highway (known as the Crowsnest Highway, of course) descends into British Columbia to the coal-mining and logging towns of Sparwood and Fernie, then on to the major population center of Cranbrook. The area is worth exploring for its natural beauty and recreation opportunities alone; the Crowsnest River reputedly offers some of Canada's best trout fishing. But a trip wouldn't be complete without visiting the historic towns and mines along the route. The Municipality of Crowsnest Pass is Alberta's only ecomuseum and was declared a Historic District in 1988, meaning that entire communities are preserved for future generations to explore.

History

The tumultuous history of the pass is one of strikes, disasters, and in more recent times, unemployment, as one by one the coal mines have closed. Coal had been reported on the eastern slopes as early as 1845, but it wasn't until the Canadian Pacific Railway opened its southern line through the pass in 1898 that the eastern slopes attracted mining companies. Mines were opened and townsites laid out, attracting workers to the area. Many of them were immigrants who brought expectations of high wages and a secure future. But the area's entire economy revolved around just one industry—coal mining. Unfortunately for the miners, the coal here turned out to be of poor quality, and located in seams at steep angles, making extraction difficult. In addition, most of the mining companies were foreign owned and severely undercapitalized, leading to serious problems. The C.P.R. was the mining companies' largest customer, but as the coal was inferior to that from the B.C. mines, the price paid was considerably less. The first mine closed in 1915 and one by one the others have followed suit. Today many of the local miners work in British Columbia, commut-

Hillcrest was devastated by a mine explosion that claimed 189 lives in 1914.

PROVINCIAL ARCHIVES OF ALBERTA

ing over the Continental Divide each day. To the residents of this job-starved valley, the tourism industry is something new, but it's catching on quickly. At present only Blairmore and Coleman have tourist services but this will certainly change.

PINCHER CREEK

This medium-sized town of 3,800 is surrounded by some of the country's best cattle land. It is reputed to be the windiest spot in Alberta. The bitter winters are tempered by chinook winds that will raise temperatures by up to 20° C in an hour. The town is located in a shallow valley in the southwest corner of the province, 211 km south of Calgary and 70 km north of the International Boundary. The town has many historic buildings, makes a good base for exploring the Castle River Valley and historic Crowsnest Pass, and is known as the gateway to Waterton Lakes National Park.

The North West Mounted Police established a horse farm at what is now known as Pincher Creek in 1876. They found that oats and hay, the horses' main source of sustenance, grew much better here in the foothills than at their newly built post at Fort Macleod. The story goes that a member of the detachment found a pair of pincers near the river—lost many years earlier by prospectors from Montana—and the name stuck. Word of this fertile agricultural land quickly spread and soon the entire area was settled. As was so often the case for towns across the west, the C.P.R. bypassed Pincher Creek and built a siding to the north called Pincher Station. Most towns either moved to the railway or struggled for a few years and died. But not Pincher Creek; it stayed put and has thrived ever since.

Sights
The **Pincher Creek Museum,** tel. (403) 627-3684, is located in **Kootenai Brown Historical Park** on James Avenue. It houses many displays associated with early pioneers of the region. Within the park are numerous historic buildings including the cabin of Kootenai Brown, a turn-of-the-century folk hero (see "Waterton Lakes National Park," above). The cabin was moved from its original site on Waterton Lakes in

1969. It's open May, June, and September daily 9 a.m.-5 p.m.; July and August daily 9 a.m.-7 p.m.; the rest of the year Tues.-Fri. 1-4 p.m. Admission is $2. Overlooking Pincher Creek's main street is **Lebel Mansion,** 696 Kettles St., tel. 627-5272, a dignified brick house that has been restored by the Allied Arts Council. Inside is a small art gallery and cultural center open weekdays 9 a.m.-5 p.m.

The **Oldman Dam** north of Pincher Creek is the latest attempt to irrigate regions of southern Alberta not normally able to produce crops. The reservoir, located just below the confluence of the Crowsnest, Castle, and Oldman rivers, is becoming a popular recreation spot for windsurfing, boating, and fishing. Just below the dam wall is a specially built kayaking course. The road to the dam (Hwy. 785) also leads to two museums. **Three Rivers' Rock and Fossil Museum,** tel. 627-2206, is a large private collection of shells, minerals, rocks, and oddities of nature. It's open May to mid-October 10 a.m.-5 p.m.; closed Monday. **Heritage Acres,** tel. 627-5212, is a museum run by the Oldman River Antique Equipment and Threshing Club. It includes a schoolhouse, Doukhobor barn, and Crystal Village—a collection of buildings made entirely from glass telephone insulators (200,000 of them). It's open May-Sept., daily 8 a.m.-6 p.m.; admission $1. The Pincher Creek **Hutterite Colony** is one of the few in Alberta that actively invites outsiders to tour the grounds and view the residents' intriguing lifestyle. This colony was the subject of an article written in the May/June 1987 issue of *Equinox*. It is located between Pincher Creek and Cowley. Turn south off Hwy. 3 at the airport sign, then turn south again at the first junction. Follow this road to a "T" intersection, then turn right. The colony comes into view after 1.5 km. Before visiting you are requested to phone ahead, tel. 627-4021.

Beauvais Lake Provincial Park
Located deep in the foothills 24 km southwest of Pincher Creek, Beauvais Lake Provincial Park is a wilderness area with a rich history of early settlement. Foundations of buildings are all that remain of the first homesteaders' efforts to survive in what was then a remote location. The park's most famous settler was James Whitford, one of General Custer's scouts at the famous Battle of Little Bighorn. He is buried at

CHINOOK WINDS

On many days in the dead of winter, a distinctive arch of clouds forms in the sky over the southwestern corner of the province as a wind peculiar to Alberta swoops down over the mountains. The warm wind raises temperatures by up to 20° C in an hour, and up to 40° C in a 24-hour period. The wind's impact on the environment is profound, its effect on the snowpack legendary. One story tells of a backcountry skier who spent the better part of a day traversing to the summit of a snow-clad peak on the front range of the Rockies. As he rested and contemplated skiing down, he realized that the slope had become completely bare!

Chinooks (a native word meaning "snow eater") originate over the Pacific Ocean as warm, moist air which is pushed eastward by prevailing westerlies. As the air crosses British Columbia's rugged interior and climbs the western side of the Rockies, it releases moisture and picks up heat. The warm, dry air then descends the eastern slopes of the Rockies and blows across the prairies. The "chinook arch" is formed as the clear air pushes the cloud cover westward. The phenomenon is most common in southern Alberta, but occurs to a lesser degree as far north as the Peace River Valley. Pincher Creek experiences around 35 chinooks each winter.

Scott's Point. A reservoir in the southeast corner of the park supplies water to Pincher Creek. The reservoir is also good for boating and fishing for trout. The campground has limited services and costs $11 per night.

Westcastle Park

Alberta's fifth-largest ski area is also one of its best-kept secrets. Westcastle Park has a vertical rise of 520 meters, and much of its 80-plus hectares (serviced by three lifts) is advanced terrain. The area is situated on a north-facing ridge 47 km southwest of Pincher Creek along highways 507 and 774. Unfortunately, chinook winds—a ski area's worst nightmare—are prevalent in this part of the Rockies, and a 20° C temperature rise can turn hard-packed snow into slush very quickly. Don't let this put you off—the skiing is usually excellent. If a $70-million development plan that has been in and out of court for years is approved, the area will be turned into a four-season resort. High-speed quad chairs will zip skiers into areas previously accessible only by backcountry touring, while con-

dos at the base will sleep hundreds, and you'll be able to come back in summer to play golf. For the time being the hill struggles on. Rumors of its closure are rife in Pincher Creek, but the locals keep coming, and Lethbridge's keen fraternity of skiers makes the trek down every weekend for some of the best skiing a $25 lift ticket can buy. That's if the lifts open and the chinooks don't blow. For more information call Westcastle Park at (403) 627-5101 or the Mountain Sno Phone in Calgary at 280-4200.

Events

Summer is busy in Pincher Creek. The town hosts three rodeos: an all-girl affair at the end of May, the **Ranchers Rodeo** on the third weekend of June, and the **Pincher Creek Fair and Rodeo** the third week of August. The Ranchers Rodeo is part of a larger celebration—the **Alberta Cowboy-Poetry Gathering and Western-Art Show.** The gathering isn't a festival or competition—just a group of cowboys who come together each year to entertain each other. Poems are recited on Friday and Saturday—

those known by heart are greeted with the most appreciation. On Saturday night a huge barbecue takes place with more beef than you could poke a brand at. This gets everyone in the mood to kick up their heels at the dance. Demonstrations and sales of traditional Western arts and crafts take place throughout the weekend.

Other annual events in Pincher Creek include the **Parade of Power and Annual Show** (including working demonstrations of farm equipment) put on by the Oldman River Antique Equipment and Threshing Club on the third weekend in July; and the following weekend, celebrations on the Piegan reservation in nearby Brocket, including traditional dancing, a rodeo, and native-food tasting.

Accommodations

Pincher Creek's motels are spread along a four-block strip of Hwy. 6 as it passes through town. Least expensive are **Parkway Motel**, 1070 Waterton Ave., tel. (403) 627-3344; **Blue Mountain Motel**, 981 Main St., tel. 627-5335; and **Stardust Motel**, 979 Waterton Ave., tel. 627-4366. Each has basic rooms with coffee-making facilities, and all are within walking distance of the excellent Swiss Alpine Restaurant. Rooms start at $30 s, $34 d. The **Foothills Motel**, 1049 Waterton Ave., tel. 627-3341, is around the same price but has a restaurant and hot tub. **Heritage Inn,** 919 Waterton Ave., tel. 627-5000, is the nicest place to stay and has a coffee shop and restaurant; $54 s, $59 d. During winter all these motels offer ski packages for only slightly more than the price of a lift ticket. **Willowback B&B,** southwest of Pincher Creek in the small mountain community of Beaver Mines, tel. 627-2434, $35 s, $40 d, has shared bathroom facilities and a family room where you can relax with a cup of tea or coffee and a good book. On the premises is a wood-carving studio and gallery. Only a few minutes' walk away is the local general store that sells excellent ice cream.

Pincher Creek Municipal Campground is in a residential area on Wentworth Ave. just off Hwy. 6. It has no services but is central to town. A short path leads to Kootenai Brown Historical Park. The fee is $4 per night. On the northeast side of town on Hwy. 6 is **Sleepy Hollow Campground,** tel. 627-2033, with lots of permanent trailers, full hookups, and showers. Unserviced sites are $10, serviced $13-15. West of town along Hwy. 3 is **Castle River Provincial Recreation Area** ($5.50), and to the southwest toward Beaver Mines is **Beauvais Lake Provincial Park** ($11). Both have pit toilets, kitchen shelters, and firewood.

Food And Drink

The **Swiss Alpine Restaurant,** 988 Main St. at Waterton Ave., tel. (403) 627-5079, is a good place for a meal, whether it's a casual lunch or an intimate dinner in a homey atmosphere. The lounge has lots of stuffed animals and a Western-style atmosphere, and the dining area has good food, including Alberta beef and lamb, delicious salads, and a number of traditional Swiss dishes such as fondue. Most entrees are over $10 but portions are generous. It's open 11 a.m.-10 p.m. for food, but the lounge stays open till the wee hours. **Seasons Eatery** in the Heritage Inn, tel. 627-5000, is slightly cheaper but lacks the atmosphere of the Swiss Alpine. It's open for breakfast, lunch, and dinner. Along Main St. are three Chinese restaurants and a **Kentucky Fried Chicken. A&W** is on Hwy. 6 at the north end of town. Also on Main St., the **King Edward Hotel** has live country music on most nights, **Leo's Marco Polo Club** has exotic dancing on weekends, and **Ezzie's** in the Heritage Inn on Waterton Ave. is where the under-20s hang out.

Services And Information

The **Greyhound Bus Depot** is at 1015 Hewetson Ave., tel. (403) 627-2716. Greyhound's summer service to Waterton Lakes National Park has recently been terminated. The only public transportation to the park is by cab, around $40 one way; call **Crystal Taxi** at 627-4262. For **Budget** car rentals call 627-2007. The **post office** is at 998 East Avenue. **Pincher Coin Wash** is on Main St. opposite the theater; open daily 8 a.m.-9 p.m. **Pincher Creek Municipal Hospital** is at 1222 Mill Ave., tel. 627-3333. For the **RCMP** call 627-4424. The **information center,** west of the Husky gas station on Hwy. 6, is open daily in summer 8 a.m.-8 p.m.; tel. 627-4313.

To Leitch Collieries

If you had an old 1894 Department of the Interior map of this area, you'd find **Massacre Butte** on it, just west of Pincher Creek. A small group of Dutch immigrants making their way to Fort Edmonton was attacked by Indians there. The only survivor was a young girl who was scalped. Many years later a local business-man, George Gill, was visiting the nearby Pie-gan Indian Reserve when he saw a white-haired scalp hanging in the home of an old In-dian. Remembering the story of the massacre and the fate of the young girl he asked for the scalp, and for some years it hung in a Pincher Creek liquor store.

Southwest of Lundbreck is **Lundbreck Falls** (signposted from Hwy. 3) where the Crowsnest River plunges 12 meters into the canyon below. The campground at the falls has pit toilets, kitchen shelters, and firewood; $7.50 per night. From Lundbreck the highway passes the junction of Hwy. 22, which heads north to Kananask-is Country and Calgary. The next community west on Hwy. 3 is **Burmis,** well known for the **Burmis Tree,** a photogenic limber pine beside the highway on the west side of town.

At the turn of the century, **Leitch Collieries** was the largest mining and coking operation in Crowsnest Pass, and the only one Canadian owned. In 1915 it became the first to cease production. Now it's a series of picturesque ruins with one of the most informative interpre-tive exhibits in the area. The collieries opened in 1907, mining a steep coal seam south of the ruins. The No. 2 Mine, beside the highway, commenced operation in 1909. To house work-ers, a town named Passburg was built east of the mine. Today this site is the most accessible of the the area's "ghost towns," although noth-ing more than a few depressions remains; most buildings were moved after the mine closed. The early development of the site included a sandstone manager's residence, a powerhouse used to supply electricity to Passburg, a row of 101 coke ovens, and a huge tipple. A board-walk through the mine ruins leads to "listening posts" (where recorded information is played) and interpretive signs. The site is open year-round, with guided tours running daily 9 a.m.-5 p.m. in summer. For more information on the site, write to Crowsnest Pass Ecomuseum

NOT TO SCALE

Trust, P.O. Box 1440, Blairmore, Alberta T0K 0E0, or call (403) 562-8831.

BELLEVUE

A French company, West Canadian Collieries, had been prospecting in the pass since 1898 and had bought up 20,000 acres of land. Fortunately, the most impressive coal seams it found were right beside the main C.P.R. line. This became the site of the **Bellevue Mine.** At 8 p.m. on 9 December 1910, an explosion rocked the mine and destroyed the ventilation fan. Thirty men died as a result. Most survived the initial blast but died after inhaling "afterdamp," a term used to describe the carbon dioxide and carbon monoxide left after fire has burned the oxygen from the air. The mine reopened soon after the tragedy and at one time employed 500 men. But the gradual decline in the demand for coal led to the mine's closure in 1962.

The original town of Bellevue was built in 1905, before the mine disaster. The townsite centered around two streets: Front St. (now 213th St.) and Main St. (now 212th St.). The earliest single-story, wood-framed buildings had false facades to make them appear taller and more important than they really were. In 1917, fire destroyed many of the town's buildings, but these were soon replaced by more permanent structures, many of which still stand today. For detailed information on the buildings, purchase *Crowsnest Pass Historical Driving Tour: Bellevue and Hillcrest* ($2.25), available from information centers and museums along the pass or by writing to Crowsnest Pass Ecomuseum Trust, P.O. Box 1440, Blairmore, Alberta T0K 0E0. On Hwy. 3 beside Bellecrest Campground is the **Wayside Chapel,** which seats eight people. Recorded sermons are held throughout summer and the doors are always open. On the last weekend in June the town celebrates Bellecrest Days with a parade, pancake breakfasts, mud-bog race, and a Jell-O–eating contest.

Bellevue Mine Tour

The Crowsnest Pass Ecomuseum Trust opened the former Bellevue Mine for underground tours in 1991. It is the only mine on the pass open to the public. The "Coal Miner" tour is as realistic as possible without actually making you shovel dirt. The mine is cold, dark, and damp. Before entering you are given a hard hat and lamp, which you can attach to your hat or carry by hand. The guides carry blankets for those who get cold—average temperature in the mine is 7° C. Tour cost is $4; look for two-for-one coupons in the local visitors guide. It's open July to early August, 10 a.m.-5:30 p.m.; tours run every half hour. For more information call (403) 564-4700, or 562-8831 in the off-season.

Practicalities
The **Bellevue Inn**, 2414 213th St., tel. (403) 564-4676, was built in 1921 to house business clients from the mine. Today it still operates as a bar and hotel, with renovated rooms for $35 s, $45 d. The **Bellecrest Campground** on Hwy. 3 at the west end of town has limited services but is free. Bellevue has only one restaurant and it's Chinese, with a limited western menu. It's located at 2438 213th St., tel. 564-4801, and open Tues.-Sun. 11 a.m.-9 p.m. A **tourist information booth** beside the campground on Hwy. 3 is open during summer.

HILLCREST

Named after Charles Plummer Hill, one of the pass's earliest prospectors, Hillcrest is best remembered for Canada's worst mine disaster. The Hillcrest Coal and Coke Company began operations in 1905 and shortly thereafter laid out a townsite. Before long the town had its own railway spur, school, hotel, and store. Then disaster struck. At 9.30 a.m. on 19 June 1914, with 235 men working underground, an explosion tore apart the tunnels of the Hillcrest Mine. The blast was so powerful that it destroyed a concrete-walled engine-house 30 meters from the mine entrance. Many of those who survived the initial explosion were subsequently asphyxiated by the afterdamp (residual carbon monoxide and carbon dioxide). Rescue teams from throughout the pass rushed to the mine but were forced back by gas and smoke. The final death toll was 189. The mine reopened and produced 250,000 tons of coal annually until closing in 1939 for economic reasons.

Many of the mine-disaster victims could not be identified. They were wrapped in white cloth and buried one foot apart in mass graves. The **Hillcrest Cemetery** off 8th Ave. is now a Provincial Historic Resource. To get there follow the signs from Hwy. 3 toward Hillcrest. Many of the original miner residences still stand in Hillcrest, now a quiet town with a population of 1,000. The **Hillcrest Mine** is accessible along a gravel road beside the trailer court. The ruins are extensive—look for the sealed mine entrance at the rear of the ruins, half hidden by trees.

To the south of Hillcrest is some good hiking and camping along the Carbondale River Rd. (also known as Adanac Rd.), which spurs south from the Hillcrest access road east of the town. The best source of detailed information regarding these hikes is *Hiking Alberta's Southwest* by Joey Ambrosi. The Frank Slide Interpretive Centre (see below) has a copy you can peruse. The town of Hillcrest has no tourist services. For information on Hillcrest and the mine write to Crowsnest Pass Ecomuseum Trust, P.O. Box 1440, Blairmore, Alberta T0K 0E0, or call (403) 562-8831.

FRANK

Frank, two km west of Bellevue, is probably the most famous (or infamous) town in the Crowsnest Pass area. In 1901, two Americans acquired mineral rights to the area directly below Turtle Mountain. Within months their company, the Canadian-American Coal and Coke Company, had established a mine and laid out the townsite of Frank. The mine, when operational, became the first to sell coal in the pass and continued to thrive along with the town of Frank, whose population swelled to 600.

29 April 1903
It was before dawn. Everything in town was quiet and the night shift was hard at work deep inside Turtle Mountain. Then, without warning, a gigantic chunk of the north face of the mountain sheared off, thundering into the valley below and burying part of Frank. It was the world's most destructive rock slide, burying 68 of the town's residents. Amazingly, none of the working coal miners were killed. After being trapped

PROVINCIAL ARCHIVES OF ALBERTA

Turtle Mountain before the slide.

for 14 hours they dug themselves out. In times of tragedy there are usually heroes, and the hero of the Frank Slide was Sid Choquette. After realizing that the rail line had been covered he scrambled over the still-moving mass of boulders and flagged down the morning express, stopping it before it reached the slide. As a token of appreciation, the C.P.R. gave Choquette $25 and a letter of commendation. Within three weeks the tracks were dug out and the railway reopened. A week later the mine reopened. Most of Frank was intact, but fear of another slide led to the relocation of all the buildings across the railway line to a safer location. The mine closed in 1917.

It is impossible to calculate the amount of rock that fell from the mountain. It has been estimated at 82 million tons by some, 30 million cubic meters by others. Looking at the north face of Turtle Mountain will give you a visual idea of the slide. But it isn't until you actually drive through the slide area, or view the fan of limestone boulders that spread over three km from the base of the mountain and over two km to the east and west that the full extent becomes apparent. Scientists to this day puzzle over what caused the slide and the vast spread. Most believe that a number of factors contributed to the initial slide, and the weakening of the mountain by mining operations was only a small part of it. As to the spread of rock, one theory put forward by scientists is "air lubrication"; as the huge mass of rock slid downward it compressed and trapped air on which it rode across the valley.

Today Turtle Mountain is monitored daily with some of the world's most advanced seismographic equipment, but has shown no sign of moving since.

Sights
The original townsite of Frank is now an industrial park. To get to it cross the rail line at 150th St. (just west of the turnoff for the interpretive center). Take the first left and look for a rusty fire hydrant to the right. This is all that remains of the ill-fated town. This hydrant once stood on Dominion Ave., Frank's main street. Directly behind it was the grand Imperial Hotel, now just a depression in the ground with a tree growing in it. This road then continues across Gold Creek and into the slide area. A memorial was erected here by Delbert Ennis, whose entire family survived the slide—and they lived on the south side of Gold Creek! This was the main route through the area before the slide and has since been cleared. It eventually joins up with the Hillcrest access road. The mine entrance is partially visible on the northern edge of the slide area, just above Frank Lake. For those with a sense of adventure it is possible to climb Turtle Mountain (2,093 meters). The trailhead is in East Blairmore on Pipeline Road. The trek to the summit is actually easier than it looks as the trail follows the mountain's northwest ridge. Only the last 20 meters along an exposed section are tricky. Allow two to three hours each way.

The **Frank Slide Interpretive Centre,** on a slight rise at the northern edge of the slide area, is an excellent place to learn more about the history of the valley, its settlers, and its tragedies. The audiovisual presentation *In The Mountain's Shadow* is a particularly moving account of the terrible working and social conditions in the valley. A 1.5-km self-guided trail leads down into the slide. Better still, scramble up the slope behind the parking lot and walk along the ridge for a view of the entire slide area. Admission to the center is $3.25. It's open mid-May through August, 9 a.m.-8 p.m.; the rest of the year 10 a.m.-4 p.m. For more information call (403) 562-7388. In the Frank Community Hall at the west end of Frank is **Crowsnest Pass Art Gallery,** tel. 562-2218, which displays local and traveling exhibitions; open Tues.-Sat. 1-5 p.m., extended hours in summer. No tourist services are available in Frank, but who wants to camp under Turtle Mountain anyway?

BLAIRMORE AND VICINITY

With a population of 1,800, Blairmore is the largest of the Crowsnest Pass communities. The town was originally known as Tenth Siding before being renamed in honor of the Federal Minister of Railways, A.G. Blair. The town had only a small mine itself, but when the Frank Mine opened in 1901, Blairmore thrived. It became a main center for the surrounding mines and a supply point for the other towns. Real-estate brokers, insurance agents, doctors, and barristers all made their home here, and in 1907, West Canadian Collieries—who owned the Lille and Bellevue mines—relocated their offices to Blairmore. A brickyard opened and many of the wooden-front buildings along the main street were replaced by impressive brick structures.

Still, it was coal mining that dictated the town's economy, and by the 1920s tensions between the workers and the mining companies had increased to the breaking point; in 1925, hundreds of miners protested on the streets of Blairmore. When the depression of 1929 set in, the companies cut wages, leading to further strikes. Communist labor leaders rallied local miners, and in February 1932 an election swept union representatives into power. The workers' town council had been elected with overwhelming support by their fellow miners. In an early act of rebellion they renamed Blairmore's main street to Tim Buck Boulevard, honoring the leader of the Communist Party of Canada.

Sights
Many of Blairmore's original buildings still stand, including the brick structures on Main St. (20th Ave.). The three-story **Cosmopolitan Hotel** is the most impressive. It was built in 1912. The bar was always full of thirsty workers whom the manager obligingly served, even after hours (leading to the hotel's liquor license being revoked many times). Opposite the hotel is a **gazebo** that was a rallying point for miners during the '20s. For detailed information on all Blairmore's early buildings purchase a copy of *Crowsnest Pass Historical Driving Tour: Blairmore,* available at information centers and museums throughout the pass.

Recreation And Events
Crowsnest Pass Golf and Country Club in Blairmore is the only golf course in the pass. Green fees on this nine-hole course are $11 weekdays, $13 weekends. **Pass Powder Keg Ski Hill,** in town on 18th Ave., has two T-bars, a day lodge, and night skiing; tel. (403) 562-8334.

The annual **Rum Runner Days** on the second weekend of July is a rip-roaring celebration of the town's seedy past. It kicks off with a pancake breakfast and parade on Saturday, followed by a barbecue and music in Bandstand Park. The weekend culminates at Leitch Collieries on Sunday with a picnic.

Accommodations
Two historic hotels on 20th Ave.—the **Cosmopolitan Inn,** 13001 20th Ave., tel. (403) 562-7321, and **Greenhill Hotel,** 12326 20th Ave., tel. 562-2232—have rooms starting at $30 s, $32 d. Ask to see them first. Some have shared bathrooms, others have TVs, all are noisy on Saturday night. At the west end of town is **Highwood Motel,** tel. 562-8888, which has a popular restaurant and pub on the premises; $38 s, $42 d. The nicest hotel is **Cedar Riverside Inn,** 11217 21st Ave., tel. 562-8851, also at the west end of town and only two blocks from Hwy. 3. It has a sauna, jacuzzi, coin laundry, and restaurant. Rooms start at $45 s or d. Rather than paying $40 for a basic, boring motel room con-

sider the **Nestle Inn B&B,** 12313 21st Ave., tel. 562-2474. The former mine-manager's residence was built in 1915 and still retains its historic charm. The rooms are cozy and the coffeepot is always on in the large guest parlor. Rates are $35 s, $40 d, which includes a good hot breakfast. **Lost Lemon Campground,** tel. 562-2932, is across the railway tracks at the west end of town. It has showers, a swimming pool, and a laundry, and is right beside the Crowsnest River; tent sites are $12, hookups $14-18.

Food And Drink
Blairmore has five restaurants on 20th Ave., none being particularly special. The **London Arms Pub,** tel. (403) 562-8888, in the Highwood Inn, provides glimpses of mountain scenery from the window tables. For breakfast expect to pay $5, lunch $7, and dinner $8 and up. It's open Mon.-Sat. 6 a.m.-10:30 p.m., Sunday 7:30 a.m.-9 p.m. The restaurant in the **Cedar Riverside Inn,** tel. 562-8851, is open daily 6 a.m.-10 p.m. and has a buffet each Sunday from 4 p.m. Opposite the Greenhill Hotel is **Yummy Inn,** tel. 562-7357, for eat-in or takeout Chinese and a buffet for Tuesday lunch and Thursday dinner. **Bandelero's,** tel. 562-8211, is a Mexican/pizza place farther east. The **Nestle Inn Tea Room,** 12313 21st Ave., tel. 562-2474, serves light snacks and lunches in a historic building; open Mon.-Sat. 11 a.m.-4 p.m.

The bar in the Cosmopolitan Inn is always busy, as is the Greenhill Hotel which has live country music on Friday and Saturday nights. Don't ask for an umbrella in your drink at either of these places. The Cedar Riverside Inn has a lounge, as does the Highwood Motel.

Services And Information
Greyhound buses head to Pincher Creek ($4.28) and on to Calgary ($29.05) twice daily. They also go west into British Columbia. The depot is at 2022 129th St., tel. (403) 562-8551. The **post office** is at 12537 20th Avenue. The only medical services on the pass are at **Crowsnest Pass Health Care Centre,** located at 2001 107th St., tel. 562-2831. For the **RCMP** call 562-2866. A good source of information on the area is the **Crowsnest Pass Ecomuseum Trust,** housed in the old **Blairmore Courthouse** on 20th Avenue. Their mailing address is P.O. Box 1440, Blairmore, Alberta T0K 0E0; tel. 562-8831.

In The Vicinity
The foundations of **Lille,** once a thriving community north of Hwy. 3, can only be accessed on foot. The hike is short but the rewards are ample. The Lille mines and townsite were run by West Canadian Collieries, the same company that owned the Bellevue Mine. Its isolation from the pass and poor quality of coal forced the mines to close in 1913. The town's population of 400 moved out and everything that could be salvaged was moved to Bellevue.

Two possible routes can be taken to Lille—the shortest is from Blairmore, the other follows Gold Creek up a valley from east of Frank. To access the shorter trail, turn north just east of the Blairmore Golf Course on Grassy Mountain Rd. and follow it for eight km to an intersection. The road to the right leads to Lille, but from here you're on foot; it's a three-km (one-hour) hike along an old railway grade to the abandoned townsite in a grassy meadow.

Most of the building materials have been salvaged through the years, leaving only foundations. To the right of your path, you'll pass an impressive row of 50 coke ovens and the foundations of a once-grand hotel. Scattered through the meadow on the left-hand side of the trail lie the ruins of the miners' cottages, schools, and even a couple of rusty fire hydrants. A 4WD drive track leads east (left) through the meadow to two of the mines, which require some bushwhacking to find. On the south (right) side of this road are the foundations of the bakery, butcher shop, general store, and hospital.

COLEMAN

The last of the Crowsnest Pass communities is Coleman, 15 km from the British Columbia border. The colliery in Coleman closed in December 1983, the last in the pass to do so. Many of the town's miners joined the ranks of the unemployed, some found work in the B.C. mines, while others packed up their belongings and left the pass completely. The effect on the town has been devastating. A walk down Coleman's 17th Avenue is like what walking down the main street of Bellevue, Frank, Passburg, and Lille must have looked like after their respective mines had closed. Most of the buildings are boarded up, all are dilapidated. Many businesses have relocated to the highway hoping to catch passing trade. Those that remain are breathing their last gasp of air.

History

Shortly after the land on which Coleman sat had been purchased by the International Coal and Coke Company, the town expanded rapidly. By 1904 it had two hotels, two churches, and a number of stores along Main Street. In 1918 the coal market collapsed and the mine closed. Still, the folks in Coleman were confident of the town's future and in due course cement side-walks were constructed. During the time leading up to WW II the mine opened, but with a scaled-down operation. The '50s was a time of amalgamation among the coal-mining companies in the pass, enabling the Coleman Colliery to remain open until 1983. Across the railway tracks at the west end of 17th Ave. are the remains of the coke ovens, the most complete in the pass. Many of the buildings that remain are of historical significance. For information pick up a copy of *Crowsnest Pass Historical Driving Tour: Coleman* ($2.25), available from the Crowsnest Museum or by writing to Crowsnest Pass Ecomuseum Trust at P.O. Box 1440, Blairmore, Alberta T0K 0E0.

Museum

Located in the old Coleman High School building is the **Crowsnest Museum,** 7701 18th Ave., tel. (403) 563-5434. The museum takes a full hour to view as it has two floors crammed with exhibits and artifacts from throughout the region. The schoolyard has displays of farming, mining, and fire-fighting equipment. It's open daily in summer 10 a.m.-noon, and 1-4 p.m.; closed weekends the rest of the year. Across the street is the ***Coleman Journal* Building.** The *Coleman Journal* was a Pulitzer Prize-winning weekly newspaper that was published until 1970. After extensive restoration, the Crowsnest Pass Ecomuseum Trust has opened the building to the public. Interpretive panels explain the slow process involved in early newspaper publishing. It's open daily in summer 10 a.m.-noon and 1-4 p.m.

Bomber Crash Site

From Coleman you can hike to the remains of a Royal Canadian Air Force Dakota which clipped the top of Andy Good Peak and crashed into the valley below in 1946. All seven airmen aboard lost their lives. The crash is on the south side of the Crowsnest River, nine km from town. Cross the railway lines at 81st St., then cross the river at 83rd St. and turn right (west) onto 13th Avenue. This road becomes gravel and fairly rough; it is only recommended for 4WDs. At the wooden bridge four km from town the road deteriorates and it's five km farther to the crash site (a 2.5-hour hike from town). Keep right at all intersections. All that remains of the plane is the tail section, wing section, and the landing gear.

THE NOT-SO-GREAT TRAIN ROBBERY

It was August 1920, and the Lethbridge-Cranbrook train had just pulled out of Coleman toward the Crowsnest Pass, loaded with passengers. Suddenly, under orders from three gun-wielding bandits, the train jerked to a halt. The trio, later identified as Aulcoff, Akroff, and Bassoff, had heard that successful local businessman Emilio Picariello—known to everyone as Emperor Pic—would be aboard carrying $10,000. The robbers' luck was short-lived from the start. They missed the wad of cash, fleeing with only $400 and several watches. After a night of drinkin' and dancin' in Coleman and evidently in no hurry, Akroff and Bassoff were spotted reading their "wanted" poster outside the Bellevue Cafe. The RCMP was alerted and confronted the pair. In the violent shoot-out that followed, Akroff and two policemen were killed. Bassoff was wounded and limped off in the direction of Frank Slide. On the run for several days he was tracked to a Pincher Creek train yard where he sat passive and composed, eating lunch. Arrested and charged, he was hanged on 22 December 1920. Three and a half years later Aulcoff was apprehended in Montana, extradited, and sentenced, but died in prison before the death sentence could be carried out. Today the only reminder of this lawless episode is a plaque at the Frank Slide Interpretive Centre remembering the slain officers (although bullet holes were visible in booths at the Bellevue Cafe for many years after the incident).

The Forestry Trunk Road

The Forestry Trunk Rd., also known as Hwy. 940 or Kananaskis Rd., is a well-graded gravel road that parallels the Rocky Mountains for over 1,000 km. The southernmost section starts in Coleman and heads north through the **Livingstone Range** to the Highwood Junction in Kananaskis Country, some 120 km to the north of Coleman. Along the way are many hiking and fishing opportunities and plenty of primitive Forest Service campgrounds. Highlights include **Livingstone Gap** (48 km north of Coleman)—where the Oldman River flows through a narrow gorge—and **Livingstone Falls** (65 km north of Coleman), which has a nearby campground.

Accommodations

Coleman has one motel, but this certainly isn't your only option. An old hotel has been restored as a youth hostel, and outside of town are cabins, a ranch, and a B&B. The **Stop Inn Motel,** tel. (403) 562-7381, is on Hwy. 3 above town. Clean, basic rooms are $35 s, $40 d. The **Grand Union International Hostel,** 7719 17th Ave., tel. 563-3433, was built in 1926. Early advertising for the hotel boasted of "thirty rooms with electric light and furnished in first class style." Substantial restoration work has been undertaken by the Southern Alberta Hostelling Association and although the rooms aren't first class they are of good hostel standard. The hostel is also central within Coleman—17th Ave. was originally the town's main street. Hostel rates are $10 members, $13 nonmembers. On Crowsnest Lake 12 km west of town is the **Rum Runner's Roost,** tel. 563-5111. Rooms in this large country home are $35 s, $45 d including a hot breakfast. A number of self-contained cabins with fantastic mountain views are also available for $50. Also on the lake is **Kosy Knest Kabins,** tel. 563-5155, where all rooms have kitchenettes and TVs; $35 s, $45 d.

Food

Most of Coleman's businesses have relocated from the main street to Hwy. 3, which bypasses town to the north. **Chris & Irvin's Cafe,** tel. (403) 563-3093, is one of the few businesses hanging on downtown. They serve hamburgers, cheeseburgers, bacon burgers, and loaded burgers. The menu might be limited but the burgers are good. They start at $2. It's open Mon.-Sat. 6 a.m.-10 p.m., Sunday 8 a.m.-8 p.m. Up on the highway is **Popiel's,** tel. 563-5555, surprisingly nice inside and with a reasonably priced steak, chicken, and seafood menu. It's open Tues.-Sat. 7 a.m.-midnight, till 10 p.m. on Sunday and Monday.

Services And Information

Greyhound stops at the Kananaskis Mohawk gas station on Hwy. 3. Beside Popiel's is a grocery store and laundromat. The **post office** on Main St. has recently closed and now houses only the residents' post boxes. The best source of information in town is the **Crowsnest Museum,** 7701 18th Ave., tel. (403) 563-5434, open daily during summer 10 a.m.-noon and 1-4 p.m.; closed weekends the rest of the year.

WEST OF COLEMAN

Crowsnest Mountain

From Coleman, the British Columbia border is only 15 km. But there's no rush, you have a mountain to climb. Crowsnest Mountain (2,785 meters) is the symbol of the pass, and although it's a fairly difficult ascent with an elevation gain of 1,030 meters, it can be hiked by anyone with a good level of fitness. Snow may be encountered until July and a certain amount of scrambling across scree slopes is required. For the most part the trail is up the north-facing slope, so don't be perturbed by the cliff faces that face the highway. The Allison Creek Rd. spurs north three km west of Coleman past one of Alberta's few outcrops of igneous rock (to the north just before the junction). Follow this road for 10.5 km, staying right at the first fork. The trailhead is marked, and a little farther is the parking lot—well, a place to park your car anyway. At first the trail climbs steadily through a subalpine forest of pine and spruce before crossing a stream. This is the last water source so fill up. At the first scree slope, below the north face of the mountain, is an impressive view of the Seven Sisters to the northeast. The trail through the scree slope is not always obvious, but try to follow it anyway—it's the easiest route. At the base of the cliff go right and climb up the wide gully to approximately 20 meters before the top of the rise, then veer sharply to the left. If you have difficulties scrambling up this section turn back;

if not, continue up three more gullies (the route is fairly obvious) from where the trail levels out and continues to the summit. The view from here is spectacular, extending well into British Columbia to the west, and to the Porcupine Hills to the east. A canister attached to one of the summit markers contains a notepad in which to sign your name and prove you made it. It is only five km to the summit but you should allow between 3.5 and five hours each way. Check the weather forecast before heading out.

To The Border

Also along Allison Creek Rd. is the **Allison Creek Brood Trout Station,** tel. (403) 563-3385, open to the public for tours and a self-guided walk. It's open daily in summer 10:30 a.m.-noon and 1-3:30 p.m., closed weekends Sept.-May. The road continues to a recreation area on **Allison Lake,** which has good fishing and nearby camping. During winter, cross-country ski trails are set around the lake. The **Travel Alberta Information Centre** on Hwy. 3 has a spectacular view of Crowsnest Mountain. The center is difficult to see coming from the east—look for a blue roof on the south side of the road opposite Crowsnest Lake. It's open mid-May to mid-June 9 a.m.-6 p.m., and mid-June to September 8 a.m.-7:30 p.m. Behind the informa-

tion center an old road now accessible only on foot leads three km (one hour each way) to an abandoned mine. The road crosses a small creek a number of times before coming to an intersection. Continue straight ahead (follow the creek) past an old car and into a grassy meadow. Head one km farther to the mine slag heap, and scramble to the top for a view of the mine and some log cabins.

Nearby are some interesting caves, also accessible by a short walk. They are not marked nor is there a set trail. The easiest way to get to them is from the roadside turnout on **Crowsnest Lake** (just west of the information center). Follow the lake's edge to the north, cross a small creek and follow the railway tracks to a point nearly opposite the roadside turnout. Look for a small stream to the north. The caves are here, and their walls bear petroglyphs (native rock carvings).

Crowsnest Lake is popular for fishing and windsurfing. From here Hwy. 3 crosses Island Lake and passes a small residential community known as **Crowsnest** before crossing the Continental Divide and entering British Columbia, which is another day and another book (Moon's *British Columbia Handbook,* by Jane King, to be precise).

KAREN MCKINLEY

CALGARY
INTRODUCTION

Calgary's nickname, Cowtown, is cherished by the city's 600,000 residents, who prefer that romantic vision of their beloved home to the city's more modern identity as a world energy and financial center. The city's rapid growth, from a NWMP post to a large and vibrant metropolis in little over 100 years, can be credited largely to the effects of resource development, particularly oil and natural gas.

Once run by gentlemen who had made their fortunes in ranching, Calgary is still an important cattle market. But the oil-and-gas bonanzas of the 1940s, '50s, and '70s changed everything. The resources discovered throughout western Canada brought enormous wealth and growth to the city, turning it into the headquarters for a burgeoning energy industry. Ignored by the eastern provinces, the city grew (at one time by 60 people a day) into a western dynamo, in constant conflict with the country's capital, Ottawa.

With the city's rapid growth came all the problems that plague major cities around the world, with one major exception—the distinct lack of manufacturing and industrial sites has meant little pollution.

Today the city is home to 20,000 Americans, many of them big oilmen with Texas twangs. Downtown is a massive cluster of modern steel-and-glass skyscrapers, a legacy of an explosion of wealth in the '70s. And in this futuristic mirage on the prairie are banks, insurance companies, investment companies, and the head offices of hundreds of oil companies. But not forgetting its roots, each July the city sets aside all the material success it's achieved as a boomtown to put on the greatest outdoor show on earth—the **Calgary Exhibition and Stampede,** a western extravaganza second to none.

HISTORY

As well as being one of Canada's largest cities, Calgary is also one of the youngest; at 120 years old it has a heritage rather than a history. Native Blackfoot moved through the area around

2,000 years ago, but had no particular interest in the direct vicinity of what is now Calgary. Around 300 years ago Sarcee and Stoney natives moved down from the north and there was continual warring between tribes. White settlers first arrived in the late 1700s. David Thompson wintered in the area, then the Palliser Expedition passed by on their way west to the Rockies. But it wasn't until the late 1860s that any real activity started. Buffalo had disappeared from the American plains and as hunters moved north so did the whiskey traders, bringing with them all the problems associated with this illegal trade.

Fort Calgary

The North West Mounted Police established a post at Fort Macleod soon after they came west to quell the whiskey trade. In 1875, a second fort was established on a terrace at the confluence of the Bow and Elbow rivers. It was named Fort Calgary after the Scottish birthplace of Inspector J.F. Macleod, who took over command of the fort in 1876. It is an apt name for a city which straddles the clear Bow River—Calgary is Gaelic for "clear, running water" a fact of which Macleod was probably well aware.

The Coming Of The Railway

For many years the Canadian Pacific Railway had planned to build a northern route across the continent through Edmonton and Yellowhead Pass. But eventually the powers in the east changed their minds and decided on a southern route through Kicking Horse Pass. This meant that the line passed right through Fort Calgary. In 1883 a station was built on an alluvial plain between the Bow and Elbow rivers. A townsite was laid out around it, settlers streamed in with the offer of free land, and nine years after the railway arrived, Calgary acquired city status—something that had taken its northern rival, Edmonton, over 100 years to obtain.

In 1886 a major fire destroyed most of the town's buildings. City planners decreed that all new structures were to be built of sandstone, which gave the fledgling town a more permanent look. The many sandstone buildings still standing today—the Palliser Hotel, Hudson's Bay Company store, and the courthouse, for example—are a legacy of this early bylaw.

Ranching

An open grazing policy, initiated by the Dominion Government, encouraged ranchers in the United States to drive their cattle from overgrazed lands to the fertile plains around Calgary. Slowly a ranching industry and local beef market developed. The first large ranch was west of Calgary, and soon many NWMP retirees, English aristocrats, and wealthy American citizens had invested in nearby land. Calgary's first millionaire was Pat Burns, who developed a meat-packing empire that still thrives today. Linked to international markets by rail and sea, Calgary's fortunes continued to rise with those of the ranching industry, receiving only a minor

Sandstone buildings gave Calgary a permanent look, even in its earliest years.

PROVINCIAL ARCHIVES OF ALBERTA

setback in 1905 when Edmonton was declared the provincial capital. During the first 10 years of this century the city's population increased 1000% and rail lines were built in all directions, radiating from the city like enormous spokes. Immigration slowed and the economy spiraled downward as the effects of WW I were felt.

Oil

The discovery of oil at Turner Valley in Calgary's backyard in 1914 signaled the start of an industry that was the making of modern Calgary. The opening of an oil refinery in 1923 and further major discoveries nearby transformed a medium-sized cowtown into a world leader in the petroleum and natural-gas industries. At its peak, the city was the headquarters of over 400 related companies. Calgary became Canada's fastest growing city, doubling its population between 1950 and 1975. During the worldwide energy crisis of the '70s, oil prices soared. Although most of the oil was extracted from farther afield, the city boomed as a world energy and financial center. Construction in the city center during this period was never ending, as many corporations from around the world moved their headquarters to Alberta. During this period Calgary had Canada's highest per capita disposable income and was home to more Americans than any other Canadian city. Much of the wealth obtained from oil and gas was channeled back into the city. Not just for office towers but for sporting facilities, cultural centers, and parks for citizens and visitors alike to enjoy. Calgary today also has tremendous civic support. Many of the city's self-made millionaires bequeath their money to the city, and the residents have always been willing to volunteer their time at events such as the Winter Olympic Games and the Calgary Exhibition and Stampede. This makes the city a great place to live and an enjoyable destination for the millions of tourists who visit each year.

1988 Winter Olympic Games

During the early '80s the province was hit by a prolonged downturn in the oil market. But good fortune prevailed when the International Olympic Committee announced that Calgary had been awarded the 1988 Winter Olympic Games. Life was injected into the economically ravaged city, construction started anew, and the high-spirited Calgarians were smiling once again.

The games are remembered for many things: the lack of snow, a bobsled team from Jamaica, the antics of English plumber/ski-jumper "Eddie the eagle," and most of all for their acclaimed success.

SIGHTS

GETTING ORIENTED

The TransCanada Hwy. (Hwy. 1) passes through the city, north of downtown, and is known as **16th Ave. N** within the city limits. Highway 2, Alberta's major north-south highway, becomes **Deerfoot Trail** as it passes through the city. Many major arteries are known as **trails,** named for their historical significance, not, as some suggest, for their condition. The main route south from downtown is **Macleod Trail,** a 10-km strip of malls, motels, restaurants, and retail stores. If you enter Calgary from the west and are heading south, a handy bypass to take is **Sarcee Trail SW,** then **Glenmore Trail,** which joins Hwy. 2 south of the city. **Crowchild Trail** starts downtown and heads northwest past the university to Cochrane.

The street numbering system is divided into four quadrants. At first it can be more confusing than the well-meaning city planner intended, but after initial disorientation, the system soon proves its usefulness. Basically the four quadrants are geographically named—northwest, northeast, southwest, and southeast. Each street address has a corresponding abbreviation tacked onto it (NW, NE, SW, and SE). The north-south division is the Bow River. The east-west division is at Macleod Trail, and north of downtown at **Centre Street.** Streets run north to south and avenues from east to west. Both streets and avenues are numbered progressively from the quadrant divisions (e.g., an address on 58th Ave. SE is the 58th street south of the Bow River, is east of Macleod Trail, and is on a street that runs east to west). Things don't get any easier in the many new subdivisions

© MOON PUBLICATIONS, INC.

that dominate the outer flanks of the city. Many street names are *very* similar to one another, so check whether you want, for example, Mackenzie Lake Bay, Mackenzie Lake Place, Mackenzie Lake Road, or Mackenzie Lake Avenue. Fill the gas tank, pack a hearty lunch, and good luck!

DOWNTOWN

The downtown core is a mass of modern steel-and-glass high-tech high-rises built during the oil boom of the '70s and early '80s. (Its ultra-modern appearance was the setting for *Superman III*.) Calgary's skyline was transformed during this period and many historic buildings were knocked down to make way for a wave of development that has slowed considerably during the last 10 years. The best way to get around is on foot or on the C-train (which is free along 7th Avenue).

Crisscrossing downtown is the Plus 15 walkway system—a series of interconnecting, enclosed sidewalks elevated at least 15 feet above road level. In total, 47 bridges and 12 km of public walkway link downtown stores, four large malls, and office buildings to give pedestrians protection from the elements. All are well signposted and wheelchair accessible. The following sights can be visited separately or seen on a walking tour (in the order presented).

Stephen Avenue Mall
The traditional center of the city is 8th Ave., between 1st St. SE and 3rd St. SW—a traffic-free zone known as Stephen Avenue Mall. This bustling tree-lined pedestrian mall has fountains, benches, cafes, restaurants, and souvenir shops. In summer the mall is full with shoppers and tourists, and at lunchtime, thousands of office workers descend from the buildings above. Many of Calgary's earliest sandstone buildings still stand along the mall on the block between 1st and 2nd streets SW. On the corner of 1st St. SW is the **Alberta Hotel,** one of the city's most popular meeting places until prohibition in 1916.

Calgary Tower
Ninth Ave. south of the mall has banks, expensive hotels, parking stations, the Glenbow Museum (see "Museums," below), and one of the city's most famous landmarks, the Calgary Tower (at the corner of Centre St.). This 190-meter tower dominated the skyline until 1985 when the nearby Petro-Canada towers went up. The observation deck affords a birds-eye view of the Rocky Mountains and the ski-jump towers at Canada Olympic Park to the west, the Olympic Saddledome (in Stampede Park) to the south, and the city below. The tower also houses the revolving **Panorama Dining Room,** a gift shop, and cocktail lounge. The one-minute elevator ride to the top costs $3.75 and runs daily, 8 a.m.-midnight. At ground level are shops, a tourist information center, and a currency exchange.

Olympic Plaza
This downtown park at the east end of Stephen Ave. Mall (on the corner of 2nd St. SE), filled with office workers each lunch hour, was used during the 1988 Winter Olympic Games for the nightly medal-presentation ceremonies. Plaques here commemorate medal winners, and the bricks on the ground are inscribed by members of the public who helped sponsor the Olympics by "purchasing" individual bricks prior to the Games. In summer, outdoor concerts are held here, and in winter, the shallow wading pool freezes over and is used as an ice-skating rink. Across 2nd St. SE from the plaza is **City Hall,** built in 1911. It still houses some city offices, although most have moved next door to the modern **Civic Complex.**

Back across 2nd St. SE is the **Calgary Centre for Performing Arts,** incorporating two of Calgary's historic sandstone buildings. The complex houses three theaters and the 1,800-seat **Jack Singer Concert Hall.** Tours of the center are offered Monday and Saturday at 11 a.m. ($2). For more information or performance schedules call (403) 294-7455.

In front of the Education Building on 1st St. SE (between 5th and 6th avenues) are the **Armengol Structures**—expressionless, raceless, humanlike forms with outstretched arms, standing over six meters tall.

Chinatown
At the east end of town on 3rd Ave. is a small Chinatown of around 2,000 residents. Chinese immigrants came to Calgary in the 1880s to work on the railroads, and stayed to establish ex-

CALGARY CITY CENTER

© MOON PUBLICATIONS, INC.

.... = C-TRAIN
O = C-TRAIN PLATFORM

KENSINGTON

MEMORIAL DR NW

BOW RIVER

PRINCE'S ISLAND PARK

CENTRE ST. BRIDGE

CHINATOWN

RIVER FRONT AVE.

CHINESE CULTURAL CENTRE

EAU CLAIRE MARKET

YMCA

WESTIN HOTEL

CENTRE ST. S

ARMENGOL STRUCTURES

DELTA BOW VALLEY INN

W.R. CASTELL CENTRAL LIBRARY

OLYMPIC PLAZA

CITY HALL

CALGARY CENTRE FOR PERFORMING ARTS

KING EDWARD HOTEL

4th AVE. SE
5th AVE. SE
6th AVE. SE
7th AVE. SE
9th AVE. SE
10th AVE. SE

5th ST. SE
4th ST. SE
3rd ST. SE
12th AVE. SE
1st ST. SE
CENTRE ST. S
1st ST. SW
2nd ST. SW
11th ST. SE

TO HOSTEL

GLENBOW MUSEUM

MACLEOD TRAIL

CALGARY TOWER

TO STAMPEDE PARK

BOW VALLEY SQUARE

BEIRUT RESTAURANT

RADISSON PLAZA HOTEL

THE BAY

STEPHEN AVE. MALL

POST OFFICE

PALLISER HOTEL

CALGARY EATON CENTRE

DEVONIAN GARDENS

CANNERY ROW/ McQUEENS UPSTAIRS

CAESAR'S STEAKHOUSE

PRINCE ROYAL INN

ENERGEUM MAP TOWN

ALBERTA SPORTS HALL OF FAME

YUZUKI JAPANESE RESTAURANT

ALBERTA BOOT CO.

ELECTRIC AVE.

2nd AVE. SW
3rd AVE. SW
4th AVE. SW
5th AVE. SW
6th AVE. SW
7th AVE. SW
8th AVE. SW
9th AVE. SW
10th AVE. SW
11th AVE. SW
12th AVE. SW

3rd ST. SW
6th ST. SW
7th ST. SW
8th ST. SW
9th ST. SW
10th ST. SW
11th ST. SW

McDOUGALL CENTRE

SUSHI HIRO

SANDMAN INN

MOUNTAIN EQUIPMENT CO-OP

TO BUS DEPOT

ALBERTA SCIENCE CENTRE

LORD NELSON INN

ROYAL PACIFIC HOTEL

NATURAL GAS MUSEUM

WEST CANADIAN COLOR

0.2 mi
0.2 km
0

The Chinese Cultural Centre is one of Calgary's many free attractions.

otic food markets, restaurants, and import stores here. Chinatown has seen its share of prejudice—from marauding whites gaining revenge for an outbreak of smallpox, to bungling city bureaucrats who demanded the streets be narrow and signs be in Chinese to give the area an authentic look. The **Calgary Chinese Cultural Centre,** 197 1st St. SW, is one of the largest such centers in Canada. It's topped by a grand central dome patterned in the same style as the Temple of Heaven in Beijing. The centerpiece of its intricate tile work is a glistening golden dragon hanging 20 meters above the floor. Within the center is a museum and gallery displaying the cultural history of the Chinese. Other facilities include a gift store and restaurant.

West On First Avenue
Eau Claire Market at the north end of 3rd St. SW is a colorful indoor market filled with stalls selling fresh fruit from B.C., seafood from the Pacific, Alberta beef, bakery items, and exotic imports. Under the same roof are a variety of specialty shops, an IMAX and regular theaters, and nine restaurants.

The northern limit of downtown is along the Bow River, where picturesque **Prince's Island Park** is linked to the mainland by a bridge at the end of 3rd St. SW. Jogging paths, tables, and grassy areas are scattered among the trees. To the east is **Centre St. Bridge,** guarded on either side by large stone lions. For a good view of the city, cross the bridge and follow the trail along the cliff to the west.

From the north end of town walk south along Barclay Mall (3rd St. SW), then west on 5th Ave. (or take the Plus 15 walkway system from the Canterra Tower) to the Energy Resources Building.

Energeum And Vicinity
One of Calgary's many free attractions, the Energeum, on the main floor of the Energy Resources Building, 640 5th Ave. SW, tel. (403) 297-4293, outlines the history and development of Alberta's largest industry. Through interpretive and hands-on displays, the story of oil, natural gas, oil sands, coal, and electricity in Alberta unfolds. The facility is operated by the Energy Resources Conservation Board, a regulatory body overseeing virtually all energy-related projects in the province. Open 10:30 a.m.-4:30 p.m., Sun.-Fri. in summer, Mon.-Fri. the rest of the year.

Just across the road is the **McDougall Centre,** 455 6th St. SW, tel. 297-8687, a Renaissance Revival building that is the southern headquarters for the Government of Alberta. It was declared a historic site in 1982. The Centre is open weekdays 8:15 a.m.-4:30 p.m.; call to arrange a tour.

One block south is the **Alberta Sports Hall of Fame,** 635 6th Ave. SW, tel. 269-6000, housing photographs, documents, and memorabilia honoring the province's sporting heroes. It's open Mon.-Fri. 8 a.m.-4 p.m.; admission is free.

Alberta Science Centre
This complex at 701 11th St. SW, tel. (403) 221-

3700, is a little farther out (you could either walk the five blocks west from 6th St. or jump aboard the C-train that runs along 7th Ave. SW and walk the last block). Among its attractions are a planetarium, theater, observatory, and science hall. The **Centennial Planetarium** features special effects shows with emphasis on different aspects of the universe. **Pleiades Theatre** has four different "mystery plays" that are presented throughout the year. For show details and ticket information call 221-3707. The **observatory** is open on clear nights, with the telescopes focused on the moon, planets, and clusters of stars. **Discovery Hall** has scientific displays and hands-on exhibits. It's open in summer, daily 10 a.m.-9 p.m.; the rest of the year, Wed.-Fri. 1-9 p.m., Saturday 10:30 a.m.-9 p.m., Sunday 10:30 a.m.-5 p.m. Admission is $4.

Devonian Gardens

The C-train will whisk you from the Alberta Science Centre back into the heart of the city to Devonian Gardens. A glass-enclosed elevator rises to the fourth floor of Toronto Dominion Square, 8th Ave. and 3rd St. SW, where a one-hectare indoor garden features 16,000 subtropical plants and 4,000 local plants—138 species in all. Within the gardens are waterfalls, fountains, pools, and bridges. Lunchtime entertainers and art exhibits can often be enjoyed in this serene environment. Admission is free, and it's open year-round, daily 9 a.m.-9 p.m.

South Of The Rail Line

South of the rail line, along 9th and 10th avenues, you'll find a smattering of restaurants, Electric Ave. nightclubs, western shops, low-rise offices, and many of Calgary's older buildings. The **Canadian Western Natural Gas, Light, Heat, and Power Co. Ltd. Museum,** 909 11th Ave. SW, tel. (403) 245-7611, is just about summed up by its long-winded name. Admission is free and it's open Mon.-Fri. 8 a.m.-4 p.m.

MUSEUMS

Glenbow Museum

This excellent museum, 130 9th Ave. SE (another entrance is on Stephen Ave. Mall), tel. (403) 268-4100, chronicles the entire history of western Canada through three floors of infor-

mative exhibits and well-displayed artifacts. The second-floor galleries display the museum's permanent collections of contemporary and Inuit art, as well as special exhibitions from national and international collections. The third floor presents historical displays on each aspect of the Canadian West; the story and traditions of the native Indian peoples unfold through displays of clothing, jewelry, ceremonial objects, and art and crafts, while other displays chronicle the fur trade, the early pioneers, the NWMP, and the ranching, oil industry, and agriculture industries. On the fourth floor is a large collection of military paraphernalia, mineralogy displays, and exhibits on the Warrior in Society and West Africa. The museum is open Tues.-Sun. 10 a.m.-6 p.m.; admission $4.50. The library and archives are open weekdays only, 10 a.m.-5 p.m.

Museum Of Movie Art

This is the only museum of its type in the world. It features over 10,000 movie and movie-star posters, many dating to 1920. The museum, 3600 21st St. NE, tel. (403) 250-7588, is open Tues.-Fri. 9:30 a.m.-5:30 p.m., Saturday 11 a.m.-5 p.m. Take the Whitehorn C-train to Barlow/Max Bell Station then hop aboard bus No. 33 (Vista Heights/Mayland Heights; weekdays only).

Aero Space Museum

This museum, 64 McTavish Place NE, tel. (403) 250-3752, traces the history of aviation in Canada through a large collection of aircraft, engines, uniforms, and old photographs dating back to the flight of one of Calgary's first aeroplanes, "West Wind," in 1913. The engine collection is one of the largest in North America. The museum, in a hangar off McKnight Blvd., also has an extensive library and archives, and a gift shop. It's open Mon.-Fri. 10 a.m.-5 p.m., Sat.-Sun. noon-5 p.m.; admission $5. Take the Whitehorn C-train to Whitehorn and then bus No. 57.

Nickle Arts Museum

This museum on the University of Calgary campus, off 32nd Ave. NW at 434 Collegiate Blvd., tel. (403) 220-7234, has a collection of coins from the Ancient World. Throughout the year more than 20 exhibitions of contemporary and historical art are displayed in one of three galleries. Hours are Tues.-Fri. 10 a.m.-5 p.m., Sat.-

Sun. 1-5 p.m.; admission $2, free on Tuesday. From downtown take the Brentwood C-train to the university or bus No. 9 (Varsity Acres).

Naval Museum Of Alberta

Canada's second-largest naval museum is located here in Calgary, over 1,000 km from the ocean. It honors those who served for Canada, many of whom were from the prairie provinces. The Royal Canadian Navy grew from humble beginnings in 1910 to become the Allied's third-largest navy in 1945. On display are three fighter aircraft that flew from the decks of aircraft carriers, as well as uniforms, models, flags, and photographs. The museum is open Tues.-Fri. 1-5 p.m., Sat.-Sun. 10 a.m.-6 p.m.; admission is free. It's located beside H.M.C.S. Tecumseh at 1820 24th St. SW; tel. (403) 242-0002. Take bus No. 2 (Killarney) from the corner of 7th Ave. and 8th St. Southwest.

Museum Of The Regiments

Opened by Queen Elizabeth in 1990, this is the largest military museum in western Canada. It highlights four regiments—Lord Strathcona's Horse Regiment, Princess Patricia's Canadian Light Infantry, the King's own Calgary Regiment, and the Calgary Highlanders—with realistic life-size figures, uniforms, badges, medals, and photographs. The museum is open daily (except Wednesday) 10 a.m.-4 p.m.; admission by donation. It's located on the Canadian Forces Base at 4520 Crowchild Trail SW, tel. (403) 240-7674. Take bus No. 13 (Mount Royal) from The Bay to 50th Ave. and walk north for five blocks.

Tsuu T'ina Museum

Commemorating the history of the Sarcee peoples, this small museum features a model tepee and two headdresses dating to the late '30s. Many displays were donated by the Provincial Museum in Edmonton. The museum is open Mon.-Fri. 8 a.m.-4 p.m.; admission by donation. It's located on the eastern flanks of the Sarcee Reserve at 3700 Anderson Rd. SW, tel. (403) 238-2677. The closest public transportation is the Anderson L.R.T. Station.

HISTORIC PARKS

Fort Calgary Historic Park

The North West Mounted Police built Fort Calgary at the confluence of the Bow and Elbow rivers in 1875. The fort is long gone but this 15-hectare park on the original site relives the earliest days of Canada's famous "Mounties"—the legacy of natives, hardy pioneers, and the wild frontier they tamed. The outline of the original fort is traced with logs, and an interpretive center has slide presentations about the NWMP every 30 minutes, and a hands-on display that follows Calgary's development. You can also try on the famous scarlet Mountie uniform or measure yourself against a plains bison. Across the Elbow River from the interpretive center is **Hunt House,** thought to be the oldest structure on its original site in Calgary. The house was built in 1876 for a Hudson's Bay Company employee. Next door is the larger **Deane House** with sweeping river views. Built in 1906 for a commanding officer of the NWMP, this is one of the oldest restored homes in the city. In the past it has been used as a stationmaster's house, boardinghouse, and artists co-op. Since being restored in 1983, it has operated as a teahouse. The menu features light lunches—mainly salads, sandwiches, and traditional English desserts. Those with a hearty appetite should try the Captain's Tea Plate ($13.95 for two).

The park is open year-round at 750 9th Ave. SE; admission $2. To get there, either walk along the river from downtown or hop aboard bus No. 1 (Forest Lawn) or No. 14 (East Calgary) from 7th Avenue. The interpretive center, tel. (403) 290-1875, is open daily 9 a.m.-5 p.m. The Deane House, tel. 269-7747, is open daily 11 a.m.-5 p.m.; call for reservations.

Heritage Park

This 26-hectare park is located on a peninsula jutting into Glenbow Reservoir southwest of downtown. Over 100 buildings and exhibits help re-create a turn-of-the-century pioneer village. Many of the buildings have been moved to the park from their original locations. Highlights include a Hudson's Bay Company fort, two-story outhouse, working blacksmith's shop, 1896 church, tepee, and an old schoolhouse with original desks. A boardwalk links stores crammed with antiques, while horse-drawn buggies carry passengers along the streets. You can also ride in authentic passenger cars pulled by a steam locomotive or enjoy a cruise in a paddlewheeler on the reservoir. A traditional bakery sells cakes and pastries, and full meals are served in the Wainwright Hotel (including an excellent Sunday brunch served 10 a.m.-2 p.m. in winter). Park admission only is $7.50; admission with all rides is $11.95. It's open mid-May to mid-October, daily 10 a.m.-4 p.m., till 6 p.m. on weekends. The park is located at 1900 Heritage Dr. SW; tel. (403) 259-1990. To get there by bus take No. 53 south from downtown or take the Anderson C-train to Heritage Station and transfer to bus No. 20 (Northmount).

Irish-born Sam Livingston was Calgary's first official settler.

CANADA OLYMPIC PARK

On the western outskirts of the city, beside the TransCanada Hwy., is 95-hectare Canada Olympic Park, developed for the '88 Winter Olympic Games. Ski jumping, luge, bobsled, freestyle skiing, and disabled events were held here. Now the park offers activities year-round, including tours of the facilities, luge rides, summer ski jumping, and sport training camps. In winter the beginner/intermediate ski slopes are filled with Calgarians who are able to ski as early as November with the help of a complex snowmaking system. Many ski jumping, bobsled, and luge events of national and international standard are held throughout winter.

Olympic Hall Of Fame
This is the largest museum devoted to the Olympic Games in the world. Three floors catalogue the entire history of the Winter Olympic Games through over 1,500 exhibits, interactive video displays, costumes and memorabilia, an athletes timeline, a bobsled and ski-jump simulator, and highlights from the last two Winter Olympic Games held at Albertville (France) and Lillehammer (Norway). The museum is open daily 10 a.m.-5 p.m.; admission $4.50.

Ski Jumping, Luge, And Bobsled Facilities
Visible from throughout the city are the 70- and 90-meter ski jump towers, synonymous with the Winter Olympic Games. These two jumps are still used for national and international competitions and training. A glass-enclosed elevator rises to the observation level. The jump complex has three additional jumps of 15, 30, and 50 meters —used for junior competitions and training. All but the 90-meter jump have a plastic-surfaced landing strip and are used during summer.

At the western end of the park are the luge and bobsled tracks. A complex refrigeration system keeps the tracks usable even on relatively hot days (up to 30° C).

Practicalities
A "Grand Olympic Tour" package that includes admission to the Hall of Fame, a trip to the observation deck of the 90-meter-ski-jump tower, a short bus ride to the luge and bobsled tracks, and a movie showing highlights from the '88 Winter Olympic Games is $10.50; half that for seniors, students, and children. On the main level of the day lodge is a gift shop selling Olympic souvenirs, books, and clothing. The former start-house for the luge is now the **Naturbahn Teahouse,** open only for Sunday brunch, 9:30 a.m.-1:30 p.m.; reservations required, call (403) 247-5465. For general information on the park call 286-2632. A **tourist information center** is located on the main level of the day lodge; open summer only, daily 9 a.m.-5 p.m.

OTHER PARKS

Calgary Zoo

The Calgary Zoo, Botanical Gardens, and Pre-historic Park, to use its full name, is one of Canada's finest zoos. It was established in 1920 near the heart of downtown on St. Georges Island and has become noted for its realistic simulation of animal habitat. Unique viewing areas have been designed to allow visitors the best look at the zoo's 1,000-plus animals. For example, underwater observation points provide a look at swimming polar bears and seals, and a darkened room allows visitors to watch nocturnal animals during their active periods (lights are turned on at night, reversing night and day). Other highlights include a section on Australian animals, a number of exotic mammals, greenhouses filled with tropical birds, and a Canadian Wilds display featuring animals of the aspen parkland. In the Prehistoric Park section, the world of dinosaurs is brought to life with 27 full-size replicas set amid plantlife and rock formations similar to that found in Alberta in prehistoric times. The zoo also has a fast-food restaurant and a number of picnic areas dotting the grounds. Admission is $7.50 for adults, $4.75 for seniors ($2 on Tuesday), and $3.75 for youths under 15. It's open in summer, daily 9 a.m.-6 p.m., the rest of the year 9 a.m.-4 p.m. The Prehistoric Park section is only open June-Sept. and is free with general grounds admission. The zoo is located at 1300 Zoo Rd. Northeast. The main parking lot is off Memorial Dr. just west of the Deerfoot Trail. For more information call (403) 232-9300 or 232-9372 (recorded message). From downtown take the Whitehorn C-train northeast.

Stampede Park

Best known for hosting the Calgary Exhibition and Stampede, these grounds south of downtown are used for a multitude of activities and events year-round. In the center of the park is the saddle-shaped **Olympic Saddledome** that has the world's largest cable-suspended roof and is one of Calgary's most impressive structures. It was used for the ice-hockey and figure-skating events during the '88 Winter Olympic Games and is home to the **Calgary Flames** of the National Hockey League. "The Dome" is constantly in use for concerts, trade shows, and entertainment events. One-hour tours of the Saddledome are given on weekdays (nonevent days). Groups are preferred, but if you're interested, and don't have a family of 10, ring ahead and try anyway; tel. (403) 261-0400. The **Grain Academy** on the Plus 15 level of the **Roundup Centre,** tel. 263-4594, is a museum cataloguing the history of agriculture in the province through working models and hands-on displays. It's open Mon.-Fri. 10 a.m.-4 p.m., Saturday noon-4 p.m. Admission is free. The Big Four Building and Agriculture Building also host trade shows and exhibitions, and thoroughbred and harness racing takes place on the grounds year-round. Stampede Park is located at 17th Ave. and 2nd St. Southeast. Take the C-train from downtown to Victoria Park/Stampede or Stampede/Erlton.

Inglewood Bird Sanctuary

Over 260 species of birds have been noted in this 32-hectare park on the bank of the Bow River, east of downtown. The land was originally owned by a member of the NWMP and was established as a park in 1929. Walking trails are open year-round. Take 9th Ave. SE to Sanctuary Rd. and follow the signs to a parking area on the south bank of the river. On weekdays bus No. 14 East turns off 9th Ave. at 17th St. SE, only a short walk from the park. Just north over the Blackfoot Trail is **Sam Livingstone Fish Hatchery,** which produces over five million fish a year,

MIDNAPORE

The last rest stop for early travelers along the Macleod Trail, linking Fort Macleod to Fort Calgary, was just south of Fish Creek. A trading post and a number of crude cabins constituted the town. The post office opened and was manned by a postmaster with dubious reading skills. One of the first parcels he received was addressed to Midnapore, India and had been misdirected through him. Fear of losing his job kept him from asking too many questions, and as the community had no official name he directed that all mail to this post be addressed to Midnapore. The name stuck and that's how a suburb of Calgary came to have the same name as an Indian city on the opposite side of the world.

used to stock rivers and streams throughout the province. This is a pleasant spot for a picnic. It's open Mon.-Sat. 10 a.m.-4 p.m., Sunday noon-6 p.m.; tel. (403) 297-6220.

Fish Creek Provincial Park
At the southern edge of the city, this 1,170-hectare park is one of the largest urban parks in North America. Many prehistoric sites have been discovered on its grounds, including campsites and buffalo jumps. In more recent times the Calgary–Fort Benton Trail passed through the park. The site—much of which was once owned by Patrick Burns, the meat magnate—was officially declared a park in 1975. Three geographical regions meet in the area, giving the park a diversity of habitat. Stands of aspen and spruce predominate, while a mixed-grass prairie, balsam, poplar, and willow can be found along the floodplains at the east end of the park. The ground is colorfully carpeted with 364 recorded species of wildflowers, and wildlife is abundant. Mule deer and ground squirrels are common, and white-tailed deer, coyotes, beavers, and the occasional moose are also present. An interpretive trail begins south of Bow Valley Ranch and leads through a grove of balsam and poplar to a shallow, conglomerate cave. An information display is located on the west side of Macleod Trail overlooking the site of Alberta's first woolen mill. To get to the main information center turn east on Canyon Meadows Dr., then south on Bow River Bottom Trail. For more information call (403) 297-5293.

RECREATION

OUTDOOR ACTIVITIES

Walking And Biking
A good way to get a feel for the city is by walking or biking along the 210 km of paved trails within city limits. The trail system is concentrated along the Bow River as it winds through the city; other options are limited. Along the riverbank the trail passes through numerous parks and older neighborhoods to various sights such as Fort Calgary and Inglewood Bird Sanctuary. From Fort Calgary a trail passes under 9th Ave. SE and follows the Elbow River, crossing it a number of times before ending at Glenmore Reservoir and Heritage Park. Ask at tourist information centers for a map detailing all trails. Bicycle rentals are available from **The Bike Shop,** 1321 1st St. SW, tel. (403) 264-0735.

Swimming
Calgary Parks & Recreation operates nine outdoor pools (open June-early Sept.) and 12 indoor pools (open year-round). Facilities at each vary. Admission at indoor pools includes the use of the sauna, jacuzzi, and exercise room. Admission to all pools is $4. For general information and pool locations call (403) 268-2300.

The **YMCA,** 101 3rd St. SW, tel. 269-6701, is a modern fitness center beside Eau Claire Market at the north end of downtown. All facilities are first class, including an Olympic-size pool, weight room, exercise room, jogging track, squash courts, a jacuzzi, and sauna. It's open Mon.-Fri. 6 a.m.-10 p.m., Sat.-Sun. 7:30 a.m.-6:30 p.m.; admission is $6.50.

Golfing
Over 20 public, semi-private, and private golf courses are located within the city limits. Many courses begin opening in April for a season that extends for up to seven months. The courses operated by Calgary Parks & Recreation are all public. Those with 18 holes include **Maple Ridge,** 1240 Maple Glade Dr. SE, tel. (403) 271-7333; **McCall Lake,** 1600 32nd Ave. NE, tel. 250-5677; and **Shaganappi Point,** 1200 26th St. SW, tel. 249-1212. Each has a pro shop with club rentals. Green fees are $24.50. **Fox Hollow Golf Club,** at the corner of Deerfoot Trail and 32nd Ave. SE, tel. 277-4653, is an inexpensive public course with an indoor full-flight driving range open year-round.

Ballooning
All summer, balloons can be seen floating peacefully over the city. Various companies offer flights but be prepared to pay for it (usually $120). One of the most professional is **Aero Dynamics,** 3413 8th St. SE, tel. (403) 287-9393. Launch sites vary depending on the wind direction, the basic aim being to float over the downtown area.

ballooning over Calgary

ALBERTA TOURISM

After making a reservation you will be contacted an hour before launch time and asked to meet at the Aero Dynamics office from where you'll be ferried to the launch site and back. Flights generally last an hour and a half and the cost includes all transportation, a drink on landing, and a framed picture of your flight.

Calaway Park

This is western Canada's largest outdoor amusement park and has many rides, including a double-loop roller coaster. Other attractions include an enormous maze, golf driving range, a zoo for the kids, live entertainment in the "Alphatheatre," and many restaurants and eateries. Admission to the park is $8.95, or $14.95 with unlimited rides. For children under six admission and unlimited rides is $8.95, seniors pay only $7.95. If you are staying in the adjacent campground, ask for free gate-admission coupons. The park is located 10 km west of the city limits on Springbank Rd., tel. (403) 240-3822. It's open in summer daily 10 a.m.-8 p.m.; in May, June, and September, Fri. 5-10 p.m. and weekends 10 a.m.-8 p.m.

Leisure Centers

The large **Family Leisure Centre,** 11150 Bonaventure Dr. SE, tel. (403) 278-7542, is an excellent facility offering a giant indoor water slide, wave pool, swimming pools, steam room and sauna, weight room, skating rink, lounge, and restaurant. It's open daily 9 a.m.-9 p.m. but there are only waves during certain sessions; ad-

mission is $6.75. Similar facilities are **Village Square Leisure Centre,** 2623 56th St. NE, tel. 280-9714, and **Southland Leisure Centre,** just off Macleod Trail at 2000 Southland Dr. SW, tel. 251-3505.

Kart Gardens has one kart track where you can reach speeds of 80 kph, and another twisting, slower one for first-time drivers. The park also has kiddy karts, mini-golf, and a snack bar. It's located off Macleod Trail at 5202 1st St. SW, tel. 253-8301. Open in summer only from 11 a.m. to dusk.

Winter Activities

When Calgarians talk about going downhill skiing for the day they are usually referring to the five world-class resorts in the Rockies, an hour and a half drive to the west. The city's only downhill facilities are at **Canada Olympic Park,** tel. (403) 286-2632. Although the park has world-class luge, bobsled, and ski-jumping facilities, snow-making capabilities, two triple chairs, and a T-bar, its vertical rise is only 150 meters. On the plus side, however, are the extensive lodge facilities, excellent teaching staff, ski rentals, and night skiing till 10 p.m. on weeknights. Lift tickets cost $16 per day or $13 for four hours.

SPECTATOR SPORTS

Ice Hockey

Calgary's favorite sports team is the **Calgary Flames,** the city's franchise in the National

Hockey League. The Olympic Saddledome in Stampede Park fills with 20,000 ice-hockey fans who follow every game with a passion; the atmosphere at a Flames' home game is electric. The season runs from October to April, and games are usually held in the early evening. Tickets aren't cheap, starting around $12.50 for nosebleed seats. For general information call (403) 261-0475; for tickets call 270-6700.

Baseball
The **Calgary Cannons** are a farm team for the National League's Seattle Mariners and play in the AAA Pacific Coast League during the regular baseball season April to October. Tickets are $5.50-7.50. Their home field is Foothills Stadium on Crowchild Trail, across from the Banff Trail L.R.T. Station. For home-game dates and ticket information call (403) 284-1111.

Football
The **Calgary Stampeders** are Calgary's franchise in the Canadian Football League, similar to the U.S.-style N.F.L. with slight modifications. The team's popularity fluctuates with its performance, but it usually does well enough to have a chance come finals time in November when the best teams compete for the Grey Cup. Later in the season, weather can be a deciding factor in both the games' results and attendance. At kick-off in the Stampeders final game of 1993 the temperature was -20° C and -33 with the wind chill, but still over 20,000 Calgarians braved the weather to attend. The season runs from July to November. Home games are played at **McMahon Stadium** at the University of Calgary, 1817 Crowchild Trail Northwest. Take the C-train to Banff Trail Station. For more information, call (403) 289-0258.

Soccer
Soccer is beginning to gain popularity in North America—especially since America hosted the recent World Cup—and Calgary is home to the only facility on the continent specially designed for playing soccer indoors. The **Calgary Soccer Centre** has four indoor fields (plus outdoor fields); games are played each evening and on weekends but the building is always open. The complex is located off Glenmore Trail and 52nd St. SE (7000 48th St. SE, tel. 403-279-8453); admission is $1.

Motor Racing
Race City Speedway has three world-class tracks and is the premier motorsport facility in western Canada. It hosts national stock-car, motorcycle, and drag-racing events. Prices vary according to event but generally run $7-15. The speedway is located at 64th St. and 114th Avenue. For upcoming events call (403) 264-6515 or 236-7223 (recorded message).

ARTS AND ENTERTAINMENT

Art Galleries
It may put a dent in Calgary's cowtown image but the city does have a remarkable number of galleries displaying and selling work by Albertan and Canadian artisans. Unfortunately they are not concentrated in any one area and most require some effort to find. **Creative Picture Gallery,** 106A 10th St. NW, tel. (403) 270-8353, features western-Canadian artists who specialize in the land and its people. **Cotton & Willow,** 313A 19th St. NW, tel. 283-8946, is similar but also makes bent-willow furniture. **Knightsbridge Fine Art,** 311 10th St. NW, tel. 270-8944, specializes in original western-Canadian paintings and photographs.

Theater
Calgary's western image belies a cultural diversity that goes further than being able to get a few foreign beers at the local dance hall. In fact, the city has 10 professional theater companies, an opera, orchestra, and a ballet troupe. The main season for performances is Sept.-May. For details on exact dates and prices contact the companies directly or pick up a copy of *City Scope* (free), available throughout the city.
    Alberta Theatre Projects, tel. (403) 294-7475, is a well-established company based in the Calgary Centre for Performing Arts at 205 8th Ave., beside the Glenbow Museum. Usual performances are of contemporary material. **Theatre Calgary,** tel. 294-7440, is also based in Calgary Centre, but performs in the city's other world-class facility, the Max Bell Theatre at 220 9th Avenue. **Loose Moose Theatre,** 2003 McKnight Blvd. NE, tel. 291-5682, offers lighthearted live entertainment on Friday and Saturday nights; tickets begin at $4. **Lunchbox Theatre,** located on the second floor of Bow Valley Square, 205

5th Ave. SW, tel. 265-4292, usually features comedy productions Mon.-Sat. at noon. Tickets are $7. For experimental productions head to **One Yellow Rabbit,** 205 8th Ave. SW, tel. 264-3707. **Storybook Theatre,** 2140 9th Ave., tel. 291-2247, specializes in children's productions.

Music And Dance

Calgary Opera, tel. (403) 262-7286, performs at the Jubilee Auditorium at 1415 14th Ave. NW, October through April. Tickets begin at $12. The Jack Singer Concert Hall at the Calgary Centre for Performing Arts is home to the **Calgary Philharmonic Orchestra,** tel. 294-7420, one of Canada's top orchestras. **Alberta Ballet** performs at locations throughout the city; for dates and ticketing details call 245-4222.

Cinemas

Most major shopping malls—including Eau Claire Market, closest to downtown—have a **Cineplex Odeon Cinema.** For information call the 24-hour film line, tel. (403) 289-7799. Also in Eau Claire Market is an **IMAX Theatre,** tel. 263-4629, with a screen five-and-a-half stories tall. Tickets are $6.50, or $9.75 for a double feature. **Uptown Screen,** 612 8th Ave. SW, tel. 265-0120, is a newly restored downtown theater featuring alternative, art, and foreign films.

Casinos

Calgary has two low-key Alberta-style casinos that have little glitz and low maximum bets. Downtown is **Tower Casino,** 501 Tower Centre, 131 9th Ave. SW, tel. (403) 262-5655, with a complimentary shuttle from major downtown hotels. Farther out is **Cash Casino,** 4040 Blackfoot Trail SE, tel. 287-1635. Both are open noon-midnight.

Bars And Nightclubs

With a nickname like "Cowtown," it's not surprising that Calgary's hottest nightspots play country music. Along Macleod Trail are three favorites. **Ranchman's,** 9615 Macleod Trail SW, tel. (403) 253-1100, is *the* place to check out first, especially during Stampede Week. Some of country's hottest stars have played this famous honky-tonk. Food is served at a bar out front all day, then at 7 p.m. the large dance hall opens. The hall is a museum of rodeo memorabilia and photographs with a chuck wagon

hanging from the ceiling. Most nights feature live performances and on Sunday mornings a church service is held. Next door is **Longhorn Dance Hall,** a spacious, two-level country-music nightspot with occasional live bands but more often piped-in contemporary country music. Toward the city is **Rockin' Horse Saloon,** 7400 Macleod Trail SE, tel. 255-4646, another popular country spot.

Eleventh Ave. SW, known locally as Electric Avenue, holds a number of dance clubs. Most are between 5th and 6th streets. Each club plays Top 40 or dance music till the early hours. Cover charges run $5-12 depending on the night.

Jazz, Blues, And Comedy

The **Classic Jazz Guild of Calgary** performs throughout the year at the Jack Singer Concert Hall. Call Ticketmaster at (403) 299-8888 for details. One of the most popular jazz clubs in town is **Kao's Cafe,** 718 17th Ave. SW, tel. 228-9997, with live performances Wed.-Sunday. Other jazz clubs are: **Bakerstreet on Fourth,** 2321 4th St. SW, tel. 228-9928, with a Sunday Jazz Brunch; and **Panchos,** 1220 Kensington Rd. NW, tel. 270-7278.

The best place to listen to blues is the **King Edward Hotel,** 438 9th Ave. SE, tel. 262-1680, with live performances most nights and jazz jams on Saturday and Sunday.

Yuk Yuk's Komedy Kabaret is located in the Blackfoot Inn, 5940 Blackfoot Trail SE, tel. 258-2028. Shows are Wed.-Sun. nights and tickets are $7-12.

SHOPPING

Plazas And Malls

The largest shopping center downtown is **Calgary Eaton Centre,** on Stephen Ave. Mall at 4th St. Southwest. This is linked to other plazas by the Plus 15 Walkway System, which provides shelter from the elements. Other downtown shopping complexes are **Eau Claire Market,** at the entrance to Prince's Island Park, where the emphasis is on fresh foods and trendy boutiques; **TD Square,** at 7th Ave. and 2nd St. SW; and **The Bay,** part of Alberta's history with its link to the Hudson's Bay Company. **Uptown 17** is a strip of over 400 retail shops, restaurants, and galleries along 17th Ave. Southwest. **Kensington,** across the Bow River from downtown, is an eclectic mix of specialty shops.

Camping Gear And Western Wear

Mountain Equipment Co-op, 1009 4th Ave. SW, tel. (403) 269-2420, is Calgary's largest camping store. On two levels is an extensive range of high-quality clothing, climbing and mountaineering equipment, tents, sleeping bags, and other accessories. The store is a co-operative owned by its members, similiar to the American R.E.I. stores, except that to purchase anything you must be a member (a once-only $5 charge). Smaller, yet with a good variety of equipment, is the **Hostel Shop,** 1414 Kensington Rd. NW, tel. 283-8311, operated by Hostelling International.

Alberta Boot Co., 614 10th Ave. SW, tel. 263-4623, within walking distance of downtown, is Alberta's only western boot manufacturer. This outlet shop has thousands of pairs for sale in all shapes and sizes, all made from leather. **Western Outfitters,** 128 8th Ave. SE, tel. 266-3656, across from the Convention Centre, has an extensive range of boots and western wear.

FESTIVALS AND EVENTS

Spring

Calgary's rodeo season kicks off with **Rodeo Royal** at the saddledome on the last weekend of March. **Calgary International Children's Festival** is the third week of May. Events include theater, puppetry, and performances by musicians from around the world. It's held in Jack Singer Concert Hall and Olympic Plaza; call (403) 294-7414 for details.

Summer

Few cities in the world are associated as closely with an event as Calgary is with the **Calgary Exhibition and Stampede.** For details of the "Greatest Outdoor Show on Earth," held each summer, see below. Island life is celebrated in the **Caribbean Festival** the third week of June. **Calgary International Jazz Festival** features various jazz and blues artists at clubs and concert halls throughout the city, the last week of June. For locations call (403) 233-2628. **Canada Day** (1 July) is celebrated in Prince's Island Park

and Heritage Park. **Calgary Folk Music Festival,** the last week of July, is an indoor and outdoor extravaganza of Canadian and international performers; tel. 233-0904. The third week of August is the **International Native Arts Festival** with performances by native dancers and musicians. Tepees are erected along Stephen Avenue Mall and workshops are held at locations throughout the city all week; tel. 233-0022.

Fall

On the second weekend of September is **Blue Mountain's Antiques, Furniture, and Collectibles Show** at the Roundup Centre, Stampede Park. The following weekend is an **artwalk** to various galleries throughout Calgary. In October **hockey** and **downhill skiing** fever hits the city as the **Calgary Flames** start their season and the first snow flies. A good place for kids on Halloween is Calgary Zoo, where **"Howl"oween** celebrations take place.

Winter

Calgary has joined other major Canadian cities by celebrating New Years Eve with a **First Night Festival.** Although severely curtailed by the weather, Calgarians enjoy the winter with the opening of the theatre, ballet, and opera seasons. National and international ski-jumping events are held at **Canada Olympic Park** Nov.-March. The 11-day **Calgary Winter Festival** takes place in late January at locations throughout the city; call (403) 268-2688 for details.

Spruce Meadows

This equestrian mecca, one of the world's greatest, is an oasis among the sprawling ranches that surround the city. An endless line of white paddock fencing surrounds the 120-hectare village that has an international-events ring the size of a football field, six warm-up rings, and a three-story tournament center. The name Spruce Meadows is marked on the calendars of all the world's best riders. Each year the site hosts 15 televised events with over $23 million in prize money. The three biggest tournaments are the **National,** during the first week of June; the **North American,** held, ironically, the same week as the Stampede, and the **Spruce Meadows Masters,** the second week of September. The Masters is the world's richest show-jumping tournament; one of its events—the du Maurier

International—has the largest purse of any single event anywhere. Up to 25,000 enthusiasts gather at the Masters each day. Entry is $5-6, making it an affordable day out. For information on Spruce Meadows write to R.R. No. 9, Calgary, Alberta T2J 5G5; tel. (403) 254-3200. To get there take Macleod Trail south to Hwy. 22X and turn right toward the mountains.

CALGARY EXHIBITION AND STAMPEDE

Every July, the city's perennial rough-and-ready cowtown image is thrust to the forefront when a fever known as Stampede hits town. For 10 days, Calgarians let their hair down—business leaders don Stetsons, bankers wear boots, half the town walks round in tight-fitting jeans, the rate of serious crime drops, and then nine months later maternity hospitals report a rise in business. For most Calgarians it is known simply as The Week (always capitalized). The stampede is many things to many people but is certainly not for the cynic. It is a celebration of the city's past—of endless sunny days when life was broncos, bulls, and steers, of cowboys riding through the streets, and saloons on every corner. But it is not just about the past. It's the cowtown image Calgarians cherish and the frontier image that visitors expect. On downtown streets everyone is your neighbor. Flapjacks and bacon are served free of charge on every corner, normally staid citizens shout "Ya-HOO!" for no particular reason, Indians ride up and down the streets on horseback, and there's dancing till dawn every night. And that's before you even arrive at the epicenter: **Stampede Park.**

Over 100,000 people converge each day on Stampede Park, just south of the city center, to watch top professionals compete in the world's richest rodeo and the just-as-spectacular chuck wagon races. These events are the nucleus of what has become a lot more than a show of cowboy skills. The gigantic midway takes at least a day to get around: a staggering number of attractions, displays, and free entertainment cost only the price of gate admission; some of the biggest stars in country music appear at the Saddledome; and a glittering grandstand show, complete with fireworks, ends each day's shenanigans.

History
Earlier this century Guy Weadick, an American cowpoke, got the idea that people would pay to see traditional cowboy skills combined with vaudeville showmanship. With the backing of four Calgarian businessmen who contributed $25,000 each, Weadick put on an inaugural show billed as the "The Last and Best Great West Frontier Days." The name was a reference to the fact that many people thought the cattle industry in Alberta was near its end, and that wheat would soon be king. On 2 September 1912 the show kicked off with a parade of cowboys and over 2,000 Indians in traditional dress.

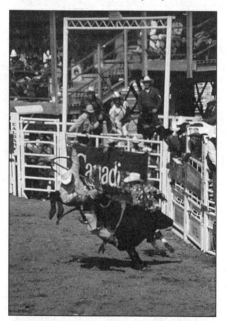

Many consider bull riding the most exciting eight seconds in sport.

Its popularity proved so immense that the competition was extended two days. Canada's governor general, the Duke of Connaught, opened the show, and enjoyed himself so much that he stayed for the duration. An estimated 60,000 people lined the streets for the parade, and 40,000 attended each day of rodeo events. Amazing, considering that barely more than 65,000 people lived in Calgary at the time. The prize money for the rodeo was an incredible $20,000. The highlight of the event was on the final day when Tom Three Persons, a little-known Blood Indian rider from southern Alberta, rode the legendary bronc "Cyclone" for eight seconds to collect the world-championship saddle and $1000.

The following year Weadick took the show to Winnipeg, then WW I intervened and it was not until 1919 that the Calgary show was revived with Weadick at the helm. In 1923 the show combined with an annual agricultural exhibition. As it turned out the inaugural show wasn't the first and last, but the beginning of an annual extravaganza that is billed, and rightly so, as "The Greatest Outdoor Show on Earth."

EVENTS

Stampede Parade
Although Stampede Park is open on Thursday evening for **Sneek-a-peek,** Stampede Week officially begins on Friday morning with a spectacular parade through the streets of downtown Calgary. It proceeds west along 6th Ave. from 2nd St. SE, then south on 10th St. SW, and east on 9th Avenue. The parade of 150 entries takes two hours to pass any one point. Starting time is 9 a.m. but crowds start gathering at six and you'll be lucky to get a front-row spot much after seven. Entries of all types take part, from Indian dancers, to Scottish bagpipers, to Buffalo Bill Cody's descendants.

Rodeo
The pinnacle of any cowboy's career is walking away with the $50,000 winner-take-all on the last day of competition in the Calgary Stampede. For the first eight days, heats are held each afternoon from 1:30 p.m., with finals held the last Saturday and Sunday. Although Stampede Week is about a lot more than the rodeo, this is the event everyone loves to watch. Cowboys compete in bronc riding, bareback riding, bull riding, calf roping, and steer wrestling, while cowgirls compete in barrel racing. Wild cow milking, a wild horse race, bull fighting, and non-stop chatter from hilarious rodeo clowns all keep the action going between the more traditional rodeo events.

Chuck Wagon Races
The **Rangeland Derby** chuck wagon races feature nine heats each evening starting at 8 p.m. At the end of the week, the top four drivers from the preliminary rounds compete in a winner-take-all, $50,000 dash-for-the-cash final. Chuck wagon racing is an exciting sport any time, but here at the Stampede the pressure is intense as drivers push themselves to stay in the running. The grandstand in the infield makes steering the chuck wagons difficult through an initial figure eight, heightening the action before they burst onto the track for what is known as the Half Mile of Hell to the finish line.

Rope Square
During the Stampede, downtown's Olympic Plaza is known as Rope Square. Every morning 8:30-10:30, free pancake breakfasts are served from the back of chuck wagons. For the rest of the morning, the square is the scene for a variety of entertainment, which might include country-music bands, native dance groups, marching bands, or mock gunfights. West along Stephen Avenue Mall, square dancing takes place each morning at 10 a.m. Also at 10, horse-drawn carriages leave the Palliser Hotel for an hour-long tour through town. Get there early to ensure seats.

OTHER ENTERTAINMENT

The cavernous **Roundup Centre** holds a variety of commercial exhibits and demonstrations (plenty of free samples), an International Photo Salon with prints submitted from around the world, Kitchen Theatre showcasing Calgary's culinary scene, and a Western Art Auction. At the front of the Roundup Centre is **Stampede Corral,** where you might find dog shows, the Calgary Stampede Show Band, or a seniors talent show. **Stampede Square** is an outdoor entertainment venue where modern rides such as a reverse bungee are set up. Also here are free phones to call anywhere in Canada, a petting zoo, and other activities for the kids. A **midway** extends along the western edge of the park with the **Safeway Skyride** overhead.

The agricultural displays are in the center of Stampede Park. **Centennial Fair** is an outdoor stage with events for children such as duck races and magicians. In the **Agricultural Building** livestock is displayed, while next door in the **John Deere Show Ring,** the World Blacksmith's Competition and horse shows take place.

At the far end of Stampede Park, across the Elbow River, is the **Indian Village.** Here, members of the five nations who signed Treaty Seven 100 years ago set up camp for the duration of the Stampede. Each tepee has its own colorful design; tours are available. Behind the village is a stage where native dance competitions are held. Also at this end of the grounds are **Penley's Academy** (for big-band dancing) and a bingo hall.

Once you've paid gate admission, all live entertainment (except in the Saddledome) is free. Top country-music acts and other well-known performers appear at the outdoor **Coca-Cola Stage** between 11 a.m. and midnight. **Nashville North** is an indoor venue with a bar, live country acts, and a dance floor; open till 2 a.m. Tickets for performances in the **Olympic Saddledome** must be bought in advance but include gate admission. Here the biggest-name country acts take the stage by night, and sporting events are held during the day.

RODEO EVENTS

For those watching for the first time, a rodeo can look like organized confusion. Although staying on the animals isn't as easy as professional cowboys make it look, learning the rules is, and it will make the events more enjoyable. The rodeo is made up of six basic events of which three are judged on points and three are timed. Other team contests are included by the organizers to liven things up even more.

Bareback Riding

In this event riders don't use a saddle or reins. They are cinched to a handhold and leather pad attached to the horse's back. The idea is to stay on the wildly bucking horse for eight seconds. As the cowboy leaves the chute he must keep both spurs above the horse's shoulders until the horse's front hooves hit the ground. Riders are judged on style and rhythm, achieved by spurring effectively and remaining in control. The cowboy is disqualified if he doesn't last eight seconds, if he loses a stirrup, or if he touches the animal with his hand. Scores above 80 (out of 100) are usually good enough to win.

Saddle Bronc Riding

This event differs from bareback riding in that (1) the horse is saddled, and (2) the rider, rather than being cinched to the animal, hangs onto a rein attached to the halter. Again, both spurs must be above the horse's shoulders after the first jump. Riders are judged by spurring action and are disqualified for falling before eight seconds have elapsed.

Bull Riding

Traditionally the last event in a rodeo, bull riding is considered to be the most exciting eight seconds in sport. The cowboy must hang onto an 1,800-pound Brahma bull for the required eight seconds with as much control as possible. No spurring is required (for obvious reasons), although if he gets the chance it will earn the cowboy extra points. Disqualification occurs if the cowboy's loose hand touches either himself or the animal, or if he doesn't last the eight seconds, which more often than not is the case. Like bareback riding, the cowboy has one hand cinched to the animal in a handhold of braided rope. Riders are tied so tightly to the animal that if they are bucked off on the side away from their riding hand they often become "hung up" and are dragged around like a rag doll until rescued by a rodeo clown.

Calf Roping

This timed event has its roots in the Old West, when calves had to be roped and tied down to receive medical treatment. The calf is released from a chute, closely followed by a mounted cowboy. The cowboy

PRACTICALITIES

Food

No chance of anyone starving to death here. Within the grounds are three restaurants, two food courts, and an endless stream of fast-food stands. The **Saddledome Restaurant** holds an all-you-can-eat buffet. The selection isn't huge but at $6.95 (around the same as a burger, fries, and a drink from a stand) it's the best deal on the grounds. Open daily 11 a.m.-9 p.m., expect a wait after 4 p.m. **O'Reillys Pub,** upstairs in the Roundup Centre, serves typical pub grub throughout the day.

Transportation

Parking around the grounds is limited; most people use public transport. The **C-train** runs from 7th Ave. downtown to the Victoria Park/ Stampede L.R.T. Station ($1.50 one way). Many hotels and campgrounds run shuttle services to the park during Stampede Week; get details before making reservations as each service is different. Generally they leave pick-up points at 11 a.m. and 6 p.m., and return at 6 p.m. and midnight. A 7 a.m. shuttle to the city center for the parade on the opening Friday is usually offered also; expect to pay $8 round trip per person. A taxi from downtown to Stampede Park runs around $5. If you decide to drive, parking close to the grounds is possible but the roads can be chaotic. Many local residents turn their gardens into parking lots—some stand out on the road waving at you like the month's rent depends on the $7-8 parking fee. The official park-

---

must lasso the calf, dismount, race to the animal, and tie a "pigging string" around any three of its legs. He then throws his hands in the air to signal the end of his run. After remounting his horse the cowboy rides forward, slackening the rope. He's disqualified if the calves legs don't remain tied for six seconds. The fastest time wins.

Steer Wrestling

This timed event is for the big boys. The steer jumps out of the chute, closely followed by a mounted cowboy who rides alongside, jumps off his horse at full speed, and slides onto the steer's back attempting to get a hold of its horns. The cowboy slows down by digging his feet into the ground, using a twisting motion to throw the steer to the ground. The fastest time wins.

Barrel Racing

This is the only rodeo event for women. Riders must guide their horse around three barrels, set in a cloverleaf pattern, before making a hat-flying dash to the finish line. The fastest time wins, and there's a five-second penalty for knocking down a barrel.

Wild Cow Milking

Although not an official rodeo event, participants in the wild cow milking are greeted with just as much hootin' and hollerin' as those in the main events. At the Stampede, 20 two-man teams race into a herd of wild cows aiming to collect a few squirts of milk in a container and race with it to the judges' table.

Wild Horse Race

In this fun event, three-man teams select a horse from among a herd in the ring. Their aim is to saddle it and have one team member ride it across the finish line.

Mutton Busting

Mutton busting is for all the little cowboys and cowgirls. Youngsters jump aboard a sheep for a wild and woolly ride across the ring.

BOB RACE

ing lots nearby charge around $7 per day, rising to $9-10 in the afternoon, depending on how busy they are.

Tickets

Advance tickets for the afternoon rodeos and evening chuck wagon races/grandstand shows go on sale a year ahead of time. These are the good seats, and are sold out by the time the event rolls around. The grandstand is divided into sections, each with a different price tag. The best views are from "A" section, closest to the infield yet high enough not to miss all the action. These sell out first. To either side are the "B" and "C" sections, also with good views. Above the main level is the **Clubhouse** level, divided into another four sections, all enclosed by glass and air-conditioned. These seats might not have the atmosphere of the lower or higher levels, but they are protected from the elements and patrons have access to a bar, full-service restaurant, and lounge area. At the top of the grandstand is the **Balcony** level, divided into two sections. Both are great for the chuck wagon races (you can see the wagons around the full circuit). Ticket prices for the first eight days of rodeo competition range $16-32 ($25 for section "A"). The evening chuck wagon races/ grandstand shows run $20-39 ($32 for section A). Tickets to both the rodeos and chuck wagon races/grandstand shows include admission to Stampede Park (normally $8). Tickets for the final two days of competition are an extra $3.

If you didn't purchase your tickets in advance, you'll need to pay the **general admission** of $8 at the gate. Once inside the park, you can purchase tickets for the afternoon's rodeo or the chuck wagon race/grandstand show from the booths behind the grandstand. Tickets are $8 to either event, and you'll only have access to either an area of the infield with poor views, or seats well away from the action. Tickets for the top country acts performing nightly at the Saddledome are about $35 (includes gate admission).

Information

An Events Schedule and map is handed out at all park gates, and the *Calgary Sun* newspaper publishes a pull-out each day during the Stampede with results of the previous day's competition and upcoming events throughout town. Thousands of volunteers (dressed in red and white) contribute to the Stampede's success. They can answer most questions or at least direct you to one of many **Howdy Folk Chuckwagons** for more information. The **Bank of Montreal** operates daily 11 a.m.-5 p.m. at the Agricultural Building, or use one of many automated banking machines located throughout the park.

In 1995, the Calgary Exhibition and Stampede will be held 7-16 July; in 1996 it's 5-14 July. For more information write to P.O. Box 1860, Station M, Calgary, Alberta T2P 2L8; or call (403) 261-0101 or (800) 661-1260 anywhere in North America.

ACCOMMODATIONS

Accommodations in Calgary vary from campgrounds, hostels, and budget motels to a broad selection of high-quality hotels catering to top-end travelers and business conventions. Many of the older, cheaper downtown hotels have been demolished in recent years to make way for office buildings. Every middle- to top-end hotel in the city was renovated for the '88 Winter Olympic Games. Most of the downtown hotels offer drastically reduced rates on weekends—Friday and Saturday nights might be half the regular room rate. During Stampede Week prices are higher than the rest of the year and many accommodations are booked-out months in advance. For further details, see the Calgary accommodations chart.

Downtown Hotels

Hotels right in the center of town are the priciest, starting at $100. Of these, **Prince Royal Inn** is the least expensive. Each room is spacious and has a kitchenette. The gracious **Palliser Hotel** was built in 1914 by the C.P.R. and is still a part of that company chain (which includes the Banff Springs Hotel and Chateau Lake Louise). The rooms may seem small by modern standards, and it lacks certain recreational facilities, but the elegance and character of this Calgary favorite is priceless. When the Queen of England visits Calgary this is where she stays. Each of the 336 rooms has been restored. The cavernous lobby has original marble columns and staircases, a magnificent chandelier, and solid-brass doors that open onto busy 9th Avenue. Also on 9th Ave., across from the Calgary Tower, is the **Radisson Plaza Hotel,** one of Calgary's newest and largest downtown hotels. It offers elegantly decorated rooms and a large indoor pool with a waterfall.

At the west end of downtown and close to C-train stations are the **Sandman Inn** and **Lord Nelson Inn.** The **Royal Pacific Hotel** is across the rail line from downtown but is excellent value. The extra-large rooms have been refurbished and each has a kitchen.

Hotels/Motels Outside Downtown

Of the many hotels close to Calgary International Airport, **Chateau Airport Hotel**—a stone's throw from the arrivals level of the main terminal—is the closest. It's another C.P.R. hotel and although not as grand as others in the chain (many of the rooms are small) it's modern and very handy for late arrivals or early departures. Most of the dozen other motels in the northeast corner of the city have shuttles to the airport and can be contacted directly by courtesy phone from the airport.

If you don't need to be close to the airport, **Motel Village** offers better value while still being close to the city and public transport. The village is not an official designation, just a dozen motels bunched together at the intersection of 16th Ave. NW and Crowchild Trail. Best value are **Red Carpet Inn, Comfort Inn** where rates include breakfast, and **Days Inn.** Another area of heavy concentration is south of the city center along Macleod Trail. For a complete listing see chart.

Bed And Breakfasts

Tourist information centers in Calgary keep a list of places offering bed-and-breakfast accommodations and will make a booking for you. The **Bed & Breakfast Association of Calgary** represents 40 homes offering rooms to visitors. Prices are $30-80 s, $40-120 d. For information write to 6016 Thornburn Drive NW, Calgary T2K 3P7; tel. (403) 531-0065. One of the nicest is **B&B on the Bow,** 23 New Bow Lane SE, Calgary T2G 5J9, tel. 263-6769, in the historic neighborhood of Inglewood. Rooms are large, each has a TV, and bathrooms are either shared or private. The city skyline and surrounding parkland can be seen from an observation tower. Downtown is a short walk along the river. Rates are $60-100.

Calgary International Hostel

At 520 7th Ave. SE, tel. (403) 269-8239, this large hostel is ideally located only two blocks east of City Hall and Stephen Ave. Mall. It has 114 beds, many in eight-bed dormitories, some in private rooms. Other facilities include a fully equipped kitchen, laundry, large common room,

(continued on page 126)

CALGARY ACCOMMODATIONS

All prices listed are for a double room during peak season.
The area code for all telephone numbers listed below is **403**.

DOWNTOWN

Hotel Regis; 124 7th Ave. SE; tel. 262-4641; $26-46; old part of town
Shamrock Hotel; 2101 11th St. SE; tel. 290-0084; $43-45; bar downstairs
Elbow River Inn & Casino; 1919 Macleod Tr. SE; tel. 269-6771 or (800) 661-1463; $49-59; near Stampede Park, full breakfast
Royal Pacific Hotel; 1330 8th St. SW; tel. 228-6900; $65-69; large rooms, each with a kitchen
Lord Nelson Inn; 1020 8th Ave. SW; tel. 269-8262 or (800) 661-6017; $65; good value
Sandman Inn; 888 7th Ave. SW; tel. 237-8626 or (800) 726-3626; $67-72; all facilities, 24 hour restaurant
Westward Inn; 119 12th Ave. SW; tel. 266-4611 or (800) 661-9378; $75-85; full facilities
Quality Hotel; 888 7th Ave. SW; tel. 237-8626 or (800) 726-3626; $80-90; one floor is for women only
Prince Royal Inn; 618 5th Ave. SW; tel. 263-0520 or (800) 661-1592; $88-95; all rooms are suites, includes breakfast
Ramada Hotel; 708 8th Ave. SW; tel. 263-7600 or (800) 661-8684; $105-125; small rooms
International Hotel; 220 4th Ave. SW; tel. 265-9600 or (800) 661-8627; $116-130; all rooms are suites, good weekend rates
Delta Bow Valley Inn; 209 4th Ave. SE; tel. 266-1980 or (800) 268-1133; $145-160; pool, spa, exercise room
Westin Hotel; 320 4th Ave. SW; tel. 266-1611 or (800) 228-3000; $153-173; full service hotel
Radisson Plaza Hotel; 110 9th Ave. SE; tel. 266-7331 or (800) 661-7776; $155-165; full service hotel
The Palliser Hotel; 133 9th Ave. SW; tel. 262-1234 or (800) 441-1414; $220-240; heritage building

NORTHEAST (AIRPORT) (most have a courtesy airport shuttle)

The Pointe Inn; 1808 19th St. NE; tel. 291-4681 or (800) 661-8164; $40-45; laundry, free coffee
Ambassador Motor Inn; 802 16th Ave. NE; tel. 276-2271 or (800) 661-1447; $49-64; outdoor pool, some kitchenettes
Travelodge Hotel Airport; 2750 Sunridge Blvd. NE; tel. 291-1260 or (800) 255-3050; $53-61; recently renovated
Best Western Airport; 1947 18th Ave. NE; tel. 250-5015 or (800) 528-1234; $56-64; free coffee
Ramada Inn Airport; 1250 McKinnon Dr. NE; tel. 230-1999 or (800) 661-5095; $58-64; 16th Ave. at 19th St.
Crossroads Hotel; 2120 16th Ave. NE; tel. 291-4666 or (800) 661-8157; $74-84
Marlborough Inn; 1316 33rd St. NE; tel. 248-8888 or (800) 661-1464; $84; exercise room
Best Western Port-o-call Inn; 1935 McKnight Blvd. NE; tel. 291-4600 or (800) 661-1161; $89; full facilities
Sheraton Cavalier; 2620 32nd Ave. NE; tel. 291-0107 or (800) 325-3535; $125-135; indoor water park
Chateau Airport Hotel; 2001 Airport Rd. NE; tel. 291-2600 or (800) 828-7447; $135-150; at airport

CALGARY ACCOMMODATIONS

NORTHWEST

Olympia Motel; 5020 16th Ave. NW; tel. 288-4461; $35-39; free local calls
Red Carpet Inn; 4635 16th Ave. NW; tel. 247-9239; $45-49; free coffee, kitchenettes
Panama Motor Inn; 2440 16th Ave. NW; tel. 289-2561; $48; whirlpool, free local calls
Avondale Motor Inn; 2231 Banff Tr. NW; tel. 289-1921; $48; free local calls, kitchenettes
Days Inn; 2369 Banff Tr. NW; tel. 289-5571 or (800) 325-2525; $49-59; whirlpool
Royal Wayne Motel; 2416 16th Ave. NW; tel. 289-6651; $50; fridges, outdoor pool
Comfort Inn; 2363 Banff Tr. NW; tel. 289-2581; $49-54; includes breakfast
Round-up Motor Inn; 1904 Crowchild Tr. NW; tel. 289-9211; $52-62
Travelodge North; 2304 16th Ave. NW; tel. 289-0211 or (800) 255-3050; $57-62; outdoor pool
Budget Host Motor Inn; 4420 16th Ave. NW; tel. 288-7115 or (800) 661-3772; $59-64; free coffee
Highlander Hotel; 1818 16th Ave. NW; tel. 289-1961 or (800) 661-9564; $59-64; all facilities, airport
   shuttle
Crowchild Inn; 5353 Crowchild Tr. NW; tel. 288-5353; $75-80; includes breakfast
Quality Inn; 2359 Banff Tr. NW; tel. 289-1973 or (800) 661-4667; $59-79; full facilities
Best Western Village Park Inn; 1804 Crowchild Tr. NW; tel. 289-0241 or (800) 528-1234; $89-99; full
   facilities, airport shuttle

SOUTH ON MACLEOD TRAIL (from north to south)

Stampeder Inn; 3828 Macleod Tr. SW; tel. tel. 243-5531; $48-50; full facilities
Holiday Inn; 4206 Macleod Tr. SW; tel. 287-2700 or (800) 661-1889; $79-99; airport shuttle, indoor
   pool
Cedar Ridge Motel; 5307 Macleod Tr. SE; tel. 258-1064; $38-46; laundry, kitchenettes
Calgary South Travelodge; 7012 Macleod Tr. SW; tel. 253-1111 or (800) 578-7878; $57-62; free
   coffee, outdoor pool
Flamingo Motor Hotel; 7505 Macleod Tr. SE; tel. 252-4401; $48-56; indoor pool, laundry
Carriage House Inn; 9030 Macleod Tr. SW; tel. 253-1101 or (800) 661-9566; $90-95; airport shuttle
Travelodge Macleod Trail; 9206 Macleod Tr. SW; tel. 253-7070 or (800) 667-3529; $68-78; full
   facilities
Best Western Hospitality Inn; 135 Southland Dr. SE; tel. 278-5050 or (800) 528-1234; $88-90; full
   facilities
Stetson Village Inn; 10002 Macleod Tr. SW; tel. 271-3210; $53-57

OTHERS

Town & Country Motor Hotel; 1825 50th St. SE; tel. 272-9881; $40-45; bar, restaurant
Westgate Motor Inn; 3440 Bow Tr. SW; tel. 249-3181 or (800) 661-1660; $45-55; nightclub
Glenmore Inn; 2720 Glenmore Tr. SE; tel. 279-8611 or (800) 661-3163; $74-82; full facilities
Blackfoot Inn; 5940 Blackfoot Tr. SE; tel. 252-2253 or (800) 661-1151; $99; full facilities

outdoor barbecue, games room, snack bar, lockers, and an information service. From the airport, shuttle buses stop two blocks away at the Delta Bow Valley Inn. A cab from the airport will run around $20. In summer, Pika Shuttle links the hostel to those in Banff and Jasper national parks. Rates are $13 for members and $18 for nonmembers. This place becomes crowded during summer so book ahead.

CAMPGROUNDS

No camping is available within the Calgary city limits, although campgrounds can be found along all major routes into the city. Shuttle buses run to and from campgrounds into Stampede Park during the Calgary Exhibition and Stampede. Reservations are necessary for this week.

West
K.O.A. Calgary West, tel. (403) 288-0411, is located on a hill a short way west of Canada Olympic Park. The modern facilities include showers, a laundry, outdoor pool, and game room. Unserviced sites are $18, hookups $18-22. **Calaway Park,** tel. 249-7372, Canada's largest amusement park, is 10 km farther west along the TransCanada Highway. It offers a large open camping area. Trees are scarce but on clear days the view of the Rockies is spectacular and prairie falcons often hover overhead. The toilets, showers, and laundry are in a trailer, but are of reasonable standard. The large overflow area is unserviced but is only needed during Stampede Week. Tent sites are $15, hookups $16-19, or $12 in the overflow. Ask for free gate-admission coupons for the amusement park.

North
Northwest of the city is **Symons Valley R.V. Park,** tel. (403) 274-4574, which has showers, laundry, and a restaurant. Unserviced sites are $8, hookups $16-18. To get there take 14th St. NW north past Nose Hill Park to Symons Valley Rd., continue northwest along W. Nose Creek to the campground at 144th Ave. Northwest. Also north of the city, but farther out, is **Whispering Spruce Campground,** tel. 226-0097, in the small town of Balzac. The campground has showers and a small grocery store. Tent sites are $10, unserviced sites $14, hookups $16-18.

East
Mountain View Farm Campgrounds, three km east of city limits on the TransCanada Hwy., tel. (403) 293-6640, doesn't have a view of the mountains, but does have a small petting farm, mini-golf, and hay rides. The sites are very close together. Facilities include showers, a grocery store, and laundry. Tent sites are $14, hookups $16-20.

South
South of Calgary on the Bow River is **Nature's Hideaway Campground,** tel. (403) 938-8185. Although farther out than all of the above, it is located in a densely wooded floodplain. Birds are abundant, and deer and coyotes are often seen. Many guests stay here for the entire summer, and the facilities are a little run down. There are showers, a grocery store, a dance hall (music on weekends), and a beach with swimming; unserviced sites $12, hookups $14-18. To get there head east from the Okotoks overpass on Hwy. 552 for 12 km, then north for one km, then east for two more. It's open year-round.

BOB RACE

FOOD

Calgary may lack the cultural trappings that Alberta's capital, Edmonton, boasts, but it gives that city a run for its money in the restaurant department. All the major high-rise buildings downtown have plazas with inexpensive food courts, coffeehouses, and cappuccino bars—the perfect places for people-watching. South of downtown, along 17th Ave. and 4th St., a once quieter part of the city has been transformed into a focal point for Calgary's restaurant scene with cuisine to suit all tastes. Familiar North American fast-food restaurants line Macleod Trail south of the city center.

DOWNTOWN DINING

Eau Claire Market

Located at the entrance to Prince's Island Park, this newly developed indoor market has a large food court as well as nine restaurants. In the food court you'll find a great seafood outlet, a bakery, and a number of Asian-food places. Across from the food court is **Wok Way,** tel. (403) 262-1133, a casual Chinese restaurant. Two enormous glass circles mark the entrance to this restaurant, which has a purple warehouse ceiling and mustard-colored walls. Lunch specials are $5. **Cajun Charlies,** tel. 233-8101, opposite the food court, is a striking orange-and-black eatery serving Louisiana Bayou dishes.

Outside the market's western entrance is **Joey Tomato's Kitchen,** tel. 263-6336, a trendy bistro-style restaurant serving moderately priced Italian food.

In the parking lot of Eau Claire Market is **1886 Cafe,** tel. 269-9255, named for the year it was built. This restaurant oozes an authentic Old-Calgary ambience. Breakfast attracts the most interesting group of diners but the place is busy all day. Portions are generous, coffee refills are free, and when you've finished your meal ask to see the museum downstairs. It's open daily 7 a.m.-3 p.m.

Japanese

Yuzuki Japanese Restaurant, 510 9th Ave. SW, tel. (403) 261-7701, is a good downtown eatery where the most expensive lunch item is the assorted sushi for $10. Excellent value considering it comes with 10 of those little rice packages and a bowl of miso soup. Less expensive items start at $6 and are priced only slightly higher at dinner.

More upscale is **Sushi Hiro,** 727 5th Ave. SW, tel. 233-0605. Sushi choices change regularly but generally include red salmon, yellowtail, sea urchin, and salmon roe. If you sit at the oak-and-green-marble sushi counter you'll be able to ask the chef what's best. Closed Sunday.

Chinese

Chinatown, along 2nd and 3rd avenues east of Centre St., naturally has the best assortment of Chinese restaurants. **Hang Fung Restaurant,** 119 3rd Ave. SE, tel. (403) 269-4646, tucked behind a Chinese grocery store, serves a variety of one-plate meals for under $7. The barbecue pork is delicious and only $4.50. Just as inexpensive is **Golden Inn Restaurant,** 107 2nd Ave. SE, tel. 269-2211, popular with the local Chinese, as well as with professionals, and shift-workers appreciate its long hours (open till 4 a.m.). The menu features mostly Cantonese-style deep-fried food. With more atmosphere is **Silver Dragon,** 106 3rd Ave. SE, tel. 264-5326, a large restaurant with subdued lighting and a relaxed and comfortable setting. **Charly Chan's,** 1140 Kensington Rd. NW, tel. 283-6165, is a yuppie Chinese restaurant on the north side of the Bow River in trendy Kensington. Chinese are not particularly fond of eating here but the Peking-style dishes are all well prepared and are popular with Calgarians.

Lebanese

The **Beirut Restaurant,** 112 8th Ave. SW, tel. (403) 264-8859, makes up for what it lacks in ambience with hearty portions of traditional middle-eastern dishes such as hummus ($4.75).

Also inexpensive are the falafel-pita sandwiches and chicken-breast sandwiches (both under $6).

Seafood

The city's best seafood is available at **Cannery Row,** 317 10th Ave. SW, tel. (403) 269-8889, and directly upstairs at the aptly named **McQueens Upstairs,** tel. 269-4722. Cannery Row is a casual affair, with an open kitchen, oyster bar, and the ambience of a San Francisco seafood restaurant. Typical fish dishes available are salmon, halibut, swordfish, and marlin. Seven southern-style entrees are also offered. The menu at McQueens Upstairs is more varied and slightly more expensive. Both restaurants are open daily for lunch (except Sunday) and dinner and are busy during office lunch hours.

Upscale

For the best steaks in the city that produces the best beef in Canada, head to **Caesar's Steakhouse,** 512 4th Ave. SW, tel. (403) 264-1222. The dimly lit, elegant restaurant is decorated in a Roman-style setting. The chef is enclosed in a glass bubble allowing diners to watch him at work. Although the menu is varied it's the juicy prime cuts that Caesar's is famous for. Entrees are $10-35. Open Mon.-Fri. noon-2 p.m. and daily 4:30 p.m.-midnight.

The **Owl's Nest,** 320 4th Ave. SW, tel. 266-1611, in the Westin Hotel is an upscale restaurant with elegant surroundings where ladies are presented with a rose and gentlemen with a cigar. Many entrees are low-cholesterol; others, such as turtle soup, quail, and beluga caviar certainly aren't. Entrees are $15-30, lunch is slightly less expensive. Open Mon.-Fri. for lunch and dinner and on Saturday for dinner only. In the Delta Bow Valley Hotel is **The Conservatory,** 209 4th Ave. SE, tel. 266-1980, a fine-dining restaurant with a French chef. Enjoy a pre-dinner drink in **The Lobby Lounge.** Other high-end restaurants in town include the **Rimrock Room,** 133 9th Ave. SW, tel. 262-1234, in the historic Palliser Hotel, and **Trader's,** 110 9th Ave. SE, tel. 266-7331, in the Radisson Plaza Hotel (where waiters wear white gloves and diners are entertained by a pianist). At the top of the Calgary Tower is **Panorama Dining Room,** 101 9th Ave. SW, tel. 266-7171, a revolving restaurant that takes one hour for a full rotation. As far as revolving restaurants go the food is excellent; the menu features mainly local game. It's open daily 7:30 a.m.-midnight.

SOUTH OF DOWNTOWN

Italian

Few restaurants in the city are as popular as **Chianti,** 1438 17th Ave. SW, tel. (403) 229-1600. Over 20 well-prepared pasta dishes are featured on the menu; all the pasta is made daily on the premises. Among many specialties are the Veal Chianti and Frutti Di Mare. Pasta entrees are all under $10 and no dish is over $13. The restaurant is dark and noisy in typical Italian style. The owner often sings with an accordionist on weekends. It's open daily till midnight.

French

The unpretentious exterior of **La Chaumiere,** 121 17th Ave. SE, tel. (403) 228-5690, belies the fact that it's one of North America's premier French restaurants. Dishes such as duck in brandy, flaming duck, and escargots are authentically prepared and the formal service is meticulous. Reservations are required for dinner. It's open for lunch Mon.-Fri. noon-2:30 p.m., and for dinner Mon.-Sat. from 5:30 p.m. Less expensive is **Entre Nous,** 2206 4th St. SW, tel. 228-5525, where a three-course lunch is under $20 per person. The tin ceiling and glass-topped tables are a legacy of the way this restaurant began—as a French bistro.

Moroccan

When you enter **Sultan's Tent,** 909 17th Ave. SW, tel. (403) 244-2333, a server appears with a silver kettle and basin filled with orange-blossom-scented water to wash your hands. It's all part of Moroccan custom and part of the fun. The restaurant features swinging lanterns, hassocks, piped-in Arabic music, and most importantly, delicious Moroccan delicacies. Try Guelli's Sultan Feast ($22.75), a six-course dinner.

Other Ethnic Restaurants

Restaurant Indonesia, 1604 14th St. SW, tel.

(403) 244-0645, is a busy, inexpensive eatery at the west end of 17th Avenue. Indonesian food is very similar to Chinese, although the sauces prepared here are usually richer. Entrees are $5-9. On 4th St. SW between 17th and 25th avenues are a number of ethnic restaurants. **Rajdoot,** 2424 4th St. SW, tel. 245-0181, has an excellent lunchtime buffet ($8.95) with around 25 different Indian dishes, each rated mild, medium, or hot. The turnover of food is fast, ensuring that items stay fresh and hot. The Sunday brunch buffet ($10.95) has even more choices. Another good place for budget-minded travelers with exotic tastes is **Cafe Med,** 2202 4th St. SW, tel. 245-0352. This restaurant has a pastel-pink interior with large windows and a relaxed atmosphere. The cuisine is Lebanese, many dishes are vegetarian. The Platter Sampler ($13.90) is a good chance to taste everything. It's open Mon.-Sat. 11 a.m.-11 p.m., Sunday 4-11 p.m. Next door is **Andrea's Taverna,** 2210 4th St. SW, tel. 244-1771, a traditional blue-and-white decorated Greek restaurant with a belly dancer on Friday nights. Entrees are $8-12; finish with Greek coffee and baklava. It's open Mon.-Fri. 11 a.m.-midnight; weekends for dinner only.

Macleod Trail South
This commercial strip from 36th Ave. to Anderson Rd. is crammed with all the familiar fast-food restaurants found everywhere in North America. Aside from these a small number of family restaurants along this stretch are worth searching for. **Cactus Club Cafe,** 7010 Macleod Trail SE, tel. (403) 255-1088, has a yuppie western atmosphere. The interior is absolutely crammed with cow-related artifacts, although the only thing that's authentic are the peanut shells on the floor. **Billy MacIntyres,** 7104 Macleod Trail SE, tel. 252-2260, features Alberta beef at reasonable prices. All entrees include an extensive salad bar that, unlike most restaurants, is tucked out of sight of other diners. For those with cash to splash try the High Roller Special that comes with a bottle of Jack Daniels. Farther south is **Fuddruckers,** 9823 Macleod

Trail SW, tel. 297-0297, a burger joint with an in-house bakery, butcher, and build-your-own burger bar.

NORTH OF DOWNTOWN

Italian
Mamma's, 320 16th Ave. NW, tel. (403) 276-9744, is the most popular Italian eatery on the northside and has been around for decades. Start with the antipasto buffet, then try one of the many veal dishes, and finish with one of their spectacular desserts, all for under $20. Closed Sunday.

Nick's Steakhouse
Whether it's professional sportsmen, their managers, or their fans, chances are if they're from Calgary they've eaten at Nick's. Its prime location directly opposite McMahon Stadium, good food, and large-screen TV all contribute to the restaurant's success. Lunch specials are $5.95, dinner specials $9.95, and charbroiled steaks begin at $10. Open daily till one or two in the morning. No reservations taken. Nick's is located at 2430 Crowchild Trail NW; tel. (403) 282-9278.

Dining With A Difference
Named after the mothballed flying machine of the late Howard Hughes, **Spruce Goose Cafe,** 1441 Aviation Park NE, tel. (403) 295-4140, is adjacent to the runways of Calgary International Airport. The building's east wall is all window, great for watching the action—perfect for kids. Breakfast costs around $5, lunch and dinner dishes start at $6. The cafe is in the Shell Aerocentre adjacent to McCall Field. Another good-value restaurant out by the airport is **Husky House,** 2525 32nd Ave. NE, tel. 291-1616, just off Barlow Trail. The white-uniformed wait staff serves up to 1,000 people a day. Servings are monstrous, soup is $1.50, burgers start at $3, and everything is deep-fried or grilled. It's open 24 hours.

TRANSPORTATION

GETTING THERE

Air

Calgary International Airport (YYC), Canada's fourth busiest, is located within the city limits northeast of downtown. It is served by 11 scheduled airlines and used by 4.6 million passengers each year. **Arrivals** is on the lower level where passengers are greeted by Welcome Hosts—dressed in traditional Western attire, they answer visitor questions about the airport, transportation, and the city. Among the baggage carousels is an information booth shaped like a chuck wagon (open daily 7 a.m.-10 p.m.). Also on the arrivals level are hotel courtesy phones, rental-car agencies, and a Brewster Transportation and Tours desk. **Chateau Airport,** connected by a skywalk, is the only hotel at the airport. A cab to the city center runs around $25, or you can catch the **Airporter** bus, tel. (403) 531-3909, to major downtown hotels for $7. Brewster Transportation and Tours offers a bus to Banff every two hours.

Scheduled airlines using Calgary International Airport include: **Air B.C.,** tel. 265-9555 or 265-3090; **Air Canada,** tel. 265-9555 or (800) 332-1080; **American Airlines,** tel. (800) 433-7300; **Canada 3000,** tel. 221-1870; **Canadian,** tel. 235-1161 or (800) 665-1177; **Canadian Regional,** tel. (800) 665-1177; **Delta,** tel. (800) 221-1212; **Northwest Airlines,** tel. (800) 225-2525; **NWT Air,** tel. 265-9555 or (800) 661-0789; **United Airlines,** tel. (800) 241-6522; and **K.L.M.,** tel. 236-2600 or (800) 361-1887.

Bus

The **Greyhound Bus Depot** is located at 850 16th St. SW, tel. (403) 265-9111. Two blocks away from the depot is the C-train stop ($1.50 into town). To walk the entire distance would take 20 minutes. A cab from the bus depot to downtown runs $5, to Calgary International Hostel $6. The depot is cavernous. It has a restaurant, Royal Bank cash machine, information boards, and lockers large enough for backpacks ($2).

Buses connect Calgary daily with Edmonton (3.5 hours, $29.96 one way), Banff (two hours, $14.71 one way), Vancouver (15 hours, $96.30 one way), and all other points within the province. No reservations are taken. Just turn up, buy your ticket, and hop aboard. If you buy your ticket seven days in advance, discounts apply. If you plan to travel extensively by bus, the Canada Travel Pass is a good deal.

Red Arrow is a more luxurious bus service that goes to Edmonton from major Calgary hotels, stopping at Red Deer. Some services continue to Fort McMurray. To Edmonton it's $31 one way. For more information call 531-0350 or (800) 232-1958.

GETTING AROUND

Bus

You can get just about everywhere in town by using the Calgary Transit System, which combines three light-rail lines with extensive bus routes. Buses are $1.50 one way to all destinations—deposit the exact change in the box beside the driver and request a transfer if you'll be changing buses. A day pass, valid for unlimited bus and rail travel, is $4.50. The best place for information and schedules is the **Calgary Transit Customer Service Centre** at 240 7th Ave. SW (opposite The Bay department store). Open Mon.-Fri. 8:30 a.m.-5 p.m. An information line is available seven days, call (403) 262-1000.

C-Train

C-train, the light-rail transit system, has three lines that converge downtown on 7th Avenue. The **Anderson C-train** parallels Macleod Trail south to Anderson Rd., **Whitehorn C-train** heads out of the city northeast, and **Brentwood C-train** heads northwest past the university. The system is operated by Calgary Transit, so fares are the same as buses, $1.50 one way or $4.50 for a day pass. Transfers in the same direction are free, as is travel on the downtown route along 7th Avenue. For route information call

(403) 276-7801. Route maps and ticket-vend-ing machines are located at all C-train stations.

Disabled Passengers
Bus No. 31 around downtown is wheelchair accessible, as are five other routes through the city. The Brentwood line (northwest) is the only fully accessible route on the L.R.T. system. For information on all wheelchair-accessible services call (403) 262-1000. **Calgary Handi-bus** provides wheelchair accessible transportation throughout the city. A book of eight tickets is $12, but visitors receive free service for a limited length of time. For more information call 276-8028. A small number of manual wheelchairs are available for loan from the **Canadian Red Cross,** tel. 541-4400.

Taxi
Flag charge for a cab in Calgary is $2.25 and it's $1.30 for every kilometer. Taxi companies include: **Associated Cabs,** tel. (403) 299-1111; **Calgary Cab Co.,** tel. 291-9100; **Checker Cabs,** tel. 299-9999; **Prestige Cabs,** tel. 974-1100; and **Yellow Cab,** tel. 974-1111.

Car Rental
If you've just arrived in Calgary, call around and compare rates. Lesser-known agencies are often cheaper, and all rates fluctuate with the season and demand. Many larger agencies have higher rates for unlimited mileage and built-in drop-off charges to nearby centers. (Drop-off charges to Banff are usually $50 extra, and to Edmonton $80 extra.) All agencies provide free pick-up and drop-off at major Calgary hotels and have outlets at Calgary International Airport. Rental agencies include **Avis,** tel. (403) 291-1475 or (800) 879-2847; **Budget,** tel. 226-1550 or (800) 268-8900; **Discount Car Rentals,** tel. 299-1222; **Dollar,** tel. 269-3777 or (800) 263-6552; **Economy Car Rentals,** tel. 291-1640; **Hertz,** tel. 221-1681 or (800) 263-0600; and **Thrifty,** tel. 262-4400 or (800) 367-2277.

Tours
Brewster Transportation and Tours, tel. (403) 221-8242, runs a City Sights tour lasting four hours. Included on the itinerary are downtown, various historic buildings, Canada Olympic Park, and Fort Calgary. The cost is $32. Pick-ups are at most major hotels. Brewster also runs tours to Banff (nine hours, $49.50), Lake Louise (nine hours, $58), and Columbia Icefields (15 hours, $69.50).

SERVICES AND INFORMATION

SERVICES

The downtown **post office** is located at 207 9th Ave. Southwest. **Calgary Foreign Exchange** is located at 407 2nd St. SW, tel. (403) 290-0330, and also has a branch at Calgary International Airport. **American Express Travel Service,** 421 7th Ave. SW, tel. 261-5982, offers all the same currency services with the advantages of also being a travel agency. Most major banks carry U.S. currency and can handle basic foreign-exchange transactions.

West Canadian Color, 1231 10th Ave. SW, tel. 244-2711, is the most efficient and reliable photo lab in town. Turnaround time on print film is an hour; on E6 slide film five hours. Drop any film off before closing time and it will be ready first thing the following day. It's open Mon.-Sat. 7 a.m.-5:30 p.m., Saturday 8 a.m.-4 p.m.

For further travel arrangements, **Travel Cuts,** 1414 Kensington Rd. NW, tel. 531-2070, is the best place to start looking for inexpensive tickets.

Handy self-service laundromats are: **Avenue Towers,** 333 17th Ave. SW; **Heritage Hill Coin Laundry,** 8228 Heritage Hill Rd. SE at the corner of Macleod Trail and Heritage Dr.; and **The Great Canadian Cleaners,** 4949 Barlow Trail Southeast.

Emergency Services
For medical emergencies call 911 or contact one of the following hospitals: **Calgary General Hospital,** 841 Centre Ave. NE, tel. (403) 268-9111; **Foothills Hospital,** 1403 29th Ave. NW, tel. 670-1110; **Holy Cross Hospital,** 2210 2nd St. SW, tel. 541-2000; **Rockyview General Hospital,** 7007 14th St. SW, tel. 541-3000; or **Alberta Children's Hospital,** 1820 Richmond Rd. SW, tel. 229-7211. For the **RCMP** call 230-6483.

INFORMATION

Libraries

The Calgary Public Library Board's 16 branch libraries are scattered throughout the city. The largest is **W.R. Castell Central Library** located at 616 Macleod Trail SE, tel. (403) 260-2600. Four floors of books, magazines, and newspapers from around the world (including the all-important *Sydney Morning Herald*) are enough to keep most people busy on a rainy afternoon. Other main branches are **Nose Hill Library** at 1530 Northmount Dr. NW, **Village Square Branch** at 2623 56th St. NE, and **Fish Creek Area Library** at 11161 Bonaventure Dr. Southeast. Hours at each are generally Mon.-Thurs. 10 a.m.-9 p.m., Fri.-Sat. 10 a.m.-5 p.m. (and on Sunday in winter only).

Bookstores

Downtown, **The Book Company** in Bankers Hall, 315 8th Ave. SW, tel. (403) 237-8344, is a good place to find books on Western Canada as well as general travel writing and nonfiction works. Another good bookshop is **Sandpiper Books,** 1145 Kensington Cr. NW, tel. 270-2115. In the same area, along Kensington Rd. are a number of secondhand and collectors bookstores. Another concentration of secondhand books is 16th Ave. Northeast. For topographical, city, and wall maps, **Map Town,** 640 6th Ave. SW, tel. 266-2241, should have what you're looking for.

Information Centers

Within the city limits are four visitor service centers operated by the Calgary Convention and Visitors Bureau. One is on the main floor of the **Calgary Tower Centre** at the corner of Centre St. and 9th Ave. Southwest. This small center is open year-round, daily 8:30 a.m.-5 p.m. On the Arrivals level at **Calgary International Airport** is another, open year-round, daily 7 a.m.-10 p.m. Seasonal locations are at **Canada Olympic Park** and on the westbound side of the Trans-Canada Hwy. between 58th and 62nd St. Northeast. Both are open June-Aug., daily 9 a.m.-5 p.m. For more information on Calgary call (403) 263-8510 or (800) 661-1678 (toll-free anywhere in North America).

KAREN MCKINLEY

VICINITY OF CALGARY

Calgary is blessed with a staggering variety of things to do and see within close proximity of the city. To the east is the **Red Deer River,** which flows past some of the world's richest dinosaur fossil beds; hundreds of museum-quality specimens from the Cretaceous period—displayed in museums throughout the world—have been unearthed along a 120-km stretch of the river valley. One spot here, **Dinosaur Provincial Park,** is the mother lode for palaeontologists— this UNESCO World Heritage Site includes a "graveyard" of over 300 dinosaurs. And the park's landforms are as enthralling as the prehistoric artifacts they entomb—spectacular badland formations make for a sight not easily forgotten.

The major city in this valley, **Drumheller,** is home to the **Royal Tyrrell Museum of Palaeontology.** The museum is a research and display center with over 50 full size dinosaurs exhibited, more than in any other museum in the world.

Although nonrenewable resources such as oil and gas are the basis of Alberta's economy today, ranching was the province's first major industry. The first ranch established in Alberta was at **Cochrane,** just west of Calgary, but the entire southern foothills have been used for running cattle for over a century. Throughout the hills are many well established towns with interesting histories, quaint teahouses, holiday ranches, and sprawling properties, all with the inspiring Rocky Mountains as a backdrop.

Kananaskis Country is a vast tract of land set aside by the Alberta government as a multiuse recreation area. It's located west of Calgary within easy day-trip distance. Although the region's emphasis is on the outdoors and camping, luxurious accommodations are available in Kananaskis Village. The village and the modern ski resort of **Nakiska** nearby were built for the 1988 Winter Olympic Games. On the northern edge of Kananaskis Country, and at the entrance to Banff National Park, is the ever-growing mountain community of **Canmore.** The town provides an inexpensive alternative to staying deeper in the mountains and is an active outdoor center in itself; many mountaineers, climbers, hikers, and skiers take advantage of the mountains surrounding town.

VICINITY OF CALGARY

© MOON PUBLICATIONS, INC.

DRUMHELLER AND DINOSAUR VALLEY

Drumheller, a small city of 6,500 in the **Red Deer River Valley** 138 km northeast of Calgary, is set in a spectacular lunarlike landscape. Ancient glacial meltwaters gouged a deep valley into the surrounding rolling prairie, and wind and water have continued the erosion process ever since. The city's proximity to some of the world's premier dinosaur fossil beds has made it a mecca for palaeontologists—scientists from around the globe come to Drumheller and environs to learn more about the prehistoric animals that roamed the earth millions of years ago.

The city was named after Samuel Drumheller, an early pioneer in the local coal industry. Coal deposits had been found in the area by early explorers, but it wasn't until 1911 that the first mine opened. In 1913, when the rail link was completed with Calgary, the town's population exploded. Coal dominated the economy until after WW II, when diesel replaced steam and demand for coal dwindled. Today the town is an agricultural and oil center, with 3,000 oil wells perforating the farmland within a close radius of town.

The Great Canadian Dinosaur Rush

Drumheller is one of Alberta's major tourist destinations. Over half a million people flock to this desolate part of Canada for one reason—dinosaurs. For generations natives had regarded the bones, which were always common in the valley, as belonging to giant buffalo. During early geographical surveys of southern Alberta by George M. Dawson, the first official dinosaur discovery was recorded. In 1884 one of Dawson's assistants, **Joseph B. Tyrrell,** collected and sent specimen bones to Ottawa for scientific investigation. Their identification initiated the first real dinosaur rush. For the first century of digging, all the dinosaur bones uncovered were transported to museums around the world for further study. But then dinosaur-hunter Dr. Phil Currie started promoting the idea of building a museum in Alberta. His efforts culminated in the 1985 opening of the **Royal Tyr-**

rell Museum of Palaeontology in Drumheller. Since then, the dinosaurs have stayed and the tourists have come.

SIGHTS

Royal Tyrrell Museum Of Palaeontology

Hidden in the badlands, six km northwest of Drumheller, is the world's largest museum devoted entirely to palaeontology. Even for those with little or no interest in dinosaurs it is easy to spend half a day in the 12,000-square-meter complex. The museum holds over 80,000 specimens, including 50 full-size dinosaur skeletons, the world's largest such display.

A "time line" of exhibits explores 4.5 billion years of life on this planet, beginning with early life forms and the development of Charles Darwin's theory. A two-story subtropical arboretum features over 100 species of plants, many of which flourished during the period that dinosaurs roamed the earth. The showpiece is Dinosaur Hall, where reconstructed skeletons and full-size replicas of dinosaurs are complemented by realistic dioramas of the habitat in which they lived. Nearing the end of the tour, the various theories for the cause of the dinosaurs' extinction are presented. The coming of the Ice Ages is described in detail, and man's appearance on earth is put into perspective.

The museum is also a major research center; a large window into the main preparation lab allows you to view the delicate work of technicians as they clear the rock away from newly unearthed bones. An interesting way to become involved in the actual digging of dinosaur bones is by participating in a museum-organized **Day Dig.** These take place at a site close to the museum. After a brief lesson in excavation techniques, you spend the rest of the day digging. Transportation and lunch are supplied. Cost is $75 (or you can watch for $8).

The museum is located in Midland Provincial Park (see below). It's open daily except Monday, 9 a.m.-9 p.m. in summer, 10 a.m.-5

at the Royal Tyrrell Museum

p.m. the rest of the year. Admission is $5. For further information, call (403) 823-7707.

Midland Provincial Park

This 595-hectare park covers the lower part of Fox Creek Coulee on the northern bank of the Red Deer River. **McMullen Island,** created by an old river meander, is a secluded day-use area shaded by willows and cottonwoods. Pathways lead along the riverbank, and barbecues and a generous supply of wood are available. On the opposite side of the highway the origins of the park become apparent. Slag heaps and building foundations are the only reminders of the three Midland Coal Mines that operated here until the late 1960s. The mine office is now the park visitor center where interpretive boards explain the history of the area and a short trail leads through the old mining sites. Many visitors to the park are not even aware that they're in it. The Royal Tyrrell Museum (see above), from where rangers conduct short hikes during summer, is at the western end of the park. For more information on the park, call (403) 823-4788.

Homestead Antique Museum

This museum, featuring mostly pioneer artifacts, is housed in a unique Quonset two km west of the city, tel. (403) 823-2600. The collection includes Indian relics, pioneer clothing, mining equipment, musical instruments, a two-headed calf, and re-creations of an early beauty parlor and barber shop. Outside is an array of farm machinery, automobiles, and a buffalo rubbing stone. The museum is open July-Aug. 9 a.m.-9 p.m.; May, June, September, and October 9 a.m.-6 p.m. Admission is $3.

Drumheller Dinosaur And Fossil Museum

This small downtown museum at 335 1st St. E, tel. (403) 823-2593, has an interesting display of privately owned and donated prehistoric pieces, most of which have been collected from the Red Deer River Valley. Exhibits include interpretive boards explaining the geography of the ancient inland sea, the process of coal formation, and the fossilization process. Two items of particular interest are the mounted 10-meter-long skeleton of an edmontosaurus and the skull of a pachyrhinosaurus, the first of its species found. The museum is open in summer, daily 10 a.m.-6 p.m.; shorter hours in May and October. Admission is $2.

Prehistoric Park

For the complete Dinosaur Valley experience you need to visit at least one gimmicky attraction and this is the best of the bunch. Life-sized dinosaur models are displayed among 50 hectares of natural badlands canyon scenery. A one-km trail leads through the park, finishing at **Ollie's Rock & Fossil Shop,** which sells stones, bones, and dinosaurs. The park is at the end of Premier Crescent off South Dinosaur Trail. It's open April-Sept., daily 10 a.m.-6 p.m.; longer hours in summer. Admission is $5.

Little Fish Lake Provincial Park

Undulating hills of northern fescue grassland and the clear waters of Little Fish Lake provide the backdrop for this small park 40 km east of Drumheller via East Coulee. (For sights along the way, see "East Coulee Drive," below.) The park is also accessible off Hwy. 9, 40 km south from Craigmyle. Both access roads are gravel. The nearby **Hand Hills** were used by both Cree and Blackfoot as a viewpoint. Many indications of the area's prehistory have been found at the southeast end of the lake—mainly tepee rings and campsites. The beach and cool water of the lake attract people from Drumheller so it can get busy on weekends. The lake is also popular with vacationing waterfowl en route to their summer homes down south or returning in the fall. The primitive campground has pit toilets, a kitchen shelter, and firewood. Sites are $7 (free to ducks).

Other Things To Do

The country's largest collection of reptiles is housed at **Reptile World** in Suncity Mall, 1222 Hwy. 9 S, tel. (403) 823-8623, where you can view and handle these much maligned creatures; admission $4. **Memory Lane Wax Gallery,** 235 3rd Ave. W, tel. 823-5159, is downtown in the Valley Plaza Mall, and the **Horn and Antler Museum and Funland Amuse-**

ment Park are located along Dinosaur Trail NW, tel. 823-5201. It's easy to spend hours in the many shops selling fossils; the best in town is **The Fossil Shop** at 61 Bridge St., tel. 823-6774. Pieces start at $10 for chunks of unidentifiable dinosaur bones and go to thousands of dollars for magnificent ammonites from the United States. The owner is a knowledgeable local man who has spent his life collecting fossils from around the world.

SCENIC DRIVES

The Dinosaur Trail

This 48-km circular route to the west of Drumheller starts and finishes in town and passes many worthwhile stops, including two spectacular viewpoints. After passing the access road to Royal Tyrrell Museum, the first point of interest

is the **Little Church,** often described as being able to seat thousands—but only six at a time. The road then climbs steeply out of the valley onto the prairie benchland. Take the first access road on the left—it doubles back to **Horsethief Canyon Lookout** from where there are spectacular views of the badlands and the multicolored walls of the canyons. Slip, slide, or somersault down the embankment here into the mysterious lunarlike landscape and it's easy to imagine why early explorers were so intrigued by the valley and how easy it was for thieves to hide stolen horses along the coulees in the early 1900s.

The halfway point of the trail is the crossing of the Red Deer River on the **Bleriot Ferry,** one of the few remaining cable ferries in Alberta. It operates April-Nov. 7 a.m.-11 p.m. On the far side of the river is a primitive campground. Upstream from the campground a major dinosaur discov-

DINOSAURS OF ALBERTA

Dinosaur bones found in the Red Deer River Valley play an important role in the understanding of our prehistoric past. The bones date from the late Cretaceous period, around 70 million years ago; for reasons that have mystified palaeontologists for over a century, dinosaurs disappeared during this period, after having roamed the earth for 150 million years. A recent theory, put together largely through work done in Alberta, suggests that while larger species disappeared, some of the smaller ones evolved into birds.

The bones of thirty-five dinosaur species—around 10% of all those currently known—have been discovered in Alberta. Like today's living creatures, they are classified in orders, families, and species. Of the two orders of dinosaurs, both have been found in the Red Deer River Valley. The bird-hipped dinosaurs (order Ornithischia) were herbivores, while the lizard-hipped dinosaurs (order Saurischia) were omnivores and carnivores. Apart from their sheer bulk, many herbivores lacked any real defenses. Others

developed their own protection; the chasmosaurus had a bony frill around its neck, the pachycephalosaurus had a 25-centimeter-thick dome-shaped skull cap fringed with spikes, and the ankylosaurus was an armored dinosaur whose back was covered in spiked plates.

Among the most common herbivores that have been found in the valley are members of the family of duck-billed hadrosaurs. Fossilized eggs of one hadrosaur, the hypacrosaurus, were unearthed still encasing intact embryos.

Another common herbivore in the valley was a member of the horned ceratops family; over 300 specimens of the centrosaurus have been discovered in one "graveyard."

Of the lizard-hipped dinosaurs, the tyrannosaurs were most feared by herbivores. The 15-meter *Tyrannosaurus rex* is most famous among *Homo sapiens.* But the smaller albertosaurus, a remarkably agile carnivore weighing many tons, was the most common tyrannosaur found in the valley.

BOB RACE

VICINITY OF DRUMHELLER

TO THREE HILLS AND RED DEER

BLERIOT FERRY

TO HANNA AND STETTLER

ORKNEY HILL LOOKOUT

HORSETHIEF CANYON LOOKOUT

TO THREE HILLS

ROYAL TYRRELL MUSEUM OF PALAEONTOLOGY

LITTLE CHURCH

DINOSAUR TRAIL GOLF AND COUNTRY CLUB

MIDLAND PROVINCIAL PARK

McMULLEN ISLAND DAY-USE AREA

DRUMHELLER

RED DEER RIVER

SUSPENSION BRIDGE

ROSEDALE

TO CALGARY

WAYNE   CAMBRIA

HOODOOS

TO DINOSAUR PROVINCIAL PARK

EAST COULEE

ATLAS COAL MINE

0   3 mi
0   3 km

ery was made in 1923 when the fossilized bones of a duck-billed edmontosaurus were unearthed. The road continues along the top of the valley to **Orkney Hill Lookout** for more panoramic views across the badlands and the lush valley floor below. A buffalo jump was nearby, where Indians once stampeded great herds of bison off the edge of the cliff. But centuries of erosion have changed the clay and sandstone landscape so dramatically that the actual position of the jump is now impossible to define.

East Coulee Drive

This 25-km road, southeast from Drumheller, passes three historic coal-mining communities in an area dotted with mine shafts and abandoned buildings. The first town along this route is **Rosedale,** which at first looks prosperous. On closer inspection, however, you'll notice the distinct lack of businesses. In fact, the town's population dropped from 3,000 to less than 100 a few years ago. The community began on the opposite side of the Red Deer River around the Star Mine, but after the combined car and rail bridge was washed out, the town was moved to its present site. For many years the mine still operated with workers crossing the river on a unique suspension bridge to get to work. The original bridge was built in 1931 but was later replaced by a cable-trolley system. Today the bridge has been upgraded and is safe for those who want to venture across.

A worthwhile detour from Rosedale is to **Wayne,** an almost-a-ghost town tucked up a valley alongside Rosebud Creek. It is nine km south of Rosedale along Hwy. 10X, which spurs away from the river just south of the town and crosses the creek 11 times. In its heyday, Wayne had 1,500 residents, most of whom worked in the Rosedeer Mine. It was never known as a law-abiding town. During Alberta's prohibition days many moonshiners operated in the surrounding hills, safe from the nearest RCMP patrol in Drumheller. By the time the mine closed in 1957 the population had dipped to 250 and today is probably a tenth of that. Many buildings remain, making it a popular setting for film crews. The only operating business in the sleepy hamlet is the **Rosedeer Hotel,** tel. (403) 823-9189, where the walls are lined with memorabilia from the town's glory days. The hotel's outside porch overlooking the creek makes a great place to grab a beer and wallow in nostalgia.

From Rosedale Hwy. 10 continues southeast, crossing the Red Deer River at the abandoned mining town of Cambria and passing hoodoos to the left. These strangely shaped rock formations along the river valley have been carved by eons of wind and rain. The harder rock on top is more resistant to erosion than the rock beneath it, resulting in the odd, mushroom-shaped pillars.

East Coulee once had a population of 3,000; now it's down to 250. Mining has taken place here since 1924, but building a rail line from Drumheller proved expensive. Eventually part of the riverbank was blasted into the river and the spur was completed in 1928. Full-time production at the main Atlas Mine ended in 1955, but the mine operated intermittently till the '70s. Most buildings remain standing but now only a hotel, grocery store, and garage are open. Through town is the **Atlas Coal Mine Museum,** a Provincial Historic Site. An ore-sorting tipple—the last one standing in Canada—towers above the mine buildings. It's a great place to just walk around, or you can go on the guided tour ($2) to learn more about the mining process. It's open in summer daily 9 a.m.-6 p.m.; tel. 823-2171. In the center of East Coulee, in the East Coulee School Museum, is a cultural center featuring a restored schoolroom, a coal-mining room, art gallery, and tearoom. It's open daily 9 a.m.-5 p.m., closed weekends in winter; tel. 822-3970.

RECREATION

Drumheller's popularity as a tourist destination is only recent and facilities for tourists reflect this. The local indoor pool is located on Riverside Dr., tel. (403) 823-1321, and has a water slide; **Dinosaur Trail Golf and Country Club,** tel. 823-5622, is past the Royal Tyrrell Museum and charges $23 for a round; and **Drumheller Valley Ski Club** is located on the opposite side of the river on 6th Ave. SW, tel. 823-2277.

hoodoos

Entertainment

The after-dark scene is not crash hot. Apart from the quiet lounge in the Drumheller Inn there is nowhere respectable to go. Many hostelers head downstairs to **The Zoo,** 30 Railway Ave. W, tel. (403) 823-2642, a lively rock 'n' roll bar where bands play most nights; cover charge Friday and Saturday. Go anywhere else and, if you're not careful, you'll finish up with more broken bones than an albertosaurus.

ACCOMMODATIONS

Motels

Outside of the cities and the Rocky Mountains, Drumheller is the province's next-largest tourist center, attracting over half a million visitors annually. Yet there are fewer than 300 motel beds in town (including the hostel). With increased demand over the last few years prices have risen, but the quality hasn't. Rooms fill up fast every day (reserve in advance during summer or try checking-in at check-out time) and are full by early afternoon. Ask about off-season rates outside of summer. The two information centers have accommodation boards which post room availability. **Rockhound Motor Inn,** P.O. Box 2350, Drumheller T0J 0Y0, tel. (403) 823-5302, has large rooms for $60 s, $70 d. **Drumheller Inn** (P.O. Box 3100, tel. 823-8400) has an indoor pool, spa, and two restaurants; $80 s, $87 d. **Badlands Motel,** P.O. Box 2217, tel. 823-5155, has a great pancake house next door; $42 s, $46 d. The best asset of **The Lodge,** P.O. Box 1810, tel. 823-3322, is that it's downtown; $60 s or d. **Dinosaur Motel,** 240 Riverside Dr., tel. 823-3381, is beside the river; $40 s or d. **Hoo-doo Motel,** P.O. Box 310, tel. 823-5662, is nothing special at $54 s, $58 d.

Each of the bed and breakfasts in town requires advance reservations. **Riverside Inn,** 501 Riverside Dr. W, tel. 823-4746, is closest to downtown; also within walking distance is **Dinosaur Valley B&B,** 1103 Riverside Dr. E, tel. 823-9250; farther out among the badlands, five minutes west of Drumheller on South Dinosaur Trail, is **Coles B&B,** tel. 823-5844. Rates for the above mentioned are $35 s, $45 d. The hotels along East Coulee Drive in **Rosedale, Wayne** (definitely worth checking out), and **East Coulee** are within 15 minutes of town and fill up last.

Hostel

After extensive renovations, a downtown hotel was reopened in 1991 as **Alexandra International Hostel.** The old hotel rooms have been given a coat of paint, and facilities include a modern kitchen area, TV room with pool table, coin laundry, and lockers. Most of the dorms are small—many have only two or four beds—and some have private bath. The downstairs hallway is lined with "things to do" brochures and schedules of current events. The hostel rents mountain bikes for $4 an hour, or $15 a day—an excellent way to get out to the museum, but take plenty of water. Hostel rates are $10 for members, $14 for nonmembers. It's located at 30 Railway Ave. W, tel. (403) 823-6337—a 20-minute walk (if you don't stop at Dairy Queen) or $5 cab ride from the bus station.

Campgrounds

Three campgrounds are located on the north side of the river. **Shady Grove Campground,** 25 Poplar St., tel. (403) 823-2576, is in a well-treed spot beside the Red Deer River and offers welcome relief from the heat of the badlands. Serviced sites are semiprivate; tenters have more options and are able to disappear among the trees. The campground offers a nice beach (by Albertan standards), mini-golf, and an arcade, and town is just a short stroll away. Tent sites are $10, hookups $12-16. On the corner of Hwy. 9 and North Dinosaur Trail is **Dinosaur Trailer Park,** tel. 823-3291. Also within walking distance of town, this private campground has full hookups, barbecues ($5 per night), and an owner who knows everything there is to know about bison—he owns the herd along Hwy. 576. Unserviced sites are $13, hookups $14-18. On the north side of the river, four km west of the Tyrrell Museum, is **Dinosaur Trail RV Resort,** tel. 823-9333, which has a heated pool, groceries, laundry, and canoe rentals. Tent sites are $14.25, hookups $16-21. All three campgrounds are open April-October.

At the end of the Dinosaur Trail is **Bleriot Ferry Provincial Recreation Area** with 35 sites, plenty of firewood, a kitchen shelter, and a small beach on the river; $5.50 per night. **Rosedale,** east of town, has a small campground (free) with pit toilets and a kitchen. It's at the back of town along the road to Wayne. **Wayne,** with a population of around 25, has two campgrounds; one beside the saloon, the other over the green bridge. Each costs $5 and has limited facilities.

FOOD

Drumheller is probably the only place in the world where you can find a Chinese restaurant called **Fred & Barney's.** It's in the Suncity Mall at 1222 Hwy. 9 S beside Reptile World, tel. (403) 823-3803. A regular Chinese menu is offered between 11 a.m. and 10:30 p.m., but most people come for the excellent buffets served daily. Lunch (11:30 a.m.-2 p.m. year-round) is $6.95 and dinner (5-9 p.m., Fri.-Sun., summer only) is $8.95. **Sizzling House,** 160 Centre St., tel. 823-8098, is a popular downtown eatery dishing up Sichuan and Bejing cuisine. Forget the lunch buffet and stick to the small (by Chinese standards) menu.

All dishes at the **Bridge Greek Restaurant–Steak & Pizza House,** 71 Bridge St. N, tel. 823-2225, are made from scratch, and everything is excellent. Appetizers are $3-7; try the lemon soup or large Greek salad. Greek entrees start at $8.95. The house specialty is *Kleftiko,* juicy spring lamb baked with herbs and spices—have it with the Greek salad for the full effect, or try the generous portion of moussaka. The atmosphere is informal, an abundance of greenery hangs from the ceiling, and later in the evening the chef can often be seen chatting with satisfied patrons. It's open 10:30 a.m.-midnight.

SERVICES AND INFORMATION

Services
Greyhound has frequent service to Calgary ($16.69 one way). The depot, 1222 Hwy. 9 S (at Suncity Mall), tel. (403) 823-7566, has a small cafe and lots of information on the area. For a cab call **Badlands Taxi,** tel. 823-0678, or **Jack's**

PRONGHORN

These agile and graceful animals (often mistakenly called antelope) that roam Alberta's short-grass prairie have made a remarkable comeback after being hunted to near extinction in the first quarter of this century. They are easily recognized by

BOB RACE

their dark muzzles, tan bodies, and large white patches on the rump, cheeks, neck and belly. Both sexes grow hollow, pronged horns that are shed annually.

Pronghorns have adapted well to life on the plains, and are endowed with incredible attributes vital for their survival. Able to sustain speeds up to 80 kph over long distances, they are one of the fastest mammals in the New World. An oversized windpipe helps them to dissipate heat quickly as they breathe, allowing for large extended outbursts of energy. Telescopic eyesight enables them to detect movement over 1.5 km away. When a member of the herd senses danger, hairs on its white rump will stand erect, silently alerting comrades of the threat.

The pronghorn's diet consists primarily of sagebrush, but they'll eat weeds and sometimes grass as well. They obtain sufficient moisture from these plants to allow them to survive hot, dry summers without much to drink. And as a guard against the long and severe prairie winters, these amazing creatures have developed hollow body hairs to insulate against the cold.

Taxi, tel. 823-2220. **Tilden** is the only car-rental agency in town, tel. 823-3371.

The **post office** is at 96 Railway Ave. East. You can wash your dusty clothes at the **laundromat** in the ESSO gas station on Hwy. 9 on the south side of town. It's open till 8 p.m. **Drumheller Regional Health Complex** is at 665 Riverside Dr. E, tel. 823-6500. For the **RCMP** call 823-2630.

Information

Drumheller has two information centers. One, operated in conjunction with the chamber of commerce, is beside the Red Deer River at the corner of Riverside Dr. and 2nd St. West. You can't miss it—look for a towering replica of a *Tyrannosaurus rex* in front. It's open daily 9 a.m.-9 p.m. during summer, Mon.-Fri. 9 a.m.-4:30 p.m. the rest of the year; tel. (403) 823-1331. The other center is in Suncity Mall on Hwy. 9 at the south end of town. This one is privately owned and run by friendly staff. The walls are lined with brochures of things to do and see, and it's open year-round, Mon.-Sat. 6 a.m.-9 p.m., Sunday 9 a.m.-9 p.m.; tel. 823-7566. **Drumheller Public Library** is at 224 Centre St., tel. 823-5382.

HIGHWAY 9 EAST

Hanna

This is the heart of goose country. Giant replicas of the Canada grey goose grace the town entrances, and in fall, the area is a mecca for hunters. **Hanna Museum,** at the east end of 4th Ave., tel. (403) 854-4244, is a re-creation of a 19th-century village with a church, railway station, jail cell, hospital, and schoolhouse. It's open daily 10 a.m.-6 p.m. during summer; admission $2.

Much of the bucking stock that throws the cowboys and woos the crowds at the Calgary Exhibition and Stampede is bred and raised at **Stampede Ranch,** 50 km south of Hanna. The ranch welcomes visitors (call ahead, tel. 566-2206), but don't let anyone talk you into going on a trail ride.

Campers have a few choices. Beside the museum are some electrical hookups ($8), north of town is **Fox Lake Campground** ($5), and 25 km south is **Prairie Oasis Park** ($5), which has a good beach and swimming. Rooms in the **Hanna Inn,** 113 Palliser Trail, tel. 854-2400, are $40 s, $48 d; a restaurant, fitness center, and laundromat are on the premises. The inn's restaurant is a popular place to eat, serving steaks, seafood, and pasta until midnight. The **information center** is in a train caboose on the highway beside Petro-Canada.

Oyen

From Hanna, Hwy. 9 continues east through many small communities to Oyen and into Saskatchewan. Pronghorn have been the most distinctive animal on this part of the prairies for thousands of years and have adapted remarkably well to the environment. Due to overhunting and particularly harsh winters in the early 1900s, their numbers were decimated until three national parks were created to protect them. When their numbers rebounded the parks were abolished and today many thousand live on the prairies. At the north end of Main St. is a replica of a pronghorn. **Oyen Crossroads Museum,** 312 1st Ave. E, tel. (403) 664-2330, has many artifacts relating to the history of the area. It's open daily 9 a.m.-5 p.m. during summer. The campground in town is opposite the golf course; most sites are free, with power $5. At the junction of Highways 9 and 41 is a **Travel Alberta Information Centre,** handy for those entering the province here (this highway is the most direct route between Calgary and Saskatoon). It's open daily 9 a.m.-7 p.m. during summer, shorter hours in May, September, and October, and closed the rest of the year.

HIGHWAY 56 NORTH

As Hwy. 56 passes out of the Red Deer River Valley on the north side of Drumheller it climbs onto the prairie benchland and heads due north for 100 km to Stettler. Along the route the towns of Rowley and Big Valley are worth investigating, and **Morrin,** just off the highway, 22 km north of Drumheller, has an interesting sod house, similar to those that many of Alberta's earliest pioneers lived in.

Rowley

The first time we visited Rowley was late one evening. The streets were empty (as they are

Rowley's main street has been featured in a number of movies and commercials.

most of the time) and yet within a few minutes we were in the community hall having coffee and apple pie with members of the town's rapidly shrinking population. It's just that sort of town. Like other prairie towns, many of its residents have moved to larger centers and their houses stand empty, but residents of Rowley have made good from bad. They actively promote the town and its empty buildings as the site for TV commercials and movies. Most of the shopfronts along the main street are locked, but someone is always around to unlock them. In the back of

the old cafe you can watch videos of clips filmed in town. A small museum is located near the rail line.

Big Valley

Located a few kilometers west of Hwy. 56, Big Valley is a quiet town of 300 with a restored Canadian Northern Railway Station that houses a museum. Farther west the Red Deer River has carved a canyon 120 meters into the surrounding prairie.

TO DINOSAUR PROVINCIAL PARK

STRATHMORE

From Calgary, the TransCanada Hwy. parallels the Bow River (although it's never in sight) 100 km to Bassano. The only town along the way is Strathmore, home to the large stockyards which are a major center for livestock auctions in southern Alberta. To catch the action head down on Thursdays in summer (weekdays in fall). The yards are located on the west side of town, tel. (403) 240-7694. Good food is served at the **Little Village Cafe,** 755 Lakeside Blvd., tel. 934-2828, next to the Shell station on the TransCanada Highway. The cafe looks like a truck stop but the fluffy omelettes and fruit pies are excellent.

Wyndham-Carseland Provincial Park
The main reason for visiting this 178-hectare park is for the fishing. Rainbow and brown trout, up to 60 cm, are caught in the Bow River where it flows through the park; the best fishing is in the deeper main channel. Also within the park is a large population of white pelicans, as well as prairie falcons, Canada geese, and great blue herons. The large campground is spread out along the river, and all sites are $11. The park is about 30 km south of Strathmore via Highways 24 or 817.

BASSANO

Bassano is located on the TransCanada Hwy. midway between Calgary and Medicine Hat. It's a thriving agricultural town of 1,200 people. Most visitors who stop in town are on their way to somewhere else.

Bassano Dam
Bassano Dam is six km southwest of town at Horseshoe Bend on the Bow River. It was built by the Canadian Pacific Railway between 1910 and 1914 to divert water from the Bow River into irrigation canals. Today those canals provide water for over 100,000 hectares of land producing crops such as wheat, hay, potatoes, and beets. At the time of construction, the dam was known as the most important structure of its type in the world because of its great length and unique foundations. It consists of a 2.3 km earthen embankment with 24 steel sluices controlling the river's flow. At the dam is a picnic area.

BROOKS

Brooks (population 9,400) is in the heart of Alberta's extensive irrigated farmlands, 160 km east of Calgary along the TransCanada Highway. The town began as a railway stop in the 1880s. Canadian Pacific Railway officials soon realized the potential for homesteading in the area and developed a major irrigation system. Today, the **Eastern Irrigation District** includes two dams, over 2,000 kilometers of canals, and 2,500 control structures. Brooks offers all tourist services and is a good base for exploring Dinosaur Provincial Park (see below).

Sights
The **Brooks Aqueduct,** three km southeast of town, was a vital link in the development of agriculture in southeastern Alberta and was used until the 1970s. It carried water across a shallow valley to a dry prairie on the other side, opening up a massive chunk of otherwise unproductive land to farming. At the time of its completion in 1914, the 3.2-km aqueduct was the longest concrete structure of its type in the world and had been designed and built using unique engineering principles. Although now replaced by an earth-filled canal, the impressive structure has been preserved as a National Historic Site, and now serves as a monument to those who developed the region.

A small interpretive center is open in summer, daily 10 a.m.-6 p.m.; tel. (403) 362-4451.

Brooks and District Museum on Sutherland Dr. catalogues the area's past from the era of dinosaurs to the heady days of a short-lived oil boom. Many restored buildings dot the grounds and the entrance is guarded by a four-ton replica of a bison. It's open in summer, daily 10 a.m.-5 p.m.; admission $1.

Budding gardeners won't want to miss the **Alberta Special Crops and Horticultural Research Centre** east of town, tel. 362-3391, where research is done on greenhouse crops, various fruits, ornamental flowers, vegetables, and weed control. The grounds are an oasis of flower beds and experimental plots, many of which are open to the public. Free guided tours are offered on weekdays throughout summer at 10:15 a.m. and 2 p.m. At **Brooks Pheasant Hatchery,** beside Tillebrook Provincial Park east of town, tel. 362-4122, ring-necked pheasants are hatched from breeding stock, raised, and released into the wild. A small visitor center is open in summer, daily 9 a.m.-4 p.m., weekdays only the rest of the year.

Kinbrook Island Provincial Park
Part of this 38-hectare park, 13 km south of Brooks, is an island in **Lake Newell,** the largest man-made body of water in Canada. Naturally, most activities revolve around the water—swimming, fishing, and boating are all popular. The large expanses of freshwater attract many species of gulls, pelicans, and cormorants that nest on the islands. The campground has firewood and picnic shelters, and a concession operates during summer. Sites are $11; reservations are taken, tel. (403) 362-2962.

Accommodations
Vacant motel rooms can be difficult to find in Brooks. During the week they are filled by work crews, and on weekends there always seems to be a wedding in town. Most motels are along 2nd St. W and the best of the bunch is **Tel Star Motor Inn,** 813 2nd St. W, tel. (403) 362-3466. Each room has a microwave and fridge; $44 s, $50 d. Other options in town are **Plains Motel,** 1004 2nd St. W, tel. 362-3367, $46 s, $50 d; and **Best Western Heritage Inn,** 1303 2nd St. W, tel. 362-6666, with an indoor pool, coffee shop, and restaurant, $55 s, $62 d. **Douglas**

Country Inn (P.O. Box 463, Brooks T0J 0J0; tel. 362-2873) is seven km north of Brooks on Hwy. 873. The large rooms are beautifully furnished, one with a fireplace and hot tub. Other amenities include a TV room, solarium, and lounge with fireplace. Rates are $65 s, $75-100 d including a hearty country breakfast.

Halfway between Brooks and Tilley is **Tillebrook Provincial Park,** one of a number of campgrounds built along the TransCanada Hwy. during that road's construction. Tillebrook is an excellent base for exploring Dinosaur Provincial Park and Lake Newell, and is one of the province's best developed parks. It has powered sites, enclosed kitchen shelters with gas stoves, showers, a laundromat, summer interpretive programs, and a trail to the aqueduct. Unserviced sites are $13, powered sites $15. It's open year-round.

Beside Brooks Museum is **Kiwanis Campground,** home to mostly permanent trailers—the closest bathrooms are in the gas station across the road. Tent sites here are $6, powered sites $7.

Food
Beda's Swiss Corral at the corner of Centre St. and 1st Ave., tel. (403) 362-7801, combines European charm with menu items from the length and breadth of the continent. Among the intriguing entrees are Alligator Schnitzel, Arctic Musk Ox, and a half dozen seafood dishes. Entrees start at $11. The restaurant is open Tues.-Sat. 5 p.m.-midnight. Next door is a quiet lounge to wash down these delicacies. **Athenai Restaurant,** 134 1st St., tel. 362-7222, serves basic Greek food starting at $9.95; the fish dishes are especially good.

Services And Information
The **Greyhound** bus depot is at 1308 2nd St. West. The **post office** is at 120 1st Avenue. The **laundromat** is on Cassils Rd. beside IGA. The **hospital** is at 410 3rd St. E, tel. (403) 362-3456, and the **RCMP** can be reached by calling 362-5535. The **information center** is open in summer, daily 8 a.m.-8 p.m. It's beside Petro-Canada on the highway.

East To Medicine Hat
Continuing southeast from Brooks on the TransCanada Hwy., it's 100-some km across the

prairies to Medicine Hat. For more information on Medicine Hat, see the Southern Alberta chapter.

DINOSAUR PROVINCIAL PARK

Badlands stretch along many river valleys throughout the North American plains, and some of the most spectacular are in 7,332-hectare Dinosaur Provincial Park, 200 km east of Calgary. But the park is best known for being one of the most important dinosaur fossil beds in the world. Thirty-five species of dinosaurs—from every known family of the Cretaceous era—have been unearthed here, along with the skeletal remains of crocodiles, turtles, fish, lizards, frogs, and flying reptiles. Not only is the diversity of specimens great, but so is the sheer volume; more than 300 museum-quality specimens have been removed and are exhibited in museums around the world.

The park's environment is extremely complex, and is unique within the surrounding prairie ecosystem. Stands of cottonwoods, a variety of animal life, and most importantly the extensive bone-beds, were instrumental in UNESCO's designation of the park as a World Heritage Site in 1979. In 1985 the opening of **The Royal Tyrrell Museum of Palaeontology,** 100 km upstream in Drumheller, meant that bones that had in the past been shipped to museums throughout the world for scientific analysis and display remained within the province. The Royal Tyrrell Museum operates a field station in the park where many of the bones are catalogued and stored. The displays, films, and interpretive programs offered at the center will best prepare you to begin your visit to the park.

Prehistory

Seventy-five million years ago during Cretaceous times, the area was a low-lying marsh at the mouth of a river flowing into the Bearpaw Sea. The Bearpaw was the last in a succession of vast seas that covered the interior plains for 30 million years. Swamp grasses and reeds

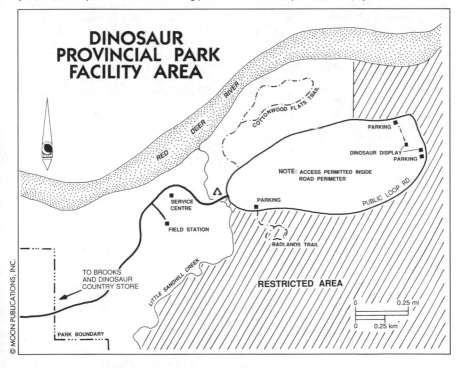

DINOSAUR PROVINCIAL PARK FACILITY AREA

RED DEER RIVER

COTTONWOOD FLATS TRAIL

PARKING

DINOSAUR DISPLAY

PARKING

NOTE: ACCESS PERMITTED INSIDE ROAD PERIMETER

PARKING

PUBLIC LOOP RD.

SERVICE CENTRE

FIELD STATION

BADLANDS TRAIL

TO BROOKS AND DINOSAUR COUNTRY STORE

LITTLE SANDHILL CREEK

RESTRICTED AREA

0   0.25 mi

0   0.25 km

PARK BOUNDARY

© MOON PUBLICATIONS, INC.

grew in the wetlands, while on higher ground, giant redwoods and palms towered over a dense forest. Dinosaurs flourished in this subtropical environment.

Over millions of years, great quantities of silt and mud were flushed downriver, building up a delta at the edge of the sea. In time this delta hardened and the countless layers formed sedimentary rock. Soon after, great pressures beneath the earth's surface pushed the crust upward, forming a jagged mountain range that we know today as the Rocky Mountains. This dramatically changed the climate of the plains region from tropical to temperate, probably killing off the dinosaurs around 63 million years ago. From then until a million years ago the climate changed many times until the first of many sheets of ice covered the plains. As the final sheet receded, around 15,000 years ago, millions of liters of sediment-laden meltwater scoured the relatively soft bedrock into an area we know as the badlands. The erosion process continues to this day, no longer by the action of glacial meltwater but by rain and wind. The carving action has created a dramatic landscape of hoodoos, pinnacles, mesas, and gorges in the sandstone here, which is 100 times softer than that of the Rockies. The hills are tiered with layers of rock in browns, reds, grays, and whites. Many are rounded, some are steep, others are ruddy and cracked, but they all have one thing in common—they are laden with dinosaur bones; for as the Red Deer River curves through the park it cuts deeply into the ancient river delta, exposing the layers of sedimentary rock and revealing the once-buried fossil treasures.

Fieldwork In The Park
Each summer palaeontologists from around the world converge on the park for an intense period of digging that starts in late June and lasts for approximately 10 weeks. Access to much of the park is restricted in order to protect the fossil beds. Digging takes place within the restricted areas. Often work is continued from the previous season, or new sites are commenced—there's never a lack of bones. New finds are often discovered with little digging at all, having been exposed by wind and rain since the previous season.

Excavating the bones is an extremely tedious procedure; therefore, only a limited number of sites are worked on at a time, with preference given to particularly important finds such as a new species. Getting the bones out of the ground is only the beginning of a long process that culminates with their scientific analysis and display by museums around the world.

Interpretive Programs And Tours
Even though much of the actual digging of bones is done away from public view, the **Field Station of the Royal Tyrrell Museum** organizes enough interesting activities and tours to keep you busy for at least a full day. The Field Station offers many interesting displays including complete dinosaur skeletons, murals, and models, and is also the departure point for tours into the park.

The **Badlands Bus Tour** takes you on a 90-minute ride around the public loop road with an interpretive guide who will point out the park's landforms and talk about its prehistoric inhabitants. This tour leaves the Field Station four to seven times daily. The **Centrosaurus Bone Bed Hike** takes visitors on a short, guided hike into a restricted area where over 300 centrosaurus skeletons have been identified. Studies have been carried out in this area for 12 years. This tour leaves from the Field Station on Tuesday, Thursday, Saturday, and Sunday at 9:15 a.m. The **Fossil Safari** is a strenuous hike into a restricted area that covers one of the many microvertebrate (small dinosaur) sites. It leaves the Field Station on Monday, Wednesday, and Friday at 9:15 a.m. Finally, a tour of the Field Station Laboratory is operated daily at 1:30. Space on all the above tours is limited. The lab tour is free. Each of the other tours costs $4.50. Tickets go on sale at the Field Station at 8:15 a.m. for the morning tours and at 12:30 p.m. for the afternoon tours.

Nights bring movies in the Field Station or special events happening somewhere in the park. The entire interpretive program operates in summer only, with certain tours offered in late May and September. The Field Station is open in summer, daily 9 a.m.-9 p.m., and weekdays only 9 a.m.-4 p.m. the rest of the year.

badlands at Dinosaur Provincial Park

On Your Own

Much of the park is off-limits to unguided visitors, but you may explore two short interpretive trails and the area bounded by the public loop road on your own. The **Badlands Trail** is a 1.5-km loop that starts just east of the campground and passes into the restricted area. It's easy to ignore the nearby floodplains, but the large stands of cottonwoods you'll see were a contributing factor in the park being designated as a World Heritage Site. The **Cottonwood Flats Trail** starts from behind the campground, leading through the trees and into old river channels that lend themselves to good birdwatching. The cabin of black cowboy John Ware has been moved to the park and is open to the public. Many regard Ware—originally a southern slave who came north on a cattle drive—as the greatest horseman ever to ride in the Canadian West. The **loop road** passes through part of the area where bones were removed during the Great Canadian Dinosaur Rush. By staying within its limits hikers are prevented from becoming lost, although the classic badlands terrain is still littered with fragments of bones, and the area is large enough to make you feel "lost in time." It's a fantastic place to explore. Of special interest are two dinosaur dig sites excavated earlier this century, one of which contains a still-intact skeleton of a duck-billed **hadrosaur.**

The restricted area protects the bone beds and the valley's fragile environment. It also serves to keep visitors from becoming disoriented in the uniform landscape and ending up spending the night among the bobcats and rattlesnakes. The area is well posted and should not be entered except on a guided tour. One other important rule: *surface collecting and digging for bones anywhere within the park is prohibited.*

Accommodations And Camping

The park's campground is in a low-lying area beside Little Sandhill Creek. It has recently been expanded and now has pit toilets, a kitchen shelter, and a limited number of powered sites. Unserviced sites cost $11, powered sites $13. The campground fills up by early afternoon. Along the access road is **Dinosaur Country Store,** which has a grassy spot for camping; tents $5, powered $8. The next closest alternative is in Brooks. **Patricia Hotel** in Patricia, 15 km from the park, tel. (403) 378-4647, is known for its Western atmosphere. Many of the cattle brands on the walls date back over 50 years. The hotel has basic rooms with private baths; $33 s, $38 d. The bar downstairs gets fairly lively and there's a barbecue every Saturday night.

Services And Information

The only commercial facility within the park is the **Dinosaur Service Centre,** a fast-food place open limited hours each day. Within the center are laundry facilities and coin showers. No groceries are available in the park.

For information write to Dinosaur Provincial Park, P.O. Box 60, Patricia, Alberta T0J 2K0; or call the park at (403) 378-4342.

RANCHLANDS

Between the snowcapped peaks of Kananaskis Country and the arid grassland of southern Alberta lies some of North America's best ranching country. From **Cochrane,** in the north, through the ranching and farming communities of **Okotoks** and **High River,** to the **Porcupine Hills** northwest of Fort Macleod—these low, rolling hills have been home to many of western Canada's cowboy heroes. Highway 2 follows the eastern flanks of these foothills south from Calgary. Other roads crisscross the region and lead to communities rich in heritage, many of which have recently been discovered by artisans and craftsmen who now call them home.

If you have ever dreamed of being a cowboy for a day or a week this is the place to do it. And the area offers enough museums, teahouses, antique emporiums, and events to keep even the most saddle-sore city-slicker busy all summer.

History

The ranching tradition that Alberta so proudly claims started in the late 1800s. The massive herds of bison that once roamed the foothills had been decimated, the indigenous peoples had been moved to reservations, and the Canadian Pacific Railway had completed linking the region to the eastern provinces. A huge tract of land in the shadow of the Rocky Mountains now stood empty, and the Canadian government decided to lease it at a cent an acre. It didn't take long for word to get out. Cowboys from Montana, Wyoming, and Texas came hootin' and hollerin' as they drove thousands of head of cattle north. They brought with them a new spirit, craving the open spaces and the hardships associated with living on the land.

Many of those who invested in the land were wealthy Americans and eastern Canadians who rarely, if ever, visited their holdings. Even English royalty became involved. Edward Prince of Wales, who abdicated the throne to marry Wallis Simpson, purchased a 10,000-hectare spread in 1919. One of the first major land holdings was at Cochrane Ranche, west of Calgary, where today a Provincial Historic Site commemorates the history of ranching in Alberta.

In 1904 a farmer found a gas seepage on his land west of Okotoks; it turned out to be petroleum gas. This first discovery of oil on the prairies led to a boom that propelled Alberta into the forefront of world oil-and-gas production—a position it still holds today.

COCHRANE

The foundation of Alberta's cattle industry was laid down here last century, when Senator Matthew Cochrane established the first of the big leasehold ranches in the province. Today's town of Cochrane is situated 22 km northwest of Calgary along Hwy. 1A in the Bow River Valley, and has a population of 5,000. Although ranching is still important to the local economy, Cochrane is growing as a "bedroom" suburb of Calgary. The business district is in the older section of town between Hwy. 1A and the rail line. The only accommodation in town is **Rivers Edge Campground** off Hwy. 22. The campground has showers, and charges $8 for unserviced sites, $12 for powered sites.

Cochrane Ranche

Although Matthew Cochrane's 76,500-hectare ranch had almost everything going for it, a number of harsh winters forced its closure in 1883. A 61-hectare site one km west of Cochrane was once the headquarters of this historic ranch and today is the site of a **Western Heritage Centre.** The facility has state-of-the-art exhibits cataloguing western Canada's cattle industry from its earliest frontier days to the world of computerized auctions. Displays are indoors and out, with interpretive programs held each day during summer and events most weekends. The site is open year-round, the heritage center summer only, daily 10 a.m.-6 p.m. Admission is $4. For more information call (403) 932-2902.

Big Hill Springs Provincial Park

This small 26-hectare park is located 16 km northeast of Cochrane and provides an example of vegetation that was once widespread across the prairies. The center of the park is a steep-walled valley with a stream flowing through it that cascades over a number of rocky terraces. The tree-lined banks of Big Hill Creek are an excellent place to escape the heat of the prairie and the roar of nearby highways. From artifacts found here it is obvious the valley was used by prehistoric people as a habitation and buffalo-kill site.

BRAGG CREEK

Bragg Creek is a rural hamlet nestled in the Rocky Mountain foothills, 40 km west of Calgary. To the east is the Sarcee Indian Reservation and to the west is Kananaskis Country. The **Stony Trail,** an Indian trading route that passed through the area, had been in use for generations when the first white people arrived in the early 1880s. Much of the surrounding forest had been cleared by fire, encouraging farmers to settle in the isolated region and eke a living from the land. Improved road access in the 1920s encouraged families from Calgary to build weekenders in town. Today many of Bragg Creek's 500 residents commute daily to nearby Calgary. The ideal location and quiet

lifestyle have attracted artists and artisans—the town claims to have more painters, potters, sculptors, and weavers than any similarly sized town in Alberta.

Sights

White Ave., also known as **Heritage Mile** and originally the main commercial strip, is lined with craft shops, antique emporiums, and restaurants. The road continues southwest to 122-hectare **Bragg Creek Provincial Park,** a day-use area alongside the Elbow River, before continuing along the Elbow Valley into East Kananaskis Country (see "Kananaskis Country," below). North of Bragg Creek is the site of southern Alberta's first church. The earliest structure, built in 1873, was a crude cabin where an Irish minister devoted his time ministering to the native Blackfoot people. A plaque, 12 km north of town along Hwy. 22, marks this historic spot. **Wintergreen Ski and Golf Area** is a year-round sporting facility six km northwest of town. In summer golfers flock to the fairways of its 18-hole championship golf course ($32). In winter a small ski area with five lifts and a vertical rise of 190 meters operates. Night skiing is offered on

Friday and Saturday. Lift tickets are $20. For more information call (403) 949-3333.

Accommodations And Food

Although lacking motels and campgrounds (closest camping is in East Kananaskis Country), Bragg Creek has a number of bed and breakfasts and a restaurant that attracts folk from Calgary. **Four Point Crossing,** tel. (403) 947-2247, is a large country-style house nestled among stands of trees, yet is within walking distance of restaurants and shops. The home has a guest lounge with fireplace and a hearty breakfast is included in the rate of $40 s, $60 d. Another, within walking distance of town, is **Bricket Wood B&B,** tel. 949-2482, where rates are a little lower.

Barbecue Steak Pit, 43 White Ave., tel. 949-3633, is a fantastic restaurant. The decor is early-Canadian style, yet realistic and elegant. The dining room decorated with hand-hewn cedar furniture is only a small part of the restaurant, which also has a cafe, lounge, sports bar, and gift shop. Eating here isn't cheap but *is* comparable to Calgary restaurants. The menu features mostly Alberta beef but has enough choices to please everyone. Open daily from 11:30 a.m.

BRAGG CREEK TO NANTON

Turner Valley

The name Turner Valley is synonymous with the oil-and-gas industry in Alberta. It was here in 1914 that Canada's first major crude-oil discovery was made. But it was gas, not oil, that first sparked interest in the valley. In 1903 a farmer named Bill Herron found gas seeping from fissures in his land. He had it tested and to his surprise was told it was petroleum gas. He was having trouble convincing anyone to back an oil-related enterprise and, so the story goes, he finally persuaded two oilmen to become involved by taking them to the site of the gas, lighting it and cooking them a fried breakfast on the flame. Shortly after, the Calgary Petroleum Products Company was formed and started sinking wells, which was the beginning of an economic boom. During the oil boom, gas was burned off in an area known as "Hell's Half Acre" northeast of Turner Valley. It is estimated that 28 billion cubic meters of excess gas was flared off in the first 10 years. Gas flares still burn 24 hours a day at an area known as the "Burning Ground." The best viewing point is from **Hell's Half Acre Bridge,** which crosses the Sheep River southwest of downtown.

Turner Valley is now a quiet town of 1,400 straddling Sheep River. **Hell's Half Acre Interpretive Centre** on the southwestern outskirts of town showcases the oil-and-gas industry in Alberta. The town has an 18-hole golf course, swimming pool, and is the gateway to the **Sheep River Valley** in Kananaskis Country.

Turner Valley Inn, 112 Flare Ave., tel. (403) 933-7878, is the town's only motel; rooms are $38 s, $44 d. **Hell's Half Acre Campground,** downtown behind the information center, has limited services; unserviced sites $6, powered sites $8. Tenters would be better off heading west into Kananaskis Country to one of two Forest Service campgrounds. Eating out is limited to the restaurant at either the Turner Valley Inn or the Turner Valley Hotel. The latter has a popular buffet every Wednesday night ($9.95) and a Sunday brunch ($8.95). **Valley Rose Tea Room,** 146 Main St., tel. 933-2972, serves breakfast (from $4) and lunch ($5-9), although most visitors stop only for tea and scones and to browse through the antiques. It's open year-round, daily 7 a.m.-5 p.m. A replica of an oil derrick on Main St. makes the **information center** highly visible.

Black Diamond

This town on the banks of the Sheep River, four km east of Turner Valley, was named for the coal once mined nearby. James A. McMillan, a government land surveyor, was digging an irrigation ditch when he uncovered a rich seam of coal. Within a few years a mine had become operational and the coal, of excellent quality, was used in households throughout the region. The coal mines have long since closed. Most residents work in the nearby oil fields or commute the 65 km to Calgary.

One of the year's highlights is the **Diamond Valley Parade** held on the first weekend of June. A colorful parade, pancake breakfast, mutton busting (a rodeo for children on wildly bucking sheep), and a fireworks display are among the event's activities. The town has limited visitor services. **Triple "A" Motel** on Hwy.

22, tel. (403) 933-4915, has basic rooms for $45 s or d. A campground in **Centennial Park** by the Sheep River has showers, a kitchen shelter, and firewood; unserviced sites $8, powered sites $10. For further information, ask at the **town office,** tel. 933-4348; open weekdays 8 a.m.-4:30 p.m.

Okotoks

The rural retreat of Okotoks is in the Sheep River Valley 34 km south of Calgary and just minutes from Hwy. 2 to the east. It is the largest population base between Calgary and Lethbridge and many of its 7,500 residents commute into Calgary to work. The name Okotoks came from the Blackfoot word "Okatak," which means rock, probably in reference to the glacial erratics west of town. The town began as a rest stop along the Macleod Trail, which linked Fort Calgary to Fort Macleod last century. Many old buildings still stand and have been incorporated in a walking tour, with maps available at the tourist information center. **Okotoks Bird Sanctuary,** east of town, attracts ducks, geese, and other waterfowl that can be watched from a raised observation deck. But the town's most popular attraction isn't a museum or a park, it's a rock, the **Big Rock,** the largest glacial erratic in the world. During the last ice age a sheet of ice up to a kilometer thick crept forward from the north. A landslide in what is now Jasper National Park deposited large boulders on top. The ice continued moving south, carrying the boulders with it. Many thousands of years later, as temperatures warmed and the ice melted, the boulders were deposited far from their source (hence the name "erratic"). Big Rock, seven km west of Okotoks, weighs 18,000 tons.

Although the town has no motels, a good campground on the south side of Sheep River is linked to town by a nearby bridge; unserviced sites $10, powered sites $12.

Ginger Tea Room and Gift Shop, 43 Riverside Dr., tel. (403) 938-2907, is a large Victorian-style mansion that has become a local landmark. Inside it's crammed with two floors of crafts and antiques. At the back is a tearoom that is always busy. Okotoks original creamery is now a restaurant, bistro, and pub all under one roof. Food in the bistro is served family-style, and although the dining room is more expensive it's still casual. The Sunday brunch is es-

pecially good. Open for lunch and dinner daily, closed in the afternoon. Called, appropriately enough, **The Creamery,** it's located at 35 Riverside Dr., tel. 938-2901.

An **information center** in a restored train station at 53 N. Railway St., tel. 938-3204, also has an interpretive display and art market. It's open in summer, daily 10 a.m.-6 p.m.

High River

In the heart of the province's ranching country, 50 km south of Calgary, High River has grown steadily from its beginnings as a rest stop on the Macleod Trail. Originally it was known as "The Crossing" as it was the only possible place to ford the Highwood River. A period of severe drought at the turn of the century was followed by many years of ample rainfall and slowly the community grew to its current population of 6,400.

The **Museum of the Highwood** is housed in a restored C.P.R. Station on 1st St. W, tel. (403) 652-7156. Its displays portray early western life. Of particular interest is the exhibit cataloguing chuck wagon racing, a sport that has special significance to locals as the area boasts many champions. If you're in town on the last weekend of June don't miss the **North American Chuckwagon Championships** at the fairgrounds. Downtown are a number of interesting shops including **Eamor's Custom Saddlery** and **Olson's Silver and Leather.** Both are on Centre Street.

Of the three motels in town, **Foothills Motel,** 67 8th Ave., tel. 652-1395, is the best value, with rooms starting at $40. Camping is in **George Lane Memorial Park** off Macleod Trail at 5th Ave. W; $10.

NANTON

In this town of 1,600, 70 km south of Calgary, Nanton Spring Water Company bottles some of Canada's finest drinking water and distributes it throughout the world. The town is also a supply center for nearby ranches and a stop along busy Hwy. 2.

Sights

The **Nanton Lancaster Society Museum,** tel. (403) 646-2270, is home to one of the few Lancaster Bombers still in existence. The Lancaster is a Canadian-built, four-engined, heavy bomber that played a major role in many of the air offensives against Nazi Germany in WW II. On the guided tour you can sit in the plane's cockpit and look through the sight of the machine gun. A replica of another classic—a Vickers Viking biplane—sits outside. Many other displays focus on Canada's role in WW II. The museum is located on the highway (southbound), and is open mid-May to October, daily 9 a.m.-5 p.m., the rest of the year, weekends only 10 a.m.-4 p.m.

A **turn-of-the-century schoolhouse** on the corner of Hwy. 2 (northbound) and 18th Ave. now hold's the town's **tourist information center.**

Events

During July and August, the **Nite Series Rodeo** is held every Friday night at the Rodeo Grounds, attracting local amateurs keen to test their skills. **Roundup Days,** held the last weekend of July, is the town's midsummer festival featuring a rodeo, beerfest, and road rally. **Shady Grove Bluegrass and Country Music Festival** attracts some of Canada's best musical talent. It's held on the third weekend of August at Broadway Farm, 13 km east of Nanton; for more information call (403) 646-2076.

Accommodations And Food

Nanton has two motels. **Ranchland Inn,** tel. (403) 646-2933, and **Double "D" Motel,** tel. 646-2170, are on Hwy. 2 (northbound). Expect to pay $40 s or d. **Nanton Campground** is east of town on 18th St., adjoining the golf course. Sites are scattered among a grove of trees and have picnic tables, a kitchen shelter, and pit toilets; $5 per night. Originally a blacksmith's shop, **Village Smithy Tea Shoppe** is the best place for lunch or a light snack. The building was constructed at the turn of the century. The forge sat in the corner near the chimney and imprints of hot horseshoes are still visible on the wooden floor. Coffee and teas are $1.50, salads and sandwiches start at $3, but leave room for desserts such as Kahlúa Chocolate Trifle topped with freshly whipped cream.

To Chain Lakes Provincial Park

Views of the Rocky Mountains are spectacular as you head west on Hwy.

533 from Nanton. An interpretive sign, 35 km outside Nanton, overlooks the old holdings of the A 7 Ranch, once one of Alberta's largest ranches. Its original owner, A.E. Cross, helped finance the first Calgary Stampede in 1912. The ranch has now been subdivided but remains in the same family. At the next rise is **Magnetic Hill.** An optical illusion here creates a bizarre misimpression: Put your car in neutral and it will slowly roll *up* the hill! The highway ends at a junction with Hwy. 22, which goes north to the Highwood region of Kananaskis Country and south to the Crowsnest Pass. **Chain Lakes Provincial Park,** west of this intersection, sits in the Willow Creek Valley between the Rocky Mountains and Porcupine Hills. It was named because of a series of spring-fed lakes that have since been dammed and stocked with rainbow trout. The park is in a transition zone; therefore, plant and animal species are varied. In the north end of the park are some high bluffs, offering good views of the surrounding land. The campground and day-use area are at the southern end of the reservoir, close to a boat launch and beach. Camping is $11.

Willow Creek Provincial Park

South of Nanton, along the eastern edge of the Porcupine Hills and only 14 km west of the constant roar of traffic on Hwy. 2, tree-lined Willow Creek flows through quiet Willow Creek Provincial Park. Generations of native tribes hunted and camped in the area; just outside the park you can find a buffalo jump and a number of tepee rings well hidden in the grass. Modern visitors go swimming in the creek and camp here. The campground has limited services; $7.50 per night.

Farther downstream on Willow Creek is another historical site. **The Leavings** was a stopover on the Macleod Trail, aptly named to remind travelers that they were leaving the last supply of water before Calgary. It was later used as a North West Mounted Police post, but was abandoned when the railway was laid farther to the east. Many of the sandstone foundations remain, as do some log cabins and a sandstone barn with tree-trunk floorboards. By road the site is seven km west of Hwy. 2 near Pultenay.

CLARESHOLM

Most people stop at Claresholm, 100 km south of Calgary, just long enough to fill up with gas, grab a burger, and stretch their legs. But the town is worth a little more time than that. Many of the buildings facing Hwy. 2 date to the early 1900s. In town are two museums and to the west the Porcupine Hills make an interesting detour.

When the Calgary and Edmonton Railway Line was extended south in 1891, a new town emerged at its southern terminus. One of the earliest settlers in town was Clare Amundsen, who decided to make it her home—that's how Claresholm got its name. Many boomtown storefronts sprung up facing the rail line, and the town quickly established a reputation as the hub of a leading grain-producing area. Many large landholdings were bought nearby and the town has prospered ever since. The airbase at Claresholm was an aircrew training center during WW II and it is still busy today hosting national and international soaring and gliding competitions.

Sights

The **Claresholm Museum,** 5126 Railway Ave., tel. (403) 625-3427, is in the C.P.R Station and holds an array of historical displays, including a dentist clinic and rail ticket office. It's open mid-May to mid-September, daily 10 a.m.-6 p.m.; admission is $1. A brochure entitled *A Walking Tour of Claresholm,* available from the museum, details the town's historic buildings and sites. The town's **tourist information center** is inside the museum.

The **Appaloosa Horse Club of Canada Museum and Archives,** 4189 3rd St. E, tel. 625-3326, is one of only two such museums in the world. The first of these spotted horses were brought over the U.S. border by Indians in the late 1800s. Displays include a 200-year-old Indian saddle. The museum is open year-round, Mon.-Fri. 8:30 a.m.-4:30 p.m.

Events

Events in Claresholm include the **South Country Hootenanny** on the Canada Day Weekend in July, attracting some of Canada's top country acts; and **Fair Days** in mid-August. And there's always something going on at the **Claresholm Agriplex.**

Accommodations And Food

Motels and fast-food restaurants line the highway as it passes through town. Nicest of the motels is **Bluebird Motel,** tel. (403) 625-3395, at the north end of town. Most rooms have refrigerators and all have coffeemakers; $40 s, $46 d. Two others to the south are slightly less expensive.

Centennial Campground, tel. 625-3830, ls ln a residential area close to the golf course. It has powered sites, showers, and kitchen shelters; tents $6.50, RVs and trailers $7.50-9. It's located on 4th St. W, north off Hwy. 520.

A&B Bakery, 129 50th Ave. W, has delicious breads, pastries, and donuts. And along the highway are a string of greasy-spoon restaurants. The **Old Fox Drive-In** is worth investigating just for the effort that's gone into the front doors; open 7 a.m.-10 p.m. **Hawleys,** 5009 1st St. W, tel. 625-3222, has an inexpensive lunch and dinner buffet.

Porcupine Hills

These hills west of Claresholm on Hwy. 520 are sandwiched between the mountains and the plains, yet are higher than the foothills to the west and are covered in vegetation from four climatic zones: grassland, parkland, subalpine forest, and montane. They are bordered to the east by Hwy. 2, to the west by Hwy. 22, extend south to Head-Smashed-In Buffalo Jump, and north past Nanton. Known to the Blackfoot as "Ky-es-kaghp-ogh-suy-is," which translates (luckily) to "porcupine tails," (describing how natives saw the forested ridges), the hills are still heavily wooded and home to a variety of wildlife including white-tailed and mule deer, elk, moose, coyote, lynx, beaver, pheasant, and wild turkey.

From Claresholm Hwy. 520 climbs slowly west for 32 km, passing through Burke Creek Ranch (one of Alberta's oldest—look for classic old buildings scattered by the creek) and continuing into the **Rocky Mountain Forest Reserve.** It eventually crests a hill with breathtaking views of the Rockies before dropping down to Hwy. 22. At this hillcrest, **Skyline Road** heads south into the hills, where rewarding trails and views await explorers. Roads through this area can take you all the way to Cowley on Hwy. 3.

HIGHWAY 23 SOUTH

An eastern alternative to four-lane Hwy. 2 between Calgary and Lethbridge is Hwy. 23. From High River it heads east past Frank Lake, continuing another 35 km before turning south and skirting the western edge of the prairies. Along the way it passes the wheat-farming towns of Vulcan, Champion, Carmangay, and Barons before finishing at Hwy. 3, 17 km west of Lethbridge.

Brant

After passing Frank Lake on Hwy. 23 east, you'll soon come to the intersection with Hwy. 804, which detours south to Brant. Named for the Brant geese that rested in the area on their migration to and from the north, Brant is a worthwhile stop not for what it is, but what it was. In 1915, Brant was a prosperous town of 125. But the Great Depression of the 1930s brought grain prices down, forcing farmers to make do with the machinery they already had. As a result, the dealerships, banks, and other businesses began to close, and many of the children of the '40s and '50s moved away. As the old-timers died and no one moved in to replace them, the town's population slowly dwindled. The railway cut back services, the general store closed, and today only empty buildings and a grain elevator remain.

Vulcan

Halfway between Calgary and Lethbridge on Hwy. 23 is Vulcan (pop. 1,400), named after the Greek god who lived on Mt. Olympus (the townsite sits on a not-so-Olympian rise above the surrounding prairie). Vulcan is also known as the "Wheat Capital of Canada" and has 12 grain elevators capable of holding over two million bushels of grain.

Little Bow Provincial Park

On the banks of Travers Reservoir east of **Champion** is Little Bow Provincial Park. It is an extremely popular place for fishing, swimming, and boating, especially on summer weekends. The park's green lawns and lush vegetation are possible because of heavy irrigation; they're a welcome sight after driving through the parched and scorched prairies. The reservoir is home to some of the province's largest pike, attracting fishermen year-round. The large campground has a beach, kitchen shelter, firewood, and a concession in the day-use area; $11 per night. On the access road to the park, 1.5 km from Hwy. 23, a stone cairn marks the site of Cleverville, a once busy town forced to move when bypassed by the Canadian Pacific Railway. The new town was named Champion and today serves as a center for the nearby wheat farms. The **Champion Inn**, tel. (403) 897-3055, has basic but clean rooms with shared bathrooms for $16 s or d, $22 with a private bathroom. Downstairs is a restaurant (open daily 7 a.m.-10 p.m.) and a bar.

Tepee Rings In A Field

In an unimposing grassy field between Hwy. 23 and Little Bow River just north of Carmangay are nine circles of stone which sit in mute testimony to the prehistoric people who once roamed throughout the plains of North America. Known as tepee rings, the stones were used to hold down the edges of natives' conical, bison-hide-covered tents. The lack of other artifacts, such as tools and bones, found here leads archaeologists to believe that this particular site was used for only a short time. A well-worn path leads from the parking lot to a ring that has been partially disturbed; better rings lay to the left of the path.

KANANASKIS COUNTRY

During Alberta's oil-and-gas boom of the 1970s, surplus oil revenues collected by the provincial government were channeled into various projects aimed at improving the lifestyle of Albertans. One lasting legacy of the boom is Kananaskis Country, a sprawling 4,250-square-km area 90 km west of Calgary that has been developed with an emphasis on providing recreation opportunities for as many people as possible.

Within the area are two distinct ecosystems: the high peaks of the Continental Divide to the west, and the lower, rolling foothills to the east. The glacier-carved **Kananaskis Valley** separates the two. The area contains three provincial parks, hundreds of kilometers of hiking trails, a complex network of bike paths, an area for horseback riding and one for ATVs, a world-class 36-hole golf course, and 40 lakes stocked with fish. The downhill-skiing events of the 1988 Winter Olympic Games were held at the specially developed **Nakiska** ski area, now open to the public. **Fortress Mountain,** located deeper in the mountains, provides more challenging skiing. And Nordic skiers can glide over hundreds of cross-country skiing trails in the region.

Although K-country, as it's best known, lacks the photogenic lakes and glaciated peaks of Banff and Jasper national parks, in many ways it rivals them. Wildlife is abundant and opportunities for observation of larger mammals are superb. The region has large populations of moose, mule and white-tailed deer, elk, black bear, bighorn sheep, and mountain goat. Wolves, grizzly bears, and cougars are present, too, but are less likely to be seen.

Services within the park include an information center at each of the main entrances, high-class accommodations in **Kananaskis Village,** camping at one of many campgrounds, bike and boat rentals, and accommodations for the physically challenged at William Watson Lodge.

The main access to K-country is 90 km west of Calgary off the TransCanada Highway. Other points of access are immediately south of Canmore; at Bragg Creek on the region's northeast border; west from Longview in the southeast; or along the Forestry Trunk Rd. from the south.

For more information write to Kananaskis Country, Suite 100, 1011 Glenmore Trail SW, Calgary, Alberta T2V 4R6; tel. (403) 297-3362.

The Old Banff Road
The original route from Calgary into the mountains has long been bypassed, but for those with a little extra time it remains as a pleasant alternative to TransCanada Highway. Also known as Hwy. 1A, the easiest place to join it is **Cochrane,** an important ranching center west of Calgary. From here Hwy. 1A follows the north side of the Bow river to Hwy. 40, the main entrance to Kananaskis Country. The first major junction is with Hwy. 940, which spurs northwest to **Ghost River Wilderness Area,** a remote reserve more easily accessible from Lake Minnewanka in Banff National Park. Soon after this junction the highway passes **Ghost Lake,** created by the damming of the Bow River for hydroelectricity. At the west end of the lake is a white church built in 1875. For the next 30 km the road passes through a large Stoney Indian Reserve and the native towns of **Morley**—where there's a handicraft store and a restaurant (Chief Chiniki's) known for traditional meals—and **Seebe,** where the road leaves the reserve. To the north is the impressive face of **Mt. Yamnuska,** a popular rock-climbing spot. From here Hwy. 1A continues west, entering the mountains (views are marred by a cement plant and limestone quarry at Exshaw) and continuing to Canmore and Banff. Along this road, at a major junction 10 km from Seebe, Hwy. 40 crosses the TransCanada Hwy. and heads south into Kananaskis Country.

Bow Valley Provincial Park
This 935-hectare park at the north end of K-country is located at the confluence of the Kananaskis and Bow rivers and is bisected by the TransCanada Highway. Calgary is 80 km to the east and Canmore is 28 km to the west. It was originally part of Rocky Mountain National Park (now Banff National Park) but the area became separated when park boundaries were reduced in 1930, excluding areas zoned for further industrial development.

TO BANFF
TO COCHRANE
1A
BOW RIVER
CANMORE
1
22
TO COCHRANE
TO CALGARY
1
8
TO CALGARY
BOW VALLEY PROVINCIAL PARK
KANANASKIS RIVER
BARRIER LAKE VISITOR INFORMATION CENTRE
ELBOW RIVER
RIBBON CREEK/SPRAY LAKES AREA
NAKISKA SKI AREA
KANANASKIS VILLAGE
40
ELBOW VALLEY VISITOR INFORMATION CENTRE
22
BRAGG CREEK
GOLF COURSE
STABLES
66
PRIDDIS
SPRAY LAKES RESERVOIR
EAST KANANASKIS COUNTRY
66
SMITH-DORRIEN/SPRAY TRAIL
FORTRESS MOUNTAIN SKI AREA
KANANASKIS COUNTRY
PARK ADMINISTRATION OFFICE
TO MILLARVILLE
549
PETER LOUGHEED PROVINCIAL PARK
VISITOR INFORMATION CENTRE
SHEEP RIVER VISITOR INFORMATION CENTRE
TO TURNER VALLEY
546
SHEEP RIVER
HIGHWOOD PASS (2227 m)
MIST CREEK
CONTINENTAL DIVIDE
40
TO LONGVIEW
541
MIST CREEK PICNIC AREA
HIGHWOOD
HIGHWOOD/CATARACT CREEK AREA
541
HIGHWOOD RIVER
BRITISH COLUMBIA
HIGHWOOD HOUSE/RANGER STATION
MOUNTAINS
CATARACT CREEK
0   6 mi
0   6 km
FORESTRY TRUNK RD.
532
940
TO CROWSNEST PASS

© MOON PUBLICATIONS, INC.

The Bow Valley was gouged by glaciers during a succession of ice ages, leaving the typical "U"-shaped glacial valley surrounded by towering peaks. Three vegetation zones are found within the park, but evergreen and aspen forest predominates. To the casual motorist driving along the highway the park seems fairly small, but over 300 species of plants have been recorded and 60 species of birds are known to nest within its boundaries. The abundance of wildflowers, birds, and smaller mammals can be enjoyed along four short interpretive trails. Other popular activities in the park include fishing for a variety of trout and whitefish in the Bow River, bicycling along the paved trail system, and attending interpretive programs presented by park staff.

Facilities at the two campgrounds within the park, **Willow Rock** and **Bow Valley,** are as good as any in the province. They both have showers, flush toilets, and kitchen shelters. Willow Rock also has powered sites, a coin laundry, and is open for winter camping, but has a distinct lack of trees. Unserviced sites are $13, powered sites $15. Reservations can be made for Bow Valley Campground only; tel. (403) 673-3663.

A **visitor information center** is located at the park entrance on Hwy. 1X. It offers general information on the park and Kananaskis Country, and interpretive displays. A 2.2-km hiking trail also begins here. The center is open in summer, Mon.-Fri. 8 a.m.-8 p.m., Sat.-Sun. 8 a.m.-6 p.m.; the rest of the year, daily 8:15 a.m.-4:30 p.m.

RIBBON CREEK/ SPRAY LAKES AREA

This is the most developed of K-country's five zones yet summer crowds are minimal compared to Banff. Highway 40 follows the Kananaskis River through the zone to **Peter Lougheed Provincial Park,** and the Smith-Dorrien/Spray Trail parallels this road to the west. At the zone's north entrance is Barrier Lake visitor information center (open in summer, daily 8 a.m.-8 p.m.; the rest of the year, daily 9 a.m.-5 p.m.), a good place to start your trip into K-country. Along Hwy. 40 are two ski areas; Kananaskis Village; horseback riding at

Boundary Stables, tel. (403) 591-7171; a 36-hole golf course; and some spectacular mountain scenery. Those keen on hiking, fishing, and boating are better off continuing to Peter Lougheed Provincial Park, although Spray Lakes Reservoir is stocked with trout.

Kananaskis Country Golf Course

This 36-hole championship course opened in 1983 at a cost of almost $1 million for each hole. Renowned golf-course architect Robert Trent-Jones, who designed the layout, described the Kananaskis River Valley as ". . . the best spot I have ever seen for a golf course." After marveling at the surrounding mountains, few will disagree with his statement. Just don't let the 136 sand traps, water which comes into play on over half the holes, or the large rolling greens distract you. Green fees are $35; for tee times call (403) 591-7070.

Nakiska

This state-of-the-art ski area was built on Mt. Allan as host site for the alpine skiing events of the 1988 Winter Olympic Games. The area has been surrounded by controversy ever since plans for the 25.3-million-dollar project were proposed. Originally the events were to be held on existing ski slopes in Banff National Park. Environmentalists succeeded in keeping the games out of the park, but the victory soon turned sour when plans for a new area on the slopes of Mt. Allan were unveiled. This was only the start of Nakiska's early problems. Anyone who had spent any time in this part of the mountains knew the effect chinook winds can have on the snow cover and how impractical it was to build a ski area there. The answer was snowmaking. A high-tech, five-million-dollar computerized snowmaking system was installed, with 40 km of piping and 343 hydrants capable of pumping 24 million liters of water a day. Great cruising and fast fall-line skiing on runs cut specially for racing will satisfy the intermediate-to-advanced crowd. And the Bronze Chairlift accesses a novice area below the main area. The area has a total of 28 runs and a vertical rise of 735 meters. Lift tickets are $35, children under 5 free. Packages are offered in Kananaskis Village, which is linked to Nakiska by shuttle from Canmore, 40 km to the northwest. For more information call (403) 591-7777.

Fortress Mountain

Fortress is a sleeping giant as ski areas go. It's a 30-minute drive farther into K-country than Nakiska but the rewards are uncrowded slopes, more snow, on-hill accommodations, and spectacular views. Runs are short, but with skiing on three distinct faces there's something for everyone. Heavy snowfalls and little grooming make it a haven for powderhounds, who with a little hiking can ski untracked snow days after a storm. Facilities include three older chairlifts, three T-bars, and a large day lodge with cafeteria, restaurant, and bar. Lift tickets are $30 per day or $23 for the afternoon; seniors and students $13. On-hill lodging is $17 in a dorm or $60 s, $70 d in motel-style rooms. For more information call (403) 591-7108.

Cross-Country Skiing

The most accessible of K-country's 200 km of cross-country trails are located in the Ribbon Creek area. Most heavily used are those radiating from Kananaskis Village, and around the base of Nakiska ski area. Most trails are easy to

fresh tracks at Fortress

intermediate, including a five km track up Ribbon Creek. Rentals are available in the Village Centre in Kananaskis Village.

Kananaskis Village

This modern alpine resort 100 km from Calgary was built for the 1988 Winter Olympic Games. Today it serves as headquarters for those who want to experience K-country while enjoying the comforts of hotels and fine restaurants. The village is located on a narrow plateau overlooking its golf course, with magnificent mountain vistas in all directions and two ski areas a short drive away. Of the three hotels in the village, **Best Western Kananaskis Inn,** tel. (403) 591-7500 or (800) 528-1234, is the least expensive. Some of the 96 rooms are bedroom lofts with fireplaces, kitchenettes, and sitting room ($165); the others are standard hotel rooms which begin at $110. The Inn also offers an exercise room, indoor pool, and the Garden Cafe. The other two accommodations in the Village—**Lodge at Kananaskis** and **Hotel Kananaskis,** tel. 591-7711 or (800) 441-1414 for both—are managed by Canadian Pacific Hotels & Resorts (which also runs the famous mountain resorts in Banff, Lake Louise, and Jasper). The Lodge has 253 moderately large rooms, many with mountain views, balconies, and fireplaces. The Hotel is much smaller and each room has a mountain view, a luxurious bathroom complete with bathrobes, and extra large beds. The Hotel also features a full-facility health club, an indoor swimming pool, whirlpool, steam room, sauna, and a beauty salon with tanning beds. Guests at both the Lodge and Hotel are welcome to use all of these facilities. Rates at both start at $150 s or d but drop dramatically outside of summer. Good ski packages are offered all winter.

Restaurants in the Lodge include **Peaks Dining Room** (open daily 6 a.m.-10 p.m.), with a casual atmosphere, floor-to-ceiling windows, and an adjoining patio used during summer; **Samurai,** with authentic Asian atmosphere for eating sushi and *shabu-shabu;* and **Obsessions,** a nonsmoking bistro. In the Hotel, **L'Escapade** is the village's most elegant restaurant. French-Canadian cuisine is served on sterling silver while a pianist plays through dinner. The Hotel's **Fireside Lounge,** is a warm, intimate bar with an Italian decor and a moderately priced pasta bar.

Village Centre in Kananaskis Village has a grocery store, post office, and health-club facilities. **Woody's Pub** in the Inn and the **Big Horn Lounge** in the Hotel offer nightly entertainment.

Hostel

Ribbon Creek Hostel is located along the access road to Kananaskis Village, within walking distance. The hostel has hot showers, a kitchen, family rooms, a lounge room with fireplace, and an outdoor barbecue. Cost to members is $10, nonmembers $15. For reservations call (403) 762-4122.

Campgrounds

Mt. Kidd RV Park, tel. (403) 591-7700, is arguably the finest in Canada. It's nestled below the sheer eastern face of Mt. Kidd in a forest of lodgepole pine. The park's showpiece is the Campers Centre. Inside are all the usual bathroom facilities as well as whirlpools, saunas, a wading pool, game room, lounge, groceries, a concession, and laundry. Outside are tennis courts, picnic areas by the river, and many paved trails. Tent sites are $14, hookups $18-23. It's open year-round.

Those who can survive without such luxuries have the choice of three other campgrounds along Hwy. 40 ($11).

PETER LOUGHEED PROVINCIAL PARK

This park, originally named Kananaskis Provincial Park, was renamed in 1986 after Peter Lougheed. Lougheed was the Albertan premier who, with the help of oil-money-based Heritage Savings and Trust Fund, began the development of Kananaskis Country as a multiuse recreation area. The 50-square-km wilderness is the largest provincial park in Alberta. The high peaks of the Continental Divide form the eastern and southern boundaries of the park, making a spectacular backdrop for the Kananaskis River and the Kananaskis Lakes. These lakes are the center of boating and fishing in the park and opportunities abound for hiking and camping nearby.

Highway 40 is the main route through the park. In the southeastern corner it climbs to **Highwood Pass** (2,227 meters), the highest

road pass in Canada. South of the park administration office, **Kananaskis Lakes Trail** heads into the main recreation area. The **Smith-Dorrien/Spray Trail** is a gravel road that follows Smith-Dorrien Creek north from Lower Kananaskis Lake to Spray Lake, descending steeply into Canmore on the TransCanada Highway.

Recreation

Hiking is the most popular activity in the park (see "Hiking in Lougheed Park," below) but by no means the only one. **Kananaskis Trail** is a 60-km paved trail designed especially for bicycles that begins behind the visitor information center and follows Lower Kananaskis Lake to Mount Sarrail Campground. Many other trails are designated for mountain bike use; inquire at the visitor information center. **Boulton Creek Trading Post,** tel. (403) 591-7058, rents mountain bikes during summer; $5 per hour, $25 per day. Upper and Lower Kananaskis lakes have fair fishing for a variety of trout and whitefish. A nightly interpretive program takes place in campground amphitheatres throughout the park. Look for schedules posted on bulletin boards or check with the visitor information center.

In winter Highwood Pass is closed to traffic, but Hwy. 40 into the park is cleared, and cross-country skiing is excellent.

William Watson Lodge

This special facility is available to disabled persons and Albertan seniors who need special accommodation while staying in the park. Guests stay in private cabins but the lodge operates like a hostel and you must supply your own bedding and food. The main lodge has a kitchen, lounge, library, laundry room, and gas barbecues on the sundeck. Disabled guests may bring up to three family members or friends. The cost is $3 per person per night. Reservations are essential and can be made up to four months in advance. Write to William Watson Lodge, Peter Lougheed Provincial Park, P.O. Box 130, Kananaskis Village, Alberta T0L 2H0, or call (403) 591-7227.

Camping

The nearest hotels are to the north in Kananaskis Village. Within the park are six auto-accessible campgrounds that have a total of 507 sites. All are on the Kananaskis Lakes Trail and are

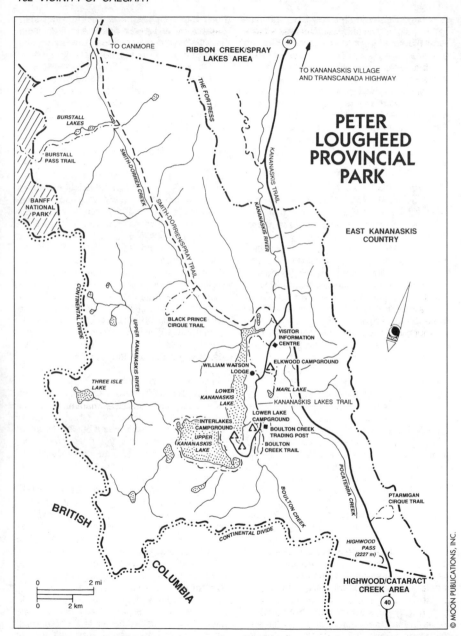

TO CANMORE

RIBBON CREEK/SPRAY
LAKES AREA

40

TO KANANASKIS VILLAGE
AND TRANSCANADA HIGHWAY

THE FORTRESS

BURSTALL
LAKES

BURSTALL
PASS TRAIL

SMITH-DORRIEN CREEK

BANFF
NATIONAL
PARK

SMITH-DORRIEN/SPRAY TRAIL

KANANASKIS TRAIL

KANANASKIS RIVER

PETER
LOUGHEED
PROVINCIAL
PARK

EAST KANANASKIS
COUNTRY

CONTINENTAL DIVIDE

UPPER KANANASKIS RIVER

BLACK PRINCE
CIRQUE TRAIL

VISITOR
INFORMATION
CENTRE

WILLIAM WATSON
LODGE

ELKWOOD CAMPGROUND

THREE ISLE
LAKE

LOWER
KANANASKIS
LAKE

MARL LAKE

KANANASKIS LAKES TRAIL

INTERLAKES
CAMPGROUND

UPPER
KANANASKIS
LAKE

LOWER LAKE
CAMPGROUND

BOULTON CREEK
TRADING POST

BOULTON
CREEK TRAIL

BOULTON CREEK

POCATERRA CREEK

PTARMIGAN
CIRQUE TRAIL

BRITISH

CONTINENTAL DIVIDE

HIGHWOOD
PASS
(2227 m)

COLUMBIA

0   2 mi

0   2 km

HIGHWOOD/CATARACT
CREEK AREA

40

© MOON PUBLICATIONS, INC.

linked by bicycle and hiking trails. **Mount Sarrail,** at the southern end of Upper Kananaskis Lake, is for tenters only and has pit toilets and firewood; $11 per night. **Canyon, Lower Lake,** and **Interlakes** have pit toilets, firewood, and kitchen shelters; $11 per night. **Elkwood** has showers, powered sites, flush toilets, an interpretive amphitheater, and a concession; unserviced sites $13, powered sites $15. **Boulton Creek** has showers, flush toilets, an interpretive amphitheater, and grocery store; $13 per night. For campground reservations call (403) 591-7226.

Services And Information

Boulton Creek Trading Post, a grocery store selling basic supplies, fishing tackle and souvenirs, is located on the Kananaskis Lakes Trail. The store also rents bikes. Next door is a small cafe serving hamburgers and light meals. The ice cream is good, although expensive.

The **visitor information center** is an excellent facility three km along Kananaskis Lakes Trail. The staff is very knowledgeable about the park and has hordes of literature hidden under their desk—but you have to ask for it. Ask them to put a movie or slide show on in the theater; most revolve around the park. The movie *Bears and Man* is a classic '70s flick dealing with public attitude to bears, one of the first documentaries to do so. A large lounge that overlooks the valley is primarily designed for winter use but is always open for trip planning or relaxing on rainy afternoons. This is also the place to pick up topographical maps, fishing licenses, and backcountry camping permits. It's open in summer, Sun.-Wed. 9:30 a.m.-5 p.m., Thurs.-Sat. 9:30 a.m.-5 p.m.; the rest of the year, Mon.-Fri. 10 a.m.-5 p.m., Sat.-Sun. 9 a.m.-5 p.m.; tel. (403) 591-7222. For more information write to Kananaskis Country, Suite 100, 1011 Glenmore Trail SW, Calgary, Alberta T2V 4R6; or call 297-3362.

HIKING IN LOUGHEED PARK

The park has a number of interesting interpretive trails and more-strenuous hikes. Most trailheads are located along Kananaskis Lakes Trail. Many trails have interpretive signs along them; others require an interpretive booklet available from the visitor information center. **Rockwall Trail,** from the visitor information center, and **Marl Lake,** from Elkwood Campground, are both wheelchair accessible. Below are some of the park's more popular interpretive and day-hikes.

Boulton Creek
- Length: 4.9 km (90 minutes) round trip
- Elevation gain: minimal
- Rating: easy

This trail starts where Kananaskis Lakes Trail crosses Boulton Creek. A booklet, available at the trailhead or at the visitor information center, corresponds with numbered posts along the trail. The highlighted stops emphasize the valley's human history. After a short climb the trail reaches a cabin built in the 1930s as a stopover for forest ranger patrols. The trail then follows a high ridge and loops back along the other side of the creek to the trailhead.

Ptarmigan Cirque
- Length: 6 km (2 hours) round trip
- Elevation gain: 230 meters
- Rating: moderate

The trailhead for this steep interpretive walk is across the road from Highwood Meadows, 17 km south of Kananaskis Lakes Rd. on Hwy 40. A booklet, available at the trailhead or at the visitor information center, corresponds with numbered posts along the trail. As it climbs into the alpine zone, magnificent panoramas of the Continental Divide unfold. Along the trail you are likely to see numerous small mammals. Columbian ground squirrels, pikas, least chipmunks, and hoary marmots are all common. At higher elevations the meadows are home to bighorn sheep, mountain goats, and grizzly bears. Another short walk two km north of Highwood Meadows leads 150 meters to a unique formation of moraine rock.

Black Prince Cirque
- Length: 5.6 km (90 minutes) round trip
- Elevation gain: 210 meters
- Rating: easy/moderate

The trailhead is eight km from Kananaskis Lakes Trail along the Smith-Dorrien/Spray Trail. Numbered posts along the trail correspond to a booklet available at the trailhead or at the visitor information center. The trail climbs steadily to an area that was logged in the early 1970s, then winds through a forest of Engelmann spruce and subalpine fir, crosses Old Creek, and emerges at a high mountain cirque scoured out by a glacier. Each spring the cirque fills with water, forming a small emerald green lake. The trail returns to the parking lot along a different route.

Burstall Pass
- Length: 7.4 km (2.5 hours) one way
- Elevation gain: 480 meters
- Rating: moderate/difficult

The trailhead is on the west side of the Smith-Dorrien/Spray Trail at the south end of Mud Lake. For the first three km it climbs an old logging road to Burstall Lakes. After traversing the willow flats it begins climbing again through heavy forest and avalanche paths to a large cirque. The final ascent to the pass is a real slog, but the view across the Upper Spray Valley (which is in Banff National Park) is worth it. From the pass it is possible to continue to Palliser Pass (two days one way) and Banff townsite (three days one way).

EAST KANANASKIS COUNTRY

East Kananaskis Country is the largest and most diverse of the zones in K-country, spanning the Elbow, Sheep, Sibbald, and Jumpingpound valleys. The valleys start in the west among the high peaks of the Rockies. As they cut east through the foothills, they gradually open up, ending at the prairie. At higher elevations elk, bighorn sheep, and bears make their home. In the foothills visitors are likely to see mule and white-tailed deer, elk, and moose. East Kananaskis also has a relatively high population of cougars, but these shy cats are rarely sighted.

The main access roads into the zone are from Bragg Creek on Hwy. 66, Millarville on Hwy. 549, and Turner Valley on Hwy. 546. **Sibbald Creek Trail** (Hwy. 68) crosses the northern reaches of the zone and is accessible from the TransCanada Hwy., intersecting Hwy. 40 south of the Barrier Lake visitor information center. Much of the zone is set aside for off-road vehicles

COUGARS

Elusive and rarely encountered by casual hikers, cougars (also known as mountain lions, pumas, or catamounts) measure up to 1.5 meters long with the average male weighing 75 kilograms and the female 40-55 kilograms. Their athletic prowess puts Olympians to shame. They can spring forward over eight meters from a standstill, leap four meters into the air, and safely jump from a height of 20 meters.

Cougars are versatile hunters whose acute vision takes in a peripheral span in excess of 200 degrees. They typically kill a large mammal such as an elk or deer every 12-14 days, eating part of it and caching the rest. Their diet also includes chipmunks, ground squirrels, snowshoe hares, and occasionally porcupines. Although attacks on humans are rare, they do occur, usually if the cougar has been surprised or if it's particularly hungry. Cases have been recorded of the animal stalking human prey, but there have been no recorded cougar attacks in Alberta for 30 years.

BOB RACE

The cougar is a solitary animal with distinct territorial boundaries. This limits its population density, which in turn means that its overall numbers are low. As is the case with all North America's large mammals, the cougar's biggest threat is man and the diminishing range of its habitat due to development and ranching. An extensive study of the cougar took place throughout the 1980s in Alberta and the good news is that although its numbers are low they remain steady.

and travel on horseback, although some hiking trails along Hwy. 66 are worthy of exploration.

Practicalities
From Bragg Creek, Hwy. 66 follows the Elbow River southwest past three campgrounds to a staging area for horses at the end of the road. Each campground is close to the river and has kitchen shelters, firewood, and picnic tables; $11-13 per night. Along Hwy. 546, west from Turner Valley, are two campgrounds. At each entrance are information centers; open in summer, daily 9 a.m.-9 p.m. For more information write to Kananaskis Country, Suite 100, 1011 Glenmore Trail SW, Calgary, Alberta T2V 4R6; or call 297-3362.

HIGHWOOD/ CATARACT CREEK AREA

The Highwood/Cataract Creek Area stretches from Peter Lougheed Provincial Park to the southern border of Kananaskis Country. This is the least developed zone in Kananaskis Country. The jagged peaks of the Highwood Mountains are its most dominant feature; high alpine meadows among the peaks are home to bighorn sheep, elk, and grizzlies. Lower down, lush spruce and lodgepole pine forests spread over most of the zone, giving way to rich grazing lands along its eastern flanks. Access to the area is via Hwy. 40 from the north, Hwy. 541 from Longview to the east, and Hwy. 940 from Crowsnest Pass to the south. In winter, the only access is from Hwy. 541.

The main summer activities are hiking, horseback riding, climbing, and fishing. Winter use is primarily by snowmobilers. Only two formal hiking trails are signposted. The rest are a complex system of traditional routes that are not well traveled; many require river crossings. One of the two marked trails, **Mist Creek Trail** starts 21 km north of Highwood Junction at Mist Creek Picnic Area. It leads seven km one way to Rickert's Pass, one of the most scenic vantage points in Kananaskis Country. The other marked route is **Cat Creek Interpretive Trail,** a short hike from Cat Creek Picnic Area. Some of the best hiking in the zone is only accessible after a difficult ford of the Highwood River, which runs parallel to Highways 40 and 541. Highlights include two Indian petroglyphs along Zephyr Creek and a number of abandoned fire lookouts along Hwy. 940. For more information contact the ranger station at Highwood Junction, tel. (403) 558-2151, or read Joey Ambrosi's *Hiking Alberta's Southwest.*

Practicalities
All four campgrounds in the zone are south of Highwood Junction on Hwy. 940. Each has water, pit toilets, firewood, fire pits, and picnic tables; $7 per night. A fifth campground at Strawberry Creek is open during the hunting season. **Highwood House** is located at Highwood Junction and has gas and a grocery store. It's open May-June, Fri.-Sun. 9 a.m.-5 p.m.; July-Sept., daily 9 a.m.-8 p.m.; and Oct.-April, weekends only 9:15 a.m.-5 p.m. The **Highwood Ranger Station,** also located at the junction, is open in summer only, Thurs.-Mon. 10-6; tel. (403) 558-2151. For more information write to Kananaskis Country, Suite 100, 1011 Glenmore Trail SW, Calgary, Alberta T2V 4R6; or call 297-3362.

CANMORE

Canmore (population 6,000) is nestled below the distinctive peaks of the Three Sisters in the Bow Valley between Calgary and Banff. It is the gateway to the mountain national parks and Kananaskis Country, and provides inexpensive lodging and dining alternatives. Its ideal mountain location and the freedom it enjoys from the strict development restrictions that apply in the nearby parks have made the town one of the fastest growing resort areas in the country. Downtown Canmore, on the southwestern side of the TransCanada Hwy., has managed to retain much of its charm. Most of the development is taking place on the outskirts. Around $2.3 billion in resort and residential projects have been planned for the next two decades, and the town's population is estimated to reach 20,000 by the end of that period. One of the largest and most controversial developments, still in its infancy, is the Three Sisters Resort. When completed, it will include 4,000 residential units, two hotels, and two golf courses on an 840-hectare parcel of land in the environmentally sensitive Wind Valley.

Apart from being a service center, the town has much to offer. Many historical buildings line the downtown streets, nearby hiking is excellent, and Mt. Yamnuska has become the most developed rock-climbing site in the Rockies. Canmore also hosted the nordic events of the 1988 Winter Olympic Games and is the home of the Alpine Club of Canada.

History

The Hudson's Bay Company explored the Bow Valley corridor and attempted, without success, to establish a fur trade with the Stoney Indians for most of the 1840s. In 1958 an expedition from the east, led by John Palliser, sent back discouraging reports about the climate and prospects of agriculture in the valley. One of the conditions of British Columbian entry into the confederation of Canada was the completion of a rail line linking them to the east by 1881. The Canadian Pacific Railway chose the Bow Valley Corridor as the route through the mountains and the first divisional point west of Calgary was established at what is now Canmore. Mining on the Three Sisters and Mount Rundle commenced soon after. Hotels and businesses were established, and a hospital, NWMP post, and opera house were built. The Canmore Opera House—reputed to be the only log movie house in the world—still stands and has been relocated to the Calgary Heritage Park. In 1899 the C.P.R. moved its divisional point to Laggan (now Lake Louise), but the mines continued to operate until 1979.

SIGHTS AND RECREATION

A number of historic buildings from the coal-mining days are being preserved at their original locations around town. The best way to get downtown from the TransCanada Hwy. is by taking Benchlands Trail from Hwy. 1A and driving down 8th St., the main drag. The first building of interest at the east end of 8th St. is Canmore's original NWMP post, built in 1892. **Ralph Connor Memorial United Church,** opposite the bakery, and a little farther down 8th St., was built in 1890 and is now a Provincial Historic Site. **Canmore Hotel** on the corner of 8th St. and 7th Ave. was built in 1891 (at a time when four hotels already operated) and is still open for thirsty travelers today. **Canmore Centennial Museum,** 801 7th Ave., tel. (403) 678-2462, has a collection of artifacts from the area's early coal-mining days and a display from the 1988 Winter Olympic Games. Open daily noon-4 p.m., extended hours in summer.

Hiking

The hiking trails around Canmore are usually passed by in favor of those of its famous neighbors. But some interesting trails do exist. Paved paths around town are suitable for walking, bicycling, and skiing in winter. They link Policeman's Creek with the golf course, nordic center, and Riverview Park on the Bow River.

Grassi Lakes Trail takes about three hours and climbs to a series of small lakes below Chinaman's Peak. To get to the trailhead follow Spray Lakes Rd. past the nordic center and take the first gravel road to the left after the reservoir. This leads to a parking lot and trail-head. The trail forks to the left by a gate and climbs to **Grassi Falls.** Stairs cut into a cliff face lead up to a bridge over Canmore Creek and to the lakes. A further scramble up a scree slope leads to four pictographs (native rock paintings) of human figures. They are on the first large boulder in the gorge.

A trail on the opposite side of the valley leads to hoodoos and a panoramic view of the Bow Valley and Canmore. To get there take the Benchlands Trail (an extension of Railway Ave.) across the TransCanada Hwy. and turn left on the first gravel road after the overpass. The trail starts at the cemetery (interesting itself with graves dating back to the 1890s) and climbs to the mysterious-looking columns carved from the soft sandstone by wind and rain. Past the hoodoos the trail continues climbing to a ridge with excellent views across the valley.

Canmore Nordic Centre
This remarkable complex was built at a cost of $15 million for the 1988 Winter Olympic Games. The cross-country skiing and biathlon (combined cross-country skiing and rifle shooting) events were held here, and today the center remains a world-class training ground for Canadian athletes. Even in summer, long after the snow has melted, the place is worth a visit. An interpretive trail leads down to the banks of the Bow River where Georgetown, an old coal-mining town, once stood. Many other trails lead around the grounds and it's possible to hike or bike to the Banff Springs Hotel. Mountain biking is extremely popular on the trails. Events are held throughout summer and bike rentals are available at **Trail Sports** at the center. The day lodge has an information rack with maps and brochures, lockers, a lounge area, and a cafeteria. It's open daily 8 a.m.-4:30 p.m. For more information call (403) 678-2400.

Other Recreation

The Bow River has good fishing for rainbow and brook trout; Gap Lake for brown and brook trout; Grotto Lake for rainbow trout; and Ghost Lake for lake, rainbow, and brown trout. **Wapiti Sports,** 704 6th Ave., tel. (403) 678-5550, stocks bait and tackle and sells fishing licenses.

Canmore is home to many qualified mountain guides who operate both in and out of Banff National Park. Basic climbing courses cost $40-70 per day, and instruction is available for all ability levels. The main guiding companies are: **The M.W. Guides Office,** P.O. Box 1913, Canmore, Alberta T0L 0M0; tel. 678-2642; **Company of Canadian Mountain Guides,** P.O. Box 1149, tel. 678-4662; and **Yamnuska,** P.O. Box 452, tel. 678-4164.

Canmore Golf Course, built in 1926, has developed into an 18-hole championship course with a clubhouse and driving range. Green fees are $29; for tee times call 678-4784.

Festivals And Events

Canmore's annual **Winter Carnival** is a two-week celebration including an ice-sculpture demonstration, ice-fishing derby, and pancake breakfasts. The highlight is the Alberta Sled Dog Championship held at Canmore Nordic Centre, where teams of four, six, eight, and 10 dogs are harnessed up and compete in various heats (organizers are always looking for volunteers, ask around if you'd like to help). **Canada Day** is celebrated with a parade, midway, and fireworks display. The first weekend in August is a busy one. **Hobie's Howler** is a nationally sanctioned mountain bike race held at Canmore Nordic Centre. Events include downhill, uphill, and cross-country. Spectators are admitted free. The same weekend is the **Heritage Day Folk Festival,** which starts on Sunday and runs through Monday evening. This event features a variety of national and international acts performing in Centennial Park. The **Canmore**

THE ALPINE CLUB OF CANADA

The Alpine Club of Canada, like similar clubs in the United States and Great Britain, is a nonprofit mountaineering organization whose objectives include the encouragement of mountaineering, the exploration and study of alpine and glacial regions, and the preservation of mountain flora and fauna.

The club was formed in 1906, mainly through the tireless campaign of its first president A.O. Wheeler. A list of early members reads like a Who's Who of the Canadian Rockies—Bill Peyto, Tom Wilson, Byron Harmon, Mary Schäffer, names familiar to all Canadian mountaineers. The original clubhouse was near the Banff Springs Hotel, but in 1980, a new clubhouse was built in Canmore which now serves as headquarters for over 3,000 members throughout Canada. The club's ongoing projects include operating the Lake Louise Hostel, maintaining a system of huts throughout the backcountry, and publishing the annual *Canadian Alpine Journal*—the country's only record of mountaineering accomplishments. A reference library of the club's history is kept at the Whyte Museum of the Canadian Rockies. For further information and membership details write to: P.O. Box 2040, Canmore, Alberta T0L 0M0; tel. (403) 678-3200.

WHYTE MUSEUM OF THE CANADIAN ROCKIES

Rodeo is held the second weekend of August. The second Sunday of September is the traditional **Highland Games,** a day of dancing, eating, and tug-of-war.

ACCOMMODATIONS

Hotels And Motels
Most lodging is located on Hwy. 1A, just off the TransCanada Hwy. between the two Canmore exits. (Mailing addresses for the following accommodations are the listed P.O. Box followed by **Canmore, Alberta T0L 0M0.**)

Akai Motel, P.O. Box 687, tel. (403) 678-4664, is a little run-down but each room has a kitchenette; $48 s, $61 d. **Rocky Mountain Ski Lodge,** P.O. Box 3000, tel. 678-5445 or (800) 665-6111, has large, modern rooms and some loft apartments with kitchenettes. Basic rooms start at $50 s, $60 d, making it the best value in town. Similarly priced are **A-1 Motel,** P.O. Box 339, tel. 678-5200; **Viscount Motor Inn,** P.O. Box 790, tel. 678-5221, $56-60 s or d; **Sundance Inn,** P.O. Box 755, tel. 678-5528, which has a restaurant, $59 s, $64 d; and **Bow Valley Motel,** P.O. Box 231, tel. 678-6560, whose large rooms are good for families, $70 s or d. **Drake Inn,** P.O. Box 2760, tel. 678-5131 or (800) 461-8730, at the end of Canmore's main street, has a sports bar, outdoor jacuzzi, and restaurant, and each room has a private balcony; $45 s, 63 d. **Rundle Mountain Motel,** P.O. Box 147, tel. 678-5322 or (800) 661-1610, has small but comfortable rooms and an indoor pool and outdoor whirlpool; $78 s or d. **Best Western Inn,** P.O. Box 520, tel. 678-5488 or (800) 661-2133, has a whirlpool in each room, private balconies, fireplaces, and a fine-dining restaurant. Rooms are $105 s or d and ski packages start at $60 per person.

Lodging in Harvie Heights, west of Canmore and closer to Banff (same Canmore postal code as above), is generally more expensive but most units have kitchens. Options are: **Cee-der Chalets,** P.O. Box 525, tel. 678-5251, from $65 s or d; **Gateway Inn,** P.O. Box 585, tel. 678-5396, $75 s, $90 d; **Rundle Ridge Chalets,** P.O. Box 1847, tel. 678-5387 or (800) 332-1299, set in a pleasant wooded area, each chalet with its own fireplace, $89 s, $99 d; and **Stockade Motel,** P.O. Box 575, tel. 678-5212, $78-120.

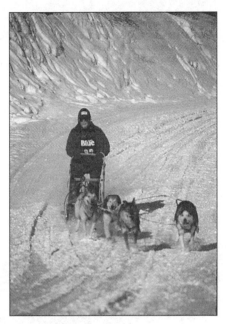

Once a traditional form of transportation, dogsledding is now a popular winter sport.

Deadman's Flats is little more than a truck stop but has two motels; **Green Acres Motel,** P.O. Box 1770, tel. 678-5344; and **Pigeon Mountain Motel,** P.O. Box 434, tel. 678-5756. Both have rooms starting at $60.

Kananaskis Guest Ranch
This historic lodge, 10 minutes east of Canmore, has been owned and operated by five generations of the Brewster family—a name synonymous with tourism in Banff. The lodge is located on a picturesque lake in the Bow Valley, close to the mountain parks. Yet a traditional western atmosphere prevails; the emphasis is on horseback riding and the outdoors, although they also have an indoor jacuzzi, dining room, and lounge. Chalets and cabins are basic, but comfortable. Rates are $85 per person per day, which includes three meals and one hour of trail riding. For more information write to Kananaskis Guest Ranch, P.O. Box 964 Banff, Alberta T0L 0C0; tel. (403) 762-5454.

Bed And Breakfasts

Over a dozen bed and breakfasts operate in Canmore. Most are small, family-run affairs, with only one or two rooms. During summer they fill every night. Largest is **Haus Alpenrose Lodge,** P.O. Box 723, Canmore, Alberta T0L 0M0, tel. (403) 678-4134, a Bavarian-style chalet that is home to the Canadian School of Mountaineering. The hosts operate an extensive mountaineering program, making this the perfect place for climbers. Rates are $50 s, $60 d.

For a full list of B&Bs in the area, ask at the tourist information center or check the *Alberta Accommodation and Visitors Guide.*

Hostel

The **Alpine Club of Canada Clubhouse** is an excellent hostel-style accommodation at the base of Grotto Mountain. The clubhouse overlooks the Bow Valley and can sleep 30 in the dormitories. It has a kitchen, excellent library, laundry, lounge area with fireplace, bar, and a sauna. Rates are $11 per night for Alpine Club members, $19 otherwise. Club membership is inexpensive and includes a discount at the Lake Louise Hostel. For reservations and more information write to Canmore Clubhouse, Alpine Club Of Canada, P.O. Box 2040, Canmore, Alberta T0L 0M0, or call (403) 678-3200. To get there from the east take the first Canmore exit and follow Hwy 1A to Exshaw (to the northeast). The clubhouse is signposted to the left.

Campgrounds

Restwell Trailer Park, off 8th St. in downtown Canmore, tel. (403) 678-5111, has showers and a laundry. It is mainly suited to RVs, but tents are allowed. Unserviced sites are $14, hookups $16-20. Behind Canmore, 16 km along the Smith-Dorrien/Spray Lakes Trail, is a primitive campground on Spray Lakes, $5.50 per night. East of Canmore are three government campgrounds, each with pit toilets, kitchen shelters, and firewood. **Bow Valley Campground** is located four km west of Dead Man's Flats, **Three Sisters Campground** is in Dead Man's Flats, and **Lac Des Arcs Campground** is seven km east. Rates are $7.50-13.

FOOD

Fireside Inn, 718 8th St., tel. (403) 678-6677, is a popular early morning hangout. Cooked breakfasts begin at $4. Open Sun.-Thurs. 6 a.m.-5 p.m., Fri.-Sat. 6 a.m.-9 p.m. Another option for breakfast is **Sherwood House,** 738 8th St., tel. 678-5211, on Canmore's busiest downtown corner. You can dine outdoor on a deck or inside in a simply furnished restaurant and lounge. The menu is mainly pasta, grills, and inexpensive fondues. Open daily 11 a.m.-10 p.m. **The Kabin,** 1702 Hwy. 1A, tel. 678-4878, is a two-story log structure at the eastern end of a strip of restaurants. Although the menu is small it is varied and should appeal to all tastes. Expect to pay $11-18 for a main meal. On Sunday, 10:30 a.m.-2 p.m., an appetizing brunch buffet is served for $11.95, which includes dessert. **Des Alpes,** 702 10th St., tel. 678-6878, is a simply furnished, upscale European restaurant. **Peppermill,** 726 9th St., tel. 678-2292, serves excellent homemade pasta and lots of beef. Try daily specials such as lamb or arctic char, and finish with a bowl of delicious homemade ice cream. It's open daily 5-10 p.m.

SERVICES AND INFORMATION

The **post office** is located on 8th St. at the corner of 7th Avenue. **Mountain Laundromat,** open 8 a.m.-9.30 p.m., is located in the mall on 7th Avenue. **Canmore Hospital** is along Hwy. 1A, tel. (403) 678-5536. For the **RCMP** call 678-5516. **Canmore Public Library,** 700 9th St., tel. 678-2468, is open Tues.-Thurs. 11 a.m.-8 p.m., Fri.-Sun. 11 a.m.-5 p.m. A **Travel Alberta Information Centre** on the west side of town, just off the TransCanada Hwy., provides plenty of information on Canmore, Calgary, and the rest of the province. Open May-Oct. 8 a.m.-8 p.m.

KAREN MCKINLEY

BANFF NATIONAL PARK
INTRODUCTION

This 6,641-square-km national park encompasses some of the world's most magnificent scenery. The snowcapped peaks of the Rocky Mountains form a spectacular backdrop for glacial lakes, fast-flowing rivers, endless forests, and two of North Americas's most famous resort towns, Banff and Lake Louise. The park's vast wilderness is home to deer, moose, elk, mountain goats, bighorn sheep, black and grizzly bears, wolves, and cougars. Many of these species are commonly sighted from roads in the park, others forage within town, and some remain deep in the backcountry. The human species is concentrated mainly in the picture-postcard town of **Banff,** located near the park's southeast gate, 128 km west of Calgary. Northwest of Banff, along the TransCanada Hwy., is **Lake Louise,** regarded as one of the seven natural wonders of the world, rivaled for sheer beauty only by **Moraine Lake,** just down the road. Just north of Lake Louise, the **Icefields Parkway** begins its spectacular course alongside the Continental Divide to Jasper National Park.

Banff National Park is only one component of a complex geological and natural area consisting of four adjacent national parks that together have been declared a World Heritage Site by UNESCO. (The others are Jasper to the north, and Kootenay and Yoho to the west in British Columbia.)

One of Banff's greatest drawcards is the accessibility of its natural wonders. Most highlights are close to the road system. For those more adventurous, an excellent system of hiking trails leads to alpine lakes, along glacial valleys, and to spectacular viewpoints where crowds are scarce and human impact has been minimal. Summer in the park is busy. In fact, the park receives nearly half of its four million annual visitors in just two months—July and August. The rest of the year crowds outside the town of Banff are minimal. In winter, three world-class ski resorts—Mystic Ridge & Norquay, Sunshine Village, and Lake Louise (Canada's largest ski area)—crank up their lifts. Being low season, hotel rates are reasonable. And if you tire of downhill skiing, you can try cross-country skiing,

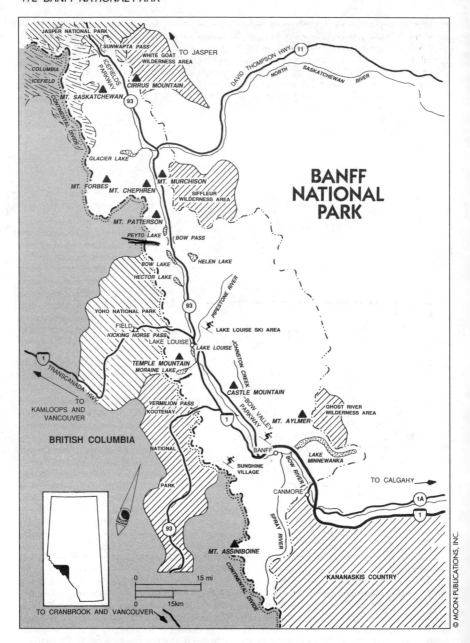

ice-skating, or snowshoeing; take a sleigh ride; soak in a hot spring; or go heli-skiing nearby.

The park is open year-round, although occasional road closures occur on mountain passes along the park's western boundary in winter, due to avalanche-control work and snowstorms.

Permits are required to enter the park, and are available from all park gates. A one-day permit is $5, a four-day is $10, and an annual pass good for all Canada's national parks is $30.

The Land

The park lies within the main and front ranges of the Rocky Mountains, a mountain range that extends the length of the North American continent. Although the mountains are composed of bedrock laid down up to one billion years ago, it wasn't until 100 million years ago that forces below the earth's surface transformed the lowland plain of what is now western Canada into the varied, mountainous topography we see today.

The **front ranges** lie to the east, bordering the foothills. These geographically complex mountains are made up of younger bedrock that has been folded, faulted, and uplifted. The **main ranges** are older and higher, lying mainly horizontal and not as severely disturbed as the front ranges. Here the pressures have been most powerful and the results most dramatic; these mountains are characterized by castle-like buttresses and pinnacles and warped waves of stratified rock. Most glaciers are found among these mighty peaks. Along the spine of the main range is the **Continental Divide.** To the east of the divide all waters flow to the Atlantic Ocean; those to the west flow into the Pacific.

Since rising above the surrounding plains these mountains have been eroding. At least four times in the last million years sheets of ice have covered much of the land, filling valleys and rounding off lower peaks such as **Tunnel Mountain.** As the ice retreated, meltwater carved deep channels into the valleys, rivers changed course, and U-shaped valleys were created of which **Bow Valley** is the most distinctive.

Many factors combine to make these mountains so beautiful. They are distinctive because the layers of drastically altered sediment are visible from miles away, especially when accentuated by the angle of sunlight or a light fall of snow. Cirques, gouged into the mountains by glacial action, fill with glacial meltwater each spring, turning them their trademark translucent green color. And fantastic views of the wide sweeping valleys are assured by the climate, which keeps the treeline low and the vegetation sparse enough so as not to hide the view.

FLORA

Nearly 700 species of plants have been recorded in the park, each falling into one of three distinct vegetation zones. The **subalpine zone** covers most of the forested area. Below it is the **montane zone** which covers the valley floor, and above it is the **alpine zone,** where climate is severe and vegetation cover limited.

Montane zone vegetation is usually found at elevations below 1,350 meters, but can grow at higher elevations on sun-drenched, south-facing slopes. As fires frequently affect this zone, **lodgepole pine** is the dominant species; its tightly sealed cones only open with the heat of a forest fire, thereby regenerating the species quickly after a blaze. **Douglas fir** is the zone's climax species and is found in open stands such as on Tunnel Mountain. **Aspen** is common in older burn areas, while **limber pine** thrives on rocky outcrops.

Dense forests of **white spruce** and **Engelmann spruce** typify the subalpine zone. White spruce dominates to 2,100 meters; above 2,100 meters to 2,400 meters, Engelmann spruce is dominant. In areas affected by fire, such as west of Castle Junction, lodgepole pine occurs in dense stands. In 1968 a fire burned 2,500 hectares near Vermilion Pass, a good area to view early stages of regeneration. **Subalpine fir** grows above 2,200 meters and is often stunted in growth, affected by the high winds experienced at such lofty elevations.

The transition from subalpine to alpine is gradual and usually occurs around 2,300 meters. The alpine has a severe climate with temperatures averaging below zero. Low temperatures, strong winds, and a very short summer force alpine plants to adapt by growing low to the ground with long roots. Mosses, mountain avens, saxifrage, and an alpine dandelion all thrive in this environment. The best place to view the brightly colored carpet of alpine flowers is Sunshine Meadows or Parker's Ridge.

FAUNA

Viewing the park's abundant and varied wildlife is one of the park's most popular activities here. During summer, with the onslaught of millions of visitors, many of the larger mammals tend to move away from the more heavily traveled areas. It then becomes a case of knowing when and where to look for them. Spring and fall are the best times of year for wildlife viewing. The big-game animals have moved below the snow cover of the higher elevations, and the crowds have thinned out. Winter also has its advantages. Although bears are hibernating, a large herd of elk winters in the town of Banff, coyotes are often seen roaming around town, bighorn sheep have descended from the heights, and wolf packs can be seen along the Bow Valley Corridor.

One of the biggest changes in the park over the last 60 years has been in the way that the complex relationship among higher-order mammals has been perceived by, and presented to, the visiting public. Only 20 years ago, hotels were taking guests to the Banff or Lake Louise dump to watch bears feeding on garbage; 30 years ago a predator-control program led to the slaughter of nearly every wolf in the park; 30-50 years ago it was deemed necessary to kill "surplus" elk; and it was only 60 years ago that Banff had a polar bear on display behind the Banff Park Museum. Amazingly enough, throughout these unsavory sagas, the park has remained a prime area for viewing the unique wildlife of the Canadian Rockies. Hopefully it will continue to be so for a long time to come.

Small Mammals

One of the first mammals you're likely to come in contact with is the **Columbian ground squirrel,** seen throughout the park's lower elevations. The **golden-mantled ground squirrel,** similar in size but with a striped back, is common at higher elevations or around rocky outcrops. The one collecting Engelmann spruce cones is the **red squirrel.** The **least chipmunk** is striped, but smaller than the golden-mantled squirrel. It lives in dry, rocky areas throughout the park. **Short-tailed weasels** are very common, **long-tailed weasels** are rare. Look for both in higher subalpine forests. **Pikas** (commonly called rock rabbits) and **hoary marmots** (well known for their shrill whistles) live among rock slides near high-country lakes—look for them around Moraine Lake and along Bow Summit Loop. **Porcupines** are widespread and are most active at night.

Vermilion Lakes is an excellent place to view the **beaver** at work; the best time is dawn or dusk. **Muskrats** and **mink** are common in all wetlands within the park. **Badgers** and **otters** are rare but do occur in the lower reaches of the Bow River watershed.

Banff's Elk

Few visitors leave Banff without having seen elk, easily distinguished by their white rump. Elk were reported passing through the park early this century but have never been indigenous. In 1917, 57 elk were moved to the park from Yellowstone National Park. Two years later 20 more were transplanted and the new herd multiplied rapidly. Coyote, cougars, and wolves were being slaughtered under a predator-control program, leaving the elk relatively free from predators. The elk proliferated and soon became a problem as they took to wintering in the range of bighorn sheep, deer, moose, and beaver. Between 1941 and 1969, controlled slaughters of elk were conducted in an attempt to reduce the population.

Today, with wolf packs returning to the park, the elk population has stabilized at about 3,500. In summer, look for them in open meadows along the Bow Valley Parkway, along the road to Two Jack Lake, or at Vermilion Lakes. In fall you'll find hundreds grazing on the golf course until the first snow flies. Fall is rutting season and the horny bull elk become dangerous as they gather their harem. In winter small herds roam in and around town. At any time of year you may see them in Central Park or walking proudly down Banff Avenue.

Other Hoofed Residents

Moose were once common around Vermilion Lakes, but competition from the expanding elk population caused their numbers to decline—now fewer than 100 live in the park. Look for them along the Icefields Parkway near Rampart Creek or at Waterfowl Lakes.

Mule deer, named for their large ears, are most common in the southern part of the park. Watch for them along the Mt. Norquay Rd. and Bow Valley Parkway. White-tailed deer are much less common but seen occasionally at Saskatchewan River Crossing. The park has a population of around 25 woodland caribou. The small herd remains in the Dolomite Pass area and Upper Pipestone Valley and is rarely seen.

Mountain goats occupy all mountain peaks in the park, living almost the entire year in the higher subalpine and alpine regions. The most accessible place to view these high-altitude hermits is along Parker's Ridge in the far northwestern corner of the park. The park's Rocky Mountain bighorn sheep have for the most part lost their fear of humans and often congregate at certain spots to lick salt from the road. Look for them at the south end of the Bow Valley Parkway, between switchbacks on the Mt. Norquay Rd., and just beyond Lake Minnewanka.

Predators
Coyotes are widespread along the entire Bow River watershed. They are attracted to Vermilion lakes by an abundance of small game, and many have permanent dens there. The lynx population fluctuates greatly; look for them in the backcountry during winter. Cougars, the largest members of the cat family, are very shy and number less than 20 in the park. They are occasionally seen along the front ranges behind Cascade Mountain. Wolves had been driven close to extinction by the early 1950s, but today at least six wolf packs have been reported in the park. One pack winters close to the townsite and is occasionally seen on Vermilion Lakes during this period.

Where Can I Go To See A Bear?
This commonly asked question doesn't have an answer, but the exhilaration of seeing one of these magnificent creatures in its natural habitat is unforgettable. From the road you're most likely to see black bears, which range in color from jet black to a cinnamon brown. Try the Bow Valley Parkway at dawn or late in the afternoon. Farther north they are often seen near the road as it passes Cirrus Mountain. Grizzly bears

spend most of the year in remote valleys, often on south-facing slopes away from the Bow Valley Corridor. During late spring they are occasionally seen in the area of Bow Pass.

The chance of encountering a bear face-to-face in the backcountry is remote. To lessen chances even further, a number of simple precautions should be taken. Never hike alone or at dusk, make lots of noise when passing through heavy vegetation, keep a clean camp, and read the pamphlet *You are in Bear Country,* available at all park visitor centers. At the Banff Visitor Centre, 224 Banff Ave., daily trail reports list all recent bear sightings. Report any bears you see to the Warden's Office, tel. (403) 762-4506.

Reptiles And Amphibians
The wandering garter snake is rare and found only near the Cave and Basin, where warm water from the mineral spring flows down a shaded slope into Vermilion Lakes. Amphibians found in the park are the widespread western toad, the wood frog, commonly found along the Bow River, the rare spotted frog, and the long-toed salamander, which spawns in shallow ponds and spends summer under logs or rocks in the vicinity of its spawning grounds.

Fish
Many of Banff's lakes and rivers have at some time been stocked with a variety of fish, usually with a low rate of success. Rainbow trout are widespread throughout most deep lakes and large streams. Lake trout to 15 kilograms are found in Lake Minnewanka. Dolly Varden (also called bull trout) are also found in most lakes. Whitefish have been introduced as have Atlantic salmon, Quebec red trout, brook trout, black bass, and golden trout.

Early residents of Banff released a variety of tropical fish into the marshes below the Cave and Basin where they quickly multiplied. Today many thrive, but the extremely rare Banff long-nose dace, found nowhere else in the world, is in danger of extinction.

Birds
Although over 240 species of birds have been recorded in the park, most are shy and live in heavily wooded areas. One species that defi-

nitely isn't shy is the fearless **gray jay** that haunts all campgrounds and picnic areas. Similar in color, but larger, is the **Clark's nutcracker** that lives in higher, subalpine forests. Another common bird is the black-and-white **magpie. Ravens** are frequently encountered, especially around campgrounds.

A number of species of **woodpeckers** live in subalpine forests. Several species of grouse are also in residence. Most common of the grouses is the **downy ruffled grouse** seen in montane forest. The **blue grouse** and **spruce grouse** are seen at higher elevations, as is the **white-tailed ptarmigan,** which lives above the treeline (watch for them in Sunshine Meadows or on the Bow Summit Loop). A colony of **black swifts** in Johnston Canyon is one of only two in Alberta.

Good spots to view **dippers** and migrating waterfowl are Hector Lake, Vermilion Lakes, and the wetland area near Muleshoe Picnic Area. A bird blind has been set up below the Cave and Basin but is only worth visiting at dawn and dusk when the hordes of human visitors aren't around. Part of the nearby marsh stays ice free during winter, attracting birds such as **killdeer.**

Although raptors are not common in the park, **bald eagles** and **golden eagles** are present part of the year, and Alberta's provincial bird, the **great horned owl,** lives in the park year-round.

HISTORY

Although the valleys of the Canadian Rockies became ice free nearly 8,000 years ago and native people periodically hunted and traded in the area since that time, the real story of the park began with the arrival of the railroad to the area.

In 1871, Canadian Prime Minister John A. MacDonald promised to build a rail line linking British Columbia to the rest of the country as a condition of the new province joining the confederation. It wasn't until early 1883 that the line reached Calgary, pushing through to **Laggan,** now known as Lake Louise, that fall. The rail line was one of the largest engineering jobs ever undertaken in Canada, eventually proving to also be one of the most costly.

On 8 November 1883, three young railway workers—Franklin McCabe, and William and Thomas McCardell—went prospecting for gold on their day off. After crossing the Bow River by raft they came across a warm stream and traced it to its source at a small log-choked basin of warm water that had a distinct smell of sulphur. Nearby, they detected the source of the foul smell coming from a hole in the ground. Nervously, one of the three men lowered himself into the hole and came across a subterranean pool of aqua-green warm water. The three men had not found gold, but something just as precious—a hot mineral spring that in time would attract wealthy customers from around the world. Word of the discovery soon got out, and the government encouraged visitors to the Cave and Basin as an ongoing source of revenue to support the new railway.

A 25-square-km reserve was established around the springs on 25 November 1885, and two years later the reserve was expanded and renamed **Rocky Mountains Park.** It was primarily a business enterprise centered around the unique springs and catering to wealthy patrons of the railway. At the turn of the century Canada had an abundance of wilderness; it certainly didn't need a park to preserve it. The only goal of Rocky Mountains Park was to generate income for the government and the Canadian Pacific Railway. Luxurious hotels such as the Banff Springs were constructed, and golf courses, the hot springs themselves, and manicured gardens were developed. It soon became Canada's best known tourist resort, attracting visitors from around the world.

In 1902 the park boundary was again expanded to include 11,440 square km of the Canadian Rockies. This dramatic expansion meant that the park became not just a tourist resort but home to existing coal-mining and logging operations, and hydroelectric dams. Government officials saw no conflict of interest, actually stating that the coal mine and township at **Bankhead** added to the park's many attractions. Many of the forests were logged, providing wood for construction, while other areas were burned to allow clear sightings for surveyors' instruments.

Most of the larger mammals were killed for food and by 1915 game was scarce. The Victo-

Feeding bears was one of the park's early attractions.

WHYTE MUSEUM OF THE CANADIAN ROCKIES

rian concept of wildlife was that it was either good or evil. Although an early park directive instructed superintendents to leave nature alone, it also told them to ". . . endeavor to exterminate all those animals which prey upon others."

As attitudes began to change, the government set up a Dominion Parks Branch whose first commissioner, J.B. Hawkins, believed that land set aside for parks should be used for recreation and education. Gradually resource industries were phased out. Hawkins's work culminated in the National Parks Act of 1930 that in turn led Rocky Mountains Park to be renamed Banff National Park. Present boundaries, encompassing 6,641 square km, were established in 1964.

TOWN OF BANFF

Many visitors to the national park don't realize that the town of Banff is a bustling commercial center with 7,000 permanent residents. The town's location is magnificent. It is spread out along the Bow River, extending to the lower slopes of **Sulphur Mountain** to the south and **Tunnel Mountain** to the east. In one direction is the towering face of **Mt. Rundle,** and in the other, framed by the buildings along Banff Ave., is **Cascade Mountain.** A strip of hotels and motels lines the north end of Banff Ave., while a profusion of shops, boutiques, cafes, and restaurants hugs the south end. Also at the south end, just over the **Bow River,** is the **Park Administration Building.** Here the road forks—to the right is the historic **Cave and Basin Hot Springs,** to the left the **Banff Springs Hotel**

If we can't export the scenery, we'll import the tourists.

—William C. Van Horne,
vice president of the
Canadian Pacific Railway

and **Sulphur Mountain Gondola.** Some people are happy walking along the crowded streets or shopping in a truly unique setting; those more interested in some peace and quiet can easily slip into pristine wilderness just a five-minute walk from town.

History
After the discovery in 1883 of the Cave and Basin, just a few kilometers from the railway station then known as **Siding 29,** many commercial facilities sprang up along what is now Banff Avenue. The general manager of the C.P.R. (later to become its vice president), William Cornelius Van Horne, was instrumental in creating a hotel business along the rail line. His most recognized achievement was the **Banff Springs**

Hotel, which opened in 1888—the world's largest hotel at the time. Enterprising locals soon realized the area's potential and began opening restaurants and offering guided hunting and boating trips. By 1900 the bustling community of Banff had eight hotels. It was named after Banffshire, the Scottish birthplace of George Stephen, the C.P.R.'s first president.

After a restriction on automobiles in the park was lifted in 1916, Canada's best known tourist resort also became its busiest. More and more commercial facilities sprang up, offering luxury and opulence among the wilderness of the Canadian Rockies. Calgarians built summer cottages and the town began advertising itself as a year-round destination.

For most of its existence, the town of Banff was run as a service center for park visitors by the Canadian Parks Service in Ottawa—a government department with plenty of economic resources, but little idea about how to handle the day-to-day running of a midsized town. Any inconvenience this caused park residents was offset by cheap rent and subsidized services.

WHYTE MUSEUM OF THE CANADIAN ROCKIES

Banff Avenue, 1888

In June 1988, Banff's residents voted to sever this tie and on 1 January 1990 Banff officially became an incorporated town, no different than any other in Alberta (except that Parks Canada controls environmental protection within the townsite).

Development And The Future
The Town of Banff is the largest urban center in any national park in the world. Demand for housing continues to grow faster than development will allow, real estate prices are high, and each summer 50,000 visitors daily converge on the town, overloading existing facilities. On the surface, Banff's commercialism seems to work against the national parks' mandate—visitors park in multistory car parks, shops sell bearskin rugs, and trees are logged for new housing estates—but as the park itself has grown from what was originally a moneymaking exercise, it is unique.

Another subject of often-heated debate is the high percentage of property in Banff owned by foreign interests, principally Japanese. Japanese investors bought into the area heavily in the '80s, today owning around a third of Banff's hotel industry, including two of the three largest hotels. Non-English-speaking salespeople are common, and over half of all jobs advertised locally require fluent Japanese.

These issues of continuing development, housing, and foreign ownership of property here in Canada's first national-park town will be debated well into the next century.

SIGHTS AND DRIVES

Sulphur Mountain Gondola
The easiest way to get high above town without raising a sweat is on this gondola, which rises 700 meters in eight minutes to an elevation of 2,285 meters. From the observation dock at the upper terminal, the breathtaking view includes the townsite, Bow Valley, Cascade Mountain, Lake Minnewanka, and the Fairholme Range. Bighorn sheep often hang around the upper terminal. The short **Vista Trail** leads along a ridge to a restored weather observatory. Between 1903 and 1931, long before the gondola was built, Norman Sanson was the meteorological observer who collected data at the station. During this period he made over 1,000 ascents of Sulphur Mountain, all in the line of duty. **Summit Restaurant** serves mediocre food, inexpensive breakfasts, and priceless views. The gondola runs in summer, 8:30 a.m.-9 p.m., shorter hours the rest of the year; closed in December. Adults pay $8.50, children $3.75; tel. (403) 762-2523. A 5.5-km trail to the summit begins from the Upper

Hot Springs parking lot. Although it's a long slog, views on the way up are good and you'll be rewarded with a free gondola ride down—they don't check tickets at the top. From downtown the gondola is three km along Mountain Avenue. In summer **Brewster Transportation and Tours** provides shuttle service to the gondola from downtown hotels ($16 includes gondola ride). For details call 762-6700.

Cave And Basin Centennial Centre

At the end of Cave Ave. is this historic site, the birthplace of Banff National Park and of the Canadian National Parks system. It was here in 1883 that three men employed by the C.P.R. stumbled upon the hot springs now known as the Cave and Basin, and were quickly lounging in the hot water—a real luxury in the wild west. They built a fence around the springs, constructed a crude cabin, and began the long process of establishing a claim to the site. But the government beat them to it, settling their claims for a few thousand dollars and acquiring the hot springs. Bathhouses were installed in

VICINITY OF BANFF

© MOON PUBLICATIONS, INC.

1887 and bathers paid 10 cents for a swim. The pools were eventually lined with concrete, and additions were built onto the original structures. Ironically, the soothing minerals in the water that had attracted millions of people to bathe here eventually caused the pools' demise. The minerals, combined with chlorine, produced sediments that ate away at the concrete structure until the pools were deemed unsafe. After closing in 1975, the pools were restored to their original look at a cost of $12 million. They reopened in 1985 only to close again in 1993 for the same reasons, coupled with flagging popularity. Although the pools are now closed for swimming, the center is still one of Banff's most popular attractions. Interpretive displays describe the how's and why's of the springs. A narrow tunnel winds into the dimly lit cave, and a number of short trails lead from the center to the entrance of the cave and through a unique environment created by the hot water from the springs. Interpretive tours begin four times daily in summer. The site is open in summer, daily 9 a.m.-7 p.m., the rest of the year, daily 9:30 a.m.-5 p.m. Admission to the center is $2. For more information, call (403) 762-1557.

Upper Hot Springs
These springs on Mountain Ave., towards Sulphur Mountain Gondola, were first developed in 1901. The present building was completed in 1935. Once considered for privatization, they are still run by Parks Canada and are popular throughout the year. Swimming is $4, lockers and towel rental extra. Therapeutic massages are available for $17 per half hour. The facility is open in summer, daily 10 a.m.-11 p.m., shorter hours the rest of the year; tel. (403) 762-2056.

Bow Falls
Small but spectacular, Bow Falls is below the Banff Springs Hotel, only a short walk from downtown. The waterfall is the result of a dramatic change in the course of the Bow River brought about by glaciation. At one time the river flowed north of Tunnel Mountain and out of the mountains via the valley of Lake Minnewanka. As the glaciers retreated they left terminal moraines, forming natural dams and changing the course of the river. Eventually the backed-up water found an outlet here between Tunnel Mountain and the northwest ridge of Mt. Rundle. From town, cross the bridge at the south end of Banff Ave., scramble down the grassy embankment to the left, and follow a pleasant trail along the Bow River to a point above the falls. This easy walk is one km (30 minutes) each way. By car, cross the bridge and follow Golf Course signs. From the falls a paved road crosses the Spray River and passes through the Banff Springs Golf Course.

Cascade Gardens
One of the earliest entrepreneurs to take advantage of the hot springs was Dr. R.G. Brett. In 1886 he opened a private spa and hospital that became known as Brett's Sanatorium. It accommodated 90 guests, drawn to Banff by the claimed healing qualities of the hot spring's water. The hotel burned down in 1933 and was replaced in 1936 by the **Park Administration Building** that stands today on the south side of the Bow River. Here you'll have a commanding view along Banff Ave. and of Cascade Mountain. And the surrounding gardens are immaculately manicured, making for enjoyable strolling on a sunny day.

Vermilion Lakes
This series of shallow lakes forms an expansive montane wetland supporting a variety of mammals and 238 species of birds. Vermilion Lakes Dr., paralleling the TransCanada Hwy. immediately west of Banff, provides the easiest access to the area. The level of **First Vermilion Lake** was once controlled by a manmade dam. Since its removal the level of the lake has dropped. This is the beginning of a long process that will eventually see the area evolve into a floodplain forest such as is found along the Fenland Trail. **Second** and **Third Vermilion lakes** have a higher water level that is controlled naturally by beaver dams. Near First Vermilion Lake is an active osprey nest. The entire area is excellent for wildlife viewing, especially in winter when it provides habitat for elk, coyote, and the occasional wolf.

Mount Norquay Road
One of the best views of town accessible by car is on this road which switchbacks steeply to the base of **Mystic Ridge & Norquay,** the local ski

Vermilion Lakes in winter

area. On the way up are several lookouts, including one near the top where bighorn sheep often graze.

To Lake Minnewanka

Lake Minnewanka Rd. begins where Banff Ave. ends at the northeast end of town. An alternative to driving along Banff Ave. is to take Buffalo St., opposite the Banff Park Museum, and follow it around Tunnel Mountain, passing the hostel, campground, and a number of viewpoints of the north face of Mt. Rundle, rising vertically from the forested valley below. This road eventually rejoins Banff Ave. at the Rocky Mountain Resort. The first road to the right after passing under the TransCanada Hwy. leads to **Cascade Ponds,** a popular day-use area. The next turnout along this road is at **Lower Bankhead.** During the early 1900s, Bankhead was a booming mining town producing 200,000 tons of coal a year. The poor quality of coal and bitter labor disputes led to the mine's closure in 1922. Soon after, all the buildings were moved or demolished. Although for many years the mine had brought prosperity to the park, peoples' perceptions changed. The National Parks Act of 1930, which prohibited the establishment of mining claims in national parks, was greeted with little animosity. From the parking lot at Lower Bankhead, a 1.1-km interpretive trail leads through the industrial section of the town and past an old mine train. The town's 1,000 residents lived on the other side of the road at **Upper Bankhead.** Just before

the Upper Bankhead turnoff the foundation of the Holy Trinity Church can be seen on the side of the hill to the right. Not much remains of Upper Bankhead. It is now a day-use area with picnic tables, kitchen shelters, and firewood. Through the meadow to the west of here are some large slag heaps, concealed mine entrances, and various stone foundations.

Lake Minnewanka

Meaning "Lake of the Water Spirit," Minnewanka is the largest body of water in Banff National Park. **Mt. Inglismaldie** (2,964 meters) and the **Fairholme Range** form an imposing backdrop. The reservoir was first constructed in 1912, and additional dams were built in 1922 and 1941 to supply hydroelectric power to Banff. Minnewanka Landing was a resort village that was submerged when the most recent dam went in. It's now a popular spot for scuba diving. The lake is great for fishing (lake trout to 15 kilograms) and is the only one in the park where motorboats are allowed. Easy walking trails lead along the western shore, and a 90-minute cruise departs from the dock every two hours. **Brewster Transportation and Tours** offers this cruise combined with a bus tour from Banff for $35 per person.

From Lake Minnewanka the road continues along the reservoir wall—passing a commemorative plaque to the Palliser Expedition and a herd of bighorn sheep—to **Johnson Lake,** with good fishing and picnic facilities.

BOW VALLEY PARKWAY

Two roads link Banff to Lake Louise. The Trans-Canada Hwy. is the quicker route, more popular with through traffic. The other is the more scenic 51-km Bow Valley Parkway, which branches off the TransCanada Hwy. five km west of Banff. Cyclists will appreciate this road's two long divided sections and low speed limit (60 kph). Along this route are a number of impressive viewpoints, interpretive displays, picnic areas, good hiking, great opportunities for viewing wildlife, a hostel, three lodges, campgrounds, and one of the park's best restaurants.

As you enter the parkway, you pass the quiet **Fireside** picnic area beside a creek and an interpretive display describing how the Bow Valley was formed. At **Backswamp Viewpoint,** you can look upstream to the site of a former dam, now a swampy wetland filled with aquatic vegetation. Farther along the road is another wetland at **Muleshoe.** This wetland consists of oxbow lakes that were formed when the Bow River changed its course and abandoned its meanders for a more direct path. Across the parkway is a one-km trail that climbs to a viewpoint overlooking the valley. (The slope around this trail is infested with wood ticks during summer so be sure to check yourself carefully after hiking in this area.) To the east, **Hole-In-the-wall** is visible. This large-mouthed cave was created by the Bow Glacier that once filled the valley and whose meltwater dissolved the soft limestone bedrock as it receded. It is known as a solution cave.

Beyond Muleshoe the road inexplicably divides for only a few meters. A large white spruce stood on the island until it blew down in 1984. The story goes that while the road was being constructed a surly foreman was asleep in the shade of the tree, and not daring to rouse him workers cleared the roadway around him. The road then passes through particularly hilly terrain, part of a mass rock slide that occurred around 8,000 years ago.

Continuing down the Parkway you'll pass the following sights:

Johnston Canyon
Johnston Creek drops over a series of spectacular waterfalls here, deep within the chasm it has carved into the limestone bedrock. The canyon is not nearly as deep as Maligne Canyon in Jasper National Park (30 meters at its deepest, compared to 50 meters at Maligne), but the raised boardwalk that leads to the falls has been built through the depths of the canyon rather than along its lip, making it seem just as spectacular. The lower falls are one km from Johnston Canyon Resort. Others falls are passed along the trail as it continues to weave its way through the canyon to the **Ink Pots,** a series of mineral springs whose sediments reflect sunlight, producing a brilliant aqua color. While in the canyon look for nesting great gray owls and black swifts.

Silver City
At the west end of **Moose Meadows** a small plaque marks the site of **Silver City.** At its peak this boomtown had a population of 2,000, more than Calgary had at the time. The city was founded by John Healy, who also founded the notorious Fort Whoop-Up in Lethbridge. During its heady days, five mines were operating, extracting not silver but ore rich in copper and lead. The town had a half dozen hotels, four or five stores, two real-estate offices, and a station on the transcontinental rail line when its demise began. Two men, named Patton and Pettigrew, salted their mine with gold and silver ore to attract investors. After selling 2,000 shares at $5 each they vanished, leaving investors with a useless mine. Investment in the town ceased, mines closed, and the people left. Only one man refused to leave. His name was James Smith but he was known to everyone as Joe. In 1887 when Silver City came under the jurisdiction of the National Parks Service, Joe was allowed to remain. And he did so, friend to everyone including Stoney Indians, Father Albert Lacombe who occasionally stopped by, well known Banff guide Tom Wilson, and of course to the animals who grazed around his cabin. By 1926 he was unable to trap or hunt due to failing eyesight, and many people tried to persuade him to leave. It wasn't until 1937 that he finally moved to a Calgary retirement home where he died soon after.

Castle Mountain To Lake Louise
After leaving the former site of Silver City, the aptly named Castle Mountain comes into view.

Castle Mountain

It's one of the park's most recognizable peaks and most interesting geographical features. The mountain consists of very old rock (approximately 500 million years old) sitting atop much younger rock (200 million years old). This unusual situation occurred as the mountains were forced upwards by pressure below the earth's surface, thrusting the older rock up and over the younger rock in places.

The road skirts the base of the mountain, passes **Castle Mountain Village,** and climbs a small hill to **Storm Mountain Viewpoint,** which provides more stunning views and a picnic area. The next commercial facility is **Baker Creek Chalets and Bistro,** an excellent spot for a meal, then another viewpoint at **Morant's Curve** from where **Temple Mountain** is visible. After passing another picnic area and a chunk of Precambrian shield, the road rejoins the TransCanada Hwy. at Lake Louise.

RAINY DAY BANFF

Banff Park Museum
Although displays of stuffed animals are not usually associated with national parks, this museum, at 93 Banff Ave., tel. (403) 762-1558, provides an insight into the park's early history. Visitors during the Victorian era were eager to see the park's animals without actually having to venture into the bush. A lack of roads and scarcity of large game due to hunting meant that the best way to see animals was either in the game paddock, the zoo, or here in the museum. It was built in 1903, before the park had electricity—hence its "railroad pagoda" design with use of skylights on all levels. Between 1904 and 1937 the grounds behind the museum were occupied by Banff Zoo and Aviary. The zoo kept over 60 species of animals, including a polar bear.

Under the supervision of a keen naturalist, Norman Sanson, the museum's extensive collection of specimens continued to grow. As times changed it was considered outdated, and plans for its demolition were put forward in the '50s. Fortunately this didn't occur and the museum was restored for the park's 100th anniversary in 1985. The exhibits are an interesting link to the park's past and provide insight into the intricate workings of various park ecosystems. The museum is open in summer, daily 10 a.m.-6 p.m.; the rest of the year it's open Mon.-Fri. 1-5 p.m., Sat.-Sun. 10 a.m.-6 p.m. Admission is $2. **Wonderful Wildlife Tours** of the museum take place in summer, daily at 4 p.m., the rest of the year at 3 p.m. The museum also has a reading room stocked with books on the park.

Luxton Museum
Looking like a stockade, this museum, to the west of the Banff Bridge at 1 Birch Ave., tel. (403) 762-2388, is dedicated to the heritage of the Indians who once inhabited the Canadian Rockies and surrounding prairies. It was named for prominent Banff resident Norman Luxton, who had a close relationship with the natives of

the area and was involved in the Banff Indian Days. He operated a trading post on the site for many years before opening the museum in 1952 with the help of the Glenbow-Alberta Institute. The museum contains memorabilia from Luxton's 60-year relationship with the Stoney Indians, as well as an elaborately decorated tepee, hunting equipment, a few stuffed animals, a realistic diorama of a buffalo jump, peace pipes, and traditional clothing. Luxton's Trading Post is now one of Banff's better gift shops and is definitely worth a browse. The museum is open in summer, daily 9 a.m.-9 p.m.; 11:30 a.m.-4:30 p.m. the rest of the year. Admission is $3.75.

Whyte Museum Of The Canadian Rockies

The Whyte Foundation was established in the mid-'50s by local artists Peter and Catherine Whyte to help preserve artistic and historical material relating to the Canadian Rockies. Their museum opened in 1968 and has continued to grow ever since. It now houses the world's largest collection of Canadian Rockies literature and art. Included in the archives are over 4,000 volumes, oral tapes of early pioneers and outfitters, antique postcards, old cameras, manuscripts, and a large photographic collection. The highlight is the photography of Byron Harmon,

WILD BILL PEYTO

" . . . rarely speaking—his forte was doing things, not talking about them." These words from a friend sum up one of Banff's earliest characters. These attributes, combined with his knowledge of the Canadian Rockies, earned Bill Peyto the status of being one of the Banff's greatest guides. In 1886, at the tender age of 18, Ebenezer William Peyto left England for Canada. After traveling extensively he settled in Banff and was hired as an apprentice guide for legendary outfitter Tom Wilson. Wearing a tilted sombrero, fringed buckskin coat, cartridge belt, hunting knife, and a six shooter he looked more like a gunslinger than a mountain man. As his reputation as a competent guide grew, so did the stories. While guiding clients on one occasion, he led them to his cabin. Before entering, Peyto threw stones in the front door until a loud snap was heard. It was a bear trap that he'd set up to catch a certain trapper who'd been stealing his food. One of the guests commented that if caught, the trapper would surely have died. "You're damned right he would have," Bill replied. "Then I'd have known for sure it was him."

In 1900 Peyto left to fight in the Boer War and was promoted to Corporal for bravery. This was revoked before it became official after they learned he'd "borrowed" an officer's jacket and several bottles of booze for the celebration. Returning to a hero's welcome in Banff he established an outfitting business and continued prospecting for copper in Simpson Pass. Although his outfitting business thrived, the death of his wife left him despondent. He built a house on Banff Avenue. Its name, "Ain't it Hell," summed up his view of life. In his later years, after being wounded in WW I, he became a warden in the Healy Creek–Sunshine district where his exploits

during the 1920s added to his already legendary name. After 20 years of service he retired and in 1943, at the age of 75, he passed away. One of the park's most beautiful lakes is named after him, as is a glacier and one of Banff's popular watering holes, **Wild Bill's**, a designation that he would have appreciated. His face also adorns the large signs welcoming visitors to Banff.

WHYTE MUSEUM OF THE CANADIAN ROCKIES

whose black-and-white studies of mountain geography have showed people around the world that the Canadian Rockies are one of the most beautiful mountain destinations in the world. The downstairs gallery features changing art and photographic exhibitions. The museum also houses the library and archives of the Alpine Club Of Canada. On the grounds are a number of heritage homes formerly occupied by local pioneers. The Whyte Museum is open in summer, daily 10 a.m.-6 p.m.; 1-5 p.m. the rest of the year; and till 9 p.m. on Thursday. Admission is $3. It's located beside the library at 111 Bear St., tel. (403) 762-2291. Don't miss this one.

Natural History Museum
Banff's smallest museum, located upstairs in the Clock Tower Mall at 112 Banff Ave., tel. (403) 762-4747, is crammed with exhibits displaying the geological evolution of the Canadian Rockies. Highlights include a replica of Castleguard Cave (one of the largest caves in North America), an interesting slide show, rock and fossil displays, and a tacky life-size model of Bigfoot—grrrr. It's open daily 10 a.m.-6 p.m., till 10 p.m. in summer. Admission is $2.50.

Banff Centre
Located on the lower slopes of Tunnel Mountain is the Banff Centre for the Arts, whose surroundings provide inspiration for some of Canada's finest postgraduate artists. Banff Centre, as it's usually called, first opened in the summer of 1933 as a theater school, and has grown to become a prestigious institution attracting artists of many disciplines from throughout Canada. The Centre's **Walter Phillips Gallery** on St. Julien Rd., tel. (403) 762-6281, has changing exhibits of visual arts from throughout the world. Activities are held on the grounds year-round. Highlights include concerts, displays, live performances, the Banff Festival of the Arts, and the Banff Festival of Mountain Films, to name a few. Call 762-6100 for a program or check the *Crag and Canyon* (published weekly on Wednesday).

Banff Springs Hotel
On a terrace above a bend in the Bow River is one of the largest, grandest, and most opulent mountain-resort hotels in the world. What better way could there be to spend a rainy afternoon

than exploring this turreted 20th-century castle—finding a writing desk overlooking one of the world's most photographed scenes and penning a long letter to the folks back home?

"The Springs" has grown with the town and is an integral part of its history. William Cornelius Van Horne, Vice President of the C.P.R., decided that the best way of encouraging customers to travel on the newly completed rail line across the Rockies was by building a series of luxurious mountain accommodations. The largest of these was begun in 1886, as close as possible to Banff's newly discovered hot springs. The location chosen had magnificent views and was only a short carriage ride from the train station. Money was no object and architect Bruce Price began designing a mountain resort the likes of which the world had never seen. At some stage of construction his plans were misinterpreted and much to Van Horne's shock the building was built back to front. The best guest rooms faced the forested slopes of Sulphur Mountain while the kitchen had panoramic views of the Bow Valley.

On 1 June 1888 it opened, the largest hotel in the world with 250 rooms beginning at $3.50 per night including meals. Water from the nearby hot springs was piped into the hotel's steam baths. Rumor has it that when the pipes blocked, water from the Bow River was used, secretly supplemented by bags of sulphur-smelling chemicals. Overnight, the quiet community of Banff became a destination resort for wealthy guests from around the world, and the hotel soon became one of North America's most popular accommodations. Every room was booked every day during the short summer seasons. In 1903 a wing was added, doubling the hotel's capacity. The following year a tower was added to each wing. Guest numbers reached 22,000 in 1911, and construction of a new hotel, designed by Walter Painter, began that year. The original design—an 11-story tower joining two wings in a baronial style—was reminiscent of a Scottish castle mixed with a French country chateau. It was completed in 1928. It is this concrete-and-rock-faced, green-roofed building that stands to this day.

Don't let the hotel's opulence put you off to spending time here. Sightseeing is actually encouraged. "The Building of Banff" tours are offered during summer, Fri.-Sun. at 2:30 p.m.

Guides take you through the hotel, explaining its history and influence on the community. Tickets are available from the Hotel Conference Centre Theatre 10 minutes before the tour starts. Call (403) 762-2291 for details. Otherwise wander through on your own (maps are available in the lobby), admiring the 5,000 pieces of furniture and antiques (most "antiques" in public areas are reproductions), paintings, prints, tapestries, and rugs. Take in the medieval atmosphere of Mt. Stephen Hall with its lime flagstone floor, enormous windows, and large oak beams, or relax in one of 16 eateries.

The hotel is a 15-minute walk southeast of town along Spray Ave., or via the trail along the south bank of the Bow River. Horse-drawn buggies take passengers from the Trail Rider Store at 132 Banff Ave. to the Springs for $8, only slightly higher than a cab; **Banff Explorer** buses leave downtown twice an hour, $1.

Gifts And Galleries

Banff has a great selection of galleries displaying the work of mostly Canadian artists. **Art Of The Wild**, tel. (403) 762-2999, and **Canada House**, 201 Bear St., tel. 762-3757, are two galleries in one, featuring Canadian landscape and wildlife works and Native art. **Arctic Art Gallery** in Cascade Plaza, 317 Banff Ave., tel. 762-0478, markets works from the Northwest Territories. **The Quest For Handcrafts**, 105 Banff Ave., tel. 762-2722, **Marika's Jewellery and Fine Art**, 94 Banff Ave., tel. 782-2678, and the smaller **The Gallery**, 210 Bear St., tel. 762-5990, contain a diverse range of affordable Canadian paintings and crafts.

HIKING

After experiencing the international thrills of Banff Avenue, many people will want to see the *real* Banff—the reason that millions of visitors flock here, thousands take low-paying jobs just to stay here, and those who become severely addicted cut ties with the outside world, raise families, and live happily ever after here. Although many landmarks can be seen from the roadside, to really experience the park's personality you'll need to go for a hike. One of the best things about Banff's 80-odd hiking trails is the variety. From short interpretive walks origi-

nating in town, to easy hikes rewarded by spectacular vistas, to a myriad of overnight backcountry opportunities—Banff's trails offer something for everyone. Before attempting any hikes you should visit the **Banff Visitor Centre,** 224 Banff Ave., tel. (403) 762-1550, where staff can advise you on the condition of trails and closures. If you are planning an overnight trip into the backcountry you *must* pick up a permit from here before heading out.

Most of the trails listed below start in or near town; the last four start out of town, on the way toward Lake Louise.

Fenland

- Length: 2 km (30 minutes) round trip
- Elevation gain: none
- Rating: easy

This short interpretive trail begins at the Forty Mile Creek Picnic Area 300 meters north of the rail line along Mt. Norquay Road. A brochure, available at the trailhead, explains the various stages in the transition between wetland and a floodplain forest of spruce as you progress around the loop. This fen environment is prime habitat for many species of birds. The work of beavers can be seen along the trail and elk are seen here during winter. This trail is also a popular shortcut for joggers and cyclists heading for Vermilion Lakes.

Tunnel Mountain

- Length: 2.3 km (30-60 minutes) one way
- Elevation gain: 300 meters
- Rating: easy/moderate

Accessible from town, this short hike is an easy climb to one of the park's lower peaks. The trailhead is on St. Julien Rd., 350 meters to the south of Wolf Street. The trail ascends the western flank of Tunnel Mountain through a forest of lodgepole pine, switchbacking past some viewpoints before reaching a ridge just below the summit. Here the trail turns northward, climbing through a forest of Douglas fir to the summit (which is partially treed, preventing 360-degree views).

Bow River/Hoodoos

- Length: 4.8 km (60-90 minutes) one way
- Elevation gain: minimal
- Rating: easy
    From the Bow River Viewpoint on Tunnel

Mountain Dr., the trail descends to the Bow River, passing under the sheer east face of Tunnel Mountain. It then follows the river for a short distance before climbing into a meadow where deer and elk often graze. From this perspective the north face of Mt. Rundle is particularly imposing. As the trail climbs you'll hear the traffic on Tunnel Mountain Rd. long before you see it. The trail ends at **hoodoos,** strange limestone-and-gravel columns jutting mysteriously out of the forest. An alternative to returning the same way is to catch the **Banff Explorer** from Tunnel Mountain Campground. It leaves every half hour ($1).

Sundance Canyon
• Length: 4.4 km (90 minutes) one way
• Elevation gain: 100 meters
• Rating: easy
   Sundance Canyon is a rewarding destination accessed from the Cave and Basin Centennial Centre. Unfortunately the first three km are along a paved road closed to traffic (but not bikes) and hard on your soles. Occasional glimpses of the Sawback Range are afforded by breaks in the forest. The road ends at a shaded picnic area from where the 2.4 km Sundance Loop begins. Sundance Creek was once a larger river whose upper drainage basin was diverted by glacial action. Its powerful waters have eroded into the soft bedrock, forming a spectacular overhanging canyon whose bed is strewn with large boulders that have tumbled in.

Spray River
• Length: 6 km (2 hours) one way
• Elevation gain: 70 meters
• Rating: easy/moderate
   This trail follows one of the many fire roads in the park. It is not particularly interesting, but it's accessible from Banff and makes a pleasant way to escape the crowds. For serious hikers this trail provides access to the rugged and remote southern reaches of the park. From the Bow Falls parking lot walk along Golf Course Rd. to the green of the first hole on the right. From there a trail heads uphill into the forest. It follows the Spray River closely—when not in sight the river can always be heard. For those so inclined, a river crossing one km from the golf course allows for a shorter loop. Continuing south, the trail climbs a bluff for a good view of

the Banff Springs Hotel and Bow Valley. The return journey is straightforward with occasional views, ending at a locked gate behind the Banff Springs Hotel, a short walk to Bow Falls.

Western Slope Of Mount Rundle
• Length: 5.4 km (2 hours) one way
• Elevation gain: 500 meters
• Rating: moderate
   At 2,950 meters, Mt. Rundle is one of the park's dominant peaks. Climbing to its summit is possible without ropes, but previous scrambling experience is advised. An alternative is to ascend the mountain's western slope along an easy-to-follow trail that ends just over 1,000 vertical meters before the summit. The trail follows the Spray River Trail (see above) before branching off left 700 meters from Golf Course Rd. and climbing steadily, breaking out of the enclosed forest after 2.5 km. The trail ends in a gully from where the undefined route to the summit begins.

Stoney Squaw
• Length: 2.4 km loop (1 hour round trip)
• Elevation gain: 180 meters
• Rating: easy
   Stoney Squaw's 1,884-meter summit is dwarfed by Cascade Mountain, directly behind it. To get to the trailhead, follow Mt. Norquay Rd. to a parking lot at the ski area. Immediately to the right of the entrance, a small sign marks the trail. The narrow trail passes through a thick forest of lodgepole pine and spruce before breaking out into the open near the summit. The sweeping panorama includes Vermilion Lakes, the Bow Valley, Banff, Spray River Valley, Mt. Rundle, Lake Minnewanka, and the imposing face of Cascade Mountain (2,998 meters). The return trail follows the northwest slope of Stoney Squaw to an old ski run at the opposite end of the parking lot.

Cascade Amphitheatre
• Length: 6.6 km (2-3 hours) one way
• Elevation gain: 610 meters
• Rating: moderate/difficult
   This enormous cirque and the subalpine meadows directly behind Cascade Mountain are one of the most rewarding destinations for hiking in the Banff area. The demanding trail begins by the Mystic Ridge & Norquay day

lodge at the end of Mt. Norquay Road. From parking lot No. 3, the trail skirts the base of a number of ski lifts, following an old road to the floor of Forty Mile Valley. Keep right at all trail junctions. One km after crossing Forty Mile Creek the trail begins switchbacking up the western flank of Cascade Mountain through a forest of lodgepole pine. Along the way are breathtaking views of Mt. Louis's sheer east face. After the trail levels off it enters a magnificent U-shaped valley and the amphitheatre begins to define itself. The trail becomes indistinct in the subalpine meadow, which is carpeted in colorful wildflowers during summer. Farther up the valley, vegetation thins out as the boulder-strewn talus slopes cover the ground. It you sit still long enough on these rocks, marmots and pikas will slowly appear, emitting shrill whistles before disappearing again.

The most popular route to the summit of 2,998-meter Cascade Mountain is along the southern ridge of the amphitheater wall. It is a long scramble up scree slopes—made more difficult by a false summit—and should be attempted only by experienced scramblers.

C Level Cirque
- Length: 4 km (90 minutes) one way
- Elevation gain: 455 meters
- Rating: moderate

This trail that begins from Upper Bankhead Picnic Area on the Lake Minnewanka Rd. is named for an abandoned mine along its route. It climbs steadily through a forest of lodgepole pine, aspen, and spruce to a pile of tailings and broken-down concrete walls. Soon after is a panoramic view of Lake Minnewanka, then the trail reenters the forest before ending in a small cirque where there are views down the Bow Valley to Canmore and beyond. The cirque is carved into the eastern face of Cascade Mountain where snow often lingers until July. When the snow melts, the lush soil is covered in a carpet of colorful wildflowers.

Aylmer Lookout
- Length: 12 km (4 hours) one way
- Elevation gain: 810 meters
- Rating: moderate/difficult

The first eight-km stretch of this trail follows the northern shore of Lake Minnewanka from the day-use area to a junction. The right fork leads to a campground, the left climbs steeply to the site of an old fire tower on top of an exposed ridge. The deep blue waters of Lake Minnewanka are visible backed by the imposing peaks of Mt. Girouard (2,995 meters) and Mt. Inglismaldie (2,964 meters). Bighorn sheep are often seen grazing in this area. From here a trail forks left and continues climbing to the alpine tundra of Aylmer Pass.

Cory Pass
- Length: 5.8 km (2.5 hours) one way
- Elevation gain: 920 meters
- Rating: moderate/difficult

This strenuous hike from the Fireside Picnic Area at the Banff end of the Bow Valley Parkway has a rewarding objective—a magnificent view of dogtoothed Mt. Louis. The towering slab of limestone rises over 500 meters from the valley below. Just over one km from the trailhead the trail divides. The left fork climbs steeply across an open slope to an uneven ridge that it follows before ascending yet another steep slope to Cory Pass—a wild, windy, desolate area surrounded in jagged peaks dominated by Mt. Louis. An alternative to returning along the same trail is continuing into **Gargoyle Valley,** following the base of Mt. Edith before ascending to Edith Pass and returning to the junction one km from the picnic area. Total distance for this trip would be 13 km, a long day considering the steep climbs and descents involved.

Bourgeau Lake
- Length: 7.6 km (2.5 hours) one way
- Elevation gain: 730 meters
- Rating: moderate

This trail follows Wolverine Creek from a parking area three km west of Sunshine Village Junction on the TransCanada Hwy. to a small subalpine lake nestled at the base of an impressive limestone amphitheatre. Although the trail is moderately steep, plenty of distractions along the way are worthy of a stop (and rest). Across the Bow Valley the Sawback Range is easy to distinguish. As the forest of lodgepole pine turns to spruce, the trail passes under the cliffs of Mt. Bourgeau and crosses Wolverine Creek (below a spot where it tumbles photogenically over exposed bedrock). After a series of strenuous switchbacks, the trail climbs into the cirque containing Bourgeau Lake. As you continue around the lake's rocky shore you'll hear the colonies of noisy pikas, even if you don't see them.

Rock Isle Lake

- Length: 8 km (2.5 hours) one way
- Elevation gain: 590 meters
- Rating: moderate

Sunshine Meadows, straddling the Continental Divide, is a unique and beautiful region of the Canadian Rockies. Large amounts of precipitation create a lush cover of vegetation during the short summer season—over 300 species of wildflowers alone have been recorded. For 60 years the meadows have been a favorite area for downhill skiing—it wasn't until 1984 that summer activities were promoted. Suddenly, instead of a few hundred adventurous souls willing to hike the 6.5-km road into the meadows, tens of thousands of visitors were whisked onto the fragile alpine tundra by gondola. In 1992 Sunshine Village terminated its summer gondola service and the meadows are quiet once again.

To get to the base station from Banff follow the TransCanada Hwy. nine km west to Sunshine Village Rd., which continues another nine km to the Gondola Base Station. The road to the meadows is closed to public traffic and climbs steadily for 6.5 km to Sunshine Village. From here the Rock Isle Lake Trail passes the Strawberry Chairlift and climbs out of the valley into an alpine meadow covered in a colorful carpet of fireweed, glacier lilies, mountain avens, white mountain heather, and forget-me-nots. Mount Assiniboine (3,611 meters), known as the "Matterhorn of the Rockies," is easily distinguished to the southeast. On the descent to the lake are various viewpoints and around the shoreline are benches and an observation deck. Expansions to Sunshine Village in 1995-96 will mean you might encounter heavy machinery on the access road.

In summer, **White Mountain Tours** offers a shuttle service for a limited number of hikers from Banff (daily at 10 a.m., $25 round trip) and the Sunshine Village parking lot (daily at 10:30 a.m. and 12:45 p.m., $14 round trip) to a small nature center at the ski area. Advance reservations are required, call (403) 678-4099.

Shadow Lake

- Length: 14.3 km (4.5 hours) one way
- Elevation gain: 440 meters
- Rating: moderate

Shadow is one of the many impressive subalpine lakes along the Continental Divide but is also popular as a base for a great variety of day-trips. The trail begins at the Redearth Creek Parking Area, 20 km west of Banff on the Trans-Canada Highway. It follows the old Redearth fire road for 11 km before forking right and climbing into the forest. The campground is two km beyond this junction and 500 meters farther is **Shadow Lake Lodge** (see "Backcountry Huts and Lodges" in the "Accommodations" section, below, for details). The lake itself is nearly two km long and from its southern shore trails lead to Ball Pass, Gibbon Pass, and Haiduk Lake.

Castle Lookout

- Length: 3.7 km (90 minutes) one way
- Elevation gain: 520 meters
- Rating: moderate

However you travel through the Bow Valley you can't help but be impressed by Castle Mountain rising proudly from the forest below. This trail takes you above the treeline on the mountain's west face to the site of Mt. Eisenhower fire lookout, abandoned in the 1970s and burned in the 1980s. The trailhead is on the Bow Valley Parkway, five km northwest of Castle Junction. The trail follows a wide pathway for 1.5 km to an abandoned cabin in a forest of lodgepole pine and spruce. It then becomes narrower and steeper, switchbacking through a meadow before climbing through a narrow band of rock and leveling off near the lookout site. From here a magnificent panorama of the Bow Valley is afforded in both directions. Storm Mountain can be seen directly across the valley.

Rockbound Lake

- Length: 8.4 km (2.5 hours) one way
- Elevation gain: 760 meters
- Rating: moderate/difficult

The trailhead for this strenuous hike is just east of Castle Junction on the Bow Valley Parkway. For the first five km it follows an old fire road along the southern flanks of Castle Mountain. Early in the season or after heavy rain, this section can be boggy. Glimpses of surrounding peaks ease the pain of the steady climb as the trail narrows. **Tower Lake** is reached after eight km. The trail skirts it to the right and climbs a steep slope. From the ridge Rockbound Lake

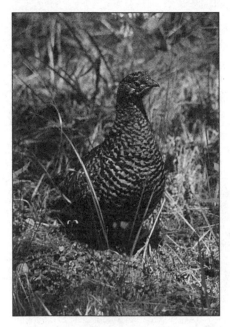

ruffed grouse, commonly seen in subalpine forests

comes into view and the reason for its name immediately becomes apparent. Good views can be achieved by scrambling up any of the nearby slopes.

OTHER RECREATION

Mountain Biking

Whether you have your own bike or you rent one from the many bicycle shops in town (see "Getting Around" in the "Transportation" section, below), cycling in the park is for everyone. The roads to Lake Minnewanka, Mt. Norquay, and along the Bow Valley Parkway are all popular routes. A number of trails radiating from Banff townsite and ending deep in the backcountry have been designated as bicycle trails. These include Sundance (3.7 km one way), Rundle Riverside (8 km one way), Spray River Loop (43 km round trip), and Cascade Trail (9 km one way). Other trails are at Redearth Creek, Lake Louise, and in the northeastern reaches of the park near Saskatchewan River Crossing.

Before heading into the backcountry, pick up the *Trail Bicycling Guide* from the Banff Visitor Centre. Riders are particularly susceptible to sudden bear encounters. Be alert and make loud noises when passing through heavy vegetation.

Horseback Riding

Jim and Bill Brewster led Banff's first paying guests into the backcountry on horseback over 100 years ago. Today visitors are still able to enjoy the park on this traditional form of transportation. **Warner Guiding & Outfitting,** P.O. Box 2280, Banff, Alberta T0L 0C0, tel. (403) 762-4551, offers a great variety of trips. Their main office is in the Trail Rider Store at 132 Banff Ave., although most trips depart from **Martin's Stables,** tel. 762-2832, behind the recreation grounds on Birch Ave., and **Banff Springs Corral,** tel. 762-2848, along Spray Avenue. One-hour rides are $18, two hours $30, three hours $38. Other day-trips include the three-hour **Mountain Breakfast Ride** that includes a hearty breakfast along the trail, $42; **Explorer,** a 6.5-hour ride up the Spray River Valley, $85; and the **Evening Steak Fry,** a three-hour ride with a steak dinner along the trail, $42. Overnight trips to established backcountry camps and lodges are also available; rates begin at $228 including all meals, one night's accommodation at Sundance Lodge, and the horse, of course.

Whitewater Rafting And Canoeing

Anyone looking for whitewater-rafting action will want to run the Kicking Horse River which flows down the western slopes of the Canadian Rockies into British Columbia. Many operators based in Banff offer a variety of exhilarating trips down this river, all of which include transportation from Banff. **Wild Water Adventures,** tel. (403) 522-2211, leads full-day trips beginning as far up river as possible. The price of $79 also includes a narrated bus trip and a gourmet lunch. Other operators are: **Kootenay River Runners,** 304 Caribou St., tel. 762-5385, and **Rocky Mountain Raft Tours,** tel. 762-3632. Rocky Mountain Raft Tours also offers one-hour ($18) and three-hour ($33) float trips down the Bow River. **Banff Canoe Rentals,** on the corner of Wolf St. and Bow Ave., rents canoes for use on the Bow River, Vermilion Lakes, or Lake Minnewanka.

Fishing And Boating

The finest fishing in the park is in Lake Minnewanka, where lake trout as large as 15 kilograms have been caught. One way to ensure a good catch is through **Minnewanka Tours,** tel. (403) 762-3473, which offers half- and full-day guided fishing expeditions. They also rent fishing boats and tackle. **Performance Ski and Sports,** 208 Bear St., tel. 762-8222, also rents tackle. Before fishing anywhere in the park you need a National Park fishing license ($6 per week, $13 per year), available from the Banff Visitor Centre and sport shops around town.

Golfing

Banff Springs Golf Course, spread out along the Bow River between Mt. Rundle and Tunnel Mountain, is considered one of the world's most scenic. The original 18 championship holes were designed by Stanley Thompson in 1928 and have been extended to 27. Not only is the course breathtakingly beautiful, it's also very challenging for all levels of golfer. Pick up a copy of the book *The World's Greatest Golf Holes,* and there'll be a picture of the fourth hole on the Rundle Nine. It's a par three, over Devil's Cauldron 70 meters below, to a small green backed by the sheer face of Mt. Rundle rising vertically over 1,000 meters above the putting surface. Another unique feature of the course is the abundance of wildlife. Each fall hundreds of elk gather on the course, and there's always the chance of seeing coyotes, deer, or black bears scurrying across in front of you.

Considering the caliber of the course, green fees are reasonable. High-season rate is $70 for 18 holes including a cart, $30 for nine holes with no cart. During May and October, the rate is $50 including a cart. Free shuttle buses run from the Banff Springs Hotel to the clubhouse, located in the middle of the course. There you'll find club rentals ($22.50), three putting greens, a driving range, pro shop, cafe, and restaurant. Booking tee times well in advance is essential; tel. (403) 762-6801.

Indoor Recreation

Banff Springs Hotel, tel. (403) 762-2211, has a four-lane bowling center; games are $2 per person. The hotel also has a mini-golf course laid out like its famous outdoor one; $3. Upstairs at 137 Banff Ave. is a large, clean pool hall. Tables are $7 per hour. The **Lux Cinema** at 229 Bear St., tel. 762-8595, shows new releases for $6.50.

Banff's only water slide is located in the Douglas Fir Resort on Tunnel Mountain Drive. The two slides are indoors and the admission price of $7.50 (under six free) includes use of a jacuzzi and exercise room. It's open Mon.-Fri. 2-9:30 p.m., Sat.-Sun. 10 a.m.-9:30 p.m. If you have energy to burn, **Banff Rocky Mountain Resort,** tel. 762-5531, has a small gym and pool open to nonguests, $6.50 per session. **Sally Borden Recreation Building** in the Banff Centre has an exercise room, gymnasium, squash courts, pool, and sauna; $10.70 per day, tel. 762-6461.

WINTERTIME

Of Alberta's six world-class ski resorts, three are in Banff National Park. **Mystic Ridge & Norquay** is a small but steep hill overlooking the town of Banff; **Sunshine Village** is located high in the mountains on the Continental Divide, catching more than its share of fluffy white powder; and **Lake Louise,** Canada's largest ski area, is spread over four distinct mountain faces providing something for everyone. Apart from an abundance of snow the resorts have something else in common—spectacular views —alone worth the price of a lift ticket.

In fact the entire park transforms itself into a winter playground covered in an impossibly white blanket of snow from November till May. You'll always find something to do: cross-country skiing, ice-skating, snowshoeing, dogsledding, or just relaxing. Crowds are nonexistent and hotels reduce rates by up to 50%—reason enough to venture into the mountains.

Mystic Ridge & Norquay

The steep eastern slopes of Mt. Norquay had been attracting local skiers for 20 years before Canada's first chairlift was installed on its face in 1948. Ever since then, the resort has had an experts-only reputation, mainly because of terrain serviced by the North American Chair including the famous double-black-diamond Lone Pine run. But an express quad installed in 1990 opened up new intermediate terrain and made the resort—located only six km from Banff—a favorite with shredders and cruisers alike. Lift tickets are $30 per day; lift, lesson, and rental packages are also $30. Night skiing is offered on Wednesday nights. A free shuttle bus picks skiers up from Banff hotels for the short ride up the hill. For more information on the resort call (403) 762-4421, or in Calgary call the 24-hour Snowphone, tel. 221-8259.

Sunshine Village

The skiing at Sunshine has lots going for it—over six meters of snow annually (no need for snowmaking up here), wide-open bowls, a season stretching for nearly 200 days, skiing in two provinces, and the only slope-side accommodation in the park.

The first people to ski the Sunshine Meadows were two local men, Cliff White and Cyril Paris, who became lost going over Citadel Pass in the spring of 1929 and returned to Banff with stories of deep snow and ideal slopes for skiing. In the following years, a C.P.R. cabin was used as a base for skiing in the area. In 1938 the Canadian National Ski Championships were held here, and in 1942 a portable lift was constructed. The White family was synonymous with the Sunshine area for many years, running the lodge and ski area while Brewster buses negotiated the steep narrow road that led to the meadows. In 1980 a gondola was installed to whisk skiers six km from the parking area in Bourgeau Valley to the alpine village.

The area has a remarkable variety of terrain serviced by 10 lifts, including the fastest chairlift in the Rockies. Lift tickets are $38 per day. Lift and lodging at slopeside Sunshine Inn is from $50 per person per day. For more information call (403) 762-6500 or (800) 661-1676. Transportation from Banff to the hill is $12 round trip; call the hill or inquire at major hotels for details.

Heli-Skiing

Although there is no heli-skiing in Banff National Park, **R.K. Heli-ski** books trips to areas outside the park from desks in the Banff Springs Hotel, 304 Caribou St., tel. (403) 762-3771, and in the Chateau Lake Louise. Each morning during winter, the company's bus leaves Banff to take skiers to Panorama in British Columbia for a day of helicopter skiing high in the Purcell Mountains. Cost is $369 per person per day. For further information call (604) 342-3889. Banff is also headquarters for the world's largest heli-skiing operation, **C.M.H. Heli-skiing,** found-

ed by Hans Gmoser. Seven-day packages in B.C.'s interior mountain ranges begin at $2568 per person. For more information write to C.M.H. Heli-skiing, P.O. Box 1660, Banff, Alberta T0L 0C0; tel. (403) 762-7100 or (800) 661-0252. **Mike Wiegele Helicopter Skiing,** whose lodge at Blue River is a base for heli-skiing in the Monashee and Cariboo Mountains, is also based in Banff. For information write to P.O. Box 249, Banff; tel. 762-5548 or drop by the shop on the corner of Banff Ave. and Caribou Street.

Cross-Country Skiing

No better way of experiencing the park's winter delights exists than skiing through the landscape on cross-country skis. Many summer hiking trails are groomed for winter travel. The most popular areas are Johnson Lake, Golf Course Rd., Spray River, Sundance Canyon, and near Lake Minnewanka. The booklet, *Cross-country Skiing—Nordic Trails in Banff National Park,* is available for $1 from the Banff Visitor Centre at 224 Banff Avenue. Weather forecasts (tel. 403-762-2088) and avalanche hazard reports (tel. 762-1460) are posted here also.

Rental packages are available from **Performance Ski & Sports** at 208 Bear St., tel. 762-8222; **Snowtips,** with outlets in the Travellers Inn, Ptarmigan Inn, and Douglas Fir Resort; and **Mountain Magic Equipment** at 224 Bear St., tel. 762-2591. Expect to pay $7-12 per day.

Ice-Skating

Rinks are located at **Banff High School** on Banff Ave. at Wolf St.; on the **Bow River** along Bow St.; and on the golf course side of the **Banff Springs Hotel.** The latter rink is lighted after dark and a raging fire is built beside it—the perfect place for a hot chocolate. Rent skates from **The Ski Stop** in the Banff Springs Hotel, tel. (403) 762-5333.

Other Winter Activities

Without the tourists, dogsledding probably wouldn't take place in the park—but there are tourists and there is dogsledding. **Mountain Mushers,** tel. (403) 762-3647, offers half-hour ($55), one-hour ($90), and half-day ($230) tours around the Banff Springs Golf Course.

Beside the Banff Springs Hotel ice-skating rink is an unofficial toboggan run; ask at your hotel for sleds. **Holiday on Horseback** has sleigh rides on the frozen Bow River throughout winter. For reservations call 762-4551 or stop by the Trail Rider Store at 132 Banff Ave. ($8 per person). **Banff Fishing Unlimited** offers ice fishing trips on nearby lakes, tel. 762-4936. Anyone interested in ice climbing must register at the national park desk in the Banff Visitor Centre or call 762-1550. The world famous (if you're an ice climber) **Terminator** is located just outside the park boundary. Curling bonspiels take place at the Banff Recreation Centre on Mt. Norquay Road. If none of the above appeals to you head to **Upper Hot Springs** for a relaxing soak; open Mon.-Fri. noon-9 p.m., Sat.-Sun. 10 a.m.-11 p.m. ($4). Camping might not be everyone's idea of a winter holiday but Tunnel Mountain Village II remains open year-round.

FESTIVALS AND EVENTS

Spring

Throughout spring the **Playbill Series** takes place at the Banff Centre, tel. (403) 762-6300. The first Saturday in May is the **Dummy Downhill**—ski racing with a difference. Enter your own dummy or just watch the fun. The **Slush Cup** takes place at Sunshine Village late in May. Events include kamikaze skiers who attempt to jump an ice-cold pit of water.

Summer

The **Banff Festival Of The Arts** is a summer-long extravaganza presented by professional artists studying at the Banff Centre. They perform dance, drama, opera, and jazz for the public at locations around town. Look for details in the *Crag and Canyon* or call (403) 762-6300. The second week of June is the **Banff Television Festival,** a meeting and international competition for the television industry with many public viewings. For information call 762-3060. Also in early June is the **Jasper-Banff Relay.** Local firefighters gather for the **Firefighters' Hose-coupling Competition,** mid-June, and late in the month is **Parks Day.** On 1 July, Banff celebrates **Canada Day** with a parade and events for all the family.

Fall

The last Saturday in September is **Melissa's Mini Marathon,** attracting over 2,000 runners. **Winterstart** runs from November to mid-December and features a host of fun events, cheap lodging, and the opening of local ski hills.

One of the year's biggest events is the **Banff Festival of Mountain Films** on the first weekend of November. Mountain-adventure-film makers from around the world submit films to be judged by a select committee. Films are then shown throughout the weekend to an enthusiastic crowd of thousands. Exhibits and seminars are also presented, and the crème de la crème of climbers and mountaineers from around the world are invited as guest speakers; the 1994 special guest was Sir Edmund Hillary.

Tickets go on sale a year in advance and sell out in advance. Tickets for daytime shows start at $20 (for up to 10 films). Night shows are more expensive, and all-weekend passes cost $95. Films are shown in the two theaters of the Banff Centre for the Arts. For more information write to Banff Festival of Mountain Films, The Banff Centre, P.O. Box 1020, Station 38, Banff, Alberta T0L 0C0; tel. (403) 762-6349.

Winter

By mid-December all local ski areas are operating. Events at the resorts continue throughout the long ski season, among them **World Cup Downhill** skiing. **Banff Winter Festival** is a two-week celebration at the end of January that has been a part of Banff's history for over 75 years. Look for ice sculpting, the Lake Louise Loppet, barn dancing, and the Town Party which takes place in the Banff Springs Hotel.

Park Interpretive Program

Each summer the national park staff presents an extensive Interpretive Program at locations in town and throughout the park. All programs are free and include guided hikes, nature tours, slide shows, campfire talks, and lectures. For details consult *The Mountain Guide* available at the Banff Visitor Centre, tel. (403) 762-1550, or look for postings at campground bulletin boards.

TOWN OF BANFF PRACTICALITIES

ACCOMMODATIONS

Finding a room in Banff in summer is nearly as hard as trying to justify its price. By late afternoon just about every room and campsite in town will be occupied, and basic hotel rooms begin at around $100. Fortunately, many alternatives are available. Rooms in private homes begin at around $30 s, $40 d. Canmore, just outside the park boundary, has many hotels and strip motels considerably cheaper than anything in Banff. Banff International Hostel has dormitory-style accommodations from $15 per night. Bungalows or cabins can be rented, which can be cost effective for families or small groups. And a thousand-odd campsites close to town accommodate campers. Wherever you decide to stay, it is vital to book well ahead during summer and the Christmas holidays. The park's off-season is from October to May, and hotels offer huge rate reductions during this period; the Banff Springs Hotel leads the way with lift and lodging packages beginning from $60 per person. Shop around and you'll find many bargains. **Summit Vacations**, tel. (403) 762-5561 or (800) 661-1676, represents most hotels in the park and can make reservations for you.

When addressing written inquiries to the establishments listed below, follow the P.O. Box provided with: **Banff, Alberta T0L 0C0**. All rates quoted below are for the high season (June-Sept.).

Banff Avenue

Spruce Grove Motel, P.O. Box 471, 545 Banff Ave., tel. (403) 762-2112, offers basic rooms for $65; kitchenettes are $85 but are larger and sleep four. **Red Carpet Inn**, P.O. Box 1800, 425 Banff Ave., tel. 762-4184 or (800) 563-4609, could do with a coat of paint; $75 s or d. **Irwin's Motor Inn**, P.O. Box 1198, 429 Banff Ave., tel. 762-4566 or (800) 661-1721, has rooms of similar standard for $80.

Banff Voyager Inn, P.O. Box 1540, 555 Banff Ave., tel. 762-3301 or (800) 372-9288, has a swimming pool and restaurant, $89 s or d. Although older, **Bow View Motor Lodge**, P.O. Box 339, 228 Bow Ave., tel. 762-2261 or (800) 661-1565, is close to town; rooms are $95, or, with a view of the river, $105. **Bumper's Inn,** P.O. Box 1328, 603 Banff Ave., tel. 762-3386, has Banff's best steakhouse; $104 s, $109 d.

Homestead Inn, P.O. Box 669, 217 Lynx St., tel. 762-4471 or (800) 661-1021, has rooms beginning at $104. **Rundle Manor Apartment Hotel,** P.O. Box 1077, 348 Marten St., tel. 762-5544 or (800) 661-1272, offers one-bedroom suites for $110, two-bedroom suites for $135, each with a full kitchen.

One of Banff's newest hotels is the **Rundlestone Lodge,** P.O. Box 489, 537 Banff Ave., tel. 762-2201 or (800) 661-8630. Its facilities include a whirlpool, sauna, and laundry, and many rooms have balconies, fireplaces, and kitchenettes. Rooms begin at $110; some are wheelchair accessible. **High Country Inn,** P.O. Box 700, 419 Banff Ave., tel. 762-2236 or (800) 661-1244, has a restaurant and pool; $115 per room.

Banff Caribou Lodge, P.O. Box 279, 521 Banff Ave., tel. 762-5887 or (800) 563-8764, opened in 1993. Its bright airy rooms go for $125 s, $140 d. The impressive log entrance is not easily missed. Close by is **Dynasty Inn,** P.O. Box 1018, at 501 Banff Ave., tel. 762-8844 or (800) 667-1464, that also opened in 1993. Each room has a log-trimmed balcony, and the facade is Rundlestone (quarried locally and named for Mt. Rundle). Rooms are $125 s, $132 d, which includes a continental breakfast.

Charlton's Evergreen Court, P.O. Box 1478, 459 Banff Ave., tel. 762-3307 or (800) 661-1379, has an outdoor pool and a limited number of kitchenettes; $125 s or d. One block north is **Charlton's Cedar Court,** P.O. Box 1478, 513 Banff Ave., tel. 762-4485 or (800) 661-1225, with an indoor pool; basic rooms are $125, loft suites with a fireplace are $140. **Traveller's Inn,** P.O. Box 1017, 401 Banff Ave., tel. 762-4401 or (800) 661-8340, has larger rooms, many with mountain views. A buffet breakfast is served for guests each morning. Rates are $130 s or d. **Best Western Siding 29 Lodge,** P.O. Box 1387, 453 Marten St., tel. 762-5575 or (800) 528-1234, is good value for small groups; rooms are $140 for up to four people.

Expensive hotels begin at $150, but between October and May it is these same lodgings that offer the deepest discounts. And you can usually receive a room upgrade for little or no extra. **Banff Ptarmigan Inn,** P.O. Box 1840, 337 Banff Ave., tel. 762-2207 or (800) 661-8310, is a full-service hotel with tastefully decorated rooms, down comforters on all beds, and mountain views. Rooms are $142 s, $152 d. **Banff International Hotel,** P.O. Box 1040, 333 Banff Ave., tel. 762-5666 or (800) 665-5666, is central to town and has high-quality rooms for $145. The much larger lofts are $165, mountain-view rooms $175. The only hotel right downtown is **Mount Royal Hotel,** P.O. Box 550, 138 Banff Ave., tel. 762-3331 or (800) 661-1528, which has a large health club and tastefully decorated rooms; $149 s or d.

One of Banff's larger hotels is **Inns of Banff Park,** P.O. Box 1077, 600 Banff Ave., tel. 762-4581 or (800) 661-1272. Each room has a mini-bar, fridge, and balcony while near the lobby is a pool, lounge, and restaurant; $150 s or d. Ask here about rooms at **Swiss Village Lodge,** part of the same complex, but less expensive. **Banff Park Lodge,** P.O. Box 2200, 222 Lynx St., tel. 762-4433 or (800) 661-9266, is a modern, full-service luxury hotel one block from Banff Avenue. Rooms begin at $185, suites with bedside jacuzzis are $240.

Banff Rocky Mountain Resort, P.O. Box 100, at the north end of Banff Ave. on the corner of Tunnel Mountain Rd., tel. 762-5531 or (800) 667-3529, is an ideal alternative for groups or families. Units are spread out across the well-manicured grounds while in the main building is a lounge, restaurant, pool, and exercise room. Tennis courts are available for guest use and cross-country ski trails are set during winter. Many of the one- and two-bedroom suites have kitchens, all have fireplaces; $170 and $210, respectively. A free shuttle runs into town from the resort each hour.

Tunnel Mountain

The four properties on Tunnel Mountain are all set on pleasant grounds and offer an alternative to the strip of hotels along Banff Avenue. Although similar in price to those on Banff Ave., all have individual chalets, making them good for families, small groups, or for those who want to cook their own meals. Town is a 15-minute

walk away, or a short ride on the **Banff Explorer** bus that runs along Tunnel Mountain Rd. twice an hour.

Douglas Fir Resort, P.O. Box 1228, tel. (403) 762-5591 or (800) 661-9267, has 133 large condo-style rooms. Each has a fully equipped kitchen and a lounge with fireplace. Facilities include an indoor pool, two water slides, a jacuzzi, weight room, squash and tennis courts, a grocery store, and laundromat. Rates begin at $120 s or d. **Hidden Ridge Chalets,** P.O. Box 519, tel. 762-3544 or (800) 661-1372, is just that, hidden. The self-contained cabins are spread among stands of Douglas fir and spruce. Each has a kitchen and fireplace; $140 per night, $160 for larger chalets on the ridge.

The first things you'll notice at **Buffalo Mountain Lodge,** P.O. Box 1326, tel. 762-2400 or (800) 661-1367, are the impressive log entrance, the hand-hewn construction of the lobby, and the huge stone fireplace. The rooms, chalets, and bungalows all have fireplaces; many have kitchens. And you won't need to go to town to eat—one of Banff's best restaurants is in the main lodge. Rooms start at $170. Across the road is **Tunnel Mountain Chalets,** P.O. Box 1137, tel. 762-4515 or (800) 661-1859. Each modern unit has a kitchenette, fireplace, and two TVs; some have a whirlpool. One-bedroom units go for $147, two-bedrooms $172.

Other Hotels

Elkhorn Lodge, P.O. Box 352, is located halfway up the hill to the Banff Springs Hotel at 124 Spray Ave., tel. (403) 762-2299. The small sleeping rooms are $75, while larger rooms with kitchens are $125. Nothing special. **Timberline Lodge,** P.O. Box 69, is located on the north side of the TransCanada Hwy. at the base of the Mystic Ridge/Norquay access road, tel. 762-2281. Standard rooms are $120-130; those on the second floor have private balconies, those on the south-facing side have excellent views. Out in back are chalets that sleep six to eight in three bedrooms. Each chalet has a kitchen and fireplace; $250 per night.

Banff Springs Hotel

This famous landmark, one of the world's great mountain resort hotels, offers 846 guest rooms in 80 different configurations. Many rooms were built in the 1920s, and as is common in older es-

Banff Springs Hotel

tablishments, many are small. But room size is only a small consideration when staying in this historic gem. With 16 eateries, a health club, pool, outdoor jacuzzi, library, 27-hole golf course, tennis courts, horseback riding, and enough twisting, turning hallways, boardwalks, towers, and shops to warrant a detailed map, you'll not be wanting to spend time in the room. Unless of course you are in the presidential suite, located in the central tower. It has eight rooms, a canopy bed, jacuzzi, baby grand piano, private pool, and your own glass elevator linking each of the three floors; $3000 per night.

For the rest of us, staying at the hotel isn't as expensive as you might think. Standard rooms begin at $100 d during the low season, $155 in high season. Those with a view are $258-325, suites begin at $376, and if you bring your pet it's $15 extra. Reserve well in advance during summer, and request "the best room available" the rest of the year. The hotel is located at the end of Spray Avenue. For reservations write to P.O. Box 960, Banff, Alberta T0L 0C0; tel. (403) 762-2211 or (800) 441-1414.

Rimrock Resort Hotel

Located on Mountain Ave. a short walk from the Upper Hot Springs is the Rimrock, P.O. Box 1110, tel. (403) 762-3356 or (800) 661-1587. The original hotel was constructed in 1903 but was fully rebuilt and opened as a 345-room full-service luxury resort in August 1993. Each well-appointed room has a king-size bed, comfortable armchair, writing desk, mini-bar, and hair dryer.

The staff is trained to pamper guests and answer all requests.

Since it's set high above the Bow Valley, views for the most part are excellent. Prices range from $210 to $260 depending solely on the views. Regular shuttle buses make the short run to town during summer.

Bow Valley Parkway

This is the original route between Banff and Lake Louise. It is a beautiful drive in all seasons and along its length are three lodges, each a viable alternative to staying in Banff. A fourth lodge is located to the west of the parkway on Hwy. 93.

Johnston Canyon Resort, P.O. Box 875, tel. (403) 762-2971, is 26 km west of Banff at the beginning of a short trail that leads to the famous canyon. The rustic cabins are older, and some have kitchenettes. On the grounds are tennis courts, a barbecue area, and restaurant. No television. Rooms start at $49 s or d, two-person cabins $58, four-person cabins $73, and chalets with a kitchen and fireplace are $84-132. It's open May-October.

Six km farther northwest is **Castle Mountain Village**, P.O. Box 1655, tel. 762-3868. Small summer cottages with kitchenettes are $55 s or d, $75 with two double beds. Log chalets that sleep four and have kitchenettes and a fireplace are $95. The newly built deluxe log chalets are one of the park's best bargains. They have high ceilings, beautifully handcrafted log interiors, three beds, stone fireplace, full kitchen with dishwasher, and a bathroom with jacuzzi; $125 for up to four people, $135 for five or six.

Six km west of Castle Mountain Junction is **Storm Mountain Lodge,** P.O. Box 670, tel. 762-4155, whose 12 original log cabins are among the nicest in the park. Each has a wood-burning fireplace, a private bathroom, cozy comforters, and antique furnishings. Only one has a kitchenette, but a restaurant is on the property. Rates are $110 s or d, extra people $10 each. The lodge is open May-September.

Baker Creek Chalets, P.O. Box 66, Lake Louise, Alberta T0L 1E0, tel. 522-3761, is the next resort along the parkway. Each of the 25 log cabins has a kitchenette, fireplace, and outside deck. Basic one-bedroom cabins are $100 for two; one-bedroom cabins with loft (sleeps six) are $125; two bedroom cabins (sleeps six) are $145 for four. Each additional person $10. The restaurant here is highly recommended.

Inexpensive Options

The Banff/Lake Louise Tourism Bureau in the Banff Visitor Centre, 224 Banff Ave., tel. (403) 762-8421, has a list of bed and breakfasts and private homes that rent rooms or cabins. Standards range from fair to good, but the prices are lower than those of the hotels. **Mrs. Cowan,** 118 Otter St., tel. 762-3696, has very sparsely furnished rooms for $25 s, $30 d, $45 s or d with a private bathroom. Continental breakfast is served in your room. Ask Mrs. Cowan about her emergency room for $10 per night—which also includes breakfast in bed. **Mr. and Mrs. Harnack** live at 338 Banff Ave., tel. 762-3619, and have two rooms, $26-31, with shared bathrooms and use of a kitchenette.

Blue Mountain Lodge, 137 Muskrat St., tel. 762-5134, has rooms for $55 and small cabins from $70. All guests have use of shared kitchen facilities. Better value is **Beaver St. Suites and Cabins,** 220 Beaver St., tel. 762-5077, with rooms beginning at $60 and cabins at $70. **Banff Mountain Academy Inn,** 121 Cave Ave., tel. 762-4101, is lived in for most of the year by skiers attending this respected academy. During July and August rooms are available from $50 s, $85 d; some have private bathrooms. Rates include a full breakfast and use of the lounge and library.

Hostels

Banff International Hostel, P.O. Box 1358, tel. (403) 762-4122 or (800) 363-0096, is located just off Tunnel Mountain Rd. three km from downtown. This large, modern hostel sleeps 154 in small two-, four-, and six-bed dormitory rooms. The large lounge area has a fireplace, and other facilities include a recreation room, bike and ski workshop, large kitchen, self-service cafe, and laundry. Members of Hostelling International pay $16 per night, nonmembers $21. During July and August reserve at least a month in advance to be assured of a bed. The hostel is open all day. To get there from town ride the **Banff Explorer** ($1), which passes the hostel twice an hour during summer. The rest of the year the only transportation is by cab, about $5 from the bus depot. Thirty-two km along the Bow Valley Parkway is **Castle Mountain Hostel,** near a number of interesting hikes. This hostel sleeps 36 and has a kitchen, common room, hot showers, and bike rentals; members $10, nonmembers $15. Make reservations through the Banff Hostel.

The **YWCA,** 102 Spray Ave., tel. 762-3560, is convenient to town, but rooms are fairly barren. Bunk beds in the dormitory are $17 per person, and you'll need a sleeping bag. Private rooms begin at $47 s or d, $49-51 with private bathroom, and $53-65 for family rooms (sleeps four to six). Between October and May all prices (except bunk bed) are reduced by $12 and everyone is treated to a full breakfast. Other facilities include kitchen, cafe, and laundry.

Backcountry Huts And Lodges

In the backcountry of the national park are two distinct types of accommodations—rustic mountain huts and lodges. Each of the often historic huts has a stove, lantern, kitchen utensils, and foam mattresses. The extensive system of huts is managed by the Alpine Club of Canada. For locations and reservations, write to P.O. Box 2040, Canmore, Alberta T0L 0M0; tel. (403) 678-3200. No huts are located in the southern end of the park.

Shadow Lake Lodge and Cabins (Brewster Rocky Mountain Adventures, P.O. Box 964, Banff, Alberta T0L 0C0; tel. 762-5454) is located 13 km from the nearest road. Access is on foot, or in winter on skis. The lodge is located near a picturesque lake of the same name, and many hiking trails are nearby. The oldest structure here has been restored as a dining area. Guests sleep in newer, more cozy cabins. All meals and afternoon tea are included in the rate of $95 per person per day. The trailhead is along the TransCanada Hwy., 19 km from Banff, at the Redearth Creek parking area.

Campgrounds

Although Banff has seven campgrounds with well over 1,000 sites in its immediate vicinity, all fill by early afternoon. Closest to town are **Tunnel Mountain Village II** and **Tunnel Mountain Trailer Court,** 3.5 km along Tunnel Mountain Road. The former has electrical hookups, and is the only campground in the park open year-round. The latter has full hookups. Both have hot showers but little privacy between sites. Sites are $15.50-17.50 and no tents are allowed. Less than one km farther along the road is **Tunnel Mountain Village I,** which has hot showers, private sites, firewood, and kitchen shelters, but no hookups. Sites are $13. Toward Lake Minnewanka northeast of town is **Two Jack Lakeside,** which has pit toilets, firewood, and lots of trees; $13 per night. In the same vicinity is **Two Jack Main,** open only Fri.-Sun. nights. Along Bow Valley Parkway you'll find **Johnston Canyon Campground, Castle Mountain Campground,** and **Protection Mountain Campground.** Generally these don't open until June, and fill up later than those in Banff; $10.50-13 per night.

FOOD

Banff has over 100 restaurants. That's more per capita than any town or city across Canada. From lobster to linguini, alligator to à la carte, and fajitas to fudge—anyone who spends time in the park will find something that suits his or her taste and budget, although not necessarily at the same place. Many have been around for decades and attract diners from as far away as Calgary (some of whom have been known to stay overnight just to eat at their favorite haunt). An eclectic mix of restaurants lines Banff Avenue—most have menus posted out front. The less adventurous can try one of the eateries at the major hotels. The Banff Springs Hotel tops the list with a choice of 16. In July and August the most popular restaurants don't take reservations and you can expect a wait at most spots. Various dining guides are available throughout town. Some, such as the Banff/Lake Louise Tourism Bureau's *Food For Thought,* list them all, while others only list those who pay.

Budget Stretchers

The best place to begin looking for cheap eats is the Food Court in the lower level of Cascade Plaza at 317 Banff Avenue. Here you'll find two bakeries and **Edo Japan,** which sells simple Japanese dishes for around $5 including a drink. A local bylaw prohibiting obtrusive signs and neon lights means that the fast food chains are easily missed. For the most expensive Big Macs this side of the Toronto Skydome, **McDonald's** is at 116 Banff Avenue. **Kentucky Fried Chicken** is at 202 Caribou St., and **Harvey's** is at 304 Caribou Street. **Smitty's,** 227 Banff Ave., tel. (403) 762-2533, is a popular breakfast spot and has many steak and chicken dishes for under $10.

Coffee Shops

The **Cake Company,** 220 Bear St., tel. (403) 762-2330, serves great coffee, as well as a delicious range of pastries, muffins, and cakes baked daily on the premises. Another Cake Company outlet is on the lower level of Cascade Plaza; look for the scrumptious $2 muffin-and-coffee deal before 11 a.m. **Evelyn's,** on Banff Ave. in the Town Centre Mall, has good coffee and huge sandwiches, and is a super place for socializing and people-watching. **Jump Start,** 206 Buffalo St., 762-0332, has a wide range of coffee concoctions as well as delicious homemade soups ($3).

Canadian

A town favorite that has faithfully served locals for many years is **Melissa's,** 218 Lynx St., tel. (403) 762-5511, housed in a log building that dates from 1928 (the original Homestead Inn). For breakfast the hotcakes piled high on your plate ($4) can't be beat. Or try the bran muffins made from scratch each morning. Lunch and dinner are casual affairs—choose from a wide variety of generously sized burgers, freshly prepared salads, and mouthwatering Alberta beef. Melissa's also features an outside patio and rustic bar with well-priced drinks. Open daily 7 a.m.-10 p.m.

Even though **Bumper's,** 603 Banff Ave., tel. 762-2622, is away from the center of Banff, it remains one of the town's busiest restaurants. And not just in summer; locals and visitors alike flock to this popular steak house year-round. Large cuts of Alberta beef, efficient service, and great prices keep people coming back. Favorite choices are the prime rib Pile-o-bones, Barbecue Beef Ribs, and of course slabs of juicy beef cooked to your taste. Main entrees are $10-18 and include a fresh salad bar. A 15% discount is offered to those seated before 5:30 p.m. Upstairs is the **Loft Lounge,** a good place to wait for a table or relax afterwards with an inexpensive drink. It's open 4:30-10 p.m.

Closer to town in the Banff Caribou Lodge is **The Keg,** 521 Banff Ave., tel. 762-4442, part of a western-Canadian chain noted for its consistently good steak, seafood, and chicken dishes at reasonable prices. All entrees include a 60-item salad bar. An all-you-can-eat buffet ($8.99) is served at breakfast and lunch. The Keg is open daily 7 a.m.-2 a.m. The familiar **Earl's,** upstairs at 229 Banff Ave., tel. 762-4414, has more of the same at slightly higher prices (but the usual parrot mascot out front is nowhere to be found). Another inexpensive choice is **Mc-Cardell & McCabe Old Time Restaurant** in Sundance Mall, 215 Banff Ave., tel. 762-3869, where good-value, home-cooked meals begin at $3 for breakfast and $5-10 the rest of the day. It's open from 7 a.m.

If you are staying in the hostel or at Tunnel Mountain campgrounds, the restaurant in **Buffalo Mountain Lodge** on Tunnel Mountain Rd., tel. 762-2400, is well worth trying. The distinctive interior of hand-hewn cedar beams and Old World elegance is the perfect setting for a moderate splurge. Expect to pay around $20 per person for soup, an entree, and dessert. Breakfast is also good. It's open daily 7 a.m.-11 p.m. One of Banff's only bistro-style restaurants is **Coyote's Deli and Grill,** 206 Caribou St., tel. 762-3963. Meals are prepared in full view of diners, and the menu emphasizes the health conscious—broiled chicken, vegetarian lasagne, and tempting desserts are favorites. Entrees are $9-18. Coyote's is open daily 8 a.m.-10 p.m.

The romantic era of the railway is relived in **The Caboose,** located in the old C.P.R. station at the corner of Elk and Lynx streets, tel. 762-3622. Although not the original station, kings, queens, and millions of other visitors have passed through the building. The walls are lined with railway memorabilia, and the elegant atmosphere makes for a memorable dining experience. Seafood and steak dominate the menu; expect to pay $12-25 for entrees and around $5 for dessert. All meals include the self-service salad cart which is wheeled to your table. The Caboose is open daily 5-10 p.m.

Mexican And Cajun

The **Magpie & Stump,** 203 Caribou St., tel. (403) 762-4067, serves no-frills authentic Mexican food at reasonable prices. It's open 11 a.m.-midnight. **The Yard,** 137 Banff Ave., tel. 762-5678, is a third-floor restaurant with clear views down Banff Ave. and out to Cascade Mountain. Beef and seafood dishes, including delicious New Orleans blackened fish, are cooked Cajun-style ($12-15). It's open daily 11 a.m.-11 p.m.

Italian

Banff is blessed with a number of fine Italian restaurants. **Guido's,** 116 Banff Ave., tel. (403) 762-4002, is known for its homemade pasta, which is cooked to perfection in a variety of sauces that appeal to all tastes and diets. Entrees are $8-17. It's open daily from 5 p.m. More trendy (reflected in the prices) is **Giorgio's,** 219 Banff Ave., tel. 762-5114, which was fully remodeled in 1994 with stylish decor. Its five fully trained chefs prepare as many as 400 meals each afternoon, and the lineup for tables is ever-present. Pasta dishes begin at $10. It's open from 4:30 p.m.

Greek

The **Balkan,** 120 Banff Ave., tel. (403) 762-3454, is run by Greeks, but the menu blends their heritage with the cuisines of Italy, China, and Canada. Select from Greek ribs (pork ribs with a lemon sauce) for $13.95, the Greek chow mein (stir-fried vegetables, fried rice, and your choice of meat) for $9, or Greek spaghetti for $8. But the most popular dishes are souvlakia ($10.95) and an enormous Greek platter that includes a leg of lamb ($32 for two). The Balkan is open daily 11 a.m.-11 p.m.

Swiss-Italian

Ticino, 205 Wolf St., tel. (403) 762-3848, is named for the southern province of Switzerland, where the cuisine has a distinctive Italian influence. The Swiss chef is best known for his beef and cheese fondues, veal dishes, and juicy steaks. Expect to pay around $6 for appetizers and from $10 for entrees; open daily 5-11 p.m.

Japanese

The large number of Japanese visitors in Banff has created the need for good Japanese restaurants. **Shiki Japanese Noodles** in Clock Tower Mall, 110 Banff Ave., tel. (403) 762-0527, has a choice of *donburi,* various meat cakes, teriyaki, and sushi. Dishes are $5-10 each. It's open daily 11 a.m.-9 p.m. A bit more expensive is **Suginoya,** 225 Banff Ave., tel. 762-4773, which has a relaxed atmosphere. Choose from the sushi bar, *ozashiki* booths, or regular tables. Traditional *shabu-shabu* and seafood teriyaki are popular. The number of Japanese diners here is indicative of the quality. Expect to pay at least $10 for entrees, $18-21 for one of the combination dinners. Suginoya is open daily 11 a.m.-10:30 p.m.

French

Le Beaujolais, 212 Buffalo St., tel. (403) 762-2712, is a Canadian leader in French cuisine and has been one of Banff's most popular fine-dining restaurants for over a decade. Its second-floor location ensures great views of Banff, especially from window tables. The dishes feature mainly Canadian ingredients, prepared and served with a French flair. Entrees begin at $18, but the extent of your final tab depends on whether you choose à la carte items, the three-course table d'hôte menu ($34-37.50), or the six-course chef's surprise ($55)—and also on how much wine you consume (at $20-250 a bottle). The restaurant is open daily from 6 p.m.; reservations are necessary.

The Grizzly House

This unique fondue restaurant at 207 Banff Ave., tel. (403) 762-4055, provides Banff's most unusual dining experience. The decor is, to say the least, eclectic (or should that be eccentric). Each table has a phone for across-table conversation, or you can call your waiter, the bar, a

cab, diners in the private booth, or even those who spend too long in the bathroom. Through all this the food is good and the service professional. Although traditional Swiss fondues are on the menu, the buffalo, seafood, oriental, rattlesnake, and alligator are the most popular. Of course it wouldn't be right to leave without having a chocolate fondue dipped with fresh fruit. Individual fondues are $17-25 (lunch a little cheaper), complete three-course dinners start at $35. Open 11:30 a.m.-midnight.

Baker Creek Bistro

Along the Bow Valley Parkway, towards Lake Louise, are the Baker Creek Chalets. The intimate restaurant here, housed in a log building, is definitely worth the drive from Banff. Next to the restaurant is a rustic lounge and large outdoor patio. The bistro is open in summer, daily 7 a.m.-10 p.m., shorter hours the rest of the year; tel. (403) 522-2182.

Banff Springs Hotel

Whether guests or not, most visitors to Banff drop by to see one of the town's biggest tourist attractions. And a meal here might not be as expensive as you think. The hotel itself has more eateries than in most small towns—from a 24-hour deli serving pizza to the finest of fine dining.

Koffie Haus Restaurant is open all day serving reliable and reasonably priced meals; **Red Terrace** features outdoor summer barbecues; **Samurai Restaurant** fills every night with Japanese guests; **Clubhouse** on the golf course serves light breakfasts, lunch, and formal dinners; **Grapes** is a small wine bar noted for its fine cheeses and pâtés; **Henry VIII Pub** serves simple meals and delicious cappuccinos with panoramic views of the Bow River; **Pavilion Restaurant** serves pasta at good prices; **Alhambra Room** is a spanish-style restaurant serving continental dishes; and the **Waldhaus** serves German specialties. The **Alberta Room** is the place to enjoy a breakfast buffet in Banff. The huge spread is $10.50 per person and definitely worth the splurge. But the most acclaimed restaurant at the hotel is the **Rob Roy Room,** named for a Scottish outlaw. This fine-dining restaurant is renowned for its excellently prepared Alberta beef (over 1,000 portions of beef are served in the hotel each day). Try the beef strip loin for two, broiled to order then carved at your table. Many lighter dishes such as chicken and seafood ($15-28) are also offered. It's open daily 6-10 p.m. For reservations call (403) 662-6860, or after 5 p.m., call 762-2211. During the summer months a desk to the left of the main lobby has all menus posted and takes reservations for the hotel restaurants.

NIGHTLIFE

Like resort towns around the world, Banff has more than its fair share of bars and nightclubs. **Wild Bill's Legendary Saloon,** upstairs at 201 Banff Ave., tel. (403) 762-0333, is named for Banff guide Bill Peyto, and is truly legendary. Music is mostly country, but bands usually play a bit of everything. The food here is excellent. Just as popular is the **Barbary Coast,** 119 Banff Ave., tel. 762-4616, which also serves good food and occasionally has live music in a clean, casual atmosphere. Across the road is the **Rose and Crown,** 202 Banff Ave., tel. 762-2121, an English-style pub serving British beers. Below the Mt. Royal Hotel is the **Buffalo Paddock,** 138 Banff Ave., tel. 762-3331, with pool tables. **Silver City,** 110 Banff Ave., tel. 762-3337, has cheap drinks and a disco open till 2 a.m. every night. **Eddy's Back Alley,** 137 Banff Ave., tel. 762-8434, also has a disco. The lounge in the **Voyager Inn,** 555 Banff Ave., tel. 762-3301, has drink specials every night. Just past the Voyager Inn is **Bumpers,** with a small bar and pool table upstairs.

Police patrol Banff all night, promptly arresting anyone who even looks like trouble, including anyone drunk or drinking on the streets.

SHOPPING

It may seem a little strange, but city folk from Calgary actually drive into Banff National Park to shop for clothes. This reflects the number of clothing shops in Banff rather than a lack of choice in one of Canada's largest cities. About the only clothing store that Banff lacks is an army-surplus outlet.

One of the best places to shop for outdoor apparel is **Outdoor Access** at 201 Banff Ave.; downstairs is a factory outlet with big savings. Other recommended stores are **Monod Sports** at 129 Banff Ave., and **Helly Hansen,** in the back of the Kirby Lane Mall at 119 Banff Avenue. Pick up your Canadian-made Tilley Hat and other Tilley Endurables from **Piccatilley Square** on the main floor of the Cascade Plaza at 317 Banff Avenue. The **Rude Boys Ski, Skate, and Shred Shop,** down an alley at 204 Caribou St., is, well, rude. Take a look—their T-shirts are hilarious (and unlike anything on Banff Ave., original), but don't expect to find anything for your grandparents here.

Camping equipment and supplies can be found in **Home Hardware** at 208 Bear St. and **The Hudson's Bay Company** at 125 Banff Ave. (downstairs). More specialized needs are catered to at **Mountain Magic Equipment** located at 224 Bear St., tel. (403) 762-2591. They have a large range of top-quality outdoor and survival gear (including climbing equipment), and they rent tents ($15 per day), sleeping bags ($8), backpacks ($7.50), and boots ($7). The largest mountain-bike shop in Banff is **Park 'N Pedal,** which has a sales outlet at 229 Wolf St., tel. 762-3190, and a service and rental branch at 226 Bear St., tel. 762-3191. Mountain Magic Equipment also sells and repairs all types of bikes.

TRANSPORTATION

Getting There

Banff has no airport and no scheduled rail service. The closest airport is an hour and a half away in Calgary. **Brewster Transportation and Tours,** tel. (403) 762-6700, operates an airporter service that leaves Calgary International Airport daily at 12:30 p.m. (summer only), 3 p.m., and 7:45 p.m.; $26 each way. This service terminates in Banff at the large **Brewster Transportation Depot** located at 100 Gopher Street. Buses leave at 8:05 a.m., noon, and 7 p.m. (summer only) for Calgary International Airport. The depot has a ticket office, lockers, cafe, and gift shop. It is open daily 7:30 a.m.-10:45 p.m. From Jasper, Brewster has an express service departing the terminal on Connaught Dr. daily at 1:30 p.m.; $37 one way. A longer alternative is the nine-hour Jasper-to-Banff tour, which stops at the Columbia Icefield and Lake Louise; $59.50 one way, $83 round trip. In spring and fall the fare is $46 one way, $59.50 round trip. No bus service runs between Banff and Jasper in winter.

Greyhound, tel. 762-6767 or (800) 661-8747, offers scheduled service from the Calgary bus depot at 877 Greyhound Way SW, five times daily to the Brewster Transportation Depot; $14.28 one way. Greyhound buses also leave Vancouver from the depot at 1150 Station St., tel. (604) 662-3222, three times daily for the scenic 14-hour ride to Banff; $92.50 one way.

From Calgary International Hostel **Pika Shuttle Co.** runs a van service to Banff International Hostel on Tunnel Mountain Rd., continuing to other hostels in the park. Fare is $15 one way. From Whistlers Hostel in Jasper the fare to Banff is $34, from Lake Louise $7. Bicycles are extra. To ride this shuttle you *must* have reservations at your destination hostel. For information and reservations call (800) 363-0096.

Getting Around
Most of the sights and many trailheads are within walking distance of town. The **Banff Explorer** is a transit service operated by the Town of Banff. Two routes are served, one from the Banff Springs Hotel to the RV and trailer drop-off at the far end of Banff Ave., the other from the Luxton Museum to the hostel and Tunnel Mountain campgrounds. Buses run June-Sept., twice an hour between 8 a.m. and 9 p.m. Fare is $1.25 (a 12-ticket book is available for $10).

Cabs around town are reasonably priced—flag drop is $2.30, then it's $1.25 per kilometer. From the bus depot to the hostel will run around $5, same to the Banff Springs Hotel, more after midnight. Companies are: **Alpine Taxi & Tours,** tel. (403) 762-3727; **Banff Taxi,** tel. 762-4444; **Taxi Taxi,** tel. 762-3111; and **Mountain Taxi,** tel. 762-3351.

THE BREWSTER BOYS

WHYTE MUSEUM OF THE CANADIAN ROCKIES

Few guides in Banff were as well known as Jim and Bill (pictured) Brewster. In 1892, aged 10 and 12, respectively, they were hired by the Banff Springs Hotel to take guests to local landmarks. As their reputation as guides grew, they built a thriving business enterprise. By 1900, they had their own livery and outfitting company, and soon expanded operations to Lake Louise. Other early business interests included a trading post, the original Mt. Royal Hotel, the first ski lodge in the Sunshine Meadows, and the hotel at the Columbia Icefield.

Today, a legacy of the boys' savvy, **Brewster Transportation and Tours,** has grown to become an integral part of many tourists' stays. The company operates some of the world's most advanced sightseeing vehicles, including a fleet of Snocoaches on Athabasca Glacier.

The days when a row of horse-drawn buggies eagerly awaited the arrival of wealthy visitors at the C.P.R. Station have long since passed, but the era is relived by the **Trail Rider Store,** 132 Banff Ave., tel. 762-4551, offering visitors rides around town in a beautifully restored carriage ($5 for 15 minutes). Expect to pay around $8 from downtown to the Banff Springs Hotel.

Banff Rent-A-Car, 230 Lynx St., tel. 762-3352, rents used cars for $50 per day with 100 free kilometers. Other agencies are **Avis** in the Cascade Plaza, tel. 762-3222 or (800) 879-2847; **Hertz** in the Banff Springs Hotel, tel. 762-2027 or (800) 263-0600; **Sears** at 204 Wolf St., tel. 762-4575; and **Tilden** at the corner of Lynx and Caribou streets, tel. 762-2688 or (800) 387-4747. Reservations for cars in Banff should be made well in advance.

Disabled Persons

The **Banff Visitor Centre** is wheelchair accessible—its washrooms, information desks, and theater are all barrier free. Once inside, use the handy Touchsource monitor for a full listing of all barrier-free services within the park. An all-terrain wheelchair is available at the Cave and Basin Centennial Centre for use on park trails. To reserve call (403) 762-1557.

Tours

Brewster Transportation and Tours, tel. (403) 762-6700, offers a three-hour Discover Banff bus tour that takes in downtown Banff, Tunnel Mountain Dr., the hoodoos, the Cave and Basin, and Sulphur Mountain Gondola (gondola fare not included). This tour runs in summer only and departs from the bus depot daily at 8:30 a.m.; call for hotel pick-up times. Adult fare is $29.50, children half price. The rest of the year this tour runs five hours and includes a trip to Lake Louise with time for lunch at the chateau; $33.50, lunch extra. During summer other tours available are: Sulphur Mountain Gondola, $16 (includes gondola ride); Lake Minnewanka, $35 (includes two-hour boat cruise); and helicopter sightseeing from Canmore, $80.25 (includes transfers).

SERVICES

The **post office** is located on the corner of Buffalo and Bear streets opposite Central Park; open Mon.-Fri. 9 a.m.-5:30 p.m. The general-delivery service here is probably among the busiest in the country, with the thousands of seasonal workers in the area, no home mail-delivery service, and a two-year wait for a post box. Address all mail to General Delivery, Banff, Alberta T0L 0C0. For all other postal services try the small and friendly full-service postal outlet in **Cascade Plaza Drug,** located in the Cascade Plaza at 317 Banff Avenue.

Major banks can be found along Banff Ave. and are generally open 9 a.m.-4 p.m. The **Bank of Montreal,** 107 Banff Ave., allows cash advances with MasterCard, while the **C.I.B.C.,** 98 Banff Ave., accepts Visa. The **Bank of America Canada Foreign Currency Service** is located at 124 Banff Ave., tel. (403) 762-4698. Other currency exchanges are located in the Clock Tower Mall at 108 Banff Ave., Cascade Plaza at 317 Banff Ave., and the Banff Springs Hotel.

Downtown laundromats are **Johnny O's Emporium,** at 223 Bear St., open Mon.-Sat. 8 a.m.-11 p.m., Sunday 10 a.m.-10 p.m., and **Cascade Coin Laundry,** on the lower level of the Cascade Plaza, open daily 7:30 a.m.-10 p.m. Located on Tunnel Mountain Rd. at the Douglas Fir Resort, and within walking distance of the hostel, is **Chalet Coin Laundry;** open daily 8 a.m.-10 p.m. **Brewster Travel,** at 130 Banff Ave., can organize travel arrangements anywhere in the world; tel. 762-3207. Along Banff Ave. are a handful of one-hour film labs; check around for the cheapest as many have special offers. The most competitive and reliable is **Miles High Image Center** at 119 Banff Ave. (beneath the Barbary Coast), tel. 762-5221. Drop slide film here on Wednesday and it will be ready for pick-up Friday morning. Get photographic supplies from **Wolf Street Cameras** in the Cascade Plaza.

Mineral Springs Hospital is at 301 Lynx St., tel. 762-2222. **Cascade Plaza Drug** on the lower level of the Cascade Plaza at 317 Banff Ave. is open till 9 p.m., as is **Harmony Drug** at 111 Banff Avenue. (Harmony Drug was once owned by noted Banff photographer Byron Harmon, whose prints, dating from around 1915, adorn the walls and adjacent mall.) **Gourlay's Pharmacy** at 229 Bear St. is open till 8 p.m. For the **RCMP** call 762-2226.

INFORMATION

Banff Public Library
Banff's library is located opposite Central Park at 101 Bear St., tel. (403) 762-2661. The extensive collection of nonfiction books, many about the park and its environs, makes it an excellent rainy-day hangout. They also have a large collection of magazines and newspapers. It's open Mon.-Sat. 11 a.m.-6 p.m. (till 9 p.m. on Tuesday and Thursday), and Sunday 1-5 p.m.

Books And Bookstores
The Rockies are one of the most written about, and definitely the most photographed, regions in Canada. As a walk along Banff Ave. will confirm, there is definitely no lack of postcards, calendars, and books. For general reading, the guides and coffee-table books produced by **Altitude Publishing** in Canmore are the best. Look for them in all Banff bookstores. Ben Gadd's *Handbook of the Canadian Rockies* is the best all-around source of information for those interested in the geology, climate, ecology, flora, and fauna of the Canadian Rockies.

Banff Book & Art Den, in the Clock Tower Mall at 110 Banff Ave., has a large collection of park literature, wilderness guides, coffee-table books, travel guides, and relevant topographical maps for backcountry trips within the park. Open in summer, daily 10 a.m.-9 p.m., till 7 p.m. rest of the year; tel. (403) 762-3919.

Look for the *Crag and Canyon* (75 cents) each Wednesday. It's been keeping Banff residents and visitors informed about park issues and town gossip for over 90 years.

Banff Visitor Centre
This large complex, at 224 Banff Ave., houses information desks for **Parks Canada** and the **Banff/Lake Louise Tourism Bureau.** The national park staff will answer all of your queries and questions regarding Banff's natural wonders and advise of trail closures. Anyone planning an overnight backcountry trip should register here and obtain a permit (free). The brochure *Banff and Vicinity Drives and Walks* is a compact guide to things to see and do around Banff. At the back of the center is a free slide show, videos, updated trail reports, and copies of the best hiking books. Across the floor is the tourism bureau, tel. (403) 762-8421, which represents businesses and commercial establishments in the park. Here you can find out about accommodations, restaurants, and have any other questions answered. To answer the most often asked question, the washrooms are downstairs. The center is open July-Aug., daily 8 a.m.-8 p.m.; June and September, daily 8 a.m.-6 p.m.; the rest of the year, daily 9 a.m.-5 p.m. For more information on the park write to: The Superintendent, Banff National Park, P.O. Box 900, Banff, Alberta T0L 0C0; tel. 762-1550. For general tourism information write to: Banff/Lake Louise Tourism Bureau, P.O. Box 1298, Banff, Alberta T0L 0C0. The **Warden's Office** is located in the industrial park, tel. 762-1470 or 762-4506.

The **weather office** is located on Bear St. opposite the library. Updated forecasts are posted daily or call 762-2088 for a 24-hour prerecorded message. A full weather synopsis is available by calling 762-3091. Tune into Channel 10 on the television for park information.

WHYTE MUSEUM OF THE CANADIAN ROCKIES

LAKE LOUISE

As the first flush of morning sun hits Victoria Glacier, and the impossibly steep northern face of Mt. Victoria is reflected in the sparkling emerald green waters of Lake Louise, you'll understand why this lake is regarded as one of the world's seven natural wonders. Overlooking the lake is one of the world's most photographed hotels, **Chateau Lake Louise.** Apart from staring, photographing, and videoing, the area has plenty to keep you busy. Some of the park's best hiking, canoeing, and horseback riding is nearby. And only a short distance away is **Moraine Lake,** not as famous as Lake Louise but rivaling it in beauty.

Lake Louise is located 51 km northwest of Banff along the TransCanada Hwy., or a little bit farther if you take the quieter Bow Valley Parkway. The hamlet of Lake Louise, comprised of a small mall, hotels, and restaurants, is located in the Bow Valley, just west of the TransCanada Highway. The lake itself is 200 vertical meters above the valley floor, along a winding four-km road. Across the valley is Canada's largest ski area, **Lake Louise,** a world-class facility renowned for its diverse terrain, abundant snow, and breathtaking views.

From Lake Louise the TransCanada Hwy. continues west, exiting the park over **Kicking Horse Pass** (1,647 meters) and passing through Yoho National Park to Golden. Highway 93, the famous **Icefields Parkway,** also begins at the townsite and heads northwest through the park's northern reaches to Jasper National Park.

History

During the summer of 1882, Tom Wilson, an outfitter, was camped near the confluence of the Bow and Pipestone rivers when he heard the distant rumblings of an avalanche. He questioned Stoney Indian guides and was told the noises originated from "Lake of Little Fishes." The following day Wilson, led by a native guide, hiked to the lake to investigate. He became the first white man to lay eyes on what he named Emerald Lake. Two years later the name was changed to Lake Louise, honoring Princess Louise Caroline Alberta, daughter of Queen Victoria.

A railway station known as Laggan was built where the rail line passed closest to the lake, six km away. Until a road was completed in 1926, everyone arrived by train. The station's name was changed to Lake Louise in 1913 to prevent confusion among visitors. In 1890 a modest two-bedroom wooden hotel replaced a crude cabin that had been built on the shore of the lake as word of its beauty spread. After many additions, a disastrous fire, and the addition of a concrete wing in 1925, the chateau of today took shape. A 51-square-mile reserve was set aside around the lake and this was incorporated as part of Rocky Mountains Park in 1902.

Recreational mountaineering has been popular in the park for over 100 years and most of the early climbing was done on peaks around Lake Louise. In 1893 Walter Wilcox and Samuel Allen, two Yale schoolmates, spent the summer climbing in the area, making two unsuccessful attempts to reach the north peak of Mt. Victoria. The following summer they made first ascents of Mt. Temple and Mt. Aberdeen, extraordinary achievements considering their lack of experience and proper equipment.

During the summer of 1896, P.S. Abbot slipped and plunged to his death attempting to climb Mt. Lefroy. In doing so he became North America's first mountaineering fatality. Following this incident, Swiss mountain guides were employed by the C.P.R. to satisfy the climbing needs of wealthy patrons of the railway and make the sport safer. During the period of their employment, successful climbs were made of Mt. Victoria, Mt. Lefroy, and Mt. Balfour.

SIGHTS AND RECREATION

Lake Louise

In summer, around 10,000 visitors a day make the journey from the Bow Valley floor up to Lake Louise. By noon the tiered parking lot is often full. An alternative to the road is one of two trails that begin at the townsite and end at the public parking lot (see "Hiking," below). From here a number of paved trails lead to the lake's eastern shore. From these vantage points the dramatic

© MOON PUBLICATIONS, INC.

setting can be fully appreciated. The lake is 2.4 km long, 500 meters wide, and up to 90 meters deep. Its cold waters reach a maximum temperature of 4° C in August.

Chateau Lake Louise is a tourist attraction in itself. Built by the C.P.R. to take the pressure off the popular Banff Springs Hotel, the chateau has seen many changes in the last 100 years and remains one of the world's great mountain resorts. No one minds the hordes of camera-toting tourists who traipse through each day—and there's really no way to avoid them. The immaculately manicured gardens between the chateau and the lake make an interesting foreground for the millions of Lake Louise photographs taken each year.

The snow-covered peak at the back of the lake is **Mt. Victoria** (3,459 meters), which sits on the Continental Divide. Amazingly, its base is over 10 km from the eastern end of the lake. Mount Victoria, first climbed in 1897, remains one of the park's most popular peaks for mountaineers. Although the difficult northeast face (facing the chateau), was first successfully ascended in 1922, the most popular and easiest route to the summit is along the southeast ridge, approached from Abbot Pass.

Take to the water for a different perspective of Moraine Lake.

Moraine Lake

Although less than half the size of Lake Louise, Moraine Lake is just as spectacular and worthy of just as much film. It is located up a winding road 12.5 km off Lake Louise Drive. Its rugged setting, nestled in the Valley of the Ten Peaks among the towering mountains of the main ranges, has provided inspiration for millions of people from around the world since Walter Wilcox became the first white man to reach its shore in 1899. Wilcox's subsequent writings, such as "no scene has given me an equal impression of inspiring solitude and rugged grandeur . . ." guaranteed its future popularity. Although Wilcox was a knowledgeable man, he named the lake on the assumption that it was dammed by a glacial moraine deposited by the retreating Wenkchemna Glacier. In fact, the large rockpile that blocks its waters was deposited by major rockfalls from the Tower of Babel to the south. The lake often remains frozen until June and the access road is closed all winter.

Lake Louise Summer Sightseeing Lift

During summer the Friendly Giant quad chairlift at Lake Louise Ski Area whisks visitors up the face of Mt. Whitehorn to Whitehorn Lodge, at an altitude of over two kilometers above sea level. The view from the lodge—of the Bow Valley, Lake Louise, and the Continental Divide—is among the most spectacular in the Canadian Rockies. Short trails lead through the forests, across open meadows, and, for the energetic, to the summit of Mt. Whitehorn over 600 vertical meters above. After working up an appetite head to the teahouse in the Whitehorn Lodge or try the outdoor barbecue. The lift operates July-Aug., daily 8:30 a.m.-7 p.m., shorter hours June and September; adults $8, seniors $7, children over five $4. An alternative is the Hiker's Special, a one-way ticket (uphill) for $5, requiring you to return the two km to the base lodge on foot. For more information call (403) 522-3555. Free shuttles run from Lake Louise accommodations to the lift.

Horseback Riding
Brewster Lake Louise Stables, tel. (403) 522-3511, has hour-long rides (departing on the hour) for $20, rides to the end of Lake Louise for $28, half-day rides for $40, and all-day rides for $80.

HIKING

The variety of hiking opportunities in the vicinity of Lake Louise and Moraine Lake is surely equal to any area on the face of the earth. The region's potential for outdoor recreation was first realized in the late 1800s and it soon became the center of hiking activity in the Canadian Rockies. This popularity continues today; trails here are among the most heavily used in the park. Hiking is best early or late in the short summer season. Head out early in the morning to miss the prams, high heels, dogs, and bear-bells that you'll surely encounter during the busiest periods.

The two main trailheads are Chateau Lake Louise and Moraine Lake. Two trails lead from the village to the chateau; a pleasant alternative to driving the steep and very busy Lake Louise Drive. Shortest is the 2.7 km **Louise Creek Trail.** It begins on the downstream side of the point where Lake Louise Dr. crosses the Bow River, crosses Louise Creek three times, and ends at the Lake Louise parking lot. The other, **Tramline,** is 4.5 km—longer but not as steep. It begins behind the railway station and follows the route of a narrow-gauge railway that once transported guests from the C.P.R. line to Chateau Lake Louise.

Bow River Loop
- Length: 7 km (1.5-2 hours)
- Elevation gain: minimal
- Rating: easy

This loop follows both banks of the Bow River southeast from the railway station. It links the station to the hostel, Post Hotel, Samson Mall, both campgrounds, and the Louise Creek and Tramline trails to Lake Louise. Interpretive signs along its length explain the ecosystem of the Bow River. It's used by joggers and cyclists to access various points in the village.

Louise Lakeshore
- Length: 2 km (30 minutes) one way
- Elevation gain: none
- Rating: easy

Probably the park's busiest trail, it follows the north shore of Lake Louise, beginning in front of the chateau and ending at the west end of the lake. Numerous braided glacial streams here empty their silt-filled waters into Lake Louise. Along its length are benches to sit and ponder what English mountaineer James Outram once described as "a gem of composition and of coloring, it is perhaps unrivalled anywhere."

Chateau Lake Louise

Plain Of The Six Glaciers

- Length: 5.3 km (90 minutes) one way
- Elevation gain: 370 meters
- Rating: easy/moderate

Hikers along this trail are not only rewarded with panoramic views of the glaciated peaks of the main range but at the end of the trail is a rustic teahouse serving homemade goodies baked on a wooden stove. For the first two km the trail follows Louise Lakeshore Trail to the western end of the lake from where it begins a steady uphill climb through a forest of spruce and alpine fir. It enters an open area where an avalanche has come tumbling down (now a colorful carpet of wildflowers), then passes through a forested area into a vast wasteland of moraines produced by the advance and retreat of Victoria Glacier. Views of surrounding peaks continue to improve until the trail switchbacks through a stunted forest before arriving at the teahouse. Built by the C.P.R. at the turn of the century, the teahouse operates as it has since it was first built. Supplies are packed in by horse and all cooking is done in its rustic kitchen. It's open July-early September. After resting, it's worthwhile continuing a further one km to the end of the trail at the top of a narrow ridge of lateral moraine. From here the trail's namesakes are visible. From left to right the glaciers are Aberdeen, Upper Lefroy, Lower Lefroy, Upper Victoria, Lower Victoria, and Pope's. Between Mt. Lefroy (3,441 meters) and Mt. Victoria (3,459 meters) is Abbot Pass where it's possible to make out Abbot Hut on the skyline. When constructed in 1922 this stone structure was the highest building in Canada. The pass and hut are named for Phillip Abbot, who died attempting to climb Mt. Lefroy in 1896.

Lake Agnes

- Length: 3.6 km (90 minutes) one way
- Elevation gain: 400 meters
- Rating: moderate

This strenuous hike is one of the park's most popular. It begins in front of the chateau, branching right near the beginning of the Louise Lakeshore Trail. For the first 2.5 km the trail climbs steeply, switchbacking through a forest of alpine fir and Engelmann spruce, crossing a horse trail, passing a lookout, and leveling out at tiny **Mirror Lake.** Here the old, traditional trail veers right (use if it's wet or snowy underfoot) while a more direct route veers left to the Plain of the Six Glaciers. Take a sharp right along a trail that climbs steeply below the Big Beehive. The final elevation gain along both trails is made easier by a flight of steps beside **Bridal Veil Falls,** ending beside a rustic teahouse that overlooks Lake Agnes, a subalpine lake nestled in a hanging valley carved out by a receding glacier. The teahouse offers homemade soups, healthy sandwiches, and a wide assortment of teas. From the teahouse a one-km trail leads to **Little Beehive** and impressive views of the Bow Valley. Another trail leads around the northern shore of Lake Agnes, climbing to **Big Beehive** (see below) or to the **Plain of the Six Glaciers Trail,** 3.2 km from the chateau and 2.1 km from the teahouse at the end of that trail.

Big Beehive

- Length: 5 km (2 hours) one way
- Elevation gain: 520 meters
- Rating: moderate

The lookout atop the larger of two "beehives" is one of the best places to admire the uniquely colored waters of Lake Louise, over half a kilometer directly below. The many variations in trails to the summit have one thing in common—all are steep. But the rewards are worth every drop of sweat along the way. The most popular route follows the Lake Agnes Trail for the first 3.6 km to Lake Agnes. From the teahouse, a trail leads to the western end of the lake, then switchbacks steeply up an exposed north-facing ridge. At the crest of the ridge, the trail forks. To the right it descends to the Plain of the Six Glaciers Trail, to the left it continues 300 meters to a log gazebo. This trail is not well defined but scrambling through the large boulders is easy. Across Lake Louise is Fairview Mountain (2,745 meters), and behind this peak is the distinctive shape of Mt. Temple (3,549 meters). Views also extend up the lake to Mt. Lefroy and northeast to Lake Louise Ski Area. Views from the edge of the cliff are spectacular but be very careful—it's a long, long way down. By returning down the Lake Louise side of the Big Beehive the loop is 11.5 km (4-5 hours).

Saddleback

- Length: 3.7 km (90 minutes) one way
- Elevation gain: 600 meters
- Rating: moderate

This trail climbs the lower slopes of Fairview Mountain from beside the boat shed on Lake Louise, ending in an alpine meadow with a view of Mt. Temple from across Paradise Valley. Four hundred meters from the trailhead the trail forks. Keep left and follow the steep switchbacks through a forest of Englemann spruce and alpine fir until reaching the flower-filled meadow. The meadow is actually a pass between Fairview Mountain (to the northwest) and Saddle Mountain (to the southeast). Although most hikers are content with the awesome views from the pass and return along the same trail, it is possible to continue to the summit of Fairview (2,745 meters), a further climb of 400 vertical meters. The barely discernible, switchbacking trail to the summit begins near a stand of larch trees above the crest of Saddleback. As you would expect, the view from the top is stupendous; Lake Louise is over one km directly below. This option is for strong, experienced hikers only. From the Saddleback the trail descends into **Sheol Valley,** then into **Paradise Valley.** The entire loop would be 15 km.

Paradise Valley

- Length: 18 km (6 hours) round trip
- Elevation gain: 380 meters
- Rating: moderate

This aptly named trail makes for a long day-hike, but it can be broken up by overnighting at the backcountry campground at the far end of the loop. The trailhead is located 3.5 km along the Moraine Lake Rd. in a heavily forested area on the right. The trail climbs steadily for the first five km, crossing **Paradise Creek** numerous times, and passing the junction of a trail that climbs the Sheol Valley to **Saddleback** (see above). After five km the trail divides again, following either side of the valley, forming a 13 km loop. **Lake Annette** is 700 meters along the left fork. It is a typical subalpine lake in a unique setting—nestled against the near-vertical 1,200-meter north face of snow- and ice-capped **Mt. Temple** (3,549 meters), one of the 10 highest peaks in the Canadian Rockies. This difficult face was successfully climbed in 1966, relatively late for mountaineering "firsts." The lake is a worthy destination in itself—allow yourself four hours round trip from the trailhead. For those completing the entire loop, continue beyond the lake into an open avalanche area that affords views across Paradise Valley. Look and listen for pikas and marmots among the boulders. The trail then passes through **Horseshoe Meadow,** crosses Paradise Creek, and begins back down the valley. Keep to the left at all trail crossings and you'll quickly arrive at a series of waterfalls known as the **Giant Steps.** From the base of these falls it is eight km back to the trailhead.

Consolation Lakes

- Length: 3 km (1 hour) one way
- Elevation gain: 65 meters
- Rating: easy/moderate

This short trail begins from the bridge over Moraine Creek near the Moraine Lake parking lot, and ends at a pleasant subalpine lake. The first section of the trail traverses a boulder-strewn rock pile—the result of rock slides on the imposing Tower of Babel (3,101 meters)—before entering a dense forest of Engelmann spruce and alpine fir and following **Babel Creek** to the lower lake. The wide valley affords 360-degree views of the surrounding jagged peaks, including Mt. Temple back down the valley and Mt. Bident and Mt. Quandra at the far end of the lakes. After lunch perched on one of many boulders, you could continue to Upper Consolation Lake by crossing Babel Creek and following a usually wet and muddy trail along the lake's eastern shore.

Larch Valley

- Length: 2.9 km (60-90 minutes) one way
- Elevation gain: 450 meters
- Rating: moderate

In autumn, when the larch trees have turned a magnificent gold and the sun is shining, few spots in the Canadian Rockies can match the beauty of this valley. But don't expect to find much solitude. Although the most popular time for visiting the valley is fall, it is a worthy destination all summer. The trail begins just past Moraine Lake Lodge and climbs fairly steeply with occasional glimpses of Moraine Lake below. After reaching the junction of the Eiffel Lake Trail, keep right, passing through an open forest of larch, and into the meadow beyond. The range of larch is restricted within the park and this is one of the few areas where they are prolific. Mt. Fay (3,235 meters) is the dominant peak on the skyline, rising above the other mountains which make up the Valley of the Ten Peaks.

Keen hikers will want to continue through the meadows to **Sentinel Pass** (2,608 meters), one of the park's highest passes. From the end of the meadow, the trail switchbacks for 1.2 km up a steep slope to the pass, sandwiched between Pinnacle Mountain (3,067 meters) and Mt. Temple (3,549 meters). From the pass most hikers opt to return along the same trail, although it is possible to continue into Paradise Valley.

Eiffel Lake
- Length: 5.6 km (2 hours) one way
- Elevation gain: 400 meters
- Rating: moderate/difficult

Eiffel Lake is small, and looks even smaller in its rugged and desolate setting, surrounded by the famed Valley of the Ten Peaks. For the first 2.4 km, follow the Larch Valley Trail (see above), then fork left. Most of the elevation gain has already been made, and the trail remains relatively level before emerging onto an open slope from where each of the 10 peaks can be seen, along with Moraine Lake far below. From left to right the peaks are: Fay, Little, Bowlen, Perren, Septa, Allen, Tuzo, Deltaform, Neptuak, and Wenkchemna. The final two peaks are divided by **Wenkchemna Pass** (2,605 meters), a further four km and 360 vertical meters above Eiffel Lake. The lake itself soon comes into view. It lies in a depression formed by a rock slide from Neptuak Mountain. The lake is named for **Eiffel Peak** (3,085 meters), a rock pinnacle behind it, that with a little imagination could be compared to the Eiffel Tower in Paris.

Skoki Lodge
- Length: 14.4 km (5 hours) one way
- Elevation gain: 775 meters
- Rating: moderate/difficult

The trail into historic Skoki Lodge is only one of the endless hiking opportunities tucked behind Lake Louise Ski Area, across the valley from all hikes detailed above. Access to the Skoki Valley is from a parking lot on a gravel road that branches right from the ski area access road. The first four km of the trail are along a gravel access road leading to Temple Lodge, part of the Lake Louise Ski Area. From here, the trail climbs to **Boulder Pass,** passing a campground and Halfway Hut, above Corral Creek. The pass harbors a large population of pikas and hoary marmots. The trail then follows the north shore of Ptarmigan Lake before climbing again to **Deception Pass,** named for its false summit. It then descends into Skoki Valley, passing the Skoki Lakes, and eventually reaching Skoki Lodge (see "Accommodations," below). Just over one km beyond the lodge is a campground, an excellent base for exploring the region.

WINTERTIME

Lake Louise is an immense winter playground offering one of the world's premier ski resorts, hundreds of kilometers of cross-country-ski trails, ice-skating, sleigh rides, nearby heli-skiing, and more. Between November and May, accommodation prices tumble by up to 70% (except Christmas holidays). Lift and lodging packages begin at $50 per person and you'll always be able to get a table at your favorite restaurant.

The most popular cross-country skiing areas are on Lake Louise, along Moraine Lake Rd., and in Skoki Valley at the back of Lake Louise Ski Area. For details and helpful trail classifications, pick up a copy of *Cross-country Skiing— Nordic Trails in Banff National Park* ($1) from the Lake Louise Visitor Centre. Before heading out check the weather forecast at the visitor center or call (403) 762-2088 for a recorded message. For avalanche reports call 762-1460. On the first Sunday in March, the long-running **Lake Louise Loppet,** a Nordic-skiing competition, is held. Races are run at 10-km and 20-km distances, with prizes in 29 age categories. For details call the Calgary Ski Club at 245-9496.

Of all the ice-skating rinks in Canada, the one on frozen Lake Louise, in front of the chateau, is surely the most spectacular. Spotlights allow skating after dark, and on special occasions hot chocolate is served. Skates are available in the chateau at **Monod Sports,** tel. 522-3628; $6 for two hours.

The closest heli-skiing is a two-hour drive away in the Purcell Mountains. A bus from **R.K. Heli-ski** leaves the chateau each morning for a day of ultimate powder skiing. Their desk in the chateau is staffed daily, 4-9 p.m. For further information call (604) 342-3889.

Brewster Lake Louise Sleigh Rides, tel. (403) 522-3511, ext. 1210, or 762-5454, offers rides in traditional horse-drawn sleighs along the shores of Lake Louise beginning from in front of the chateau. Although blankets are supplied, you should still bundle up. The one-hour ride is $10 per person, $7 for children. Reservations are necessary. The rides are scheduled hourly from 11 a.m. on weekends, from 3 p.m. weekdays.

Lake Louise Ski Area
Canada's answer to the United States mega-resorts such as Vail and Killington is Lake Louise. The nation's largest ski area is comprised of 40 square kilometers of gentle trails, mogul fields, long cruising runs, steep chutes, and vast bowls filled with famous Rocky Mountain powder.

The earliest skiing undertaken in the Lake Louise area was in the 1920s when groups from Banff went backcountry touring in the Skoki Valley. In 1930, Cliff White and Cyril Paris built a small ski chalet in the valley. The location of this chalet, 20 km from the nearest road, turned out not to be practical, so another, closer one was built on the site of today's Temple Lodge. In 1954, a lift was constructed next to Temple Lodge's back door, opening the slopes of Larch Mountain to the ever-increasing number of downhill enthusiasts in the area. A young Englishman who had inherited a fortune from his father saw the potential for a world-class ski resort here and made the completion of his dream a lifelong obsession. Norman Watson, known as the "Barmy Baronet," pulled together a group of financiers and constructed a gondola up the slopes of Whitehorn in 1958. More lifts were constructed and two runs—Olympic Men's Downhill and Olympic Ladies' Downhill—were cut on the south face of Whitehorn in anticipation of a successful bid for the 1968 Winter Olympics. The bid eventually failed due to the opposition of environmentalists (the same reasons that the alpine events of the Calgary Winter Olympics were held on a specially built hill outside of the park boundary). Huge development plans for the base area that included rooms for 6,500 guests were scuttled in 1972, but under the supervision of one-time local mountain guide Charlie Locke, the area has continued to improve and grow, and often hosts World Cup skiing events.

The resort is made up of four distinct faces. The front side has a vertical drop of 1,000 meters and is served by eight lifts, including two high-speed quads. The four back bowls are each as big as many midsize ski areas and are all well above the treeline. Larch and Ptarmigan faces have a variety of terrain, allowing you to follow the sun as it moves across the sky or escape into trees for protection on windy days.

Each of the three day lodges has a restaurant and bar. Ski rentals, clothing, and souvenirs are available at the base area. Lift tickets are $39.50 per day, children and seniors $35. Lifts are open from early November to early May, 9 a.m.-4 p.m. Free guided tours of the mountain are available three times daily—inquire at customer service. Free shuttle buses run regularly from Lake Louise accommodations to the hill. From Banff you pay $12 round trip for transportation to Lake Louise. For more information on the ski area call (403) 522-3555.

ACCOMMODATIONS

In summer, for the price of the cheapest room in town, you could buy a tent, pay your campground fee with a smile, and sit around a campfire telling bear stories. If you must stay indoors it's essential to make reservations well in advance. Any rooms not taken by early afternoon will be the expensive ones. When making reservations for all lodging listed below, write to the establishment's P.O. Box followed by: **Lake Louise, Alberta, T0L 1E0.**

Hotels
Originally called Lake Louise Ski Lodge, the **Post Hotel,** P.O. Box 69, tel. (403) 522-3989 or (800) 661-1586, is bordered to the east and south by the Pipestone River. It may lack views of Lake Louise, but it is as elegant, in a modern, woodsy way, as the chateau. Each bungalow-style room is furnished with Canadian pine and has a balcony. Many have whirlpools and fireplaces, while some have kitchens. Other facilities include an indoor pool, steam room, and library. High tea is served in the lobby each afternoon. The hotel has 17 different room types, with 26 different rates depending on the view. Rates start at $135 s or d per night.

Across the road from the Post Hotel is **Lake Louise Inn,** P.O. Box 209, tel. 522-3791 or (800) 661-9237, where rooms start at $120 per night. **Mountaineer Lodge,** P.O. Box 150, tel. 522-3844, close to everything, is open in summer only. Rates start at $110 s or d. The historic

Deer Lodge, P.O. Box 100, tel. 522-3747 or (800) 661-1595, is located along Lake Louise Dr., just below Chateau Lake Louise, and has a good restaurant; $110-150. **Moraine Lake Lodge,** P.O. Box 70, tel. 522-3733 or (800) 661-8340, is located on the lake of the same name. Rooms are $145 per night; cabins with fireplaces start at $185.

Paradise Lodge And Bungalows

A much better deal, especially for those who like privacy or for families and small groups, is Paradise Lodge and Bungalows, P.O. Box 7; tel. (403) 522-3595. Spread out around the well-manicured gardens are self-contained cabins beginning at $105 per night. Bungalows with kitchens are $115 for one bedroom and $120 for two bedrooms. Newly built suites, each with a fireplace, TV, two rooms, and fabulous mountain view start at $150, $165 with a kitchen. The lodge is open May-October. To get there from the valley floor, follow Lake Louise Dr. toward Chateau Lake Louise for two kilometers.

Paradise Lodge and Bungalows

Chateau Lake Louise

This historic 520-room hotel, on the shore of Lake Louise, has views equal to any mountain resort in the world. But all this historic charm and mountain scenery comes at a price. During the summer season (June to mid-October), a standard room is $244, and lakeside $333. Rates drop 40% outside of summer and many ski packages are advertised in winter. Children under 17 sharing with parents are free, but if you bring a pet it'll be an extra $20. For reservations—and you'll need one— write to P.O. Box 96; tel. (403) 522-3511 or (800) 441-1414.

Skoki Lodge

Skoki is a rustic lodge, deep in the backcountry, north of Lake Louise Ski Area. Getting there requires an 11-km hike or ski depending on the season. The lodge is an excellent base for exploring nearby valleys and mountains. For information and reservations write to P.O. Box 5; tel. (403) 522-3555.

Hostel

At around $90 less than any other bed in town **Lake Louise International Hostel** fills up quickly each day. Of log construction, with large windows and high vaulted ceilings, the hostel was a joint venture between the Alpine Club of Canada and the Southern Alberta Hostelling Association. It opened early in the summer of 1992. Downstairs is a large reception area and **Bill Peyto's Cafe,** the least expensive place to eat in Lake Louise. Upstairs is a large lounge area and guides room—a quiet place to plan your next hike or browse through the large collection of mountain literature. Hostel members pay $15 per night in a four- or six-bed dorm, or $19.50 in a two-bed dorm. Nonmembers pay $22 and $24.50, respectively. The hostel is open year-round. In summer and on weekends during the ski season, advance bookings (up to six months) are essential. Write P.O. Box 115, Lake Louise, Alberta, T0L 1E0; tel. (403) 522-2200. The hostel is located along Village Rd., one km from Samson Mall.

Campgrounds

Lake Louise Campground, within easy walking distance of the village, is divided into two areas by the Bow River. One side has unserviced sites, the other serviced. Individual sites are close together, but some privacy and shade is provided by towering lodgepole pines. The unserviced (tent camping) sites have flush toilets, kitchen shelters, fire rings, and free firewood; $11.75 per night. Serviced (trailer camping) sites have power and flush toilets; $14. A dump station is located near the entrance to the campground. An interpretive program runs throughout summer, nightly at 9 p.m. in the outdoor theater. **Bow River Loop** leads into the village along either side of the Bow River, crossing at the southern end of the serviced sites and again behind Samson Mall. To get to the campground take Lake Louise Dr. under the railway bridge, turn left on Fairview Dr., and continue past the impressive log staff accommodations to the fee station. The campground is open year-round.

FOOD AND DRINK

On The Cheap
Samson Mall is the center of much activity each afternoon as campers descend on the grocery store to stock up on supplies for the evening meal. Prices are high and by the end of the day stocks are low. **Laggan's Mountain Bakery,** in the mall, is *the* place to hang out with a coffee and one of their delicious freshly baked cakes or muffins. If the tables are full and you manage to somehow reach the cake cabinet, order takeout and enjoy your feast on the grassy bank behind the mall. The chocolate brownie ($1) is delicious. Order two slices to save having to line up again. It's open daily 6 a.m.-7 p.m.

Forget the Bar and Grill in the mall—much better is **Bill Peyto's Cafe** in the hostel on Village Road. The food is consistent and well priced. A huge portion of nachos is $6. You don't have to be staying in the hostel to eat here. Open daily 7 a.m.-9 p.m. The **Lake Louise Inn,** tel. (403) 522-3791, has a barbecue buffet in a gazebo (7-8 p.m.), $15 per person. Other inexpensive alternatives are the **Mountain Restaurant,** in the ESSO station, and **Lake Louise Trading Post,** beside Deer Lodge on Lake Louise Drive.

Railway Station Restaurant
One hundred years ago visitors departing trains at Laggan Station were keen to get to the Chateau Lake Louise as quickly as possible to begin their adventure. Today, guests from the chateau, other hotels, and even people from as far away as Banff are returning to the restored station to dine in this unique restaurant. Although the menu is not extensive, the ample variety satisfies most tastes. Open for lunch and dinner. For reservations call (403) 522-2386.

Chateau Lake Louise
Within this famous hotel are a choice of eateries and an ice-cream shop. The **Poppy Room** has obscured lake views and is the most casual place for a meal. A continental buffet breakfast is served 7-9 a.m.; $8. For dinner a pizza and pasta buffet is offered ($13) or order off the menu. It's open till 8:30 p.m. **Walliser Stube** is an elegant two-story wine bar decorated with oak furniture. It offers a simple menu of German dishes from $13 and cheese fondue for $32. **Victoria Dining Room** features a large buffet lunch $15.95. **Lakeside Terrace** is an open-front grill. Victorian high tea of crumpets, sandwiches, desserts, and drinks is served each afternoon; $12. **Glacier Saloon** is a western-style saloon serving light meals; open noon-1 a.m. **Edelweiss Room** has the best view of Lake Louise and offers the chateau's most elegant dining. Appetizers start at $4.50 while entrees from the fish, game, chicken, and meat menu start at $17.

Post Hotel
In 1987, the Post Hotel was expanded to include a luxurious new wing. The original log building was renovated as a rustic, timbered, dining room, linked to the rest of the hotel by an intimate bar. Although eating here is not cheap, it's a favorite of locals and visitors alike. The chef specializes in European cuisine—preparing a number of Swiss dishes (such as veal Zurichoise) to make owner George Schwarz feel homesick—but he's also renowned for his presentation of Alberta beef, Pacific salmon, and Peking duck. Main meals start at $21. The restaurant is open daily 7 a.m.-2 p.m. and 5-9:30 p.m. Reservations are essential for dinner; call (403) 522-3989.

Drink
Hang out with seasonal workers at **Lake Louise Bar and Grill,** upstairs in Samson Mall, or head

to rowdy **Charlie's Pub** in the Lake Louise Inn for dancing to recorded music. Although the bar in the Post Hotel doesn't have mountain views, it has light food, a fireplace, and a distinctive mountain atmosphere. In the Chateau Lake Louise is **The Glacier Saloon**, where on most summer nights, a DJ plays music ranging from pop to western.

TRANSPORTATION

Getting There
Calgary International Airport is the closest major airport to Lake Louise. **Brewster Transportation and Tours,** tel. (403) 762-6700, operates a bus service leaving the airport three times daily, stopping at Banff, Samson Mall, and the chateau. The bus arriving at 1:10 p.m. continues to Jasper (April-Oct. only). The earliest service back to the airport departs at 7:15 a.m. Lake Louise to Banff is $11.50, to Calgary and Jasper $32.

    Greyhound, tel. (403) 522-2121 or (800) 661-8747, leaves the Calgary Bus Depot at 877 Greyhound Way SW five times daily for Banff and Lake Louise, $17.35. Banff to Lake Louise is $6.20. Buses leave Vancouver from 1150 Station St., tel. (604) 662-3222, three times daily for the 13-hour haul to Lake Louise; $89.24.

    Pika Shuttle links Calgary International Hostel to hostels in Banff, Lake Louise, and those along the Icefields Parkway every second day. Lake Louise to Calgary is $21, to Banff $7, and to Whistler's Hostel in Jasper $37. To ride this shuttle you *must* have advance reservations at your destination hostel. For further information call (800) 363-0096.

Getting Around
The campground, hostel, and hotels are all within easy walking distance of Samson Mall. Chateau Lake Louise is a 2.7 km walk from the valley floor. The only car-rental agency in the village is **Tilden,** tel. (403) 522-3870 or (800) 387-4747. They don't have many cars; you'd be better off picking one up in Banff or at Calgary International Airport. **Lake Louise Taxi & Tours** is located in Samson Mall, tel. 522-2020; flag drop is $2.30, then $1.25 per km. From the mall to Chateau Lake Louise runs around $9, to Moraine Lake $16, and to Banff $85. **Wilson Mountain**

Sports, in Samson Mall, tel. 522-3636, has mountain bikes for rent for $6 per hour or $24 per day (includes a helmet, bike lock, and water bottle). Inquire here about canoe rentals for float trips along the Bow River to Banff.

Tours
No tours of the area are offered for visitors staying in Lake Louise. For those staying in Banff, **Brewster Transportation and Tours,** tel. (403) 762-6700, has a four-hour tour departing select Banff hotels daily 1:15-1:40 p.m. to Lake Louise; $35. In winter this tour departs in the morning, runs five hours, and includes Banff sights; $33.50.

SERVICES AND INFORMATION

Services
Located in Samson Mall is a small postal outlet serving as a bus depot and car-rental agency. Although Lake Louise has no banks, there's a currency exchange in the Chateau Lake Louise and a cash machine in the grocery store. The mall also has a laundromat that's always busy, and downstairs are military-style showers; $2.50. Open in summer, daily 8 a.m.-8 p.m., shorter hours the rest of the year. Camping supplies are available from **Wilson Mountain Sports** and photographic supplies from **Pipestone Photo.** Pipestone has a one-hour photo-developing service and is the only place in the park offering overnight slide developing; tel. (403) 522-3617. The closest **hospital** is in Banff, tel. 762-2222. For the **RCMP** call 522-3811.

Information
Woodruff & Blum, located in the Samson Mall, tel. (403) 522-3842, has an excellent selection of books on the natural and human history of the park, animal field guides, hiking guides, and general Western Canadiana.

    The **Lake Louise Visitor Centre,** tel. 522-3833, is located beside Samson Mall on Village Road. This excellent facility has interpretive displays, slide and video displays, and park staff on hand to answer questions, issue backcountry camping permits, and recommend hikes suited to your ability. Look for the stuffed (literally) female grizzly and read her fascinating, but sad, story.

ICEFIELDS PARKWAY/BANFF

The 230-km Icefields Parkway, between Lake Louise and Jasper, is one of the most scenic, exciting, and inspiring mountain roads ever built. From Lake Louise it parallels the Continental Divide, following in the shadow of the highest, most rugged mountains in the Canadian Rockies. The first 122 km to Sunwapta Pass (the boundary between Banff and Jasper national parks) can be driven in two hours, and the entire parkway in four. But it's likely you'll want to spend at least a day, probably more, stopping at each of the 13 viewpoints, hiking the trails, watching the abundant wildlife, and just generally enjoying one of the world's most magnificent landscapes. Along the section within Banff National Park are two lodges, three hostels, four campgrounds, and one gas station.

Although the road is steep and winding in places, it has a wide shoulder, making it ideal for an extended bike trip. Allow seven days to pedal north from Banff to Jasper, staying at hostels or camping along the route. This is the preferable direction to travel by bike as the elevation of Jasper townsite is more than 500 meters lower than either Banff townsite or Lake Louise.

History

Natives and early explorers found the swampy nature of the Bow Valley difficult for foot and horse travel. They used instead the Pipestone River Valley, farther east, when heading north. Banff guide Bill Peyto lead American explorer Walter Wilcox up the Bow Valley in 1896, to the high peaks along the Continental Divide northeast of Lake Louise. The first complete journey along this route was made by Jim Brewster in 1904. Soon after, A.P. Coleman made the arduous journey, becoming a strong supporter for the route aptly known as "The Wonder Trail." During the Great Depression of the 1930s, as part of a relief-work project, construction began on what was to become the Icefields Parkway. It was completed in 1939 and the first car traveled the route in 1940. In tribute to the excellence of the road's early construction, when upgraded to its present standard in 1961, the original roadbed was followed nearly the entire way.

The parkway remains open year-round, although winter brings with it some special considerations. The road is often closed for short periods for avalanche control—check road conditions in Banff or Lake Louise before setting out. And fill up with gas—no services are available between November and April.

SIGHTS

The Icefields Parkway forks right from the Trans-Canada Hwy. just north of Lake Louise. The impressive scenery begins immediately. Just three km from the junction is **Herbert Lake,** formed during the last ice age when retreating glaciers deposited a pile of rubble—known as a moraine—across a shallow valley and water filled in behind it. The lake is a perfect place for early morning or evening photography when the **Waputik Range** and distinctively shaped **Mt. Temple** are reflected in its waters.

Traveling north, you'll notice numerous depressions in the steep, shaded, slopes of the Waputik Range across the Bow Valley. The cooler climate on these north-facing slopes makes them prone to glaciation. Cirques were cut by small "local glaciers." On the opposite side of the road, **Mt. Hector** (3,394 meters), easily recognized by its layered peak, soon comes into view.

Hector Lake Viewpoint is 16 km from the junction. Although the view is partially obscured by trees, the emerald green waters nestled below a massive wall of limestone form a breathtaking scene. **Bow Peak,** seen looking northward along the highway, is only 2,868 meters high, but is completely detached from the Waputik Range, making it a popular destination for mountain climbers. As you leave this viewpoint look across the northeast end of Hector Lake for glimpses of **Mt. Balfour** (3,246 meters) on the distant skyline.

Crowfoot Glacier

The aptly named Crowfoot Glacier can best be appreciated from north of Bow Lake. From the

JASPER NATIONAL PARK

NIGEL PASS

SUNWAPTA PASS
HILDA CREEK HOSTEL

WHITE GOAT WILDERNESS AREA

TO ROCKY MOUNTAIN HOUSE AND RED DEER

11

COLUMBIA ICEFIELD

MT. ATHABASCA

NIGEL CREEK

SILVERHORN

CIRRUS MOUNTAIN

ABRAHAM LAKE

CASTLEGUARD MOUNTAIN

NORTH SASKATCHEWAN RIVER

93 PARKWAY

ICEFIELDS

RAMPART CREEK HOSTEL

MT. AMERY

RAMPART CREEK

MT. WILSON

THE CROSSING

SASKATCHEWAN RIVER CROSSING

NORTH SASKATCHEWAN RIVER

BANFF NATIONAL PARK

MISTAYA CANYON

CONTINENTAL DIVIDE

GLACIER LAKE

MT. OUTRAM

MT. FORBES

HOWSE RIVER

MT. SARBACH

MT. MURCHISON

SIFFLEUR WILDERNESS AREA

MT. CHEPHREN

WATERFOWL LAKES

HOWSE PEAK

MISTAYA LAKE

SIFFLEUR RIVER

MT. PATTERSON

BOW SUMMIT

DOLOMITE PASS

KATHERINE LAKE

BRITISH COLUMBIA

PEYTO LAKE

NUM-TI-JAH LODGE

HELEN LAKE

BOW LAKE

ICEFIELDS PARKWAY

CONTINENTAL DIVIDE

MOSQUITO CREEK

MOSQUITO CREEK HOSTEL

CROWFOOT MOUNTAIN

BOW PEAK

HECTOR LAKE

WAPUTIK RANGE

BOW RIVER

ICEFIELDS PARKWAY

93

MT. BALFOUR

YOHO NATIONAL PARK

PIPESTONE RIVER

HERBERT LAKE

0   10 km

0   10 mi

TO KAMLOOPS

TRANSCANADA HWY.

1

LAKE LOUISE

TO BANFF

1

© MOON PUBLICATIONS, INC.

viewpoint, 17 km north of Hector Lake, it is easy to see how this and other glaciers are formed. It sits on a wide ledge near the top of Crowfoot Mountain from where its glacial "claws" cling to the mountain's steep slopes. The retreat of this glacier has been dramatic. It was only 50 years ago that two of the claws extended to the base of the lower cliff.

Bow Lake

The sparkling, translucent waters of Bow Lake are among the most beautiful that can be seen from the Icefields Parkway. The lake was created when moraines, left behind by retreating glaciers, dammed subsequent meltwater. On still days, the water reflects the snowy peaks, their sheer cliffs, and the scree slopes that run into the lake. You don't need to take a photography class to take good pictures here! At the southeast end of the lake is a day-use area with waterfront picnic tables and a trail that leads to a swampy area at the lake's outlet. At the upper end of the lake is a lodge and the trailhead for a walk to Bow Glacier Falls (see "Hiking," below).

The road leaves Bow Lake and climbs to **Bow Summit.** Looking back, the true color of Bow Lake becomes apparent and the Crowfoot Glacier reveals its unique shape. At an elevation of 2,069 meters, this pass is one of the highest points crossed by a public road in Canada. It is also the beginning of the Bow River, the one you camped beside at Lake Louise, photo-graphed flowing through the town of Banff, and strolled along in downtown Calgary.

Peyto Lake

From the parking lot at Bow Summit, a short paved trail leads to one of the most breathtaking views that you could ever imagine. Far below the viewpoint is Peyto Lake, an impossibly intense green-colored lake whose hues change according to season. Before heavy melting of nearby glaciers begins (June-early July), the lake is dark blue. As summer progresses, meltwater flows across a delta and into the lake. This water is laden with fine particles of ground rock-debris known as "rock flour" that remains suspended in the water. It is not the mineral content of the rock flour that is responsible for the lakes unique color, but rather the particles reflecting the blue-green sector of the light spectrum. Hence, as the amount of suspended rock flour changes, so does the color of the lake.

The lake is one of many park landmarks named for early outfitter Bill Peyto. In 1898 he was part of an expedition camped at Bow Lake. Seeking solitude (as he was wont to do), he slipped off during the night to sleep near this lake. Other members of the party coined the name "Peyto's Lake," and it stuck.

A further three km along the parkway is a viewpoint from where **Peyto Glacier** is visible at the far end of Peyto Lake Valley. This glacier is part of the extensive **Wapta Icefield** that straddles the Continental Divide and extends into

NADINA PURDON

spectacular Bow Lake and Crowfoot Glacier

the northern reaches of **Yoho National Park** in British Columbia.

Beside The Continental Divide

From Bow Pass the parkway descends to a viewpoint directly across the Mistaya River from **Mt. Patterson** (3,197 meters). **Snowbird Glacier** clings precariously to the mountain's steep northeast face, and the mountain's lower, wooded slopes are heavily scarred where rock and ice slides have swept down the mountainside.

As the parkway continues to descend and crosses **Silverhorn Creek,** the jagged limestone peaks of the Continental Divide can be seen to the west. **Mistaya Lake** is a three-km-long body of water that sits at the bottom of the valley between the road and the divide, but can't be seen from the parkway. The best place to view this panorama is from the **Howse Peak Viewpoint** at Upper Waterfowl Lake. From here the high ridge that forms the Continental Divide is easily distinguishable. Seven peaks can be seen from here including **Howse Peak** (3,290 meters). At no point along this ridge does the elevation drop below 2,750 meters. From Howse Peak the Continental Divide makes a 90-degree turn to the west. One dominant peak that can be seen from Bow Pass to north of Saskatchewan River Crossing is **Mt. Chephren** (3,268 meters). Its distinctive shape and position away from the main ridge of the Continental Divide make it easy to distinguish (directly north of Howse Peak).

To Saskatchewan River Crossing

Numerous trails lead around the swampy shores of **Upper** and **Lower Waterfowl lakes,** providing one of the park's best opportunities to view moose, who feed on the abundant aquatic vegetation that grows in Upper Waterfowl Lake. Rock and other debris that has been carried down nearby valley systems has built up, forming a wide alluvial fan, nearly blocking the **Mistaya River** and creating Upper Waterfowl Lake.

Continuing north is **Mt. Murchison** (3,337 meters), on the east side of the parkway. Although not one of the park's highest mountains, this gray-and-yellow massif of Cambrian rock includes 10 individual peaks, covering an area of 30 square km.

From a parking lot 14 km northeast of Waterfowl Lake Campground, a short trail descends into the montane forest to **Mistaya Canyon.**

Here, the effects of erosion can be appreciated as the Mistaya River leaves the floor of Mistaya Valley, plunging through a narrow-walled canyon into the North Saskatchewan Valley. The area is scarred with potholes where boulders have been whirled around by the action of fast-flowing water, carving deep depressions into the softer limestone bedrock below.

The **North Saskatchewan River** posed a major problem for early travelers and later for the builders of the Icefields Parkway. This swiftly running river eventually drains into Hudson Bay. In 1989 it was named a Canadian Heritage River. A panoramic viewpoint of the entire valley is located one km past the bridge. From here the Howse and Mistaya rivers can be seen converging with the North Saskatchewan at a silt-laden delta. This is also a junction with Hwy. 11 (also known as David Thompson Hwy.), which follows the North Saskatchewan River to Rocky Mountain House and Red Deer. From this viewpoint numerous peaks can be seen to the west. Two sharp peaks are distinctive. **Mount Outram** (3,254 meters) is the closer. The farther is **Mt. Forbes** (3,630 meters), highest peak in Banff National Park (and sixth-highest in the Canadian Rockies).

To Sunwapta Pass

On the north side of the North Saskatchewan River is the towering hulk of **Mt. Wilson** (3,261 meters), named for Banff outfitter Tom Wilson. The Icefields Parkway passes this massif on its western flanks. A pullout, just past Rampart Creek Campground, has good views of Mt. Amery to the west and Mounts Sarbach, Chephren, and Murchison to the south. Beyond here is the **Weeping Wall,** a long cliff of gray limestone where a series of waterfalls tumbles over 100 meters down the steep slopes of **Cirrus Mountain.** In winter this wall of water freezes, a mecca for ice climbers. After climbing quickly, the road drops again, before beginning the long climb to Sunwapta Pass. Before ascending to the pass the road makes a sweeping curve over an alluvial plain of the North Saskatchewan River. Halfway up the 360-vertical-meter climb is a viewpoint well worth stopping for. Cyclists will definitely appreciate a rest. From here views extend down the valley to the slopes of Mt. Saskatchewan and, on the other side of the parkway, Cirrus Mountain. Another viewpoint, farther up the road, has the added attraction of **Panther Falls** across the valley. A cairn at **Sunwapta Pass** (2,023 meters) marks the boundary between Banff and Jasper national parks. It also marks the divide between the North Saskatchewan and Sunwapta rivers, whose waters drain into the Atlantic and Arctic oceans, respectively.

HIKING

Helen Lake
- Length: 6 km (2.5 hours) one way
- Elevation gain: 455 meters
- Rating: moderate

The trail to Helen Lake is one of the easiest ways to access true alpine environment from the southern end of the Icefields Parkway. The trailhead is opposite Crowfoot Glacier Lookout, 33 km from the junction with the TransCanada Highway. The trail climbs steadily through a forest of Engelmann spruce and alpine fir for the first 2.5 km to an avalanche slope, reaching the treeline after three km. The view across the valley is spectacular, with Crowfoot Glacier visible to the southwest. As the trail reaches a ridge, it turns 180 degrees and descends into the glacial cirque where Helen Lake lies. Listen and look for hoary marmots around the scree slopes along the lakeshore. For those with the time and energy, it's possible to continue an additional three km to **Dolomite Pass.** The trail to the pass switchbacks steeply a further 100 vertical meters before descending to Katherine Lake and Dolomite Pass.

Bow Glacier Falls
- Length: 3.4 km (1 hour) one way
- Elevation gain: 130 meters
- Rating: easy/moderate

This hike skirts one of the most beautiful lakes in the Canadian Rockies before ending at a narrow but spectacular waterfall. The trail begins beside Num-ti-jah Lodge at the north end of Bow Lake and follows the shore through Willow Flats to a gravel outwash area at the end of the lake. Across the lake are reflected views of Crowfoot Mountain and, farther west, a glimpse of Bow Glacier among the jagged peaks of the Waputik Range. The trail then begins a short but steep climb up the rim of a canyon before leveling out at the edge of a vast moraine of gravel, scree,

and boulders. This is the end of the trail, although it's possible to reach the base of Bow Glacier Falls by picking your way through the 800 meters of rough ground that remains.

Peyto Lake
- Length: 1.4 km (30 minutes) one way
- Elevation loss: 100 meters
- Rating: easy

Without doubt the best place to view Peyto Lake is from the popular viewpoint accessible via a short trail from Bow Summit. From here a trail drops nearly 300 meters in 2.4 km to the lake. For those wanting to reach the lake's shore there is an easier alternative. From a small parking lot 2.4 km north of Bow Summit an unmarked trail leads 1.4 km to the shore of this famous lake. The pebbled beach, strewn with driftwood, is the perfect setting for picnicking, painting, or admiring the lake's quieter side.

Chephren Lake
- Length: 4 km (60-90 minutes) one way
- Elevation gain: 100 meters
- Rating: easy/moderate

This pale green body of water is hidden from sight of those traveling the Icefields Parkway. The trailhead is located within **Waterfowl Lakes Campground,** where the Mistaya River flows into the lake. The trail crosses the Mistaya River, 400 meters from the trailhead, then dives headlong into a subalpine forest until reaching the lake, nestled under the buttresses of Mt. Chephren. To the left is Howse Peak. The trail to **Cirque Lake** (4.5 km from trailhead) branches left after 1.7 km and is less heavily used.

Glacier Lake
- Length: 9 km (2.5-3 hours) one way
- Elevation gain: 220 meters
- Rating: moderate

This three-km-long lake is one of the largest backcountry lakes in the park. Although not as scenic as the more accessible lakes along the parkway, it's a pleasant destination for a full-day or overnight trip. The trailhead is in an old gravel pit on the west side of the highway, one km north of the Saskatchewan River Crossing service center. For the first kilometer the trail passes through an open forest of lodgepole pine to a fancy footbridge across the rushing North Saskatchewan River. It then climbs gradually to a viewpoint overlooking Howse River and the valley beyond before turning away from the river for a long slog through a dense forest to Glacier Lake. A primitive campground is located just over 300 meters from where the trail emerges at the lake.

Saskatchewan Glacier
- Length: 7.3 km (2 hours) one way
- Elevation gain: 150 meters
- Rating: moderate

The Saskatchewan Glacier, a tongue of ice from the great Columbia Icefield, is visible from various points along the Icefields Parkway. This hike will take you right to the toe of the glacier. The trailhead is an old concrete bridge located on the gravel flats just before the road begins its "big bend," 35 km north of the Saskatchewan River Crossing service center. The trail begins across the bridge, disappearing into the forest to the right, joining an old access road, and continuing up the valley along the south bank of the river. When the toe of the glacier first comes into sight it looks deceivingly close. It is still a long hike over rough terrain to the actual glacier.

Nigel Pass
- Length: 7.4 km (2.5 hours) one way
- Elevation gain: 365 meters
- Rating: moderate/difficult

On the east side of the Icefields Parkway, 2.5 km north of the switchback on the "big bend," is a gravel road that leads to a locked gate. Turn right here and cross Nigel Creek on the bridge. The trail is obvious, following open avalanche paths up the east side of the valley. In a stand of Engelmann spruce and alpine fir two km from the trailhead is an old campsite used first by native hunting parties, then by mountaineers exploring the area around the Columbia Icefield. Look for carvings on trees recording these early visitors. From here the trail continues to climb steadily, only increasing in gradient for the last one km to the pass. The pass (2,195 meters) marks the boundary between Banff and Jasper national parks. For the best view, scramble over the rocks to the left. To the north, the view extends down the Brazeau River Valley, surrounded by a mass of peaks. To the west (left) is **Nigel Peak** (3,211 meters) and southwest are views of Parker's Ridge and the glaciated peaks of Mt. Athabasca.

Parker's Ridge
- Length: 2.4 km (1 hour) one way
- Elevation gain: 210 meters
- Rating: easy/moderate

This short trail into the alpine begins from a parking lot at the north end of the park, just four km south of Sunwapta Pass. From the trailhead on the west side of the road, the wide path gains elevation quickly through open meadows and scattered stands of alpine fir. This fragile environment is easily destroyed, so it's very important that you stay on the trail. During the short alpine summer, these meadows are carpeted with red heather, white mountain avens, and blue alpine forget-me-nots. From the summit of the ridge, you look down on the two-km-wide Saskatchewan Glacier spreading out below. Beyond is **Castleguard Mountain,** renowned for its extensive cave system.

ACCOMMODATIONS

Lodging
Pioneer guide and outfitter Jimmy Simpson built **Num-ti-jah Lodge** on the north shore of Bow Lake in 1920. In those days, the route north from Lake Louise was nothing more than a horse trail. The desire to build a large structure when only short timbers were available led to the unusual octagonal shape of the main lodge. Simpson remained at Bow Lake, a living legend, until his death in 1972. Today the lodge continues to offer facilities for travelers along the highway. Rooms here cost $65 s, $95 d; most units have private bath. A small coffee shop is open daily 9 a.m.-5:30 p.m., and **Elkhorn Dining Room** is open for dinner. Horseback rides are offered for guests and nonguests. A one-hour ride along Bow Lake is $16, a three-hour ride to Peyto Lake is $30, and a full-day ride to Helen Lake is $70. Write to the lodge at P.O. Box 39, Lake Louise, Alberta T0L 1E0; tel. (403) 522-2167.

Just north of Saskatchewan River Crossing, 45 km south of the Columbia Icefield, is **The Crossing** (Mail Bag 333, Lake Louise T0L 1E0; tel. 761-7000), with rooms for $68 s, $73 d (40% discount in spring and fall), a restaurant, cafeteria with buffet, lounge, large gift shop, and gas.

Hostels

From Lake Louise, hostels are located at Km 24, 88, and 118 of the Icefields Parkway. The first is **Mosquito Creek Hostel,** which has good hiking nearby, accommodations for 38 in four cabins, and a large common room with fireplace, a kitchen, and a wood-heated sauna. **Rampart Creek Hostel** is located 12 km north of Saskatchewan River Crossing, a long day's bike ride from Mosquito Creek. Accommodation for 30 is in two cabins, and there's a kitchen, sauna, and good hiking nearby. After the long climb up to Sunwapta Pass, **Hilda Creek Hostel** will be a welcome sight for cyclists. This hostel is located just below the glacial moraines left by the retreating Columbia Icefield and has a variety of hikes beginning from the doorstep. It has 21 dorm beds, kitchen, sauna, and a common room. All the above hostels are open year-round, with Rampart Creek requiring reservations between November and May. Members $10, nonmembers $14. It is recommended to book ahead during July and August as these hostels fill each night. Reservations can be made at the hostels in Banff (403-762-4122), Lake Louise (522-2200), or Calgary (800-363-0096). **Pika Shuttle Co.,** tel. (800) 363-0096, runs from Calgary through Banff to all hostels along the Icefields Parkway every second day stopping at all the hostels. You must have advance reservations.

Campgrounds

Campgrounds are located at **Mosquito Creek** (Km 24), **Silverhorn** (Km 103), **Waterfowl Lake** (Km 57), and **Rampart Creek** (Km 88). Each has pit toilets, kitchen shelters, firewood, and fire rings, but no showers or hookups, and each is open from mid-June to early September. Mosquito Creek also remains open for winter camping.

KAREN MCKINLEY

JASPER NATIONAL PARK

INTRODUCTION

Snowcapped peaks, vast icefields, beautiful glacial lakes, soothing hot springs, thundering rivers, and the most extensive backcountry trail system of any Canadian national park make Jasper a stunning counterpart to its sister park, Banff. A 3.5-hour drive west of the provincial capital of Edmonton, Jasper extends from the headwaters of the Smoky River in the north to the Columbia Icefield (and Banff National Park) in the south. To the east are the foothills; to the west, the Continental Divide (which marks the Alberta/British Columbia border). This 10,900-square-km wilderness is a haven for wildlife; much of the park is traveled only by wolves and grizzlies.

The park's most spectacular natural landmarks can be admired from two major roads. The **Yellowhead Highway** runs east-west from Edmonton to British Columbia through the park. The **Icefields Parkway,** regarded as one of the world's great mountain drives, runs north-south, connecting Jasper to Banff. The main service center in the park is the town of **Jasper,** a smaller, less-commercial version of Banff, where you'll find a number of motels and restaurants. Many of the park's campgrounds are accessible by road, while others are located throughout the backcountry. Also popular in the park are fishing, boating, downhill skiing, golfing, horseback riding, and whitewater rafting.

The park is open year-round, although road closures do occur on the Icefields Parkway during winter months due to avalanche-control work and snowstorms.

Permits are required for entry into the park; they're available from all park gates. A one-day permit is $5, four days $10, and an annual pass good for all Canada's national parks is $30.

The Land
The Rocky Mountains, extending from the Arctic to the jungles of central Mexico, form the backbone of North America. Although the peaks of Jasper National Park are not particularly high, they are among the most spectacular along the range's entire length. About 100 million years ago, layers of sedimentary rock—laid down here up to a billion years ago—were forced upward,

folded, and twisted under tremendous pressure into the mountains seen today. The land's contours were further altered during four ice ages that began around a million years ago. The last ice age ended about 10,000 years ago, and the vast glaciers began to retreat. A remnant of this final sheet of ice is the huge **Columbia Icefield;** approximately 325 square km and up to 400 meters deep, it's the most extensive icefield in the Rocky Mountains. As the glaciers retreated, piles of rock melted out and were left behind. Meltwater from the glaciers flowed down the valleys and was dammed up behind the moraines. **Maligne Lake,** like many other lakes in the park, was created by this process. The glacial silt suspended in the lake's waters produces amazing emerald, turquoise, and amethyst colors; early artists who painted these lakes had trouble convincing people that their images were real.

In addition to creating the park's gemlike lakes, the retreating glaciers carved out the valleys that they ever-so-slowly flowed through. The **Athabasca River Valley** is the park's largest watershed and a typical example of a U-shaped, glacier-carved valley. The Athabasca River flows north through the valley into the Mackenzie River system and ultimately into the Arctic Ocean. The glacial silt that paints the park's lakes is also carried down streams into the Athabasca, giving the river a pale green "milky" look. Another beautiful aspect of the park's scenery is its abundance of waterfalls. They vary from the sparkling tumble of Mountain Creek as it cascades down a limestone cliff into a picturesque pool at **Punchbowl Falls,** to the roar of **Athabasca Falls** where the river is forced through a narrow gorge.

FLORA

Vegetation zones in the park range from montane in the valleys, through subalpine evergreen forests higher up, to alpine tundra above the treeline.

Only a small part of the park is **montane.** It is characterized by stands of Douglas fir, as well as savannah-like grasslands that occur on drier sites in valley bottoms. Well-developed stretches of montane can be found along the floors of the Athabasca and Miette river valleys, providing winter habitat for larger mammals such as elk.

The **subalpine** zone, heavily forested with evergreens, extends from the lower valley slopes up to the treeline. The dominant species in this zone is lodgepole pine, although Engelmann spruce, alpine fir, poplar, and aspen grow here. Lodgepole pine has adapted to make use of fire. Its hard seed cones are sealed by a resin which is melted only at high temperatures. When fire races through the forest, the resin melts and the cones release their seeds. As a result, these are the first conifers to regenerate in burned-out areas. The park's extensive stands of lodgepole pine are inhabited by few large mammals as the understory is minimal. Wildflowers are common in this zone, and can be found by the roadside, in clearings, or on riverbanks.

Timberline here lies at an elevation between 2,050 and 2,400 meters above sea level. At this height, only a few stunted trees survive. Above this point is the **alpine** zone, where the climate is severe; the average yearly temperature is below freezing, and summer is brief. The zone's plant species grow low to the ground, with extensive root systems to protect them during high winds and through the deep snow cover of winter. During the short summer these open slopes and meadows are carpeted with a profusion of flowers such as golden arnicas, bluebells, pale columbines, and red and yellow paintbrush. Higher still are brightly colored heathers, buttercups, and alpine forget-me-nots.

FAUNA

Wildlife is abundant in the park, and can be seen throughout the year. During winter many larger mammals move to lower elevations where food is accessible. February and March are particularly good for looking for animal tracks in the snow. By June most of the snow cover at lower elevations has melted, the crowds haven't arrived, and animals can be seen feeding along the valley floor. In fall, tourists move to warmer climates, the rutting season begins, bears go into hibernation, and a herd of elk moves into Jasper townsite for the winter.

While the park provides ample opportunities for seeing numerous animals in their natural habitat, it also leads to human/animal encounters that are not always positive. For example, less than 10% of the park is made up of well-vegetated valleys. These lower areas are essential to the larger mammals for food and shelter but are also the most heavily traveled by visitors. Game trails used for thousands of years are often bisected by roads—hundreds of animals are killed each year by speeding motorists. Please drive slowly in the park.

Another problem occurs when people leave food where animals can get at it (inside a cooler isn't secure enough), or try to feed them directly —a well-meaning gesture that creates as much of a problem for the animals as does traffic. Some of them become accustomed to the taste of human food and become reliant on this easily obtained food source. Then after summer, when everyone has gone home, they have no supply of food. Some of these animals lose their fear of humans and start demanding or stealing food. The familiar moral of the story is: Please Don't Feed the Animals.

Campground Critters
Several species of small mammals thrive around campgrounds, thanks to an abundance of humans who are careless with their food. **Columbian ground squirrels** are very bold

and will demand scraps of your lunch. **Golden-mantled ground squirrels** and **red squirrels** are also common. The **least chipmunk** (often confused with the golden-mantled ground squirrel thanks to similar stripes) can also be seen in campgrounds; they'll often scamper across your hiking trail, then sit boldly on a rock waiting for you to pass.

Aquatic Species

Beaver dams are common between the townsite and the park's east gate. Dawn and dusk are the best times to watch these intriguing crea-tures at work. Also common in the park's wet-lands are **mink** and **muskrat**.

On The Hoof

Five species of deer inhabit the park. The large-eared **mule deer** is commonly seen around the edge of the townsite or grazing along the road. **White-tailed deer** can be seen throughout the park. A small herd of **woodland caribou** roams throughout the park; they are most commonly seen during late spring, feeding in river deltas. The town of Jasper is in the home range of around 500 **elk,** which can be seen most of the year around the townsite or along the highway northeast and south of town. **Moose,** although not common, can be seen along the major drainage systems feeding on aquatic plants.

In summer, **mountain goats** can often be seen feeding in alpine meadows. A good place for goat watching is Goat Lookout on the Icefields Parkway. Unlike most of the park's large mammals, these surefooted creatures don't migrate to lower elevations in winter, but stay sheltered on rocky crags where wind and sun keep the vegetation snow free. Often confused with the goat is the darker **bighorn sheep.** The horns on the males of this species are very thick and often curl 360 degrees. Bighorns are common in the east of the park at Disaster Point, and will often approach cars.

Reclusive Residents
Several of the park's resident species keep a low profile, usually out of sight of humans. Populations of the shy and elusive **lynx** fluctuate with that of their primary food source, the snowshoe hare. The largest of the big cats in the park is the **cougar** (also called the mountain lion), a solitary carnivore that inhabits remote valleys. Jasper's **wolves** are one of the park's success stories. After being driven to near extinction, the species has rebounded. Five packs now roam the park, but they are rarely seen—keeping to the deep wilderness rarely traveled by people. While not common in the park, **coyotes** can be seen in cleared areas alongside the roads; usually at dawn and dusk.

Bears
Black bears are common throughout the park and occasionally wander into campgrounds looking for food. Grizzly bears are occasionally seen crossing the Icefields Parkway at higher elevations early in summer. For the most part they remain in remote mountain valleys, and if they do see, smell, or hear you they'll generally move away.

Each summer, human–bear encounters occur within the park, with the most common outcome being that the bear will amble away. Very few attacks have been recorded within the park and there has been only one fatality in recent years. The best ways to avoid trouble? Don't hike alone or at dusk; make lots of noise when passing dense brush; and keep a clean camp. It is imperative that you read *You are in Bear Country* before setting out; the pamphlet is available at campgrounds and information centers throughout the park.

Other Mammals
The **pine marten** is common, but shy; look for them in subalpine forests. The **short-tailed weasel**—a relative of the marten—is also common, while the **long-tailed weasel** is rare. At higher elevations look for **pikas** in piles of fallen rock. **Hoary marmots** live near the upper limits of vegetation growth, where their shrill warning whistles carry across the open meadows. **Porcupines** are widespread in all valleys and are most active at night.

Birds
The extensive tree cover in the lower valleys hides many species of birds, making them seem less abundant than they are. A total of 248 species has been recorded. The two you're most likely to see are the **gray jay** and **Clark's nutcracker,** which regularly joins picnickers for lunch. Also common are black-and-white **magpies,** raucous **ravens,** and several species of **ducks,** which can be seen around lakes in the Athabasca River Valley. **Harlequin ducks** nest in the park during early summer. A stretch of the Maligne River is closed during this season to prevent human interference.

The colony of **black swifts** in Maligne Canyon is one of only two in Alberta. Their poorly developed legs make it difficult for them to take off from their nests in the canyon walls—they literally fall before becoming airborne. High alpine slopes are home to **white-tailed ptarmigans,** a type of grouse that turns white in winter. Also at this elevation are flocks of **rosy finches** that live under overhanging cliffs. In subalpine forests the songs of **thrushes** and the tapping of **woodpeckers** can be heard.

At dusk, **great horned owls** swoop silently through the trees, their eerie call echoing through the forest. **Golden eagles** and **bald eagles** can be seen soaring high above the forests, and 12 pairs of **ospreys** are known to nest in the park, many along the Athabasca River between town and the east park gate.

Coast Hotels
& Resorts

HISTORY

The first white man to enter the Athabasca River Valley was David Thompson, one of Canada's greatest explorers. He was looking for a pass through the mountains to use as access to the Pacific Ocean. The gap he eventually found—**Athabasca Pass,** south of Mt. Edith Cavell—became famous as the route used by the North West and Hudson's Bay companies to cross the Rockies.

Meanwhile, the North West Company built a post named Jasper's House near the present townsite of Jasper. In time, an easier passage through the mountains was discovered farther north (at what is now called **Yellowhead Pass**), displacing Thompson's original, more difficult route to the south.

Leading up to the end of the fur-trading era, many visitors to the area returned home with accounts of the region's natural splendor. In 1858, Irish-Canadian artist Paul Kane published the book *Wanderings of an Artist,* which gave the outside world its first glimpse of the Jasper area.

At the turn of this century only seven homesteaders lived in the valley, but the Grand Trunk Pacific Railway was pushing westward, bringing with it the possibility of multitudes of settlers coming to live there. In 1907, the federal government officially declared the boundaries of Jasper Forest Park and bought all the land within, save for one homestead owned by Lewis Swift. (This parcel remained privately owned until 1962, long after the stubborn Mr. Swift had passed away.) The threat of oversettlement of the valley had been abated, but as a designated forest park, mining and logging were still allowed. In 1908, Jasper Park Collieries staked claims in the park. By the time the railway came through in 1910, mining activity was centered at **Pocahontas** (near the park's east gate), where a township was established and thrived. During an extended miners' strike, the men spent their spare time constructing log pools at Miette Hot Springs, which were heavily promoted to early park visitors. The mine closed in 1921 and many families relocated to Jasper, which had grown from a railway camp into a popular tourist destination. Jasper was officially designated a national park in 1930. This was followed by the construction of many roads including the Icefields Parkway, which opened in 1940.

ICEFIELDS PARKWAY/JASPER

Sunwapta Pass, at the boundary between Banff and Jasper national parks, is just over halfway between Lake Louise and Jasper townsite along the 230-km Icefields Parkway, one of the world's great mountain drives. From the pass it is 108 km to Jasper, passing first the **Columbia Icefield** then following the **Athabasca River** for the rest of the way. The scenery along this stretch of road is no less spectacular than the other half through Banff National Park, and it's easy to spend a few days en route. Along this section of the parkway are two lodges, three hostels, six campgrounds, and one gas station.

SIGHTS

Columbia Icefield

The largest and most accessible of 17 glacial areas along the Icefields Parkway is 325-square-km Columbia Icefield at the south end of the park. It's a remnant of the last major glaciation that covered most of Canada 20,000 years ago, and has survived because of the elevation (1,900-2,800 meters above sea level), cold temperatures, and heavy snowfalls. From the main body of the ice cap, which sits astride the Continental Divide, glaciers creep down three main valleys. Of these, **Athabasca Glacier** is the most accessible and can be seen from the Icefields Parkway. A path to the toe of the glacier traverses a mixture of rock, sand, and gravel, known as *till,* deposited by the glacier as it retreats. The speed at which glaciers advance and retreat varies with the long-term climate. Athabasca Glacier has retreated to its current position from across the highway, a distance of over 1.5 km, in 100 years. Currently it retreats two to three meters per year.

Brewster's Snocoaches drive right onto the icefield for a close look.

BREWSTER TRANSPORTATION AND TOURS

The icefield is made more spectacular by the impressive peaks that surround it. **Mt. Athabasca** (3,491 meters) dominates the skyline, and three glaciers cling to its flanks. **Dome Glacier** is also visible from the highway. Although part of Columbia Icefield it is not actually connected. It is made of ice that breaks off the icefield 300 meters above, supplemented by the large quantities of snow the area receives each winter.

Exploring The Icefield

The icefield can be very dangerous for unprepared visitors, especially the broken surface of Athabasca Glacier where often-deep crevasses are uncovered as the winter snows melt. The safest way to experience it firsthand is on specially developed vehicles with balloon tires that can travel over its crevassed surface. These Snocoaches are operated by **Brewster Transportation and Tours.** The 90-minute tour of Athabasca Glacier includes time spent walking on the surface of the glacier. The tour, which begins from the terminal opposite the icefield, is $19.50 and operates from May to early October. Early in the season the glacier is still covered in a layer of snow and is therefore not as spectacular as during the summer months.

On the same side of the road as the Snocoach Terminal is the **Icefield Information Centre.** It's open May and September, daily 10 a.m.-5 p.m.; June-Aug., daily 10 a.m.-7 p.m.

To Sunwapta Falls

Sunwapta Lake—at the toe of the Athabasca Glacier—is the source of the **Sunwapta River,** which the Icefields Parkway follows for 48 km to Sunwapta Falls. Eight km north from the Icefield Information Centre, the road descends to a viewpoint for **Stutfield Glacier.** Most of the glacier is hidden from view by a densely wooded ridge, but at its toe, till left by the glacier's retreat litters the valley floor. The main body of the Columbia Icefield can be seen along the clifftop high above. To the south of the glacier is **Mt. Kitchener.** Six km farther down the road is **Tangle Ridge,** a grayish brown wall of limestone over which Beauty Creek cascades.

A further 40 km along the road a one-km gravel spur to the left leads to **Sunwapta Falls.** Here, the Sunwapta River changes direction sharply and drops into a deep canyon. Two km downstream the river flows into the much-wider Athabasca Valley.

Goat Lookout

After following the Athabasca River for 17 km, the road ascends to a lookout. Below the lookout is a steep bank of glacially ground material containing natural deposits of salt. The local mountain goats spend most of their time on the steep slopes of Mt. Kerkeslin, to the northeast, but occasionally cross the road and can be seen searching for the salt licks along the riverbank.

Athabasca Falls

At Athabasca Falls, the Athabasca River is forced through a narrow gorge and over a cliff into a cauldron of roaring water below. Old river channels can be seen along the west bank. As the river slowly erodes the center of the riverbed, the falls will move upstream. Trails lead from a day-use area to various viewpoints above and below the falls. From the falls it is 31 km to Jasper townsite.

Mount Edith Cavell

The original Icefields Parkway (Hwy. 93A) that followed the southeast bank of the Athabasca River has now been bypassed by a more direct route on the other side of the river. Along the original route, known also as the Athabasca Parkway, a 14.5-km road leads to a parking area below the northeast face of Mt. Edith Cavell (3,363 meters). This peak can be seen from many vantage points in the north end of the park,

including the townsite, but none is more impressive than directly below it. On this face, **Angel Glacier** lies in a saddle on the mountain's lower slopes. From the parking area the **Path of the Glacier Trail** (one hour round trip) traverses moraines deposited by the receding Angel Glacier and leads to some great viewpoints.

HIKES ALONG ICEFIELDS PARKWAY

Wilcox Pass

- Length: 4 km (90 minutes) one way
- Elevation gain: 340 meters
- Rating: moderate

This trail was once used by northbound outfitters because, 100 years ago, Athabasca Gla-

COLUMBIA ICEFIELD

TO JASPER TOWNSITE

JASPER NATIONAL PARK

SUNWAPTA RIVER

93

WILCOX PASS TRAIL

MT. WILCOX

NIGEL PEAK

BRAZEAU RIVER

MT. KITCHENER (3511 m)

COLUMBIA ICEFIELD CHALET

COLUMBIA ICEFIELD CAMPGROUND

WILCOX CREEK CAMPGROUND

ICEFIELD INFORMATION CENTRE

SUNWAPTA LAKE

SUNWAPTA PASS (2023 m)

NIGEL CREEK

DOME GLACIER

SNOW DOME (3460 m)

ATHABASCA GLACIER

HILDA CREEK HOSTEL

PARKER'S RIDGE

ICEFIELDS PARKWAY

PANTHER FALLS

MT. ATHABASCA (3491 m)

BANFF NATIONAL PARK

MT. ANDROMEDA (3442 m)

NORTH SASKATCHEWAN RIVER

TO BANFF

93

SASKATCHEWAN GLACIER

ALBERTA BRITISH COLUMBIA

COLUMBIA ICEFIELD

0   2 mi

0   2 km

© MOON PUBLICATIONS, INC.

cier covered the valley floor and had to be by-passed. The trail begins from the north side of Wilcox Creek Campground, three km south of the Icefield Information Centre. It climbs through a forest of Engelmann spruce and alpine fir to a ridge with panoramic views of the valley, Columbia Icefield, and surrounding peaks. Ascending gradually from there, the trail enters a fragile environment of alpine meadows. From the pass, most hikers return along the same trail, although it is possible to continue north, descending to the Icefields Parkway at Tangle Ridge, 11.5 km from the trailhead.

Fortress Lake
- Length: 24 km (7-8 hours) one way
- Elevation gain: minimal
- Rating: moderate

The trail to this seldom-visited lake straddling the Continental Divide begins from the Sunwapta Falls parking lot. For the first 15 km the trail meanders along the east bank of the Athabasca River, then crosses it. Beyond the main bridge you'll need to ford the braided Chaba River, then continue southwest along the river flats for six km to the east end of Fortress Lake. The lake lies within British Columbia in Hamber Provincial Park. Its shores are difficult to traverse as they lack established trails.

Geraldine Lakes
- Length: 5 km (2 hours) one way
- Elevation gain: 410 meters
- Rating: moderate

The first of the four Geraldine Lakes is an easy two-km hike from the trailhead (located 5.5 km along the Geraldine Fire Rd., which spurs south off Hwy. 93A west of Athabasca Falls). The forest-encircled lake reflects the north face of Mt. Fryatt (3,361 meters). The trail continues along the northwest shore, climbs steeply past a scenic 100-meter waterfall, and traverses some rough terrain where the trail becomes indistinct; follow the cairns. At the end of the valley is another waterfall. The trail climbs east of the waterfall to a ridge above the second of the lakes, five km from the trailhead. Although the trail officially ends here, it does continue to a campground at the south end of the lake. Two other lakes, accessible only by bush-bashing, are located farther up the valley.

HIKES NEAR MOUNT EDITH CAVELL

Mount Edith Cavell Rd. begins from Hwy. 93A and winds through a subalpine forest, ascending 300 meters in 14.5 km. Trailheads are located at the end of the road (Cavell Meadows Trail and a short interpretive trail) and across from the hostel two km from the end (Astoria River Trail). A third trailhead is on Marmot Basin Rd. where it crosses Portal Creek (Maccarib Pass Trail).

Cavell Meadows
- Length: 4 km (1 hour) one way
- Elevation gain: 350 meters
- Rating: easy/moderate

This trail, beginning from the parking lot beneath Mt. Edith Cavell, provides easy access to an alpine meadow and panoramic views of Angel Glacier. The trail climbs steadily through a subalpine forest of Engelmann spruce and alpine fir to emerge facing the northeast face of Mt. Edith Cavell and Angel Glacier. The trail continues to higher viewpoints and an alpine meadow which, in mid-July, is filled with wildflowers.

Astoria River
- Length: 19 km (6-7 hours) one way
- Elevation gain: 450 meters
- Rating: moderate

Beginning opposite the hostel on Mt. Edith Cavell Rd., this trail descends through a forest on the north side of Mt. Edith Cavell for five km, then crosses the Astoria River and begins a long ascent into spectacular Tonquin Valley. Amethyst Lakes and the 1,000-meter cliffs of the Ramparts first come into view after 13 km. At the 17-km mark the trail divides. To the left it climbs into Eremite Valley where there is a campground. The right fork continues following Astoria River to Tonquin Valley, Amethyst Lakes, and a choice of four campgrounds.

Maccarib Pass
- Length: 21 km (7-8 hours) one way
- Elevation gain: 730 meters
- Rating: moderate

This trail is slightly longer and gains more elevation than the trail along Astoria River but is more spectacular. From 6.5 km up Marmot Basin Rd., the trail strikes out to the southwest. It follows Portal Creek and passes under Peveril Peak before making a steep approach to Maccarib Pass, 12.5 km from the trailhead. The full panorama of the Tonquin Valley can be appreciated as the path gradually descends from the pass. At Amethyst Lakes it links up with the Astoria River Trail, and many options for day-hikes head out from campgrounds at the lakes.

ACCOMMODATIONS

Lodging
Sunwapta Falls Resort, P.O. Box 97, Jasper, Alberta T0E 1E0, tel. (403) 852-4852, is located 55 km south of Jasper townsite. It has 40 rooms, a restaurant, and a gift shop; $115 s or d. **Becker's Chalets,** P.O. Box 579, tel. 852-3779, just six km from the townsite, was established in the 1940s. One-bed sleeping rooms are $57, chalets—each with a kitchenette, fireplace, and double bed—are $81 (or $87 for those on the riverfront).

Hostels
Along this section of the Icefields Parkway, hostels are located at Km 144 and 198 (from Lake Louise). **Beauty Creek Hostel,** located 14 km from Columbia Icefield, overlooks the Sunwapta River. It has two separate male and female cabins; each sleeps 12 and has a woodstove. A third building holds a well-equipped kit. dining area. Members of Hostelling Interna. al pay $8, nonmembers $13. **Athabasca Fal:** **Hostel** is a further 60 km toward Jasper townsite. It is larger and has electricity. Athabasca Falls is only a few minutes' walk away; members $9, nonmembers $14.

Mt. Edith Cavell Hostel has a million-dollar view for the price of a dorm bed. It's located 13 km up Mt. Edith Cavell Road. Because of the location there's usually a spare bed. Opposite the hostel are trailheads for hiking in the Tonquin Valley, and it's just a short walk to the base of Mt. Edith Cavell. The hostel is rustic but has a kitchen, dining area, and outdoor wood sauna. It's closed November to mid-June. **Hiker's Wheels** leaves Hava Java House at 407 Patricia St. in Jasper daily at 5 p.m. for the hostel; reservations are necessary, call (403) 852-2188.

Reservations for the above hostels can be made at all major hostels or by calling 439-3139.

Campgrounds
Wilcox Creek and **Columbia Icefield campgrounds** are within two km of each other at the extreme southern end of the park. Both are primitive campgrounds with toilets, cooking shelters, and fire rings; sites are $7.25. Traveling north, **Jonas Creek, Honeymoon Lake,** and **Mt. Kerkeslin campgrounds** are located along the next 50 km stretch of road. Each is $7.25 per site, per night. **Wabasso Campground** is located along Hwy. 93A; $9.25.

JASPER TOWNSITE

The townsite of Jasper is Banff's northern counterpart, linked to its neighbor by a similar history and, today, by the Icefields Parkway. The town—run by Parks Canada—has just over half the population of Banff, and its setting is less dramatic. But it's also less commercialized than Banff and its streets a little quieter. Part of the town's charm is its location at the confluence of the Athabasca and Miette rivers, surrounded by the rugged, snowcapped peaks of Jasper National Park. From town it's a 3.5-hour drive to Edmonton, the closest city. The town of Banff is 280 km to the southeast, and to the west is the vast wilderness of the Monashee, Cariboo, and Columbia ranges of the British Columbia interior.

Connaught Dr., the town's main street, parallels the rail line as it curves through town. Along here you'll find the park information center, bus depot, rail terminal, restaurants, motels, and a parking lot. Behind Connaught Dr. is Patricia St. (one way), which has more restaurants and services and leads to more hotels and motels on Geikie Street. Behind this main core are rows of neat houses—much less pretentious than those in Banff—and all the facilities of a regular town, including a library, school, post office, museum, swimming pool, and hospital.

JASPER TOWNSITE

TO PYRAMID LAKE

SAWRIDGE HOTEL

MARMOT LODGE

TO HWY. 16
TO MALIGNE CANYON
AND MIETTE
HOT SPRINGS

16

LOBSTICK LODGE

TONQUIN INN

CHATEAU JASPER

JUNIPER ST.

JASPER INN

BONHOMME BUNGALOWS

ASPEN AVE.

AMETHYST LODGE

GEKIE ST.

BONHOMME ST.

PATRICIA ST.

PYRAMID LAKE RD.

PYRAMID LAKE LOOP

CEDAR AVE.

AQUATIC CENTRE

TOKYO TOM'S PLACE

JASPER-YELLOWHEAD MUSEUM

ASTORIA HOTEL

HAVA JAVA HOUSE

PAPA GEORGE'S

ELM AVE.

PARK INFORMATION CENTRE

LIBRARY

POST OFFICE

WHISTLERS INN

ATHABASCA HOTEL

VIA RAIL STATION

HOSPITAL

CHABA THEATRE

SOMETHING ELSE RESTAURANT

CANTONESE RESTAURANT

CONNAUGHT SQUARE

MIETTE AVE.

MALIGNE TOURS

JASPER TOURISM INFORMATION CENTRE

L & W RESTAURANT

YELLOWHEAD HWY.

ATHABASCA RIVER

CABIN CREEK RD.

WILLOW AVE.

PINE AVE.

CONNAUGHT DR.

TO OLD FORT POINT

MOUNT ROBSON INN

MALIGNE LODGE

93A

93

TO PRINCE GEORGE

16

TO ICEFIELDS PARKWAY AND BANFF

MOON

MIETTE RIVER

NOT TO SCALE

© MOON PUBLICATIONS, INC.

History

In the winter of 1810-11, when David Thompson was making the first successful crossing of the Continental Divide, some of his party remained in the Athabasca River Valley and constructed a small settlement east of the present townsite. The settlement was named Henry House and was used for many years by the North West Company as a supply depot for fur traders. The post was run by a clerk named Jasper Hawes, and in time the settlement became known as Jasper's House. Over the years, stories of the area's natural beauty filtered east. Gold seekers commonly stopped by on their way to the Cariboo Goldfields. But when the fur-trading era ended in the mid-1880s, the post closed.

In 1911 a construction camp was established for the Grand Trunk Pacific Railway near the present townsite of Jasper. The company had dreamed of a transcontinental rail line to rival the C.P.R. line that crossed the Rockies farther south. When the northern line was completed, visitors flocked into the remote mountain settlement, and its future was assured. The first accommodation for tourists was 10 tents on the shore of Lac Beauvert that became known as Jasper Park Camp. In 1921 the tents were replaced and the original Jasper Park Lodge was constructed. By the summer of 1928, a road was completed from Edmonton and a golf course was built. As the number of tourists to the park continued to increase, existing facilities were expanded. In 1940 the Icefields Parkway opened and in the '60s Marmot Basin Ski Area opened and the downtown core of the townsite was developed.

SIGHTS AND DRIVES

Downtown

With all the things to do and see in the park it's amazing how many people hang out in town. July and August are especially busy; much-needed improvements to the parking problem have had little impact on the traffic. The best way to avoid the problem is to avoid town during the day. The park information center, on Connaught Dr., is the only real reason to be in town. The shaded park in front of the center is a good place for people-watching—but you may get clobbered by a wayward Hacky Sack.

At the back of town is the excellent, relatively new **Jasper-Yellowhead Museum and Archives,** 400 Pyramid Lake Rd., tel. (403) 852-3013, which has a collection of artifacts cataloguing the human history of the park. The museum also features extensive archives, including photos, documents, and maps. It's open June-Sept., daily 1-9 p.m.

If you like taxidermy, visit **The Den Wildlife Museum,** which exhibits stuffed animals in their "natural setting." It's located down a dark stairway beneath the Whistlers Inn. Yep, they even charge you for it; $2.50. Open year-round, daily 9 a.m.-10 p.m.

Jasper Tramway

This tramway climbs over 1,000 vertical meters up the steep north face of **The Whistlers,** named after the hoary marmots that live on the summit. The tramway operates two 30-passenger cars that take seven minutes to reach the upper terminal, during which time the conductor gives a narrated lecture about the mountain and its environment. From the upper terminal, a one-km trail leads to the summit (2,470 meters). The view is breathtaking; to the south is the Columbia Icefield, and on a clear day you can see Mt. Robson (3,954 meters)—the highest peak in the Canadian Rockies—to the northwest. Round-trip fare is $9.65; allow two hours on top and, on a clear summer's day, two more hours in line at the bottom. The tramway is located three km south of town on Hwy. 93 (Icefields Parkway) and then three km up Whistlers Road. It operates in summer, daily 8 a.m.-10 p.m., shorter hours April-May and Sept.-Oct., closed the rest of the year. For more information call (403) 852-3093. A shuttle bus runs from major Jasper hotels to the tramway; inquire at hotel desks for times.

Patricia And Pyramid Lakes

A winding road heads through the hills at the back of town to these two picturesque lakes, formed when glacial moraines dammed shallow valleys. The first, to the left is Patricia, the second, farther along the road, is Pyramid, backed by **Pyramid Mountain** (2,765 meters). Both lakes are popular spots for picnicking, fishing, and boating. Boat rentals are available at **Pyramid Lake Resort Bungalows,** tel. (403) 852-4900. Canoes, rowboats, paddleboats, and kayaks are $10 for the first hour and $7 for each additional hour. They also rent sailboards ($15 per hour), motorboats and catamarans ($20 per hour), and Jet Skis ($60 per hour). From the bungalows the road continues around the lake to a bridge, which leads to an island popular with picnickers. The road ends at the quieter end of the lake.

Edith And Annette Lakes

These two lakes along the road to Jasper Park Lodge—across the Athabasca River from town—are the perfect place for a picnic, swim, or pleasant walk. They are remnants of a much larger lake that once covered the entire valley floor. The lakes are relatively shallow, therefore the sun warms the water to a bearable temperature; in fact they have the warmest waters of any lakes in the park. The 2.5-km **Lee Foundation Trail** encircles Lake Annette and is wheelchair accessible. Both lakes have day-use areas with man-made beaches and picnic areas.

Jasper Park Lodge

Accommodations are not usually considered "sights" but then this is the Rockies, where three grand railway hotels attract as many visitors as the more legitimate natural attractions. Jasper Park Lodge has been the premier accommodation in the park since it opened in 1921. Back then it was a single-story structure, reputed to be the largest log building in the world. It burned to the ground in 1952, but was rebuilt. Additional bungalows were erected along Lac Beauvert, forming a basis for today's lodge. Rows of cabins radiate from the main lodge, which contains restaurants, lounges, and the town's only covered shopping arcade. Today up to 900 guests can be accommodated in 437 rooms. A large parking area for nonguests is located on Lodge Rd., behind the golf clubhouse; you're welcome to walk around the resort, play golf, dine in the restaurants, and of course, browse through the shopping promenade—even if you're not a registered guest. From the main lodge, a hiking trail follows the shoreline of Lac Beauvert and links up with other trails from Old Fort Point. To walk from town will take one hour.

Maligne Canyon

To get here head northeast from town and turn right onto Maligne Lake Road. The canyon access road veers left, 11 km from Jasper. This unique geological feature has been eroded out of the easily dissolved limestone bedrock by the fast-flowing Maligne River. Surface water here is augmented by underground springs, therefore it seems that more water flows out of the canyon than into it. The canyon is up to 50 meters deep, yet so narrow that squirrels often jump across. At the top of the canyon, opposite the teahouse, are large potholes in the riverbed. These potholes are created when rocks and pebbles become trapped in what begins as a shallow depression, and under the force of the rushing water carve jug-shaped hollows into the soft bedrock.

An interpretive trail winds down from the parking lot, crossing the canyon six times. The most spectacular sections of the canyon can be seen from the first two bridges, at the upper end of the trail. In summer a teahouse operates at the top of the canyon. To avoid the crowds at the upper end of the canyon, an alternative would be to park at Sixth Bridge, near the confluence of the Maligne and Athabasca rivers, and walk *up* the canyon (see "Hiking Around Town," below). The **Maligne Lake Shuttle** stops at the canyon eight times daily. For reservations call (403) 852-3370; fare is $6 one way from town. In winter guided tours of the frozen canyon are an experience you'll never forget (see "Wintertime" below).

To Maligne Lake

From the canyon, Maligne Lake Rd. climbs to **Medicine Lake,** which does a disappearing act each year. The water level fluctuates due to an underground drainage system. At the northwest end of the lake, where the outlet should be, the riverbed is often dry. In fall, when runoff from the mountains is minimal, the water level drops and, by November, the lake has almost completely dried up. Early Indians believed that spirits were responsible for the phenomenon, hence the name.

At the end of the road, 48 km from Jasper, is Maligne Lake, the largest glacier-fed lake in the Canadian Rockies and second-largest in the world. The first paying visitors were brought to the lake in 1929, and it has been a mecca for camera-toting tourists from around the world ever since. Once at the lake, activities are plentiful. But other than taking in the spectacular

TO MIETTE HOT SPRINGS AND EDMONTON

PYRAMID LAKE

MALIGNE CANYON

16

MALIGNE CANYON HOSTEL

PYRAMID LAKE RESORT BUNGALOWS

MALIGNE LAKE RD.

EDITH LAKE

PATRICIA LAKE

ANNETTE LAKE

PATRICIA LAKE BUNGALOWS

PYRAMID RIDING STABLES

PINE BUNGALOWS

COTTONWOOD SLOUGH

JASPER PARK LODGE

LAC BEAUVERT

YELLOWHEAD HWY.

JASPER TOWNSITE

VICINITY
OF
JASPER

OLD FORT POINT

TEKARRA LODGE

93A

MIETTE RIVER

TO VALLEY OF THE FIVE LAKES

16 TO PRINCE GEORGE

ATHABASCA RIVER

WHISTLERS MOUNTAIN HOSTEL

WHISTLERS CAMPGROUND

93

JASPER TRAMWAY

WAPITI CAMPGROUND

ICEFIELDS PARKWAY

0   1 mi

0   1 km

TO BANFF

THE WHISTLERS (2470 m)

© MOON PUBLICATIONS, INC.

vistas, the only thing you won't need your wallet for is hiking one of the numerous trails in the area.

The most popular tourist activity at the lake is a 90-minute narrated cruise on a glass-enclosed boat up the lake to oft-photographed **Spirit Island.** Cruises leave in summer, every hour on the hour 10 a.m.-5 p.m., with fewer sailings in May and September; $30 per person. Many time slots are block-booked by tour companies, therefore reservations are suggested; make them at the Maligne Tours office, 626 Connaught Dr., tel. (403) 852-3370. The lake also has excellent trout fishing; Alberta's record rainbow trout was caught here. Fishing tackle and bait is available at the Boathouse, by Parking Lot 2. The Boathouse also rents rowboats and canoes for $10 the first hour, $6 each additional hour. Again, for reservations contact Maligne Tours in Jasper. Horseback riding is also available at the lake.

The Maligne River, a class III river and the wildest whitewater trip in the park, is run by two companies. **Maligne River Adventures,** tel. 852-3370, and **White Water Rafting,** tel. 852-7238, offer two-hour trips, including transfers from Jasper for $45.

The **Maligne Lake Shuttle** runs from the Maligne Tours office at 626 Connaught Dr., tel. 852-3370, and from various hotels out to the lake. Tickets can be bought in conjunction with a cruise ($45), raft trip ($65), or horseback ride ($65), or for the bus only ($20 round trip). The shuttle makes eight trips daily.

Miette Hot Springs

Near the park's east gate is Miette Hot Springs Rd., which leads to the warmest springs in the Canadian Rockies. One km along the road is **Punchbowl Falls,** where a small river cascades through a narrow crevice in a cliff to a pool of turbulent water. After curving, swerving, rising, and falling many times the road ends at the hot springs. In the early 1900s, the springs were one of the park's biggest attractions. In 1910, a packhorse trail was built up the valley and the government constructed a bathhouse. The original hand-hewn log structure was replaced in the '30s with pools that remained in use until new facilities were built in 1985. Water that flows into the pools is artificially cooled from 54° C to a soothing 39°. A swim in the pools is $3.50, a

towel $1, and lockers 25 cents. It's open mid-May to mid-June, daily 10:30 a.m.-9 p.m.; mid-June to September, daily 8:30 a.m.-10:30 p.m. Many hiking trails begin from the hot springs complex; the shortest is from the picnic area to the source of the springs (200 meters). Below the springs is a restaurant and lodging.

HIKING AROUND TOWN

The 1,000 kilometers of hiking trails in Jasper are significantly different than those in the other mountain national parks. The park has an extensive system of interconnecting backcountry trails that, for experienced hikers, can provide a wilderness adventure rivaled by few areas on the face of this earth. For casual day-hikers, on the other hand, opportunities are more limited. Most trails in the immediate vicinity of the townsite have little elevation gain and lead through montane forest to lakes. The trails around Maligne Lake, in the Tonquin Valley, at the base of Mt. Edith Cavell, and along the Icefields Parkway have more rewarding objectives and are more challenging.

The most popular trails for extended backcountry trips are the **Skyline Trail,** between the townsite and Maligne Lake (44.5 km, three days each way); the trails to **Amethyst Lakes** in the Tonquin Valley (19 km, one day each way) and **Athabasca Pass** (50 km, three days each way), which was used by fur traders for 40 years as the main route across the Rockies; and the **South Boundary Trail,** which traverses a remote section of the front ranges into Banff National Park (160 km, 10 days each way).

Before setting off on any hikes, whatever the length, go to the **park information center** in Jasper townsite for trail maps, trail conditions, and trail closures. To prevent overuse, many longer trails operate on a quota system and you *must* pick up a permit before heading out.

Pyramid Lake Loop

- Length: 17 km (5 hours) round trip
- Elevation gain: 150 meters
- Rating: easy/moderate

A myriad of official and unofficial hiking trails is located on the benchland immediately west of Jasper townsite. From the parking lot opposite the Aquatic Centre on Pyramid Lake Rd., a well-marked trail climbs onto the benchland. Keep right, crossing Pyramid Lake Rd., and you'll emerge on a bluff overlooking the Athabasca River Valley. Bighorn sheep can often be seen grazing here. If you return to the trailhead from here, you will have hiked seven km. The trail continues north, disappearing into the montane forest until arriving at Pyramid Lake. Various trails can be taken to return to town; ask for a map of the entire area before setting out at the park information center.

Patricia Lake Circle
- Length: 5 km loop (90 minutes round trip)
- Elevation gain: minimal
- Rating: easy

This trail begins across the road from the riding stables on Pyramid Lake Road. It traverses a mixed forest of aspen and lodgepole pine; prime habitat for a variety of larger mammals such as elk, deer, and moose. The second half of the trail skirts Cottonwood Slough where you'll see a number of beaver ponds.

The Whistlers
- Length: 8 km (2.5-3 hours) one way
- Elevation gain: 1,220 meters
- Rating: moderate/difficult

This steep ascent, one of the most arduous in the park, is unique in that it passes through three distinct vegetation zones in a relatively short distance. From the trailhead on Whistlers Rd., 200 meters below the hostel, the trail begins climbing and doesn't let up until you merge with the crowds getting off the tramway at the top. The trail begins in a montane forest of aspen and white birch, climbs through a subalpine forest of Engelmann spruce and alpine fir, then emerges onto the open, treeless tundra, inhabited by pikas, hoary marmots, and a few hardy plants. Carry water—none is available before the upper tramway terminal.

Old Fort Point
- Length: 6.5 km loop (2 hours round trip)
- Elevation gain: 60 meters
- Rating: easy

Old Fort Point is a moderately sized knoll above the Athabasca River, to the east of Jasper townsite. Although it is not likely a fort was ever

BOB RACE

BIGHORN SHEEP

Bighorn sheep are some of the most distinctive mammals of the Canadian Rockies. Easily recognized by their impressive horns, they are often seen grazing on grassy mountain slopes or at salt licks beside the road. The color of their coat varies with the season; in summer it is a brownish gray with a cream-colored belly and rump, turning lighter in winter. At seven years of age, males are fully grown and can weigh up to 120 kilograms. Females generally weigh around 80 kilograms.

Both sexes possess horns, rather than antlers like moose, elk, and deer. Unlike antlers, horns are not shed each year, and can grow to astounding sizes. The horns of rams are larger than those of ewes, and curve up to 360 degrees. The spiraled horns of an older ram can measure 115 cm and weigh as much as 15 kilograms. As the horns grow, they become marked by an annual growth ring. By counting the rings it is possible to determine the approximate age of the animal. In fall, during the mating season, a hierarchy is established among them for the right to breed ewes. As the males face off against each other to establish dominance, their horns act as both a weapon and a buffer against the head-butting of other rams. The skull structure of the bighorn, rams in particular, has become adapted to these clashes, avoiding heavy concussion.

These animals are particularly tolerant of humans and often approach parked vehicles; although they are not dangerous, as with all mammals in the park, you should not approach or feed them.

located here, the first fur-trading post in the Rockies, Henry House, was located just downstream, and it is easy to imagine fur traders and early explorers climbing to this summit for 360-degree views of the Athabasca and Miette rivers. To get to the trailhead from town, take Hwy. 93A and turn left to Lac Beauvert. The trail begins just over the Athabasca River. Climb the wooden stairs, take the left trail to the top of the knoll, then continue back to the parking lot along the north flank of the hill.

Valley Of The Five Lakes
- Length: 2.3 km (1 hour) one way
- Elevation gain: 60 meters
- Rating: easy

These lakes, nestled in an open valley, are small, but make a worthwhile destination. From the trailhead, 10 km south of Jasper townsite along the Icefields Parkway, the trail passes through a forest of lodgepole pine, crosses a stream, and climbs a ridge from where you'll have a panoramic view of surrounding peaks. As the trail descends to the lakes, turn left at the first intersection to a point between two of the lakes. These lakes are linked to Old Fort Point by a tedious 10-km trail through montane forest.

Maligne Canyon
- Length: 3.7 km (90 minutes) one way
- Elevation gain: 125 meters
- Rating: moderate

Maligne Canyon is one of the busiest places in the park, yet few visitors hike the entire length of the canyon trail. By starting from the lower end of the canyon, at the confluence of the Maligne and Athabasca rivers, you'll avoid starting your hike alongside the masses and you'll get to hike downhill on your return (when you're tired). To get to the trailhead head east from the townsite, turn right on Maligne Lake Rd., and follow it 2.5 km to the warden's office, from where a one-km access road leads to Sixth Bridge. Crowds will be minimal for the first three km, to Fourth Bridge, where the trail starts climbing. By the time you get to Third Bridge, you start encountering "adventurous" hikers coming down the canyon, and soon thereafter you'll meet the real crowds, bear-bells and all. Upstream of here the canyon is deepest and most spectacular. See "Maligne Canyon" under "Sights and Drives," above, for details of the hike starting from the *top* of the canyon.

HIKING IN THE MALIGNE LAKE AREA

Maligne Lake, 48 km from Jasper townsite, provides more easy hiking with many opportunities to view the lake and explore its environs. The first two hikes detailed are along the access road to the lake; the others leave from various parking lots located at the northwest end of the lake.

Watchtower Basin
- Length: 10 km (3.5 hours) one way
- Elevation gain: 630 meters
- Rating: moderate/difficult

Watchtower is a wide, open basin high above the crowds of Maligne Lake Road. The trailhead is 24 km from Jasper townsite. All the elevation gain is made during the first six km, through a dense forest of lodgepole pine and white spruce. As the trail levels off and enters the basin it continues to follow the west bank of a stream, crossing it at km 10, and officially ending at a campground. To the west and south the **Maligne Range** rises to a crest three km beyond the campground. From the top of this ridge, at the intersection with the **Skyline Trail**, it is 17.5 km northwest to Maligne Canyon, or 27 km southeast to Maligne Lake. By camping at Watchtower Campground, day trips can be made to a small lake in the basin or to highlights of the Skyline Trail such as the Snowbowl, Curator Lake, and Shovel Pass.

Jacques Lake
- Length: 12 km (3-3.5 hours) one way
- Elevation gain: 100 meters
- Rating: moderate

The appeal of this trail, which begins from a parking lot at the southeast end of Medicine Lake, is its lack of elevation gain and the numerous small lakes it skirts as it travels through a narrow valley. On either side, the severely faulted mountains of the Queen Elizabeth Ranges rise steeply above the valley floor, their strata tilted nearly vertical.

Lake Trail (East Side)
- Length: 3.2-km loop (1 hour round trip)
- Elevation gain: minimal
- Rating: easy

This short trail begins from the back of Parking Lot 2, following the eastern shore of Maligne Lake to a point known as **Schäffer Viewpoint,** named for the first white person to see the valley. After dragging yourself away from the spectacular panorama, follow the trail into a forest of spruce and subalpine fir before looping back to the trailhead.

Opal Hills
- Length: 8.2-km loop (3 hours round trip)
- Elevation gain: 455 meters
- Rating: moderate

This trail begins at the back of Parking Lot 1, climbing steeply for 1.5 km to a point where it divides. Both options end in the high alpine mead-

---

MARY SCHÄFFER

In the early 1900s, exploration of mountain wilderness areas was considered a man's domain. However, a spirited and tenacious woman entered that domain and went on to explore areas of the Canadian Rockies that no white man ever had. Mary Sharples was born in 1861 in Pennsylvania and raised in a strict Quaker family. Mary was introduced to Dr. Charles Schäffer on a trip to the Rockies and, in 1889, they were married. His interest in botany drew them back to the Rockies, where Charles collected, documented, and photographed specimens until his death in 1903. Mary also became apt at these skills. After hearing Sir James Hector (the geologist on the Palliser Expedition) reciting tales of the mountains, her zest to explore the wilderness returned. In 1908, with Billy Warren guiding, Mary, her dog, and a small party set out for a lake that no white man had ever seen but that the Stoney Indians knew as "Chaba Imne," or Beaver Lake. After initial difficulties, they succeeded in finding the elusive body of water now known as Maligne Lake. In Mary's words, "there burst upon us . . . the finest view any of us have ever beheld in the Rockies . . . " In 1915 Mary married Billy Warren, continuing to explore the mountains until her death in 1939. Her success as a photographer, artist, and writer were equal to any of her male counterparts. But it was her unwavering love of the Rockies—her "heaven of the hills . . . "—for which she is best remembered.

---

ows of the Opal Hills; the trail to the right is shorter and steeper. Once in the meadow, the entire Maligne Valley can be seen below. Across Maligne Lake are the rounded Bald Hills, the Maligne Range, and to the southwest, the distinctive twin peaks of Mt. Unwin (3,268 meters) and Mt. Charlton (3,217 meters).

Bald Hills
- Length: 5.2 km (2 hours) one way
- Elevation gain: 495 meters
- Rating: moderate

From a picnic area at the very end of Maligne Lake Rd., this trail follows an old fire road for its entire distance, entering an open meadow near the end. This was once the site of a fire lookout. The 360-degree view includes the jade green waters of Maligne Lake, the Queen Elizabeth Ranges and the twin peaks of Mt. Unwin and Mt. Charlton. The Bald Hills extend for seven km, their highest summit not exceeding 2,600 meters. A herd of caribou summers in the hills.

Moose Lake
- Length: 1.4 km (30 minutes) one way
- Elevation gain: minimal
- Rating: easy

This trail begins 200 meters along the Bald Hills trail, spurring left along the Maligne Pass Trail (signposted). One km along this trail a rough track branches left, leading 100 meters to Moose Lake—a quiet body of water where moose are sometimes seen. To return, continue along the trail as it descends to the shore of Maligne Lake, a short stroll from the picnic area.

OTHER RECREATION

Mountain Biking
Bicycling in the park is continuing to grow in popularity; the ride between Banff and Jasper, along the Icefields Parkway, attracts riders from around the world. As well as riding along the paved roads, many designated unpaved bicycle trails radiate from the town. One of the most popular is the Athabasca River Trail, which begins at Old Fort Point and follows the river to a point below Maligne Canyon. Cyclists are particularly prone to sudden bear encounters—a couple of years ago a rider was pulled from his

Maligne Lake

BREWSTER TRANSPORTATION AND TOURS

bike by a grizzly, within screaming distance of Jasper Park Lodge. Fit bear-bells to your bike, or make noises when passing through heavily wooded areas. The brochure *Trail Bicycling Guide* lists designated trails and is available from Freewheel Cycle at 611 Patricia St., tel. (403) 852-3898.

Horseback Riding
Pyramid Riding Stables is on Pyramid Lake Rd., tel. 852-3562. They offer one-, two-, and three-hour guided rides for $18.50, $30, and $40, respectively. The one-hour trip follows a ridge high above town, providing excellent views of the Athabasca River Valley. **Sunrider Stables,** at the Jasper Park Lodge, tel. 852-3363, offers guided rides around Lake Annette; the one hour trip is $20. **Ridgeline Riders,** at Maligne Lake, offers 3.5-hour guided rides high into the Bald Hills for $45. Book through Maligne Tours at 626 Connaught Dr., tel. 852-3370.

Overnight pack trips consist of four to six hours of riding per day, with a few nights spent at a remote mountain lodge where you can hike, boat, fish, or ride. Rates start at $120 per person per day. For details write to Skyline Trail Rides, P.O. Box 207, Jasper, Alberta T0E 1E0, tel. 852-4215; or Tonquin Valley Amethyst Lakes Pack Trips, P.O. Box 23, Brûlé, Alberta T0E 0C0, tel. 865-4417.

Canoeing And Whitewater Rafting
Running Jasper's raging rivers is the newest "in" thing to do. Half a dozen outfitters offer trips ranging from an easy float down the Athabasca River to shooting the boulder-strewn rapids of the Maligne River. Most companies offer a choice of rivers and provide transportation to and from downtown hotels. Expect to pay $30-40 for a two-hour trip on the Athabasca and $45 for a two-hour trip on the Maligne. For details and reservations contact **Maligne Tours,** tel. (403) 852-3370, **White Water Rafting,** tel. 852-7238, or **Tickets Please** in the Chaba Theatre, tel. 895-5595.

For a different, more relaxing, and historically linked adventure, try a trip down the Athabasca River in a stable 10-meter voyageur canoe, similar to those used by early explorers and fur traders. These trips are offered by **Rocky Mountain Voyageurs** starting at Old Fort Point and floating downstream for two to three hours. The cost, including transfers, is $35. For reservations call 852-3343 or drop by **Tickets Please** in the Chaba Theatre.

Fishing
Fishing in the many alpine lakes—for rainbow, brook, cutthroat, and lake trout, as well as pike, whitefish, and Dolly Varden—is excellent. Guided fishing trips are offered by many outfitters. Whether you fish with a guide or by yourself, you'll need a National Park fishing license ($6 per week, $13 per year), available from the park information center or On-line Sport & Tackle at 600 Patricia Street. Maligne Lake is the most popular fishing hole; in 1981 a 10-kilogram rainbow trout was caught in its deep waters, a

provincial record. Boats, bait, and tackle are available from the Boathouse at Maligne Lake, tel. (403) 852-3370. Guided fishing trips on the lake are offered by **Maligne Tours,** tel. 852-3370; half day $80, full day $150. **Currie's Guided Fishing,** 416 Connaught Dr., tel. 852-5650, offers trips to Maligne Lake (full day $139) and other lakes requiring a 30-60 minute hike to access (from $130). Their shop on Connaught Dr. sells and rents tackle and also has canoe and boat rentals. **On-line Sport & Tackle,** 600 Patricia St., tel. 852-3630, offers similar trips, sells tackle, and rents canoes and boats.

Climbing And Mountaineering

Jasper Climbing Schools & Guide Service runs two-day beginner's rock-climbing classes that deal with use of equipment, technique, and safety. Everything is supplied except lunch, gloves, boots, and Band-Aids; $80. They also lead two-day courses for intermediates ($110), snow- and ice-climbing trips to Columbia Icefields ($90), and various courses that include climbs of nearby summits. For dates and details write to Hans Schwarz, P.O. Box 452, Jasper, Alberta T0E 1E0; tel.(403) 852-3964.

Golfing

The world-famous **Jasper Park Lodge Golf Course** was designed by renowned golf-course architect Stanley Thompson. The 18-hole championship course takes in the contours of the Athabasca River Valley as it hugs the banks of turquoise-colored Lac Beauvert. The 6,598-

meter course is a true test of accuracy, and with holes named "The Maze," "The Bad Baby," and "The Bay" you'll need lots of balls, literally. The green fee for 18 holes is $48; playing after 5 p.m. reduces the price to $36 (don't forget it doesn't get dark till 10 p.m. midsummer), as does playing early in the season (May). Tee times can be reserved by calling (403) 852-6090. The pro shop has electric carts, handcarts, and club rentals.

Indoor Recreation

The **Aquatic Centre,** with an olympic-size swimming pool, is at 401 Pyramid Lake Rd., tel. (403) 852-3663; admission is $4.28. The **Activity Centre,** at 303 Pyramid Lake Rd., tel. 852-3381, has squash courts, indoor and outdoor tennis courts, and a weight room; admission $5.35.

WINTERTIME

Winter is certainly a quiet time in the park, but that doesn't mean there's a lack of things to do: Marmot Basin offers world-class alpine skiing; many snow-covered hiking trails are groomed for cross-country skiing; portions of Lac Beauvert and Pyramid Lake are cleared for ice-skating; horse-drawn sleighs travel around town; and Maligne Canyon is transformed into a magical, frozen world. Hotels reduce rates by 40-70% through winter and many offer lodging and lift tickets for under $50 per person.

ALBERTA TOURISM

Maligne Canyon in winter

Marmot Basin Ski Area

The skiing at Marmot Basin is highly underrated; the terrain is good, there's plenty of the dry fluffy stuff, and the mountain scenery is breathtaking, to say the least. A fellow by the name of Joe Weiss saw the potential for skiing in the basin in the 1920s and began bringing skiers up from the valley. A road was constructed from the highway in the early '50s and the first paying skiers were transported up to the slopes in a Sno-Cat. The first lift, a 700-meter rope tow, was installed on the Paradise face in 1961 and the area has continued to expand ever since. Marmot Basin now has seven lifts servicing 400 hectares of terrain and a vertical rise of 701 meters. It doesn't get the crowds of Banff, so lift lines are uncommon. The season runs from early December to late April. Lift tickets are $35. Rentals are available at the resort or in town at **Totem Ski Shop,** 408 Connaught Dr., tel. (403) 852-3078. For more information on the resort write to Marmot Basin Ski-lifts, P.O. Box 1300, Jasper, Alberta T0E 1E0; tel. 852-3816 or, from Edmonton, call 488-5909.

Cross-Country Skiing

For many, traveling Jasper's hiking trails on skis is just as exhilarating as on foot. An extensive network of summer hiking trails is groomed for cross-country skiing. The four main areas of trails are: along Pyramid Lake Rd., around Maligne Lake, the Athabasca Falls area, and in Whistlers Campground. The booklet *Cross-country Skiing in Jasper National Park,* available at the park information center, details each trail and its difficulty. Weather forecasts and avalanche-hazard reports are posted here also.

Rental packages are available from **First Run Ski Rental & Repair** at 402 Connaught Dr., tel. (403) 852-4144; or **Spirit of Skiing Ski Rentals** in the Jasper Park Lodge, tel. 852-3433. **Totem Ski Shop** has rentals, repairs, and sales; located at 408 Connaught Dr., tel. 852-3078.

Maligne Canyon

By late December the torrent that is the Maligne River has frozen solid. Where it cascades down through Maligne Canyon the river is temporarily stalled for the winter, creating remarkable formations through the deep limestone canyon. **Maligne Winter Tours,** 626 Connaught Dr., tel. (403) 852-3370, offers exciting two-hour guided tours into the depths of the canyon throughout winter, daily at 9 a.m. and 1 p.m.; $20 per person.

FESTIVALS AND EVENTS

Summer is prime time on the park's events calendar. The first weekend of June is the **Jasper to Banff Relay,** while the first weekend of July **Canada Day Celebrations** are held, including a parade down Connaught Drive. Every second year (even years) Jasper hosts a **Heritage Folk Festival.** The **Jasper Lions Pro Indoor Rodeo,** on the third weekend of August, dates back 60 years and attracts pro cowboys from across North America. Apart from the traditional rodeo events, the fun includes dances, a casino, the Miss Jasper contest, and jail-and-bail, where pedestrians are thrown in the slammer until friends bail them out. On the other side of the calendar, winter is not totally partyless—**Jasper in January** is a two-week celebration that includes fireworks, special evenings at local restaurants, and all the activities associated with winter.

Park Interpretive Program

Parks Canada offers a wide range of interpretive talks and hikes throughout summer. Each night in the **Whistlers Campground Outdoor Theatre** a different slide and movie program is shown. The theater is located near the shower block. The **Wilcox Campground Campfire Talk** takes place each Tuesday and Friday at 8 p.m.; hot tea is supplied while wardens and various speakers talk about the park. Each Wednesday at 7:30 p.m. a slide show on hiking in Jasper is shown at the museum located at 400 Pyramid Lake Road. Many different guided hikes are offered (all free) throughout summer; check bulletin boards at the park information center, at campgrounds, or call (403) 852-6176.

ACCOMMODATIONS

Motel and hotel rooms here are expensive. Most of the motels and lodges have indoor pools, a restaurant, and are within walking distance of town. Luckily, alternatives to staying in $100-

plus places do exist. Many private residences have rooms for rent in summer; two hostels are close to town (and many more are down the Icefields Parkway), bungalows are available that can be a good deal for families or small groups, and there's always camping in the good ol' outdoors. The park has nearly 2,000 campsites, and camping is virtually unlimited in the backcountry. When addressing written inquiries to the establishments listed below, follow the listed P.O. Box with **Jasper, Alberta T0E 1E0.**

Hotels And Motels

The least expensive is the **Athabasca Hotel,** P.O. Box 1420, tel. (403) 852-3386, with rooms above a honky-tonk bar. Some of the rooms have private bathrooms, but most share one down the hall. Rates are $46-69 s, $48-71 d. **Astoria Hotel,** P.O. Box 1710, tel. 852-3351 or (800) 661-7343, is a European-style lodging built in 1924 and kept in the same family since. It is close to town, and all rooms have a fridge; $81 s, $89 d. **Pyramid Lake Resort Bungalows,** P.O. Box 338, tel. 852-4900, overlooks the lake of the same name, a few kilometers from town. Plenty of water-based activities here make the resort a good choice for families; $94-176 per unit.

Maligne Lodge, P.O. Box 757, tel. 852-3143 or (800) 661-1315, has medium-size rooms; $104 s or d. **The Whistlers Inn,** P.O. Box 250, tel. 852-3361 or (800) 282-9919, is right downtown and has spacious rooms and a rooftop jacuzzi; $109 s, $119 d. Rooms at **Marmot Lodge,** P.O. Box 687, tel. 852-4471 or (800) 661-6521, are modern and stylishly decorated, many with mountain views. On the main level is a good restaurant. Some rooms and the indoor pool are fully wheelchair accessible. In summer, rates begin at $110 s or d, from $70 the rest of the year.

Tonquin Inn, P.O. Box 658, tel. 852-4987 or (800) 661-1315, has luxurious rooms, a beautiful indoor pool, an outdoor hot tub, and laundry facilities; $114 s or d. **Mount Robson Inn,** P.O. Box 88, tel. 852-3327, has a fridge in each room; $115-140 s or d. **Sawridge Hotel,** P.O. Box 2080, tel. 852-5111 or (800) 661-6427, is an older-style lodging with a large indoor atrium and indoor pool; rooms start at $117 s or d (discounts here in the off-season aren't as large as other lodgings).

Jasper Inn, P.O. Box 879, tel. 852-4461 or (800) 661-1933, is a modern chateau-style lodging of brick and red cedar. Many rooms have kitchenettes and fireplaces; $119 s, $129 d, chalet with kitchen $131. **Amethyst Lodge,** P.O. Box 1200, tel. 852-3394 or (800) 661-9935, named after a lake in the Tonquin Valley, has large rooms and an outdoor hot tub; $126 s, $131 d. **Lobstick Lodge,** P.O. Box 1200, tel. 852-4431 or (800) 661-9317, has extra-large, simply furnished rooms and a range of modern amenities; $126 s, $131 d. **Chateau Jasper,** P.O. Box 1418, tel. 852-5644 or (800) 661-9323, is one of Jasper's nicest lodgings. Rooms are large and the low ceilings give them a cozy feel. Downstairs is an excellent restaurant; $189-280 s or d.

Jasper Park Lodge, P.O. Box 40, tel. 852-3301 or (800) 441-1414, on Lac Beauvert, is the park's original resort and its most famous. It has four restaurants, three lounges, horseback riding, tennis courts, a championship golf course, and Jasper's only covered shopping arcade. The main lodge features stone floors, carved wooden pillars, and a high ceiling. The 437 rooms vary in configuration; some are modern while others are elegantly rustic. Most are in cottages spread around Lac Beauvert, each with a porch or balcony; basic rooms start at $259 s or d; off-season rates begin at $87.

Summer Lodging

The following lodgings all open for the summer months only (generally May to late September), and with one exception are away from the townsite. **Patricia Lake Bungalows,** P.O. Box 657, tel. (403) 852-3560, is located on the lake of the same name, a five-minute drive from Jasper along Pyramid Lake Road. Small motel-style rooms are $54, cottages with kitchens are $80-117 depending on the size. **Pine Bungalows,** P.O. Box 7, tel. 852-3491, is on a secluded section of the Athabasca River. Motel-style units with kitchenettes are $58 s or d, individual cabins with fireplaces begin at $75. **Jasper House Bungalows,** P.O. Box 817, tel. 852-4535, four km south of the townsite on Hwy. 93, has basic sleeping units for $82; those with cooking facilities begin at $99. **Miette Hot Springs Bungalows,** P.O. Box 907, tel. 866-3750, is located northeast of Jasper within walking distance of the park's only hot springs. Motel units are $59 s or d, $67 with a kitchenette; bungalows begin at $75. **Pocahontas Bungalows,** P.O. Box 820, tel. 866-3732, are near the park's east gate at the bottom of the road that leads to Miette Hot Springs; $60-69 s or d. **Bonhomme Bungalows,** on Bonhomme St., P.O. Box 700, tel. 852-3209, offers the only accommodation of this type in the townsite. Cabins are basic, but each has a TV, bathroom, and coffee-making facilities; $68-80 s or d. **Tekarra Lodge,** P.O. Box 669, tel. 852-3058, is located 1.5 km south of the townsite at the confluence of the Miette and Athabasca rivers. Rooms in the lodge are $62 s or d; cabins, each with a kitchenette and wood-burning fireplace, begin at $79. Many Canadians will recognize the lodge as the setting for the weekly television drama "Destiny Ridge."

The only backcountry accommodation in the park is **Tonquin Valley Lodge,** P.O. Box 550, tel. 852-3909, southwest of Jasper in the Tonquin Valley. Getting there involves a 23-km hike from a trailhead opposite Edith Cavell Hostel. Cabins have wood-burning heaters, bunk beds, oil lanterns, and a spectacular view. The rate, $90 per person per night, includes accommodations, three meals, and use of small boats.

Private Suites/Bed And Breakfasts

At last count, Jasper had 60 private-home accommodations. Often they offer nothing more than a room with a bed, but the price is right; $25-50 s or d. Usually the bathroom is shared with other guests or the family; few have kitchens, and breakfast is not included. The positive side, apart from the price, is that your hosts are usually knowledgeable locals and town is only a short walk away. The Jasper Tourism and Commerce Information Centre has a board listing each accommodation, but in summer, by early afternoon, there is a big red "full" plastered across it. Most have signs out front so you could cruise the streets (try Connaught, Patricia, and Geikie), but checking with the information center is easier. For a full listing that includes the facilities at each, write to Jasper Home Accommodation Association, P.O. Box 758, Jasper, Alberta T0E 1E0; use their brochure to book ahead.

Hostels

On the road to the Jasper Tramway is **Whistlers Mountain Hostel,** which has 70 beds in men's and women's dorms, a large kitchen, a common room, showers, an outdoor barbecue area, and mountain bike rentals. Members of Hostelling International pay $13, nonmembers $17. For hostel reservations call (403) 852-3215 or 439-3139 in Edmonton. In the summer months this hostel fills up every night. Check-in time is in the evening, but the hostel is open all day. It is located five km from Jasper; the only public transportation is the Pika Shuttle, which stops on its way to Banff every second day.

Maligne Canyon Hostel is on Maligne Lake Rd., beside the Maligne River and a short walk from the canyon. Although rustic, it is in a beautiful setting. The 24 beds are in two cabins; other facilities include a kitchen and dining area. Rates are members $9, nonmembers $13. For reservations call 852-3584 or 439-3139 in Edmonton. The hostel is closed Wednesday Oct.-April. The **Maligne Lake Shuttle,** 626 Connaught Dr., tel. 852-3370, costs $6 from town. It makes eight trips daily.

Campgrounds

Whistlers Campground, at the base of Whistlers Rd., three km south of Jasper townsite, has 781 sites, making it the largest campground in the Canadian Rockies. It is divided into three sections; prices vary with the services available—unserviced sites $12, powered sites $14.50, full hookups $16.50. Each section has showers. The campground is open May to mid-October. A further two km south is **Wapiti Campground,** which stays open year-round and has showers; unserviced sites $12, powered sites $14. Northeast of the townsite, along Hwy. 16, are two smaller, more primitive campgrounds. **Snaring River Campground,** 17 km from Jasper, is $7.25; **Pocahontas Campground,** 45 km northeast, is $9.25. Both are open June to early September.

Backcountry campgrounds are located throughout the park. For a full list (as well as a camping permit) head for the park information center.

FOOD AND DRINK

Coffeehouses And Cafes

Hava Java House, 407 Patricia St., tel. (403) 852-5727, is a popular coffeehouse with tables in the garden out front. Besides coffee, they serve a selection of healthy sandwiches and light lunches. If you've become addicted to the pastries at Laggan's Mountain Bakery in Lake Louise, you've come to the right place—they're delivered to Hava Java fresh every day. It's open 7:30 a.m.-9 p.m. **Soft Rock Cafe,** in Connaught Square at 622 Connaught Dr., tel. 852-5850, starts the day by dishing up plates of waffles for $3.95. If the cinnamon buns are still in the oven you'll have to come back later in the day—they're gigantic! The variety of coffee concoctions here is mind boggling; prices are reasonable. It's open 7 a.m.-11 p.m. **Dano's,** 604 Patricia St., tel. 852-3322, will stifle any ice cream or cappuccino cravings. The cappuccino bar in the Athabasca Hotel is also a good hangout on rainy days.

Cool And Casual

The best Greek meals in town are served at **Something Else Restaurant,** 621 Patricia St., tel. (403) 852-3850. Portions are generous, service is friendly, the prices are right, and you'll find plenty of alternatives if the Greek dishes don't appeal to you. Greek favorites are $10-15, pasta dishes $10-13, pizza from $10. It's open daily 11 a.m.-midnight. **Papa George's,** 406 Connaught Dr., tel. 852-3351, is a locals' favorite and one of Jasper's oldest restaurants. Breakfast is $3-6, lunch and dinner feature burgers, pasta, and steaks; daily specials are $10-15 and include soup and salad. Hours are 7 a.m.-11:30 p.m. **O'Shea's Restaurant,** 510 Patricia St., tel. 852-4229, also has a good selection of pasta dishes.

L&W Restaurant, on the corner of Hazel and Patricia streets, tel. 852-4114, has an outside patio, a strangely sloping roof, and plenty of greenery that brings to life an otherwise ordinary restaurant; a good place to take the family for an inexpensive meal. **Tramway Restaurant,** tel. 852-5352, high above town on The Whistlers has, without a doubt, the best views in town. Daily lunch and dinner buffets complement the à la carte menu.

Middle Of The Road

The Cantonese Restaurant, 608 Connaught Dr., tel. (403) 852-3559, is the place to go for Chinese; combo specials are $9-12 and set menus for two start at $22. It's open daily 11 a.m.-10 p.m. The place to go for Alberta beef is **Tonquin Prime Rib Village,** on Juniper St. be-side the Tonquin Inn, tel. 852-4966, which specializes in charbroiled steaks and prime rib but also offers a good choice of seafood. Five km south of town is **Becker's Gourmet Restaurant,** tel. 852-3535, where the atmosphere is intimate and relaxing, the views of Mt. Kerkeslin and the Athabasca River are inspiring, and the steak and seafood dishes are well prepared. With a bottle of wine expect to pay $70 for two. **Tokyo Tom's Place,** 410 Connaught Dr., tel. 852-3780, features a traditional sushi bar and eight tatami booths for eating the very best Japanese cuisine. It's open 5-11:30 p.m. **Walter's Dining Room** in the Sawridge Hotel, 82 Connaught Dr., tel. 852-5111, features a menu of Alberta beef, Rocky Mountain trout, and B.C. salmon in an elegant but relaxed atmosphere.

Top End

The **Inn Restaurant** in the Jasper Inn, tel. (403) 852-3232, sits within a glass-enclosed atrium and features a menu of Alberta beef, ribs, fondue, and seafood. Entrees start at $15. Diners are offered complimentary limo service to the restaurant. The same menu is served in the just-as-elegant lounge for half the price. **Fiddle River Seafood Company,** 620 Connaught Dr., tel. 852-3032, upstairs in Connaught Square, has fresh seafood, but expect to pay around $40 per person for a three-course meal. If you can't afford to eat here, at least stick your head in the door and admire the decor. The award-winning **Beavallon Dining Room** at Chateau Jasper, tel. 852-5644, ext. 179, offers an extensive menu emphasizing continental cuisine prepared by a Swiss chef. All the chairs are upholstered, and the blue tablecloths and wood-trimmed crimson walls provide an air of elegance—elegance you pay for. It's expensive. The Sunday brunch here is worth the splurge.

Jasper Park Lodge

The lodge offers a choice of casual or elegant dining in four restaurants and three lounges. **Meadows Cafe,** in the Beauvert Shopping Promenade, is open for breakfast, lunch, and dinner. **Obsessions,** also in the arcade, has tempting French pastries, gourmet coffee, and homemade truffles and chocolates. Drinks and light snacks are served at the **Spike Lounge Deck** overlooking the golf course. At lunchtime the smell of sizzling steaks from **La Terrasse**

Early guests to the Jasper Park Lodge, then a remote mountain retreat, were treated to all the luxuries of the day.

WHYTE MUSEUM OF THE CANADIAN ROCKIES

wafts across Lac Beauvert; this outdoor eatery is only open in summer. The least expensive dining room is **Moose's Nook,** whose rustic atmosphere serves as a good place to enjoy some fine Canadian fare. **Beauvert Room,** a huge dining room overlooking Lac Beauvert, features a menu of European cuisine. The **Edith Cavell Room** is the finest fine-dining restaurant in Jasper. Its dark oak walls are contrasted by white linens and large, bright windows overlooking Lac Beauvert and the mountains beyond. The classic cuisine is served with a French flair and price tag; if you need to ask the price you can't afford it. For all lodge restaurant reservations call (403) 852-3301.

Drinking And Dancing

The most popular nightspot in town is the **Atha-b,** in the Athabasca Hotel. Bands play most nights and it gets pretty rowdy with all the seasonal workers but is still enjoyable; minimal cover charge. **The Pub,** in the Whistlers Inn, has great atmosphere with a classic wooden bar and memorabilia everywhere. Most of Jasper's larger hotels have lounges.

TRANSPORTATION

Getting There

The closest domestic and international airports are in Edmonton, 3.5 hours to the east. The **VIA rail station** and the **bus depot** are in the same building, central to town at 607 Connaught Drive. The building is open in summer, daily 24 hours; the rest of the year, Mon.-Sat. 7:30 a.m.-

10:30 p.m., Sunday 7:30-11 a.m. and 6:30-10:30 p.m. Lockers are available for $1 per day, and also here are a travel agent and a Tilden car-rental agency. A cab to Whistlers Mountain Hostel is $10.

Jasper is on the "Canadian" route, the only remaining transcontinental passenger rail service in the country. Trains run either way three times weekly. To the west the line divides going to both Prince Rupert and Vancouver; to the east it passes through Edmonton and all points beyond. For all rail information call (800) 561-8630.

Greyhound, tel. (800) 661-8747, offers buses departing Jasper for all points in Canada, including Vancouver (three times daily, 12-13 hours, $82.50 one way), Edmonton (five times daily, 4.5 hours, $42.50 one way) with connections to Calgary, and Prince Rupert (once daily, 18 hours, $120 one way).

Brewster Transportation and Tours, tel. (403) 762-6700, operates an airporter service to Jasper from Calgary International Airport, departing the airport daily at 12:30 p.m. ($49.50 one way to Jasper), Banff at 3:15 p.m. ($37 one way to Jasper), and Lake Louise at 4:15 p.m. ($32 one way to Jasper), arriving in Jasper at 8 p.m. The return service departs daily from Jasper Park Lodge at 12:50 p.m. and from the bus depot at 1:30 p.m. They also have a nine-hour (one way) tour between Banff and Jasper that departs May-Oct. daily from Banff at 8 a.m.; $59.50 one way, $83 round trip. The round trip requires an overnight in Jasper. No bus service between Banff and Jasper is available Nov.-April.

Pika Shuttle Co. is a van service that operates in the summer months between Calgary International Hostel and hostels in Banff and Jasper national parks. The fare from Calgary to Jasper is $45 one way, from Banff $34. Bicycles are extra. To ride this shuttle you *must* have reservations at your destination hostel. For information and reservations call (800) 363-0096.

Getting Around

Although the town is compact, getting out to see the sights can be a problem without your own transportation. **Hiker's Wheels** is a shuttle service to popular trailheads, but they also do pick-ups and drop-offs at hostels and campgrounds. The departure point in town is Hava Java House at 407 Patricia Street. For details and reservations call (403) 852-2188.

The **Maligne Lake Shuttle** runs out to Maligne Lake eight times daily ($20 round trip) and will make drops at Maligne Canyon and Maligne Canyon Hostel ($6 one way); tel. 852-3370.

Rental cars start at $50 per day with 100 free kilometers. The following companies have agencies in town: **Avis,** tel. 852-3970; **Budget,** tel. 852-3222; and **Tilden,** tel. 852-4972.

Mountain bikes can be rented from: **On-line Sport & Tackle,** 600 Patricia St., tel. 852-3630; **Beyond Bikes,** 14 Cedar Ave., tel. 852-5922; **The Sports Shop,** 416 Connaught Dr., tel. 852-3654; **Freewheel Cycle,** 611 Patricia St., tel. 852-3898; and **Sandy's at Jasper Park Lodge** (tel. 852-3301). Expect to pay $4-5 per hour or $12-20 per day.

Cabs in town are not cheap; most drivers will take you on a private sightseeing tour or to trailheads if requested, try: **Jasper Taxi,** tel. 852-3600 or 852-3146. **Heritage Cabs,** tel. 852-5558, has a fleet of antique cars.

Tours

Brewster Transportation and Tours has a three-hour General Drive Tour taking in Patricia and Pyramid lakes, Maligne Canyon, and Jasper Tramway (ride not included in fare). It departs April-Oct., daily at 8:30 a.m.; $29.50. **Maligne Lake Tours** has a variety of tours including one to Maligne Lake ($47, includes cruise); the office is at 626 Connaught Dr., tel. (403) 852-3370. **Mountain Meadow Tours** offers narrated trips to Maligne Canyon (three hours), Mount Edith Cavell (three hours), Athabasca Falls (2.5 hours), and Miette Hot Springs (four hours); $28 per person per tour. Book through **Tickets Please,** 604 Connaught Dr., tel. 852-5595. Tickets Please is also a booking agent for Brewster Transportation and Tours, rafting trips, guided hikes, heli-hiking, fishing trips, and just about everything else. Look for their signs outside the Chaba Theatre; open in summer, daily 7:30 a.m.-9 p.m.

SERVICES AND INFORMATION

Services

The **post office** is at 502 Patricia St., opposite the park information center. Mail to be picked up here should be addressed General Delivery, Jasper, Alberta T0E 1E0. The two laundromats on Patricia St. are open 6 a.m.-11 p.m. and offer showers that cost $2 for 10 minutes (quarters). **On-line Sport & Tackle** sells a wide range of camping gear and fishing tackle. It's located at 600 Patricia St., tel. (403) 852-3630. The **hospital** is at 518 Robson St., tel. 852-3344. For the RCMP call 852-4848.

Books And Bookstores

The small **Jasper Municipal Library,** on Elm Ave., tel. (403) 852-3652, holds just about everything ever written about the park. It's open Mon.-Thurs. 2-4 p.m. and 7-9 p.m., Fri.-Sat. 2-4 p.m. only.

Jasper has a number of excellent bookstores. **Reader's Choice,** 610 Connaught Dr., tel. 852-4028, next to the Cantonese Restaurant, has the widest choice of park and Canadiana books; open daily 9 a.m.-10 p.m. The park information center and museum both have a good selection of books on the park's natural and human history. **Maligne Lake Books,** in the Jasper Park Lodge, has a good selection of coffee-table books.

Information

The Parks Canada **Park Information Centre** is in a beautiful old stone building in Athabasca Park on Connaught Drive. The staff at the first desk provides general information on the park and can direct you to hikes in the immediate vicinity. Then they whip out another map and a fluorescent marker and quicker than you can say "bear-bells" they've marked all the trail closures. The next desk is for those going into the backcountry—save your questions that you don't want a canned answer to for here. This is also the place to register for backcountry camping permits. In the far corner is a **Parks and People** outlet selling maps, books, and local publications. Look out for notices posted out front with the day's interpretive programs. The center is open in summer, daily 8 a.m.-8 p.m., the rest of the year, daily 9 a.m.-5 p.m.; tel. (403) 852-6786.

At 632 Connaught Dr. is the **Jasper Tourism and Commerce Information Centre,** tel. 852-3858, where the friendly staff never seems to tire of explaining that all the rooms in town are full. They will happily ring around to find accommo-dations for you, and can provide general information on the town. They also have a large collection of brochures on activities, shopping, and restaurants in town. It's open in summer, daily 8 a.m.-8 p.m., the rest of the year, Mon.-Fri. 9 a.m.-5 p.m. Jasper's weekly newspaper *The Booster* (65 cents) is available throughout town on Wednesday. For a list of park-related items including publications and topographic maps write to Parks and People, P.O. Box 992, Jasper, Alberta T0E 1E0; or call 852-4767. For more information on the park write to The Superintendent, P.O. Box 10, Jasper, Alberta T0E 1E0. For general tourist information write to Jasper Tourism and Commerce, P.O. Box 98, Jasper T0E 1E0, or call 852-3858. **Jasper National Park Radio** is on the AM band at 1490.

BOB RACE

KAREN MCKINLEY

CENTRAL ALBERTA

The central sector of the province is a diverse region extending from the peaks of the Canadian Rockies in the west through the foothills and aspen parkland to the prairies in the east. **Rocky Mountain Forest Reserve** occupies much of the the the heavily forested western foothills, nestled against the folded and faulted front ranges of the Rocky Mountains. Most of this large coniferous forest is committed for nonrenewable resource development, although two designated wilderness areas in the reserve are totally protected from development. The entire reserve is a recreation playground; perfect for camping, fishing, hiking, and other outdoor activities. **Rocky Mountain House,** a medium-sized town on Hwy. 11, is the gateway to the foothills. The North West and Hudson's Bay companies once used trading posts here as a jumping-off point into the mountain wilderness to the west. The original site of these posts is now Alberta's only National Historic Park.

The 290-km road between Calgary and Edmonton through central Alberta on Hwy. 2 takes about three hours to drive straight through. Those with a little more time can explore the many historic towns along the way, or visit a buffalo jump used by natives to stampede herds of bison to their deaths. Halfway between Calgary and Edmonton is **Red Deer,** a city of 58,000 that was once an important way station for travelers on the Calgary Trail (or Edmonton Trail, depending on which direction they were going).

North and east of Red Deer is the **aspen parkland,** a biome with characteristics unique to Canada's prairie provinces. Long, straight country roads link primarily agricultural towns along three main highways that extend into the neighboring province of Saskatchewan. Highlights of this section of parkland include five provincial parks, one of Canada's last remaining passenger steam trains at **Stettler,** and a fantastic museum dedicated to machinery at **Wetaskiwin.**

© MOON PUBLICATIONS, INC.

WEST-CENTRAL ALBERTA

Highway 2 between Calgary and Edmonton skirts the edge of the prairie—just west of the highway a region of foothills begins. The hills rise gradually, eventually reaching the lofty peaks of the front ranges adjoining Banff and Jasper national parks. Several rivers—among them the North Saskatchewan, Red Deer, Clearwater, and Brazeau—slice through the foothills on their cascading descent from sources high in the Rockies. Fur trading was once a booming industry here, but the greatest human impact on the area came from coal mining earlier this century. Rocky Mountain House, located on the bank of the North Saskatchewan River, is the largest town in the region and a good base for exploring. The cities of Calgary and Edmonton are also close by.

This little-traveled region of the Canadian Rockies attracts outdoor enthusiasts year-round. Here you can hike in two wilderness areas, camp in many Forest Service campgrounds, fish in fish-filled lakes and rivers, explore historic sites, run the North Saskatchewan River, take horseback trips into the hills, cross-country ski in winter, or just admire the spectacular mountain scenery. For a full list of all adventure outfitters write to **West-central Adventurers,** P.O. Box 5008, Red Deer, Alberta T4N 3T4; tel. (403) 346-0180.

HIGHWAY 22 NORTH

This highway follows the eastern flanks of the foothills from Cochrane, northwest of Calgary, through the small communities of Cremona, Sundre, and Caroline, and the larger town of Rocky Mountain House. The Rockies dominate the western horizon for much of the route and are especially imposing around Sundre.

Sundre
This town of 1,800, on the banks of the Red Deer River, is a good jumping-off point for trips into the Rocky Mountain Forest Reserve. Nearby rivers provide excellent whitewater-rafting opportunities for those with their own craft. Highway 584, heading west from town, links up with Forestry Trunk Rd., providing access to many campgrounds and fishing spots. In town, Sundre's **Pioneer Museum,** 130 Centre St., tel. (403) 638-4768, displays a large collection of artifacts from early pioneer days, including farm machinery, a blacksmith shop, and an old schoolhouse. It's open in summer, Wed.-Sat. 10 a.m.-4:30 p.m. and Sunday noon-4:30 p.m. A canoe race is held on the Red Deer River on the last weekend of May, and the **Sundre Professional Rodeo** comes to town on the third weekend of June.

Sundre has four motels, all on Main Ave.; the least expensive is **Bulldog Inn,** tel. 638-4748, $35 s or d. **Greenwood Park,** on the west bank of the Red Deer River, has no hookups, but has clean facilities with showers; $7.50. East of town is **Tall Timber Leisure Park,** tel. 638-3555, a full-service RV park where tenters aren't welcome; powered sites $17, full hookups $19. **Outlaw's Bar and Grill,** 250 Main Ave., tel. 638-2882, is the only place in town to get a decent meal. Lunch specials are $5-7 including a salad bar, and the weekend hot breakfast buffet, served till noon, is $5.95. The **tourist information center** is located on the east bank of the Red Deer River; open in summer, Thurs.-Mon. 10 a.m.-8 p.m.

Caroline
Named after the daughter of one of the town's earliest settlers, Caroline depended on agriculture and forestry to support its economy until recently, when Alberta's largest sour gas discovery was made south of town. Now Shell Canada's plant at the site also contributes to the area's economy.

Multiple-time world figure-skating champion Kurt Browning was born and raised on a ranch just west of town. His portrait adorns local tourist literature, and the town's Kurt Browning Arena houses the Kurt Browning Memorabilia and Viewing Room (open weekdays).

The two motels in town are inexpensive, and **Caroline Municipal Campground,** located at the east end of town, has showers, kitchen shelters, and firewood. Unserviced sites are $10 a night, powered sites are $12.

The Forestry Trunk Road

At regular intervals along Hwy. 22, gravel roads lead west to the **Forestry Trunk Rd.**—a well-graded gravel road that parallels the Rockies for over 1,000 km. Along the route are plenty of campgrounds, beautiful scenery, and a degree of solitude not found along roads through the national parks farther west. The middle section of the trunk road begins at its intersection with Hwy. 1A, 13 km west of Cochrane. Heading north from there, the first services available are 265 km away at Nordegg, on Hwy. 11. But opportunities to exit and enter the road are found west of Cremona, Sundre, Caroline, and Rocky Mountain House.

ROCKY MOUNTAIN HOUSE

This town of 5,500, best known simply as "Rocky," straddles the North Saskatchewan River. It's surrounded by gently rolling hills in a transition zone between aspen parkland and mountains. Highway 11 (also known as David Thompson Hwy.) passes through town on its way east to Red Deer (82 km) and west to Banff National Park (170 km).

History

Between 1799 and 1875, four fur-trading posts were built at the confluence of the Clearwater and North Saskatchewan rivers, west of the present townsite. The forts were used not only for trading but as bases for exploring the nearby mountains. David Thompson, one of western Canada's greatest explorers, was a regular visitor. In 1821, after the two major fur-trading companies merged, the community that had grown around the forts was christened Rocky Mountain House. At the beginning of the 20th century, settlers began arriving. Today the town's economy relies on forestry, natural-gas processing, agriculture, and tourism.

Rocky Mountain House
National Historic Park

Alberta's only national historic park commemorates the important role fur trading played in Canada's history. The first trading post, or fort, was built on the site in 1799. By the 1830s beaver felt was out of fashion in Europe and traders turned to buffalo robes. By the 1870s, the massive herds of buffalo that had roamed the plains for thousands of years were gone. This signaled an end to the fur trade—an industry that had opened up the West and had been the Indians' main source of European goods such as clothing, horses, and guns. The last post at Rocky Mountain House closed soon after and, by the early 1900s, was reduced to two brick chimneys. In 1926 the forts were declared National Historic Sites. Today the protected areas include the sites of four forts, a buffalo paddock, and a stretch of riverbank where the large voyageur canoes would have come ashore to be loaded with furs bound for Europe.

The **visitor center** is the best place to begin a visit to the site; its interpretive displays detail the history of the forts, the fur trade, and exploration of the West. Two trails lead along the north bank of the river. The longer of the two, a 3.2-km loop, passes the site of the two original forts. Frequent "listening posts" along the trail play a lively recorded commentary on life in the early 1800s. All that remains of the forts are depressions in the ground, but through the commentary and interpretive displays it is easy to get a good idea of what the forts looked like. To the north of the fort site is an observation deck for viewing a herd of 25 buffalo that may, or may not, be visible. The other trail leads to two chimneys, remnants of the later forts.

The park is open year-round, although the visitor center is only open May-Sept., daily 10 a.m.-8 p.m. It's located five km west of Rocky Mountain House on Hwy. 11A. Admission is by donation. For more information write to P.O. Box 2130, Rocky Mountain House, Alberta T0M 1T0; tel. (403) 845-2412.

Other Sights

The **Rocky Mountain House Museum,** 4604 49th Ave., tel. (403) 845-2332, located in a 1927 schoolhouse, exhibits an array of pioneer artifacts, including an early Forest Service cabin. It's open in summer, Mon.-Sat. 10 a.m.-7 p.m. and Sunday 1-7 p.m. Admission is $2. Another collection of pioneer memorabilia is housed at **Mandelin Antique Museum,** tel. 845-6144, 15 km southwest of Rocky on Hwy. 752; admission $2. It's open in summer, Thurs.-Mon. 10 a.m.-6 p.m. The Canadian chapter of the **Rocky Mountain Elk Foundation** is based in Rocky. The foundation's main objective is to preserve critical wildlife habitat by buying large chunks of land; members are mostly hunters. It's located in the Big Horn Plaza; tel. 845-6492.

Recreation

The best way to appreciate the history of the area, see some great river scenery, and generally have a good time is by taking a float trip with **Voyageur Adventure Tours,** 4804 63rd St., tel. (403) 845-7878, on the North Saskatchewan River. The voyageur canoes used are replicas of those used by early explorers; they

Natives built dome-shaped sweat lodges out of brush and covered them in buffalo robes.

are large and stable, requiring little paddling skill. Half-day trips, which include a stop at the National Historic Park and lunch, are $40; a full day with cooked lunch—prepared along the riverbank while you take a short hike or rest in the sun—is $60. Overnight tours start at $140, and a five-day trip—including three days on horseback—is $395. For a faster-paced river adventure, **D&B River Runners,** tel. 845-4085, offers river trips by jet boat.

Pine Hills Golf Course offers linksters an 18-hole course eight km west of town, tel. 845-7400; green fees are $22.

Accommodations

Many motels are spread out along Hwy. 11 east of town, among them: **Voyageur Motel,** tel. (403) 845-3381, which has large, clean rooms for $36 s, $40 d; **Big Horn Motel,** tel. 845-2871, in the Big Horn Plaza, $35 s, $39 d; and **Walking Eagle Motor Inn,** tel. 845-2804, easily recognized by its striking log exterior, $53 s, $59 d. Downtown, **Cosy Roomettes,** 4917 49th St., tel. 845-2270, has cheap backpacker rooms, each with a kitchenette, cable TV, and shared bathroom; $25 s, $28 d.

Two municipal campgrounds within town limits both have toilets, showers, and firewood; $10 per night. **Aspen Park,** behind the tourist information center, is the larger of the two. The other, **Centennial Park,** is along 54th Street. **Riverview Campground,** tel. 845-4422, on the North Saskatchewan River is the only commercial facility in town. The unserviced sites are tucked in among a grove of trees on the riverbank and above them are serviced sites, with spectacular views along the valley. The campground has a small grocery store, laundromat, showers, and free firewood; unserviced sites $8.50, full hookups $14.

Northwest of town along an access road off Hwy. 11, campgrounds are available at both **Crimson Lake Provincial Park** and **Twin Lakes** (good rainbow trout fishing).

Food And Drink

The only restaurants in town are those in the strip of family-style and fast-food places along Hwy. 11 and 52nd Avenue. **Walking Eagle Motor Inn,** on the east side of the highway, serves a good lunch buffet for $8.95. A wild honky-tonk bar in the **David Thompson Hotel,** 4834 50th St., tel. (403) 845-3123, cranks out live music most nights.

Services And Information

The **Greyhound Bus Depot** is in the Shell gas station at 4504 47th Ave., tel. (403) 845-2650. For a cab call **D&L Taxi,** at 845-6199.

The **post office** is downtown at 5011 50th Avenue. **Happy's Laundromat** is located at 4507 47th Ave., open daily 8 a.m.-10 p.m. **Rocky Mountain House General Hospital** is at 5016 52nd Ave., tel. 845-3347. For the **RCMP** call 845-2881 and if you spot a forest fire call 845-8211.

The **tourist information center,** located in a small trailer north of town on Hwy. 11, offers free coffee and good information on the forestry roads farther west. Don't buy the town map—many shops in town give them away. The center is open in summer, daily 9 a.m.-8 p.m.; tel. 845-2414. The chamber of commerce, located in the Town Hall, also has information; open year-round, weekdays only, tel. 845-5450.

NORDEGG

Westbound Hwy. 11 climbs slowly from the aspen parkland around Rocky Mountain House into the dense forests on the eastern slopes of the Rockies. The only community between Rocky and Banff National Park is Nordegg, 85 km west of Rocky. Nordegg was once a booming coal-mining town of 3,500. But the town was abandoned when the mines closed; now fewer than 100 hardy souls call the town home. Below the old townsite, just off Hwy. 11, various tourist facilities have sprung up, including an excellent museum. And the town is near many fine fishing rivers and the Forestry Trunk Road.

History

Early this century, Martin Nordegg staked a claim at a site near where his namesake town is today. Soon after, he established **Brazeau Collieries** and struck a deal with the Canadian National Railway; if they would extend the line to his mines, he would have 100,000 tons of coal waiting. He kept his side of the deal and the railway kept theirs, completing the rail line in 1914. Until then, miners had been housed in makeshift quarters. But the railway brought construction supplies, and permanent structures were soon erected. The town of Nordegg became the first "planned" mining town in Alberta. The streets were built in a semicircular pattern, centered around the railroad station and shops. Fifty miners' cottages were built, all painted in pastel colors. Gardens were planted and two churches and a modern hospital were built; miners had never had it better. In 1923 production peaked at nearly half a million tons of coal. By the '30s, most of the coal was being converted to briquettes, which were easy to handle and burned better than raw coal. By the early '40s, with four briquette presses, Nordegg had one of the largest such operations in North America. But the success soon turned to ash. In 1941 an explosion killed 29 men, and in 1950 fire destroyed many structures. Then trains began converting to diesel fuel and home heating went to natural gas. Brazeau Collieries ceased operations in January 1955. Many miners had spent their entire lives working the mine and had raised families in the remote mining community. By the summer of '55, the town had been abandoned. A minimum security prison has operated on the site since 1963 and only a few of the original buildings remain.

The recently formed **Nordegg Historic Heritage Interest Group,** made up of many former residents of the mining community, has commenced restoration of some of the buildings. The townsite is not open to the general public. To visit the area, you must either take a guided tour or do a short stint in the slammer. We recommend the tour. For more information, write to the group at P.O. Box 2039, Rocky Mountain House, Alberta T0M 1T0.

In Town

Tourist services are on an access road south of Hwy. 11. The **Nordegg Museum** is housed in the old schoolhouse, just up the hill from "downtown." Among many interesting displays are newspaper articles telling of the town's ups and downs. Tours of the abandoned townsite and mine leave from here in summer, daily at 1 p.m. They last about 2.5 hours and cost $4. The museum, tel. (403) 721-3950, is open in summer, daily 9 a.m.-5 p.m., and is a good source of information about the area. The **Fish and Wildlife office,** tel. 721-3949, has information on current road conditions. The office is open year-round, Mon.-Fri. 8:30 a.m.-midday.

Recreation

Nearby fishing is excellent—inquire at the **Fish and Wildlife office,** tel. (403) 721-3949, for details. Nordegg, with a population of under 100, has a nine-hole golf course; $5. **Baldy Mountain Trail Rides,** tel. 721-2030, offers guided horseback rides into the hills. The one-hour ride is $12, two-hour $22, and the full-day ride to the top of Coliseum Mountain is $75, including lunch and dinner.

Accommodations And Food

Nordegg Resort Lodge, tel. (403) 721-3757, is the town's only motel, but it's usually full with mineral exploration crews (so much so that there's a temporary helipad beside it); basic rooms are $35 s, $45 d. If you must have a roof over your head, don't despair; Nordegg has its own hostel. **Shunda Creek Hostel** is a huge log chalet in a bush setting that has a fully equipped kitchen, dining room, fireplace, hot showers, and some private rooms. Members of Hostelling International pay $12 per night, nonmembers $17. For reservations call 721-2140, or book through the Edmonton Hostel at 439-3139. The hostel is located along Shunda Creek Recreation Rd., just west of Nordegg; closed Tuesday and Wednesday. If you've never stayed in a hostel, check this one out.

Campers are spoiled for choice with Forest Service campgrounds north and south along the Forestry Trunk Road, and provincial recreation areas east and west along Hwy. 11. All are primitive but have pit toilets, firewood, kitchen shelters, and are usually beside a creek or lake. Expect to pay $5.50-7.50 per night. Closest to town is **Upper Shunda Creek,** west of Nordegg.

The only place to eat in town is the restaurant in the **Nordegg Resort Lodge,** open 7 a.m.-9 p.m.

WEST FROM NORDEGG

The **Forestry Trunk Rd.** crosses Hwy. 11 three km west of Nordegg. This road, used mainly to maintain the forest, is well traveled by those going fishing, hiking, and camping. From Hwy. 11 it is 190 km north to Hinton and 265 km south to Cochrane. There are no services along either route but the scenery is spectacular, the fishing great, and the crowds nonexistent.

From this junction Hwy. 11 veers southwest. Twenty-three km from Nordegg it passes a gravel parking area at the trailhead for **Crescent Falls** and **Bighorn Canyon**. A further five km, a gravel road leads south to the eastern end of **Abraham Lake** on the North Saskatchewan River, one of Alberta's largest reservoirs. An information center at the dam is open in summer, daily 8:30 a.m.-4:30 p.m.; tel. (403) 721-3952. Back on the highway, the main body of Abraham Lake quickly comes into view, its brilliant turquoise water reflecting the front ranges of the Rockies. Don't stop for a photo session just yet—the views improve farther west. Across the lake is **Michener Mountain** (2,337 meters).

David Thompson Resort, tel. 721-2103, provides the only services along the highway west of Nordegg. Its full-service RV park charges $13 for unserviced sites, $15-17 for hookups. Motel rooms are available for $58 s, $65 d. A cafe serves hearty breakfasts from $4, lunch and dinner from $6. The resort also rents bikes for $10 per day, and has a heated pool and a Frisbee golf course. **Helicopter Adventures** is based at the resort and takes people on a seven-minute spin for $25, worthwhile if it's clear. To the south of the resort is the main access point into White Goat Wilderness Area (see below).

Kootenay Plains Ecological Reserve/Siffleur Falls

Located at the south end of Abraham Lake, this reserve protects a unique area of dry grasslands in the mountains. The climate in this section of the valley is unusually moderate, the warmest in the Rockies. Vegetation such as June grass and wheat grass, usually associated with the prairies of southeastern Alberta, thrives here. The valley is a prime wintering area for elk, but due to the dry microclimate and its associated vegetation, mammals are not abundant in summer.

Two km farther west along the highway is the trailhead for a five-km hike (allow 1.5 hours one way) to spectacular **Siffleur Falls.** Along the first section the trail crosses the North Saskatchewan River via a swinging bridge. From the falls, this trail continues into the Siffleur Wilderness Area (see below).

Highway 11 then continues climbing, past a parking area (from where a trail leads to a

DAVID THOMPSON

David Thompson, one of Canada's greatest explorers, was a quiet, courageous, and energetic man who drafted the first comprehensive and accurate map of western Canada. He arrived in Canada from England as a 14-year-old apprentice clerk for the Hudson's Bay Company. With an inquisitive nature and a talent for wilderness navigation, he quickly acquired the skills of surveying and mapmaking. Natives called him "Koo-koo-sint," which translates as "the man who looks at stars."

Between 1786 and 1808 Thompson led four major expeditions into what is now Alberta—the first for the Hudson's Bay Company and the last three for its rival, the North West Company. The most important one was the fourth, from 1806-08, during which he traveled up the North Saskatchewan River and discovered the Athabasca Pass through the Continental Divide. For many years, this was the main route across the Rockies to the Pacific Ocean.

In 1813 Thompson began work on a master map covering the entire territory that the North West Company controlled. It was four meters long and two meters wide, detailing over 1.5 million square miles. On completion it was hung out of public view in the council hall of a company fort in the east. It was years later, after his death in 1857, that the map was "discovered" and Thompson became recognized as one of the world's greatest land geographers.

whirlpool on the North Saskatchewan River) and on into Banff National Park at Saskatchewan River Crossing. From here it is 153 km north to Jasper and 127 km south to Banff.

White Goat Wilderness Area

The region's three designated wilderness areas—White Goat, Siffleur to the south, and Willmore to the north, afford hikers the chance to enjoy the natural beauty and wildlife of the Canadian Rockies away from the crowds associated with the mountain national parks. No horses or motorized vehicles are allowed within wilderness area boundaries; hunting and fishing are prohibited, as is all construction. This, ironically, gives these lightly traveled regions (an unnamed 15-year resident of adjoining Banff National Park had never heard of them) more protection than national parks. The drawback, and the reason so few people explore these areas, is that wilderness really means *wilderness,* sans roads, bridges, or campsites. With one exception at Willmore, no roads even lead to the areas' boundaries; the only access is on foot.

White Goat is the largest of the three wilderness areas, comprising 445 square km of high mountain ranges, wide valleys, hanging glaciers, waterfalls, and high alpine lakes. The area's vegetation zones are easily recognizable: subalpine forests of Engelmann spruce, subalpine fir, and lodgepole pine; alpine tundra higher up. Large mammals here include a large population of bighorn sheep, as well as mountain goats, deer, elk, woodland caribou, moose, cougars, wolves, coyotes, black bears, and grizzly bears.

The most popular hike is the **McDonald Creek Trail,** which first follows the Cline River, then McDonald Creek to the creek's source in the heart of the wilderness area. McDonald Creek is approximately 12 km from the parking area on Hwy. 11 but a full day should be allowed for this section as the trail crosses many streams. From where McDonald Creek flows into the Cline River it is 19 km to the McDonald Lakes but allow another two full days; the total elevation gain for the hike is 1,224 meters. Other hiking possibilities include following the Cline River to its source and crossing Sunset Pass into Banff National Park, 17 km north of the Saskatchewan River Crossing, or heading up Cataract Creek and linking up with the trails in the Brazeau River area of Jasper National Park. White Goat Wilderness Area has no services and is for experienced hikers only. For more information write to Alberta Environmental Protection, Maps Alberta, 9945 108th St. 2nd Floor, Edmonton, Alberta T5K 2C9; tel. (403) 427-3520. The park is covered by topographic maps 83 C/2 and 83 C/7 and, for those traveling in the remote northwestern corner of the area, 83 C/6.

Siffleur Wilderness Area

Siffleur, like White Goat Wilderness Area, is a remote region of the Canadian Rockies, completely protected from any activities that could have an impact on the area's fragile ecosystems, including road and trail development. No bridges have been built over the area's many fast-flowing streams, and the few old trails that do exist are not maintained. Elk, deer, moose, cougars, wolverines, wolves, coyotes, black bears, and grizzly bears roam the area's four main valleys, while higher, alpine elevations harbor mountain goats and bighorn sheep.

The area is located on the opposite (south) side of Hwy. 11 from White Goat Wilderness and borders Banff National Park to the west and south. The main trail into the 412-square-km wilderness begins from a parking area two km south of the Two O'clock Creek Campground at Kootenay Plains (see above). The area's northeastern boundary is a seven km hike from here. Once inside the wilderness area, the trail climbs steadily alongside the Siffleur River and into the heart of the wilderness. Ambitious hikers can continue through to the Dolomite Creek Area of Banff National Park, finishing at the Icefields Parkway, seven km south of Bow Summit. Total length of this trail is 68 km (5-7 days). Another access point for the area is opposite Waterfowl Lakes Campground in Banff National Park. From here it is six km up Noyes Creek to the wilderness area boundary; the trail peters out after 4.5 km and requires some serious scrambling before descending into Siffleur. This trail—as with all others in the wilderness area—is for experienced hikers only. For more information write to Alberta Environmental Protection, Maps Alberta, 9945 108th St. 2nd Floor, Edmonton, Alberta T5K 2C9; tel. (403) 427-3520. Siffleur Wilderness Area is covered by topographic maps 82 N/15 and 82 N/16.

NORTH FROM ROCKY MOUNTAIN HOUSE

Alder Flats

Alder Flats is 61 km north of Rocky and six km west of Hwy. 22. Through town, along a gravel road, is Alberta's only privately owned ghost town, **Em-te.** It was built completely from scratch and includes a saloon, jailhouse, harness shop, stables, a bank, emporium, and a church. Rose's Cantina serves meals throughout the day. A campground at the ghost town has hot showers, but sites are unserviced; $8.60 per night. Admission to Em-te is $4.25; tel. (403) 388-2166.

Pigeon Lake Provincial Park

On the shore of Pigeon Lake east of Alder Flats, this park is a popular recreation area for residents of Edmonton (60 km to the northwest). The lake is reputed to be the best swimming lake in Alberta, and offers good fishing for walleye, pike, and whitefish. At the main campground you'll find a beach, showers, kitchen shelters, firewood, and the start of a short hiking trail; unserviced sites $13. **Zeiner Campground,** a little farther north, has powered sites, kitchen shelters, firewood, and canoe rentals, but no showers; unserviced sites $13, powered sites $15. Reservations are taken for both these campgrounds, call (403) 586-2644. Also on Pigeon Lake is Alberta's smallest provincial park, **Ma-me-o Provincial Park** (1.5 hectares), which sits at the southeastern end of the lake among a colorful array of summer cottages. It is a day-use area only.

Drayton Valley And Vicinity

Drayton Valley is a town of 5,000 at the base of the foothills and at the western edge of Alberta's extensive oil- and gas fields, 110 km north of Rocky Mountain House. It is located on what is known as the **subcontinental divide;** a high point of land dividing the Arctic Ocean–bound Pembina River system from the Atlantic-bound North Saskatchewan River System. To the southwest, along Hwy. 620, is **Brazeau Reservoir,** whose waters are used to supply hydroelectric power to nearby industry. To the east, 40 km along Hwy. 39, then 25 km north on Hwy. 770, are the **Genesee Fossil Beds.** Each year the North Saskatchewan River erodes its banks here, exposing often perfectly preserved 60-million-year-old fossilized plants. To get to the site from the hamlet of Genesee head west three km, south 1.5 km, then west again 1.5 km to a small creek. A partially defined trail leads down to the much larger river and to the fossil beds.

CALGARY TO RED DEER

The main route out of Calgary is the Deerfoot Trail, which becomes Hwy. 2 as it heads through outlying suburbs and onto the prairies. To the west are the foothills and, over 100 km away, dominating the horizon, the Canadian Rockies. They remain in view for much of the 145-km run to the city of Red Deer, located halfway to Edmonton. The Calgary and Edmonton Railway Company built the first permanent link between Alberta's two largest centers in 1891, following a trail used for generations by natives, early explorers, traders, and missionaries. With the coming of the automobile, a road was built. The original road (Hwy. 2A) is now paralleled the entire length by Hwy. 2, a four-lane divided highway that makes the trip an easy three-hour drive. Highway 2A is still maintained in some sections, passing through small ranching and farming communities. A longer but more interesting alternative is to take Highways 9 and 21, to the east of Hwy. 2, passing through the southern edge of the aspen parkland to a buffalo jump used by natives 2,000 years ago.

VIA HIGHWAY 2A

Airdrie

This fast-growing city is mostly residential. Folks from Calgary who become disenchanted with city living need only move to this rural town—only 10 minutes from Calgary International Airport—to escape the hustle. It began as the first stopping house on the Calgary and Edmonton Railway and has grown ever since. The town's **Nose Creek Valley Museum,** 1701 Main St. S, tel. (403) 948-6685, has an interesting exhibit of artifacts from the Blackfoot and Shoshoni tribes who fought many battles in the area, vying for dominance as buffalo herds declined. It's open in summer, daily 10 a.m.-5 p.m.

Beside the main highway is **Airdrie Driftwood Inn,** 121 Edmonton Trail, tel. 948-3838, convenient to Calgary International Airport and a handy alternative to Calgary lodgings during Stampede Week. Rooms are $48 s, $52 d and there is a restaurant on site.

Carstairs

Carstairs is a farming, dairy, and ranching center 67 km north of Calgary. The town's tree-lined streets are dotted with grand old houses, while the grain elevators associated with all prairie towns stand silhouetted against the skyline. Although there is a small museum at 1138 Nanton St., the main attractions are outside of town. **Pasu Farm,** located 10 km west of town (follow the signs), displays a wide variety of sheepskin, Albertan wool products, and weavings from Africa. The farm's Devonshire Tea Room serves scones, homemade apple pie, and various teas each afternoon. The farm is open year-round, Tues.-Sat. 10 a.m.-5 p.m., Sunday noon-5 p.m.; tel. (403) 337-2800. On the other side of Carstairs, 20 km east on Hwy. 581 and 4.5 km north on Hwy. 791, is **Custom Woollen Mills,** tel. 337-2221. Here raw wool is processed on strange-looking machines—some of which date to the mid-1800s—into the finished product ready for knitting. Call ahead to arrange a tour.

Didsbury

From its beginnings as a Dutch Mennonite settlement, Didsbury has grown into a thriving agricultural community. Cheese lovers should stop for a tour of **Neapolis Dairy Products,** tel. (403) 335-4485. You can camp on the east side of town at **Rosebud Valley Park,** which has showers and kitchen shelters; unserviced sites $8, powered sites $10.

Olds

Olds is located just over halfway between Calgary and Red Deer. Surrounded by rich farmland, it's the home of **Olds Agriculture College,** which has been a leader in the development of Canadian agriculture for most of this century. The school's landscaped gardens provide a welcome break from the seemingly endless farms that surround the town. The campus is located between Highways 2 and 2A.

Red Lodge Provincial Park

This small park is located 14 km west of **Bowden** on the **Little Red Deer River.** An English settler built a large log house on the river's edge and then painted the logs red, hence the name. The park is within a heavily wooded strip of land that extends east from the foothills well into central Alberta, an ideal habitat for deer and moose.

The campground has a kitchen shelter and firewood, and the river is good for swimming. It can get busy on weekends; $13.

Innisfail

Innisfail (population 5,800) is the largest town between Calgary and Red Deer. From Antler Ridge, north of town, Anthony Henday in 1754 became the first white man to see the Canadian Rockies. Highway 54, named the Anthony Henday Hwy. in his honor, begins in town and branches west, passing the turnoff to Markerville and continuing to Caroline and the Forestry Trunk Road. The **Hereford Breeding Test Centre,** at the southern edge of town, tel. (403) 227-5246, is designed to improve the Hereford breed and holds up to 200 head of cattle at one time; open for tours Nov.-April, Mon.-Fri. 8 a.m.-5 p.m. The large **Innisfail Historical Village,** in the fairgrounds at 42nd St. and 52nd Ave., tel. 227-2906, has re-created a variety of historic buildings including a stopping house, school, store, C.P.R. Station, and blacksmith's shop. It's open in summer, daily 8 a.m.-5 p.m. Afternoon tea is served on Friday afternoons ($1.50). The **RCMP Dog Training Centre,** located four km south of town on the east side of the highway, is the only one of its type in Canada. Canine cops receive training here in obedience, agility, and criminal apprehension. Tours of the facility are given year-round, weekdays 9 a.m.-4 p.m.; tel. 227-3346.

Innisfail has two inexpensive motels, and just west of town is **Anthony Henday Campground,** with showers and kitchen shelters but no hookups; $7.

Stephansson House

Markerville, 16 km west then three km north of Innisfail, was originally settled by Icelandic people in the late 1800s; today their heritage lives on through the work of the local Icelandic Society. In town is the **Markerville Historic Creamery Museum.** Between 1897 and the time of its closure in 1972, the creamery won many awards for its fine quality butters. Tours of the factory explain how butter is made. It's open in summer, daily 10 a.m.-5:30 p.m.; tel. (403) 728-3006. Just north of Markerville is **Stephansson House,** once home to Stephan A. Stephansson, one of the western world's most prolific poets. He spent the early part of his life in Iceland but most of his poetry was written here. The house has been restored with displays about the man and his work. Open May-Sept., daily 10 a.m.-6 p.m. For more information call 932-2902.

THE BACK WAY

The area east of Hwy. 2, immediately north of Calgary, was once covered in aspen. But over time, the trees have given way to cereal agriculture and a number of large dairy farms. Stands of trees are now limited to the valleys of tributaries of the Red Deer River, the region's main watershed. The landscape is generally flat, but along the main route north (via Highways 9 and 21) are a number of interesting towns and a buffalo jump.

To Three Hills
Highway 9 intersects Hwy. 1, 31 km east of Calgary, and heads north to **Irricana.** Two km northwest of town, **Pioneer Acres** displays a large collection of working farm machinery, and holds a festival the second weekend each August, with demonstrations of pioneer farming and homemaking activities. It's open May to early September, Tues.-Sun. 9 a.m.-6 p.m. Admission is $3. For more information call (403) 823-2214.

North of Irricana is **Beiseker,** where a C.P.R. Station, built in 1910, has been restored and now houses a museum. From here Hwy. 9 heads east, passing the junction with Hwy. 21 and continuing on to Drumheller (see the Vicinity of Calgary chapter). North up Hwy. 21 is **Three Hills,** home of **GuZoo Animal Farm.** The farm, tel. 443-7463, keeps a collection of exotic animals such as Siberian tigers, as well as cougars and bobcats—native to Alberta but rarely seen. It's open year-round, daily from 9 a.m. Admission is $4. To get there from Three Hills head 1.5 km west, then six km north.

Trochu
The **Arboretum,** just off Hwy. 21, showcases the flora of southern Alberta.

Pathways lead through the gardens, where over 100 different plant species attract a variety of birds. The arboretum is open in summer, daily 10 a.m.-6 p.m.; tel. (403) 442-2111. **St. Ann Ranch Trading Co.** was established in 1905 by a group of aristocratic French settlers and is now a Provincial Historic Site. A French settlement including a school, church, and post office grew around it. The thriving community suffered a blow during WW II when many townsmen returned to France to defend their country. Descendants of one of the men now operate the ranch, which has been partly restored. A small museum displays many historic items, and a large tearoom and bed-and-breakfast inn serve visitors. The teahouse is open in summer, daily 2-5 p.m., and offers lots of great desserts. For information or reservations at the B&B call 442-3924.

Dry Island Buffalo Jump
This 1,180-hectare park is named for both an isolated mesa in the Red Deer River Valley and the site where natives stampeded bison over a cliff around 2,000 years ago. The buffalo jump—a 50-meter drop—is much higher than other jumps in Alberta, and is in an ideal location; the approach to the jump is uphill, masking the presence of a cliff until the final few meters. Below the prairie benchland, clifflike valley walls and banks of sandstone have been carved into strange-looking badlands by wind and water erosion. A great diversity of plantlife grows in the valley; over 400 species of flowering plants have been recorded. The park is a day-use area only—apart from a picnic area and a few trails, it is undeveloped. Access is along a gravel road, east from Huxley on Hwy. 21. From the park entrance, at the top of the buffalo drop, the road descends steeply into the valley. (It can be extremely slippery after rain.)

RED DEER

This city of 58,000 is located on a bend of the Red Deer River, halfway between the cities of Calgary and Edmonton (which are 145 km

The bison was once king of the plains.

south and 148 km north, respectively). From the highway, Red Deer seems all industrial estates and suburban sprawl. But an extensive park system runs through the city and many historic buildings have been restored.

History

The name Red Deer was mentioned on maps by explorer David Thompson in the early 1800s. The Cree name for the river is "Waskasoo," which means "elk"; scholars believe Thompson translated the word incorrectly, confusing these animals with the red deer of Scotland.

Permanent settlement began in 1882 at a site where the busy trail linking Calgary to Edmonton crossed the Red Deer River. Most of the early settlement was centered around Fort Normandeau, at the river crossing. But the Calgary and Edmonton Railway Company built its line and a station farther east, and the town slowly grew in around it. Initially the economy was based on agriculture, but it enjoyed the oil-and-gas boom after WW II. By the '70s, Red Deer was one of Canada's fastest growing cities.

RED DEER

THE CANADA GOOSE

Each spring and fall the skies of central Alberta come alive with the honking of the Canada goose, a remarkable bird whose migratory path takes it clear across the North American continent. Each spring family units migrate north to the same nesting site, year after year. These are spread throughout Canada, from remote wetlands of northern Alberta to desolate islands in the Arctic Ocean. Groups of families migrate together in flocks, the size of the flock varying according to the region, subspecies, and season. Preparation for long flights includes hours of preening and flexing of wings. Once in the air they navigate by the sun, moon, and stars, often becoming disoriented in fog or heavy cloud cover. They are intensely aware of air pressure and humidity. In spring Canada geese hitch a ride north on the strong winds produced by low-pressure systems rolling up from the southwest. In fall they take advantage of Arctic fronts that roar south. If weather conditions aren't right, the geese will rest for a while, usually in farmers' fields (taking advantage of freshly sown crops). The "V" formation, for which the geese are famous, serves a very specific purpose. Each bird positions itself behind and slightly to

BOB RACE

the side of the bird immediately ahead. In this way every goose in the flock has a clear view, and all but the leader benefit from the slipstream of the birds ahead.

If, during migration, a goose becomes ill or is crippled by a hunter's bullet, family members will remain with the bird, delaying their flight and only leaving the injured bird if it dies or if their own survival is in jeopardy.

Waskasoo Park And Fort Normandeau

Red Deer's sights are spread out along the Red Deer River, connected by 11-km-long, 1,000-hectare Waskasoo Park. The park has an extensive trail system, good for walking or biking in summer and cross-country skiing in winter. The best place to start is **Heritage Ranch,** tel. (403) 346-0180, located at the end of Cronquist Drive. To get there from Hwy. 2 take the 32nd St. exit, then take the first left. The ranch is primarily an equestrian center offering trail rides, but is also a year-round tourist information center. From the ranch, walk upstream through the wooded river valley, or drive back out along 32nd St., crossing Hwy. 2, to **Fort Normandeau.** This replica is built on the site of the original fort, constructed in the spring of 1885 in anticipation of the Reil Rebellion—a Cree uprising led by Louis Reil. As protection against marauding natives, a hotel by the river crossing was heavily fortified. Its walls were reinforced, lookout towers were erected, and the entire building was palisaded. The fort was never attacked and was moved to an outlying farm in 1899. Beside the

fort is an interpretive center with displays depicting early settlement at the crossing. The center is open May-Sept., Mon.-Sat. noon-8 p.m., Sunday 1-4 p.m.; tel. 346-2010.

Other Sights

The **Red Deer and District Museum and Archives,** 4525 47A Ave., tel. (403) 343-6844, tells the story of the area from prehistoric times to the present, with emphasis on the growth and development of the last 100 years. It's open July-Aug., Mon.-Thurs. 10 a.m.-9 p.m., Friday 10 a.m.-5 p.m., Sat.-Sun. 1-5 p.m.; the rest of the year, daily 1-5 p.m. The museum is also the starting point for two historical walking tours—ask here for a map. Adjacent to the museum is **Heritage Square,** a collection of historic structures including the Stevenson-Hall Block, Red Deer's oldest building, and a re-created Norwegian sod farmhouse, typical of those lived in by many early settlers in Alberta. One block north, on Ross St., is **City Hall Park,** where 45,000 flowering plants create the perfect spot for a relaxing stroll.

On the opposite side of the river from downtown (take 55th St. then Taylor Dr.) is **Cronquist House.** This 1911 three-story Victorian farmhouse overlooks Bower Ponds. When threatened with demolition, enterprising locals waited until winter and moved it piece by piece across the frozen lake to its present site.

Kerry Wood Nature Centre is located north of downtown at 6300 45th Ave., tel. 346-2010. The center has various exhibits and videos on the natural history of the river valley, and provides access to the adjacent **Gaetz Lakes Sanctuary,** home to 128 species of birds and 25 species of mammals. On the east side of town, at the junction of 30th Ave. and Ross St., is the distinctively shaped **St. Mary's Church,** designed by renowned architect Douglas Cardinal. The church is open to the public weekday afternoons, 2-5 p.m.

Recreation

The city's park system provides a range of recreational facilities. Paddleboats and canoes can be rented at Bower Ponds; tel. (403) 347-9777. At Heritage Ranch, trail riding, horseback riding lessons, and wagon and sleigh rides are offered; tel. 347-8058. **River Bend Golf Course** (tel. 343-8311) couples an 18-hole championship course with a driving range, pro shop, and club rentals; green fees are $22. To get there follow 30th Ave. four km north of the city.

Canyon Ski Area, nine km east of town along Hwy. 11, tel. 346-5589, has 11 runs, and night skiing on weekday nights. Lift tickets are $22.50 for adults, $16 for children 6-12, and $5 for toddlers five and under. Half-day rates are available.

Sylvan Lake

This lake, 16 km west of Red Deer, has been a popular summer resort since the turn of the century. It has sandy beaches, a large marina, and plenty of recreation facilities. **Wild Rapids Waterslides,** on Lakeshore Dr., tel. (403) 887-3636, offers two 110-meter-long water slides, nine other slides, a heated pool, and sailboard and paddleboat rentals; admission $15, children under 12, $11. Other facilities at the lake include bike rentals from **The Pedal Shop,** tel. 887-2778; boat rentals from **Rev's Hover Sports,** tel. 887-2220, or **Sylvan Marina,** tel. 887-2950; three golf courses; and a greyhound racetrack (racing each Saturday), tel. 887-5782.

Festivals And Events

The **Silver Buckle Rodeo,** held the third week of April, kicks off Red Deer's summer festival season and attracts rodeo stars from throughout North America. For more information call (403) 343-7800. The town celebrates **Canada Day** (1 July) with a parade and the **International Folk Festival. Westerner Days** begin in mid-July, the weekend the Calgary Stampede ends; festivities include a parade, midway, livestock displays, chuck wagon races, an art display, and a casino. Most events are held at the Agriplex, tel. 343-7800. The **Red Deer International Air Show** on the last weekend of July is one of Canada's most spectacular aerial events. For information call 340-2333.

Accommodations

Red Deer's location between Alberta's two largest cities makes it a popular location for conventions and conferences. As a result, the city has a large number of hotels. On the south side of the city are some inexpensive strip motels; try **Holiday House Motel,** tel. (403) 346-4188, $34 s, $42 d; or **Rest E-Z Inn,** tel. 343-8444, $37 s, $42 d; where a continental breakfast is included in the price.

Other clusters of motels are located south and north of the city along Gaetz Avenue. Better ones are: **Red Deer Inn,** 4217 Gaetz Ave., tel. 346-6671, with a restaurant and lounge, $36 s, $44 d; **City Centre Motel,** 4124 Gaetz Ave., tel. 342-6969, $38 s, $44 d; and **Renford Inn,** 2803 Gaetz Ave., tel. 343-2112 or (800) 661-6498, which has nicer rooms than the above, many of which are nonsmoking, $46 s, $51 d. The following hotels are generally full of conventioneers during the week; ask about reduced rates on weekends. **North Hill Inn,** 7150 Gaetz Ave., tel. 343-8800, has a restaurant, lounge, and indoor pool; $48 s or d, $61 with a kitchenette. **Great West Inn,** 6500 67th St., tel. 342-6567 or (800) 661-4961, has slightly larger rooms and similar facilities as well as an exercise room; $51 s, $55 d. The city's largest hotel, with over 200 rooms, is **Red Deer Lodge,** 4311 49th Ave., tel. 346-8841 or (800) 661-1657, a full-service establishment with rooms beginning at $80 s or d.

Lions Municipal Campground is located on the west side of the river at 3753 43A Ave., tel. 342-8183. To get there follow Gaetz Ave. north through town and turn right after crossing the

Red Deer River. The campground has showers, full hookups, and a laundry; unserviced sites $10, hookups $12-15.

Food And Drink

Fast-food restaurants line Hwy. 2 as it passes by town; Gaetz Ave. has additional fast-food choices, as well as a range of family-style dining places. **Willy's Hamburgers,** on the east side of Hwy. 2 South, tel. (403) 347-5444, has daily breakfast specials and is open from 6:30 a.m. The best of a handful of cafes downtown is **Judge's Court Coffee Shop** in the Old Courthouse, tel. 342-1117. Light meals are served Mon.-Fri. 9:30 a.m.-4:30 p.m. with afternoon tea offered after 2 p.m. **Club Cherry's Restaurant,** 4605 Gaetz Ave., tel. 340-8787, has a colorful decor and lively servers who actually seem to enjoy themselves. Chinese dishes are offered but stick to the western part of the menu (from $8). **Snifters Dining Lounge,** in the Red Deer Lodge, opens daily at 5 p.m. for fine dining.

Silver Buckle Dance Hall, in the North Hill Inn, plays recorded country music seven nights a week, while **Club Cherry's** at 4605 Gaetz Ave., favors rock.

Transportation

Two scheduled bus services link Red Deer to Calgary and Edmonton. **Greyhound** departs from the depot at 4303 Gaetz Ave., tel. (403) 343-8866, throughout the day for both cities; $17.28 one way to either one. **Red Arrow** offers a more luxurious service with fewer departures but with free onboard beverages and snacks. Their buses depart Red Deer Lodge four times daily for Calgary and Edmonton; $18.75 one way. For more information call 343-2356 or (800) 232-1958.

For a cab call **City Cabs,** tel. 346-4444, or **Red Deer Cabs,** tel. 347-1110.

Services And Information

The **post office** is at 4909 50th Street. The **Laundry Basket,** at 5511 50th Ave., is open Mon.-Fri. 8 a.m.-10 p.m. and Sat.-Sun. 8 a.m.-9 p.m. **Red Deer Regional Hospital** is at 3942 50th Ave., tel. (403) 343-4422 (for emergencies, call 343-4448). For the **RCMP** call 341-2000.

Red Deer Book Exchange features a wide variety of used books and magazines at 6791 50th Ave., tel. 342-4883. For a good place to laze away a rainy afternoon head to **Red Deer Public Library** at 4818 49th St., tel. 346-4576. A **tourist information center** is located at Heritage Ranch. To get there from Hwy. 2 take the 32nd St. exit, turn left, then left again on Cronquist Drive. It's open year-round, Mon.-Fri. 9 a.m.-6 p.m., Sat.-Sun. 10 a.m.-6 p.m.; tel. 346-0180.

EAST OF HIGHWAY 2: THE ASPEN PARKLAND

The aspen parkland lying east of Hwy. 2, between Red Deer and Edmonton, is a transition zone between the prairies to the south and the boreal forest to the north. Here groves of aspen and, to a lesser degree, balsam poplar, grow around sloughs and pothole-like depressions left by the retreating ice sheet at the end of the last ice age. Much of the original vegetation was burned by native peoples in order to attract grazing bison. And in the last 100 years, the land has been given over to agriculture, changing its ecological makeup forever. Although much of the forest has been cleared and cultivated, the region is still home to mammals such as fox, coyote, lynx, white-tailed deer, beaver, and muskrat. The lakes and sloughs attract over 200 species of birds, including literally millions of ducks that can be seen in almost all bodies of water.

From Red Deer, halfway between Calgary and Edmonton, Hwy. 2 continues north, providing access to outdoor recreation opportunities along the way. Sylvan, Gull, and Pigeon lakes are popular summer resort areas west of the highway. To the east are the historic towns of Lacombe, Ponoka, and Wetaskiwin, home of the large Reynolds-Alberta Museum. Highways 12, 13, and 14 are the main routes east. Along each are many small towns with interesting museums and quiet provincial parks. **Camrose,** on Hwy. 13, hosts one of North America's largest gatherings of country-music superstars each August.

HIGHWAY 12 EAST

Lacombe

Lacombe, located 30 km north of Red Deer, is a historic town of 6,500 that is the site of provincial and federal agricultural stations. At the turn of the century, the town was a bustling commercial center of 1,000 where an important spur of the Calgary and Edmonton Railway headed east. Today many Edwardian buildings from this era stand in the main business district. One block from the main street (50th Ave.) is the **Roland Mitchener Museum,** birthplace of a former Canadian governor-general. It's open in summer, Wed.-Sun. 10 a.m.-4 p.m.; tel. (403) 782-4300.

Rochon Sands Provincial Park

This small 99-hectare park is located on a peninsula on the south shore of Buffalo Lake, 14 km north of Erskine. The lake is used by migrating waterfowl each spring and fall and also supports a large population of northern pike. Camping is $11 per night. The west side of the lake is part of the Buffalo Lake Moraine, a hummocky area created by receding ice during the last ice age.

Stettler

Stettler (population 5,200) is located 72 km east of Hwy. 2 in the middle of a farming and ranching area well known for its purebred livestock. One of Canada's last remaining passenger steam trains operates from a historic railway station at the end of the main street. **Alberta Prairie Railway Excursions** runs these trains each weekend throughout the summer to small prairie towns such as Big Valley, Rowley, Donalda, and Consort. Onboard entertainment is provided, and a hearty smorgasbord lunch or dinner is served at the destination.

northern phalarope

The fare is adults $45, children $30. For more information call (403) 742-2811. Stettler also offers the **Stettler Museum,** spread over three hectares along 44th Ave., tel. 742-4534.

The best of six motels in town is **Grandview Motel,** 5720 44th Ave. (at the south end of town), tel. 742-3391; $36 s, $44 d. **Stettler Lions Campground** is located on the west side of town off Hwy. 12 on 62nd Street. It has showers and hookups for $8-10 per night. Most restaurants are along Hwy. 12; try **White Goose Restaurant,** tel. 742-2544, a family-style eatery with inexpensive seafood dishes. **Kalamata,** 4922 50th St., tel. 742-3520, is a pleasant downtown Greek restaurant; entrees are $10-13. The **tourist information center** is at the junction of Highways 12 and 56.

Big Knife Provincial Park

Legend has it that Big Knife Creek was named after a fight between two long-standing enemies—one Cree, the other Blackfoot—that resulted in the death of both men. Recent history is no less colorful. A local farmer named One-eyed Nelson ran a moonshine operation here. His hooch was in demand the length of the prairies; he even exported his popular brew to Montana. Thirty years after he'd left the area, park rangers found the remains of his still in the side of the creek bank.

The small campground at the park has no services, but the Battle River flows through the park making for good swimming and boating. Sites are $11. The park is located 29 km north of **Halkirk** on Hwy. 855.

Coronation

The town of Coronation lies halfway between Stettler and the Alberta/Saskatchewan border. **Bullicks Museum,** at 5005 Imperial Ave., maintains an interesting collection of Indian artifacts; it's open by appointment only, call (403) 578-3936. **Amco Canada** offers tours of its refinery, 27 km north of town; call 578-4010.

Gooseberry Lake Provincial Park

This small park, 14 km north of **Consort,** is located on the shore of a tree-encircled lake and is made up of rolling grassland and a series of alkaline ponds. Many birds—including the northern phalarope—use the lake as a staging area along their migratory paths. The campground is between the lake and a nine-hole golf course and has powered sites, a kitchen shelter, and firewood. Unserviced sites are $11, powered sites $15. To the north are the **Neutral Hills,** which, according to legend, the Great Spirit raised to prevent Cree and Blackfoot from fighting. Nearby **Consort** is the birthplace of country music star K.D. Lang.

WETASKIWIN

This town, located halfway between Red Deer and Edmonton on Hwy. 2A, was founded as a siding on the Calgary and Edmonton Railway and has developed into a wheat-farming and cattle-ranching center of 10,500. In the language of the Cree, Wetaskiwin means "Hills of Peace," a reference to nearby hills where a treaty between Cree and Blackfoot was signed in 1867.

Although the Reynolds-Alberta Museum (see below) is the town's biggest drawcard, other sights include another, smaller museum at 4118 57th St. and a replica of a railway station—with a number of rail cars in the yard—10 km southeast of town. A number of restored buildings on the main route through town (50th Ave.) house arts-and-crafts shops and antique emporiums.

The **tourist information center** is located in the chamber of commerce at the corner of 55A St. and 49th Avenue. It's open in summer, daily 9 a.m.-5 p.m.; the rest of the year, Mon.-Fri. 9 a.m.-4 p.m.

Reynolds-Alberta Museum

Usually museums of this caliber are located in major cities. But here in the rolling hills two km west of Wetaskiwin, a world-class facility cataloguing the history of all types of machinery has been developed. In the main exhibition hall are over 100 major displays and demonstrations, and regular parades of vintage cars and farm machinery. The museum is also home to the **Canadian Aviation Hall of Fame,** recognizing those that have made contributions to the history of aviation. The Hall of Fame and a number of vintage aircraft are housed in a large hangar.

The museum is open year-round, daily 9 a.m.-5 p.m. Admission is $5. For further information call (403) 361-1351.

Accommodations And Food

The least expensive motel in town is **Rose Country Inn,** 4820 50th St., tel. (403) 352-7444, with microwaves in each room; $39 s, $49 d including breakfast. The other two are: **Fort Ethier Lodge,** 3802 56th St., tel. 352-9161, $48 s or d; and **Wayside Inn,** 4103 56th St., tel. 352-6681, which has a restaurant, $50 s, $54 d. **Wetaskiwin Community Campground,** located 2.5 km east of town along Hwy. 13, has showers, a laundry, and mini-golf; unserviced sites $10, hookups $14.

MacEachern Tea House, 4719 50th Ave., tel. 352-8308, built by one of the district's early pioneers, is open for breakfast, lunch, and afternoon tea. Everything served is made on the premises, including delicious cheesecakes ($4 per slice). It's open Mon.-Sat. 9 a.m.-5 p.m. **Blair Originals,** 5116 50th Ave., tel. 352-6035, is a European-style cafe serving coffees and desserts. Other restaurants can be found along all main routes into town.

CAMROSE

Camrose, 40 km east of Wetaskiwin, is a town of 13,000 that has greatly benefited from the oil-and-gas boom yet retained its agricultural base. The area was first settled by Scandinavians, primarily Norwegians, late last century. As a tribute to their success in breaking the land and developing the community, a 10-meter Viking longship is on display in the **Bill Fowler Centre,** 5402 48th Ave. overlooking Mirror Lake. A **tourist information center,** tel. (403) 672-4217, is also in the Fowler Centre. It's open in summer, daily 9 a.m.-9 p.m.; the rest of the year, Mon.-Fri. 8:30 a.m.-4:30 p.m.

Sights

One of western Canada's most recognizable breakfast cereals is Sunny Boy, manufactured here in Camrose by **Prairie Grain Cereals.** The mill is located at 4601 51st Ave., tel. (403) 672-3675. Tours are given and are not very official; call ahead or just roll up and you'll be taken

© MOON PUBLICATIONS, INC.

through each process of the 50-year-old operation, then given some samples to try. **Camrose & District Centennial Museum** on 53rd St. at 46th Ave., tel. 672-5456, presents a working model of a steam threshing machine and many other outdoor displays; it's open in summer, daily 10 a.m.-6 p.m.

Accommodations

Camrose Motel, 6116 48th Ave., tel. (403) 672-3364, has newly renovated rooms, each with a fridge; $34 s, $36 d. The much larger **Camrose Country Inn,** 3911 48th Ave., tel. 672-7741, has large rooms, a cafe, restaurant, and lounge. The rate, $35 s or d, includes one full breakfast.

Valleyview Campground has powered sites, showers, a kitchen shelter, and firewood. Sites overlook the ski hill and ski jump, and a trail links the campground to Mirror Lake. Unser-

viced sites are $9, powered $11. To get there follow 53rd St. two km and turn left on 39th Avenue.

Food

The **Feed Mill Dining Lounge,** 4919 47th St., tel. (403) 672-9502, is in a historic building downtown. The relaxed atmosphere and excellent food are popular with locals and visitors alike. The menu is fairly standard and prices are good; entrees range $9.75-15. It's open daily 11 a.m.-10 p.m. Downtown, a two-tiered movie theater has been transformed into a unique restaurant called **The Old Cinema,** 4917 48th St., tel. 672-4809. Downstairs is a lounge and stage where live entertainment is presented on weekends. The dining area is upstairs on the balcony, surrounded in greenery. Expect to pay $20 for a three-course meal.

HIGHWAY 13 EAST

This part of Alberta is known as the **Battle River Region** for the river that flows from Pigeon Lake, in the foothills west of Wetaskiwin, through heavily developed agricultural land to Wainwright, then into Saskatchewan where it drains into the North Saskatchewan River. Buffalo herds once congregated along the banks of the river, drawing Cree from the north and Blackfoot from the south, who fought over the right to hunt them, hence the river's name.

In **Strome**, the **Sodbuster's Museum**, on Main St., tel. (403) 376-3688, is dedicated to the ingenuity of pioneer families who homesteaded the region. The museum also has various Indian artifacts and a six-meter-long chunk of petrified wood. It's open in summer, daily 9 a.m.-4 p.m. **Hardisty** is located in the Battle River Valley, just north of Hwy. 13. Two local companies offer tours of their plants; in each case you should call ahead. **Home Oil Ltd.,** tel. 888-3565, liquefies petroleum gas, while **Higrade Feed Lot,** tel. 888-3540, is the largest feedlot in the province with the capacity to feed 15,000 cattle. **Hardisty Lake** at the west edge of town is stocked with rainbow trout and has a beach and campground; $8.

From Hardisty the highway continues east through **Amisk** (a nearby Hutterite colony welcomes visitors) to **Czar** and the **Prairie Panorama Museum**, tel. 857-2155, which is known throughout the land for its collection of over 1,000 salt and pepper shakers; open Sunday 2-6 p.m. The town of **Provost** (population 1,800) is 20 km from the Alberta/Saskatchewan Border. Ten km south of town is **St. Norbert's Church,** a magnificent Gothic structure built in 1926. If viewing the church from the outside doesn't satisfy you, call 753-6687 or 753-6503 to get a key.

HIGHWAY 14 EAST

Miquelon Lake Provincial Park

Originally a bird sanctuary, this 906-hectare park lies 30 km north of Camrose on Hwy. 833. It is part of the 650-square-km Cooking Lake Moraine, a hummocky, forested region dotted with lakes that extends north to Elk Island National Park. At the end of the last ice age, as the sheet of ice that covered much of the continent receded, it occasionally stalled, as it did in this area. Chunks of ice then broke off and melted, depositing glacial till in mounds. Between the mounds are hollows, known as kettles, that have filled with water. The **Knob and Kettle Trail System** is a series of short interconnecting trails through this remarkable landscape that starts behind the baseball diamond. Being heavily wooded, the area attracts many birds and animals; most ponds house a resident beaver family, and moose and deer can often be seen feeding at dawn and dusk. The main body of water is fed by underground springs and has no streams running into it. This means that the level of the lake in summer is largely dependent on winter snowfall which, in recent years, has been low. During summer, rangers conduct guided hikes (Thurs.-Sun. at 10:30 a.m.) and present evening shows in the amphitheater (Wed.-Sat.). A visitor center is open in summer, Wed.-Sun. 1-5 p.m. The campground has showers, kitchen shelters, and firewood; unserviced sites $13, powered sites $15. For more information on the park, or to reserve a campsite, call (403) 672-7308.

Tofield

Western Canada's only shorebird reserve, **Beaverhill Natural Area,** is located 10 km east of Tofield. Beaverhill Lake, with its unspoiled islands and rich marshes, is a haven for over 250 species of birds. Many species use the lake as a stopover on their migratory path, attracting birders from around Canada during spring and fall. The natural area is relatively undeveloped. A paved road from Tofield turns to gravel four km from town and ends at **Beaverhill Bird Observatory,** operated by the Edmonton Bird Club; biologists and club members are often present, feel free to ask questions. Before the road turns to gravel you'll see a turnoff to the north (left). At the end of this road a short trail leads to **Francis Viewpoint** and a bird blind on the lakeshore. On the eastern shore of the lake is another undeveloped area with access to a beach. Walking north along the beach you can see pelicans, cormorants, and swans on **Pelican Island.** Farther north are the **Dekker Islands,** another nesting area for a variety of bird species.

With all this great birdwatching, you'd expect a bird-related celebration at some point. The last weekend of April is the **Snow Goose Festival,** a celebration of the town's ornithological neighbors.

Beaverhill Motel, tel. (403) 662-3396, has basic rooms for $36 s, $44 d. The closest campground is in Ryley, east of town (free), or at **Ministik Recreation Area,** on the highway 24 km west of town (much nicer, $5.50). **That Place** on 50th St. is where the locals gather to eat and gossip; not necessarily in that order. At the entrance to the town of Tofield is the **Beaverhill Lake Nature Centre,** an interpretive center which has maps of the area and bird checklists. It's open in summer, daily 8 a.m.-8 p.m.; tel. 662-3191.

Ryley

If you need an excuse to stop in Ryley, visit **George's Harness & Saddlery,** tel. (403) 663-3611, a working museum that produces saddles, chuck wagon harnesses, and other equine accessories. Most artifacts are made with antique tools and stitching machines. The goings-on in the large workshop are visible from the shop, but if George isn't busy filling orders he'll happily show you around. The store is on the main street; closed Sunday.

Viking

Southeast of Viking in a farmer's field are the **rib stones,** two stones carved with a design resembling bison ribs. The stones held special significance for generations of plains Indians, whose lives revolved around the movement of bison herds. They believed that by conducting certain ceremonial rites and by leaving gifts of beads or tobacco around the stones their luck in hunting would improve. The site is not well marked. Fourteen km east of Viking on Hwy. 14 is a historical sign. A little farther east is a gravel road to the south; follow this road a short way to Hwy. 615, turn east (left), then take the first gravel road to the south (right) and follow it for three km. A provincial historic cairn marks the site.

Wainwright

Best known for a large combined forces base, Wainwright is the last town along Hwy. 14 before Saskatchewan. The military's **Camp Wainwright** is on the site of what once was Buffalo National Park, the site of probably the most unusual chain of events ever to take place in a Canadian national park. Originally created in 1908 to protect 3,000 plains bison, Buffalo National Park was also home to elk, moose, and deer. Experiments within the park cross-bred bison with cattle, trying to create a more resilient farm stock; meanwhile bison parts were sold for pemmican. All that may seem odd enough to begin with. But then a Hollywood film crew paid officials to stampede a herd of bison and slaughter part of the herd for a movie scene. Shortly afterward the bison were struck by tuberculosis and were secretly shot along with every ungulate in the park. This sad and sorry story ended with the land being handed over to the Department of National Defence. Today it is Canada's second-largest military training facility, able to house 15,000 troops at one time. On its 400 square kilometers are 22 weapons ranges, two airfields, and yes, a small herd of bison, which can be viewed in **Bud Cotton Buffalo Paddock** beside the base's main gate. The base is two km south of town along 1st Street.

Also in Wainwright, the Canadian Wildlife Service operates a **Peregrine Falcon Hatchery,** where individuals of the endangered species are raised and released into the wild. During summer, tours can be arranged through the tourist information center at the west end of town; the rest of the year contact the facility, tel. (403) 842-3115. **Wainwright Museum** is a restored Canadian National Station at the end of Main St., with displays on the railway and the ill-fated national park. Open daily 9 a.m.-5 p.m.; tel. 842-3115.

Dillberry Lake Provincial Park

This park is on the Alberta/Saskatchewan border, 50 km southeast of Wainwright in the transition zone between aspen parkland and prairie. Of the many lakes within the park, Dillberry is the largest. It's surrounded by sandy beaches and low sand dunes (the biggest dunes are at the southeastern end of the lake), and its clear spring-fed waters are good for swimming. The diverse habitat creates excellent birdwatching opportunities—140 species have been recorded. The large campground is right by the best beach and has showers, kitchen shelters, and firewood; unserviced sites $13, powered sites $15. For more information on the park or to reserve a site call (403) 858-3824.

KAREN MCKINLEY

EDMONTON
INTRODUCTION

Edmonton sits in the center of Alberta, surrounded by the vast natural resources that have made the city unabashedly wealthy. It's a vibrant cultural center and a gateway to the north, but its reputation as a boomtown may be its defining characteristic. Boomtowns are a phenomenon unique to the West—cities that have risen from the surrounding wilderness, oblivious to hardship, pushed forward by dreams of the incredible wealth to be made overnight by pulling riches from the earth. Most boomtowns disappear as quickly as they rise, but not Edmonton. The proud city has seen not one, but three major booms in the past century and has grown to become one of the world's largest northerly cities. Its population has mushroomed 800% in 50 years to 800,000, making it the fifth-largest city in Canada. While Calgary is the administrative and business center of the province's billion-dollar petroleum industry, Edmonton is the technological, service, and supply center.

The **North Saskatchewan River Valley** winding through the city has been largely preserved as a 27-km greenbelt of parks—the largest urban park system in Canada. Rather than the hodgepodge of slums and streets you might expect in a boomtown, the modern city of Edmonton has been extremely well designed and built, with an eye toward the future. The downtown area sits on a spectacular bluff overlooking the river valley park system. Silhouetted against the deep blue sky a cluster of modern glass-and-steel high-rises makes a dynamic contrast to the historic granite Alberta Legislature Building and lush valley floor below.

Edmonton is the capital of Alberta, it's home to the University of Alberta, and it's hosted events such as the 1978 Commonwealth Games and 1983 World University Games. So it comes as no surprise that Edmonton has some of Canada's best cultural facilities. Each week during summer, a festival of some sort takes place within the city. But the city's biggest attraction is the ultimate shopping mecca, **West Edmonton Mall,** the world's largest shopping and amusement complex.

© MOON PUBLICATIONS, INC.

Getting Oriented

Highway 2 from Calgary enters Edmonton from the south and divides just north of Gateway Park Tourist Information Centre. At that point it becomes known as **Calgary Trail.** To make this even more confusing, northbound Calgary Trail is also known as **103rd St.,** while southbound is **104th Street.** From the south you can get to West Edmonton Mall and Hwy. 16 West, without going through downtown, by taking **Whitemud Drive.** Whitemud crosses the North Saskatchewan River southwest of downtown. From the Whitemud Dr. intersection, Calgary Trail continues north through **Old Strathcona,** crossing the North Saskatchewan River directly south of downtown.

The **Yellowhead Hwy.** passes through the city east to west, north of downtown. To get downtown from the east, take 97th Street. From downtown, Jasper Ave. changes to Stony Plain Rd. as it heads west, eventually joining Hwy. 16 at the city's western limits.

Since the turn of the century Edmonton streets have been numbered. Avenues run east to west, numbered from 1st Ave. in the south to 259th Ave. in the north. Streets run north to south, numbered from 1st St. in the east to 231st St. in the west. Even-numbered addresses are on the north sides of the avenues and west sides of the streets. The center of the city is crossed by both 101st St. and 101st Ave., the latter having retained its original name of **Jasper Avenue.**

When vast outlying areas were annexed by the city in 1982, new additions had to be made to the street numbering system. First St. was renamed Meridian St. and 1st Ave. was renamed Quadrant Avenue. The entire existing city now lies within the northwest quadrant, allowing for easy numbering of new streets as the city grows to the south and east.

HISTORY

For at least 3,000 years natives came to the river valley where Edmonton now stands, searching for quartzite to make stone tools. They had no knowledge of, or use for, the vast underground resources that in time would cause a city to rise from the middle of the wilderness.

Fort Edmonton

European fur traders, canoeing along the North Saskatchewan River, found the area where Edmonton now stands to be one of the richest fur-bearing areas on the continent. Large populations of beavers and muskrats lived in the surrounding spruce, poplar, and aspen forest. In 1795, a Scotsman, William Tomison, built a sturdy log building beside the North West Company's Fort Augustus. He named it Fort Edmonton after an estate owned by Sir James Winter Lake, Deputy Governor of the Hudson's Bay Company. Both forts stood on the site of the present Legislature Building grounds. It was an ideal location for trading. Cree and Assiniboine could trade beaver, otter, and marten pelts in safety, without encroaching on the territory of fierce plains Indians, such as the Blackfoot. Yet the fort was far enough south to be within range of the Blackfoot—peaceable when outside their own territory—who came north to buy muskrat, buffalo meat, and other natural resources, which they later traded with Europeans.

The Klondike Gold Rush

The most common images of the Klondike Gold Rush in the Yukon are of miners climbing the Chilkoot or White Pass trails in a desperate attempt to reach Dawson City. Often for financial reasons, various other routes were promoted as being superior. The merchants of Edmonton led a patriot cry to try the "All-Canadian Route," which would allow prospectors to buy their supplies in a Canadian city rather than Seattle. The proposed route followed the Athabasca Landing Trail north to Athabasca, continued by boat down the Athabasca, Slave, and Mackenzie rivers to just south of the Mackenzie Delta, and ended with a short overland trip to the goldfields. The route was impractical and very difficult. About 1,600 people were persuaded to attempt the route. Of these, 50 died, many turned back, and only 700 reached the Yukon. None reached the goldfields before 1899 when the main rush was over, and few, if any, found gold. It is this slim connection to the gold rush that is now celebrated in the annual **Edmonton's Klondike Days,** much to the displeasure of Yukoners.

Selecting The Capital

The provinces of Alberta and Saskatchewan

PROVINCIAL ARCHIVES OF ALBERTA

Fort Edmonton, on the bank of the North Saskatchewan River, 1902

were both inaugurated on 1 September 1905. As Regina had been the capital of the Northwest Territories, it was only natural that it continued as the capital of Saskatchewan. The decision on Alberta's capital did not come as easily. The Alberta Act made Edmonton the temporary capital but it had plenty of competition. Other contenders were Athabasca Landing, Banff, Calgary, Cochrane, Lacombe, Red Deer, Vegreville, and Wetaskiwin. Each thought it had a rightful claim: Banff because it could be fortified if war ever broke out; Vegreville for the clean air and a climate free of chinook winds. But the strongest claims were from the citizens of Calgary, who believed their city to be the financial and transportation center of the province. Heated debates on the subject took place in the Canadian capital of Ottawa and between rival newspaper editors, but Edmonton has remained the capital to this day. In 1912 Edmonton merged with Strathcona, giving the city a total population of 55,000. For the next 35 years the city grew and declined, according to the fortunes of agriculture.

Oil And A Growing City

Fur was Edmonton's first industry and coal was its second. Commercial coal-mining operations began as early as 1880, with mining concentrated in three areas of the city. The last of over 150 operations closed in 1970, and much of the coal seam remains unmined below the downtown area. But Edmonton's future lay not in coal, but oil. Since the discovery of "black gold" in 1947 at nearby **Leduc,** Edmonton has been one of Canada's fastest growing cities. The building of pipelines and refineries created many jobs and the city became the center of western Canada's petrochemical industry. As demand continued to rise, hundreds of wildcat wells were drilled around Edmonton. Farmers' fields were filled with derricks, valves, and oil tanks, and by 1956 over 3,000 producing wells were pumping within 100 km of the city.

Edmonton experienced the same postwar boom of most major North American cities, as a major population shift from rural areas to the city began. By 1956 Edmonton's population had grown to 254,800, doubling in size since 1946. A 20-square-km area east of the city was filled with huge oil tanks, refineries, and petrochemical plants. Changes were also taking place within the city as the wealth of the oil boom began to take hold. Restaurants improved and cultural life flourished. The city's businesses were jazzed up, and the expanding business community began moving into the glass-and-steel skyscrapers that form the city skyline today. Although the boom is over, oil is still a major part of the city's economy. Also important are the various service industries; West Edmonton Mall alone employs 15,000 people.

SIGHTS

DOWNTOWN

Looking at Edmonton's dynamic skyline, it's hard to believe that less than 100 years ago the main drag was lined with dingy saloons and rowdy dance halls. Since those heady days, the city has seen many ups and downs—its present look being a legacy of the 1970s oil boom. The well-planned city center, on the northern bank of the Northern Saskatchewan River, is a conglomeration of skyscrapers that seemingly rose overnight when oil money flooded the city. The downtown core is fairly compact and is within walking distance of many hotels, the bus depot, and the train station. **Jasper Ave.** (101st Ave.) is downtown's main thoroughfare, lined with restaurants and shops. One block north is the large and popular **Eaton Centre** shopping complex. On 102nd St. is 36-story ManuLife Place, Edmonton's tallest building. A few blocks east are the provincial government buildings, including the futuristic **City Hall,** which opened in August 1992.

The **pedway** system is unique and necessary this far north. It's a complex system of enclosed walkways linking office buildings, hotels, plazas, the Civic Centre, and public transportation stops. Using the pedways, you can get virtually anywhere downtown, without ever having to step outside into the elements. At first it all seems a bit complicated, but armed with a map, the system soon becomes second nature. Pedways are below, above, or at street level and the excellent signage makes it easy to find your way. The walkways are spotlessly clean, well lit, and relatively safe, although you wouldn't want to loiter around the Central LRT (Light Rail Transit) Station at night.

Secondhand stores and pawnshops line 97th St. between 102A Ave. and 104th Avenue. This is skid row with sleazy bars and suspicious looking characters—not the place to linger at night.

Throughout all the development, a number of historic buildings managed to survive. Many can be seen along **Heritage Trail,** a route taken by early fur traders that linked the old town to Fort Edmonton. Today the trail begins at the Convention Centre, at the corner of Jasper Ave. and 97th St., and ends at the legislature grounds. The route is easy to follow—the sidewalk is paved with red bricks and lined with period benches, replica lampposts, and old-fashioned street signs. The **High Level Bridge** crosses the North Saskatchewan River at the bottom end of 109th Street. It was built in 1913, linking the new capital to Strathcona. The bridge is 775 meters long and 53 meters above the river. It has been used as a tramway, railway, sidewalk, and roadway. In 1980, the **Great Divide Waterfall** was added to the bridge. When turned on, a man-made curtain of water, higher than Niagara Falls, cascades down along the entire length of the bridge. It usually operates during special events such as Edmonton's Klondike Days. For operating times call (403) 496-8416.

Edmonton Civic Centre

This complex, in the heart of downtown, occupies six square blocks and is one of the city's showcases. Within its limits are the Centennial Library, Edmonton Art Gallery, Sir Winston Churchill Square, City Hall, the Law Courts Building, Convention Centre, and the performing arts community's pride and joy, the magnificent Citadel Theatre.

The **Edmonton Art Gallery** houses an extensive collection of modern Canadian paintings as well as historical and contemporary art in all media. Various traveling exhibitions are presented throughout the year. The exhibit *From Sea to Sea: The Development of Canadian Art* catalogues the entire history of the country's art through well-laid-out displays. The gallery is open Mon.-Wed. 10:30 a.m.-5 p.m., Thurs.-Fri. 10:30 a.m.-8 p.m., and Sat.-Sun. 11 a.m.-5 p.m. Admission is $3, free on Thursday after 4 p.m. The gallery is located northeast of Sir Winston Churchill Square on 99th St.; tel. (403) 472-6223.

The new **City Hall,** built on the site of the old, is designed to be the centerpiece of the Civic Centre. The main public areas are located on the main floor. An Edmonton Tourist Information Centre is in the South Plaza. Tours of City Hall leave from this center Monday, Wednesday, and Friday at 10:30 a.m. and 2:30 p.m. Immediately behind this area is the City Room, the building's main focal point. Its ceiling is a glass pyramid that rises eight stories. To the east are various displays cataloguing the city's short but colorful history.

On the lower pedway level of the Convention Centre is the **Canadian Country Music Hall Of Honour** with plaques and memorabilia in recognition of Canadian entertainers who have made contributions to the development of this popular style of music.

Chinatown

An elaborate gateway designed by a master architect from China welcomes visitors to Edmonton's small Chinatown. The gate spans 23 meters across 102nd Ave. (also known as Harbin Rd.) at 97th Street. It is supported by eight steel columns painted in the traditional Chinese color of red. Stretched across the center of the arch's roof is a row of ornamental tiles featuring two dragons, the symbol of power in China. The 11,000 tiles used in the gate were each handcrafted and glazed in China. Originally Chinatown extended north along 97th St. to around 108th Ave., but many new restaurants and shops selling exotic imports and fresh groceries are spread east along 102nd Ave. and, to a lesser degree, south to Jasper Avenue.

Edmonton Police Museum

This museum is located on the second floor of the Police Service Headquarters at 9620 103A Ave., tel. (403) 421-2274. Displays of uniforms, photographs, and equipment tell the story of the Royal Canadian Mounted Police (originally called the North West Mounted Police) and the now defunct Alberta Provincial Police who existed 1917-32. The museum is open Mon.-Sat. 9 a.m.-3 p.m. Admission is free.

Hotel Macdonald

This hotel overlooking the river valley, at 10065 100th St., has long been regarded as Edmonton's premier luxury accommodation. For many years it was the social center of the city. It was built in 1915 by the Grand Trunk Railway in the same Chateau-style used for many of the Canadian Pacific hotels across the country. After closing in 1983, plans to tear it down were aborted. After $28 million was spent on refurbishing, the hotel reopened, as grand and elegant as ever. The main lobby has been totally restored and opens to the Confederation Lounge and The Library, a bar overlooking the river that has the feel of an Edwardian gentlemen's club. Ask at reception for a map of the hotel.

Edmonton Public Schools Archives And Museum

Built in 1904, McKay Avenue School is Edmonton's oldest standing brick schoolhouse. It was the venue of the first two sittings of the provincial legislature in 1906. The building contains reconstructions of early classrooms and of the historic legislature assembly. Also on the grounds is Edmonton's first schoolhouse, built in 1881 and looking much as it would have looked to 19th-century students. Admission to both is free. The school is located on Edmonton's Heritage Trail at 10425 99th Ave., tel. (403) 422-1970. It's open Tues.-Fri. 12:30-4 p.m., Sunday 1-4 p.m.

Alberta Legislature Building

Home of the provincial government, this elegant Edwardian building overlooking the North Saskatchewan River Valley is surrounded by formal gardens and manicured lawns. It officially opened in 1912 and for many years stood beside the original Fort Edmonton. Today it remains as one of western Canada's best examples of architecture from that era. Its 16-story vaulted dome is one of Edmonton's most recognizable landmarks. Many materials used in its construction were imported; sandstone from near Calgary, granite from Vancouver; marble from Quebec, Pennsylvania, and Italy; and mahogany from Belize. The interior features a wide marble staircase that leads from the spacious rotunda in the lobby to the chamber and is surrounded by stained-glass windows and bronze statues. Free tours are offered every half hour; in summer, weekdays 9 a.m.-8:30 p.m., weekends 9 a.m.-4:30 p.m.; the rest of the year, weekdays 9 a.m.-3 p.m., and weekends noon-4 p.m. For details call (403) 427-7362. The Legislature Building is part of a complex known as Government Centre on the southwest side of downtown at 109th St. and 97th Avenue. Also of interest is the **Legislature Display,** a series of boards depicting the early history, culture, and technology

EDMONTON POLICE MUSEUM

VIA RAIL

POST OFFICE

104th AVE.

103A AVE.

TO HOSTEL

103rd AVE.

CITY HALL

ITALIAN GARDENS

EDMONTON ART GALLERY

102A AVE.

GREYHOUND BUS DEPOT

HILTON

YMCA

CHINATOWN GATE

102nd

EATON CENTRE THE CREPERIE

CENTENNIAL LIBRARY

101A AVE.

102nd AVE.

MANULIFE PLACE

THE SHERLOCK HOLMES

CITADEL THEATRE

MONGOLIAN FOOD EXPERIENCE

HY'S STEAK LOFT

WESTIN HOTEL

CANADA PLACE

JASPER AVE. (101st AVE.)

HUDSON'S BAY CENTRE

CONVENTION CENTRE

ALBERTA PLACE SUITE HOTEL

HOTEL MACDONALD

GRIERSON HILL DR.

NORTH SASKATCHEWAN RIVER

HOLIDAY INN

YWCA

EDMONTON HOUSE SUITE HOTEL

TO MUTTART CONSERVATORY

LOW LEVEL BRIDGE

103rd ST.

98th AVE.

JAMES MACDONALD BRIDGE

101st ST.

96th AVE.

JOHN DUCEY PARK

102nd ST.

100th ST.

99th ST.

97th ST.

96th ST.

101st ST.

0   100 yd
0   100 m

© MOON PUBLICATIONS, INC.

St. Josephat's Ukrainian Catholic Cathedral

in the province. It's located along a pedway linking the Legislature Building to three other government buildings.

Ukrainian Museums
Two museums, just to the north of the city center, honor Albertans of Ukrainian descent. The **Ukrainian Museum of Canada,** 10611 110th Ave., tel. (403) 483-5932, displays costumes from throughout the Ukraine, as well as woodcarvings, tapestries, and a small collection of Easter eggs. It's open May-Aug., Mon.-Fri. 9 a.m.-4 p.m., Sunday 2-5 p.m. The **Ukrainian Canadian Archives and Museum of Alberta,** 9543 110th Ave., tel. 424-7580, exhibits artifacts from the lives of Ukrainian Pioneers in Canada and has one of the largest archives in the country. It's open year-round, Tues.-Sat. noon-4 p.m. Admission is by donation. Edmonton has a number of Ukrainian churches. One of the most impressive is **St. Josephat's Ukrainian Catholic Cathedral** on 97th St. at 108th Ave., well worth a look for its elaborate decorations and pastel wall paintings.

SOUTHSIDE

Muttart Conservatory
Nestled in the valley on the south side of the North Saskatchewan River are four large pyramid-shaped greenhouses that make up the Muttart Conservatory. Three contain the flora of specific climates. In the arid pyramid are cacti and other hardy plants found in desertlike conditions. The tropical pyramid holds a humid jungle, home to colorful (and raucous) exotic birds that live among the palms. The temperate pyramid features plant species from four continents—none of which would grow naturally in Edmonton's harsh environment. Displays in the fourth pyramid change with the season, but always feature colorful floral displays such as red, white, and yellow poinsettias at Christmastime. The conservatory is located at 9626 96A St. off 98th Ave.; tel. (403) 496-8755. Take bus No. 45 or 51 south along 100th Street. It's open year-round, Sun.-Wed. 11 a.m.-9 p.m., Thurs.-Sat. 11 a.m.-6 p.m. Admission is $4.

John Walter Museum
This historic site located near the Kinsmen Sports Centre consists of three houses—dating from 1875, 1884, and 1900—that were built by John Walter for his family. The first house was a stopping point for travelers using Walter's ferry service to cross the river. Walter also opened a carriage works, lumber mill, coal mine, and at one time even built a steamship. For a time the area was known as Walterdale, but with the completion of the High Level Bridge, the need for a ferry service ended. Today, all that remains are Walter's houses. Each house holds exhibits corresponding to the period of its construction, and depicts the growth of Edmonton and the importance of the North Saskatchewan River. The buildings are only open in summer, Sunday noon-5 p.m., but the grounds are pleasant to walk through at any time. The museum is located at 10627 93rd Avenue. From downtown, take 101st St. south down Bellamy Hill and cross the river at the Walterdale Bridge. On foot allow 30-60 minutes. By bus, jump aboard No. 43 west along 102nd Ave. or south along 103rd Street.

ALBERTA TOURISM

Muttart Conservatory

Rutherford House

This elegant Edwardian mansion was built in 1911 for Alexander C. Rutherford, Alberta's first premier. The Rutherford family lived in this house for 30 years. It was then used as a University of Alberta frat house before being restored to its original condition and furnished with antiques from the Edwardian period. You can wander throughout the two-story house and ask questions of the costumed interpreters. The covered sunporch operates as a tearoom in summer (Wed.-Sun.), serving lunch ($7) and afternoon tea (from $4), using historical recipes from 1915 or earlier. The house is open in summer, daily 10 a.m.-6 p.m., the rest of the year, daily noon-5 p.m. It's located on the University of Alberta campus at 11153 Saskatchewan Dr., tel. (403) 427-3995. Admission is free. The easiest way to get here by public transport is on the LRT from downtown.

Fort Edmonton Park

An authentic reconstruction of the early trading post from which Edmonton grew is only a small part of this exciting park, Canada's largest historic park. From the entrance, a 1919 steam locomotive takes you through the park to the Hudson's Bay Company Fort, which has been built much as the original fort would have looked in 1846—right down to the methods of carpentry used in its construction. Outside the fort is 1885 St., re-creating downtown Edmonton between

1871 and 1891 when the west was opened up to settlers. The street is lined with wooden-facaded shops such as a bakery, blacksmith, and Egges Stopping House (where there is always a game of horseshoes on). As you continue down the road, you round a corner and are on 1905 St., in the time period 1892-1914 when the railway had arrived and Edmonton was proclaimed provincial capital. **Reed's Tea Room,** near the far end of the street, serves English teas and scones from 12:30-5 p.m. in a traditional atmosphere. By this time you're nearly on 1920 St., representing the years 1914-1929—a period of social changes when the business community was developing and the city's industrial base was expanding.

A constant variety of activities is offered; a weekly program is available from the main entrance or by calling (403) 428-2992. An authentic streetcar travels the park picking up passengers along the way. You can take a wagon ride or a pony ride, or rent a canoe.

The park is located in the North Saskatchewan River Valley off the Whitemud Freeway near Fox Drive. By public transport, take the LRT to the University Transit Centre, then bus No. 32 or 132. It's open May-June, Mon.-Fri. 10 a.m.-4 p.m., Sat.-Sun. 10 a.m.-6 p.m.; July-Sept., daily 10 a.m.-6 p.m.; closed in winter except for special events (such as sleigh rides) over the Christmas break. Admission is $6.25 adults, $4.75 seniors, $3 children.

John Janzen Nature Centre

Beside Fort Edmonton Park (use the same parking lot) is John Janzen Nature Centre, which has a number of hands-on exhibits, displays of local flora and fauna—both dead and alive—and a four-km self-guided interpretive trail that leads through the river valley and loops back to the center. In one room various natural environments have been simulated with displays of frogs, fish, snakes, salamanders, and a working beehive made from glass. Throughout the year special events are held, films are shown, and Sunday nature walks are conducted. The center is open year-round, Mon.-Fri. 9 a.m.-4 p.m., longer hours and weekends in summer. Admission is free. For more information call (403) 496-2939.

Valley Zoo

Across the river from Fort Edmonton Park is the city zoo, which holds around 350 animals, representing all seven continents. It is designed mainly for kids, with a petting zoo, camel and pony rides, a miniature train, and cut-out storybook characters. The zoo is open daily, May-June 10 a.m.-6 p.m., July-Aug. 10 a.m.-9 p.m.; the rest of the year, weekends only, noon-4 p.m. It's located at the end of Buena Vista Rd., off 142nd Street. To get there by bus take No. 12 from west along 102nd Ave. to Buena Vista Rd. and walk 1.5 km down to the park. On Sunday, buses leave on the hour from the University Transit Centre and go right to the zoo. Admission is $4.75 adults, $2.50 children.

OLD STRATHCONA

When the Calgary and Edmonton Railway Company completed a rail line between the province's two largest cities, it decided to end it south of the North Saskatchewan River and establish a townsite there, rather than build a bridge and end the line in Edmonton. The town was named Strathcona, and it grew to a population of 7,500 before merging with Edmonton in 1912. Because of an early fire-prevention bylaw, buildings were built of brick. Today many still remain, looking much as they did at the turn of the century. Old Strathcona is Edmonton's best-preserved historical district. In addition to the old brick buildings, the area has been refurbished with brick sidewalks and replica lampposts. The commercial core of Old Strathcona is centered along Whyte (82nd) Ave. west of the rail line. Over 75 residential houses built prior to 1926 are scattered to the north and west of Whyte Avenue. The easiest way to get around is on foot and the best place to start walking is from the **Caboose Tourist Information Centre** on the corner of Whyte Ave. and 103rd Street. Opposite is the **Strathcona Hotel,** one of the few wood-framed buildings surviving from the pre-1900 period. Before Strathcona had permanent churches, congregations worshipped in the hotel, and during prohibition it was used as a ladies' college. One block north, on 83rd Ave., is **Old Strathcona Farmer's Market** with plenty of fresh produce, crafts, and homemade goodies for sale. It's open year-round, Saturday 8 a.m.-3 p.m., and in summer, Tuesday 1-6 p.m. Many of the historic buildings have plaques at street level but the brochures *A Walk through Old Strathcona* and *Historical Walking and Driving Tour: Strathcona,* available at the information center, make a stroll much more interesting. The caboose is open in summer, Wed.-Sun. 10 a.m.-6 p.m. For more information on the district write to Old Strathcona Foundation, 8331 104th St., Edmonton, Alberta T6E 4E9; tel. (403) 433-5866. Within walking distance of Whyte Ave. are several small museums detailed below. By public transportation take the LRT to the University Transit Centre, then bus No. 8 or 46 east along 82nd Avenue.

C&E Railway Museum

Strathcona's original railway station was located just north of the C.P.R. Station. It was later moved farther along the line, then demolished, and replaced with a partial replica that houses a railway museum. The museum, at 10447 86th Ave., tel. (403) 433-9739, relives the days of steam engines and settlers, when people streamed into the newly opened Canadian West from around the world. It's open in summer, Tues.-Sat. 10 a.m.-4 p.m.; admission by donation.

Strathcona Model And Toy Museum

Unlike other toy museums, all exhibits here are made entirely of paper and card from kits that have been collected from around the world. The exhibits include scale models of famous build-

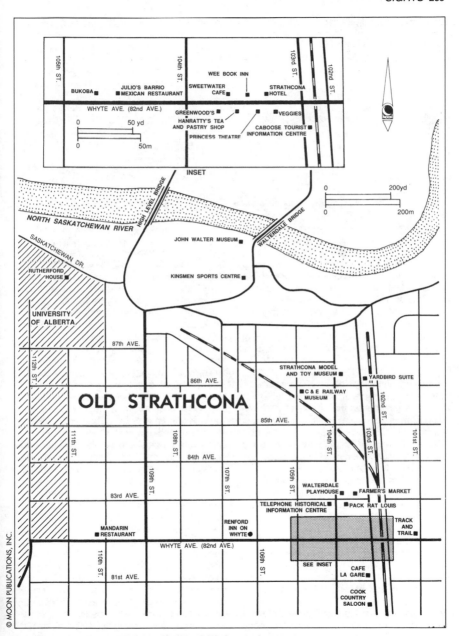

INSET

NORTH SASKATCHEWAN RIVER

HIGH LEVEL BRIDGE

WALTERDALE BRIDGE

SASKATCHEWAN DR.

RUTHERFORD HOUSE ■

UNIVERSITY OF ALBERTA

JOHN WALTER MUSEUM ■

KINSMEN SPORTS CENTRE ■

OLD STRATHCONA

STRATHCONA MODEL AND TOY MUSEUM ■

■ C & E RAILWAY MUSEUM

■ YARDBIRD SUITE

WALTERDALE PLAYHOUSE ■

■ FARMER'S MARKET

TELEPHONE HISTORICAL INFORMATION CENTRE ■

■ PACK RAT LOUIS

TRACK AND TRAIL ■

MANDARIN ■ RESTAURANT

RENFORD INN ON WHYTE ●

WHYTE AVE. (82nd AVE.)

SEE INSET

CAFE LA GARE ■

COOK COUNTRY SALOON ■

105th ST. 104th ST. 103rd ST. 102nd ST. 112th ST. 111th ST. 110th ST. 109th ST. 108th ST. 107th ST. 106th ST. 105th ST. 104th ST. 103rd ST. 102nd ST. 101st ST.

87th AVE. 86th AVE. 85th AVE. 84th AVE. 83rd AVE. 81st AVE.

INSET:

BUKOBA ■ JULIO'S BARRIO ■ MEXICAN RESTAURANT

WEE BOOK INN

SWEETWATER CAFE ■

STRATHCONA HOTEL ■

WHYTE AVE. (82nd AVE.)

GREENWOOD'S ■ ■ VEGGIES

HANRATTY'S TEA AND PASTRY SHOP ■

PRINCESS THEATRE

CABOOSE TOURIST INFORMATION CENTRE ■

0   50 yd
0   50m

0   200yd
0   200m

© MOON PUBLICATIONS, INC.

Looking west along Whyte Ave. in 1903. The large building on the right is the Strathcona Hotel, which still stands.

ings, planes, trains, boats, and animals. Also on display are children's card games and paper dolls from last century. The museum is located at 8603 104th St., tel. (403) 433-4512, in the 1907 McKenzie Residence, one of the best preserved examples of Edwardian architecture in Old Strathcona. It's open in summer, Wed.-Fri. noon-8 p.m., Saturday 10 a.m.-6 p.m., and Sunday 1-5 p.m.

Telephone Historical Information Centre

This museum, at 10437 83rd Ave., tel. (403) 441-2077, catalogues the history of telecommunications in Edmonton from the introduction of telephones in 1885 to the present. It is housed in Strathcona's original telephone exchange and has many hands-on exhibits including an early switchboard where you can make your own connections. Current technology is also displayed with exhibits of digital switching, fiber-optic cables, and cellular phones. A multimedia presentation in the small **Alex Taylor Theatre** traces telecommunications technology from its earliest days. The center is open Mon.-Fri. 10 a.m.-4 p.m., and Saturday noon-4 p.m. Admission is $1.

WEST EDMONTON

From the city center, Jasper Ave. (101st Ave.) goes west through **West End**—where many residential and commercial buildings date from the boom years of 1912-1914—and continues to **Glenora,** one of the city's oldest and most sought-after neighborhoods. Many streets are lined with elegant two-story mansions from the early 1900s. The neighborhood fountain in Alexander Circle, at 103rd Ave. and 133rd St., is the center of the area.

Provincial Museum Of Alberta

The provincial museum, 12845 102nd Ave., tel. (403) 453-9100, overlooks the river valley in the historic neighborhood of Glenora. The museum's exhibits catalogue a billion years of natural and human history. In the habitat gallery Alberta's four natural regions—mountain, prairie, parkland, and boreal forest—are re-created with incredible accuracy. The natural-history section explains the forces that have shaped Alberta's land, describes the dinosaurs of the Cretaceous period and mammals of the Ice Age (such as the woolly mammoth), and has a large collection of rocks and gems. Other sections detail Alberta's indigenous peoples, its earliest explorers, and the settlers who came from around the world to eke out a living in the harsh environment. The museum also has a gift shop and cafeteria. It's open in summer, daily 9 a.m.-8 p.m.; the rest of the year, Tues.-Sun. 9 a.m.-5 p.m. Admission is $3.25; free on Tuesday in winter. To get there, take bus No. 1, 2, or 10 along Jasper Ave; or bus No. 115, 116, or 120 west along 102nd Avenue.

The museum houses the **Provincial Archives,** containing photographs, maps, government records, and other documents pertaining to Alberta's history. The archives are open to the public, Tues.-Sat. 9 a.m.-5 p.m.; for more information call 428-3033. Beside the museum is **Government House,** an impressive structure used for conferences.

Edmonton Space And Science Centre
Completed in 1984, this multipurpose complex in Coronation Park at 11211 142nd St., tel. (403) 452-9100 (weekdays) or 451-7722 (recorded information), is one of Edmonton's major attractions and most recognizable landmarks. It houses various science displays including an IMAX Theatre, Planetarium Star Theatre, observatory, Challenger Centre, and a science shop. The science displays are in three galleries; **Lower Gallery** focuses on the human body and medicinal technology, **Middle Gallery** looks into the future of communications and displays a chunk of the moon, and **Upper Gallery** is home to the **Challenger Centre,** where you can make a simulated mini-mission through the universe. Times for missions vary, adults $7, children $4.50. Laser light shows are presented in the **Magret Zeidler Theatre,** daily 11 a.m.-7 p.m. with a different show each hour. A day pass includes all shows in this theater and admission to the Lower and Middle galleries. Laser light shows featuring music of the world's most popular bands are presented each evening at 8 p.m., with three later shows on Friday and Saturday nights; $4.95-11 per show. The IMAX Theatre presents spectacular video productions —seemingly always of an interesting nature— projected onto a 12- by 20-meter screen; adults $7, children $4.50. **Science Demonstrations** take place all day at the NOVA Science Carnival; it's free with a day pass. Combination tickets for various shows save a couple of bucks.

Beside the complex is an **observatory,** open to the public daily 1 p.m.-midnight (weather permitting) for star-, moon-, and planet-gazing; no charge.

By bus, from downtown, take No. 5 or 22 west along Jasper Ave. to the Westmount Transfer Centre and hoof it through Coronation Park or transfer to bus No. 96.

West Edmonton Mall
Feel like a trip to the beach to do some sunbaking and surfing? Would you like to play a round of golf? How about a submarine trip through a coral reef? Do you like eating at Parisian cafes? Does watching a National Hockey League team in training seem like a good way to spend the afternoon? Do the kids like dolphin shows? And at the end of the day would you like to sink into a jacuzzi, surrounded by a lush tropical forest? This is all possible under one roof at West Edmonton Mall, the largest shopping and indoor amusement complex in the whole wide world. Calgary may have the greatest *outdoor* show on earth but Edmonton

Edmonton Space and Science Center

has what can surely be billed as the greatest *indoor* show on earth, a place that attracts 20 million people a year. Much more than an over-sized shopping mall, Edmonton's top tourist attraction is a shop-and-play four-season wonderland, where many visitors check into the 355-room luxury Fantasyland Hotel, stay a weekend, and never step a foot outside the mall's 58 entrances.

Shopping is only one part of the mall's universal appeal. Prices are no less than anywhere else in the city, but the experience of having over 800 stores (including over 200 women's-wear stores) under one roof is unique. Aside from the shops, five other major attractions fill the mall. **Fantasyland Theme Park** is the world's largest indoor amusement park, with 22 rides including "Mindbender"—a fourteen-story, triple-loop roller coaster (world's largest indoor roller coaster)—and "Drop of Doom," where you're strapped into a cage, hauled up thirteen stories, then dropped, free falling back to earth in seconds. Admission to Fantasyland Theme Park is free and an All Day Ride Pass is $19.95 (dis-

counts for seniors, disabled persons, and those under 48 inches).

In the two-hectare **World Waterpark** you almost feel as though you're at the beach; the temperature is set at a balmy 30° C, and a long sandy beach (with special nonslip sand), tropical palms, change houses, a beach bar, and waves crashing on the shore all emulate the real thing. The computerized wave pool holds 12.3 million liters of water and is programmed by computer to eject "sets" of waves at regular intervals. Behind the beach are 22 water slides that rise to a height of 26 meters. The World Waterpark also has the world's only indoor bungee jump, three whirlpools, and a volleyball court. On the second floor of the mall is a water park viewpoint. Admission to World Waterpark is $18.95 general, $7.95 seniors, $15.95 children under 10. All prices drop after 4 p.m.

At the same end of the mall as World Waterpark is the world's largest indoor lake and a series of attractions, known collectively as **Deep Sea Adventure.** You can gawk at the area along its entire 122-meter length from either the main or second floors of the mall. The most dominant feature of the lagoon is a full-size replica of Christopher Columbus's flagship, *Santa Maria.* It was built in False Creek, Vancouver, and shipped across the Rockies to its new indoor home. You can descend into the depths in one of four self-propelled submarines that cruise the lake, passing 200 different types of marine life, including real coral (adults $10, children under 10 $5). The lake is also the site of regular dolphin shows ($1, or watch from above for free), scuba-diving courses, canoe rentals, and an underwater aquarium with seals, penguins, and sharks ($2.50).

Other major attractions in the mall include a mini-golf version of Pebble Beach Golf Course ($7.50) and, smack in the middle of the mall, **The Ice Palace.** This NHL-size skating rink is the second home of the Edmonton Oilers, who often practice here. It's open to the public year-round; $4.25 per session, seniors $2.25, children $2.50, skate rentals $2.25.

WEST EDMONTON MALL TRIVIA

West Edmonton Mall is:
- the world's largest shopping and amusement complex, encompassing 483,000 square meters (that's equivalent to 48 city blocks)

West Edmonton Mall has:
- over 800 stores
- over 100 eateries
- 58 entrances
- 19 movie theaters
- 235,000 light bulbs
- five postal codes
- the world's largest car park (parking for 20,000 vehicles)
- the world's largest indoor amusement park
- the world's largest water park, covering two hectares and containing 50 million liters of water
- the world's largest indoor lake (122 meters long)
- the world's only indoor bungee jump
- more submarines than the Canadian Navy

West Edmonton Mall:
- cost over a billion dollars to construct
- employs 15,000 people
- uses the same amount of power as a city of 50,000
- attracts 20 million people a year (nearly 55,000 per day)

Other sights include an aviary with various exotic birds, a Chinese pagoda hand-carved by four generations of the same family, replicas of the British crown jewels, bronze statues commissioned especially for the mall, and a couple of aquariums. Two theme streets, **Europa Boulevard** and the glitzy New Orleans-style **Bourbon Street** hold some of the mall's 110 restaurants and eateries.

Throughout the mall, information booths can supply maps and answer all commonly asked questions. When your legs tire, **scooter rentals** are available; $5.50 for the first hour, $3.25 for each additional hour.

The mall is located on 170th St., between 87th and 90th avenues. Parking is usually not a problem, but finding your car again can be, so remember which of the 58 entrances you parked near. From downtown take bus No. 12, 115, or 10. For information on West Edmonton Mall write to #1784, 8770 170th Street, Edmonton, Alberta T5T 4J2, or call (403) 444-5200 or (800) 661-8890 (toll free within North America). Shopping hours vary seasonally, but are generally Mon.-Fri. 10 a.m.-9 p.m., Saturday 10 a.m.-6 p.m., and Sunday noon-5 p.m. Hours of the various attractions and restaurants vary. Many restaurants stay open later, and the nightclubs stay open to the early hours of the morning.

VICINITY OF EDMONTON

Devonian Botanic Garden

These gardens developed by the University of Alberta are southwest of the city and five km north of the small town of Devon, which was named for the Devonian rock formation in which nearby oil strikes were made during the late 1940s. The 70-hectare site has been developed around the natural contours of the land. The highlight is **Kurimoto Japanese Garden,** one of

WEST EDMONTON MALL

the world's northernmost authentic Japanese gardens. The various natural elements are complemented by an ornamental gate, arched bridge, and a number of ornamental lanterns. Other features are the large Alpine Garden, with examples of plants from mountainous regions; the Herb Garden, where in August the aroma is almost overpowering; the Peony Collection, at its most colorful in July; a greenhouse filled with plants unique to the Southern Hemisphere; and the Native People's Garden, surrounded by water and showcasing plants used by the native people of Alberta. The gardens are open May-Sept., daily 10 a.m.-6 p.m., till 8 p.m. in July and August. General admission is $4, seniors $3, children $2. For more information call (403) 987-3054.

Stony Plain Multicultural Heritage Centre

The streets of Stony Plain, which was home-steaded before 1900, are lined with historic buildings, but the best place to learn more about the community's history is this living museum located at 5411 51st Street. On the grounds, the town's first high school houses a museum, craft store, library and archives, candy store, and **Homesteaders Kitchen**—a basement restaurant serving pioneer-style home-cooked meals at reasonable prices. Housed next door, in the historic residence of an early pioneer, is the **Oppertshauser Gallery,** Alberta's first rural public art gallery. Admission to both buildings is free. The Centre is open year-round, Mon.-Sat. 10 a.m.-4 p.m., and Sunday 10 a.m.-6:30 p.m.; tel. (403) 963-2777.

Andrew Wolf Wine Cellars

Known to the French as a *négociant,* this winery, at Stony Plain west of the city, imports wines in bulk from California, which it further ages in handcrafted oak vats, then bottles and distributes throughout the province. Skip the self-guided tour and head to the winetasting bar for samples of the remarkably well-rounded wines. Bottles in the gift store are priced from $5.50—as inexpensive as you'll find anywhere in Canada. It's open in summer, Mon.-Fri. 10 a.m.-8 p.m., Saturday 10 a.m.-6 p.m., Sunday noon-5 p.m.; tel. (403) 963-7717.

Saint Albert

The city of St. Albert (population 42,000)—northwest of Edmonton along the St. Albert Trail—is one of Alberta's oldest settlements, but has today become part of Edmonton's sprawl. Albert Lacombe, a pioneering Western Canadian priest, built a mansion overlooking the Sturgeon River in 1861, when Fort Edmonton was only a small trading post. A sawmill and gristmill were constructed, and by 1870, St. Albert was the largest agricultural community west of Winnipeg. Father Lacombe's first log chapel, built in 1861, had a brick structure built around it in 1927. It was used as a museum until the mid-'70s when it was declared a provincial historical site and restored to its original appearance. The chapel, west of Hwy. 2 on St. Vital Ave., tel. (403) 427-3995, is open in summer, daily 10 a.m.-6 p.m. Beside the chapel is a cast-iron statue of Father Lacombe that was made in France and brought to Canada in 1929. Also on Mission Hill is **Grandin House,** an imposing three-story structure built in 1887 as a hospital.

In stark contrast to the historic buildings overlooking the Sturgeon River is City Hall in **St. Albert Place** on St. Anne Street, a contoured brick building designed by Douglas Cardinal. Inside is the **Musée Heritage Museum,** tel. 459-1528, with displays telling the story of St. Albert's history and the people that made it happen. It's open in summer, daily 9:30 a.m.-8 p.m.; the rest of the year, Tues.-Sun. noon-5 p.m.

It is worth traveling to St. Albert just to eat at the elegant **Boardwalk Cafe,** on the corner of Perron St. and Mission Avenue. It's housed in a beautifully restored residence overlooking the Sturgeon River. The refined atmosphere is upstaged by excellently prepared dishes ranging from pasta to stir-fry. Expect to pay $5-12 for a main meal—but no one minds if you just stop by for coffee. Sunday brunch here (10 a.m.-3 p.m.) is accompanied by live music.

A **tourist information center** is located in a log cabin by the river, just off Hwy. 2 at Sturgeon Road. It's open in summer, Mon.-Tues. 9 a.m.-6 p.m., Wed.-Fri. 9 a.m.-8 p.m., and Sat.-Sun. 11 a.m.-8 p.m.; weekdays only the rest of the year. From downtown Edmonton, take the St. Albert bus east along 102nd Avenue.

Alberta Railway Museum

Featuring Canada's largest collection of N.A.R. (Northern Alberta Railway) equipment, this museum also has rolling stock from C.N. (Canadian National) and C.P. (Canadian Pacific). Over 70 locomotive, passenger, and freight cars from 1877-1950 are displayed. Also exhibited are various railway artifacts, equipment, and machinery. Admission is $3, and train rides ($1) are offered on long weekends. The museum, tel. (403) 472-6229, is open in summer, Tues.-Sun. 10 a.m.-6 p.m. To get there, take 97th St. (Hwy. 28) north to Namao, turn east on Hwy. 37 for seven km, then south on 34th St. for two km. It is well signposted.

Fort Saskatchewan

In 1875—long after the fur-trading post of Fort Edmonton had been established—the NWMP marched north and established its northern divisional fort on the North Saskatchewan River, 30 km northeast of Fort Edmonton. **Fort Saskatchewan Historic Site** overlooks the river from along 101st St. in the present-day town of Fort Saskatchewan. It consists of various historic buildings moved to this picturesque site where the original post was situated. Structures include Fort Saskatchewan's first courthouse, a restored log homestead, a blacksmith shop, and a one-room schoolhouse. A cairn marking the site of the NWMP guard room has been built from stones used in the original structure. It's open July-Aug., daily 10 a.m.-6 p.m.; the rest of the year, daily 11 a.m.-3 p.m. For more information call (403) 998-1750.

Polar Park

Located 22 km east of the city on Hwy. 14, Polar Park, tel. 922-3401, is a 600-hectare park designed to preserve and breed cold-climate animals, many of which are endangered. All animals are outdoors, so the park is open year-round. Hay rides are offered on summer weekends, sleigh rides during winter. Extensive cross-country-ski trails are set during winter. Also within the park are a restaurant (summer only), picnic area, and hiking trails. It's open daily 8 a.m. till dusk. Admission is $4 adults, $3 seniors, $2 children.

RECREATION

OUTDOOR ACTIVITIES

River Valley Park System

One of the first things you'll notice about Edmonton is its large amount of parkland. The city has more land set aside for parks, per capita, than any other city in the country. Most parks interconnect along the banks of the North Saskatchewan River and in adjoining ravines, encompassing 7,400 hectares and comprising the largest stretch of urban parkland in North America. Within these parks are picnic areas, swimming pools, historic sites, golf courses, and many kilometers of walking and biking trails. The map *Cycle Edmonton*, available from tourist information centers, details all routes and trail lengths. One of the larger individual parks is **William Hawrelak Park**, which has a man-made lake with boat rentals and fishing. It is west of the university along Groat Road. **River Valley Cycle**, 9124 82nd Ave., tel. (403) 465-3863, rents mountain bikes for $7 per hour, $28 per day, and leads guided tours during summer. **Sport & Ski Rentals**, 6430 104th St., tel. 435-7547, also rents bikes at similar rates.

Swimming

Edmonton's outdoor swimming season lasts around three months beginning at the end of May. Of the five outdoor pools owned by the city, the one in **Queen Elizabeth Park** is in a particularly picturesque location among poplar trees and with a view of the city skyline over the river; access is from 90th Avenue. Another, close to the city center, is in **Mill Creek Park,** north of Whyte Ave. (82nd Ave.) on 95A Street. Admission to all outdoor pools is $3.50. When the weather gets cooler, or to take advantage of more facilities, head to one of the city's many indoor pools, where admission includes the use of saunas, a jacuzzi, weight rooms, and water slides. The most famous of these is **World Waterpark** in the West Edmonton Mall, which has

22 water slides, a wave pool, a nonslip sandy beach, and bungee jump (additional cost); admission is $18.95. Swimming events of the 1978 Commonwealth Games were held at the **Kinsmen Sports Centre,** 9100 Walterdale Hill, tel. (403) 496-7300, in Kinsmen Park on the south bank of the North Saskatchewan River. Admission of $3.60 includes use of the pools, fitness center, sauna, and jogging track. Towel rental is $1.10. The cafeteria here has reasonably priced meals. For information on all outdoor and indoor pools call the Swim Line at 428-7946.

Golfing

Edmonton has so many golf courses you could play a different one each day for a month. Three are within a five iron of the city center while others are located along the North Saskatchewan River Valley and throughout outlying suburbs. The municipal **Victoria Golf Course,** tel. (403) 428-8002, is a challenging 18-hole course, over 6,000 meters in length, located just west of the Legislature Building along River Road. Green fees are $18 weekdays, $21 weekends. Slightly longer and situated on a sweeping bend of the river is **Riverside Golf Course** at 8630 Rowland Rd., tel. 428-5330; weekdays $18, weekends $21. **Kinsmen Pitch & Putt** is located behind the Kinsmen Sports Centre, a tree-covered area close to the city; 18 holes $8.50, seniors $4.50. For tee times call 432-1626.

Ballooning And Skydiving

Recreational and competition ballooning is popular in Edmonton throughout the year. One company offering flights is **Windship Aviation,** 5615 103rd St., tel. (403) 438-0111. Flights depend entirely on weather conditions. Launch sites and landing sites change with the wind direction; most often the grounds of Muttart Conservatory are used for launching. Flight time is 60-90 minutes and the $150 cost includes transportation back to the launch site, a celebration drink on landing, and a framed picture of your flight.

Edmonton Skydive Centre has a shop at 10588 109th St., but they do their jumping from the small airport at Westlock, 85 km north of the city. Experienced skydivers pay $16-21.50 per jump, depending on the altitude; $35-39 with gear rental. A six-hour training program for first-timers includes a jump from 1,200 meters and costs $120. These courses begin each Sat-

urday and Sunday at 9 a.m. For more information contact the center at P.O. Box 358, Morinville, Alberta T0G 1P0, tel. 444-5867, or drop into their Edmonton shop.

WINTERTIME

Downhill Skiing

Edmonton has three ski hills within the city limits and one just outside. All are small and great for beginners but won't hold the interest of other skiers for very long. **Edmonton Ski Club** runs the hill closest to the city at 9613 96th Ave., tel. (403) 465-0852. It's on the south side of the North Saskatchewan River, facing downtown. Lift tickets are $8 midweek, $12 on weekends. It's open from December to early March, Mon.-Thurs. 9 a.m.-9 p.m., Fri.-Sun. 9 a.m.-5:30 p.m. To get there follow signs to the Muttart Conservatory. Farther upstream, where Whitemud Dr. crosses the river, is **Snow Valley,** which has a chairlift, T-bar, and rope tow. Lift tickets are $15, $13 half day. Hours are weekdays 9:30 a.m.-9:30 p.m., weekends 9 a.m.-6 p.m. For information call 434-3991. **Sunridge Ski Area** is downstream of downtown in Strathcona Science Park and has four lifts. Tickets are $16 per day, $13 half day. It's open Mon.-Fri. 9:30 a.m.-10 p.m., Sat.-Sun. 9:30 a.m.-5 p.m.; tel. 449-6555. To get there follow the Yellowhead Hwy. to 17th St., then turn south and follow the signs. **Rabbit Hill Ski Area** is south of Edmonton. Take Calgary Trail south to Nisku, then follow the signs west for 13 km. The hill has a chairlift, two T-bars, and four rope tows. Lift tickets are $18 per day, $12 after 6 p.m. It's open Mon.-Fri. 10 a.m.-10 p.m., Sat.-Sun. 9 a.m.-6 p.m.; tel. 955-2440.

Cross-Country Skiing

The River Valley Park System provides ample opportunity for cross-country skiing. Over 75 km of trails are groomed from December to early March. The most popular areas are in William Hawrelak Park, up Mill Creek Ravine, and through Capilano Park. For details of trails pick up the brochure *Cross-country Ski Edmonton* from tourist information centers or call (403) 493-9000 and enter the code 3446. The **Kinsmen Sports Centre** has cross-country ski rentals, $8 for two hours, or $12 per day including boots and poles. **Sport & Ski Rentals,** 6430 104th St., tel. 435-7547, has similar packages for $11 per day and $23 for three days.

SPECTATOR SPORTS

Ice Hockey
Alberta's first major-league hockey team was the Alberta Oilers, who played in both Calgary and Edmonton. The team finally settled in Edmonton permanently for the '73-74 season. During the '80s, when Wayne Gretzky was leading the **Edmonton Oilers,** the National Hockey League's Stanley Cup resided just as permanently in Edmonton, "City of Champions." Since 1988, when Gretzky was sold to the L.A. Kings, the team has floundered. Most talk on the streets these days is about the politics of the team rather than performances on the ice. Home games are played Sept.-May in the coliseum at **Edmonton Northlands,** 7300 116th Avenue. Tickets cost $12-40. For more information call (403) 471-2191 or Ticketmaster at 451-8000.

Baseball
The **Edmonton Trappers** are a farm team for the Florida Marlins. They play in the AAA, Pacific Coast League. Home games are played April-Sept. at **John Ducey Park,** 10233 96th Avenue. Tickets are priced from $6.75; for details call (403) 429-2934 or Ticketmaster at 451-8000.

Football
The **Edmonton Eskimos** have a distinguished record in the Canadian Football League (C.F.L.), having won the Grey Cup 11 times—including five straight (1978-82)—since joining the league in 1910. "Eskimos" was originally an insult, given to the team by a Calgary sportswriter in its early days. But the name stuck. Since 1948 the team has played in, and won, more Grey Cup games than any other team in the league. Two former Albertan premiers, Peter Lougheed and Don Getty, once starred for the team. The "Esks" play June-Nov. at Commonwealth Stadium, 9021 111th Avenue. Tickets are $18-28. For more information call (403) 448-3757 or Ticketmaster at 451-8000.

Horse Racing
Harness racing takes place at Edmonton North-

lands from spring to mid-December. Thoroughbred racing takes place throughout summer at the same track. During Edmonton's Klondike Days, a full racing program is presented. General admission is $2, $3.25 for the Clubhouse. The track is located at 7300 116th Ave.; for information call (403) 471-7210 or the Event Hotline at 471-8111.

ARTS AND ENTERTAINMENT

Art Galleries
Scattered throughout the city are a number of commercial art galleries, many of which exhibit and sell Canadian and native art. A group of galleries close together on Jasper Ave. between 123rd and 124th streets downtown form what is known as **The Gallery Walk.** Other galleries of note include **Northern Images,** 8770 170th St., tel. (403) 444-1995, with a good collection of native and northern arts and crafts, and **Bearclaw Gallery,** 9724 111th Ave., tel. 479-8502. Both are closed Sunday.

Theater
Edmonton's 13 professional theater companies present productions at various locations all year long. For most companies, Sept.-May is the main season. For information on theater events throughout the city pick up a free copy of *Billy's Guide* or *Culture Shock.* Both are available all around town.

The **Citadel Theatre,** 9828 101A Ave., tel. (403) 426-4811 or 425-1820, is Canada's largest theater facility, taking up an entire downtown block. From the outside it looks like a gigantic greenhouse; one entire side is glass, enclosing a magnificent indoor garden complete with waterfall. The complex houses five theaters: the Maclab Theatre showcases the work of teens and children; the Rice Theatre features mainly experimental and innovative productions; Zeidler Hall hosts films, lectures, and children's theater; Tucker Amphitheatre presents concerts and recitals, and often puts on small lunchtime stage productions; and Shoctor Theatre is the main stage for the Citadel's long-running subscription program ($15-35 per production). Tickets are available from the Citadel Box Office.

The **Phoenix Theatre** company, 9638 101A Ave., tel. 429-4015, typically stages powerful and thought-provoking productions at the Kaasa Theatre in the University of Alberta's Jubilee Auditorium. Their season runs Sept.-June. For tickets call Ticketmaster, tel. 451-8000. For slightly more adventurous productions and occasional international imports, see what's on at the **Northern Light Theatre,** 11516 103rd St., tel. 471-1586. Tickets are $9-18. Edmonton's oldest theater is **Walterdale Playhouse,** 10322 83rd Ave., tel. 439-2845, located in the heart of Old Strathcona, which presents historical and humorous material throughout the year. Ticket prices begin at $8. **Celebrations,** 102-13103 Fort Rd., tel. 448-9339, is a popular dinner theater; the ticket price of $40 includes dinner. Open Wed.-Sun., reservations necessary, no jeans, and you must be seated by 6 p.m.

Music And Dance
Edmonton Opera, tel. (403) 429-1000, **Edmonton Symphony Orchestra,** tel. 428-1414, and **Alberta Ballet,** tel. 428-6839, all perform at the Jubilee Auditorium in the University of Alberta, 11455 87th Ave., between October and March. For performance dates and ticket information call the above numbers or Ticketmaster, tel. 451-8000.

Cinemas
Famous Players Cinemas are located throughout the city, including 10233 Jasper Ave., tel. (403) 428-1307, and 2950 Calgary Trail Southbound, tel. 436-6977. The historic **Princess Theatre,** 10337 82nd Ave., tel. (403) 433-5785, is an old-time movie house showing revivals, experiments, and foreign films. **Metro Cinema,** 10136 100th St., tel. 425-9212, in Canada Place, shows classics, imports, and brave new films.

Casinos
Casinos in Alberta are strange places. They are all privately owned, lack the glamour of Las Vegas, and all the profits must go to charity. They offer blackjack, roulette, baccarat, Red Dog, and Sic Bo—no slot machines. **Casino A.B.S.** has locations at 10549 102nd St., tel. (403) 424-9467, and on the south side at 7055 Argyll Rd., tel. 466-0199. **Casino Palace,** in West Edmonton Mall, is located by Entrance 45, tel. 444-2112. All casinos are open daily, noon-midnight.

Bars And Nightclubs
The **Sidetrack Cafe,** 10333 112th St., tel. (403) 421-1326, is central to downtown, serves excellent food, and presents live entertainment nightly from 9 p.m. Shows change dramatically —one night it might be stand-up comedians, the next a blues band, then jazz—the only thing you can rely on is that it will be busy. Monday is usually comedy night and Sunday variety night. Cover charges vary, $3-8 is normal. Downtown, the **Sherlock Holmes,** 10012 101A Ave., tel. 426-7784, serves a large selection of British and Irish ales and is the place to head on St. Patrick's Day (17 March). The rest of the year, drinkers are encouraged to join in nightly sing-a-longs with the pianist. **The Rose And Crown,** 10235 101st St., tel. 428-7111, in the Hilton Hotel, is another English-style pub with a great atmosphere and evening sing-a-longs.

Cook Country Saloon, 80100 103rd St., tel. 432-2665, is consistently voted Canada's No. 1 Country Nightclub by the Canadian Country Music Association. Its mellow honky-tonk ambience draws crowds, and Canadian and international performers occasionally perform here. Free two-step lessons are offered on Tuesday and Thursday nights, while on Wednesday and Thursday nights, "Twister" the mechanical bull bucks into action. On Friday and Saturday nights the action really cranks up with live entertainment and a DJ spinning country Top 40 discs. On these two nights, the cover is $3 before 8 p.m. and $6 after. Other country nightclubs are **Denim And Diamonds,** 10812 Kingsway Rd., tel. 479-4266; **Longriders Saloon,** 11733 78th St., tel. 479-8700, which has a jam session on Wednesday, cheap drinks for the ladies on Thursday, and a cover charge of $5 after 9 p.m. on Friday and Saturday nights; and **Tumbleweeds,** 17512 Stony Plain Rd., tel. 484-3388, featuring live country acts most nights.

Top 40 and dance nightclubs change names, reputations, and locations regularly. But some are reliable fixtures. **The Chase,** downstairs in the Scotia Centre at 10060 Jasper Ave., tel. 426-0728, plays Top 40, and is one of the busiest clubs in the city. **Club Malibu** attracts the under-25's to its two locations at 10310 85th Ave., tel. 432-7300 ($4 cover charge), and 10045 109th St., tel. 429-0404 ($3 cover charge). **Barry T's,** 6111 104th St., tel. 438-2582, plays a unique cross of Top 40 and country.

Jazz, Blues, And Comedy

The Edmonton Jazz Society is based at the **Yardbird Suite** at 10203 86th Ave., tel. (403) 432-0428. Live jazz fills the air every night of the week 10 p.m.-2 a.m. Tuesday night jam sessions are $2, other nights admission is $5-18. Friday is nonsmoking night.

Downtown Blues Club Upstairs at Smokey Joe's, 11607 Jasper Ave., tel. 488-7538, is a small lounge with pool tables and small four- to five-piece blues bands playing on Friday and Saturday nights; no cover charge. **Blues on Whyte,** 10329 82nd Ave., tel. 439-5058, has live entertainment most nights; minimal cover charge.

Yuk Yuk's Komedy Kabaret is located at West Edmonton Mall, tel. 481-9857. Show times vary, but generally there are two shows nightly Thursday through Saturday. Sunday is variety night, and Wednesday is amateur night. Tickets are $7-11.

SHOPPING

Plazas And Malls

Downtown's major shopping centers are **Eaton Centre, Edmonton Centre, and ManuLife Place.** Apart from **West Edmonton Mall** at 87th Ave. and 170th St. other malls are located along Stony Plain Rd., Calgary Trail South, and north of the city at 137th Ave. and 66th St. (Londonderry Mall).

Camping Gear And Western Wear

Across the railway tracks from Old Strathcona is **Track and Trail,** 10148 82nd Ave., tel. (403) 432-1707, which carries a wide variety of camping and climbing gear. In the same general area is **Totem Outdoor Outfitters,** 7430 99th St., tel. 432-1223, with more of the same as well as kayaks, canoes, and some secondhand gear. **Gear up for the Outdoors,** 17309 107th Ave., tel. 484-3066, is a climbing specialty store with a climbing wall; lessons are $20 per person per hour. Nearby is the large **Campers Village,** 10951 170th St., tel. 484-2700, with camping equipment, fishing tackle, books, boots, and scuba diving equipment. **Budget Sports Rentals,** 10344 63rd Ave., tel. 434-3808, rents backpacks, tents, sleeping bags, and canoes.

The **Western Boot Factory,** 10007 167th St., tel. 489-0594, stocks thousands of styles of cowboy boots. You can't miss it—out front is the world's largest cowboy boot. This store has another location at 3414 Calgary Trail Northbound, tel. 435-3702. High-quality boots are also sold by **Diablo Boots,** next door to Foody Goody Chinese buffet, at 3440 Calgary Trail Northbound, tel. 435-2592. **J.R. Austin Western Wear** in the lower level of West Edmonton Mall (near the entrance to Bourbon St.), tel. 444-1511, always has specials on their extensive range of western wear.

the world's largest cowboy boot

FESTIVALS AND EVENTS

Spring

Mid-March is the **Alberta Book Festival**, a three-day event with public workshops, readings, book signings, and a small midway. Many of the events are held in the Convention Centre. For details call (403) 426-5892. The **World Figure Skating Championships** will take place at Northlands Coliseum 19-25 March 1996. **Edmonton International Children's Festival** takes place the third week of May in the Citadel Theatre. Acts from around the world include theater, music, dance, storytelling, and puppetry; tel. 426-4811.

Edmonton's Klondike Days

This 10-day event beginning on the third Thursday of each July celebrates a somewhat infamous chapter in Edmonton's history. In 1898, when the rush to the Yukon goldfields was in full swing, city merchants persuaded around 1,600 miners that the best route north was to Edmonton and north along the Mackenzie River. The route turned out to be an impractical and difficult one. Few made it, many died trying, and when they reached the Klondike the rush was nearly over. Today that rush for gold is relived on the streets of the city. Events include a massive parade through downtown, an 1890s-style he-man contest at Hawrelak Park, the World Championship Sourdough Raft Race down the river, nonstop entertainment on downtown streets, and a bathtub road-race that always creates a laugh. Edmonton's finest restaurants offer samples of their cuisine in a Taste of Edmonton, and each morning, throughout the city, pancake breakfasts are given away. At Edmonton Northlands, 7300 116th St., is the Edmonton's Klondike Days Exposition, open every day, featuring a midway, Klondike Days Casino, a British Pavilion, free concerts, racing pigs, vaudeville shows, thoroughbred racing, and a crafts and country fair. Northlands hosts the **World Wheelchair Basketball Championship** during the festival. For more information write to Edmonton's Klondike Days, P.O. Box 1480, Edmonton, Alberta T5J 2N5; tel. (403) 471-7335.

Other Summer Festivals

During the last week of June the **Jazz City International Festival** is held at various indoor and outdoor venues. Many foreign stars make special appearances. Call (403) 432-7166 for details. **The Works: A Visual Arts Celebration** features art exhibitions on downtown streets, in parks, and in art galleries for two weeks from late June; tel. 426-2122. For 10 days in early July the streets and parks come alive during the **Edmonton International Street Performers Festival,** with nearly 1,000 performances by magicians, comics, jugglers, musicians, and mimes; tel. 425-5162. Fifty outdoor ethnic pavilions are just a small part of the **Edmonton Heritage Festival,** on the last weekend of July. Visitors to the festival have the opportunity to experience international singing and dancing, arts and crafts displays, costumes, and cuisine from around the world; tel. 488-3378. During the **Edmonton Folk Music Festival** the first weekend of August, Gallagher Park comes alive with the sound of blues, jazz, country, celtic, traditional, and bluegrass music. Tickets are cheaper if bought in advance; tel. 429-1999.

Quickly becoming one of the city's most popular events is the 10-day **Fringe Theatre Festival,** which begins on the second Friday in August. It is held in parks, on the streets, in parkades, and in theaters throughout Old Strathcona. With over 1,200 performances, the festival has become North America's largest alternative-theater event, attracting artists from around the world. Tickets are generally inexpensive; for details call 448-9000. **Dreamspeakers Festival,** on the last weekend of August, is the last gasp in Edmonton's busy summer festival schedule. It celebrates the art, culture, and film-making of the First Nation's People—the native Canadians. For more information call 439-3456.

Winter

Farmfair brings livestock exhibits to Edmonton Northlands the second week of November. Call (403) 471-7210 for details. The city celebrates the end of the year during **First Night Festival,** an alcohol-free celebration on the streets of downtown Edmonton; tel. 448-9200.

ACCOMMODATIONS

Nearly all of Edmonton's best hotels are located downtown. Motels can be found along Calgary Trail (south from downtown), scattered along Stony Plain Rd. in the west, and around the municipal airport. The towns of Leduc and Nisku have a number of motels close to Edmonton International Airport. Other options include many bed and breakfasts, a centrally located hostel, and camping (just five minutes from downtown, or in campgrounds west, east, or south of the city).

HOTELS AND MOTELS

Downtown

Downtown's suite hotels (also called apartment hotels) offer rooms with cooking facilities for lower prices than regular hotels. **Alberta Place Suite Hotel** is one of the best. The rooms are large and each has a well-equipped kitchen. Continental breakfast and daily papers are complimentary and Jasper Ave. is only half a block away. **Edmonton House Suite Hotel** is similarly priced and each room has a balcony with views of the valley or city.

Generally, midpriced downtown hotels are a few blocks from the core of the city. Try **Renford Inn at Fifth,** which has an indoor pool and lounge; **River Valley Inn,** with kitchenettes; or the newly renovated **Howard Johnson Plaza Hotel.**

If you're on a bigger budget, you can choose from several more luxurious lodgings downtown. The 24-story **Holiday Inn Crowne Plaza** sits on Bellamy Hill, its unusual cylindrical design making it recognizable against the skyline. Facilities include a fitness center, boutiques, a cocktail lounge, and a revolving restaurant. The **Hilton International** is in the financial district, linked to other buildings by the pedway system. All rooms have bay windows and are elegantly furnished with marble tabletops, walnut furniture, and brass trimmings. Nearby is **The Westin Hotel,** which has large comfortable rooms, a luxurious indoor pool, and a shopping complex below. **Hotel Macdonald** is an Edmonton land-mark and has the same historic charm as other Canadian Pacific hotels such as the Palliser in Calgary. The smallish rooms are decorated with a subtle elegance and the hotel has an excellent restaurant, a health club, and a beautiful lounge overlooking the river valley.

Away From Downtown

Prices at the 20-odd motels south of downtown along Calgary Trail begin at $40 s, $45 d. Those at city limits, such as **Ellerslie Motel,** are slightly cheaper, but are a 15-minute drive from downtown. Others recommended in this part of the city are **Cedar Park Inn,** a Best Western hotel with well furnished rooms, a restaurant, and airport shuttles; **Travelodge South;** and **Renford Inn on Whyte,** in the heart of Old Strathcona.

In the northwest of the city, along Stony Plain Rd., are more similarly priced motels. **West Harvest Inn** is a clean, modern, three-story motel with large rooms. For a complete listing of Edmonton accommodations see the chart.

Fantasyland Hotel And Resort

Within West Edmonton Mall is 355-room Fantasyland Hotel and Resort, famous for theme rooms that attract folks from around the world. No catching a cab back to your hotel after a day shopping here—just ride the elevator to the room of your wildest fantasy. The lavish marble-floored lobby and two life-size lion statues surrounded by glittering lights are only a taste of what's to come upstairs.

Each floor has a theme; the choice is yours—Hollywood, Roman, Polynesian, Victorian, African, Arabian, Igloo, Canadian Rail, or Truck. Each theme is carried out in minute detail. The Polynesian-room fantasy, for example, begins as you walk along a hallway lined with murals depicting a tropical beach, floored with grass matting. You'll walk through a grove of palm trees before reaching your room. In the room, an enormous jacuzzi is nestled in a rocky grotto, and the bed is shaped like a warrior's catamaran, with a sail as the headboard.

EDMONTON ACCOMMODATIONS

All prices listed are for a double room during peak season.
The area code for all telephone numbers listed below is **403**.

DOWNTOWN

Ambassador Motor Inn; 10041 106th St.; tel. 423-1925; $40-45

Quality Inn; 10209 100th Ave.; tel. 428-6442 or (800) 221-2222; $49-54; restaurant

Mayfair Hotel; 10815 Jasper Ave.; tel. 423-1650 or (800) 463-7666; $59; restaurant, sauna

Renford Inn at Fifth; 10425 100th Ave.; tel. 423-5611 or (800) 661-6498; $59; good value

Best Western City Centre Inn; 11310 109th St.; tel. 479-2042 or (800) 528-1234; $62-68

Alberta Place Suite Hotel; 10049 103rd St.; tel. 423-1565 or (800) 661-3982; $75; large rooms, kitchens

Delta Edmonton Centre Suite Hotel; 10222 102nd St.; tel. 429-3900 or (800) 661-6655; $79; private lounge for guests

River Valley Inn; 9710 105th St.; tel. 428-7133 or (800) 661-7385; $79; exercise room

Edmonton House Suite Hotel; 10205 100th Ave.; tel. 424-5555 or (800) 661-6562; $87; kitchenettes

Howard Johnson Plaza Hotel; 10010 104th St.; tel. 423-2450 or (800) 446-4656; $90; recently renovated

Tower on the Park; 9715 110th St.; tel. 488-1626 or (800) 661-6454; $90; includes breakfast

Hilton International Edmonton; 10235 101 St.; tel. 428-7111 or (800) 263-9030; $99-135; full facilities

The Westin Hotel; 10135 100th St.; tel. 426-3636 or (800) 228-3000; $99; excellent restaurant

Inn on 7th; 10001 107th St.; tel. 429-2861 or (800) 661-7327; $99-109

Holiday Inn Crowne Plaza; 10111 Bellamy Hill; tel. 428-6611 or (800) 465-4329; $99-114; all rooms have views

Edmonton Renaissance Hotel; 10155 105th St.; tel. 423-4811 or (800) 268-8998; $120-140; full facilities

Hotel MacDonald; 10065 100th St.; tel. 424-5181 or (800) 441-1414; $129; an unbeatable historic charm

SOUTH

Note: Calgary Trail N is northbound Calgary Trail; Calgary Trail S is southbound.

Patricia Motel; 7730 101st Ave.; tel. 469-2317; $32-34

Trailway Motor Inn; 3815 Calgary Trail N; tel. 435-3863; $32-34; laundry

Ellerslie Motel; 1304 Calgary Trail S; tel. 988-6406; $32-35

Roadrunner Motel; 6622 104th St.; tel. 434-8741; $33-36

Southbend Motel; 5130 Calgary Trail N; tel. 434-1418; $34-37; can use facilities at Cedar Park Inn

Derrick Motel; 3925 Calgary Trail N; tel. 434-1402; $32-38

Southgate Motor Inn; 4805 Calgary Trail N; tel. 435-3511; $33-40

South Centre Motel; 4009 Calgary Trail N; tel. 435-4877; $37-41

Chateau Motel; 1414 Calgary Trail S; tel. 988-6661; $35-45; laundry

Travelodge South; 10320 45th Ave.; tel. 436-9770 or (800) 661-9563; $42-46

Highway Motor Inn; 4520 76th Ave.; tel. 468-5400; $49

Regency Hotel; 7230 Argyll Rd.; tel. 465-7931 or (800) 465-3648; $49; indoor pool

Argyll Plaza Hotel; 9933 63rd Ave.; tel. 438-5876 or (800) 661-6454; $50; complimentary breakfast

Renford Inn on Whyte; 10620 82nd Ave.; tel. 433-9411 or (800) 661-6498; $52; in the heart of Old Strathcona

Riviera Hotel; 5359 Calgary Trail N; tel. 434-3431 or (800) 661-9030; $55-59; indoor water slide
Best Western Cedar Park Inn; 5116 Calgary Trail N; tel. 434-7411 or (800) 528-1234; $65-70; shuttle to West Edmonton Mall, restaurant
Palace Inn; 4235 Calgary Trail N; tel. 438-1222 or (800) 565-1222; $75; large rooms, restaurant
Campus Tower Hotel; 11145 87th Ave.; tel. 439-6060 or (800) 661-6562; $64-78; at the University of Alberta
Convention Inn; 4404 Calgary Trail N; tel. 434-6415 or (800) 661-1122; 85; restaurant, indoor pool
Coast Terrace Inn; 4440 Calgary Trail N; tel. 437-6010 or (800) 222-6405; $150-160; full facilities

NORTHWEST

Royal Western Motel; 15335 111th Ave.; tel. 489-4911; $29-40
Aurora Motel; 15145 111th Ave.; tel. 489-2581; $30-35
Yellowhead Motor Hotel; 15004 Yellowhead Trail; tel. 447-2400; $35; restaurant
Rest E-Z Inn; 21640 Stony Plain Rd.; tel. 447-4455; $35-38; some kitchenettes
Algonquin Motor Lodge; 10401 Mayfield Rd.; tel. 489-4901; $36-38
Lodge Motor Inn; 18125 Stony Plain Rd.; tel. 489-3321; $37-45
Rosslyn Motor Inn; 13620 97th St.; tel. 476-6241; $38-43; bar
Aladdin Motel; 15425 111th Ave.; tel. 484-0071; $40-45
Travelodge West; 18320 Stony Plain Rd.; tel. 483-6031; $42-46; indoor pool
Continental Inn; 16625 Stony Plain Rd.; tel. 484-7751; $45-50; comfortable rooms
Comfort Inn West; 18245 Stony Plain Rd.; tel. 484-1136; $45-55; close to mall
Chateau Louis Hotel; 11727 Kingsway Ave.; tel. 452-7770 or (800) 661-9843; $50-56; at Municipal Airport
West Harvest Inn; 17803 Stony Plain Rd.; tel. 484-8000 or (800) 661-6993; $53-63; clean, large rooms
Sandman Inn; 17635 Stony Plain Rd.; tel. 483-1385 or (800) 726-3626; $56-60; restaurant, indoor pool
Comfort Inn By Journey's End; 17610 100th Ave.; tel. 484-4415 or (800) 668-4200; $57-65
Royal West Inn; 10010 178th St.; tel. 484-6000 or (800) 661-4879; $58; restaurant, indoor pool
Best Western Westwood Inn; 18035 Stony Plain Rd.; tel. 483-7770 or (800) 528-1234; $62-69; full facilities
Edmonton Inn; 11830 Kingsway Ave.; tel. 454-9521 or (800) 661-7264; $65; shuttle to Municipal Airport
Mayfield Inn; 16615 109th Ave.; tel. 484-0821 or (800) 661-9804; $83; restaurant, many two-room suites
Fantasyland Hotel And Resort; 17700 87th Ave.; tel. 444-3000 or (800) 661-6454; $118; in West Edmonton Mall, theme rooms

NORTHEAST

Beverly Motel; 4403 118th Ave.; tel. 479-3923; $30-40
Eastglen Motor Inn; 6918 118th Ave.; tel. 471-2610; $36-42
Jockey Motel; 3604 118th Ave.; tel. 479-5981; $38-44; near Edmonton Northlands
Sands Motor Hotel; 12340 Fort Rd.; tel. 474-5476; $40-46
Beverly Crest Travelodge; 3414 118th Ave.; tel. 474-0456 or (800) 255-3050; $47-51; restaurant, bar
Forum Inn; 11845 73rd St.; tel. 471-1231; $49
Neighbourhood Inn; 13103 Fort Rd.; tel. 478-2971; $52; English-style pub

All of this escapism comes at a cost, with the theme rooms ranging $195-225 per night. Regular guest rooms—without jacuzzis and mirrors on the ceiling—are $130 per night. Despite the price, the theme rooms are very popular and book up far in advance. Make reservations early.

BED-AND-BREAKFAST INNS

B&Bs start at $35 s, $45 d and are scattered throughout the city. Tourist information centers keep current listings, and you can make bookings through **Edmonton Bed & Breakfast,** 13824 110A Ave., Edmonton, Alberta T5M 2M9; tel. (403) 455-2297.

La Boheme, 6427 112th Ave., tel. 474-5693, is located in the historic Gibbard building, which originally held Edmonton's first luxury apartments. Today, the La Boheme restaurant downstairs is one of the city's best, and a number of upstairs rooms have been refurnished and are run as a B&B. The building is certainly charming, right down to its creaky floors. Each of the simply furnished rooms has a kitchenette. Rates are $45-70 s or d.

HOSTELS

Edmonton International Hostel, 10422 91st St., tel. (403) 429-0140, is located in a suburban cul-de-sac, a few blocks east of downtown. It has 58 beds in male and female dorms and a number of couples rooms with two beds. Facilities include a large kitchen and a laundry. The hostel rents bikes and issues bus passes. It's only open 8 a.m.-midnight but the curfew isn't strictly enforced. Rates are $13 for members and $18 for nonmembers.

The **YMCA** has an outstanding location, right downtown at 10030 102A Ave.; tel. 421-9622. The rooms are small and sparsely furnished, and are available to men, women, couples, and families. Also here is a cafe and fitness center. Rooms are $37 s, $42 d. The **YWCA,** 10305 100th Ave., tel. 429-8707, is for women only and has an exercise room and cafe. Dorm beds are $12, private rooms $35.

CAMPGROUNDS

The only camping within city limits is at **Rainbow Valley Campground,** 14340 56th Ave., tel. (403) 434-1621. The location is excellent and, as far as city camping goes, the setting pleasant. Facilities include showers, laundry, barbecue, and cooking shelter. In summer all sites are full by midday; phone reservations aren't taken. Grassed tent sites are $13, powered sites $16. To get there, turn south off Whitemud Freeway at 119th St., then take the first right and follow it into the valley. It's open April 15-Oct. 15.

West

Shakers Acres, 21530 103rd Ave., tel. (403) 447-3564, on the north side of Stony Plain Rd., is fairly unprotected if the wind blows but has the advantage of being open year-round. Unserviced sites are $12 and full hookups are $18. Farther out, in Spruce Grove, is **Glowing Embers Travel Centre,** 26309 Hwy. 16, tel. 962-8100. All facilities are modern and, although tents are allowed, they may look out of place among the satellite-toting RVs; all sites are $18.

East

Half Moon Lake Resort, 21524 Hwy. 520, tel. (403) 922-3045, is on the shore of a shallow lake, 30 km from Edmonton. It has a large area set aside for tents ($12) and RVs and trailers ($15-18), but the emphasis is mainly on activities such as fishing, swimming, boating, and horseback riding. To get there, head east on 82nd Ave. to Hwy. 21, three km east of Sherwood Park, then south to Hwy. 520, then 10 km east.

South

Klondike Valley, 1660 Calgary Trail SW, tel. (403) 988-5067, is located along Blackmud Creek, to the west of Hwy. 2, at the southern edge of city limits. The sites are large and all facilities modern. Walk-in tent sites are $12.50, hookups $15-17. In the town of Devon, a 20-minute drive southwest of the city, is **River Valley Lions Campground,** tel. 987-4777; sites are $11-17.

FOOD

Eating out in Edmonton had always been identified with the aroma of good ol' Alberta beef wafting from the city's many restaurants. But things are changing. Today, 2,000 restaurants offer a balance of international cuisine and local favorites in all price brackets. From the legendary home-style cooking of Barb and Ernie's to the French sophistication of Claude's, there's something to suit everyone's taste and budget. Restaurants are concentrated in a few main areas. **Downtown** in the plazas are food courts that fill with office workers, shoppers, and tourists each lunchtime. This part of the city also has some of Edmonton's finest dining establishments. **Old Strathcona** offers a smorgasbord of choices, with cuisine from all corners of the world. Southbound and northbound along **Calgary Trail** are a variety of family restaurants, buffets, and inexpensive steak houses.

DOWNTOWN

Cheap Eats
Most of the city's downtown high-rises have food courts on their lower levels, where lunch dishes offered by many ethnic outlets begin at around $3. For the widest choice try the food courts in the Eaton Centre, Edmonton Centre, or Canada Place.

Zenari's in ManuLife Plaza East, at 10180 101st St., is a trendy lunchtime hangout known for its variety of sandwiches and freshly prepared soups, as well as coffee, ground fresh to order. It's closed Sunday. Surrounded by the city's highest high-rises is the **Sherlock Holmes,** 10012 101A Ave., tel. (403) 426-7784, a charming English-style pub with a shingled roof, whitewashed walls with black trim, and a white picket fence surrounding it. At lunchtime it is packed with the office crowd from above. Try traditional British dishes such as Mrs. Hudson's Steak and Kidney Pie ($6), ploughmans ($6.50), liver and onions ($7), and fish and chips ($7), washed down with a pint of English ale or Guinness stout. It's open Mon.-Sat., from 11:30 a.m.

A Real Experience
Most people are familiar with the name Mongolia, but few could find it on a map, and even fewer can claim to have tasted its food. Here in Edmonton you have this opportunity at **Mongolian Food Experience,** which has four locations throughout the city. Its downtown location is at 10160 100A St., tel. (403) 426-6806. As you walk in the door, the first thing you'll notice is the vast buffet of raw beef, chicken, and seafood. You simply gather what takes your fancy, add some vegetables, choose from the sweet, spicy, or salty sauces, and within minutes the chef will have barbecued your selection to perfection. Cost of the buffet is $1.80 per 100 grams. If you prefer, there's a regular menu too, with dishes ranging $7.50-11. The restaurant is open daily 11:30 a.m.-2:30 p.m. and 5-10:30 p.m. Other locations are near the Provincial Museum at 12520 102nd Ave., tel. 452-7367; in St. Albert at 3880 St. Albert Rd., tel. 459-8883; and east of the city in Sherwood Park at 933 Fir St., tel. 449-6928.

Italian
Among the dozens of Italian restaurants in the city, one of the most highly regarded is **Italian Gardens,** 10015 103rd Ave., tel. (403) 424-5454, tucked away down a lane beside the Centennial Building. All the pasta is made daily, in time for the regular lunchtime crush. Pastas on the regular dinner menu are $6.50-11, specialties begin at $9, and the lunch menu is slightly less expensive. Anything the chef puts out as a daily special will always be good—many of the regulars don't even bother looking at the menu, opting always for the special. It's closed on Sunday.

The Creperie
As you descend the stairs to this restaurant below the Boardwalk Market, 10220 103rd St., tel. (403) 420-6656, a great smell, wafting from somewhere in the depths of this historic building, hits you in the face. It will take a minute for your eyes to adjust to the softly lit dining area, but

once you do, its inviting atmosphere will become apparent. Entree crepes begin at $8, including rice and vegetables. Dessert crepes begin at $5. It's open weekdays for lunch, and daily for dinner.

Oysters At Midnight
Cafe Select, 10018 106th St., tel. (403) 423-0419, nestled below a parkade just off Jasper Ave., gives the first impression of being an upscale, trendy eatery, and to a degree it is. The restaurant is elegant, soft music is played, and a bunch of intellectuals sip wine and eat oysters till two in the morning. But the food is well priced ($10-15 for pasta, steak, or fondue dishes) and no one seems to mind if you stick to just coffee and dessert. Try the chocolate torte ($4). The cafe is open daily till 2 a.m.

Upscale
Located at the lower pedway level of the Convention Centre, **Claude's on the River,** 9797 Jasper Ave., tel. (403) 429-2900, overlooks the North Saskatchewan River. The formal service, warm and comfortable atmosphere, soft music, well-prepared French dishes, and a long and informative wine list make this restaurant a city favorite. Entrees are $18-26, a five-course table d'hôte is $35. Claude's is open Mon.-Fri. for lunch and Mon.-Sat. for dinner.

One of Canada's most renowned steak houses, **Hy's Steak Loft,** 10013 101A Ave., tel. 424-4444, is probably also one of Canada's most expensive. The elegant setting, centered around a Tiffany-styled skylight, is the perfect place for a splurge. The house specialty is New York strip steaks ($22); only the chicken dishes are less expensive. It's closed on Sunday. **The Carvery,** 10135 100th St., tel. 426-3636, in the Westin Hotel, is another popular steak house at the top end of the market. **La Ronde,** 10111 Bellamy Hill, tel. 428-6611, atop the Holiday Inn Crowne Plaza, is the city's only revolving restaurant.

WEST END

Vi's Restaurant
This popular eatery is located in a refurbished house overlooking the North Saskatchewan River at 9712 111th St., tel. (403) 482-6402. Small groups of tables are located in various rooms throughout the house; many tables have river views. Upstairs is a lounge with a number of outside tables. Start with one of the thick homemade soups ($3.95), or a fresh salad (from $3.25). The wide variety of entrees ($8-14) should suit everyone's taste, and you'd better save room for a piece of chocolate glazed pecan pie ($3). Vi's is open daily 11:30 a.m.-midnight.

A Southern Delight
Louisiana Purchase, 10320 111th St., tel. (403) 420-6779, serves Cajun and Creole cuisine without overdoing the blackened bit. All the fish and meat are carefully trimmed, doing away with the fat that is so much a part of Southern cooking. Prices are reasonable; entrees begin at $8. Open Mon.-Sat. 11:30 a.m.-midnight and Sunday 5 p.m.-midnight.

Sidetrack Cafe
Directly behind Louisiana Purchase is the Sidetrack Cafe, 10333 112th St., tel. (403) 421-1326. In addition to some of the city's best live entertainment, the cafe has a reputation for excellent food. Big, hearty breakfasts cost $3-7. Soups, salads, burgers, sandwiches, pizza, and world fare are all on the menu. The soup-and-sandwich lunch deal includes a bottomless bowl of soup. Dinners are served 5-10 p.m., and include such delicacies as Buffalo Meatloaf ($7.95). The cafe is open daily from 7 a.m.; expect a wait for a table on Saturday and Sunday mornings and most nights.

Smokey Joe's Hickory Smokehouse
This down-home restaurant at 11607 Jasper Ave., tel. (403) 488-7538, is Edmonton's only authentic American-style pit barbecue. The owners are a family from Oklahoma who brought their favorite recipes north. The meats are smoked over a pit barbecue for up to 24 hours, then served—in huge portions—with beans, French toast, and a thick chunk of garlic bread. On each table are hotter-than-hot Oklahoma crude sauces and *super*-hot jalapeño peppers pickled in a Cajun brine; use at your own risk! Most people end the feast with a piece of Smokey Joe's famous three-layered banana- and pecan-filled hummingbird cake. Entrees range $10-20. The combo dinners are a good deal, beginning at $28 for two. Desserts are around $4.

OLD STRATHCONA

Coffeehouses
Cafe La Gare, 10308 81st Ave., is beside Calgary Trail South on one of the busiest sidewalks in Old Strathcona, making it a prime people-watching location. It is bright, airy, gets the morning sun, and is nonsmoking. Other popular spots for coffee are **Hanratty's Tea and Pastry Shop,** 10341 82nd Ave., where the walls are covered in antiques, and light meals such as soup and corn bread are $3.75; and **Bukoba,** 10460 82nd Ave., tel. (403) 433-1848, which has a large, antique coffee-bean roaster in the front and a long coffee bar extending way down the back. Try an oatmeal cookie with your coffee.

Sweetwater Cafe
An unobtrusive, poster-covered entrance, opening to a flight of rickety stairs, leads to Sweetwater Cafe, 10360 82nd Ave., tel. 433-1244, one of Old Strathcona's favorite eateries. The food is excellent. Breakfast consists of all the usual fare (starting at $4.25), including delicious three-egg omelettes ($6). The rest of the day it's southwestern-style cooking. The black-bean soup with cheese biscuits on the side is a good way to start, then it's pasta, pizza, Tex-Mex, and vegetarian dishes. The cafe is open daily 9 a.m.-10 p.m.

Pack Rat Louis
Located in a renovated warehouse, one block off Whyte Ave., is Pack Rat Louis, 10335 83rd Ave., tel. (403) 433-8494, where butcher paper covers the tables, daily specials are chalked onto the pillars, and an open kitchen lets you watch your meal being cooked. The atmosphere is social, casual, and usually crowded. Lunch is mostly Italian pastas and pizza for $6-10; the dinner menu is more extensive, with entrees ranging $8-16. The restaurant is open Mon.-Sat. 11 a.m.-midnight, Sunday 4-10 p.m.

Mexican
Julio's Barrio Mexican Restaurant, 10450 Whyte Ave., tel. (403) 431-0774, is decorated with earthy colors and southwestern-style furniture, and has a true south-of-the-border ambience. The menu is appealing but limited. If you just want a light snack, try the warm corn chips with Jack cheese and freshly made Ultimate Salsa for $4.95. Main meals are $8.50-14. The only thing out of place is the selection of yuppie coffee drinks, which you certainly wouldn't find in a Mexican cantina. Julio's is open daily till midnight.

A Chinese Favorite
West of Old Strathcona, towards the University of Alberta, is **Mandarin Restaurant,** 11044 82nd Ave., tel. (403) 433-8494, consistently voted as having the best Chinese food in the city. You'd never know by looking at it. It's informal, noisy, family-style dining, and the walls are plastered with sporting memorabilia donated by diners. Most dishes are from northern China, known for traditionally hot food. But enough Cantonese dishes are offered to please all tastes. Expect to pay under $20 per person for a three-course meal. It's open daily 11:30 a.m.-2 p.m. and 4:30-10 p.m.

Vegetarian
The dishes at **Veggies,** 10331 82nd Ave., tel. (403) 432-7560, should intrigue even the most ardent meat eaters. The choice is extreme—Eggplant Enchilada's Oriental Stir Fry, Hummus Ieladel (pureed chickpeas seasoned with garlic and lemon juice) from Arabia, or the more traditional tofu burgers. Dishes begin at $6. Veggies is open Sun.-Thurs. 11 a.m.-9 p.m., Fri.-Sat. 11 a.m.-10 p.m.

The Unheardof
This unusual restaurant has no windows, and no regular menu. Despite this, it's harder to get a table here than just about anywhere else in town. The Unheardof, 9602 82nd Ave., tel. (403) 432-0480, is located in a renovated house filled with Victorian antiques. The seven-course table d'hôte costs $42.50 per person. The menu changes weekly, featuring fresh game, homemade chutneys, and relishes during fall, and chicken and beef dishes the rest of the year. Desserts such as Grapefruit Cheesecake with Grand Marnier top it off. The food is absolutely mouthwatering. Hours are Tues.-Sat. 6:30-8:30 p.m. Reservations are essential.

CALGARY TRAIL

Buffets

Everything a buffet lacks in atmosphere it usually makes up for in value. Along the city's main southern artery are two excellent Chinese buffets within a block of each other. **Foody Goody,** 3318 Calgary Trail Northbound, tel. (403) 998-8113, and **Buffet King,** 10150 34th Ave., tel. 437-7677, are huge restaurants that offer over 100 choices, including all the usual Chinese fare, fried chicken, pizza, and a wide variety of desserts including a dozen or so flavors of ice cream. Dinner is more expensive, but includes salmon, roast beef, and mussels or prawns. The food is never very hot, so only take small portions (easier said than done). Weekdays the lunch buffet is $6, dinner $10, weekend brunch $7, and weekend dinner $11. Drinks are extra, but wine and beer are well priced. Both are open daily 11 a.m.-10 p.m., closed 3-4 p.m. to prepare for the evening crush. At **Southpark Buffet,** 3921 Calgary Trail Southbound, tel. 437-5862, the choice is smaller, but the food is usually hot, there are more Canadian dishes, nonalcoholic drinks are included in the price, and most importantly, they have a soft-serve ice cream machine. Lunch is $6, dinner $9, and Sunday brunch $8.50. Children are 50 cents per year of their lives. It's open daily 11 a.m.-3:30 p.m. and 4-9 p.m.

The World's Best Hamburgers?

This is the claim made by **Fuddrucker's** 4804 Calgary Trail Southbound, tel. (403) 437-3535. Even if you have had better hamburgers, you probably haven't eaten in a place like this. In one corner is a glassed-in butcher shop where you watch the steaks being cut and meat being ground, and a bakery where the hamburger buns are baked daily. Across the restaurant is the fresh produce area where crates of tomatoes and lettuce are stacked. You get to build your own hamburger here with selections from the Fresh Produce Bar. Burgers start at $4, steak sandwiches at $6, salads at $5, and plenty of alternatives are offered for non-meat eaters.

Sawmill Dining Room And Pub

The menu at this popular south-of-the-river eatery, 4745 Calgary Trail Northbound, tel. (403) 436-1950, will suit everyone. An array of seafood, beef, chicken, and pasta dishes (from $10) is complemented by one of the city's best small salad and oyster bars (an extra $3.95). Most tables are partitioned from each other, and the restaurant is filled with antiques and greenery. The pub next door has live entertainment Thurs.-Saturday. The Sawmill is open Mon.-Thurs. 11:30 a.m.-2:30 p.m. and 4:30-10 p.m.; Fri.-Sat. till midnight; and for Sunday brunch 10:30 a.m.-2 p.m.

OTHER PARTS OF THE CITY

La Boheme

La Boheme, 6427 112 Ave., tel. (403) 474-5693, seems a little out of place, being in the same part of town where Wayne Gretzky made the Edmonton Oilers famous. But here just a five-minute drive east of the city center is one of Edmonton's best restaurants. The restaurant is an ever-changing gallery of French prints. Fresh flowers are placed on every table, the windows are bordered by lace curtains, and above are Edwardian tin ceilings. The classic French menu features fresh game; appetizers begin at $3 (for the thick, healthy soups) or $4 (for the salads); entrees are $8-16. The six-course table d'hôte is $30 per person. The restaurant is open daily 11:30 a.m.-10:30 p.m.

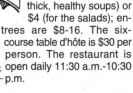

BOB RACE

Does Fuddrucker's make the world's best burgers?

Cheesecake Cafe

Anyone with a sweet tooth would be proud to be seen at this restaurant. The long, well presented menu is fine, and many come for the main meals, but to our way of thinking, the main meals here are the desserts. A cabinet is filled with mouthwatering cheesecakes ($3.95 per slice) and foot-high cakes that come in all imaginable flavors ($4.25 per slice). Like all the good spots in town, expect a wait during the usual busy periods. It's open daily 11 a.m.-11 p.m., till 1 a.m. Fri.-Saturday. The cafe's two locations are 17011 100th Ave., tel. (403) 486-0440, and 10390 51st Ave., tel. 437-5011.

A Greek Restaurant Worth Looking For

Syrtaki Greek Restaurant, 16313 111th Ave., tel. (403) 484-2473, is bright and airy, with four split-level dining areas, whitewashed walls, and a colorful Greek village mural encompassing one wall. A belly dancer dances up the aisles on Friday and Saturday nights. The extensive menu features dishes from northern Greece and Crete with entree prices ranging $8-17.50. Combination platters for two begin at $24. It's open for lunch and dinner, Mon.-Saturday.

Barb And Ernie's: A Local Legend

It's hard to believe that here in the cultural capital of Canada, getting a table at this restaurant sandwiched between auto-body shops and backing onto an abandoned rail line nearly always entails a wait. But such is the case at Barb And Ernie's, 9906 72nd Ave., tel. (403) 433-3242, an unpretentious southside restaurant with vinyl seats, hearty home-style cooking, hot coffee, and reasonable prices. Ernie will always make you feel welcome. Breakfast is the busiest time of day; omelettes begin at $4 and weekend breakfast specials are $4.50. The rest of the day hamburgers begin at $2.50, main meals such as halibut steak and shrimp creole are all under $10. It's open Mon.-Fri. 6 a.m.-8 p.m., Sat.-Sun. 9 a.m.-8 p.m.

TRANSPORTATION

GETTING THERE

Air

The city has two airports: **Edmonton International Airport,** 29 km south of the city center along Calgary Trail (Hwy. 2); and **Edmonton Municipal Airport,** located on Airport Rd. off Kingsway Ave., north of the city center.

The International Airport is open 24 hours (the observation platform is a good place to catch some z's). On the **arrivals** level is a small information booth; open year-round, daily 7 a.m.-11 p.m. Also at the airport are car-rental desks, hotel courtesy phones, a restaurant, and a currency exchange. The **Grey Goose** airporter service leaves for downtown hotels every 20 minutes and for Edmonton Municipal Airport (Muni) every two hours; tel. (403) 463-7520. One way to Muni is $11, round trip $18. A cab to downtown runs $30-35, but if trade is slow, haggling the price is worthwhile. Long-term parking is possible at a number of places nearby. For a regular-size car, **Car Park-n-go** charges $4.55 per day, $30 per week, and $107 per month; tel. 890-7690.

A few years ago the International Airport was a busy hub, with all international, most domestic, and some interprovincial flights using its large and modern facilities. Today it is only a shadow of its former self. Major domestic carriers (Canadian Regional and Air B.C.) have moved operations to "Muni." Airlines still using the International Airport are: **Air Canada,** tel. 423-1222 or (800) 332-1080; **American Airlines,** tel. (800) 433-7300; **Canadian,** tel. 421-1414 or (800) 372-9508; **Delta,** tel. (800) 221-1212; **Lufthansa,** tel. 424-6303 or (800) 665-2282; **NWT Air,** tel. 423-1222 or (800) 661-0789; and **Northwest Airlines,** tel. (800) 225-2525.

Edmonton Municipal Airport is smaller than the International but handles more flights, including most short-haul domestic service. It began as Blanchford Field in 1927, used by bush pilots such as the famous "Wop" May. Scheduled flights started in the 1950s. On the departures level is a gift shop, restaurant, and lounge. On the arrivals level are car-rental desks, a cafe, and large lockers ($1). Covered parking is 50 cents per half hour, $9 per day, or $30 per month. A cab downtown will be around $9, to West Edmonton Mall $14, and to the International Airport $37. It is also possible to get downtown by taking bus No. 23 from the terminal and changing at Kingsway Transfer Centre to bus No. 27, 41, 42, or 109. The **Grey Goose** airporter leaves every two hours from 10:30 a.m. for the International Airport, $11 one way, $18 round trip.

Rail

The **VIA Rail Station** is located close to the city center, downstairs in the CN Tower at 10004 104th Ave., tel. (800) 561-8630. The ticket office is generally open 8 a.m.-3:30 p.m., later when trains are due. Trains leave Vancouver (1150 Station St.) and Prince Rupert three times weekly for the grueling 23.5-hour trip to Edmonton (via Jasper), continuing on the "Canadian" route to the eastern provinces. Before paying full price for your ticket inquire about off-season discounts and the Canrailpass.

Bus

The **Greyhound Bus Depot** is located at 10324 103rd St., tel. (403) 421-4211, within walking distance of the city center, VIA Rail Station, and many hotels. A cab to Edmonton International Hostel from the depot is $5. Within the depot is an A&W Restaurant, a small paper shop, cash machine, and large lockers ($2). The depot is open 5:30 a.m.-midnight. Buses leave daily for all points in Canada including Vancouver (15-17 hours, $107 one way), Calgary (3.5 hours, $29.96 one way), and Jasper (4.5 hours, $41.46 one way). No reservations are taken—just turn up, buy your ticket, and hop aboard. Discounts apply if tickets are bought seven days in advance. For extensive travel, the Canada Travel Pass is a good deal (see "Transportation—Getting There" in the On the Road chapter).

Red Arrow buses leave Edmonton four times daily for Red Deer ($18.75) and Calgary ($31) and once daily for Fort McMurray ($39). Buses leave Edmonton from the Howard Johnson Plaza Hotel at 10014 104th St. and on southbound runs pick up at the Riviera Hotel on Calgary Trail. For more information call (403) 424-3339 or (800) 232-1958.

GETTING AROUND

Bus

Edmonton Transit System operates an extensive bus system that links the city center to all parts of the city and many major sights. Not all routes operate on Sunday. For many destinations south of the North Saskatchewan River you'll need to jump aboard the LRT to the University Transfer Point. Bus fare anywhere within the city is $1.60 during peak hours (5-9 a.m. and 3-6 p.m.), $1.35 at other times; exact fare only. Transfers are available on boarding and can be used for additional travel in any direction within 90 minutes. A day pass good for one day's unlimited travel is $4.25. For more information and passes, go to the Customer Services Outlet at Churchill LRT Station on 99th St. (weekdays 8:30 a.m.-4:30 p.m.) or the tourist information center in City Hall. For route and schedule information and a list of locations where day passes are sold, call (403) 421-4636.

Light Rail Transit

The LRT has 10 stops (Canada's smallest subway system) running east-west along Jasper Ave. (101st Ave.), south to the University, and northeast as far as 139th Street. The LRT runs underground through the city center, connecting with many pedways. Travel between Grandin and Churchill is free, Mon.-Fri. 9 a.m.-3 p.m. and Saturday 9 a.m.-6 p.m. LRT tickets are the same price as the bus, and tickets, transfers, and day passes are valid for travel on either the LRT or bus system.

Disabled Passengers

Edmonton Transit operates Disabled Adult Transportation System (D.A.T.S.), which provides access to various points of the city for physically disabled passengers who are unable to use the regular transit system. The door-to-door service costs the same as Edmonton Transit adult tickets. Priority is given to those heading to work or for medical trips; tel. (403) 496-4567. At the beginning of the Edmonton White Pages is an **Accessibility Guide,** listing all wheelchair accessible facilities within the city.

Taxi

Standard flag charge for cabs is $2.25 plus $1.30 per km but most companies have flat rates for major destinations within the city. Major companies are: **Checker Cabs,** tel. (403) 455-2211; **Co-op Taxi Line,** tel. 425-8310; **Skyline Cabs,** tel. 468-4646; and **Yellow Cab,** tel. 462-3456.

Car Rental

If you've just arrived in Edmonton, call around and compare rates. Lesser-known agencies are often cheaper, and all rates fluctuate with the season and demand. Many larger agencies have higher rates for unlimited mileage and built-in drop-off charges to nearby centers (otherwise to drop in Jasper is usually $70 extra, and Calgary $80 extra). All agencies provide free pick-up and drop-off at major Edmonton hotels and have outlets at both airports. Rental agencies are: **Avis,** tel. (403) 423-2847 or (800) 879-2847; **Budget,** tel. 448-2000 or (800) 268-8900; **Discount Car Rentals,** tel. 448-3892 or (800) 263-2355; **Dollar,** tel. 420-0581 or (800) 800-4000; **Hertz,** tel. 423-3431 or (800) 263-0600; **Rent-A-Wreck,** tel. 448-1234 or (800) 327-0116; **Thrifty,** tel. 428-8555 or (800) 367-2277; and **Tilden,** tel. 422-6097 or (800) 387-4747.

Tours

If you are short on time, or just want to see Edmonton's major attractions, **Royal Tours** has just the answer. The 2.5-hour Ecological Tour (Provincial Museum, University of Alberta, river valley, downtown, and West Edmonton Mall; $18) and 3.5-hour Historical Tour (Legislature Building, river valley, and Fort Edmonton Park; $21) leave between 8:30 and 9:30 a.m. during summer from all major hotels. For more information and details of ticketing call 488-9040. **Nite Tours,** tel. 453-2134, has theme tours—such as comedy, country, dance, and pub crawls—of the city's nightlife in English double-decker buses; $18.50 per person.

SERVICES AND INFORMATION

SERVICES

The main **post office** is downtown at 9808 103A Avenue. Main branches of most banks in the downtown area will handle common foreign-currency exchange transactions. **Thomas Cook Foreign Exchange,** tel. (403) 448-3660, is located at 10180 101st St. in ManuLife Place. **Bank of America Foreign Currency Services,** tel. 444-3072, is located in West Edmonton Mall at Entrance Nine beside the Fantasyland Hotel lobby. Edmonton International Airport has a foreign exchange on the departures level. **Carousel Photographics,** 10525 Jasper Ave., tel. 424-7161, develops print film in an hour and E6 slide film in five hours; it's open Mon.-Fri. 7 a.m.-5:30 p.m. and Saturday 10 a.m.-4 p.m. For onward travel plans, **Travel Cuts,** at 12304 Jasper Ave., tel. 488-8487, has the best deals.

On the south side of the river is **Clean Easy,** 10441 80th Ave., tel. 439-5012, one of Edmonton's largest laundromats. On the west side of the city is **LaPerle Homestyle Laundry,** 9756 182nd St., tel. 483-9200, handy to the hotels in the area and with large washers and dryers for sleeping bags. Toward the city is **Silver Coin Laundry,** at 15220 Stony Plain Rd., tel. 481-9455. **Soaptime Laundromat,** 7626 104th St., tel. 439-3599, is open till 11:30 p.m.

Emergency Services

For medical emergencies call 911 or one of the following hospitals: **Edmonton General Hospital,** 11111 Jasper Ave., tel. (403) 482-8111; **Charles Camsell Provincial General Hospital,** 12804 114th Ave., tel. 453-5311; **Royal Alexandra Hospital,** 10240 Kingsway Ave., tel. 477-4111; **University of Alberta Hospital,** 8440 112th St., tel. 492-8822. For the **RCMP** call 945-5330.

INFORMATION

Downtown Bookstores

Audrey's, 10702 Jasper Ave., tel. (403) 423-3487, has the city's largest collection of travel guides, western Canadiana, and general travel writing on two vast floors. Open weekdays till 9 p.m., till five on weekends. Closer to the city center, in the Hudson's Bay Centre, is **The Book Company,** 10230 Jasper Ave., tel. 424-5887. **Map Town,** 10815 100th Ave., tel. 429-2600, stocks the provincial 1:50,000 and 1:250,000 topographical map series along with city maps, world maps, Alberta wall maps, travel guides, atlases, and a huge selection of specialty maps. It's open Mon.-Fri. 9 a.m.-6 p.m., Saturday 10 a.m.-2 p.m.

Old Strathcona Bookstores

Old Strathcona is an excellent place for browsing through secondhand bookstores. **Wee Book Inn,** 10310 82nd Ave., tel. (403) 432-7230, is the largest, and stocks more recent titles and a large collection of magazines. **Varscona Books,** 10309 82nd Ave., tel. 439-4195, specializes in Canadiana and has an extensive collection of Albertan material, including pamphlets and newspapers. **Athabasca Books,** 8228 105th St., tel. 431-1776, stocks mostly history and literature books. **Bjarne's Books** has older books, including a large selection of hard-to-find Western Canadiana and Arctic region material. **Edmonton Bookstore,** 8530 109th St., tel. 433-1781, also has a large stock of out-of-print books from the region.

Old Strathcona's lone new-book store is **Greenwood's,** 10355 82nd Ave., tel. 439-2005, which stocks a lot of everything.

Libraries

The Edmonton Public Library System has 13 libraries spread throughout the city. Largest is **Centennial Library** located at 7 Sir Winston Churchill Square, tel. (403) 423-2331. It's open Mon.-Fri. 9 a.m.-9 p.m., Saturday 9 a.m.-6 p.m., and Sunday 1-5 p.m. This large two-story facility, connected to the downtown core by pedways, is a great place to spend a rainy afternoon. It carries newspapers, magazines, and phone books from all corners of the globe, as well as rows and rows of Western Canadiana. Throughout the week, author readings take place on the main level. Other locations are: **Jasper Place Library,** 9010 156th St.; **Mill Woods Library,** 2331 66th St.; **Strathcona Library,** 8331 104th St. (closed Wednesday); and **Highlands Library,** 6710 118th Avenue.

Information Centers

Edmonton Tourism has information centers at five locations in the city. The most central is in City Hall at 1 Sir Winston Churchill Square; open in summer, daily 8:30 a.m.-4:30 p.m., weekdays only the rest of the year. In Gateway Park, south of town on Calgary Trail (Hwy. 2), is the largest center; open in summer, daily 8 a.m.-9 p.m., the rest of the year, Mon.-Fri. 8:30 a.m.-4:30 p.m., Sat.-Sun. 9 a.m.-5 p.m. On the arrivals level of Edmonton International Airport is a small booth open year-round, daily 7 a.m.-11 p.m. Seasonal centers are located along the Yellowhead Trail, east of the city, and at 19001 Stony Plain Road. Both are open summer only, daily 9 a.m.-5 p.m. For more information on the city write to Edmonton Tourism, 9797 Jasper Ave., No. 104, Edmonton, Alberta T5J 1N9, tel. (403) 496-8400 or (800) 463-4667.

Alberta Tourism runs an information center at 10155 102nd St. that has general information on the province, including maps and guides to camping and accommodations. It's open in summer, Mon.-Fri. 8:15 a.m.-4:30 p.m.; tel. 427-4321 or (800) 661-8888.

BOB RACE

KAREN MCKINLEY

NORTHERN ALBERTA

The northern half of Alberta, from Hwy. 16 north to the 60th Parallel, is a sparsely populated land of unspoiled wilderness, home to deer, moose, coyotes, foxes, lynx, black bears, and the elusive Swan Hills grizzly bear. For the most part it is heavily forested, part of the boreal forest eco-region that sweeps around the Northern Hemisphere broken only by the Atlantic and Pacific oceans. Much of the world's boreal forest has been devastated by logging. But here in northern Alberta, a good portion of the land is muskeg—low-lying bogs and marshes that make logging difficult and expensive. Only a few species of trees are adapted to the long, cold winters and short summer growing seasons characteristic to these northern latitudes. Conifers such as white spruce, black spruce, jack pine, fir, and larch are the most common.

This vast expanse of land is relatively flat, the only exceptions being the **Swan Hills**—which rise to 1,200 meters—and, farther north, the **Birch** and **Caribou mountains.** The **Athabasca** and **Peace** river systems are the region's largest waterways. Carrying water from hundreds of tributaries, they merge in the far northeastern corner of the province and flow

north into the Arctic Ocean. A third major watercourse, the **North Saskatchewan River,** flows east from the Continental Divide, crossing northern Alberta on its way to Hudson Bay. It was along these rivers that Alberta's earliest explorers arrived, opening up the Canadian west to the trappers, missionaries, and settlers who followed.

Northeast of Edmonton is the **Lakeland** region, where many early fur-trading posts were established. From there, Hwy. 63 heads north through boreal forest to **Fort McMurray,** an isolated city of 36,000, 437 km north of its closest sizable neighbor, Edmonton. Oil is Fort McMurray's raison d'être—oil sands, to be precise. The **Athabasca Oil Sands** are the world's largest such deposit. To extract just 33 billion barrels will take 500 years at current extraction rates.

Alberta's **Northern Heartland** extends from Edmonton's outer suburbs north to the towns of **Athabasca** and **Slave Lake,** jumping-off points into the vast boreal forest. This area is a paradise for birdwatchers; it's at the confluence of three major flyways.

NORTHERN ALBERTA

NORTHWEST TERRITORIES
ALBERTA

BRITISH COLUMBIA
ALBERTA

SASKATCHEWAN
ALBERTA

0   70 mi
0   70 km

FORT SMITH

WOOD BUFFALO
NATIONAL PARK

LAKE ATHABASCA

CARIBOU MOUNTAINS

MEANDER RIVER

HAY RIVER

HIGH LEVEL

FORT CHIPEWYAN

RAINBOW LAKE

FORT VERMILION

BIRCH MOUNTAINS

ATHABASCA RIVER

MACKENZIE HIGHWAY

BICENTENNIAL HIGHWAY

MANNING

FORT McKAY

FORT McMURRAY

PEACE RIVER

PEACE RIVER

DAWSON CREEK

LESSER SLAVE LAKE

SLAVE LAKE

GRANDE PRAIRIE

HIGH PRAIRIE

LAC LA BICHE

LAC LA BICHE

COLD LAKE

VALLEYVIEW

SWAN HILLS

SWAN HILLS

ATHABASCA

SMOKY RIVER

BARRHEAD

GRANDE CACHE

WHITECOURT

WESTLOCK

ST. PAUL

WILLMORE WILDERNESS PARK

YELLOWHEAD HIGHWAY

ELK ISLAND NATIONAL PARK

HINTON

EDMONTON

LLOYDMINSTER

JASPER NATIONAL PARK

JASPER

TO RED DEER AND CALGARY

SASKATCHEWAN RIVER

NORTH

TO BANFF

© MOON PUBLICATIONS, INC.

West of Edmonton the Yellowhead Hwy. climbs into the Rockies, through **Evergreen County** and past **Hinton,** a town surrounded by natural wonders. From Hinton, travelers can continue on Hwy. 16 into Jasper National Park, or take Hwy. 40 northwest to **Willmore Wilderness Park,** a park usually ignored by tourists in favor of the neighboring national parks to the south. Continuing north on Hwy. 4 you come to **Grande Prairie,** one of northern Alberta's largest cities and a regional agriculture and service center. The **Peace River Valley,** north of Grande Prairie, leads travelers into the Northwest Territories via the **Mackenzie Hwy.** (Hwy. 35), which parallels the Peace and Hay rivers.

With few regular "sights," northern Alberta receives fewer tourists than the rest of the province. Those who do venture north find solitude in a vast, untapped wilderness with abundant wildlife and plenty of recreation—lakes and rivers to fish, historic sites to explore, rivers to float, and gravel roads to drive just for the sake of it.

LAKELAND

Highway 16, east from Edmonton, follows the southern flanks of a region containing hundreds of lakes formed at the end of the last ice age by a retreating sheet of ice nearly one km thick. From its headwaters beneath the Columbia Icefield on the Continental Divide, the **North Saskatchewan River** flows east through Edmonton and the Lakeland region before eventually draining into Hudson Bay.

History buffs appreciate the legacies of early white man that dot the landscape here—restored fur-trading posts, missions, and the Ukrainian Village near Vegreville. Other visitors are attracted by the region's vast areas of unspoiled wilderness, including seven provincial parks. Anglers will feel right at home among the area's countless lakes, and wildlife watchers are drawn to **Elk Island National Park,** which rivals Tanzania's Serengeti Plains for the population densities of its animal inhabitants.

The region's major population centers are **Lloydminster** (250 km east of Edmonton), Canada's only town in two provinces; **St. Paul,** which has the world's only UFO landing pad; and the tri-towns of **Grand Centre, Medley,** and **Cold Lake,** at the edge of the boreal forest, surrounded by vast reserves of untapped oil.

ELK ISLAND NATIONAL PARK

Heading east from Edmonton on Hwy. 16, you'll soon come to Elk Island National Park. This small, fenced 194-square-km park preserves a remnant of the transitional grassland ecoregion—the aspen parkland—that once covered the entire northern flank of the prairie. It's also one of the best spots in Alberta for wildlife watching; with around 3,000 large mammals, the park has one of the highest concentrations of big game in the world.

The park was originally set aside in 1906 to protect a herd of elk; it's Canada's only national park formed to protect a native species. The elk here have never been crossbred and are probably the most genetically pure in the world. In addition to the elk, resident mammals include moose, two species of bison, white-tailed and mule deer, coyotes, beavers, muskrats, mink, and porcupines. The many lakes and wetland areas in the park serve as nesting sites for waterfowl, and around 230 species of birds have been observed here.

A mosaic of mixed-wood forest—predominantly aspen and balsam poplar—covers the low, rolling Beaver Hills here, slowly taking over the grassland. One slow-moving stream winds its way throught the park, and many shallow lakes dot the landscape.

Bison In The Park

Two different species of bison inhabit the park, and to prevent interbreeding they are separated. All bison on the north side of Hwy. 16 are **plains bison,** while those on the south side are **wood bison.**

Before the late 1700s, 60 million plains bison lived on the North American plains. In less than a century man brought these shaggy beasts to the brink of extinction. By 1880, incredibly, only a few hundred plains bison remained. A small herd, owned by ranchers in Montana, was brought north in 1907. They were held at what was then Elk Island Reserve until Buffalo National Park (since closed) at Wainwright was fenced. When it came time to move the animals from Elk Island, some couldn't be found—today's herd descended from those well-hidden progenitors. A small part of the herd is kept in a large enclosure just north of the park information center while others are free to roam through the north section of the park.

The wood bison, largest native land mammal in North America, was for many years thought to be extinct—a victim of hunting, severe winters, and interbreeding with its close rela-

tive, the plains bison. In 1957 a herd of 200 was discovered in the remote northwestern corner of Wood Buffalo National Park. Some were captured and transported to the Mackenzie Bison Sanctuary in the Northwest Territories and to Elk Island National Park. The herd at Elk Island has ensured the survival of the species and today it is the purest herd in the world. It is used as breeding stock for several captive herds throughout North America. To view the herd, look south from Hwy. 16 or hike the Wood Bison Trail (see below).

© MOON PUBLICATIONS, INC.

Hiking

Twelve trails, ranging in length from 3.5 to 18.5 km, cover all areas of the park and provide excellent opportunities to view wildlife. A park information sheet details each one. Make sure to carry water with you—surface water in the park is not suitable for drinking. The **Shoreline Trail** (three km one way) follows the shore of Astotin Lake from the golf-course parking lot. The **Lakeview Trail** (3.3 km round trip) begins from the northern end of the recreation area and also provides good views of the lake. Hike this trail in the evening for a chance to see beavers. The only trail on the south side of Hwy. 16 is the **Wood Bison Trail** (18.5 km round trip), which has an interpretive display at the trailhead. In winter the trails provide excellent cross-country skiing and snowshoeing.

Other Recreation And Events

Canoes, rowboats, sailboards, and small sailboats can be rented at Astotin Lake. **Elk Island Golf Course,** an interesting nine-hole layout, is located beside Astotin Lake. Green fees are $18 for 18 holes; call (403) 998-3161 for reservations.

In summer an array of interpretive talks and walks are held at various locations; ask for details at the park information center or Astotin Interpretive Centre. Early August brings the **Great Buffalo-Chip Flip,** where contestants throw the organic frisbees and win prizes for accuracy and distance.

Practicalities

Sandy Beach Campground is the only overnight facility within the park. It has firepits, picnic tables, flush toilets, and showers; $11 per night. This facility is open in summer only; the rest of the year primitive camping (no water, chemical toilets) is available at the boat-launch area. A concession selling fast food and basic camping supplies operates May-Oct. at Astotin Lake, and the golf course has a restaurant; tel. (403) 998-3161.

The **park information center,** tel. 992-5790, is located 0.8 km north of Hwy. 16 on the Elk Island Parkway; it's open in summer, Mon.-Sat. 10 a.m.-6 p.m., Sunday 8 a.m.-8 p.m. The **Astotin Interpretive Centre,** tel. 992-6392, farther

ELK ISLAND NATIONAL PARK

© MOON PUBLICATIONS, INC.

along the parkway, has interpretive programs; open daily in summer, weekends only the rest of the year. Another source of information is the park radio station (1540 AM). For further information on the park write: Superintendent, Elk Island National Park, R.R. No. 1, Site 4, Fort Saskatchewan, Alberta T8L 2N7.

EAST ALONG
THE YELLOWHEAD HIGHWAY

Blackfoot Recreation Area

South of Elk Island National Park is the 97-square-km Cooking Lake–Blackfoot Recreation, Wildlife, and Grazing Area. It is an integrated resource management unit, meaning that it can be used for many purposes, including grazing, mineral exploration, hunting, and recreation. It is part of the massive Cooking Lake Moraine, formed during the last ice age as the retreating sheet of ice stalled for a time, leaving mounds and hollows which have since filled with water. Large natural areas of wetland and forest provide habitat for abundant wildlife including moose, elk, white-tailed deer, coyotes, beavers, and over 200 species of birds. Much of the well-posted trail system is for hikers only, but some parts are open to horses and mountain bikes. **Blackfoot Staging Area,** off Hwy. 16, is the trailhead for a good selection of short hiking trails, but to really get into the heart of the area head south along the southwestern border of Elk Island National Park to three other staging areas.

Ukrainian Cultural Heritage Village

This site, 50 km east of Edmonton, is a realistic replica of a Ukrainian settlement, common in the rural areas of east-central Alberta at the turn of the century. It was in this region that the first, and largest, Ukrainian settlement in Canada was located. Driven from their homeland in Eastern Europe, Ukrainians fled to the Canadian prairies where for many years they dressed and worked in the ways of the Old World. These traditions are kept alive at the heritage village. It's open in summer, daily 10 a.m.-6 p.m. Admission is $5.50. For more information call (403) 662-3640.

Vegreville

Although first settled by French farmers from Kansas, this town of 5,200 is best known for its Ukrainian heritage. Today Vegreville's biggest attraction is the world's largest *pysanka,* a giant, traditionally decorated Ukranian Easter egg, located at the east end of town. It measures eight meters long, weighs 2,270 kilograms, and can turn in the wind like a giant weathervane.

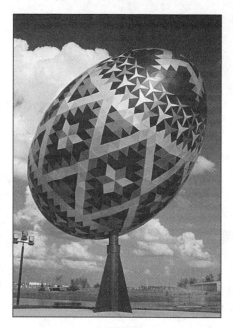

the world's largest pysanka

Vermilion

The reddish-colored iron deposits in a nearby river gave this town of 4,200 at the junction of Highways 16 and 41 its name. **Vermilion Provincial Park** is one of only two urban-area provincial parks in Alberta. The park encompasses 771 hectares of aspen parkland and grassland along the banks of the Vermilion River, an ancient glacial meltwater channel. To date, 20 species of mammals and 110 species of birds have been documented here. The park also has 15 km of hiking trails and a campground. **Vermilion Heritage Museum,** on 50th Ave., tel. (403) 853-6211, features a pioneer home, an extensive photographic collection, and native artifacts; it's open in summer, daily 1-5 p.m. Across from the town office is a cast-iron mill wheel, one of the only relics retrieved from the Frog Lake Settlement after the massacre in 1885 (see "Southeast to St. Paul and Beyond," below).

LLOYDMINSTER

North America has a number of "twin cities" that straddle borders (such as Minneapolis and St. Paul) but Lloydminster is the only one that has a single corporate body in two provinces (or states, depending on the case). About 60% of the city's 18,000 residents live on the Alberta side, separated from their Saskatchewan neighbors by the main street.

Lloydminster was settled in 1903 by 500 immigrants from Britain, who followed the Reverend George Lloyd to the site of Lloydminster.

The community thrived, and when the provinces of Alberta and Saskatchewan were created out of the Northwest Territories in 1905, the town was divided by the new border, which ran along the fourth meridian. It functioned as two separate communities until 1930, when community leaders requested that the two halves be amalgamated into the City of Lloydminster. Farming and cattle ranching form the base of the regional economy, although oil and natural gas play an important role in the city's future.

Sights
Barr Colony Heritage Cultural Centre, tel.

(403) 825-5655, in Weaver Park on Hwy. 16, houses the Richard Larsen Museum featuring a collection of artifacts and antiques used by early settlers. Also here, the Imhoff Art Gallery contains the work of early-1900s artist Count Berthold Von Imhoff. In an adjoining wing is a taxidermy display. The center is open in summer, daily 10 a.m.-7 p.m.; admission $2.75.

The 81-hectare **Bud Miller Park** offers a number of nature trails winding around a two-hectare lake and through stands of aspen. Canada's largest sundial, a tree maze, formal gardens, an arboretum, a nature center, and boat rentals can also be found here. The park is open year-round, daily 7 a.m.-11 p.m. It's located south of Hwy. 16 along 59th Ave.; tel. 875-4497.

Events And Recreation
On the second weekend of July, Lloydminster hosts **Colonial Days.** Its **Heritage Day Festival** takes place mid-August, and the last week of October is the **Canadian Cowboys Association Rodeo Finals.** All winter you can go downhill skiing, prairie-style, south of town at **Mt. Joy Ski Hill;** tel. (403) 745-2547.

Accommodations
Motels are located along Hwy. 16 (44th St.), mostly on the Alberta side of the border. **Cedar Inn Motel,** on the Saskatchewan side, 4526 44th St., tel. (403) 825-6155, is the least expensive; $25 s, $30 d. **Lodge Motel,** 6301 44th St., tel. 875-1919, has large clean rooms; $37 s, $43 d including breakfast. **Tropical Inn,** 5621 44th St., tel. 825-7000, and **West Harvest Inn,** 5614 44th St., tel. 875-6113, are larger, with more facilities, but are more expensive.

Weaver Park Campsite, tel. 825-3726, located behind the Barr Colony Centre, has showers and a grocery store; unserviced sites $10, hookups $13.50-15. Much nicer is **Rolling Green Fairways,** tel. 875-4653, located two km west of city on Hwy. 16, then one km north. Facilities include showers, laundry, and an adjacent golf course; tents $8, hookups $14-16.

Food
Country at Heart Antiques and Teahouse, tel. (403) 825-9498, is located on the south side of Hwy. 16, just east of the border post. The teahouse was built in 1942 and is surrounded by a variety of well-established gardens. Afternoon tea and light lunches are served April-Dec., Tues.-Sat. 10 a.m.-6 p.m. **Lunch at Lorna's Cafe,** 5008 50th St., tel. 875-1152, has hearty breakfasts and healthy sandwiches. At the opposite end of the cholesterol scale is **Digger's Roadhouse,** 4301 49th Ave., tel. 825-7979, where, although it may seem so at first, you don't have to wear a cap saying "I Love My Mother-in-law" to be served promptly.

Information
The **Saskatchewan Information Centre,** located beside the Barr Colony Centre, has information on the town but is mainly a source of information for those heading east; open in summer, daily 8 a.m.-8 p.m. A **Travel Alberta Information Centre,** for those entering the province from the east, is located one km east of town; it's open in summer, daily 8 a.m.-8 p.m.

LIVING IN LLOYDMINSTER

Living in a town in two provinces can be confusing. The liquor store on the Alberta side is always busier—Alberta's booze is cheaper—except, of course, during one of Alberta's all-too-frequent beer strikes, when the Saskatchewan store gets the trade. The minimum drinking age is 19 in Saskatchewan, but 18-year-olds can just cross the road into Alberta to drink. The minimum wage is higher in Saskatchewan and vacations are longer, but income tax is higher. In theory Saskatchewan retailers charge five percent tax on many goods, unless of course you can prove they will be used or consumed outside of the province. Telephones are serviced by an Albertan company. Power is supplied by two companies; those on the Alberta side get a rebate. Albertans pay a monthly fee for health care, even though the hospital is in Saskatchewan. The best strategy might be to live in Alberta and work in Saskatchewan; houses on the Alberta side are up to 30% more expensive, but the province has lower taxes, and with a job in Saskatchewan—where the benefits are better—you'd come out in front eventually.

HIGHWAY 28 TO ASHMONT

Highway 28 leaves Edmonton heading north through the suburbs. After a series of 90-degree turns—first one way, then the other, then back again—it comes to **Waskatenau,** where it straightens out to pursue an easterly heading toward Cold Lake.

Long Lake Provincial Park

During the last ice age, the low-lying area occupied by this 764-hectare park was a part of a glacial meltwater channel. Today it's surrounded by boreal forest, though aspens predominate in the park because of fires over the years. Fishing is great here; the main body of water holds some lunker northern pike. Right on the lake is a campground with flush toilets, showers, a grocery store, and canoe rentals; unserviced sites $13; powered sites $15. To get there from Hwy. 28 head north from Wasketenau on Hwy. 831 for 48 km.

Immediately to the south of the park is **White Earth Valley Natural Area,** a 2,055-hectare tract of land set aside to protect the habitat of the abundant wildlife and waterfowl.

Smoky Lake

Named for a lake where natives once rested and smoked pipes during hunts, this small community is located 93 km west of St. Paul. **Pine Ridge Forest Nursery,** tel. (403) 656-4130, 12 km east, then five km south of town, is a 113-hectare site with 20 greenhouses full of white spruce and lodgepole pine seedlings used for reforestation throughout the province. The **World Championship Pumpkin Weigh-in** takes place in the center of town on the first weekend of October.

Victoria Settlement

Victoria Settlement is 21 km south and east of Smoky Lake, on the north bank of the North Saskatchewan River. Founded as a mission in 1862, the settlement originally consisted of a small house, church, and school. In 1864 the Hudson's Bay Company established a fur-trading post at the site. The clerk's 1864 log house still stands, 100 years after the last beaver pelt changed hands. The trading post closed in 1897 and was abandoned until early this century, when groups of Ukrainian settlers moved to the area and the settlement became known as Victoria-Pakan. When the railway bypassed the settlement in 1918, businesses moved north to Smoky Lake and the area was abandoned once again. The Pakan Church is open in summer, daily 10 a.m.-6 p.m., and presents a short slide show about the settlement. Paved trails lead to the clerk's house, to the river (where traders came ashore), and to the site of the McDougall Mission and the graves of the founder's three daughters. Picnic tables are set among broad maple trees, planted during the fur-trading days. For more information on the site call (403) 656-2333.

From Victoria Settlement, you can continue south on Hwy. 855, which eventually intersects Hwy. 16 west of Vegreville. Along the way, you'll pass by **Andrew,** home of the world's largest mallard duck. Careful you don't rip your jeans climbing the fence to touch it.

East To Ashmont

East from Smoky Lake, Hwy. 28 passes **Vilna**— home of the world's largest mushrooms—and skirts many lakes with excellent swimming, fishing, and boating. Garner Lake Provincial Park, four km north of Spedden, is a 74-hectare park with a sandy beach and fishing for northern pike, perch, and pickerel; camping is $11. At **Ashmont,** Highways 28 and 28A split, with Hwy. 28 dipping south to St. Paul, and 28A continuing east to Bonnyville and Cold Lake (see "Northeast Toward Cold Lake," below).

SOUTHEAST TO ST. PAUL AND BEYOND

Saint Paul

This town of 5,000 gets very few visitors from outer space. Ordinarily, that wouldn't be surprising—except that here they are encouraged to drop by. You guessed it (or maybe you didn't), St. Paul has the world's only UFO landing pad— a raised platform beside the main road forlornly waiting for its first visitor. The town's origins date to 1896 when Father Albert Lacombe, the famed western missionary, established a settlement where Métis people—who had been largely ignored by the government during treaty talks—could live and learn farming skills. Lacombe extended an open invitation to all Métis in western Canada, but fewer than 300 responded. After 10 years of hardship he opened the settlement to whites, attracting people from many cultures. The town's diverse background is catalogued at the **St. Paul Culture Centre,** 4537 50th Ave., tel. (403) 645-4800; open in summer, Mon.-Sat. 9 a.m.-5 p.m. The **Old Rectory,** at 5015 47th St., looks much as it would have when built in 1896. At the south end of town (head down 47th St.) is **Upper Therien Lake.** Over 200 species of birds have been recorded around this and other nearby lakes. A large stretch of land along Lakeshore Dr. has been set aside as a park with picnic shelters and paths leading out to the lake.

The **King's Motel,** 5638 50th Ave., tel. 645-5656, has good rooms for $36 s, $40 d; ask if that includes breakfast at the restaurant next door. The **Municipal Campground,** which has showers, is located on 55th St. at 49th Ave., a short walk from the golf course; unserviced sites $6, powered sites $9. **Westcove Municipal Recreation Area,** 16 km north of St. Paul, is beside a beach and has all facilities; unserviced sites $5-7, powered sites $9; tel. 645-6688.

Corfou Restaurant, 5010 50th Ave., tel. 645-2948, has a pleasant atmosphere and is managed by a friendly character. Pasta and other southern-European dishes range $6.85-13.95; seafood and grills start at $8.75 but tend to be smaller portions. The **tourist information center** is located on 50th Ave. at 53rd St., tel. 645-6800. It's a raised, circular structure behind the UFO landing pad; if approaching from outer space, look for the green flashing light on top. Hours are daily 9 a.m.-5 p.m.

Twenty-eight km east of St. Paul, Hwy. 28 makes a 90-degree left turn at its junction with Hwy. 41 and resumes its northeasterly course toward Cold Lake (see "Northeast Toward Cold Lake," below). Those heading back to Hwy. 16 can turn right at this junction and either beeline directly south on Hwy. 41 to Vermilion, or wind around the backwoods to Lloydminster, taking in the following sights.

Fort George–Buckingham House

Nine km south of Hwy. 28 is the junction of Highways 41 and 646 at **Elk Point** (look for a large mural outlining the history of the area along 50th Ave., and an 11-meter statue of explorer Peter Fidler at the north end of town). Turn left (east) onto Hwy. 646 and soon you'll come to Fort George and the Buckingham House.

The site of these two fur-trading posts on the north bank of the North Saskatchewan River, 13 km east of Elk Point, has been designated a provincial historical site. In 1792, soon after the North West Company had established Fort George, the Hudson's Bay Company followed suit a few hundred meters away with Buckingham House. Both posts were abandoned in the early 1800s and have long since been destroyed; depressions in the ground, piles of stone, and indistinct pathways are all that remain. Above the site is an interpretive center with audio and visual presentations explaining the rivalry between the two companies and the history of the forts. Interpretive trails lead from the center down to the river. It's open mid-May to September, daily 10 a.m.-6 p.m. Admission is $2.25. For more information call (403) 724-2611.

Whitney Lakes Provincial Park

Whitney, Ross, Laurier, and Borden lakes are the namesake attractions at this 1,490-hectare park on Hwy. 646. The fishing is excellent in all but Borden. Because the park is located in a transition zone, plant, mammal, and bird species are diverse. A mixed forest of aspen, white spruce, balsam poplar, and jack pine grows on the uplands while black spruce and tamarack grow in lower, wetter areas. Beavers are common—look for their ponds on the north side of Laurier Lake. Other resident mammals include porcupines, white-tailed deer, coyotes, and, during berry season, black bears. Birds are abundant, especially waterfowl and shorebirds. A 1.5-km interpretive trail starts at the day-use area at the northeast corner of Ross Lake. Fishing is best for northern pike, perch, and pickerel. **Ross Lake Campground** has 149 sites ($13 per night) on six short loops around the south and eastern shore of the lake. A trail along the shore links each loop. Showers are located between loops "A" and "B".

Vast reserves of salt, west of Whitney Lakes, are harvested by the **Canadian Salt Company,** based at Lindbergh. Tours of the factory are available on weekdays; call ahead, (403) 724-3745.

Frog Lake Massacre

On 2 April 1885, a band of Cree led by Chief Big Bear massacred nine whites in a remote Hudson's Bay Company post on Frog Lake. It was an act of desperation on the part of the Cree. The great buffalo herds had been decimated and the fur trade was coming to an end. Big Bear had been forced into signing land treaties to prevent his people from starving. Life on reserves didn't suit the nomadic Cree and they yearned to return to the old ways. Exactly what sparked the massacre remains unknown, but word of confrontations farther east must have encouraged the Cree. Historians believe the natives originally planned to take hostages, but when Tom Quinn, the post's Indian agent, refused native orders a shooting spree took place.

The site is marked by a small graveyard and a series of interpretive panels outlining the events leading up to the massacre. To get there from Whitney Lakes, continue east on Hwy. 646 to its junction with Hwy. 897. Follow 897 north to the small hamlet of **Frog Lake.** At the Frog Lake General Store head east for three km to a slight rise, then south at the crest.

To Lloydminster

From Frog Lake get back on Hwy. 641 and follow it east to Hwy. 17 at the native community of **Onion Lake.** Highway 17 parallels the border 26 km south to Lloydminster.

NORTHEAST TOWARD COLD LAKE

Highway 28A

Highway 28A leaves Ashmont and bisects Upper and Lower Mann lakes (best fishing is in Upper Mann Lake on the *south* side of the road).

A farther 25 km east is a turnoff to **Glendon.** Glendon's claim to fame takes the cake, or actually the *pyrogy*—it has the world's largest *pyrogy.* This indigestible part of the Ukrainian diet —something like boiled potato- or onion-filled ravioli—can be sampled next to Pyrogy Park in the Pyrogy Park Cafe, opposite the Pyrogy Motel on Pyrogy Drive.

Bonnyville

Originally called St. Louis de Moose Lake, this town of 5,000 is an agriculture center surrounded by many good fishing and swimming lakes including **Moose Lake,** to the west, and **Muriel Lake,** to the south. The town is located on the north shore of **Jessie Lake,** where over 300 species of waterfowl and shorebirds have been recorded. Spring and fall are the best viewing times although many species are present year-round, nesting in the marshes and aspen parkland surrounding the lake. Numerous viewing platforms, linked by the **Wetlands Nature Trail,** are scattered along Lakeshore Dr. and Hwy. 41.

All Bonnyville's tourist facilities, including a number of motels, are located along the main highway. The **tourist information center** is located at the west end of town. It's open in summer, Mon.-Sat. 10 a.m.-8 p.m., Sunday 10 a.m.-5 p.m.; tel. (403) 826-7807.

Moose Lake Provincial Park

Moose Lake is a large, shallow body of water between Highways 28A and 660. One of Alberta's earliest trading posts was built in 1789 on the shore of Moose Lake by Angus Shaw, of the North West Company. All that remains of the post is a pile of rocks and a depression just west of Moose Lake River. In 1870 a smallpox epidemic wiped out the local Cree—they're buried on the west side of Deadman's Point. Access to the lake is possible from many directions, but the 736-hectare provincial park is on the lake's north shore. All but Deadman's Point has been affected by fire and is reforested with jack pine and dense forests of aspen and birch. Ground squirrels and coyotes are common and occasionally black bears wander through. The lakeshore is a good place to explore, with trails leading either way from the day-use area to good sandy beaches. Another trail leads to the tip of Deadman's Point and to a bog that is home to many species of birds. Fishing in the lake is best for pike, perch, and walleye. The small campground has 59 sites on two loops, both which have access to the beach; $11.

TRI-TOWN AREA

At the end of Hwy. 28, a little under 300 km northwest of Edmonton, are **Cold Lake, Grand Centre,** and **Medley.** The only one of these you'll want to visit is Cold Lake, located on the south shore of Alberta's seventh-largest lake. This historic town has a large marina and is close to **Cold Lake Provincial Park.** The town marked on most maps as "Medley" is, in fact, only the name of the post office at **Canadian Forces Base Cold Lake**—Canada's largest jet-fighter base whose training range occupies a large tract of wilderness to the north. Over 5,000 military personnel and their families live on the base. Grand Centre, at the entrance to the base, is a service center consisting of a long strip of modern shopping facilities and industrial estates. At the town's main intersection is a CF-104 Starfighter donated by the base in recognition of the ties between the communities.

Generations of Chipewyan Indians hunted and trapped in the area and both major fur-trading companies had established posts on the lake, but it wasn't until after WW II that the population boomed. In 1952 C.F.B. Cold Lake was established. The base continues to expand, but the area's future economic growth is tied to its large deposits of oil sands.

Cold Lake Oil Sands

The heavy oil found northwest of Cold Lake is similar to that of the Athabasca Oil Sands at Fort McMurray, but the extraction process is different. The oil-rich sands lie in a 50-meter-thick band nearly a half km underground, making surface mining impractical. Instead, steam is pumped into the reservoir, thinning out the tar-like bitumen which is then pumped to the surface and piped to Edmonton. This process, known as cyclic-steam simulation, is still in its developmental stages and is very expensive, but many of the major players in the North American oil market have leases around Cold Lake.

Alberta's Seventh-Largest Lake

Cold Lake is part of what was once a much larger lake, a remnant of the last ice age. Today the lake is approximately 22 km wide, 27 km long, has a surface area of 370 square km, and reaches depths of 100 meters. Its surface is frozen for five months of the year and doesn't break up till early May; the tackle shop at the marina has a sheet pinned to the wall showing break-up dates for the last 50 years.

The town of Cold Lake, on the south shore, is the center of most activity on the lake. The marina at the end of the main street rents boats

and fishing tackle; four-meter boats with outboard engines are $10 per hour and $70 per day; tel. (403) 639-3535. Fishing in the lake is best for northern pike, lake trout, and walleye. The best beaches are on the northwestern shore of the lake at **English Bay. Kinosoo Beach,** along Lakeshore Dr., is also popular.

Cold Lake Fish Hatchery is one of five facilities in Alberta that hatches fish eggs for the stocking of lakes throughout the province. It's open for self-guided tours, daily 10 a.m.-3 p.m.; tel. 639-4087. To get there, take Hwy. 55 eight km west of Cold Lake, then Primrose Rd. 15 km north, then head two km east.

Cold Lake Provincial Park

This 399-hectare park is located on a low isthmus of land east of town along 16th Avenue. Although the beaches are much nicer on the northwestern shore of the lake, fishing is excellent here and the park holds many interesting places to explore. A diversity of plant species grows in the park, thanks to its location in a transition zone between boreal forest and aspen parkland. Balsam fir and white spruce dominate the northern end of the peninsula while stands of aspen and birch can be found to the south. The dominant natural feature of the park is **Hall's Lagoon,** on the northwest side of the isthmus. The lagoon is very shallow and thick vegetation lines its banks. This is the best place for viewing birdlife. Over 40 species of mammals also inhabit the area, including muskrats, mink, water shrews, and moose. Within the park are many short hiking trails, most radiating from the campground and day-use area. The campground has showers, a beach, summer interpretive programs, and is open year-round; unserviced sites $13, powered sites $15.

Accommodations

On the shore of Cold Lake, a short stroll from town, is **Harbour House Bed & Breakfast Inn,** one of Alberta's finest B&Bs. Each room is tastefully decorated in a unique theme. The Hearts Afire room is decorated in pastel colors and has a lake view, a fireplace, bath, and a magnificent mahogany canopy bed that you need a stepping stool to get into. Rooms range $50-70 s, $60-80 d; you'll need reservations in summer. The Harbour House is located at 615 Lakeshore Dr., tel. (403) 639-2337.

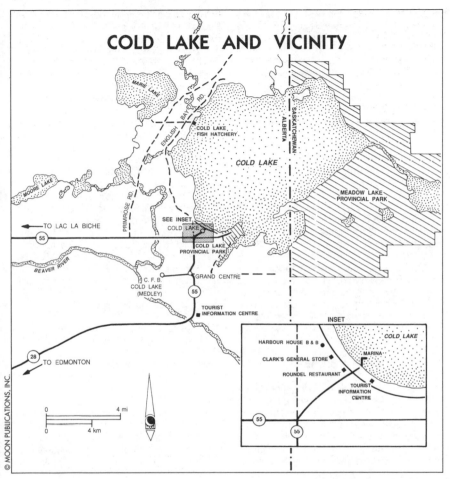

COLD LAKE AND VICINITY

MARIE LAKE

COLD LAKE FISH HATCHERY

COLD LAKE

SASKATCHEWAN-ALBERTA

ENGLISH BAY RD.

MOORE LAKE

MEADOW LAKE PROVINCIAL PARK

PRIMROSE RD.

SEE INSET COLD LAKE

← TO LAC LA BICHE

55

COLD LAKE PROVINCIAL PARK

BEAVER RIVER

C.F.B. COLD LAKE (MEDLEY)

GRAND CENTRE

55

TOURIST INFORMATION CENTRE

28 TO EDMONTON

© MOON PUBLICATIONS, INC.

0   4 mi
0   4 km

INSET

HARBOUR HOUSE B & B

CLARK'S GENERAL STORE

ROUNDEL RESTAURANT

MARINA

COLD LAKE

TOURIST INFORMATION CENTRE

55

55

For a different kind of hospitality stay at **Roundel Hotel,** 902 8th Ave., tel. 639-3261, opposite the marina. If there is no one in the lobby, head past the exotic dancer posters to the bar to check in. Basic rooms are $22 s, $26 d, and it's a couple of bucks extra for a private bathroom. **New Frontier Motel,** 1002 8th Ave., tel. 639-3030, has rooms for $30 s, $36 d.

Along 1st Ave., past Kinosoo Beach, is **Cold Lake Municipal Campground,** tel. 639-4121, a resort-style place where most sites are taken by families who stay the summer; unserviced sites $11, powered sites $13, lakefront sites with power $15. Other options are east at **Cold Lake Provincial Park** and west along Hwy. 55, where numerous gravel roads head north to primitive campgrounds (kitchen shelters, firewood, pit toilets); best of the bunch is at **English Bay** on the northwest shore of Cold Lake.

Food

For a bit of nostalgia head to **Clark's General Store,** a 50s-style diner at 701 Lakeshore Drive. Many of the furnishings are from the original store, built in 1927. Light lunches are served, a cappuccino machine churns out a variety of delicious coffees, and the old-fashioned hard ice cream is a great way to finish lunch; open daily 10 a.m.-10 p.m. **Harbour House B&B Inn,** farther along Lakeshore Dr., has an adjoining teahouse open each afternoon with a changing menu of mouthwatering desserts to accompany tea and coffee.

The only place serving full meals is **Roundel Restaurant,** 902 8th Ave., tel. (403) 639-3261. Breakfast starts at $3, main meals at $6, and a huge bowl of clam chowder is $2.50. It's open daily 6 a.m.-10 p.m.

Services And Information
Greyhound buses depart daily from the Roundel Hotel for the five-hour run to Edmonton. The **post office** is at 913 8th Avenue. The closest **laundromat** is at the Husky gas station in Grand Centre. The **hospital** is at 314 25th St., through town to the west; tel. (403) 639-3322.

As you enter the tri-town area along Hwy. 28 the **Cold Lake/Grand Centre Tourist Information Centre** is signposted at the crest of a hill; open July-Aug., daily 10 a.m.-6 p.m. Cold Lake has its own information center located in an A-frame building on Lakeshore Dr.; open in summer, daily 9 a.m.-8 p.m., tel. 639-2999.

LAC LA BICHE

The historic town of Lac La Biche (population 2,600) is located on the southern flanks of the boreal forest, 225 km northeast of Edmonton. The town itself has little of interest, but nearby you'll find a restored mission, two interesting provincial parks, many excellent fishing lakes, one of northern Alberta's finest golf courses, and a gravel road that may, or may not, get you to Fort McMurray.

The town lies on a divide that separates the Athabasca River system (which drains into the Arctic Ocean) from the Churchill River system (which drains into Hudson Bay). The historic Portage La Biche, across this strip of land, was a vital link in the transcontinental route taken by the early fur traders. Voyageurs would paddle up the Beaver River from the east to Beaver Lake and portage the five kilometers to Lac La Biche, from where passage could be made to the rich fur-trapping regions along the Athabasca River.

In 1798 David Thompson built Red Deer Lake House for the North West Company at the southeast end of the lake. Soon after, Peter Fidler built Greenwich House nearby for the Hudson's Bay Company. By the early 1820s this northern route across the continent was virtually abandoned for a shorter route along the North Saskatchewan River via Edmonton House.

Lac La Biche Mission
The mission was established beside the Hudson's Bay Company post in 1853 and was moved to its present site, 11 km northwest of Lac La Biche, in 1855. It became a base for priests who had missions along the Athabasca, Peace, and Mackenzie rivers and was used as a supply depot for voyageurs still using the northern trade route. The parish expanded, adding a sawmill, gristmill, printing press, and boat-building yard. Today the original buildings still stand, and services take place each Sunday in the church. A free guided tour takes an hour, or you can wander around the buildings yourself. It's open in summer, daily 10 a.m.-6 p.m.; for more information call (403) 623-3274.

Sir Winston Churchill Provincial Park
Located on the largest of nine islands in Lac La Biche, this unique 239-hectare park was linked to the mainland by a 2.5 km causeway in 1968. A road around the island leads through a lush, old-growth coniferous forest. The trees on the island are much larger than those found on the mainland, due to little disturbance from man and no major fires in over 300 years. As they come to the end of their 65-year lifespan, the aspen and poplar that dominate younger boreal forests are replaced by balsam fir. Many fir trees are 150 years old and reach a height of 23 meters. Along the loop road short trails lead to sandy beaches (best on the northeast side of the island), marshes rich with birdlife, and a bird-viewing platform where a mounted telescope lets you watch white pelicans and double-crested cormorants resting on a gravel bar. A campground is located on the south side of the island; $13.

Lakeland Provincial Park
Encompassing 60,000 hectares of boreal forest that, for the most part, remains in its natural

state, this park and an adjacent recreation area are a wildlife-watcher's paradise. Deer, moose, beavers, red foxes, lynx, coyotes, small numbers of wolves and black bears, and over 200 species of birds can be spotted in the area. A colony of great blue herons, Alberta's largest wading birds, lives at **Pinehurst Lake,** 27 km off Hwy. 55. Fishing in the lakes is excellent for northern pike and walleye. Those with their own canoes can get out on the water for a real wilderness experience.

Campgrounds are located at **Pinehurst, Ironwood, Seibert,** and **Touchwood lakes.** Each has pit toilets, kitchen shelter, and firewood; $5.50 per night, except Touchwood Lakes, $7.50. Several routes access the two area; head either east from Lac La Biche or north from Hwy. 55.

Practicalities

Lac La Biche Inn, 101st Ave., tel. (403) 623-4427, has a restaurant and a nightclub where the disc jockey sits in a big rig; $45 s, $51 d; The closest campgrounds are east and north of town in the two provincial parks (see above). **Spruce Point Resort,** tel. 623-3330, is a full-service RV park on Beaver Lake, three km east and nine km south of town. One block west of the Almac Motor Hotel is a small **tourist information center.** It's open in summer, daily 10 a.m.-6 p.m.; tel. 623-4804.

FORT MCMURRAY AND VICINITY

This city of 36,000, 450 km north of Edmonton, has grown around the **Athabasca Oil Sands,** the largest deposit of oil in the world—more than all the proven reserves of Saudi Arabia, the United States, and Western Europe combined. The oil is not conventional oil but a heavy oil, commonly called bitumen. To extract it is expensive, and once on the surface it must be chemically altered to produce a lighter, more useful oil. This process, in stark contrast to other operations where the oil is simply brought to the surface and shipped or piped around the world, requires an enormous amount of machinery and manpower.

Fort McMurray is a long drive from anywhere else and has little of interest except for the mining operation, but it is surrounded by a wilderness that would be difficult to access without the services of the city.

To Fort McMurray

For many years the only way to get to Fort McMurray was by airplane or the Muskeg Express, a rail service to Edmonton. Today a paved highway (Hwy. 63), as good as any in the province, has replaced the rail line. It parallels, but never crosses, the **Athabasca River,** which cuts deeply into the boreal forest covering the entire northern half of the province. From its southern terminus (at the junction of Hwy. 55, between Lac La Biche and Athabasca) to Fort McMurray, only two small communities hug the highway. The first is **Wandering River,** a small lumber and service town with gas, a motel, and a 24-hour restaurant. The Alberta Forest Service maintains campgrounds 13, 58, and 76 km north of Wandering River. Each has a water source, pit toilets, kitchen shelter, and firewood; $5.50 a night. Along the route are many roadside fens and areas ravished by fire, where the cycle of natural reforestation has just begun.

Mariana Lake, a little over halfway to Fort McMurray, has the same services as Wandering River. Just south of town is **Mariana Lake Recreation Area,** which, although beside the highway, has a good campground; also $5.50 per night.

History

Natives and early explorers first reported oil oozing from the sand here, but it took a long time for anyone to gain commercial success from extracting it. Fort McMurray started out as a trading post along the Athabasca River, and for the first half of this century, the town experienced little growth. But in 1964, the first oilsands plant was built, and 10 years later a second company began operation. Between 1974 and 1994, the population mushroomed from 1,500 to 36,000 as personnel from around the world came to work at the plants, attracted by high wages. At first the population was young and transient; they made their money then left. But today the city has an air of permanence about it. As new subdivisions are carved into the boreal forest, suburbs of respectable three-bedroom homes are springing up, and downtown looks similar to hundreds of midsize cities across Canada.

Athabasca Oil Sands

Only 800 billion barrels of conventional crude oil are known to remain on this planet. But trapped in the Athabasca Oil Sands surrounding Fort McMurray are one trillion barrels of bitumen. As conventional crude-oil reserves are depleted the sands will become essential to the world's future energy needs. At current production rates (187,000 barrels a day or 15% of Canada's petroleum needs) it will take 500 years to extract just three percent of the deposit.

As the name implies, the deposits are of highly compacted sand containing heavy oil or bitumen. The oil-rich sand is found both close to the surface—beneath a layer of clay and silt—and deeper down, requiring a more expensive extraction technique. Rather than drilling for oil, the sands are mined. Once on the surface, hot water and steam are used to separate the sand from the bitumen, which is then diluted with naphtha to make it flow more easily. The bitumen is heated to 500° C, producing vapors that, when cooled, condense at three levels. While the sulphur and the gases produced during the process are all drawn off and put to use, it is the liquid products that are the most precious. By blending them and increasing the hydrogen content of the mix to make it "lighter," a high-quality synthetic crude oil is produced. This is piped to Edmonton and distributed around North America for use in cars, airplanes, and derivative products such as plastics.

Two companies are involved in the mining of the oil sands. **Suncor Inc.,** the smaller of the two, began production in 1967 after taking over the company that had initiated mining in the area three years earlier. The Suncor operation became the world's first commercially successful oil-sands plant. **Syncrude Canada Ltd.,** the world's largest producer of synthetic crude oil, was established in 1978. Both operations are located north of Fort McMurray. The size of machinery used to scrape off the surface layer of muskeg and excavate the oil sands below it is mind-boggling. Syncrude's walking draglines are the largest land-based machinery in the

world. Each moves slowly, dropping buckets as large as a two-car garage into the ground and dragging them back on a boom the length of a football field. The process continues around the clock with a constant stream of 170-ton heavy haulers taking the overburden to reclamation sites and the oil sands to conveyor belts bound for the processing plants.

SIGHTS

Oil Sands Interpretive Centre

For an insight into the history, geology, and technology of the Athabasca Oil Sands mining process, head to this large interpretive center at the south end of the city (on the corner of Hwy. 63 and Mackenzie Blvd.). Start your visit by watching *Quest for Energy,* a multimedia, big-screen presentation about the industry that has grown around the resource. The center houses an interesting collection of machinery and has interactive displays, hands-on exhibits, and interpretive presentations. Outside is the Industrial Equipment Garden where an older-style bucket-wheel excavator and other machinery is displayed. To move the excavator to this site it had to be disassembled, with some sections requiring a 144-wheel 45-meter-long trailer for the 45-km trip from the mine. The center is open in summer, daily 10 a.m.-6 p.m.; the rest of the year, daily 10 a.m.-4 p.m. Admission is $2.25. For information call (403) 743-7167.

Syncrude/Suncor Plant Tours

Touring the oil-sands plants is the best way to experience the operation firsthand. Syncrude is the larger, more imposing operation of the two, but imposes more rules and keeps you farther from the action; tours depart July-Aug., Wed.-Sun. at 9 a.m. The Suncor tour gives you a better feel for the sheer size of the equipment; tours depart mid-June to August, Sat.-Tues. at 9 a.m. Both tours are operated by the Fort McMurray Visitors Bureau and depart from the Oil Sands Interpretive Centre. Tour cost is $8.50; reservations are essential and can be made at the visitors bureau or by calling (403) 791-4336.

To Fort McKay

Fort McKay is a small native settlement on the

TO FORT McKAY

THICKWOOD BLVD.

FORT McMURRAY
GOLF CLUB

ATHABASCA RIVER

FORT McMURRAY

MISKANAW
GOLF COURSE
MACDONALD ISLAND

CLEARWATER RIVER

MAIN ST.

SEE INSET

FRANKLIN AVE.

PARK PLAZA MALL

ABASAND DR.

HOSPITAL

HOSPITAL ST.

CENTENNIAL DR.

TOLEN DR.

RED ARROW

GREYHOUND BUS DEPOT

HERITAGE PARK

KEYANO
COLLEGE

INSET

FABLED TABLE BUFFET

MORRISON ST.

FRAZER AVE.

MacDONALD AVE.

FRANKLIN AVE.

MAIN ST.

MANNING AVE.

OIL CAN
TAVERN

TWIN PINE
MOTOR INN

NOMAD
MOTOR INN

CEDAR
STEAK
HOUSE

BIGGS AVE.

LIBRARY

GARDEN
CAFE

POST OFFICE

HARDIN ST.

PETER POND
SHOPPING
CENTRE

PETER POND INN

BEACON HILL DR.

63

CENTENNIAL PARK

MACKENZIE PARK INN

RUSTY'S MOTOR INN

GREGOIRE DR.

ALBERTA FORESTRY
RANGER STATION

VISITORS BUREAU

SAWRIDGE HOTEL

OIL SANDS
INTERPRETIVE CENTRE

MACKENZIE BLVD.

0   0.5 mi

0   0.5 km

TO AIRPORT AND ROTARY PARK CAMPGROUND

TO GREGOIRE LAKE P. P. AND EDMONTON

63   69

west bank of the **Athabasca River.** The town itself has little of interest (and no services) but the drive out to the end of Hwy. 63 is pleasant and gives you a chance to view the mining operations, albeit at a distance. The **Oil Sands Viewpoint** is 40 km from Fort McMurray and looks out over tailing ponds and reclaimed land from the Suncor operation. The road north of the viewpoint has been rerouted so that Syncrude can continue work at what is known as East Mine. In the next stage of mining, the road will again be rerouted along a causeway over **Mildred Lake,** Canada's largest man-made reservoir.

A farther five km north and the road forks. To the left is **Fort McKay** and to the right Hwy. 63 crosses the Athabasca River and continues 10 km to a dock. Here, supplies such as petroleum and building materials are loaded onto barges and transported downstream (north) to the communities of Fort Chipewyan, Uranium City, and Fond-du-lac on Lake Athabasca.

This is the end of the summer road. Between December and March a winter road is built over the frozen muskeg and river 225 km to Fort Chipewyan and up the Slave River to Fort Smith in the Northwest Territories.

Heritage Park

This village, 1 Tolen Dr., tel. (403) 791-7575, is made up of historic buildings housing artifacts that reflect the importance of fishing, trapping, and transportation to the city. Other displays include boats used on the river, a Northern Alberta Railway passenger car, and an early log mission. The park is open in summer, Mon.-Fri. 10 a.m.-5 p.m., Sat.-Sun. 1-5 p.m. Admission is by donation.

Gregoire Lake Provincial Park

Southeast of the city 34 km is **Gregoire Lake,** the only accessible lake in the Fort McMurray area. The 690-hectare park on the lake's west shore is a typical boreal forest of mixed woods and black-spruce bogs. Many species of waterfowl nest on the lake and mammals such as moose and black bears are relatively common. Some short hiking trails wind through the park and canoes are rented in the day-use area.

Farther around the lake is the small community of **Anzac;** many people camp free on the beach here.

RECREATION AND EVENTS

Hiking

An extensive network of trails links downtown to all parts of the city, the Athabasca River, small parks, and picnic areas; ask for a map at the visitors bureau.

A self-guided interpretive trail demonstrating forestry management practices begins at the Alberta Forestry Ranger Station across the highway from the Fort McMurray Visitors Bureau.

In summer, each Sunday at 1 p.m., members of the **Field Naturalists Society** lead a walk through the nearby wilderness, pointing out the flora and fauna of the area. The walk starts from Heritage Park and ends with a slide show.

Wilderness Tours

Majic Country Wilderness Adventures offers a variety of tours from Fort McMurray. The most popular are their jet boat tours to a wilderness camp along the river for fishing or birdwatching. Three-night packages, including accommodations, transportation, and meals, start at $350 per person. Other options include overnight horseback trips, fishing and sightseeing charters on the Athabasca River, and floats by canoe down the Clearwater River. For details write to Chuck Graves, P.O. Box 5242, Fort McMurray, Alberta T9H 3G3; tel. (403) 743-0766.

Other Recreation

Over 60 sports, ranging from scuba diving to skydiving, are organized locally. The city's original golf course, **Miskanaw,** is located on MacDonald Island, north of downtown. It's a challenging 18-hole course with plenty of hazards. Green fees are $25; tel. (403) 790-1812. **Fort McMurray Golf Club,** located on the north side of the Athabasca River off Thickwood Blvd., is a new course carved out of the forest. Green fees are $24; tel. 743-5577.

MacDonald Island Recreation Complex, tel. 791-0070, north of downtown, has a modern exercise room, tennis courts, squash courts, and a swimming pool; it's open daily 8 a.m.-11 p.m.

Wintertime

Spruce Valley Ski Hill, tel. (403) 791-0796, is located along Hwy. 69, six km beyond the airport turnoff. It has two small lifts and five runs; lift tickets are $22.

Entertainment And Events

Fort McMurray has over 20 bars and lounges. The legendary **Oil Can Tavern**, 10007 Franklin Ave., tel. (403) 791-1300, occasionally presents live entertainment but is best known as a hard-drinking pub. At **Bronco Billy's**, in the Mackenzie Park Inn, 424 Gregoire Dr., tel. 791-4770, a DJ plays country tunes Tues.-Saturday. Another popular hangout is the **Longhorn Saloon**, 8124 Franklin Ave., tel. 743-2711. **Keyano Theatre** puts on a season of live performances Sept.-March, with top country and pop acts appearing throughout the year. It's located in Keyano College at 8115 Franklin Ave.; tel. 791-4990.

Canada Day is celebrated on MacDonald Island with multicultural performers and ethnic foods. At **Heritage Park** on the second Sunday of each month you'll find a barbecue and displays of pioneer arts and crafts. A **Beerfest** takes place on MacDonald Island on the last Saturday in July; many out-of-town musicians perform in an outdoor concert.

ACCOMMODATIONS AND FOOD

Hotels And Motels

Peter Pond Inn, 9713 Hardin St., tel. (403) 743-3301, has small, basic rooms but is right downtown; $40 s, $45 d. **Twin Pine Motor Inn**, 10024 Biggs Ave., tel. 743-3391, is also downtown and many rooms have a fridge; $44 s or d. **Nomad Motor Inn**, 10006 MacDonald Ave., tel. 791-4770, has well-kept rooms and a restaurant and lively bar; $56 s or d.

Sawridge Hotel, 530 Mackenzie Blvd., tel. 791-7900, is geared for business travelers but usually has rooms on the weekend; $64 s or d. **Mackenzie Park Inn**, 424 Gregoire Dr., tel. 791-7200 or (800) 582-3273, is the pick of the bunch but is four km south of downtown. It features a good restaurant, lounge, and indoor swimming pool; $64 s or d. **Rusty's Motor Inn**, 385 Gregoire Dr., tel. 791-4646, is across the road from the Mackenzie Park Inn; $45 s or d.

Campgrounds

Two campgrounds are located south of the city limits. **Rotary Park Campground**, tel. (403) 790-1581, 11 km south, offers showers and cooking facilities and is open year-round; unserviced sites $8, powered sites $12. The park is signposted, but easy to miss; turn east along Hwy. 69 and look for the entrance to the left. **Fort McMurray Centennial Park**, 9909 Franklin Ave., tel. 743-7925, doesn't have showers or hookups but is along Hwy. 63, closer to the city. Sites are $7.

Food

Peter Pond Shopping Centre has a fast-food court, while **Grandma Lee's Bakery** slaps up a daily breakfast special of bacon, eggs, hash browns, and toast for $3.75. The **Mapletrees Pancake House**, in the Mackenzie Park Inn, 424 Gregoire Dr., tel. (403) 791-7200, serves well-prepared dishes at reasonable prices and offers the best Sunday brunch buffet in town ($8). Daily dinner specials, which include soup or salad, run around $8; open daily 6 a.m.-11 p.m. For a variety of steaks try **Cedar Steak House**, 10020 Biggs Ave., tel. 743-1717, where entrees start at $10. The **Garden Cafe**, 9924 Biggs Ave., tel. 791-6665, is bright, full of greenery, and always busy; it's open 24 hours. **Fabled Table Buffet**, 10202 MacDonald Ave., tel. 790-9333, lays out a buffet spread for lunch ($6.50) and dinner ($9.50).

TRANSPORTATION

Getting There

Although the road out of Fort McMurray is excellent and always seems to be busy, many people prefer to fly. The **airport** is located nine km south then six km east of downtown. **Canadian Regional**, tel. (403) 743-4188 or (800) 665-1177, and **Air B.C.**, tel. 790-1373 or (800) 222-6596, fly daily to Edmonton; $119 one way, $211 round trip if purchased 14 days in advance. A cab from the airport to downtown runs around $15.

Greyhound has services three times daily to Edmonton ($39.86). The depot is located at 8220 Manning Ave., tel. 791-3664. **Red Arrow**, 10002 Queen St., tel. 791-2990 or (800) 232-1958, offers a more luxurious service than Greyhound, with fewer stops, more legroom, and free coffee and snacks ($39 one way). Either way, it's a five hour trip to Edmonton.

Getting Around

Diversified Transportation, 460 MacAlpine Crescent, tel. (403) 743-9100, operates a transit service around town and to outlying suburbs; $1.10 per sector. From downtown, a cab will run $7 to the Oil Sands Interpretive Centre and $15 to the airport. Taxi companies include: **Class Cabs,** tel. 743-9100; **Sun Taxi,** tel. 743-5050; and **United Thickwood Cabs,** tel. 743-1234. The following car rentals are available in town and all have airport counters: **Avis,** tel. 743-4773; **Budget,** tel. 743-8215; **Hertz,** tel. 743-4047; and **Tilden,** tel. 743-6393.

SERVICES AND INFORMATION

The **post office** is at 9702 Hardin Street. **D Laundromat** is in the Park Plaza Mall on Franklin Ave.; open daily 8 a.m.-10:30 p.m. **Fort McMurray Public Library** is housed in a large, rust-colored building at 9907 Franklin Ave., tel. (403) 743-7800; closed Monday. **Fort McMurray Regional Hospital** is at 7 Hospital St., tel. 791-6161. For the **RCMP** call 799-8888.

   Fort McMurray Visitors Bureau is located south of downtown, just north of the Oil Sands Interpretive Centre, tel. 791-4336. It's open May-Aug., Mon.-Fri. 9 a.m.-7 p.m., Sat.-Sun. 10 a.m.-7 p.m.; the rest of the year, Mon.-Fri. 9 a.m.-5 p.m.

FORT CHIPEWYAN

When the Hudson's Bay Company established a post on the west shore of Lake Athabasca in 1788, what is now Alberta was a wild land with no white settlers. Today Fort Chipewyan, on the site of the original trading post, holds the title of Alberta's most remote community. In summer, the only access is by river or air. After freeze-up, a winter road connects the community to the outside world. For fur traders, Fort Chip, as it's best known, was the ideal location for a post. The confluence of the Athabasca and Peace rivers was nearby and to the north were the Slave and Mackenzie rivers. It became a way station for some of Canada's great explorers—Alexander Mackenzie, David Thompson, Simon Fraser, and Sir John Franklin—who rested and replenished supplies at the post.

Things To See And Do

Perched on a south-facing slope overlooking the lake, the town itself is not particularly inspiring but is a good base for trips into nearby **Wood Buffalo National Park** and fishing on the lake and nearby rivers. In town, on Mackenzie Ave., is **Bicentennial Museum,** tel. (403) 697-3011, modeled on the original fur-trading post. The second floor is dedicated to the fur trade, while the lower floor catalogues the native history of the region, the RCMP, and local industries. Open year-round, Mon.-Fri. 9 a.m.-5:30 p.m., Sat.-Sun. 1-5 p.m.

Originally, fur-trading posts were heavily fortified, hence the name "fort." Later, the fortifications weren't necessary, but the name stuck. Today the names of many northern towns reflect this early heritage.

PROVINCIAL ARCHIVES OF ALBERTA

Athabasca Interpretive Tours, P.O. Box 178, Fort Chipewyan, Alberta T0P 1B0, tel. 697-3604, operates a lodge a short boat ride from Fort Chip on Jackfish Lake. The emphasis is on the traditional lifestyle of the local Dene people; activities include wilderness trips, fishing, wildlife viewing, and native cooking. Rates are $160 per person per day or $1570 for a seven-day package departing from Fort McMurray.

Practicalities

The only accommodation in town is **Fort**

Chipewyan Adventure Lodge, P.O. Box 347, Fort Chipewyan, Alberta T0P 1B0, tel. (403) 697-3679. The lodge has 10 rooms and a spectacular view over the lake. Rates are $85 s, $95 d, but many package deals, including meals and tours into the delta, are offered. The closest camping is 17 km northeast of town at **Dore Lake.**

Contact Air, tel. 697-3753, departs twice daily from Fort McMurray for Fort Chipewyan. The 50-minute flight is $125 one way, $225 round trip.

NORTHERN HEARTLAND

Alberta's Northern Heartland is a varied region that extends north out of Edmonton's suburbs through rich agricultural land and into the wilderness of the boreal forest. The **Athabasca River** flows southwest to northeast through the region. It is linked to Edmonton by Hwy. 2, which follows the historic **Athabasca Landing Trail**— a supply route used by early explorers and traders for travel between the North Saskatchewan and Athabasca river systems. From **Athabasca,** Hwy. 2 heads northwest to the city of **Slave Lake,** on the southeast shore of **Lesser Slave Lake.** From there it continues along the lake's southern shore to **High Prairie** and into the Peace River Valley. Other major roads in the region include: Hwy. 18, which runs east-west through the southern portion of the region and through the farming and oil towns of **Westlock** and **Barrhead;** Hwy. 33, which climbs into the **Swan Hills,** home to a subspecies of the now-extinct plains grizzly bear; and Hwy. 43, the main thoroughfare northwest from Edmonton to Grande Prairie. Adventurous souls driving to the Northwest Territories will want to travel the **Bicentennial Highway** (Hwy. 88) at least one way. This gravel road opens up a remote part of the province otherwise accessible only by floatplane.

EDMONTON TO ATHABASCA

From downtown Edmonton, Hwy. 2 (called the "St. Albert Trail" in the vicinity of Edmonton) heads north into a once-forested land, now

heavily developed as farm and ranch country. The first town north of the city limits is **Morinville,** a farming community founded by French and German settlers over 100 years ago. **St. Jean Baptiste Church,** built by the town's founders, is an imposing structure that has been declared a Provincial Historical Site. **Heritage Lake,** at the junction of Highways 2 and 642, is a popular recreation and camping area.

Athabasca Landing Trail

The Athabasca Landing Trail was a historic trade route plied first by indigenous people and later used by the Hudson's Bay Company to carry goods between Fort Saskatchewan and Athabasca. Bits and pieces of the original trail can still be seen today, interspersed among the small towns and hamlets east of Hwy. 2. Travelers wandering through this area will find a variety of other sights in addition to the old trail.

At one time the trail passed through **Gibbons,** a small town of 2,800 on the banks of the Sturgeon River. Sites of interest here include **Gibbons Anglican Church,** whose unique interior is shaped like a ship, and **Sturgeon River Historical Museum,** located in Oliver Park, which features a two-story log house. The museum is open in summer, daily noon-8 p.m. Golfers will want to head to **Goose Hummock Golf Course,** four km north of town, one of Alberta's better courses. Green fees are $20-25; tel. (403) 921-2444.

Old St. Mary's Ukrainian Catholic Church is 1.5 km west of the hamlet of **Waugh.** It was the first church of its denomination to be built

NORTHERN HEARTLAND

TO NORTHWEST TERRITORIES

TO FORT VERMILION

MANNING

PEERLESS LAKE

88

RED EARTH CREEK

TROUT LAKE

PEACE RIVER

WABASCA-DESMARAIS

FALHER

McLENNAN

UTIKUMA LAKE

PELICAN MOUNTAINS

49

DONNELLY

WINIGAMI LAKE P.P.

GROUARD MISSION

HILLIARD'S BAY P.P.

88

LESSER SLAVE LAKE P.P.

TO DAWSON CREEK, B.C.

HIGH PRAIRIE

LESSER SLAVE LAKE

CALLING LAKE

KINUSO

CALLING LAKE P.P.

WILLIAMSON P.P.

34

VALLEYVIEW

SLAVE LAKE

HONDO

2

43

SWAN HILLS

TO GRANDE PRAIRIE

33

TO LAC LA BICHE

LITTLE SMOKY

44

CROSS LAKE P.P.

55

SWAN HILLS

ATHABASCA

FAWCETT

2

FOX CREEK

33

FERRY

ROCHESTER

43

32

FORT ASSINIBOINE

NEERLANDIA

TAWATINAW

CARSON-PEGASUS P.P.

WHITECOURT

THUNDER LAKE P.P.

BARRHEAD

WESTLOCK

18

ATHABASCA

18

WAUGH

32

43

33

GIBBONS

EDSON

McLEOD

MORINVILLE

FORT SASKATCHEWAN

16

37

21

16

TO JASPER N.P.

EDMONTON

TO LLOYDMINSTER

SASKATCHEWAN RIVER

N.

2

21

0   30 mi

0   30 km

© MOON PUBLICATIONS, INC.

north of Edmonton, and is located adjacent to the original trail. The trail disappears north of Hwy. 18 but historic markers and buildings are accessible by following gravel roads east through **Tawatinaw** and **Rochester** (look for historic markers and log buildings on the roadside approaching the crest of the first ridge east of these towns).

ATHABASCA AND VICINITY

Located on the banks of the Athabasca River, 147 km north of Edmonton, this town of 2,000 was probably the most famous of the many communities that formed vital links to the north. The town is on a gently sloping hill on the river's south bank with the steep-sided Muskeg Creek Valley on one side and the Tawatinaw River on the other. Many historic buildings still stand in town and the surrounding area is pristine wilderness, excellent for fishing, boating, and camping.

History
Athabasca Landing was founded by the Hudson's Bay Company in 1874 on the southernmost bend of the Athabasca River. Goods from the east were shipped to Fort Saskatchewan and transported north along the Athabasca Landing Trail from where they were distributed throughout northern Canada. A thriving boat-building business began at the landing. Once the paddlewheelers and scows reached their destination along the river system many were broken up and used for housing, others were loaded with furs for the return journey. Passengers who boarded the paddlewheelers from the landing were from all walks of life—traders, trappers, land speculators, settlers, North West Mounted Police, geologists, missionaries, and anyone looking for a new life and adventure in Canada's great northern wilderness. Robert Service, the renowned poet, lived at Athabasca Landing for a time; much of his early work was about trappers and people of the Athabasca River.

Sights
Although the Hudson's Bay Company buildings have long since disappeared, many later buildings from the days of the paddlewheelers remain. On the riverfront is the railway station, built in 1912. Next to it is a 1915 steam engine. The Union Hotel, overlooking the river, was built in 1913. Behind it, up the hill on 48th St., is an old brick schoolhouse. Next door is the library that houses the Athabasca Archives, a comprehensive collection of photographs and newspapers.

Muskeg Creek Park, on the west side of town, offers hiking trails and good fishing during spring. The creek flows through a heavily forested ravine into a floodplain, then drains into the Athabasca River. Wildlife abounds, berry picking is good in late summer, and cross-country skiing trails are laid in winter. Access to the park is from the elementary school on 48th Avenue.

PROVINCIAL ARCHIVES OF ALBERTA

Athabasca Landing in 1898

Athabasca University has a 12,000-square-meter facility on a 180-hectare site, with a staff of over 500, a library with 100,000 books, and an annual budget exceeding $22 million—but no on-campus students. It's one of the largest correspondence universities in North America, open to students regardless of their geographical location or previous academic levels. The 12,000 enrolled students work from home, communicating with their tutors through the post and by phone. The campus is open to the public and has some unique artworks commissioned especially for the building. For more information call (403) 675-6111.

Accommodations And Food

A number of motels are located on Hwy. 2, south of town. Try **Athabasca Hillside Motel,** tel. (403) 675-5111, with good views of the river and kitchenettes in each room; $42 s, $46 d. **Our Log Cabin,** tel. 675-3381, a bed and breakfast 12 km south of town, has a pleasant outdoor area in quiet surroundings; from $45 s, $55 d. **River's**

Edge Campground, on 50th Ave. where the Tawatinaw River drains into the Athabasca, is the site of the original landing; sites are $7.

Green Spot, 4820 51st St., tel. 675-3040, serves breakfast for under $5 and sandwiches, hamburgers, and a variety of other dishes the rest of the day. **Giorgio's,** 4910 49th St., tel. 675-5418, is a pizza, pasta, and steak place; the pizza is especially well priced. **Le Bar** is a tiny drinking hole upstairs at 4915 49th St., tel. 675-5650, with a relaxed atmosphere and a small food menu.

Services And Information

Greyhound, tel. (403) 675-2294, stops three times daily at the Athabasca Inn on its run between Edmonton and Fort McMurray. The **tourist information center** is beside the railway station on 50th Ave., tel. 675-2055; it's open in summer, daily 10 a.m.-6 p.m.

Calling Lake Provincial Park

Lying along the south shore of one of Alberta's

larger lakes, this 741-hectare park is on Hwy. 813, 55 km north of Athabasca. A boreal forest of aspen surrounds the lake, giving way to a marshy area nearer the shore. Look for deer, moose, and black bears, as well as the occasional white pelican and blue heron. Fishing for northern pike, walleye, perch, and whitefish is the park's main attraction, although swimming and canoeing on the lake is also possible. Camping is $10.75.

From the park, Hwy. 813 follows the east shore of Calling Lake to a hamlet of the same name. The road turns to gravel and continues 130 km north to **Wabasca-Desmarais**, a native settlement between South and North Wabasca lakes, then loops back and follows the Willow River for much of the way to Lesser Slave Lake. This is a remote region of Alberta, services are few and far between. But wildlife is abundant and fishing is excellent in the many roadside lakes and rivers.

Amber Valley

This small hamlet just east of Athabasca was first settled in 1910 by 200 blacks from Oklahoma. They moved from their homeland to escape racial persecution, led north by 22-year-old Jefferson Davis Edwards. The prejudice continued in Alberta with locals suggesting they should head south because the climate wouldn't suit them. Despite the hard times, the community thrived and remained virtually all black. Since WW II the population has declined and today only a few black families remain.

ATHABASCA TO SLAVE LAKE

From Athabasca, Hwy. 2 heads northwest to Slave Lake, passing many summer communities along the shores of **Baptiste** and **Island lakes.** This section of the highway is known as the **Northern Woods and Water Route.** Just before **Hondo,** the route intersects **Hwy. 44,** which heads south 106 km to Westlock and Hwy. 18 (see "Highway 18 West," below). At Hondo, 72 km from Athabasca, Hwy. 2A leads to **Fawcett Lake,** known for its good walleye fishing. At the lake are two campgrounds, cabins, and boat rentals.

SLAVE LAKE

The town of Slave Lake (population 5,600) is located on the southeastern shore of **Lesser Slave Lake,** 250 km northwest of Edmonton. It began as an important staging point for steamboat freight and passengers heading for the Peace River Country and Yukon goldfields. The arrival of a rail line in 1914 meant a boom time for the fledgling community and the beginning of a lumber industry that continues today. In 1935 disastrous floods destroyed many of the buildings on the main street. Following that debacle, the town was relocated, 3.5 km to the south. Only a few foundations remain of the original settlement. Today the town has little to interest the visitor, but Lesser Slave Lake has some of the best fishing in the province with northern pike to 10 kilograms, walleye to five kilograms, whitefish to 2.5 kilograms, and perch to one kilogram—enough to make any self-respecting fisherman quit his job, pack the rod and reel, and head north.

But Isn't Slave Lake In The Arctic?

Well, no, but an explanation is in order. Lesser Slave Lake is one of *two* Slave lakes in northwestern Canada. Both lakes are at the same longitude, but they're about 600 km apart as the crow flies. The bigger one—the one that many people *think* is in the Arctic—is north of Alberta in the Northwest Territories (but still south of the Arctic Circle). The smaller, more southerly of the two is here in northern Alberta. Both are named after the Slavey Indians who traveled south up the Athabasca River from the big Slave Lake to the smaller Slave Lake on hunting and fishing expeditions. In early writings, and on maps, both lakes were denoted as Slave Lake. This led to confusion, especially since both were in what was then the Northwest Territories. To remedy the problem, the larger, northern body of water was renamed Great Slave Lake, and its Albertan counterpart, Lesser Slave Lake. Lesser Slave Lake is the third largest in Alberta (only Athabasca and Claire are larger) and the largest accessible by road. It is 90 km long, 20 km wide, has an area of 1,150 square km, and is relatively shallow.

Fishing in northern lakes is nearly always productive.

ALBERTA TOURISM

And Why Are So Many Things Named "Sawridge"?

The original settlement on Lesser Slave Lake was named Sawridge, for the jagged range of hills to the north. Many prominent residents didn't like the name; in 1922 they changed it to Slave Lake. But the original name lives on. Today it's the name of the local Indian band and a creek flowing through town. And many local businesses use the name as well.

Lesser Slave Lake Provincial Park

At this 7,290-hectare park north of town you'll find a campground (see "Accommodations," below), long sandy beaches, unique sand dunes, and wetland and boreal forest habitats supporting diverse wildlife. Offshore is **Dog Island,** the lake's only island, home to a pair of bald eagles, pelicans, and other shorebirds. North of the Lesser Slave River are many access roads leading to **Devonshire Beach,** a seven-km stretch of sandy beach popular for sunbaking and swimming. The sunsets from this beach are spectacular. The **North Shore,** to the north of Devonshire Beach, has a picnic area and provides access to the 23-km **Freighter Lakeshore Trail,** which runs the entire length of the park. North Shore beaches are nonexistent, but a gravel road heading back toward Devonshire leads to a quiet one. **Gilwood Golf Club,** tel. (403) 849-4389, with a challenging nine-hole course, is also on the North Shore. Green fees are $13 per round. At the north end of the park a steep eight-km road leads through a dense forest of lodgepole pine to the plateaulike summit of 1,030-meter Marten Mountain. The views are spectacular from this vantage point 500 meters above the lake. A three-km trail from the summit winds through an old-growth forest of balsam fir that has escaped major fires. The trail ends up at **Lily Lake,** a small, secluded lake from where Lily Creek flows into Lesser Slave Lake.

Fishing

Although fishing from the lake's edge and in nearby rivers can be productive, the big ones are hooked out on the lake. Sawridge Recreation Area, on Caribou Trail, rents small motorboats for $20 per hour, $50 half day, or $100 full day. **Oglow Tours,** tel. (403) 849-4045, takes guided fishing and sightseeing tours onto the lake; call for rates.

Slave Air, tel. 849-5353, based at the airport in town, will fly you to their favorite fishing lakes. Orloff Lake is a half-hour to the east and has a campsite ($183 for up to five people), and Gods Lake is one hour north ($394). If the pilot knows that the fishing is good he won't charge you ground time.

Accommodations

Highway Motor Inn, on Hwy. 2 by the tourist information center, 600 14th Ave. SW, tel. (403) 849-2400, has basic rooms for $42.50 s, $47.50 d. **Sawridge Hotel** 200 Main St. S, tel. 849-4101 or (800) 661-6657, has rooms in an older section ($50 s, $55 d) and larger ones in a new wing ($57 s, $62 d). Just down Main St. is

Northwest Inn, 801 Main St., tel. 849-3300, which offers an exercise room and indoor pool; rates are $57 s, $67 d.

Lesser Slave Lake Provincial Park's **Marten River Campground** (at the extreme northern end of the park) has showers, a beach, and a summer interpretive program; unserviced sites $11, powered sites $13. Immediately north, outside the park boundary, is **Diamond Willow Resort,** tel. 849-2292, a private campground with coin showers, a grocery store, pitch-and-putt golf course, and nature trail; unserviced sites $12, powered sites $15. **Sawridge Recreation Area,** in town, is used mainly by noisy families who stay the entire summer.

Food

The **Sunrise Cafe** in the Sawridge Hotel, tel. (403) 849-4101, serves a good lunch buffet with a wide selection of dishes; $7. Also in the hotel is **Sweet Grass Cafe,** tel. 849-4101, a casual dining room with bright decor and a great atmosphere. Expect to pay $5-7 for lunch and a few dollars more for the pasta, ribs, steak, and chicken on the dinner menu. The **Sawridge Truckstop** on the corner of Hwy. 88 and Caribou Trail NE, tel. 849-4030, is just that—a truckstop with vinyl seats, hearty meals, inexpensive prices, and waitresses as busy as Beirut bricklayers. It's open 24 hours.

© MOON PUBLICATIONS, INC.

Services And Information
The **Greyhound Bus Depot,** tel. (403) 849-4003, is in the Sawridge Truckstop on Hwy. 88 at the east end of town. The **post office** is on 2nd St. Northeast. **Allarie Laundromat,** at 116 3rd Ave. NE, is open 8:30 a.m.-10 p.m.

The **tourist information center** is located on Hwy. 2, just west of Main Street. It's open May-Sept., daily 9 a.m.-8 p.m.; tel. 849-4611 or (800) 661-2594.

Bicentennial Highway
This 430-km road (also known as Hwy. 88) connects Slave Lake with Fort Vermilion to the north and is an excellent alternative to the Mackenzie Hwy. for those traveling in that direction. It was renamed and renumbered to commemorate the bicentenary of Fort Vermilion in 1988. Services (gas, rooms, and restaurant) are available at the only community along the road, **Red Earth Creek**—a semipermanent oil-fields town 130 km north of Slave Lake. From here, Hwy. 686 heads east to **Peerless** and **Trout lakes,** named for the excellent fishing, and west to the town of Peace River.

At Red Earth Creek, the Bicentennial Hwy. turns to gravel and parallels the Loon and Wabasca rivers, following the eastern flanks of the **Buffalo Head Hills.** Seventy km from Fort Vermilion a turnoff to the west leads to **Wadlin Lake,** home to one of Alberta's few colonies of white pelicans. They nest on an island and should not be disturbed during the breeding season as they are prone to abandoning their nests if approached. The lake has good fishing for northern pike and whitefish, and a primitive campground with sites for $5 a night.

(For Fort Vermilion see "Peace River Valley," later in this chapter.)

TO THE PEACE RIVER

From Slave Lake, Hwy. 2 follows the southern shore of Lesser Slave Lake past the small resort towns of Widewater and Canyon Creek. Take the turnoff to Wagner to follow the historic route to High Prairie along the lake. Mink farming was big business in the early 1900s and many mink cages remain, scattered along the shore. The hotel at Canyon Creek was once a fish hatchery where fish were raised as food for the mink. At **Kinuso** there is a museum with a stuffed grizzly bear that stands over 2.5 meters tall; the museum is open Mon.-Fri. 10 a.m.-4 p.m. A little farther along the highway, a nine-km gravel road leads to a marina, camping, and a beach at **Spruce Point Park.**

Grouard
A town of 350 near the west end of Lesser Slave Lake, Grouard grew up around the St. Bernard Mission, founded in 1884 by Father Emile Grouard. The town was destined to become the center of the north. It had a few thousand people and a rail line on the way when, due to an unfortunate set of circumstances, everything changed. A sample of water from a nearby lake was sent to the railway headquarters to ensure that it was fit for the steam engines. Along the way it was either dropped, lost, or emptied and replaced by a sample of water from muskeg wetland. The new sample was tested and found to be of poor quality. The proposed route for the railway changed and the once-thriving town collapsed. **Grouard Native Arts Museum** is dedicated to promoting a better understanding of North American native cultures through exhibition of native arts, crafts, and historic artifacts. It's open Mon.-Fri. 10 a.m.-4 p.m. in the Moosehorn Lodge Building of the Alberta Vocational Centre; tel. (403) 751-3915.

Hilliard's Bay Provincial Park is 13 km east of Grouard on the northwest shore of Lesser Slave Lake. It is a 2,330 hectare park with mixed woods, two sandy beaches, and a one-km spit framed by a stand of gnarled paper birches. The **Boreal Forest Interpretive Trail** meanders through a forest habitat where many species of mammals are present—look for tracks along the top of the ridges at the east end of the park. The campground has pit toilets, kitchen shelters, and firewood; sites are $11 a night.

Shaw's Point Lakeside Resort, tel. 751-3900, is a full-service campground located just outside the provincial park. It caters mainly to families and fishing enthusiasts. Facilities include showers, laundry, general store, two marinas, boat launches, and boat rentals; unserviced sites $11, powered sites $13.

FATHER ALBERT LACOMBE

Dressed in a tattered black robe and brandishing a cross, Father Albert Lacombe, known to natives as "The Man With The Good Heart," dedicated his life to those with native blood—to the Assiniboine, Blackfoot, Cree, and, in particular, to the Métis. His travels, mainly associated with northern Alberta, took him as far south as Calgary, but his reputation extended to every corner of the province. He was a spokesman for the church, an effective influence on government policies, and, most importantly, he had a hand in just about every advance in the often-tense relationship between warring tribes and white men.

Father Lacombe originally came to what is now Alberta in 1852 to serve the Métis and natives who had moved to Fort Edmonton. In his time there he founded missions at what are now St. Albert and Brosseau. After returning from a short stint in Manitoba, he returned as a traveling missionary, instigating Canada's first industrial school for natives. He also mediated a dispute between the C.P.R. and angry leaders of the Blackfoot over rights to build a rail line through a reserve, and wrote the first Cree dictionary. The trust he built up with native leaders was great; during one rebellion of the Blackfoot Confederacy, it is claimed that his influence prevented the slaughter of every white man on the prairies.

PROVINCIAL ARCHIVES OF ALBERTA

High Prairie

This town of 3,000 hosts the **Golden Walleye Classic** the third week of August. It is North America's richest walleye tournament boasting $100,000 in prize money. Walleye fishing is not the world's most exciting spectator sport, but amateur anglers are welcome to enter. For details call (403) 751-2241.

High Prairie and District Museum, tel. 523-2601, has some material on the early settlement of Grouard. The museum is located in the library on 53rd Ave.; open Tues.-Sat. 9:30 a.m.-5 p.m.

High Prairie Lions Campground, at the east end of town, has showers; unserviced sites $9, powered sites $12. The **tourist information center** is open in summer, daily 9 a.m.-5 p.m.

Winigami Lake Provincial Park

Winigami Lake, north of High Prairie on Hwy. 749, is ringed by a riot of paper birch, aspen, balsam fir, and poplar trees. The park is on the lake's eastern shore and is an excellent place for birdwatching; two platforms have been built for this purpose (the best time of year is May-June). The day-use area has been planted with ornamental shrubs, and a short hiking trail leads along the lakeshore. The campground has pit toilets, firewood, and kitchen shelters; sites are $11.

Winigami Conservation Area, located along the northeastern arm of the lake (turn off nine km south of McLennan), is also good for birdwatching. It's undeveloped except for a number of short trails.

McLennan

Known as the "Bird Capital of Canada," this town of 1,000 is located on **Kimiwan Lake** at the confluence of three major bird migration paths—the Mississippi, Pacific, and Central. An estimated 27,000 shorebirds and 250,000 waterfowl reside or pass through here; over 200 different species are sighted annually. An excellent interpretive center overlooking the lake has information on the many species sighted and comprehensive bird lists; it's open in summer, daily 10 a.m.-7 p.m. From the center, **Kimiwan Boardwalk** leads through a wetland area to a gazebo and a bird blind. Panels along the boardwalk provide pictures and descriptions of commonly sighted species. For more information write to P.O. Box 489, McLennan, Alberta T0H 2L0; tel. (403) 324-2004.

Continuing West

The small hamlet of **Donnelly,** 14 km west of McLennan, is best known for the annual **Smoky River Agriculture Society Fair** on the first weekend of August. The fair features home cooking, a parade, demonstrations of country skills, a country-style beauty contest (the best looking tractor wins), and the highlight of the weekend—the Antique Tractor Pull.

From west of Donnelly, Hwy. 2 heads north 63 km to the town of Peace River. Highway 49 continues west to Spirit River and the turnoff to Grande Prairie. The first town along this route is **Falher,** known as the "Honey Capital of Canada." One million bees in 25,000 hives produce 2.5 million kilograms of honey annually. Naturally, this industry has created a need for the town to construct the world's largest honey bee; located in a small park on Third Avenue. At the east end of town are two strange-smelling alfalfa-processing plants. The alfalfa is dehydrated and pressed into pellets—over 50,000 tons-worth annually. You can watch all the action from across the road.

HIGHWAY 18 WEST

Seventy-three km north of Edmonton on Hwy. 2, Hwy. 18 heads west through some of Canada's most productive mixed farming land. Major crops include wheat, barley, oats, canola, and hay. Livestock operations include cattle, hogs, poultry, dairy cows, and sheep; the area is home to several large feedlots and Alberta's two largest livestock auctions. At the junction of Highways 2 and 18, a gravel road leads north to **Nilsson Bros. Inc.,** Canada's largest privately owned cattle exchange. Live auctions are held in summer on Tuesday and Thursday mornings, more frequently the rest of the year. Buyers come from throughout North America but anyone is welcome to attend. The auctioneer is lightning

fast—Alberta's best beef cattle are sold hundreds at a time by gross weight. The facility is open every day; ask to have a look around. The staff restaurant, open for an hour at lunchtime, serves hearty meat-and-potato meals for a reasonable price. Just don't ask for lamb. For details and auction times call (403) 348-5893.

Westlock

Westlock is an agricultural service center 11 km west of Hwy. 2. The small **District Museum** is at 10216 100th St., tel. (403) 349-2887 (open Fri.-Sun. 1-5 p.m.), and a private museum is located on the south side of Hwy. 18, just west of town. Look for colorful wooden animals alongside the road and head down the driveway to a collection of antiques collected over many years by the friendly owner. **Tawatinaw Ski Hill** is a small, municipally operated ski club 31 km northeast of town with one rope tow, two T-bars, and groomed cross-country trails. The town also has a good golf course. One of the best-value motels in the entire province is **Southview Motel,** 9919 100th St., tel. 349-2700, which has rooms with bath, kitchen, and cable TV for $24 s or d, and is only one hour from West Edmonton Mall.

Highway 44 North

From Westlock it is 106 km north along Hwy. 44 to Hondo, halfway between Athabasca and Slave Lake. Along the way are two worthwhile detours. **Long Island Lake Municipal Park** (go 22 km north from Westlock, then turn right at Dapp Corner and follow the signs) is a recreation area with fishing, swimming, canoeing, and camping; sites are $8. Farther north, near the hamlet of Fawcett, is a turnoff to 2,068-hectare **Cross Lake Provincial Park.** Deer and moose are common here, and in late summer black bears often feed among the berry patches. The shallow lake is good for swimming, canoeing, and fishing for northern pike. The campground has pit toilets, firewood, kitchen shelters, and a concession; sites are $11.

Barrhead And Vicinity

Continuing west on Hwy. 18 takes you to Barrhead, an agriculture and lumber town of 4,100 located an hour and a half northwest of Edmonton. **Centennial Museum,** with displays depicting the town's agricultural past, is located along Hwy. 33 at 57th Avenue. The museum is open in summer, Mon.-Sat. 10 a.m.-4 p.m., Sunday 1-5 p.m. The town's symbol is the great blue heron; you can see a model of one at the top end of 50th St., or head out to Thunder Lake Provincial Park (see below) for the chance to see a real one. The biggest event of the year is the **Wildrose Rodeo Association Finals** in mid-September.

Barrhead has many motels; most are on Hwy. 33 at the north end of town. Camping is free at **Rotary Park,** on the south side of town. The **tourist information center** is located in the museum.

An interesting loop drive from Barrhead is to take Hwy. 769 north to **Neerlandia** (settled by the Dutch in 1912 and named after their homeland), the small hamlet of **Vega,** and the Athabasca River. On the bank of the river is **Misty Ridge Ski Hill,** tel. (403) 674-4242, with a rope tow and T-bar. The river crossing is on the **Klondike Ferry,** one of the province's few remaining ferries. The next community along this route is **Fort Assiniboine,** which was a vital link in the Hudson's Bay Company chain of fur-trading posts. The original fort was built in 1824, making it one of the oldest settlements in Alberta. Although furs were traded at the fort, its main role was as a transportation link across the then-uncharted wilderness. A reconstruction of the original fur-trading post is located in the center of town; open in summer, daily 1-5 p.m. From Fort Assinboine it is 38 km southeast back to Barrhead, completing the loop, or 62 km northwest to Swan Hills.

Thunder Lake Provincial Park

Colonies of great blue herons reside at this 208-hectare park 21 km west of Barrhead on Hwy. 18. The park is on the northeast shore of Thunder Lake, set among stands of aspen and balsam fir. Birdwatching, especially for waterfowl, is excellent; look for herons on the islands in the quiet northwest corner of the lake. Grebes and black terns are also common. The lake's water level is artificially controlled to prevent flooding of cottages and beaches. This results in poor fishing, although the lake is stocked annually with northern pike and perch. Four short hiking trails begin from the day-use area including one along the lakeshore. The campground is beside the beach and is open year-round. It has pit toilets, firewood, and kitchen shelters; unserviced sites $11, powered sites $13.

SWAN HILLS

The town of Swan Hills (population 2,400) is located in the hills of the same name 100 km northwest of Barrhead. The hills were named, according to Indian legend, for giant swans that nested in a nearby river estuary. Oil was discovered in 1957 and the town grew quickly thereafter. Today, five major companies extract 260,000 barrels of oil and 250 million cubic meters of gas daily from 2,000 wells. North of town is the world's most modern special-waste treatment plant, which treats material that cannot be disposed of in a landfill, incinerator, or sewage system. Corrosive, combustible, and environmentally unfriendly materials such as lead, mercury, and pesticides are broken down into nontoxic compounds and either burned off or safely stored. Tours of the plant are available, call (403) 333-4197 for details. The surrounding hills are wetter than the Rocky Mountain Foothills, creating a unique environment of rainforest, boreal, and subarctic zones. The best place to observe this blend is at **Goose Mountain Ecological Reserve,** 24 km west of town. Hiking and fishing are popular activities throughout the hills; the easiest area to access is **Krause Lake Recreation Area,** south of town. Old logging roads crisscross the entire region, making exploration (with a full tank of gas and a map from the Alberta Forest Service Office) easy. Moose, deer, and coyotes are common, while the **Swan Hills grizzly bear,** a subspecies of the now-extinct plains grizzly, is rare.

The **Grizzly Trail** (Hwy. 33), linking Barrhead and Swan Hills, offers two interesting stops along its route. **Trapper Lea's Cabin** is 30 km southeast of Swan Hills. It consists of two buildings constructed on the trapline of the "Wolf King of Alberta," the man who trapped the largest number of wolves in the province during the early '40s. Five km farther south is a highway rest area from where a three-km trail leads to the geographic center of Alberta. Follow the brown and yellow signs along an old seismic road to the center, marked by an orange marker.

Accommodations And Food

Swan Hills has a number of motels, but each is usually full with work crews. Try **Derrick Motor Inn,** tel. (403) 333-4405, in the plaza; $40 s, $45 d. Instead of staying at the unappealing campground in town, head southeast to Trapper Lea's Cabin ($5.50), 15 km north to Chystina Lake ($5.50), or 16 km south to Freeman River ($7.50). The only place to get a meal in town is the Chinese place in the plaza.

Information

The **tourist information center** is located on Hwy. 33, opposite the Grizzly Motel; open in summer, daily 9 a.m.-5 p.m. For a good map of the surrounding area go to the **Alberta Forest Service Office** at 4831 Plaza Ave.; tel. (403) 333-2229.

Carson-Pegasus Provincial Park

This 1,178 hectare park is located on the southern edge of the Swan Hills, 49 km south of the town of Swan Hills and 25 km north of Whitecourt. Because of its location in a transition zone, it contains forest typical of both the foothills (lodgepole pine and spruce) and the boreal forest (aspen, poplar, birch, and fir). Over 40 species of mammals have been recorded here including deer, moose, and black bear. Fishing is excellent for rainbow trout, and northern pike and whitefish are also caught. The day-use area offers canoe, rowboat, and motorboat rentals ($6, $7, and $11 per hour, respectively) and a sandy beach. The general store sells groceries, fishing tackle, bait, and hot food, and has a laundry; it's open in summer, daily 9 a.m.-9 p.m. The campground has flush toilets, showers, firewood, and kitchen shelters; unserviced sites $13, powered sites $15.

WHITECOURT

Many of Whitecourt's earliest settlers had been Yukon-bound in search of gold when they reached this lushly forested region and decided to settle here instead. To them, the area held plenty of opportunities that wouldn't require an arduous trek to the Klondike. When the railroad arrived, so did many homesteaders. They took to cutting down trees to sell for firewood and railroad ties. Thus began Whitecourt's lumber industry; today the town is the "Forest Centre of Alberta."

Whitecourt sits at the confluence of the Athabasca, McLeod, and Sakwatamau rivers on Hwy. 43, 177 km northwest of Edmonton and 341 km southeast of Grande Prairie. Highway 32 also passes through town; Swan Hills is 74 km north, and the Yellowhead Hwy. is 72 km south. If you're coming in from the southeast, you'll pass a strip of motels and restaurants before descending to the Athabasca River and the older part of town, off to the right. The **tourist information center** is located by the traffic lights at the top of the hill, tel. (403) 778-5363; it's open in summer, daily 8 a.m.-7 p.m.; the rest of the year, Mon.-Fri. 9 a.m.-5 p.m.

Sights

Industrial tours are run by the chamber of commerce Mon.-Fri. in summer. Each of the four tours is to a forestry-related industry—a pulp mill, newsprint plant, sawmill, and a medium-density fiberboard plant. For reservations call the tourist information center, tel. (403) 778-5362.

Medi-save Drugs, in Valley Centre Mall on 51st St., has North America's longest suspended railway, a large display of Coca-Cola memorabilia, a fudge machine, and a '50s-style diner.

The **E.S. Huestis Demonstration Forest,** five km north of Hwy. 43 on Hwy. 32, contains several stages of forest development. A seven-km road leads through various ecosystems including an old-growth coniferous forest and a deciduous forest, and past aspen and spruce cut blocks, a beaver dam, and an exotic plantation. Each site has interpretive signs; additional information is available from a kiosk at the entrance to the forest.

Accommodations And Food

Most of Whitecourt's dozen motels are on Hwy. 43 as it enters town from the southeast. All are priced $30-45 s, $35-55 d. Best value of the bunch is **Glenview Motel,** tel. (403) 778-2276. **Green Gables Inn,** tel. 778-4537, at the top end of the scale, has large, modern rooms and a good restaurant. **Lions Club Campground,** at the south end of the service strip, is set in a heavily forested area and has a laundry and showers; unserviced sites $8, powered sites $11. On the opposite side of town, one km along Hwy. 43, is the full-service **Sagitawah Tourist Park,** tel. 778-3734. Sites with hookups are $15-17.

Mountain Pizza & Steak House, tel. 778-3600, has great pizza from $6.25 and broiled steaks from $10. Next to the tourist information center is **Ken's Kitchen,** tel. 778-4338. It is small, but the meals are excellent and all breads and pastries are baked on the premises. The Green Gables Inn has a cafe open all day and a restaurant with dishes starting at $10, which includes a salad bar.

HIGHWAY 43 WEST

From Whitecourt, Hwy. 43 continues northeast to **Fox Creek,** a small town surrounded by a wilderness where wildlife is abundant and the fishing legendary. If you don't believe the local fishing stories, head to the Home Hardware Store to see a 12-kilogram northern pike caught in a nearby lake. **Smoke** and **Iosegun** lakes are two of the most accessible and offer excellent fishing for northern pike, walleye, perch, and whitefish.

Moose are abundant between Fox Creek and **Little Smoky,** 47 km northwest, from where gravel roads lead to a number of small lakes. This area is not noted for fossils, but a few years back, a mammoth tusk was found in Waskahigan River, west of Little Smoky.

Valleyview

Valleyview is an agricultural and oil-and-gas center that also serves travelers who pass through heading north to the Northwest Territories and west to Alaska. It is also one of the largest towns in Alberta without a pioneer museum. Instead, it has **Text Garden,** a series of miniature gardens with paths, benches, and a small chapel. It's located beside the Four Seasons Flower Centre at 4909 50th St.; open daily 10 a.m.-6 p.m.

The town's four motels fill up each night with road-weary travelers. **Horizon Motel,** tel. (403) 524-3904, has large rooms, a laundry, and restaurant; $42 s, $47 d. The **Lions Den Campground** is on Hwy. 34, just west of Hwy. 43, and has showers; sites are $8. **Sherk's RV Park,** tel. 524-4949, is a full-service campground on the south side of town (head west from ESSO); full hookups $17. The large **tourist information center,** located five km south of town in a shaded rest area, is open in summer, daily 8 a.m.-9 p.m.

Sturgeon Lake

Sturgeon Lake, west of Valleyview, is known for its excellent northern pike, perch, and walleye fishing, and two interesting provincial parks. Located along the south side of the lake is the **Sturgeon Lake Indian Band Reserve** whose members are from the Cree Nation. While many still pursue a traditional lifestyle, the band has built, of all things, a chopstick factory, from where the finished product is exported throughout the world, including to China.

Williamson Provincial Park is only 17 hectares but has a sandy beach, good swimming, and a campground with flush toilets and showers; unserviced sites $11, powered sites $13.

On the lake's northwest shore is 1,090-hectare **Young's Point Provincial Park.** Here you'll find good birdwatching for forest birds and waterfowl, and good fishing among the dense aquatic growth close to the shore. Much of the park is forested with a blend of aspen, white spruce, and lodgepole pine. Porcupines, deer, and coyotes wander the woods here, and if you're lucky, you might see red foxes, lynx, and black bears. Hiking trails begin at the day-use area and lead along the lake and to an active beaver pond. The campground has flush toilets, showers, and is near a sandy beach; unserviced sites $11, powered sites $13.

EVERGREEN COUNTRY

The Evergreen Country extends along the Yellowhead Hwy. (Hwy. 16) from the parkland and lakes region west of Edmonton through the Rocky Mountain Foothills to the border of Jasper National Park, and north along Hwy. 40 to Grande Cache and Willmore Wilderness Park. An area of frenzied oil activity during the early 1970s, today it's the center for a large petroleum industry, as well as for farming, coal mining, forestry, and the production of electricity. The major service centers are **Edson** and **Hinton,** both on the Yellowhead Highway.

FROM EDMONTON TO EDSON

Long after leaving Edmonton's city limits, the Yellowhead Hwy. is lined with motels, industrial parks, and housing estates. The towns of Spruce Grove and Stony Plain (see "Sights" in the Edmonton Chapter) flash by and farming begins to dominate the landscape.

Wabamun And Nearby Lakes

Wabamun is the name of a town, lake, and provincial park 32 km west of Stony Plain. The skyline around Wabamun Lake is dominated by high-voltage power lines coming from the three coal-fired generating plants that supply over two-thirds of Alberta's electrical requirements. Fuel for the plants is supplied by nearby mining operations—the largest coal extraction sites in Canada. Tours of the plants, mines, and the relocated hamlet of **Keephills** can be arranged through TransAlta Utilities, tel. (403) 498-7020 (Edmonton).

  Wabamun Lake Provincial Park is located on Moonlight Bay at the lake's eastern end. The fishing is good, a manmade beach is the perfect spot for a swim, and the hiking trail is a good spot for wildlife viewing. Two

geothermal outlets create a perfect environment for waterfowl in winter; expect to see up to 40 species at each. The easiest to get to is at the end of the wharf. The campground has showers, firewood, kitchen shelters, and is close to the beach; $13 per night.

  On the west side of Wabamun Lake is the busy resort community of **Seba Beach. Pier Boat Rentals,** on the main pier, rents canoes, paddleboats, and fishing boats. Seba Beach has no motels. Those red-backed, inflatable-toy-waving crowds either come out from Edmonton for the day or own a cottage in town. **Shady Brook Campground,** tel. 797-5433, south of town, is a good place to escape the mob. It has showers, groceries, and is close to the lake for fishing; unserviced sites $10.50, with power and water $15. North of the Yellowhead Hwy. are numerous other lakes good for swimming, boating, and fishing including **Lac Ste. Anne.**

Pembina River Provincial Park And Vicinity

The Pembina River Valley is the first true wilderness area west of Edmonton. The small towns of Entwistle and Evansburg straddle either side of the valley where the park lies. The only man-made structures you'll see in this 167-hectare park are an old single-lane road bridge and the concrete foundations of what once was a railroad trestle. White spruce and aspen blanket the park and provide a habitat for many mammals including beavers, mule deer, white-tailed deer, and moose. Fishing in the river is particularly good for northern pike and walleye, and those who don't fish might appreciate the deep swimming hole behind a weir, or the hiking trails in the northern part of the park. The campground, on the eastern side of the river, has flush toilets, showers, kitchen shelters, and firewood; sites are $11.

Waterfowl flock to Wabamun Lake.

BOB RACE

EVERGREEN COUNTRY

© MOON PUBLICATIONS, INC.

Highway 16 bypasses **Entwistle,** but the town's main street is worth a look for its historic buildings. Out on the highway are all the services you'll need; motels ($30-33 s, $32-36 d), restaurants, gas, and, of course, mini-golf.

Continuing west on Hwy. 16 toward Edson, you'll pass **Chip Lake,** interesting primarily for the scatological story behind its name. It used to be called Buffalo Chip Lake, but the name was shortened for aesthetic reasons.

Edson

The site of today's town of Edson was once the starting point of a trail early settlers used to access the Peace River Valley to the north. Later, the site was picked as a divisional point of the Grand Trunk Pacific Railway and the town sprang up around it. Today this town of 7,500, 199 km west of Edmonton, relies on natural-resource-based industries such as forestry and oil-and-gas to fuel its economy.

The **Galloway Station Museum** is in RCMP Centennial Park at 5433 3rd Avenue. The museum houses artifacts reflecting the importance of transportation and industry to the town's growth. Also on display in the park are a restored caboose and a 1964 Lockheed jet. The museum is open in summer, daily 9:30 a.m.-4:30 p.m. **Silver Summit Ski Resort,** 51 km north of town, has a rope tow, T-bar, and chairlift. Lift tickets are $22. The ski area is open Thurs.-Sun.; tel. (800) 667-2546.

Most motels are along 2nd Ave. (heading west) and 4th Ave. (heading east). **Yellowhead Motel,** 5207 4th Ave., tel. (403) 723-4242, is a bargain; $25 s or d. **Lions Park Campground,** tel. 723-3169, at the east end of town, has treed sites far enough from the highway to be relatively quiet. Facilities include extra hot (and fast) showers and plenty of free firewood, which is just as well—you need a bonfire to cook anything on the oversized fire rings; unserviced sites $10, powered sites $12. Primitive campgrounds are signposted east and west of town; most are a short drive from Hwy. 16 along gravel roads and have a water source, pit toilets, and firewood.

Ernie O's, 4340 2nd Ave., tel. 723-3600, is one of the best places in town to eat breakfast ($3-7). Nightly specials are $10. **Mountain Pizza & Steakhouse,** 5102 4th Ave., tel. 723-3900, is a classy pizza joint where the food and prices are excellent. The Mountain Extra Special Pizza ($15) is worth the extra bucks.

The **tourist information center** is in RCMP Centennial Park at 5433 3rd Ave., tel. 723-3339. It's open in summer, daily 8 a.m.-6 p.m., the rest of the year, weekdays 9 a.m.-5 p.m.

HINTON AND VICINITY

Located on the south bank of the Athabasca River, at the base of the front ranges of the Canadian Rockies, this town of 9,800 makes an ideal base for exploring the northern reaches of Jasper National Park. But before speeding off into the mountains, take time out to explore Hinton's immediate vicinity. To the south are well-maintained roads leading into the historic Coal Branch; to the north, lakes, streams, canyons, hoodoos, and sand dunes. The town itself has some interesting sights and the motels and restaurants have prices you'll appreciate after spending time in Jasper.

Hinton began as a coal-mining and forestry town. These industries still play a major role in the town's economy, although the town now also benefits from being an important service along the Yellowhead Highway.

On the campus of the **Environmental Training Centre,** 1176 Switzer Dr., tel. 865-8236, you'll find a small museum dedicated to the history of forestry in the province. It's open year-round, weekdays 8:15 a.m.-4:30 p.m. Outside, the **Forestry School Trail**—a 1.5-km interpretive path—winds around the perimeter of the school, passing various forest environments, an old rangers' cabin, Edna the erratic, and a viewpoint with magnificent views of the Athabasca River Valley and Rocky Mountains.

The Coal Branch

An area of heavily forested foothills south of Hinton has been the scene of feverish coal-mining activity for 80 years. Most of the mines, along with the towns of Mountain Park, Luscar, Leyland, Coal Spur, and Mercoal, have been abandoned. Two mines still operate, and two towns survive, although the populations of **Cadomin** and **Robb** have dwindled to around 100 apiece. This area, so rich in history, is also a wilderness offering hiking, fishing, and spectacular views of the Rockies. The best way to access the region, known as the Coal Branch, is via Hwy. 40. The active mines are Cardinal River Coal's pit-mining operation and another at Gregg River. A viewpoint overlooks one of the largest pits. Look for bighorn sheep at natural salt deposits on the cliff above the viewpoint, oblivious to the rumbling trucks below. As the highway approaches Cadomin, Genstar Cement's Cadomin Quarry and its "giant's staircase" come into view. The quarry is the only thing that keeps Cadomin—once a town of 2,500—alive. The town has a motel (tel. 403-692-3663), restaurant, and general store.

From the highway, **Cadomin Caves** can be seen in the mountain face west of town. These caves are the best known and most accessible in Alberta. A short trail leads up to them. Anyone serious about exploring the caves can find out more from the tourist information center in Hinton.

Camping is available at **Whitehorse Creek Campground,** five km south of Cadomin at the base of a sheer rock wall. Sites are $7.50 per night. A trail from this campground leads 10 km to **Whitehorse Falls,** another four km to **Whitehorse Pass,** then continues to Miette Hot Springs in Jasper National Park, a total of 40 km one way. Farther along the road, above the treeline, lies what's left of **Mountain Park,** once a thriving community of 1,000 connected by rail to Coal Spur to the east. The mine at Mountain Park closed in 1950 and residents dismantled their houses and moved to new locations. Today all that remains is a cemetery, some foundations, and remnants of the narrow-gauge railway.

From here you can continue south to Nordegg, across the Cardinal Divide (the division between the Athabasca River system, which flows north, and the North Saskatchewan River system, which flows east). Or you can return to Cadomin and take Hwy. 40 northeast to Hwy. 47, passing through the coal-mining hamlet of Robb and rejoining Hwy. 16 just west of Edson. This 250-km loop through the Coal Branch will take at least one day.

Ogre Canyon

This unique natural feature, between **Brûlé Lake** and the front ranges of the Rockies, was created by underground streams that dried up, creating sinkholes. Huge chunks of the treed surface above have dropped down, just like an elevator. In most cases the trees have continued growing, their tops barely reaching the level of the surrounding ground. Between the canyon and the lake is an old packhorse trail that switchbacks steeply up a hill (look for it near the C.P.R. tunnel). At the top of the ridge a cairn marks the boundary of Jasper National Park. The trail continues into a lush valley and to a hidden stream that cascades into a canyon below. A dry gully of eroded rock, across the canyon, marks the stream's former route. Camping is possible at Brûlé Lake although there are no facilities. To get to Ogre Canyon head north of Hwy. 16 on Hwy. 40 and take the first left after crossing the Athabasca River. Continue through Brûlé; the road is rough but passable, and ends by Brûlé Lake. The canyon, at the base of the cliffs, is obvious.

Athabasca Tower

Fire towers are spread at regular intervals throughout the foothills. The Athabasca Tower is one of the few that can be reached by two-wheel drive. The access road turns west off of Hwy. 40, 14 km north of Hwy. 16. The gravel road passes a nordic center and finishes at the tower. Before attempting to climb the structure, holler for the warden or call (403) 865-2400 in advance. The 360-degree view from the 15-meter tower is fantastic. Anyone who doesn't like heights can appreciate the view from a platform a little farther up the road. This is also a popular hang-gliding spot—many record-breaking flights have been made here, thanks to the updrafts that sweep through the valley.

Emerson Creek Road

Of the many logging roads that radiate from Hinton, Emerson Creek Rd. is one of the most interesting. It passes a small canyon, hoodoos similar to those found in the badlands, and a series of emerald green lakes stocked with fish, before eventually rejoining Hwy. 16 at Edson. To access the road from Hinton, take Switzer Dr. and turn left on Weldwood Bridge Access Rd., then cross the Athabasca River and continue for five km. The Emerson Creek Rd. to the east (right) is marked by a sign. It is maintained primarily as a logging road so drive with care and yield to trucks. (Yellow signs along the road are not kilometer markers.) A short hiking trail, between signs 18 and 19, follows **Canyon Creek** to a point where it cascades dramatically into a series of canyons. **Emerson Lakes,** at sign 52 (around 55 km from Hinton), were formed as the sheet of ice from the last ice age receded. A nature trail winds around the lakes to an old trapper's cabin and past some active beaver dams. A small campground at the lakes has sites with no services for $7.50. At sign 60 is **Wild Sculpture Trail,** where wind and rain have carved mysterious-looking hoodoos into the sandstone cliffs. Along the trail are three glacial lakes, each with a campground.

Accommodations

The strip of motels, hotels, restaurants, fast-food places, and gas stations along Hwy. 16 reflects the importance of Hinton as a service center. The cost of motel rooms here is considerably less than in Jasper, an hour west, making the town an ideal alternative for budget-conscious travelers. The **Hinton Hotel,** tel. (403) 865-2658, has the least expensive rooms in town, above the loudest bar in town; $32 s, $38 d with shared bathrooms. The dowdy-looking **Big Horn Motel,** tel. 865-1555, beside the Husky gas station, has surprisingly good rooms, some larger than others; $40 s, $45 d, kitchenettes an extra $10. Other choices are **Pines Motel,** tel. 865-2624, beside the golf course, $55 s or d; **Tara Vista Motel,** tel. 865-3391, with the best views in town, $65 s, $68 d; and, in the Jasper price range, **Greentree Lodge,** tel. 865-3321, which has a restaurant, pool, and jacuzzi, $70 s, $75 d.

   Black Cat Guest Ranch, P.O. Box 6267, Hinton, Alberta T7V 1X6, tel. 865-3084, is a mountain retreat west of Hinton. All the rooms have private bath and views of the mountains.

Elk are frequently seen in Switzer Provincial Park.

Horseback riding is available during the day ($10-12 per hour), and in the evening, guests can relax in the large living room or hot tub. The rate, $67 per person, includes three delicious home-cooked meals. To get to the ranch take Hwy. 40 north for six km, turn left to Brûlé and continue for 11 km, then turn right and follow the signs.

   Hinton Campground, at 813 Switzer Dr., has flush toilets, kitchen shelters, and firewood; $8 per night. A much nicer alternative is to stay at a forest service campground (Emerson Lakes or along the Coal Branch Rd.) or in William A. Switzer Provincial Park toward Grande Cache.

Food

Apart from the fast-food restaurants that line the highway from one end of town to the other, Hinton has little to offer the hungry traveler. The **Husky Restaurant** does, as usual, serve filling meals at good prices; open 24 hours. If gas-station dining isn't your style, try **Greentree Cafe** in the Greentree Lodge. Continental breakfast is $2.75, the lumberjack breakfast of steak, bacon, eggs, and hotcakes is $8.50. Lunch specials are $4-5 and dinner specials start at $7. Also in the Lodge is the elegant **Fireside Dining Room,** tel. (403) 865-3321. **Athens Corner,** tel. 865-3956, in the Hill Shopping Centre, serves reasonable Greek, Italian, and Western food.

Services And Information

The **Greyhound Bus Depot,** 128 North St., tel. (403) 865-2367, is served daily by buses from Edmonton and Jasper. **Tilden** car rental has an office in the Greentree Lodge, tel. 865-3321. For **Hinton Taxi** call 865-5500.

   The **post office** is on Park Street. **Koin Clean and Dry Laundromat** is at 220 Pembina Avenue. The **tourist information center** is on Gregg Ave., which parallels the highway, tel. 865-2777; open in summer, daily 8 a.m.-7 p.m., the rest of the year, weekdays 8 a.m.-4 p.m.

William A. Switzer Provincial Park

This 2,688-hectare park, in the foothills northwest of Hinton on Hwy. 40, encompasses a series of shallow lakes linked by Jarvis Creek. Most of the park is heavily forested with lodgepole pine, spruce, and aspen. The northern section, however, is more wide open and elk and deer can often be seen grazing there. An ill-

BOB RACE

deer can often be seen grazing there. An ill-fated attempt at beaver ranching was made in the 1940s (cement lodges built for the purpose can be seen near Beaver Ranch Campground). Soon after, Entrance Provincial Park was established, renamed Switzer in 1958. The lakes are excellent for canoeing and bird and wildlife viewing; fishing is considered average. The park has various hiking trails, four day-use areas, and five campgrounds. Sites at **Graveyard, Halfway,** and **Cache campgrounds** are $7.50 per night, **Jarvis Lake Campground** is $11, and **Gregg Lake Campground**—which has showers, powered sites, winter camping, and an interpretive program—is $11-15. For more infor-

mation on the park call (403) 865-5600.

On To Grande Cache

From Switzer park it is 118 km to Grande Cache. A 32-km gravel spur to **Rock Lake,** a staging area for hikes into Jasper National Park and a worthwhile destination in itself, is 15 km north of the park. Ever since a Hudson's Bay Company post was established at the lake the area has drawn hikers and anglers, attracted by mountain scenery, the chance of viewing abundant big game, and the remote location. Hiking trails lead around the lake and three km to the remote northern reaches of Jasper National Park. Fortunately you don't have to travel far to appreciate the rugged beauty of the lake and surrounding kitchen shelters, firewood, and pit toilets; sites are $7.50 a night.

From Rock Lake Rd., Hwy. 40 continues to climb steadily, crossing Pinto Creek and Berland River (small campground), then following Muskeg River for a short while. The road passes **Pierie Grey Lakes** (fishing, boating, and camping) before making an arc around the shoulder of Grande Mountain and entering downtown Grande Cache, one of the most remote towns in the Canadian Rockies.

GRANDE CACHE

Grande Cache is a remote town of 3,700, 450 km west of Edmonton and 182 km south of Grande Prairie. The surrounding wilderness is totally undeveloped, offering endless opportunities for hiking, canoeing, kayaking, fishing, and horseback riding. Immediately to the south is **Willmore Wilderness Park,** an unspoiled region of snowcapped mountains, rivers, and over 700 km of hiking trails. The town is located on the side of **Grande Mountain** above the **Smoky River.** This river flows from its source in Jasper National Park through Willmore Wilderness Park and north, through the valley in which Grande Cache lies, to the Peace River whose waters drain into the Arctic Ocean.

The first Europeans to explore the area were fur trappers and traders. They cached furs near the site of the present town before taking them to major trading posts. At one point there was a small trading post on a lake south of town, remains of which can still be found.

Grande Cache is a planned town. Construction started in 1969 in response to a need for services and housing for miners and their families working at the McIntyre Porcupine Coal Mine. The town was developed 20 km south of the mine to maintain a scenic environment.

Hiking

The main attraction of the Grande Cache area is the great outdoors. Hiking is excellent both inside and outside Willmore Wilderness Park—many short trails lead to lakes or along the banks of mountain rivers. Climbing the surrounding peaks usually requires at least a half-day of walking, and to access the most spectacular areas of Willmore will require an overnight trip. The tourist

information center has brochures detailing each hike. Below are a few favorites.

Grande Mountain
- Length: 3.5 km (90 minutes) one way
- Elevation gain: 730 meters
- Rating: moderate

The town of Grande Cache sits on the southern shoulder of Grande Mountain, which, at 2,000 meters, is not particularly imposing. But from the summit, the view across the Smoky River Valley to the Rocky Mountains is spectacular. The trail follows a power line the entire way to the peak and is easy to follow. To get to the trailhead, head northwest of town one km and turn right at the cemetery gate. Park here, walk along the road to the power line, veer right, and start the long slog to the summit.

Muskeg Falls Trail
- Length: 1.5 km (30 minutes) one way
- Elevation gain: minimal
- Rating: easy

The trailhead for this pleasant, easy hike to Muskeg Falls is 16 km east of Grande Cache. The gravel parking lot on the north side of Hwy. 40 is easy to miss. It's two km before the airport. The first half of the trail, through lodgepole pine and aspen, is relatively flat. The trail then forks; to the right is the preferred route which will take you to the top of the falls, to the left the trail descends steeply to below the falls. In both cases the trail can be wet and slippery, so stay away from the edge.

Mount Hamel
- Length: 7.5 km (2-3 hours) one way
- Elevation gain: 1,110 meters
- Rating: moderate/difficult

Mount Hamel is the peak north of Grande Cache on the west side of the Smoky River Valley. The hike to the summit is a long haul up an old logging road. To get to the trailhead, drive 10 km north of town on Hwy. 40 and turn west at the far end of a grassy meadow. Park in an area just before the road enters the forest. Start hiking up the road to the right, past a No Trespassing sign. Take a left at the first junction from where the road quickly switchbacks to the right. The road climbs slowly around the southern and western flanks of the mountain. From the summit, where there is a cabin, the 360-

GRANDE CACHE

TO HELL'S GATE
AND GRANDE PRAIRIE

40

MARV MOORE

SHAND AVE.

97th ST.

HOPPE AVE.

BIG HORN MOTEL

GRANDE CACHE HOTEL

ALPINE LODGE MOTEL

ACORN MOTEL

VEGAS PIZZA

PINE PLAZA

TO HINTON

TOURIST INFORMATION CENTRE

40

103rd ST.

ALBERTA FOREST SERVICE

TOWN OFFICE

104th ST.

SHAND AVE.

HOPPE AVE.

NOT TO SCALE

© MOON PUBLICATIONS, INC.

the summit, where there is a cabin, the 360-degree view is breathtaking. On a clear day Mt. Robson, the highest peak in the Canadian Rockies, can be seen to the south.

Other Recreation And Events

The many rivers that come churning out of the Rocky Mountains provide some exciting kayaking and rafting possibilities. The most popular rivers are Muskeg River (class I-II), Sheep Creek (class III-V), and the Smoky River (class I-II). The first two flow into the Smoky, which can be navigated on a multiday trip to Grande Prairie, Peace River, or even to Inuvik and the Arctic Ocean. For guided tours contact **Wilderness River Adventure Tours,** tel. (403) 827-3377. For those who don't need an adrenaline rush to enjoy themselves, the lakes to the south of town

are good for exploring by canoe and harbor large populations of waterfowl. These same lakes are good for fishing, with rainbow and brook trout, whitefish, and arctic grayling commonly caught. Many of the forestry roads are suitable for mountain biking; **Grande Cache Adventure Sports,** tel. 827-3764, rents bikes. Day and overnight horse-packing trips are offered by **Diamond G.,** tel. 827-3503, and **Leonard Outfitting,** tel. 827-3246. Grande Mountain is a popular spot for hang gliding or you can go windsurfing on the nearby lakes. **Grande Cache Golf Course** is only nine holes, but you'll want to go around twice, however badly you're playing—the scenery is distracting to say the least; tel. 827-5151. In winter many of the hiking trails echo with the swishing of cross-country skiers, while telemarkers whoop it up in fresh powder on the

The whole town celebrates **Coal Dust Daze** in June, a jet boat race thunders through in July, and a hang-gliding competition and mountain-bike race take place in September.

Willmore Wilderness Park

To the west and south of Grande Cache is Willmore Wilderness Park, 4,600 square km of foothill and mountain wilderness accessible only on foot, horseback, or, in winter, on skis. It is totally undeveloped—the trails that do exist are not maintained, and in most cases are those once used by trappers. The park is divided roughly in half by the Smoky River. The area west of the river is reached from Hell's Gate (see below). The east side is far less traveled—the terrain is rougher and wetter.

The park is made up of a number of long, green ridges above the treeline and, farther west, wide passes and expansive basins along the Continental Divide. Lower elevations are covered in lodgepole pine and spruce, while at higher elevations the cover changes to fir. The diverse wildlife is one of the park's main attractions; white-tailed and mule deer, mountain goats, bighorn sheep, moose, elk, caribou, and black bears are all common. The park is also home to wolves, cougars, and grizzly bears.

The easiest way to access the park is from Hell's Gate Staging Area, six km north of town off Hwy. 40. From there, follow a gravel road the same distance farther in. Even for those not planning a trip into the park, the cliffs at **Hell's Gate** are only a short walk. These 70-meter cliffs are at the confluence of the Sulphur and Smoky rivers. The color difference between the glacial-fed Smoky River and spring-fed Sulphur River is apparent as they merge. One of the most popular overnight trips is to Clarke's Cache, an easy 16-km hike to the remains of a cabin where the original Grande Cache fur caches were made. Anyone planning an extended trip into the park should be aware that no services are available within the park, most trails are unmarked, and certain areas are heavily used by horse-packers. Topographical maps

Black bears inhabit the Willmore Wilderness Park.

are available from **Alberta Forest Service** on Shand Avenue. The book *Willmore Wilderness Park,* published by the Alberta Wilderness Association, is available at **Grande Books** in the Pine Plaza Shopper's Mall on Hoppe Avenue. Two outfitters offer trips into the park on horseback: **Leonard Outfitting,** tel. (403) 827-3246, and **Sheep Creek Backcountry Experience,** tel. 827-2829.

Accommodations

Most motels are busy in summer so make reservations in advance. All addresses below are Grande Cache, Alberta T0E 0Y0. **Big Horn Motel,** P.O. Box 208, tel. (403) 827-3744, is the best value. Each room has a fridge, some have kitchenettes, and a laundry and restaurant are on the premises; $35 s, $40 d. The other choices are **Alpine Lodge Motel,** P.O. Box 1379, tel. 827-2450, $32 s, $35 d; **Acorn Motel,** P.O. Box 188, tel. 827-2412, $32 s, $40 d; and **Grande Cache Hotel,** beside the mall, P.O. Box 600, tel. 827-3377, which has suites, a restaurant, and a lounge with country bands on weekends; $39 s, $48 d.

Marv Moore Campground, tel. 827-2404, has semiprivate, well-treed sites and showers, kitchen shelters, and firewood; unserviced sites $8, hookups $11-13. It's located at the north end of town on Shand Ave. beside the golf course. Forest service campgrounds are located at regular intervals the entire length of Hwy 40. Of special note are the ones at **Hell's Gate Staging Area,** north of town, which makes a good base for exploring Willmore Wilderness Park ($5.50), and on **Grande Cache Lake**, five km south of town, which has good swimming, canoeing, and fishing ($5.50).

Food

On a clear day, the view from **Mountainview Cafe,** in the Grande Cache Hotel, is worth at least the price of a coffee. Soup and sandwich lunch specials are around $6 and pizza and pasta dishes start at $7. A dining room in the hotel opens at 5 p.m.; dinner entrees range $10-14, and on Friday night there's a prime rib buffet. Call (403) 827-3377 for reservations and information.

BOB RACE

Vegas Pizza and Spaghetti House, 207 Pine Plaza, tel. 827-5444, is an inexpensive place to go for a meal; portions are large and the atmosphere pleasant.

Services And Information
The **post office** is in the plaza, as is a **laundromat** (beside IGA). **Home Hardware,** in the Pine Plaza, stocks camping and fishing gear. The **tourist information center** is east of town, toward Hinton; open in summer, daily 8 a.m.-8 p.m. The **town office,** in the provincial building, is another good source of information. It's open year-round, weekdays 9 a.m.-4 p.m.

To Grande Prairie
From Grande Cache a 181-km gravel road follows the Smoky River out of the foothills and into the wide valley in which Grande Prairie lies. Along the route are a number of forest service campgrounds and good opportunities for wildlife viewing.

GRANDE PRAIRIE AND VICINITY

Grande Prairie, a city of 28,000, is located in a wide, gently rolling valley surrounded by large areas of natural grasslands. Such grasslands are something of an anomaly at such a northern latitude. To the south and west are heavily forested mountains and to the north and east are boreal forests and wetlands. But it was the grasslands here, *la grande prairie,* that provided the stimulus for growth in the region. While so many of Alberta's northern towns began and grew as trading posts beside rivers, Grande Prairie grew as a result of the land's agricultural potential.

In the late 1800s, when the first settlers began making the arduous journey north to Peace River Country, the area had no roads and no communication to the outside world. Families had to be entirely self-sufficient. But that didn't deter the first immigrants from journeying through 300 km of dense forests and boggy muskeg to the prairie—isolated from southern farmland, but highly suited to agriculture. When the Grand Trunk Pacific Railway reached Edson, to the south, settlers arrived over the **Edson Trail.** When the railway arrived from Dunvegan in 1916, the settlement—then on the floodplains of Bear Creek—boomed. The population continued to climb slowly but steadily until 1976, when the discovery of Alberta's largest gas reserve nearby boosted it to over 20,000. Now the largest city in northwestern Alberta, Grande Prairie is a major service, cultural, and transportation center.

SIGHTS

Although malls, motels, restaurants, and other services are spread out along Hwy. 2 west and north of town, the center of the city has managed to retain much of its original charm. A short walk west of downtown on 100th Ave. is **Bear Creek,** along which most of Grande Prairie's sights lie.

Pioneer Museum
Located overlooking Bear Creek, this excellent museum, tel. (403) 532-5482, houses artifacts from the area's early development, a wildlife display, and dinosaur bones from a nearby dig site. Outside are a number of historic buildings including a church, schoolhouse, blacksmith shop, and fire station. It's open in summer, daily 10 a.m.-6 p.m.; admission $2. The easiest access from downtown is east along 102nd Avenue.

Muskoseepi Park
The name of this 446-hectare city park means "Bear Creek" in the Cree language. The valley through which Bear Creek flows has always been used for recreation and is now preserved as a natural area within city limits. At the north end of the park is **Bear Creek Reservoir,** the focal point of the park. Here you'll find an interpretive pavilion, outdoor pool, tennis courts, mini-golf, and canoe rentals. From the lake, 40 km of hiking and biking trails follow both sides of Bear Creek to the city's outer edge.

Overlooking the reservoir (access from the Hwy. 2 bypass) is **Grande Prairie Regional College.** Designed by renowned architect Douglas Cardinal, the flowing curves of this brick building are the city's most distinctive landmark.

Prairie Art Gallery
Housed in the original Grande Prairie High School, 10209 99th St., tel. (403) 532-8111, this large fa-

GRANDE PRAIRIE

BEAR CREEK

CRYSTAL LAKE

TO HWY. 34 AND EDMONTON

APPLE BETTY'S

GREYHOUND BUS DEPOT

TRUMPETER MOTOR INN

SILVER CREST LODGE

IGLOO INN

116th AVE.

HWY. 2 BYPASS

TOURIST INFORMATION CENTRE

ROTARY PARK CAMPGROUND

MUSKOSEEPI PARK

BEAR CREEK RESERVOIR

SEE INSET

108th AVE.

GRANDE PRAIRIE REGIONAL COLLEGE

HOSPITAL

TO AIRPORT, BEAVERLODGE, AND DAWSON CREEK (B.C.)

PIONEER MUSEUM

100th AVE.

STANFORD INN

WESTPORT INN

TRAX

ECONO-LODGE

99th AVE.

96th AVE.

92nd AVE.

116th ST.

WAPITI RD.

108th ST.

100th ST.

84th AVE.

84th AVE.

92nd ST.

102nd ST.

100th ST.

96th ST.

RESOURCES RD.

68th AVE.

WEE LINKS GOLF CAMPGROUND

SOUTH BEAR CREEK PARK

GRANDE PRAIRIE GOLF AND COUNTRY CLUB

TO EVERGREEN PARK

BEAR CREEK

INSET

CHAMBER OF COMMERCE

103rd AVE.

102nd AVE.

101st AVE.

100th AVE.

99th AVE.

98th AVE.

97th AVE.

102nd ST.

101st ST.

100th ST.

98th ST.

99th ST.

97th ST.

103rd AVE.

PRAIRIE ART GALLERY

ABERDEEN PUB & RESTAURANT

POST OFFICE

BOOKS ABOUND

JAVA JUNCTION

LIBRARY

TOWNE CENTRE MALL

0   0.5 mi
0   0.5 km

TO GRANDE CACHE

40

cility has three main galleries displaying permanent and temporary exhibitions of work by artists from throughout Canada. It's open year-round, Tues.-Fri. 10 a.m.-6 p.m., Sat.-Sun. 1-5 p.m.

Kleskun Hill Natural Area

Kleskun Hill is located 20 km east of Grande Prairie along Hwy. 34. It rises 100 meters above the surrounding prairie and is the most northern badlands in North America. Plant species normally associated with southern latitudes, such as prickly-pear cactus, are found here. The only facility is a picnic area at the south end.

RECREATION AND EVENTS

Golfing

Grande Prairie has a number of challenging golf courses. South of downtown is **Grande Prairie Golf and Country Club,** tel. (403) 532-0340. Farther south is **Bear Creek Golf Club,** tel. 538-3393, a difficult 18-hole course, and **Dunes Golf Club,** tel. 538-4333.

Theater

Two theaters offer performances Sept.-April. **Grande Prairie Little Theatre,** based at the newly renovated Second Street Theatre, is small but all productions are popular; call (403) 538-1616 for details. **Grande Prairie Regional College Theatre** hosts a variety of amateur dramas as well as touring performers and country-music stars; call 539-2957 for details.

Events

Evergreen Park, south of downtown, is a 200-hectare site that hosts many of the city's larger events including horse racing and a farmer's market each Saturday during summer. The first weekend of June is **Stompede,** a gathering of North America's best cowboys and chuck wagon drivers. On the following weekend are the **Highland Games,** including zany events such as the North American Haggis Hurling Championship. The last weekend of July is the regional fair with a livestock show, chuck wagon races, and a midway.

Grande Prairie's climate is perfect for **hot air balloning** and every couple of years the city plays host to a national or international competition.

ACCOMMODATIONS AND FOOD

Hotels And Motels

All motels are located west and north of downtown along Hwy. 2. **Westport Inn,** 11301 100th Ave., tel. (403) 532-4100, is the least expensive; $32 s, $34 d. **Econo-lodge,** 10909 100th Ave., tel. 539-4700, has slightly larger rooms; $34 s, $44 d. **Stanford Inn,** 11401 100th Ave., tel. 539-5670 or (800) 661-8160, is better value. Each room has a kitchenette with coffee supplied; $35 s, $40 d. **Silver Crest Lodge,** north of downtown at 11902 100th St., tel. 532-1040 or (800) 422-7791, has clean, modern rooms; $38 s, $40 d. Nearby, **Igloo Inn,** 11724 100th St., tel. 539-5314, has a laundry and exercise room; $40 s, $45 d. And **Trumpeter Motor Inn,** 12102 100th St., tel. 539-5561 or (800) 661-9435, has a good restaurant and an indoor pool; $50 s, $55 d.

Campgrounds

Rotary Park Campground, located along the Hwy. 2 bypass, tel. (403) 532-1137, overlooks Bear Creek and is a short walk from downtown through Muskoseepi Park. It has showers and a laundry but few trees; tent sites are $10, hookups $13-15. At the south end of town, along 68th Ave., is **Wee Links Golf Campground,** tel. 538-4501, at a pitch-and-putt golf course; $13-15.

Food

Downtown is **Java Junction,** 9931 100th Ave., tel. (403) 539-5070, a small coffee shop with friendly staff; coffee and a muffin is $1.50, and soup, sandwich, and coffee is $4. **Trax Dining Room,** 11001 100th Ave., tel. 532-0776, is open daily 6 a.m.-11 p.m. and has good breakfasts from $4 and lunch and dinner from $8. This joint is always busy. **Apple Betty's,** 12309 100th St., tel. 538-1600, is a reasonable buffet restaurant although the choice of hot dishes is not great; lunch is $6, dinner $8. **Aberdeen Pub & Restaurant,** 9728 Montrose Ave., tel. 539-4720, has a warm, cozy atmosphere and reasonably priced steak and seafood dishes ($10-17). The lounge next door is open till 2 a.m. The restaurant **The Golden Inn,** 11201 100th Ave., opens at 5:30 a.m. and is popular for breakfast. The cafeteria in Grande Prairie Regional College has inexpensive meals from $4.

SERVICES AND INFORMATION

Transportation
Grande Prairie Regional Airport is located two km west of downtown, then north along Airport Road. It is served by **Air B.C.,** tel. (403) 539-1700 or (800) 222-6596, and **Canadian Regional,** tel. 532-9616 or (800) 665-1177, who both have daily flights to Edmonton.

The **Greyhound Bus Depot,** 9918 121st Ave., tel. 539-1111, has a cafe and lockers. Buses leave four times daily to Edmonton ($47.19 one way), once daily to Peace River ($15.78), and twice daily to Dawson Creek in British Columbia ($14.28).

For a taxi call **Prairie Cabs,** tel. 532-1060, or **Swan Taxi,** tel. 539-4000.

Other Services
The **post office** is at 10001 101st Avenue. **Towne Centre Laundry** is in the Towne Centre Mall on 99th Ave. (another is located to the north in the Prairie Haven Motel at 12002 100th St.). **Queen Elizabeth II Hospital** is at 10409 98th St., tel. (403) 538-7100.

Information
Grande Prairie Public Library, 9910 99th Ave., tel. (403) 532-3580, is an excellent facility open Tues.-Fri. 10 a.m.-9 p.m., Saturday 10 a.m.-6 p.m., and Sunday 1-5 p.m. **Books Abound,** at 10017A 100th Ave., has a good selection of books about western Canada.

The **tourist information center** is located off the Hwy. 2 bypass on 106th Street. It's open in summer, daily 9 a.m.-9 p.m. The **chamber of commerce,** 10011 103rd Ave., tel. 532-5340, is open year-round, Mon.-Fri. 8:30 a.m.-4:30 p.m.

VICINITY OF GRANDE PRAIRIE

Saskatoon Island Provincial Park
For thousands of years natives have come to this area to collect, as the name suggests, saskatoons (serviceberries). The berries are still abundant and cover nearly a third of the 102-hectare park. Late July and August are the best times for berry picking (although park rangers don't encourage the activity). **Little Lake,** with its abundant aquatic vegetation, provides ideal habitat for **trumpeter swans,** North America's largest waterfowl. This park is one of the few areas in Canada where the majestic bird can be viewed during the nesting season. Vegetation in the park is classified as northern aspen parkland, the only park in Alberta to be representative of this biome.

The campground has showers, groceries, a food concession, mini-golf, and is beside a beach; unserviced sites are $11, powered sites $13. The park is located 19 km west of Grande Prairie on Hwy. 2, then three km north.

Beaverlodge And Vicinity
This small town, 40 km west of Grande Prairie along Hwy. 2, is a northern agricultural center at the gateway to **Monkman Pass,** a pass through the Canadian Rockies found earlier this century. The only access to the pass is by 4WD. **Beaverlodge Hotel** houses a collection of over 20,000 historical artifacts, including a mechanical stuffed animal. **South Peace Centennial Museum,** tel. (403) 354-8869, started as a farmer's hobby and has grown into a working museum cataloguing the agricultural history of Alberta with displays housed in 15 buildings. It's open in summer, daily 10 a.m.-6 p.m.; admission is $2. On **Pioneer Day,** the third Sunday of July, all the farm machinery is started up and operated.

West of Beaverlodge on Hwy. 671, just west of **Goodfare,** is **Driftwood Exotic Ranch and Wildlife Haven.** The ranch functions as both an animal sanctuary and a working farm of exotic animals. Among the odd creatures are a joose (a cross between a Jersey cow and a moose); llamas; Vietnamese pigs; highland cattle; Siberian tigers, one of which appeared in the movie *Bird on a Wire;* and a jaguar. Part of the farm is a Ducks Unlimited bird sanctuary where many shorebirds and waterfowl nest. The farm is open in summer, daily 10 a.m.-6 p.m.; tel. 356-3769.

Sexsmith
North of Grande Prairie, the small town of Sexsmith—once known as "Grain Capital of the

British Empire"—has undergone extensive restoration. Its main street is now a pleasant place to stop. One block off the main street is the **Sexsmith Blacksmith Shop,** tel. (403) 568-3668, a working shop restored to its original 1916 condition. Inside the log structure are over 10,000 artifacts including caches of moonshine, hidden in the log walls to prevent detection by the North West Mounted Police. The shop is open in summer, daily 9 a.m.-5 p.m.

From Sexsmith, Hwy. 2 climbs slowly through a mixed-wood forest connecting the **Saddle Hills,** to the west, and the **Birch Hills,** to the northeast. After crossing a low, indistinguishable summit the road begins descending into the Peace River Valley.

THE PEACE RIVER VALLEY

From its source in the interior of British Columbia, the Peace River has carved a majestic swath across the northwestern corner of Alberta's boreal forest. Explorers, trappers, settlers, and missionaries traveled upstream from Fort Chipewyan on Lake Athabasca and established trading posts along the fertile valley and surrounding plains. The posts at **Fort Vermilion** and **Dunvegan** have slipped into oblivion and are now designated historical sites, but the town of **Peace River** has grown from a small post into an agriculture and distribution center that serves the entire Peace River region. The river—so named because on its banks peace was made between warring Cree and Beaver Indians—and the surrounding land is often referred to as Peace Country. This moniker is a throwback to the 1930s when the government refused to build a rail link and many local residents favored ceding from Alberta and creating their own country.

UPPER PEACE VALLEY

The Upper Peace Valley extends 230 km from the Alberta/British Columbia border to the town of Peace River. From Hwy. 49, on the south side of the river, and Highways 64 and 2 on the north side, roads lead down to the river and nine recreation and camping areas, initially developed for the bicentennial of Alexander Mackenzie's historical passage to the Pacific Ocean. The best way to start a visit to the region is by visiting **Courtesy Corner,** at the junction of Highways 2 and 49. An enormous red-and-white tepee houses a tourist information center and sells local arts and crafts; open in summer, daily 9 a.m.-8 p.m.

Moonshine Lake Provincial Park And Vicinity

Over 100 species of birds and, in winter, high concentrations of moose call Moonshine Lake Provincial Park home. Occupying 850 hectares 42 km west of Courtesy Corner, the park is best known for its rainbow trout fishing. Some people claim the lake is named for the moon's reflection on its still water, although it more likely came

from a fellow who sold moonshine to travelers en route to Dawson Creek. Campsites are scattered among stands of aspen, poplar, and white spruce, and have pit toilets, kitchen shelters, and firewood; unserviced sites $11, powered sites $13.

From south of the park, Hwy. 49 continues 54 km to the Alberta/B.C. border and a further 19 km to Dawson Creek at Mile Zero of the Alaska Highway. **Cotillion Park,** on the southern banks of the Peace River, is accessible along 35-km Pillsworth Rd. (Hwy. 719), eight km from the border. Many large mammals frequent this secluded park, and sandstone cliffs here have been eroded into strange-looking pinnacles called hoodoos. Camping, with showers, is $7.50.

Historic Dunvegan

As Hwy. 2 descends into the Peace River Valley from the south, it crosses Alberta's longest suspension bridge at Dunvegan—a point that has been the site of many trading posts and an Anglican mission. On the east side of the road are the restored buildings of St. Charles Roman Catholic Mission, built in 1885. A gravel road leads under the bridge to the site of the original settlement. Just past the bridge are truck farms that date back over 100 years. Beside them, hidden in the trees, the Hudson's Bay Company factor's house dates to the fur-trading era. A small provincial park on the east side of the bridge has a campground; unserviced sites $11, powered sites $13.

Highway 64

From **Fairview,** 26 km northeast of Dunvegan, Hwy. 64 heads north then west, roughly following the Peace River into British Columbia. To the west, on the banks of the Peace River, are two campgrounds that form part of the Upper Peace Valley Recreation Area. **Pratt's Landing** is along Hwy. 682, and to the north, at the mouth of Montagneuse River, is **Carter Camp.** Back on Hwy. 64 is the town of **Hines Creek** and its **End of Steel Heritage Park and Museum** featuring a caboose, church, trapper's cabin, and a Russian pioneer home; open in summer, Mon.-Fri. 9 a.m.-

Before 1916, Peace River had no rail line, and was just one of many remote posts throughout the north.

PROVINCIAL ARCHIVES OF ALBERTA

5 p.m., weekends 1-7 p.m. From Hines Creek it is 98 km to the border. To the north rise the flat-topped **Clear Hills,** which offer a number of forest-service campgrounds, and **Whispering Pines,** a small ski hill with one lift and a vertical rise of 140 meters.

PEACE RIVER

From all directions, the final approach into the town of Peace River is breathtaking. This town of 6,700 straddles the majestic Peace River below the confluence of two other rivers, the Smoky and Heart. Alexander Mackenzie was one of the earliest white men to visit the region. He established a post, named Fort Forks, on the south bank of the river, upstream of the present town. It was from here, after the winter of 1792-93, that he completed his historic journey to the Pacific Ocean—the first person to cross the North American continent north of Mexico. The first permanent settlers were missionaries who, apart from their zealous religious work, promoted the region for its agricultural potential and as a service center and distribution point for river transportation. When the rail link with Edmonton was completed in 1916, land was opened for homesteading and settlers poured into town. The farming traditions they began continue today.

Sights

High above town (access from 100th Ave., and under Hwy. 2), at a lookout overlooking the valley, is the grave of **12 Foot Davis.** Davis was not a giant of a man. In fact, he was short. But he got his name from a claim he staked in the Cariboo Goldfields in British Columbia. He noticed that two very successful claims had a 12-foot strip between them, so he staked the area and made a fortune. He then headed to Peace River Country and opened up trading posts along the river. Another excellent view is afforded from **Sagitawa Lookout** on Judah Hill. From here you can see town, valley, and the confluence of the Peace and Smoky rivers.

Many historic buildings line the main street (100th St.) and many have plaques with historical facts. The wide street is typical of early boomtowns; its width allowed wagons to turn around. At the southern end of the street, across the mouth of the Heart River is **Peace River Centennial Museum,** which has displays on native clothing, the fur trade, early explorers, the development of the town, and an extensive photo collection and archives. It's open in summer, daily noon-5 p.m.; tel. (403) 624-4261. Admission is $2.

On the west side of the river is the site of **Shaftesbury,** a settlement that grew around an Anglican mission founded in 1887. From the

PEACE RIVER

73rd AVE.

PEACE REGIONAL POOL

77th AVE.

RIVER RD.

84th AVE.

PEACE RIVER

90th AVE.

TO GOLF COURSES AND GRIMSHAW

2

LIONS CLUB CAMPGROUND

SHAFTESBURY TRAIL

98th ST.

96th AVE.

SILVER SPUR SALOON

SEE INSET

98th AVE.

99th AVE.

100th ST.

101st AVE.

103rd AVE.

12 FOOT DAVIS HISTORICAL SITE

MISERY MOUNTAIN

TO SHAFTESBURY FERRY

684

107th AVE.

101st ST.

HOSPITAL

JUDAH HILL RD.

HEART RIVER

TO DONNELLY AND EDMONTON

2

TO SAGITAWA LOOKOUT

744

NOT TO SCALE

INSET

TRAVELLERS MOTOR HOTEL

TOURIST INFORMATION CENTRE

96th AVE.

PEACE VALLEY INNS

97th AVE.

BUS DEPOT

98th AVE.

CRESCENT MOTEL

99th AVE.

100th AVE.

98th ST.

99th ST.

100th ST.

101st ST.

POST OFFICE

101st AVE.

LAUNDROMAT

CHUCK'S PLACE

THE MET

T.J'S RESTAURANT

PEACE RIVER CENTENNIAL MUSEUM

103rd AVE.

© MOON PUBLICATIONS, INC.

site, Hwy. 684 follows the historic Shaftesbury Trail—used for hundreds of years by natives, explorers, traders, missionaries, and Klondikers—to Blakely's Landing from where the **Shaftesbury Ferry** now crosses the river all summer, daily 7 a.m.-midnight.

Recreation And Events

The nine-hole **Peace View Golf Course,** tel. (403) 624-1164, is along Weberville Rd., west of town. Farther west is **Mighty Peace Golf and Country Club,** tel. 332-4885, an 18-hole championship course; green fees $20. **Peace Regional Pool,** 9810 73rd Ave., tel. 624-3720, opens for public swimming each day; $3.50.

Misery Mountain Ski Hill, tel. 624-4881, off Hwy. 684, is visible from most points in town. It's the largest non-mountain ski area in Alberta. Although the lifts don't operate in summer, views from the summit are well worth the one-hour walk from the base area. In winter lift tickets are $13.

In March, on the first Saturday following St. Patrick's Day, the **pig races** come to town—two-man teams race prized porkers down the main street. The third weekend of July, the **Jaywalkers Jamboree** brings parades and a street dance to town. And **River Daze** floats by the second weekend of August, featuring a variety of wild and wet activities on the Peace River.

Accommodations

All motels are located at the north end of downtown, but still within walking distance of shops and restaurants. Least expensive is **Crescent Motel,** tel. (403) 624-2586, $40 s, $44 d. Kitchenettes are an extra $6. **Peace Valley Inns,** tel. 624-2020, is beside a 24-hour Smitty's Restaurant, $39 s, $49 d. The last option is **Travellers Motor Hotel,** tel. 624-3621 or (800) 661-3227, which has a sauna, restaurant, and lounge; $44 s, $49 d.

Lions Club Campground on the west side of the river, tel. 624-2120, has well-treed sites, showers, laundry, and groceries; unserviced sites $10, powered sites $12. Other places where you ought to be able to pitch a tent without a hassle include **Tangent Park,** beside the Shaftesbury Ferry south of town; at both golf courses (west of town); and west of town off Hwy. 2 at **Queen Elizabeth Provincial Park.**

Food

Restaurants are limited. Try **Chuck's Place,** 10107 100th St., where large portions make up for a distinct lack of atmosphere. Another busy place is **TJ's Restaurant,** 10011 102nd Ave., tel. (403) 624-3427, where the Chinese dishes are better than the Canadian. Especially delicious is the Seafood Hotpot, $14. **The Met** department store, 10010 102nd Ave., has an inexpensive cafe where two eggs and bacon is under two bucks. Along River Rd. is the **Silver Spur Saloon,** tel. 624-5007, which has live country music most nights.

Transportation And Tours

The **airport,** 13 km west of town, is served by **Canadian Regional,** tel. (403) 624-1777 or (800) 665-1177. The **Greyhound Bus Depot** is downtown at 9801 97th Ave., tel. 624-2558, with daily services to Edmonton ($47.19 one way), Grande Prairie ($15.78 one way), and Hay River in the Northwest Territories ($69.44 one way). For **Peace River Taxi** call 624-3020. **Town & Country Bus Tours,** tel. 624-2554, runs a variety of tours around town and to nearby attractions and will pick up at the Lions Club Campground; $18-33. **Tar Island River Cruise** operates jet boat trips down the Peace River to a small island with log cabins. The overnight journey, including three meals, the boat ride, and lodging, is $117 per person. For more information call 624-4295.

Services And Information

The **post office** is at 10031 100th Street. **Conveno Laundromat** is in the River Drive Mall on 100th Street. **Peace River Municipal Hospital** is located at 10915 99th St., tel. (403) 624-7500. For the **RCMP** call 624-6611. The **tourist information center** is located in a log building at 9309 100th St., tel. 624-4042; it's open in summer, daily 8:30 a.m.-4:30 p.m.

MACKENZIE HIGHWAY

Named for 18th-century explorer Alexander Mackenzie, this route, also known as Hwy. 35, extends from **Grimshaw,** 24 km west of Peace River, for 473 km north to the Northwest Territories. It passes through a vast, empty land,

NORTHWEST TERRITORIES
ALBERTA

INDIAN CABINS

TO HAY RIVER

BISTCHO LAKE

CAMERON HILLS

BRITISH COLUMBIA
ALBERTA

1

35

STEEN RIVER

HAY RIVER

WOOD BUFFALO NATIONAL PARK

MACKENZIE HIGHWAY

ZAMA CITY

MEANDER RIVER

CARIBOU MOUNTAINS

HAY RIVER

HAY-ZAMA LAKES

MARGARET LAKE

RAINBOW LAKE

58

HIGH LEVEL

58

FORT VERMILION

LA CRETE

PEACE RIVER

88

PADDLE PRAIRIE

697

FERRY

MACKENZIE HIGHWAY

BUFFALO

CHINCHAGA RIVER

MOON

HEAD

35

HILLS

0   20 mi
0   20 km

HOTCHKISS

692

NOTIKEWAN PROVINCIAL PARK

MANNING

NOTIKEWAN

RIVER

NORTH STAR

690

DEADWOOD

DIXONVILLE

689

743

686

TO FORT ST. JOHN

64

QUEEN ELIZABETH PROVINCIAL PARK

737

686

PEACE RIVER

688

TO SLAVE LAKE AND HIGH PRAIRIE

685

732

2

TO GRAND PRAIRIE

2

GRIMSHAW

TO WHITECOURT AND EDMONTON

2

88

© MOON PUBLICATIONS, INC.

dominated by the Peace River and a seemingly endless forest of spruce, poplar, and jack pine. The main population centers are **Manning** and **High Level.** Along the way are many stump-filled fields, carved out of the boreal forest by farmers who, for the last 100 years, have eked a living from some of the world's northernmost farmland. The only access to the Peace River is at **Notikewin Provincial Park** and at **Tompkin's Landing,** a ferry crossing east of Paddle Prairie.

When you're through exploring this wild northland, you have two alternatives to backtracking along Mackenzie Highway. One is to continue into the Northwest Territories and complete what is known as the **Deh Cho Connection,** which links the Mackenzie with the Liard and Alaska highways—an 1,800-km loop that finishes in Dawson Creek, British Columbia. The other option is to follow Hwy. 58 east from High Level and head south on the Bicentennial Hwy. 430 km to Slave Lake (see "Slave Lake" in the "Northern Heartland" section above).

Grimshaw

Best known as Mile Zero of the Mackenzie Hwy., this town of 2,700 has grown around the railway as a farming center. For many years after the railway arrived it was a jumping-off point for farmers, trappers, and homesteaders in Peace Valley Country. Northwest of Grimshaw, on the eastern shore of Lac Cardinal, is **Queen Elizabeth Provincial Park.** The lake is very shallow and no streams flow from it. This creates an ideal habitat for many species of waterfowl. Beavers, moose, and black bears are also present. The camping area has pit toilets, kitchen shelters, and firewood; sites are $11.

To Manning

From Grimshaw it is 40 km north to the small hamlet of **Dixonville.** Here you'll find a trading post and the turnoff to Sulphur Lake (55 km northwest along Hwy. 689), where camping is available. A further 23 km north, along the access road to Deadwood, a turnoff south leads to **Bradshaw Bird Sanctuary,** a privately owned exotic bird farm with geese, peacocks, pheasants, and a pair of trumpeter swans. The Bradshaws also sell crafts made from bird feathers.

A homestead built by a Latvian settler in 1918 is located three km south of **North Star,** on the

old Hwy. 35. It has been declared a Provincial Historical Site and, although locked, you can stick your nose against the windows and see homemade wooden beds and a sauna, and appreciate the work that has gone into the hand-hewn log buildings.

Manning

As the highway descends into the picturesque Notikewin Valley it passes through the relatively new town of Manning. Formerly called Aurora, this town of 1,100 is a service center for the region's agricultural and petroleum industries. At the south end of town, one km east on Hwy. 691, is the excellent **Battle River Pioneer Museum,** which has a large collection of antique wrenches, stuffed animals (including a rare albino moose), carriages and buggies, farm machinery, a birch necklace carved out of a single piece of wood, and a collection of prehistoric arrowheads—ask to see the one embedded in a whalebone. The museum is open in summer, daily 10 a.m.-6 p.m.; tel. (403) 836-2374.

The **Hillcrest Motel,** tel. 836-3381, $40 s, $45 d, and **Manning Motor Inn,** tel. 836-2801, $45 s, $50 d, are both located at the south end of town and both have restaurants. **Manning Municipal Campground** is located just west of the tourist information center in a shaded spot beside the Notikewin River. The campground is small but has showers, powered sites, and is free. It is also possible to camp at the golf course, north of town, which offers powered sites ($7-10 per night) and a restaurant. The **tourist information center,** tel. 836-3875, is located on the main street, by the river; it's open from May to mid-September, daily 9 a.m.-5 p.m.

Notikewin Provincial Park

Twenty-one km north of Hotchkiss, Hwy. 692 turns east off Hwy. 35 and leads to Notikewin Provincial Park, a 970-hectare preserve at the confluence of the Notikewin and Peace rivers. The 30-km road to the park is partly paved and occasionally steep. "Notikewin" is the Cree word for battle—many were fought in the region. Here a stand of 200-year-old spruce presides over Spruce Island, at the mouth of the Notikewin River. The island also supports an abundance of ostrich ferns growing to a height of two meters. Beavers, mule deer, moose, and the occasional black bear can be seen in the area. Bird species are diverse and include sandhill cranes, which rest at the mouth of the Notikewin River on their southern migration in September. The river offers good fishing for gold-eye, walleye, and northern pike. Camping is $7.50.

A Short Detour
The largest of eight Métis settlements, established throughout the province during the 1930s, is **Paddle Prairie,** 65 km north of Twin Lakes. From 10 km north of here a gravel road (Hwy. 697) leads east to Tomkin's Landing and one of

---

AURORA BOREALIS

The aurora borealis, or northern lights, is an emotional experience for some, spiritual for others, and without exception is unforgettable—an exhibition of color that dances across the sky like a kaleidoscope.

Auroral light is created through a complex process that occurs within the earth's atmosphere—a spontaneous phenomenon with no pattern and no "season," that starts with the sun. Essentially a huge, atomic fusion reactor, the sun emits the heat and light that keep us alive, and also emits electronically charged ions that are thrust through space at high speeds. When these ions reach the earth's rarefied upper atmosphere—about 180 km above the earth's surface—they are captured by the earth's magnetic field and accelerated toward the poles. Along the way they collide with the atoms and molecules of the gases in the atmosphere, which in turn become temporarily charged or "ionized." This absorbed energy is then released by the ionized gases, often in the form of light. The color of the light varies from red to yellow to green, depending on the gas; nitrogen atoms produce a violet and sometimes red color, oxygen a green and, at higher altitudes, an orange.

Because the magnetic field is more intense near the north and south magnetic poles the lights are best seen at high latitudes. In northern Alberta the light show takes place up to 160 nights annually, with displays best north of Peace River. They generally start as a faint glow on the northeastern horizon after the sun has set, improving as the sky becomes darker.

---

only eight ferry crossings in the province (operates in summer, daily 24 hours). It then continues to La Crete and Fort Vermilion, crosses the Peace River, and intersects Hwy. 58, which heads west, rejoining the Mackenzie Hwy. at High Level.

La Crete has grown into an agricultural center on the northern fringe of the continent's arable land. Most residents are Mennonites who moved to the region in the 1930s. They are from a traditional Protestant sect originating in Holland, whose members settled in remote regions throughout the world and established self-sufficient agricultural lifestyles, in hopes of being left to practice their faith in peace. On the streets and in the local restaurants you'll hear their language, Plattdeutsch (Low German), which is spoken by Mennonites throughout the world.

To the east of this flat, prairielike area, the **Buffalo Head Hills** rise nearly 700 meters above the surrounding land. To the west, an eight km road from town leads past a golf course to one of the Peace River's many natural sandbars, and to Etna's Landing where there is good swimming.

Fort Vermilion
This town of 800, on the south bank of the Peace River, 77 km east of High Level, vies with Fort Chipewyan as the oldest settlement in Alberta. It was named for the red clay deposits present in the banks of the river. The first trading post here was established a few kilometers downstream of present-day Fort Vermilion by the North West Company in 1788. Trade with Beaver, Cree, and Dene Indians was brisk, and by 1802 the Hudson's Bay Company had also established a post. In 1821 the companies merged, and in 1830, they moved operations to the town's present site. The area's agricultural potential gained worldwide attention when locally grown wheat, transported along the river highway, won a gold medal at the 1876 World Fair in Philadelphia. For 150 years, supplies arrived by riverboat or were hauled overland from the town of Peace River. When the Mackenzie Hwy. was completed the river highway became obsolete. The last riverboat arrived in Fort Vermilion in 1952 but it wasn't until 1974, when a bridge was built across the Peace River, that the town was linked to the outside

world. Many old buildings and cabins, in varying states of disrepair, still stand. Pick up a *Fort Vermilion Heritage Guide* from the tourist information center to help identify the many historical sites in town. The **Mary Batt & Son General Store** was constructed from logs removed from the 1897 Hudson's Bay Company post. The **Sheridan Lawrence Hotel**, tel. (403) 927-4400, is the only place to stay in town and has a small restaurant and bar; $45 s, $50 d. North and west of town are campgrounds. The summer-only **tourist information center** is located in a dove-tailed log home built by hand in 1923; tel. 927-3216.

High Level

Located 279 km north of Grimshaw, this town of 3,000 is situated at the center of a vast region rich in natural resources. The town expanded during the oil boom of the 1960s and has prospered ever since. The grain elevators, serving agricultural communities to the east, are the northernmost in the world. Forestry is also a major local industry; the town boasts one of the world's most productive logging and sawmill operations, turning out over 250 million board feet of lumber annually.

Fortunately, much of the surrounding forest is safe from loggers; the 7.5-million-hectare **Footner Lake Forest** has poor drainage, forming major bogs and permafrost that make timber harvest commercially unviable. The forest encompasses the entire northern part of the province west of Wood Buffalo National Park.

Northeast of High Level are the **Caribou Mountains,** which rise to a plateau 800 meters above the Peace River. At that altitude, and being so far north, the fragile environment is easily disturbed. The mountains are blanketed in white spruce, aspen, and pine, and two major lakes—Margaret and Wentzel—offer excellent fishing and sandy beaches. Northwest of High Level are the **Cameron Hills** and **Bistcho Lake** (where many Albertan fish hatcheries harvest walleye spawn). The most accessible part of the forest is **Hutch Lake,** 32 km north of town. The lake is surrounded by aspen and poplar and is the source of the **Meander River.** The dominant feature here is **Watt Mountain** (780 meters), which you can see to the northwest of High Level. From Hutch Lake, a service road

leads 11 km to the summit. The recreation area at the north end of the lake has a large picnic area, an interpretive trail, and camping. Maps are available at the tourist information center.

Motel prices in High Level are just a warm-up for those in the NWT, so don't be surprised at $60 rooms that you'd prefer to pay $30 for. The six motels in town are usually full throughout the year with work crews. Least expensive is **Sweet Dreams Motel,** tel. (403) 926-3395, $35 s, $40 d. The largest is **Sunset Motor Inn,** tel. 926-2272, which has a restaurant and bar, $53 s, $64 d. A free municipal campground is located east of town on Hwy. 35, and a primitive campground lies farther north at **Hutch Lake Recreation Area,** $7.50 per night. **Aspen Ridge Campground,** tel. 926-4540, three km south of town, is privately owned and has coin showers and a laundry; unserviced sites $13, powered sites $16.

The only facade on 100th Ave. (the main street) not painted shades of brown or gray is **The Lunch Counter.** The specialties are large, healthy sandwiches and freshly prepared salads. Expect to pay around $4 for breakfast and $5-6 for lunch. Across the road is **The Canton Restaurant,** tel. 926-3053; the combo dinners seem like a good deal, but portions are small— stick to the main meals. The restaurant in the Sunset Motor Inn serves dishes starting at $10 including a salad bar (that also offers soup and a variety of fresh fruit). Also here is a lounge and nightclub open Friday and Saturday nights with occasional live bands.

Footner Lake Airport, north of town, is served by **Canadian Regional;** tel. 926-3031 or (800) 665-1177. The **Greyhound Bus Depot** is located at 10101 95th St., tel. 926-3233. Buses depart daily for Peace River ($34.12), continuing to Edmonton ($81.32).

The post office, banks, library, and a number of laundromats are located on 100th Street. The large **tourist information center,** tel. 926-4811, is located at the south end of town. It's open in summer, daily 9 a.m.-5 p.m., weekdays only the rest of the year.

Rainbow Lake

Rainbow Lake is an oil field community of 1,100, 141 km west of High Level along Hwy. 58. The town grew around oil-and-gas exploration during the 1960s. Vast reservoirs of these resources still lie underneath the ground, untapped until oil prices rise. The town has a golf course, two motels, and two restaurants. A campground 45 km south of town has sites for $7.50 per night.

Hay-Zama Lakes
This complex network of lakes, marshes, and streams is one of Canada's largest freshwater wetlands. It covers 800 square km and is home to over 200 species of birds. It's also the main source of the Hay River, which flows north to Great Slave Lake. This fragile ecosystem, 160 km northwest of High Level, is relatively remote, and would have remained that way except for the large reservoirs of oil that lay beneath its surface. Oil and birds do not mix, but drilling has gone ahead and the small community of **Zama City,** north of the lakes, has grown around the drilling project. The town is also the southern terminus for an interprovincial pipeline from the oil fields at Norman Wells (NWT). Strict environmental guidelines mean that most of the mining activity takes place during winter, after the many thousands of geese, ducks, and other shorebirds have migrated south. Although there are no designated roads or camping areas around the lakes, many gravel roads used by the natives and oil-exploration personnel lead through the area.

The Border Or Bust
From High Level it is 191 km to the Alberta/ Northwest Territories border. The road follows the Meander River to a town of the same name at the confluence of the Hay River which the road then parallels to the border. The settlement of **Meander River** is on a Dene Tha Indian Reserve and is noted for its many local artists. Watch for the local rabbit population living beside the road. North of the community, where the highway crosses the Hay River, a gravel road leads 63 km to the oil town of Zama City. Campgrounds are located north of Meander River and just south of the small community of **Steen River,** a base for forest-fire-fighting planes. Alberta's northernmost community is **Indian Cabins,** 14 km from the border. The cabins that gave the town its name are gone but a traditional native cemetery with spirit houses covering the graves is located 200 meters north of the gas station. In the trees is the scaffold burial site of a child whose body was placed in a hollowed-out log and hung between the limbs of two trees.

BOB RACE

KAREN MCKINLEY

NORTHWEST TERRITORIES
INTRODUCTION

As the world's last great wilderness frontiers slowly disappear, Canada's vast northlands—north of the 60th Parallel—remain relatively untouched, unspoiled, and uninhabited. Once these lands were home only to small populations of indigenous Dene and Inuit people who had adapted to the harsh environment. But explorers, whalers, missionaries, and governments eventually found their way here, bringing rapid changes to native lifestyles. Today, travelers, adventurers, writers, artists, and scientists come in search of the territories' unlimited opportunities for naturalist and wilderness pursuits.

Within the region's borders are two of the world's 10 largest lakes, one of the world's longest rivers, a waterfall twice the height of Niagara, two UNESCO World Heritage Sites, five national parks, the glaciated peaks of Baffin and Ellesmere islands, and an amazing abundance of wildlife.

THE LAND

The territories' 3.3 million square km take up a third of Canada—an area nearly half the size of the United States, with a population of only 63,000. Its borders stretch from the 60th Parallel to the 84th, and from the Yukon to Davis Strait (just 50 km from Greenland)—over 3,200 km in each direction. The land can be divided into two regions—below the treeline and above it. The treeline is marked on most NWT maps as a single line that snakes from the southern reaches of Hudson Bay northwest to the Mackenzie Delta near Inuvik. The "line" provides a rough idea of where the boreal forest stops and the treeless tundra starts. But the actual transition takes place gradually across many kilometers, and varies in latitude depending on the topography and climate of the particular area.

NORTHWEST TERRITORIES

Apart from the **Mackenzie Mountains** that form the NWT/Yukon border, the dominant natural feature of the mainland is the glacially scarred bedrock of the Canadian Shield. As ice from four or five ice ages receded north, it scoured the bedrock, carving hundreds of depressions—now lakes—and creating meltwater streams that today flow throughout the land. In the west is the **Mackenzie River,** tenth-longest river in the world. North and east of the Mackenzie River Valley the land is relatively flat. Only lakes, rivers, and low rolling hills break the monotonous landscape, which ends at the west coast of Hudson Bay and, farther north, at the Arctic coast. The tidal zone here is devoid of sessile life, which would be crushed by annual movement of pack ice. North of the Arctic coast are the lower Arctic islands, which are generally less than 300 meters above sea level, their gently rolling landscapes broken only by occasional bluffs. Finally, to the northeast are the islands of the high Arctic, where you'll find the classic Arctic landscape of mountains, icefields, glaciers, and icebergs. Here sheer cliffs rise thousands of meters out of the ice-choked waters of **Baffin Bay,** incised by steep-walled fiords that end at massive glaciers spilling over from the inland ice cap.

Climate

In general, the human species lives in the middle latitudes and is accustomed to the particular set of natural phenomena common to those latitudes—the sun rises in the east each morning and sets in the west each evening; night follows day; vegetation is lush; and water most often occurs as a liquid. But here in the north, these comfortable patterns don't exist. Here in winter, the sun doesn't rise for days (or, in some places, even months), while in summer, it circles endlessly around the horizon. And for over half the year, lakes, rivers, and the ocean aren't free-flowing water but solid ice.

The region's climate is harsh, but the image of the Canadian North being a land of eternal ice and snow is a misconception. During the summer months, from late May to September, the weather can be quite pleasant. Precipitation is slight, and the average July temperature in Yellowknife is 16° C—only three degrees cooler than Calgary. Farther north, the average July

temperature in Inuvik is 13° C, and in Iqaluit 8° C. The highest temperature recorded in the territories was 41° C in Coppermine; the lowest, -57° C in Inuvik. In January, Yellowknife's average of -28° C is colder than that of Iqaluit, -26° C.

Much of the north is covered by **permafrost**—ground with an average annual temperature below freezing. In much of the mainland the topsoil melts each summer. This is known as an active layer of permafrost. But farther north, and in the Arctic archipelago, the ground remains continuously frozen in a layer 2-500 meters deep. This is called continuous permafrost.

Parks

Many of the territories' most spectacular landscapes, wildlife concentrations, and sites of historical importance have been set aside as national, territorial, and historic parks. The five national parks include **Wood Buffalo,** in the Big River Region (second-largest national park in the world); **Nahanni,** in the rugged Mackenzie Mountains; **Aulavik,** on Banks Island, representative of Canada's Arctic lowlands and supporting one of the world's greatest concentrations of musk oxen; **Auyuittuq** in the rugged mountains of Baffin Island; and **Ellesmere,** the world's northernmost national park, at the tip of the North American continent. Proposals are currently under consideration to protect several additional areas as national parks, including the breeding ground of the **Bluenose caribou herd,** the dramatic **East Arm of Great Slave Lake,** wildlife-rich **Wager Bay** in the Keewatin, and the nesting grounds of millions of seabirds on **North Baffin Island.**

Territorial parks preserve and protect sites with historic or scenic value. The largest is **Katannilik,** stretching across Baffin Island's Meta Incognita Peninsula. The **Soper River** running through the park has been designated a **Canadian Heritage River.**

Among the 17 migratory bird sanctuaries in the territories are **Queen Maud Gulf,** the world's largest such sanctuary, and **McConnell River,** where one million lesser snow geese gather during the fall migration. **Thelon Game Sanctuary,** the only such area in Canada, is primarily for the conservation of wildlife but is also a popular area for wilderness river trips.

NORTHWEST TERRITORIES REGIONS

GREENLAND

0   200 mi
0   200 km

ELLESMERE ISLAND

BAFFIN AND BEYOND

BAFFIN BAY

BEAUFORT SEA

ALASKA

WESTERN ARCTIC

BAFFIN ISLAND

VICTORIA ISLAND

ARCTIC CIRCLE

ARCTIC COAST

GREAT BEAR LAKE

YUKON

MACKENZIE RIVER VALLEY

YELLOWKNIFE AND VICINITY

RIVERS OF MYTH, MOUNTAINS OF MYSTERY

KEEWATIN

60th PARALLEL

GREAT SLAVE LAKE

BIG RIVER

HUDSON BAY

BELCHER ISLANDS

BRITISH COLUMBIA

ALBERTA

SASKATCHEWAN

MANITOBA

QUEBEC

© MOON PUBLICATIONS, INC.

The Regions

This chapter divides the Northwest Territories into eight regions. **Big River** is immediately north of Alberta and has a good road system linking Hay River, on the south shore of Great Slave Lake, to Fort Smith and Wood Buffalo National Park. Across the lake to the north is the territorial capital, **Yellowknife,** and outlying Dene communities. The spectacular mountainous region in the southwest corner of the NWT, including Nahanni National Park, has for generations been known as **Rivers of Myth, Mountains of Mystery.** These mountains and Great Slave Lake form part of the watershed that drains into the **Mackenzie River Valley.** The Mackenzie flows into the Arctic Ocean in the **Western Arctic,** north of Inuvik, at the end of North America's northernmost public road. To the east is the **Arctic coast,** a barren, treeless land where small Inuit communities rely on the abundance of marine mammals and arctic char for survival. The west coast of Hudson Bay and an area rich in wildlife farther inland is the **Keewatin.** Finally, the mountainous islands of the eastern and high Arctic, including Baffin and Ellesmere, offer some of the continent's premier wilderness adventures, and are covered in this chapter under **Baffin and Beyond.**

FLORA

The Northwest Territories include two main biomes. The **subarctic** biome, below the treeline, is predominately evergreens interspersed with tundra vegetation. **Black spruce, white spruce, jack pine** (most northerly of the pines), and **aspen** are the most common trees found here. **White birch** is the only deciduous tree able to withstand the region's climate. Due to little precipitation and a short growing season (70-80 frost-free days annually), tree growth is slow and stunted, especially closer to the treeline.

Above the treeline, in an area of continuous permafrost, is the **arctic** biome—the tundra. Here a unique selection of vegetation has successfully adapted to the region's extreme seasonal changes of temperature and sunlight, and its lack of precipitation (less than the Sahara Desert). Where water and wind have deposited soil—usually in depressions or along the banks of rivers—the vegetation is more varied. Almost all plants are perennials, able to spring to life quickly after a winter of hibernation. Brightly colored flowers such as **yellow arctic poppies, purple saxifrage, pink rhododendrons,** and **white heather** carpet entire landscapes during the short summer. **Willows** are one of the few woody plants to survive on the otherwise treeless tundra—they're found across the Arctic mainland along with **ground birch** and **Labrador tea.** Other areas are almost completely void of soil, supporting little more than **arctic ferns, lichens,** and **mosses.** Low temperatures here restrict bacterial action, and as a result, the soil is lacking in the nitrogen necessary for plant growth. Occasional oases of lush vegetation mark spots where the soil received a nitrogen boost—as

from a rotting animal carcass or the detritus of an ancient Inuit campsite.

The sparse plantlife of the Arctic is inadequate as a human food source, but all the region's plants are edible. A popular Inuit drink is made by boiling **sorrel grass** then adding sugar. When chilled, this concoction is cool and refreshing.

FAUNA

Species *diversity* in the Northwest Territories is relatively low compared to other parts of the world. Species *concentrations* here, however, are enormous, including some of the world's largest populations of caribou, musk oxen, polar bears, whales, and seabirds. The same species are found below the treeline in the Mackenzie River Basin as are found in the mountainous and northern parts of Alberta. Of note are the high numbers of **black bears** and **moose,** especially prevalent along the Liard Hwy.; the **Dall's sheep** that roam the Mackenzie Mountains; and the hybrid **bison** of Wood Buffalo National Park.

Caribou
Caribou, standing 1.5 meters tall at the shoulder, seem ungainly but have adapted superbly to life in the Arctic. Those on the mainland normally live in small groups, but congregate each fall for a migration west to the boreal forest. As many as 400,000 of the animals may band together into a single herd. Each spring the process is reversed as they head east to summer calving grounds, high above the treeline. Caribou are also found on islands of the Arctic archipelago, as far north as Ellesmere Island.

Grizzly Bears
Although there is only one species of grizzly bear—whether they be on the tundra of the Northwest Territories, on Alaska's Kodiak Island, or in the forests of northern Russia—populations in different parts of the world have each made unique adaptations to their particular environment. The grizzlies inhabiting lands north of the treeline feed mostly on the vegetation alongside Arctic streams, but occasionally hunt down other animals. One was spotted hunting seals on pack ice north of Victoria Island, 500 km north of the bears' usual range.

grizzly bear

MIKE WELLINS

Musk Oxen

These shaggy beasts, hunted to near extinction by 1900, are now restricted to the Arctic archipelago and Thelon Game Sanctuary and number approximately 80,000. The image of them in a defensive circle, protecting the young from predators or the cold, is an endearing symbol of the north. Known to the Inuit as "oomingmak," meaning "bearded one," they are covered with an underlayer of short, fine wool, and a topcoat of shaggy hair up to 60 centimeters long. This gives the animals their characteristic prehistoric appearance and helps protect them from frequent blizzards and winter temperatures that in some areas average -30° C.

Polar Bears

Evolving from the grizzly bear 250,000-400,000 years ago, the polar bear may weigh up to 600 kilograms and measure 3.5 meters from head to tail. Its most distinctive feature is a pure-white coat, but it also has a long body with a large neck.

The bear's scientific name, *Ursus maritimus,* aptly describes its habitat, that of the permanent pack ice of the Arctic Ocean and the eastern coastline down to Hudson Bay. Polar bears are at home in the sea and have been known to swim hundreds of kilometers. Their most common hunting strategy is to wait at a hole in the ice, days at a time, for a seal who needs to take a breath.

Whales

Only three of the world's 80 species of whales are widespread in the waters of the Canadian Arctic. **Belugas**—also called white whales for their coloring—are most common. They winter in the Bering Sea and off the west coast of Greenland, and migrate to estuarine areas such as the Mackenzie Delta in the western Arctic for summer calving season. **Bowheads** were the most intensely hunted of all whales, mainly due to their slow speed and great yield of blubber. The bowhead weighs as much as 50,000 kilograms and may reach 20 meters in length. Two separate populations inhabit these waters—one spends summer in the Beaufort Sea, the other in Lancaster Sound and Davis Strait.

The **narwhal** got its name from the Old Norse word "nar," meaning "corpse"—a reference to the whale's mottled gray color. Distinguished

by an ivory tusk that spirals from the male's head—an extension of a tooth—it was probably from this mammal that the European legend of the unicorn was born. It is one of the least understood of all whale species, wintering under the pack ice of Baffin Bay and Davis Strait, and migrating north in pods of up to 300 each spring. Its remarkable circulatory system allows it to dive to great depths without suffering from the bends upon surfacing.

A fourth species, the **killer whale,** is occasionally seen in the Beaufort Sea and Davis Strait.

Walruses

With its massive build and sabrelike tusks, the walrus presents a formidable and intriguing sight. They spend the summer months sunning themselves on pack ice or on isolated shorelines, and spend winter at the edge of the pack ice, or at recurring polynyas in the high Arctic. Their main diet consists of mollusks, but they've also been known to eat fish and seals. Males can weigh up to 1,400 kilograms.

Seals

Five types of seals inhabit the Canadian Arctic. The most abundant, smallest, and most important to the Inuit are **ringed seals,** the name referring to the cream-colored circular markings on their back. Largest are the **bearded seals,** which weigh up to 250 kilograms and have facial whiskers resembling a beard. **Harp seals** are found primarily around the coastline of Baffin Island. In the early 1980s, they were the focus of an emotional campaign aimed at ending hunting of the species. **Harbour seals** and **hooded seals,** although common, are found only in Hudson Bay and the waters of Davis Strait.

Fish

Arctic grayling is found in all watersheds on the mainland and is particularly common in the Mackenzie River Basin. **Inconnu,** a member of the whitefish family, inhabit the Hay River and are occasionally caught in the Big Buffalo and Taltson rivers. **Lake whitefish** occur mainly in lakes and are bottom feeders. They are also the most valuable commercial fish in the territories; Great Slave Lake is the center of the industry. **Pickerel,** known as walleye in the south, inhabits small lakes in the southwest. **North-**

ern pike live around aquatic vegetation in slow-moving rivers and have been recorded up to 18 kilograms. **Lake trout** are common in Great Slave and Great Bear lakes but also occur in fast-flowing rivers and small lakes.

The most dominant fish of the Arctic is the **arctic char,** a member of the salmon family. It weighs an average of three to four kilograms but can grow to seven. The char spends most of its life in the freshwater of inland lakes, but each summer makes a run to the ocean, returning

BOB RACE

WHOOPING CRANES

The whooping crane, *Grus americana,* has become a symbol of human efforts to protect endangered species in North America. Whoopers, as they are commonly called, have never been prolific. Their naturally low reproduction rate, coupled with severe degradation of their habitat, caused their numbers at one point to dip as low as 21. This small flock wintered along the Texas coast in Aransas National Wildlife Refuge, but no one knew where their summer breeding grounds were. The last time infant whoopers had been seen in the wild was 1922 when a Saskatchewan game warden found a nesting couple and preserved a newly hatched chick for posterity. The mystery was solved in 1954 when a helicopter pilot spotted nesting whoopers in Wood Buffalo National Park. Ever since, a concerted effort has been made to increase their population, including an intense captive-breeding program. The birds arrive in the park in late April, with some pairs nesting in the same area for up to 15 years. Each pair produces two eggs but raises only one chick, leaving the other to die. By late September the young chicks have learned to fly and the flock migrates south, taking 20-40 days to cover the 4,000 km to the Texas coast.

after only a few weeks. They occur throughout the Arctic archipelago and in rivers and lakes along the coast.

Birds

Around 280 species of birds have been recorded in the territories, of which 70 nest exclusively north of the 60th Parallel. These figures do no justice to the many millions of shorebirds, waterfowl, and seabirds that migrate north each spring to breed. Birds from six continents and 30 countries flock here each year, including species such as **gulls, kittiwakes, terns, fulmars, eiders,** and **geese.** Other species, such as **ptarmigan** and **ravens,** spend all year in the region. The winner for the longest migration goes to the **arctic tern,** which flies here from Antarctica. Many of Canada's endangered species spend summer here; the **Ross gull** prefers Queen Maud Gulf, while the **whooping crane,** for many years thought to be extinct, nests in Wood Buffalo National Park.

HISTORY

Prehistory

Two distinct groups of natives lived in the Canadian north for thousands of years before European exploration in the region. About 15,000 years ago, at the end of the last ice age, a group of people migrated from Siberia across the Bering Strait—then solid ice—and fanned out across North and South America. At first, the northern extent of their range was limited by the polar ice cap. But as the ice cap retreated, the people spread north. Over the generations, some of them eventually found their way to the Mackenzie River Basin, where they lived as hunters and gatherers. These people were known as the **Dene.**

The second group crossed the Bering ice bridge much later—around 10,000 years ago—and settled in Alaska. Eventually, people from this group would migrate across the Arctic coast in two major waves. The first wave occurred around 4,000 years ago when the people known as the **Dorset culture** began to move east. They lived in skin tents in summer, and snow houses—previously unknown in Alaska—in winter. The second eastward migration, that of the **Thule culture,** occurred about 1,000 years ago, and picked up elements of the Dorset culture—such as snow houses and intricate carvings—as it progressed. The Thule lived in semipermanent villages and specialized in hunting sea mammals. It is the Thule who are ancestors of the Inuit.

European Contact
The first European contact with the Inuit was recorded by expeditions searching for the **Northwest Passage.** (Vikings probably encountered the Inuit earlier, but no written record is available to prove it.) European contact with the Dene occurred much later, but was more extensive and the results more dramatic. Many Dene died of diseases brought by the white man, and the Dene lifestyle changed forever as they gave up their nomadic existence to settle around the white man's trading posts. Rivalry between the Hudson's Bay Company and the North West Company pushed traders farther north in search of furs. By 1900, the whaling industry was in decline and the fur trade of the Mackenzie was finished, but posts remained throughout the north. In 1905, when the provinces of Alberta and Saskatchewan were created, administration of the NWT remained with Ottawa. Local issues were left to the RCMP while the church was responsible for medical and education services.

The Twentieth Century
While many Inuit and Dene continued a nomadic way of life into the 20th century, rapid changes were soon to come. The WW II-instigated construction of military installations such as airfields and Distant Early Warning Line stations created an economic boom and a wage economy for many natives, while the construction of schools and hospitals throughout the 1950s gradually led natives to move into towns.

Mining has played an important role in the development of the north since Martin Frobisher took 1,000 tons of fool's gold back to England in 1576. Mineral and oil exploration had taken place for decades, but the introduction of aircraft opened the north up for mining. In the last 60 years, versatile bush planes—capable of carrying heavy loads and landing on short strips—have contributed to the expansion of the north.

GOVERNMENT

The NWT is one of Canada's two territories (the other is the Yukon). Its government is led by a commissioner with the advice of a legislative assembly. Unlike in Canada's provinces, natural resources remain sole responsibility of the federal government. The legislative assembly does not operate on a party system and a majority of members are of Dene or Inuit descent.

Nunavut
On 1 April 1999 the map of Canada will have to be redrawn when Canada's third territory, Nunavut, is born. Nunavut, meaning "our land," encompasses the Keewatin, Arctic Coast, and

PROVINCIAL ARCHIVES OF ALBERTA

The first bank in the NWT was erected at Fort Smith in the 1870s.

Baffin regions—over two million square km—and is home to 22,000 people, of whom 17,500 are Inuit. While native groups around the world dragged issues of land claims through courts, held demonstrations, and, in parts of Canada, took up arms, the Inuit led a low-profile 15-year campaign that culminated in the historic bill that created Nunavut being passed in Canadian Parliament in July 1993. But Nunavut is a lot more than the world's largest land claim. It is an enormous step for the Inuit. One hundred years ago, many of them had never seen a white man; now they will assume responsibility for a chunk of land twice as big as Ontario—Canada's largest province—and will have outright ownership of about 18% of the land, including subsurface mineral rights. The working language of the government will be **Inuktitut.**

Although Nunavut is a victory for the Inuit, it won't automatically solve the many social problems experienced in the region—unemployment is three times the national average, cost of living is twice the national average. Only 21 km of government-maintained roads cross the region, and only five percent of its population has completed high school. Nevertheless, after 100 years, the Inuit will once again have control of their land.

ECONOMY

Those communities accessible by road have a cost of living comparable to other areas of Canada, while those in the remote Arctic regions are up to 100% higher. Most consumer goods are imported from other parts of Canada, and all transportation costs must be added. Higher prices are offset by higher wages for local workers, but visitors should arrive well prepared. The economy of the Northwest Territories relies heavily on nonrenewable resources and less so on renewable resources. Although the federal and territorial governments are the largest employers, mining is the mainstay of the economy. Seven mines in the territories produce $1 billion worth of minerals annually. The principal minerals extracted are zinc and gold, with yields totaling 25% and 10%, respectively, of all Canadian production. Although Yellowknife has two gold mines within its city limits, **Lupin,** on the barrenlands 400 km northeast, is Canada's largest gold mine. Rumors of diamonds on the

barrenlands have been rife for many years; a rush to stake 2.5 million hectares by 20 companies in 1991-92 confirmed that the gems are here. Time will tell if it is economically viable to start mining them.

The largest oil field in the NWT is at **Norman Wells,** from where oil is piped south to Alberta. But the oil there is only a tiny fraction of the vast reserves located in the Mackenzie Delta and islands of the high Arctic. In the future, as oil prices rise and supplies elsewhere in the world decline, extraction will become commercially viable.

Tourism has grown quickly to become the second-largest slice in the NWT economic pie. Its importance to the economy will continue to rise as more people become aware of the region's potential. Fishing, hunting, and trapping had, until WW II, been the staple of the territorial economy; today they remain an important part of native lifestyles.

PEOPLE

In 1994 the population of the Northwest Territories was 63,000, and it's been growing in recent years at four percent annually. Roughly half the population is of native descent. Three groups of indigenous northerners inhabit the NWT. The **Dene** and **Métis** peoples are found along the Mackenzie River Basin, while the **Inuit** live north of the treeline, along the Arctic coast, and in the Arctic archipelago.

The native peoples of the Arctic are often called Eskimos. This term comes from the French *esquimau,* a word derived from the Algonquin *esquimantsic* meaning "eater of raw fish." Although not derogatory, the natives of the Arctic feel it puts them in poor light. They prefer to use more specific terms. The most widely used of these is "Inuit," referring to those people of the Arctic coast and eastern Arctic regions of Canada. "Inuvialuit" refers to people of the Mackenzie Delta, and "Inupiat" and "Yup'ik" to those of the Alaskan coastlines.

Dene
The Dene (DEN-ay) people are comprised of seven groups—Chipewyan, Dogrib, Gwich'in, Hare, Loucheux, Nahanni, and Slavey—that are part of the Athabascan family. As ice from

the last ice age receded, North American Indians whose ancestors had migrated from Siberia moved north in small groups. They were nomadic hunters whose survival depended on their ability to fish and hunt in a harsh environment. This pattern of life changed dramatically with the coming of white man; the old trading systems and nomadic lifestyles were given up for life in settlements around trading posts. Today many Dene live a traditional lifestyle, while others have moved into a wage economy. All have developed influential political organizations such as the Dene Nation to seek increased control of their own affairs.

Métis

The Métis, numbering around 7,000 in the territories, are of mixed French Canadian and Cree or Dene descent. They were traditionally employed as workers for the major fur-trading companies and settled along the Mackenzie and Slave rivers in the 18th and 19th centuries. They were well suited for positions with trading companies as they were bilingual. The Métis were responsible for bringing commerce to the north, and they continue to play an integral role in the territories' commercial world today. Like the Dene, culture plays an important role in their lives and they have formed a political organization known as the Métis Nation.

Inuit

The Inuit live mainly above the treeline and along the coast and are the largest group of native people in the NWT, numbering around 19,000. Their distant ancestors, the Thule, specialized in hunting whales. While the Inuit's physical adaptation to Arctic conditions has been phenomenal, their recent Asian origins can be seen in the epicanthic eyefold. They are a short, stocky people, with small hands and feet. Their survival depended on insulated clothing and a diet high in saturated fats. Traditionally the Inuit hunted marine mammals in the spring, moved inland to hunt caribou in summer, and spent fall preparing for the long winter. By the end of the 1800s they had developed a dependence on white men's goods, brought by whalers. Diseases decimated their numbers in the 1940s and when the fur-trading economy collapsed, the federal government began settling the Inuit in communities. Today, most still have strong ties to the land, living a traditional lifestyle hunting and fishing as well as being involved in their own political and economic future.

RECREATION

Although the vast wilderness of the NWT is the perfect destination for a variety of adventures, the climate can be unpredictable, severe, and dangerous for the ill-prepared. Help may be hundreds of kilometers away; you must be able to take care of yourself. Before setting out you should file travel plans with local authorities. In some areas, you are required to travel with a local guide—these arrangements should be made well in advance. Those planning their own adventure should first write to Arctic Expeditions Secretariat, Circumpolar and Scientific Affairs, Department of Indian and Northern Affairs Canada, Ottawa, Ontario K1A 0H4, for their booklet *Guide for Expeditions to Northern and Arctic Canada.*

Hiking

For all the wilderness in the north, opportunities for extended hikes along established trails are limited. The **Canol Heritage Trail** is a 372-km hike from the NWT/Yukon border to the Mackenzie River along a service road established in WW II. The most popular area for wilderness hiking is **Auyuittuq National Park** on Baffin Island. To explore either of these areas requires much advance planning and a big budget. **Katannilik Territorial Park**, near Lake Harbour, also has excellent hiking.

Canoeing And Kayaking

A number of adventure outfitters offer whitewater trips down some of the territories' most exciting rivers. For those with experience in both river *and* wilderness travel there are some excellent opportunities for extended river trips. The legendary **Nahanni River** is at the top of many people's to-do list. It provides unrivaled wildlife viewing, the excitement of fast-flowing water, and beautiful scenery. Other popular rivers include the **Burnside,** which bisects the vast barrenlands; the **Coppermine,** which combines isolation, wildlife, and history; the **Thomsen,** the world's northernmost navigable river; and the **Soper,** on Baffin Island. All of these rivers are run by outfitters. Experienced paddlers who can handle the challenging logistics can organize their own expedition and save some money. A compromise is offered by **Great Canadian Ecoventures** (P.O. Box 25181, Winnipeg, MB R2V 4C8, Canada; tel. 800-667-9453), which offers drop-offs and pick-ups, canoe and equipment rentals, and air transportation from Winnipeg to a base camp at **Kasba Lake,** south of Thelon Game Sanctuary.

Fishing

The NWT has countless rivers, streams, and lakes teeming with fish that are both exciting to catch and delicious to eat. Inland lakes and rivers are the domain of trophy-size **lake trout, arctic grayling, pickerel,** and **northern pike.** Great Bear Lake holds world records in *every* class of lake trout and arctic grayling. The **arctic char,** caught in rivers, lakes, and the open ocean of the Arctic coast and Arctic archipelago, is famous as a fighting fish and as an acclaimed northern delicacy. The NWT also holds the overall world record for this species—an arctic char weighing a whopping 14.7 kilograms was caught in the Tree River.

Before fishing you'll need a license, available from sport stores, co-ops, and outfitters. A three-day license will cost $15 for Canadians, $30 for nonresidents. An annual license is $20 and $40, respectively. A separate license is required for fishing in national parks. For the *NWT Sport Fishing Guide* write to Fisheries and Oceans, P.O. Box 2310, Yellowknife, NT X1A 2P7.

ACCOMMODATIONS AND FOOD

Indoor Accommodations

Every community has at least one hotel, often run by the local native co-op. Prices in Yellowknife and southern towns begin at around $100 s or d for a basic room. Farther north, and in those communities without road access, prices are generally quoted per person, ranging $90-170. Often, the hotel offers the only restaurant in town and meals will be included in the rate ($50-80 per person per day). In smaller communities you will be asked to share your room if it's busy and it is standard practice to accept. Bed and breakfasts, starting at $55 s, $65 d, operate in Yellowknife, Inuvik, and Iqaluit.

Campgrounds

Camping is the only way to stay cheaply in the north. Territorial campgrounds are located at regular intervals along the road system. Some are very basic, others—usually those on the outskirts of towns—have showers. All have bug-proof kitchen shelters. They are $10 per night or $100 for a 14-night pass. Payment is often on an honor system. Many of the more remote communities have an area designated for campers, often a short walk from the airport. Always make a point of asking at the hamlet office before pitching a tent away from a designated area. In national parks and other wilderness areas campers should practice no-trace camping and pack out all rubbish. North of the treeline there is no source of firewood (although driftwood can often be found on beaches). This means that a lightweight campstove is indispensable. White gas, known as naphtha in the north, is not allowed on scheduled flights but is available in most Northern stores and co-ops. If it's late in the season, call ahead to check availability—some communities only receive supplies once a year.

Food

Part of the northern experience is tasting local foods. Most restaurants serve these dishes when availability allows. Favorites are musk ox, caribou, and arctic char, all of which can be bought as jerky or, from meat co-ops, as steaks. When meals are part of an accommodations package, they are usually served cafeteria-style and offer little or no choice.

GETTING THERE

Air

The main air route into the NWT is from Edmonton or Calgary, in Alberta, to the capital Yellowknife, from where easy connections can be made throughout the north. Airlines flying this route are: **Canadian North,** tel. (800) 665-1177 or, in the U.S., (800) 426-7000, and **NWT Air,** tel. (800) 661-0789. From Edmonton, both charge $372 one way, $409 for a 14-day APEX round trip. Fares from Calgary are only slightly higher. For destinations in the eastern Arctic and high Arctic, **Canadian North** and **First Air,** tel. (800) 267-1247, fly at least once daily to

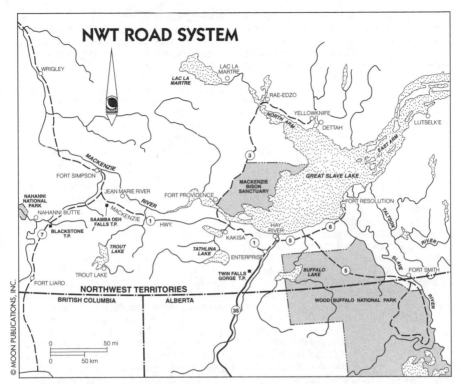

NWT ROAD SYSTEM

Iqaluit from Ottawa and Montreal; $715 one way, $807 for a 14-day APEX round trip with taxes being less from Montreal. From Whitehorse (Yukon), **Alkan Air,** tel. (403) 668-2107, flies four times weekly to Inuvik; $290 one way, $580 round trip.

For those keen on circumpolar travel **First Air** flies to Iqaluit from Nuuk (Greenland) twice weekly; $323 one way, $528 for a 14-day APEX round trip. This could, conceivably, be linked with an **SAS** flight from Copenhagen or an **Icelandair** flight from New York or Luxembourg via Reykjavik. The best people to contact for travel in this part of the world are at Arctic Experience, 29 Nork Way, Banstead, Surrey SM7 1PB, England; tel. 0737-362321.

Bus

From Edmonton, **Greyhound,** tel. (403) 265-9111, or, in Canada only, (800) 661-8747, goes as far north as Hay River ($116.63 one way), just over the NWT border.

Car

Driving is the most popular way to come north. The main route is the **Mackenzie Hwy.,** which begins northwest of Edmonton at Grimshaw. From Grimshaw the road is paved beyond the 60th Parallel to Hay River. From there, gravel highways lead east to Fort Smith and Wood Buffalo National Park, northwest to Yellowknife, and west to Fort Simpson. A loop known as the **Deh-Cho Connection** can be made by taking the **Liard Hwy.** from southeast of Fort Simpson, south to Fort Nelson (British Columbia) and back to Edmonton. The other route north is the **Dempster Hwy.** from Dawson City (Yukon) to Inuvik in the western Arctic. This is the northernmost public road on the continent.

GETTING AROUND

Air

In many cases, the only way to get from place to place is by plane. If you are flying into the NWT make reservations for all onward flights before coming north; this works out much cheaper than buying flight sectors separately. If round-trip tickets are bought 14 days in advance, and you meet certain requirements, they will be similar in price to one-way tickets bought on the spot. Student standby tickets (anyone under 25) will save 30-60% of regular ticket prices. Officially, stops are not permitted on regular fares, but if you buy the tickets in the north, and have some skill at negotiation, you may be able to work something out. The only other money-saving possibility is a travel pass available from **First Air.** Two coupons cost $700 ($600 before June 15), with additional coupons $100. Each is valid for one-way travel anywhere on the First Air system, which serves the Baffin and Arctic coast regions with connections to Yellowknife; tel. (800) 267-1247.

The other major carriers are: **Canadian North,** tel. (800) 665-1177, serving all major centers in the NWT; and **NWT Air,** tel. (800) 661-0789, serving Inuvik, Cambridge Bay, and Iqaluit. Each of the above has affiliated connector airlines serving smaller communities.

Bus

Frontier Coachlines, tel. (403) 873-4892, continues to Fort Smith and Yellowknife from Hay River (the end of the line for Greyhound).

Tours

The *Northwest Territories Explorer's Guide* provides a full listing of all tour operators and outfitters in the territories. **Touch the Arctic Adventure Tours** offers a cross-section of tours to suit all tastes. They include air transportation on NWT Air from Yellowknife or Edmonton, accommodations, and services of local outfitters. The tours offer exceptional value, as the included airfares are at a reduced rate. For example, the Midnight Sun Tour, including round-trip airfare from Edmonton to Tuktoyaktuk, dinner, and a tour, is $299. For details call (800) 661-0894.

INFORMATION

Money

All prices quoted in this book are in the local currency, **Canadian dollars.** As this book went to press, one American dollar would buy you $1.40 Canadian. Banks are located in all major centers and you should check with hotels and outfitters before expecting them to accept U.S. dollars or credit cards. The NWT is liable to the same taxes as Alberta, including the seven percent Goods and Services Tax (GST) which ap-

Floatplanes are an integral mode of transportation in the north.

plies to all goods and services, including hotel accommodations.

Other Information
For detailed information on accommodations and outfitters write to NWT Economic Development and Tourism, Yellowknife, NT X1A 2L9,

Canada; tel. (800) 661-0788. For ferry information call (800) 661-0751. For highway information call (800) 661-0750. The NWT has two area codes: **403** is used for all phone numbers except those in the Keewatin and Baffin regions, where the area code is **819.**

BIG RIVER: THE ACCESSIBLE NORTH

Whether it's your first time or your fortieth, crossing the 60th Parallel marks the beginning of a new adventure. And the adventure starts in the Big River Travel Zone, a vast expanse of spruce, poplar, and aspen forests, stunted in growth by the harsh climate and scarred by wildfires that sweep unforgivingly through the region every few years. Two of North America's largest rivers, the **Slave** and **Mackenzie,** flow through the area en route to the Arctic Ocean. Many of their smaller tributaries are perfect for wilderness canoe trips, and offer streamside hiking and some of the world's best fly-fishing. To the north lies **Great Slave Lake,** named for the Slavey Dene who have trapped and fished along its southern shores for thousands of years. This vast inland sea of freshwater is the world's tenth-largest lake. It covers an area of 28,438 square km and is 456 km in length. It is also the world's sixth-deepest lake (615 meters), meaning water temperatures remain cold year-round and ice is present for at least five months of the year. The lake remains frozen long after the rivers flowing into it have broken up, creating an annual cycle of flooding at rivermouths.

The region's main communities are **Hay River,** on the south shore of Great Slave Lake, and **Fort Smith,** gateway to Wood Buffalo National Park, the second-largest national park in the world. Paved roads and improved gravel roads link the two towns, and continue around the west and north sides of Great Slave Lake to the territorial capital, Yellowknife.

For more information on the region write to Big River Tourism Association, P.O. Box 185, Hay River, NT X0E 0R0, Canada; tel. (403) 874-2422 or (800) 661-0788.

60TH PARALLEL TO HAY RIVER

The wood-and-stone structure marking the 60th Parallel is a welcome sight after the long drive north through Alberta up the Mackenzie Highway. North of the border, the highway number changes from 35 to 1, and follows the Hay River 118 km to Great Slave Lake. This stretch of road is known as the **Waterfalls Route,** for the impressive falls along the way.

Just beyond the border is the **60th Parallel Visitors Centre,** tel. (403) 920-1021, well worth a stop just to have a chat with the friendly hosts. The center offers maps and brochures, camping permits, fishing licenses, and displays of local arts and crafts. And the coffeepot is always on, accompanied by freshly made scones if you're lucky. Behind the center is **60th Parallel Campground,** a small facility overlooking the Hay River; $12. The visitors center is open May to mid-September, daily 10 a.m.-10 p.m. But with the long hours of daylight, the staff often chats with visitors until midnight.

Twin Falls Gorge Territorial Park
North of the border, the Hay River has carved a deep gorge into the limestone bedrock. Punctuating the river's flow are two dramatic waterfalls that formed a major barrier for early river travelers, forcing a portage along the west bank. Encompassing both falls, and the equally impressive **Escarpment Creek,** is Twin Falls Gorge Territorial Park. From the first day-use area a short trail leads to a viewing platform overlooking **Alexandra Falls,** where the peat-colored Hay River tumbles 34 meters. **Louise Falls,** three km downstream, is not as high, but its intriguing steps make it just as interesting.

A walking trail through jack pine, aspen, and white spruce links the two sets of falls. Escarpment Creek (also known as Twin Falls Creek) flows into the Hay River a further three km downstream and has some smaller falls worthy of the short walk. **Louise Falls Campground** has water, pit toilets, and bug-proof kitchen shelters; $12.

Enterprise

Following the completion of the Mackenzie Hwy. in 1948, two gas stations opened here, marking the beginning of this small community of 55. The community had hoped to become a transportation hub for freight heading north, but nothing materialized. Today with a gas station, restaurant, a few motel rooms, and a highway-maintenance depot, it just manages to hang on. East of the highway are excellent views of the Hay River Gorge. Located at the junction of Highways 1 and 2 is **Ed's Place,** tel. (403) 984-3181, where basic rooms are $48 s, $53 d. Ask about inexpensive (with good reason) dormitory beds. Also at Ed's Place is a popular restaurant. A **tourist information center** is located in the ESSO Station; open in summer, daily 8 a.m.-9 p.m.

HAY RIVER

This town of 3,100 is a vital transportation link for waterborne freight bound for communities along the Mackenzie River and throughout the western and central Arctic. Within town limits, a number of distinct communities surround the delta, which was formed where the Hay River flows into Great Slave Lake. Most modern development—including motels, restaurants, and government offices—is located in **New Town,** on the west bank of the Hay River. A bridge links New Town to **Vale Island,** where the airport, campground, and excellent beaches are located. Also on the island are the communities of **Old Town,** partially destroyed by flooding in 1963, and **West Channel Village,** which grew around the commercial fishing industry. Across the mouth of Hay River is the **Hay River Dene Reserve,** the only Indian reserve in the NWT. Farther upstream are **Delancey Estates,** a modern subdivision, and **Paradise Gardens,** where at a wide, sweeping curve of the river the particularly rich soil has sprouted the territories' largest

truck-farm operation. Follow a gravel road down to this small community, 24 km south of Hay River, to a sign advertising fresh produce. Look around for the Greenfields, who will no doubt be in their extensive gardens, toiling away as they have done for years. Many of their customers come from Hay River, although any self-respecting Yellowknife resident returning from a trip south will stop by for the freshest and best-priced produce north of the 60th Parallel.

History

For thousands of years Slavey Dene inhabited the area. Their nomadic lifestyle required no permanent settlements. Rival fur-trading companies had opened posts along the Hay River as early as 1806, but it wasn't until 1868 that the Hudson's Bay Company built a post on the east bank at the river's mouth. It closed after 10 years of poor trade. Soon after, Chief Chatla of the Slavey Dene constructed some log cabins near the defunct post and asked church officials to build a small mission to serve his people. The community grew and by the turn of the century had a school, boatyard, and vegetable gardens. The traditional transportation route north to Slave Lake, along the Athabasca and Slave rivers and through Fort Smith, was superseded in 1939 by an overland route from Grimshaw, following the west bank of the Hay River to Vale Island at the mouth. Before long, the west side of the island was crisscrossed with streets lined with shops, and the waterfront was alive with tugs and barges being loaded with goods for the long trip north.

In 1945 Great Slave Lake was opened to commercial fishing, and a community known as **West Channel Village** was established on the west side of the island. Fishing soon became the town's leading employer, with 10 companies and eight processing plants harvesting up to eight million tons of fish annually, including the whitefish for which Great Slave Lake is renowned. Vale Island was once linked to the mainland by a man-made causeway, removed each spring to prevent flooding during break-up. But in 1963, the causeway was left in place and the fast-flowing Hay River—which breaks up well before the lake—flooded much of the island. As a result, the town was moved to the mainland and a permanent bridge was built over the channel.

New Town Sights

With the opening of the Pine Point Mine and arrival of the railway in the 1960s, and general economic growth of the western Arctic in the '70s, the new townsite grew at a rapid pace. In anticipation of further growth, the 17-story **Mackenzie Place Apartment Building** was constructed in the center of town. Grab a key from the manager's office (second floor) and ride the claustrophobic elevator to the roof, from where panoramic views of the Great Slave Lake, Hay River, and the boreal forest extend to the horizon. The **Diamond Jenness High School,** on Riverview Dr., was named for a famed north-

ern anthropologist and is without a doubt the town's most unique structure. It was designed by Douglas Cardinal, an Albertan architect whose distinctive work is found throughout that province. Its unique curved walls alone would have made it a northern landmark, but the choice of color for the entire exterior was left to the students—and they chose purple! Behind the school, the **Kiwanis Nature Trail** leads along the banks of Hay River (look for fossils) to various signposted points of interest.

Vale Island

The boarded-up shop fronts, dusty streets, and

empty houses of Vale Island belie the activity that still takes place along the waterfront. The large **Canadian Coastguard Base** is responsible for all search-and-rescue operations in the western Arctic. And the facilities of **Northern Transportation Co.,** a large shipping concern, include shipyards, a dry dock, freight-storage areas, and a syncrolift—a hydraulic device that removes vessels from the water for easy maintenance (it's one of only four in Canada, and can be seen to the right along 106th Ave.).

From Old Town, Mackenzie Dr.—the island's main thoroughfare—continues past a popular swimming beach and a radio observatory before it dead-ends in **West Channel Village.** This once-prosperous fishing community is a shadow of its former self, since processing is now done at the Freshwater Fish Marketing Board Plant in New Town.

Hay River Dene Reserve

Across East Channel from Vale Island is the site of Hay River's first permanent settlement. To get there, backtrack to the Fort Smith turnoff and head north (turn left) shortly after crossing the Hay River. Indian Village Rd. follows the river to New Indian Village, which, through the work of a dedicated Band Council, has a school, new houses, a grocery store, and scheduled bus service to Hay River. The road continues through the community to the original site of the village. Here you will see early churches and the remains of the Hudson's Bay Company post, sitting in mute testimony to the two major influences on early life in the north.

Recreation

The beaches of Vale Island are very popular during summer, even if the water may be a little cold for most. The best beach is at the end of 106th Ave.; those farther around the island will be quieter. Located 15 km south of town is the territories' finest golf course. It has nine holes with artificial greens, a driving range, and a superbly crafted log clubhouse (well worth a look, even for nongolfers). A round of golf (18 holes) is $22 and club rentals are available. The clubhouse is used as a base for cross-country skiers who set tracks around the course in winter.

The best way of getting onto Great Slave Lake is with **Arctic Star Tours,** which offers a charter service using an 11-meter Bayliner. Various tours are available at a rate of $125 per hour, per boat. For more information call (403) 874-2628. Anglers will find plentiful northern pike and pickerel in the Hay River.

Festivals And Events

Winter carnivals are held on the first weekends of March and April, and the **Kelly King 250 Jet Boat Race** comes to town in early August. With the best golf course in the north, it's natural that the town is host to many tournaments throughout the summer. The most important of these is the **NWT Open Championship** on the Labour Day weekend in September. This fully sanctioned event attracts golfers from throughout the north but everyone is welcome to enter. The entry fee of $60 includes green fees and two evening meals. Book well in advance; tel. (403) 874-6290.

Accommodations

The least expensive rooms in town are at **Hay River Hotel** on Vale Island, tel. (403) 874-6022, and you'll see why before you've taken a step inside. The medium-sized, self-contained rooms are $45 s, $55 d. Common sense dictates that you ask for one in the back—as far away from Vale Island's only bar as is possible. Other motels are located along the highway in New Town. **Migrator Motel,** tel. 874-6792, has rooms for $60 s, $65 d; similar in standard is the **Caribou Motor Inn,** tel. 874-6706, $70 s, $75 d; and one step up, with a restaurant and lounge, is the **Ptarmigan Inn,** tel. 874-6781, in the center of town, with rooms for $95 s, $108 d.

Hay River Campground, on Vale Island, is a short walk from the beach and seven km from downtown. The sites are very private, a few have power, and all have picnic tables and fire rings. It's open mid-May to mid-September; $12. South of town is **Paradise Garden Campground,** which has showers and an enclosed cooking shelter with a woodstove. The camping area is operated by farmers whose delicious vegetables are a welcome and inexpensive addition to any meal; unserviced sites $7.50, powered sites $10.

Food

Worth the effort to find is **Back Eddy Restaurant,** tel. (403) 874-6680. It's above Rings Drug Store on Capital Crescent. Meals are served in the lounge or, for families, in a separate dining area. Expect to pay $6-10 for lunch and a few dollars more for dinner. **The Keys,** tel. 874-6781, in the Ptarmigan Inn, is popular with locals, especially at lunchtime—but it can get very smoky. Beside Northern, **Hay River Bakery,** tel. 874-2322, has a wide variety of cakes and pastries and is a good place for an inexpensive lunch. Ignore the unappealing decor at the **Kishu Canada Restaurant,** tel. 874-6923, to sample some good (for this far north) Japanese dishes starting at $6. It's beside the Caribou Motor Inn. Chinese meals at **The Board Room,** tel. 874-2111, are also well priced, if a bit small. The restaurant is located on the road toward Old Town.

Transportation
Hay River Airport is located on Vale Island, a $10 cab ride from town. During freeze-up and break-up of the Mackenzie River, road traffic through to Yellowknife is blocked and Hay River Airport becomes the center of frenzied activity; freight and passengers arriving by road from the south transfer to planes for the short hop over Great Slave Lake. **Canadian North,** tel. (403) 874-2435 or (800) 665-1177, has daily flights to Hay River from Edmonton Municipal Airport (via Fort Smith and continuing to Yellowknife). **Buffalo Airways,** tel. 874-3333, a connector airline for NWT Air, flies daily to Yellowknife for $102 one way, $169 round trip. Local flightseeing is done by **Landa Aviation,** tel. 874-3500. A flight over the Hay River Delta and Louise and Alexandra falls costs $40 per person, three-person minimum; flights to view bison in Wood Buffalo National Park are $90 per person.

The bus depot is located at the south end of Vale Island. **Greyhound** departs daily for Edmonton (16 hours, $116.63 one way). **Frontier Coachlines,** using the same depot, runs to Yellowknife ($64.50) and Fort Smith ($46.55). For all bus times call 874-6966, or (800) 661-8747 in Canada only.

Services And Information
The **post office** is located on Capital Crescent. Just around the corner, at the base of Mackenzie Place Apartment Building, is a **laundromat;** open daily 8 a.m.-8 p.m. **Centennial Library,** opposite Northern on Woodland Dr., is head-

quarters for the NWT library system. Books are transported by road, air, and sea to 18 other libraries, including those in the most remote communities. The library has a reasonable selection of books and magazines, including material on the north; open Mon.-Thurs. 11 a.m.-9 p.m., Fri.-Sat. 1-5 p.m. **Raven's Nest Arts and Crafts,** tel. (403) 874-3570, on the highway south of town, has a large collection of prints, paintings, and moose-hair tufting, for which the region is famous. They also have a limited number of topographical maps and marine charts. The **hospital** is located along Woodland Dr., tel. 874-6512. The **visitors center,** located at the south entrance to town, has bundles of literature, books to read, and the coffeepot is always on; open in summer, daily 9 a.m.-9 p.m.; tel. 874-3180.

TO FORT SMITH

The 270-km road linking Hay River to Fort Smith (Hwy. 5) is paved for the first 60 km then turns to improved gravel. No services are available along this route. The road bisects a typical boreal forest of stunted spruce and aspen. Jack pine dominates areas scorched in a disastrous fire that consumed 160,000 hectares in 1981. The fire burned for three months and pockets continued to smolder under the snow until the following spring. Visible to the north along the paved section of road is a rail bed used by the Great Slave Lake Railway to link the now-abandoned mine at Pine Point to Roma, Alberta, 680 km to the south. A gravel road to the north, 49 km from Hwy. 2, leads two km to **Polar Lake,** a camping and picnic area developed by the community of Pine Lake. The lake is stocked with rainbow trout and has good birdwatching around the shoreline. Camping is $5. A further 11 km, the road divides; the right fork continues to Fort Smith, the left to Pine Point and Fort Resolution.

Pine Point
Early prospectors interested in gold and silver largely ignored the area east of Hay River. But in 1951, Pine Point Mines Limited, owned by Cominco, began extracting lead and zinc from an open-pit mine at a site known as Pine Point. In 1965 the Great Slave Lake Railway was built,

linking the mine to outside markets. With production on the increase, a town was built, at one time boasting over 2,000 residents. Low lead and zinc prices, coupled with rising operational costs, forced Cominco to close the mine in 1988. One of the lease conditions was that Cominco was to restore the land to its original condition when it left. As a result, the whole town—a school, hospital, supermarket, and hundreds of houses—had to be moved. After standing empty for a few years, the buildings were moved to various locations throughout the north. Today all that remains are tailing piles from the mine, paved streets, sidewalks, and an overgrown golf course.

Fort Resolution

This historic community of 500 is located in a forested area on the southeastern shore of Great Slave Lake at the end of Hwy. 6, 170 km east of Hay River. The original fort, built by the North West Company in 1786, was to the east, on the Slave River delta. When the post was moved, a Chipewyan Dene settlement grew around it, and in 1852, Roman Catholic missionaries arrived, building a school and hospital. A road connecting the town to Pine Point was completed in the '60s and today the mainly Chipewyan and Métis population relies on trapping and a sawmill operation as an economic base.

Walking tours through town can be arranged through the Community Office on the main road. Also ask here about walking along the lakeshore to the site of the original fort. The town is a good jumping-off point for exploring the spectacular East Arm of Great Slave Lake. **Res Delta Tours,** tel. (403) 394-3141, offers a variety of excursions including 2.5-hour tours of the delta ($60 per person) and overnight trips along the East Arm and to Fort Smith. **Dave's B&B,** tel. 392-5215, is the only accommodation in town; the street it's on doesn't have a name; ask at the general store for directions. If no one is home, head back to the store and ask where the owner, Dave McNabb, is. He's one of the north's true characters and well worth meeting, just for a rundown on the town. It's $85 s or d, including breakfast. Another option is to camp down a gravel road just west of town where there appears to have been a campground at one time. Also in town is a gas station, cafe, and a community hall where evening meals are served for reasonable prices. The only scheduled transportation is from Yellowknife on **Ptarmigan Airways,** tel. 873-4461 or (800) 661-0808.

Continuing To Fort Smith On Highway 5

From the Fort Smith/Fort Resolution junction, 60 km east of Hay River, it is 210 km southeast to Fort Smith. For much of the way the highway is paralleled by power lines. A hydroelectric plant was built on the Taltson River, east of Slave River, in the 1960s to provide electricity to Pine Point. Now it runs well below capacity, supplying towns in the Big River region. Many of the power line's towers are capped by masses of sticks and twigs—the nesting sites of ravens. Twenty-seven km from the Fort Resolution junction is a 13 km road to **Sandy Lake,** which has a good beach, swimming, and fishing for northern pike, but no camping.

The road then enters **Wood Buffalo National Park,** the largest national park in North America. Five km beyond the park entrance sign is the **Angus Fire Tower.** Behind the tower is one of many sinkholes found in the northern reaches of the park. This example of karst topography occurs when underground caves collapse, creating a craterlike depression. This one is 26 meters deep and 40 meters across. The next worthwhile stop is at **Nyarling River,** 14 km farther east. The dried-up riverbed is actually the path of an underground river, hence the name Nyarling, meaning "underground" in the Slavey language.

Little Buffalo Falls Territorial Park

As the highway continues east it enters an area where the Precambrian Shield is exposed, making for a rocky landscape where stunted trees cling to shallow depressions that have filled with soil. After crossing the **Sass River,** the road passes an area of shallow lakes and marshes where whooping cranes—one of North America's rarest birds—nest. As the road crosses **Little Buffalo River** it leaves the park. To the north, an access road leads to a series of small waterfalls in Little Buffalo Falls Territorial Park. This was only a small part of an enormous area affected by fire in 1981. An interpretive trail follows the cycle of regeneration from stands of aspen and spruce to jack pine, whose seeds are released at high temperatures. Near the end of the access road is a campground with pit toilets, a kitchen shelter, and firewood; $10.

FORT SMITH

Until 1967, this town of 2,500 on the west bank of the Slave River was the territorial capital. It still functions as an administrative center for various governmental offices and is the educational center for the western Arctic, with students from throughout the territories studying at the Thebacha Campus of Arctic College. But its glory days are over. The transportation routes upon which the town was built have long been abandoned and the governmental hierarchy that once resided here is long gone. Rapids in the Slave River, below town, are the nesting grounds of white pelicans—a unique location considering its northern latitude, and considering that the pelicans somehow manage to raise young among the fast-flowing waters of the river.

History

It was because of the formidable rapids that the town was established. The Slave River was a vital link for all travelers heading north, but rapids here and upstream necessitated a 25-km portage around them. In 1872 the Hudson's Bay Company opened a post, later known as Fort Fitzgerald, at the southern end of the rapids. Two years later the company established a fort near the northern end of the portage route, at Fort Smith. Occasionally the brave attempted to run the rapids. In 1876 five paddlers for the North West Company successfully negotiated the three upstream sets but then misinterpreted instructions and perished on the rapids in front of Fort Smith. Their misfortune won't be forgotten; these rapids are now known as Rapids of the Drowned. Around this time, sternwheelers began replacing the slower and more cumbersome

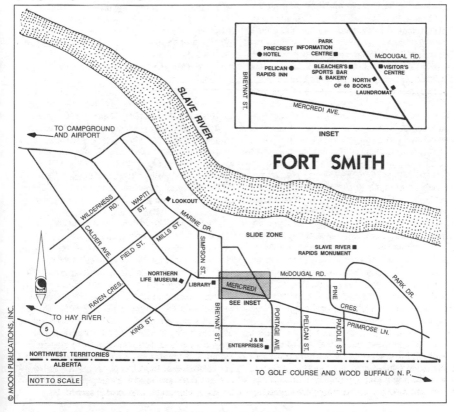

INSET

FORT SMITH

TO CAMPGROUND AND AIRPORT

SLAVE RIVER

SLIDE ZONE

SLAVE RIVER RAPIDS MONUMENT

McDOUGAL RD.

NORTHERN LIFE MUSEUM

LIBRARY

MERCREDI

SEE INSET

TO HAY RIVER

5

NORTHWEST TERRITORIES
ALBERTA

NOT TO SCALE

J & M ENTERPRISES

TO GOLF COURSE AND WOOD BUFFALO N. P.

© MOON PUBLICATIONS, INC.

voyageur canoes and larger York boats. Red River carts, drawn by oxen, replaced human portagers, and were in turn replaced by tractors in 1919. By this time Fort Smith had become the administrative center of the NWT. It remained so until an all-weather road was built from Peace River to Hay River and through to Yellowknife, and river transportation slid into oblivion.

Sights

Most people who venture to Fort Smith do so to visit Wood Buffalo National Park, although it is possible, at a stretch, to spend a half day sightseeing in town. **Northern Life Museum,** 110 King St., tel. (403) 872-2859, is shaped like a fort and houses a large collection of artifacts from the days of the fur trade, as well as mushing equipment, Inuit carvings, the first printing press in the north, and displays on bison; open in summer, Mon.-Fri. 9 a.m.-5 p.m., Sat.-Sun. 1-5 p.m. At the end of Breynat St., signs indicate the **slide zone,** where many of Fort Smith's riverfront buildings once stood. Continue downstream and onto Marine Dr. to **Slave River Lookout,** a gazebo with a telescope through which you can watch the pelicans. Overlooking the rapids (the view is slightly marred by trees) is the **Slave River Rapids Monument,** dedicated to the explorers and riverboat guides of the 1800s who courageously tackled the river. To get there follow McDougal Rd. east through town and turn left on Park Dr.; the monument is off to the left in the trees.

Fort Fitzgerald, 25 km upstream of Fort Smith, was once a hive of activity at the beginning of the north's most notorious portage. Today, all that remains are abandoned houses, a deserted mission, and, down on the river, rotting docks.

Recreation And Tours

Pelican Rapids Golf Course, through town to the southeast, has been carved out of the forest by the town's surprisingly large golfing population. If you don't have clubs, head to Bleacher's Sports Bar and someone will rustle up a set for you; green fees are $5; slip it in the box beside the first tee.

Subarctic Wilderness Adventures offers a

Rather than portaging the rapids, some brave souls attempted to run them in scows.

PROVINCIAL ARCHIVES OF ALBERTA

multitude of one-day and overnight tours throughout the area, including into Wood Buffalo National Park. Day-trips include rafting on the Slave River (five hours, $49 per person), bus tours into the national park (six hours, $80 per person), and flightseeing tours (one hour, $65 per person). For details on these and longer excursions write to P.O. Box 685, Fort Smith, NT X0E 0P0; tel. (403) 872-2467.

Accommodations

The least expensive motel is **Pinecrest Hotel,** 163 McDougal Rd., tel. (403) 872-2104; $50 s, $60 d. Much nicer is **Pelican Rapids Inn,** 152 McDougal Rd., tel. 872-2789, with large rooms for $90 s, $95 d, $15 extra for kitchenettes; call in advance, this place fills up fast.

The only campground close to town is **Queen Elizabeth Campground,** four km west toward the airport; turn north on Teepee Trail Road. Sites cost $10 per night, and are spread out and private with pit toilets and cooking shelters. Showers and flush toilets are in the warden's compound. Alternatives are **Thebacha Campground** 16 km west of Fort Smith on Hwy. 5, or **Pine Lake,** 60 km south in Wood Buffalo National Park.

Food And Drink

The **Old Skillet Restaurant** in the Pinecrest Hotel, tel. (403) 872-3161, may look a mess from the outside but inside it's clean and it comes highly recommended by locals; open from 7 a.m. **J-bell Bakery,** corner of McDougal Rd. and Portage Ave., serves hot and cold lunches and great pastries. For a chance to meet a few colorful locals and exchange golf stories that get better as the night goes on, head to **Bleacher's Sports Bar,** next to J-bell Bakery.

Transportation

The **airport** is located five km west of town along McDougal Road. **Canadian North,** tel. (403) 872-2057 or (800) 661-1505, flies daily to Edmonton ($306 one way, $337 for a 14-day APEX round trip), Hay River ($148 one way, $163 round trip), and Yellowknife ($174 one way, $191 round trip). **Northwestern Air,** tel. 872-2216, operates a scheduled air service to and from Fort Chipewyan; $95 one way, $190 round trip. **Loon Air,** tel. 872-3030, is a charter air service operating out of Fort Smith; $325 gets you a one-way flight to Fort Chipewyan in a small Cessna that seats five. **Frontier Coachlines,** tel. 872-2031, runs a passenger service between Fort Smith and Yellowknife. **J & M Enterprises** on Portage Ave., tel. 872-2221, is open daily 8 a.m.-midnight and has a mechanic, car wash, and car rentals. For a taxi, call **Slave River Cabs** at 872-3333.

Information

Mary Kaeser Library is at 170 McDougal Rd., and **North of 60 Books,** across from the visitors center, offers a great selection of books, maps, and souvenirs. The **visitors center** is on Portage Rd., open in summer, daily 10 a.m.-10 p.m.

WOOD BUFFALO NATIONAL PARK

The sheer size of Wood Buffalo National Park, second-largest national park in the world (the largest is in Greenland), can be overwhelming at first. With few conventional "sights," many first-time visitors leave disillusioned. The park really is a place where you must stop, pause, and take it all in. Through this 45,000-square-km chunk of boreal forest, boreal plains, shallow lakes, and bogs flow two major rivers—the Peace and Athabasca. These drain into **Lake Claire,** forming one of the world's largest freshwater deltas. The Peace-Athabasca Delta is a mass of confusing channels, shallow lakes, and sedge meadows, surrounded by a wetland that is prime wintering range for bison, rich in waterfowl, and home to beavers, muskrats, moose, lynx, wolves, and black bears. From the delta, the Slave River—which forms the park's eastern boundary—flows north into Great Slave Lake.

Probably best known for being the last natural nesting habitat of the rare whooping crane, the park is also home to the world's largest free-roaming herd of bison. It has extensive salt plains and North America's finest example of gypsum karst topography—a phenomenon created by underground water activity. For all these reasons, and as an intact example of the boreal forest that once circled the entire Northern Hemisphere, the park was declared a UNESCO World Heritage Site in December 1983.

On the surface, Wood Buffalo epitomizes everything that a national park should be—little development and stable wildlife populations—so it is ironic that the park has faced ongoing problems with diseased bison and clear-cut logging, and currently faces the prospect of a collapse of the entire delta ecosystem because of a dam built over 1,000 km away. But let's start at the beginning.

Bison: The Good Times And The Bad

Wood Buffalo National Park was created by the Dominion Government in 1922 to protect 1,500 wood bison that were scattered through the region. At the time, the wood bison—a larger subspecies of plains bison—were being heavily hunted and their future was in jeopardy. In the years that followed, their numbers were supplemented with nearly 6,000 plains bison from Buffalo National Park near Wainwright, in Alberta. Unfortunately, the imported plains bison were carrying tuberculosis and brucellosis, which have remained in the park's now hybrid population of bison for 70 years. In the early 1950s, large-scale bison roundups took place in the Sweetgrass area of the delta and large numbers of diseased bison were slaughtered. Park administrators set up a small settlement at

The bison is North America's largest land mammal.

Sweetgrass and constructed over 30 km of corrals to hold the diseased animals. The last slaughter took place in 1967, and the corrals were last used in 1976 to vaccinate the bison against anthrax—an infectious disease that can kill bison in a few days. For the most part, these diseases lie dormant in the ecosystem; bison generally show no outward effects of illness, and the diseases are not easily transmitted to humans. In late 1990, an Environmental Advisory Board recommended that the entire bison population be slaughtered, eradicating the diseases once and for all. Currently the government is considering all options and, as yet, no action has been taken. Each spring hundreds of calves are born and bison numbers remain steady at around 3,500. No reported cases of disease transfer to humans have been reported in the park's history.

Timber Berth 408

Logging in most national parks would raise a few eyebrows, clear-cut logging of a 500-square-kilometer old-growth spruce forest would cre-

ate a furor, and, if foreign interests were involved, you'd think there would be a riot—but not in Wood Buffalo. For the last 30 years a number of companies have held leases to harvest timber in "Timber Berth 408," a remote region of the park along the Peace River. Through the years, many infractions were made on the leases, but they were always extended. The final lease was held by Canadian Forest Products Ltd. (Canfor), whose logging operations feed a sawmill in High Level owned by Diashowa Canada Co. Ltd., a Japanese multinational corporation. On 7 March 1991 the operation was shut down after further violating its lease. No further logging has taken place within the park.

Peace-Athabasca Delta

For thousands of years, the silt-laden waters of the Peace and Athabasca rivers flowed into Lake Claire, forming a delta rich in vegetation that provided diverse habitats for larger mammals and a traditional hunting ground for Chipewyan and Cree natives. Each spring a natural cycle of flooding would take place when the Peace River would break its banks, replenishing sloughs and marshes. This created hundreds of square kilometers of wetland, vital to the millions of birds that use the delta as a stopover on their annual migratory path and to the fur-bearing mammals whose survival is dependent on this annual cycle.

That age-old natural cycle was broken in the 1980s by the construction of the W.A.C. Bennett Dam, on the Peace River over 1,000 km upstream in British Columbia. Since the river was dammed, the flow has been regulated and the flood-cycle ended. Now the delta is slowly drying up. Protein-rich sedges along the sloughs have been replaced by silverweed and thistle, and large areas of once-rich marshland are now dried-up mudflats, severely affecting the wintering range of bison. In an attempt to return the delta to its natural state, several groups, including the federal government and local native associations, are developing plans to artificially flood the delta. Adding to the tarnished image of the park are worries about water contamination from mills upstream on the Peace and Athabasca rivers and the threat of a dam on the Lower Slave River, which would flood northern sections of the park, including the salt plains.

Whooping Cranes:
A Park Success Story

When, in 1954, a flock of 21 whooping cranes was discovered nesting in the park, the species was on the verge of extinction. Today, the population of the highly publicized and heavily studied flock has increased to over 100 and is growing slightly each year. The birds nest in a remote area of marshes and bogs in the northern reaches of Wood Buffalo far from human contact. They stand 1.3 meters, have a wing span of 2.4 meters, and are pure white, with long black legs. They are often confused with the slightly smaller, reddish-brown-colored sandhill crane which is quite common in the park.

Salt Plains

The expansive salt-encrusted plains located in the northeast of the park are one of Wood Buffalo's dominant natural features. Underground water flows through deposits of salt left behind by an ancient saltwater ocean, emerging in the form of salt springs. Large white mounds form at their source, and where the water has evaporated the ground is covered in a fine layer of salt. The best place to view this phenomenon is from the **Salt Plains Overlook,** 35 km west of Fort Smith, then 10 km south on Parson's Lake Road. The panoramic view of the plains is spectacular from this spot but **Salt Plains Trail** (one km each way), which leads to the bottom of the hill, is well worth the effort. If you decide to go beyond the trail take your shoes and socks off (squishing through the mud is good fun—and you'll appreciate clean shoes back at the car). The salt attracts many mammals including bison, wolves, foxes, and black bears. Their tracks can often be seen in the mud, along with those of various birds who feed on the aquatic vegetation unique to the plains.

Gypsum Karst

A gypsum bedrock underlies many areas of the northeast corner of the park. Gypsum is a soft, white rock that slowly dissolves in water. Underground water here has created large cavities beneath this fragile mantle. This type of terrain is known as karst, and this area is the best example of karst terrain in North America.

As the bedrock continues to dissolve, the underground caves enlarge, eventually collapsing under their own weight, forming large de-

pressions known as **sinkholes.** The thousands of sinkholes here vary in size from a few meters to 100 meters across. The most accessible large sinkhole is behind the Angus Fire Tower, 150 km west of Fort Smith. The short **Karstland Trail,** which begins behind the Salt River Picnic Area, 24 km south of Fort Smith, passes several smaller sinkholes. The **North Loop Trail,** which starts as part of the Karstland Trail but branches right, off the gravel trail, is a longer hike through typical gypsum karst terrain ending on the main road a short walk from the picnic area. The total loop is nine km; allow 2.5 hours. **Pine Lake,** 60 km south of Fort Smith, is a sinkhole that formed beneath the water table. This deep, clear lake is excellent for canoeing and fishing. A trail follows the southern shore or you can continue south to **Lane Lake,** a 6.5 km (one way) hike.

Sweetgrass

The Peace-Athabasca Delta is in a remote part of this remote park and is therefore rarely visited. Getting to the delta requires some planning as no roads access the area. The most popular visitor destination on the delta is **Sweetgrass Station,** located 12 km south of the Peace River. The site is on the edge of a vast meadow that extends around the north and west shore of Lake Claire, providing summer range for most of the park's bison. The corrals at Sweetgrass Station were built in 1954 to help the fight against diseased bison. Although now abandoned, facilities remain to vaccinate the herd if the need ever arises. A cabin with bunks and a woodstove is available for visitors to the area at no charge, although reservations at the park information center are required. The cabin is an excellent base for exploring the meadows around Lake Claire and viewing the abundant wildlife. Drinking water can be obtained from Sweetgrass Creek but should be filtered and boiled.

Park Practicalities

Park headquarters is located in Fort Smith at 126 McDougal Road. There the excellent **park information center,** tel. (403) 872-2349, offers current park information, a short slide display, and an exhibit room. The center is open in summer, Mon.-Fri. 8:30 a.m.-5 p.m., Sat.-Sun. 10 a.m.-5 p.m., the rest of the year, Mon.-Fri. only. Another small park office is located in Fort Chipewyan. It has an interesting exhibit on the

Peace River, and is open year-round, Mon.-Fri. 8:30 a.m.-5 p.m.; tel. 697-3662.

The park's only developed facilities are at **Pine Lake,** 60 km south of Fort Smith. The lake has a campground with pit toilets, covered kitchen shelters, and firewood; sites $6.50. The park staff presents a summer interpretive program at various locations—check the schedule at the park information center or on the campground notice board.

For further information write to: Superintendent, Wood Buffalo National Park, P.O. Box 750, Fort Smith, NT X0E 0P0. Seven 1:250,000 topographic maps are needed to cover the entire park. For details write to the Canada Map Office, 615 Booth St., Ottawa, Ontario K1A 0E9, or pick them up from North of 60 Books in Fort Smith.

HAY RIVER TO YELLOWKNIFE

Yellowknife, located on the north shore of the Great Slave Lake, is a long 480-km haul from Hay River, through a monotonous boreal forest of spruce, poplar, and jack pine. The trees diminish in size as the road heads north. The gravel road is slowly being replaced, but it will be many years before the territorial capital is linked to the outside world by a paved road. Twice a year, for three to six weeks in spring and again in late fall (at break-up and freeze-up, respectively, of the Mackenzie River), the road to Yellowknife is not passable.

Lady Evelyn Falls
From **Enterprise,** south of Hay River, Hwy. 1 heads northwest, coming to Lady Evelyn Falls after 53 km. These falls, where the wide **Kakisa River** cascades off a 15-meter escarpment, are easily accessible from the highway, seven km down a gravel road. A short trail leads from the day-use area down to a platform overlooking the falls. A path continues upstream past a different view of the falls, to a miniature version of the larger falls downstream. The falls are part of a territorial park that has a campground with pit toilets, bug-proof kitchen shelters, and firewood; sites $10.

Kakisa
Kakisa is a small Slavey community on Kakisa Lake at the end of the Lady Evelyn Falls access road. It was established in 1962 when the community, then located farther south on Tathlina Lake, moved to have access to the newly constructed highway. Kakisa has no services, although the lake is known for good pickerel and whitefish fishing.

Fort Providence
Eighty-five km from Enterprise the highway forks. To the left Hwy. 1 continues west to Fort Simpson, while Hwy. 3 heads north toward Yellowknife. Highway 3 crosses the **Mackenzie River,** via a ferry, 24 km from the junction. Across the river and just up the highway, a spur road leads eight km to the Slavey Dene community of Fort Providence, perched high above

Lady Evelyn Falls

the river on its steep northern bank. A Roman Catholic mission was established here in 1861, attracting natives from nearby communities. The mission continued to play an important role in the area, encouraging agriculture and operating a school. Some of the town's older residents can speak French, a legacy of the French-speaking Catholic missionaries who taught at the school. Local artisans are known for moose-hair tufting and intricate porcupine-quill weaving. On the riverfront is a **visitors center**, and farther along, historical markers honoring the roles played by Alexander Mackenzie and the church in the region's history. Fishing in the Mackenzie River is excellent, with catches of northern pike up to 12 kilograms—ask a local where the best spots are. You can rent a boat from **Aurora Sport Fishing**, tel. (403) 699-3551. **Snowshoe Inn**, tel. 699-3511, on the riverfront, has basic rooms; $70 s, $90 d. Out on the highway you'll find a gas station, a cafe with reasonable food, and a few motel rooms in ATCO trailers ($60 per night). The cafe is open till 10 p.m. and the gas station till midnight. A **campground** is located along the Fort Providence access road; sites $6.50.

Mackenzie Bison Sanctuary

Many years after the wood and plains bison in Wood Buffalo National Park had interbred, a small herd of pure wood bison was found in a remote corner of the park. In 1963, 18 of these animals were moved to the northwest side of Great Slave Lake. The herd has now grown to 2,000, occupying an area of around 10,000 square km. The region between the highway and Great Slave Lake is a bison sanctuary, although their range extends well beyond these boundaries. The animals were thought to be disease-free, but in August 1993, an outbreak of anthrax killed over 100 bison before it was quelled.

Rae-Edzo

Rae-Edzo, 214 km north of Fort Providence, is the largest Dene community in the Northwest Territories with a population of 1,500 Dogrib Dene. Dogrib have hunted and trapped in the area for centuries, but a permanent settlement wasn't established until 1852 when Dr. John Rae—an early explorer who had adopted the Indians' way of life—built a Hudson's Bay Company post nearby. Soon after, the post was moved to the present site of Rae on Marian Lake, an extension of the North Arm of Great Slave Lake.

The Dogrib were severely affected by measles, tuberculosis, and influenza—diseases brought by traders and explorers. The spread of disease was exacerbated by the poor drainage at Rae, which caused sanitation problems that continue to affect the community. By the 1940s, the Dogribs' survival was in doubt. In 1965 the government began developing a new townsite, Edzo, closer to the highway. The school at Rae was closed and a new one opened at Edzo. But despite outbreaks of disease, most of the community continued living at Rae where the water access is better for fishing and hunting.

The 10-km side trip to Rae is worthwhile. The resilient community is perched on a rocky outcrop jutting into **Marian Lake.** The main road through town leads to a small island where the rocky beaches are littered with boats, fishing nets, and dogs tied up waiting for snow. Apart from the snowmobiles, the village looks much as it did 100 years ago. **Rae Industrial Lodge,** tel. (403) 392-6044, is an alternative to the higher prices of Yellowknife, 100 km away. The rate of $85 per person includes three meals in the adjoining cafe.

North of Rae-Edzo are the remote communities of Lac La Martre, Rae Lakes, and Snare Lakes, accessible only by plane from Yellowknife (see "Communities in the Vicinity of Yellowknife" under "Yellowknife and Vicinity," below).

YELLOWKNIFE AND VICINITY

Built on dreams, perseverance, and the ingenuity of a small group of pioneers who came in search of gold, the territorial capital of Yellowknife has grown into a modern urban center of 18,000. Its frontier-town flavor and independent spirit distinguish it from all other Canadian cities. It's the northernmost city in Canada, the *only* city in the NWT, and the only predominately nonnative community in the territories. Located on the North Arm of the Great Slave Lake, the city clings precariously to the ancient, glacial-scarred rock of the Canadian Shield. Edmonton is 1,524 km south by road, 965 km by air. The Arctic Circle is 442 km north. At first, Yellowknife looks little different from other small Canadian cities, but unique contrasts soon become apparent. While some residents are writing computer programs, others are preparing caribou hides; architect-designed houses are scattered among squatters' log cabins; and the roads are seemingly always under repair, a legacy of permafrost.

History

Samuel Hearne dubbed the local Dene natives the Yellowknife for the copper knifes they used. Their numbers were decimated by disease and warring with the Dogrib who had traditionally hunted in the area. Miners on their way to the Klondike were the first to discover gold in the area, but didn't rush in to stake claims due to the area's remote location and the difficulty of extracting the mineral from the hard bedrock. But as airplanes began opening up the north, the area became more attractive to gold-seekers. Hundreds of claims were staked between 1934 and 1936, and a boomtown sprang up along the shore of Yellowknife Bay. Very few struck it rich, but the rush continued until WW II with miners coming north in scows, barges, floatplanes, and a sternwheeler that plied the lake from Fort Smith. After the war, growth continued and soon the original townsite around the bay was at full capacity. A new town, just up the hill, was surveyed and by 1947 the city center of today began taking shape. In 1967 a road was completed to the outside and the city came to rely less on air travel. The city was named terri-

torial capital the same year. As the white-collar population grew, houses went up and more sophisticated services became available. Although the federal and territorial governments are Yellowknife's biggest employers, several producing gold mines have kept the economy alive.

In the late 1980s, a general downturn in the price of gold along with union demands for better and safer conditions led to a general strike that became the most vicious in Canada's history. The strike was violent from the start, with security guards protecting the mine and scab workers, brawls in bars, and daily battles at the picket line. The strike's darkest hour was the morning of 18 September 1992 when a bomb planted by a striking miner exploded 150 meters underground, killing nine miners. It was the worst crime in Canadian labor history. The strike continued for another 18 months.

SIGHTS

Prince Of Wales Northern Heritage Centre

The entire history of the territories is catalogued at this modern facility on the shore of Frame Lake. The South Gallery displays a collection of Dene and Inuit artifacts. The North Gallery catalogues the arrival of white man and his impact on the environment. The Aviation Gallery presents a realistic display of a bush pilot and his plane and a wall of fame for the pilots who helped opened up the north. Also here is a live hookup to the traffic controllers at Yellowknife Airport. The center houses the NWT Archives of maps, photographs, books, and manuscripts available for public examination. The center is open in summer, daily 10:30 a.m.-5:30 p.m.; the rest of the year, Mon.-Fri. 10:30 a.m.-4:30 p.m.; tel. (403) 873-7551.

Old Town

From the city center, Franklin Ave. (50th Ave.) descends a long, dusty hill to Yellowknife's Old Town. It was here, in the 1930s, that the first log and frame buildings were erected. Along the narrow streets, Quonset huts, original set-

YELLOWKNIFE

YELLOWKNIFE BAY

LATHAM ISLAND

BLUE RAVEN B & B

BACK BAY

OTTO DR.

CAPTAIN RON'S B & B

WILDCAT CAFE

THE ROCK

JOLLIFFE ISLAND

BUSH PILOTS BREW PUB

SAIL NORTH

NORTH WEST CO. TRADING POST

WILLOW FLATS

TO TIBBIT LAKE (DEAD END)
INGRAHAM TRAIL

4

3

IGLOO INN

SCHOOL DRAW AVE.

LAUNDROMAT

NIVEN LAKE

JACKFISH LAKE

EXPLORER HOTEL

VISITORS CENTRE

NORTHERN HERITAGE CENTRE

52nd ST.
48th ST.
51st AVE.
50th AVE.
49th AVE.
FRANKLIN AVE.

SEE INSET

PROSPECTOR'S TRAIL

LONG LAKE

CAMPGROUND

FRED HENNE T. P.

TO GOLF COURSE

3

OLD AIRPORT RD.

FRAME LAKE

THE SPORTS TRADERS

FORREST DR.

YELLOWKNIFE AIRPORT

STANTON YELLOWKNIFE HOSPITAL

RANGE LAKE RD.

SAM'S MONKEY TREE

RANGE LAKE

KAM LAKE RD.

KAM LAKE

© MOON PUBLICATIONS, INC.

INSET

47th ST.
51st AVE.
DISCOVERY INN
48th ST.
ARCTIC ART GALLERY
49th ST.
YELLOWKNIFE INN
CENTRE SQUARE MALL
BISTRO ON FRANKLIN
OUR PLACE
THE OFFICE
50th ST.
POST OFFICE
GOLD RANGE
51st ST.
FRANKLIN AVE.
OVERLANDER SPORTS
OUTCROP
52nd ST.
49th AVE.
53rd ST.
NORTHWEST MEATS
54th ST.
YWCA

tlers' homes, converted buses, old boats, and tin shanties look incongruous to a Canadian capital city. Some of the most unusual housing is in **Willow Flats,** east of Franklin Avenue. **Ragged Ass Rd.,** named for a mine claim, has the most unusual houses, many posting signs telling the story of the building. Across Franklin Ave. is **Peace River Flats** where a few original buildings remain. Farther north along Franklin Ave. is an area known simply as **The Rock,** for the huge chunk of Canadian Shield that towers above the surrounding landscape. At the top of The Rock is the **Pilot's Monument,** dedicated to the bush pilots who opened up the north. At the corner of Pilots Lane and Wiley Rd. is **Weaver & Devore,** an old-time general store selling just about everything. Many of their larger orders have to be flown in to buyers scattered through the north. Farther around Wiley Rd., overlooking Back Bay, is the **Wildcat Cafe,** one of the city's landmarks. East of The Rock, in Yellowknife Bay, is **Jolliffe Island,** once a fuel depot but now a residential area. The homes are reached by boat or canoe in summer and by road in winter. At the north end of The Rock a causeway, built in 1948, connects **Latham Island** to the mainland. At the south end of the island are floatplane bases where the constant buzz of small planes taking off and landing symbolizes the north.

Fred Henne Territorial Park
Forest-encircled **Long Lake,** opposite Yellowknife Airport, is mainly used by visitors for the excellent camping facilities. But it's also a good example of the wilderness surrounding the city. The four-km **Prospector's Trail,** which begins from the campground, is a good way to experience the unique landscape. You can hike to the park from the city center along the trails around **Frame Lake.**

Ingraham Trail
Apart from Hwy. 3 from the south, the Ingraham Trail (Hwy. 4 East) is the only route out of the city. The road passes a string of lakes—great for fishing, boating, and swimming—and the **Royal Oak Mine.** It then crosses the Yellowknife River and passes **Prosperous, Pontoon,** and **Prelude lakes,** each with day-use areas. Continuing east, the road parallels the **Cameron River.** A number of trails lead down to

the riverbank and waterfalls dot the route. The road ends at **Tibbit Lake,** 71 km from Yellowknife.

Dettah
This community, originally a seasonal fish camp for the Dogrib Dene, is located east of Yellowknife across Yellowknife Bay. As Yellowknife grew, the Dogrib people settled here permanently to take advantage of the growing services of the new city, while maintaining a traditional way of life. Today the 150 residents continue a lifestyle of fishing, hunting, and trapping.

RECREATION

Great Slave Lake
North Arm Adventures, tel. (403) 873-8533, offers two- and four-hour fishing trips on the North Arm of Great Slave Lake ($75 and $95, respectively). **Vern's Venture,** tel. 873-6234, also leads fishing trips that work out slightly cheaper with four or more people.

Sail North, P.O. Box 2497, Yellowknife, NT X1A 2P8, tel. 873-8019, charters motorboats and sailboats. Motorboats start at $20 per hour for a four-meter boat and $80 per hour for a 12-meter boat. Per week, the same boats are $500-2699. Sailboats ranging 8-14 meters rent for $275-549 per day or $1099-2699 per week, and make a great way to explore the hundreds of uncharted bays on the East Arm. You can sail yourself or hire a skipper ($85 extra per day).

Golf
Yellowknife Golf Course is located west of downtown along Hwy. 3. The greens of this nine-hole course have always been oil-soaked sand but are gradually being replaced by artificial grass. One thing that won't change is the rock and gravel fairways. Each shot must be hit from a small mat that players carry around the course. The club has a pro shop with rentals, a restaurant, and some great photos of the course's early days. For details call (403) 873-4326.

Entertainment
Entertainment at the **Gold Range Hotel,** 5010 50th St., tel. 873-4441, best known as the **Strange Range,** is like no other in the country. Don't be put off by the unusual characters, hun-

The eclectic housing of Ragged Ass Road is a reminder of the city's earliest days.

dreds of empty beer glasses, and bouncers with legs like tree trunks; it isn't as rowdy as it seems. There's live entertainment on weekends, including one bloke who, in the winter months, rides 50 km on his snowmobile from his remote trapper's cabin to perform. If you like to mix with the locals this is the place to do it, and you may help them claim the title of highest beer sales per capita in Canada; so far they only run second. On Franklin Ave. **The Gallery,** tel. 873-2651, also has live entertainment but is rougher.

Down in Old Town, overlooking Back Bay, is the **Bush Pilots Brew Pub,** 3502 Wiley Rd., tel. 920-2739, home to **Arctic Brewing Co.,** the territories' only brewery (tours available). A casual bar here serves the beer and light meals. The bar top is the wing of a DeHaviland Beaver that crashed nearby. Beer is $5 a pint. Out front is a rusty plane engine that spent three years on the bottom of the bay. The pub is open Mon.-Sat. 11:30 a.m.-midnight.

Shopping
Yellowknife has many arts and crafts shops but the best place for browsing is the **North West Co. Trading Post,** 5005 Bryson Dr., tel. (403) 873-8064. The store sells native arts, warm clothing, northern literature, and a variety of tacky souvenirs. It's a replica of trading posts that once dotted the north; open daily 10 a.m.-9 p.m. Also down at this end of town is **The Mission,** beside the Wildcat Cafe, selling a wide range of souvenirs. For limited-edition prints, paintings and carvings from throughout the north

head to the **Arctic Art Gallery,** 4801 Franklin Ave., tel. 873-5666.

Festivals And Events
Not many visitors are around for the **Caribou Carnival,** the last weekend of March. Events include bingo on ice, and log-sawing, flour-packing, igloo-building, and dog-mushing contests. The weekend closest to Summer Solstice (21 June) is **Raven Mad Daze,** featuring street entertainment and a midnight-sun golf tournament (this event is popular with visitors, make reservations in advance, tel. (403) 920-5647). **Folk on the Rocks,** the third weekend of July, takes place on the shore of Long Lake and attracts northern and southern performers.

ACCOMMODATIONS

Hotels And Motels
The **YWCA,** 5004 54th St., tel. (403) 920-2777, is close to downtown and has private rooms for men and women, each with a kitchenette and access to a laundry and health club; $70 s, $85 d. Dorm beds are only available by the month. **Yellowknife Inn,** P.O. Box 490, Yellowknife, NT X1A 2N4, tel. 873-2601, is right in the center of the city. Each room has a mini-bar and is well decorated. Guests have use of a health club, laundry, and an airport shuttle; $125 s, $130 d. Other hotels are: **Igloo Inn,** 4115 Franklin Ave., P.O. Box 596, NT X1A 2N4, tel. 873-8511, halfway to Old Town, $95 s, $100 d, extra for

kitchenettes; **Discovery Inn,** 4701 Franklin Ave., P.O. Box 784, NT X1A 2N6, tel. 873-4151, simply furnished with older-style rooms and a bar downstairs, $105 s, $115 d; and **Explorer Hotel** on 47th St., Postal Service 7000, NT X1A 2R3; tel. 873-3531 or (800) 661-0892, an eight-story luxury hotel with air-conditioned rooms, many with views of Old Town and the rolling tundra beyond, $140 s, $150 d.

Bed And Breakfasts
Ask at the visitors center for a current list of B&Bs. **Captain Ron's,** 8 Lessard Dr., Yellowknife, NT X1A 2G5, tel. (403) 873-3746, overlooking the floatplane base, has four rooms, a sundeck, library, and guest lounge; $70 s, $86 d. **Blue Raven B&B,** 37B Otto Dr., NT X1A 2T9, tel. 873-6328, on top of a hill on Latham Island, overlooks Great Slave Lake; $60 s, $75 d. For a full listing write to Yellowknife B&Bs, 22 Otto Dr., Yellowknife, NT X1A 2T8, or call 873-6238.

Lodges
Of the many wilderness lodges surrounding the city, the only one accessible by road is **Prelude Lake Lodge,** P.O. Box 2548, Yellowknife, NT X1A 2P8, tel. (403) 920-2525. It's 32 km east of town along the Ingraham Trail, and offers a number of cabins, beginning from $55, spread along the lakeshore. Boats are available for rent and fishing is good in the lake. **Enodah Wilderness Travel,** P.O. Box 2382, NT X1A 2P8, tel. 873-4334, has a lodge on Trout Rock, a two-square-km island 30 km west of Yellowknife that was once the site of a Dogrib community. The lodge specializes in fishing; three-day fishing trips start at $675 per person. **Plummer's Great Slave Lake Lodge,** 950 Bradford St., Winnipeg, MB R3H 0N5, tel. (204) 774-5775 or (800) 665-0240, is located at Taltheilei Narrows on the northeast corner of the lake at a point of fish migration. The lodge offers a number of cabins (each with private bathroom), a trading post, restaurant, and fishing from six-meter boats. Access is from Winnipeg—aboard a Boeing 737 each Saturday, or smaller planes from Yellowknife during the week.

Campgrounds
The city's only campground is at **Fred Henne Territorial Park,** tel. (403) 920-2472, across from the airport and a one-hour walk from downtown. Facilities include bug-proof kitchen shelters, woodstoves, showers, and some powered sites; $10 per night. Along the Ingraham Trail, at Reid Lake, is a primitive campground. Both are open late May-September.

FOOD

Cheap Eats
Fortunately, you need not spend a fortune to experience true northern cuisine or hospitality. The **Wildcat Cafe,** 3904 Wiley Rd., tel. (403) 873-8850, has been famous since it was opened by Willy Wiley and Smoky Stout in 1937, becoming the first place in Yellowknife to sell ice cream. The cafe closed its doors in 1959, but reopened with some remodeling in 1979. It only has a few tables and is perpetually full—chances are you'll end up sharing a table. The menu features mostly northern dishes from $12. It's open in summer only, Mon.-Sat. 7 a.m.-10 p.m., Sunday 10 a.m.-9 p.m. **Northwest Meats,** 5012 53rd St., tel. 920-4924, sells a variety of northern delicacies for the campfire. Or try the buffalo, caribou, and musk ox jerky. **McDonald's** and **KFC** (once voted the national dish of the NWT) have only one franchise each in the territories, and here in the north, take-away really means take-away; when people from outlying communities visit Yellowknife they often take a large supply home with them to microwave. KFC has even developed special boxes that will fit under airplane seats.

Red Apple in the Discovery Inn, tel. 873-2324, opens at 6 a.m., and is a popular spot for breakfast. It also serves a variety of dishes the rest of the day starting at $7.50. Farther out is **Sam's Monkey Tree,** 483 Range Lake Rd., tel. 920-4914, a good, clean, family-style restaurant.

Other Restaurants
A number of upscale restaurants in Yellowknife serve northern specialties. Small and dimly lit, **The Office,** 4915 50th St., tel. (403) 873-3750, serves delicious arctic char and other seafood dishes from $18. **Bistro on Franklin,** 4910 Franklin Ave., tel. 873-3991, is similarly priced but with a more intimate atmosphere. **Our Place** in the 50/50 Mini Mall Building on Franklin Ave., tel. 920-2265, is a well-decorated cocktail lounge serving meals.

TRANSPORTATION

Air
Yellowknife Airport, five km west of the city along Hwy. 3, is the hub of air travel in the NWT. It is open daily 24 hours, has an inexpensive cafe (5:30 a.m.-10 p.m.), a bar, lockers, and rental cars. Airlines with scheduled flights to Yellowknife from Edmonton include: **Canadian North,** tel. (403) 873-4484, (800) 665-1177, or, in the U.S., (800) 426-7000; and **NWT Air,** tel. (403) 920-2500 or (800) 661-0789. Both these airlines provide scheduled services from Yellowknife to points throughout the Arctic. Other scheduled airlines flying to Yellowknife include: **Alkan Air,** from Whitehorse, tel. (403) 668-2107; **First Air,** from the Baffin region, tel. (819) 873-6884 or (800) 267-1247; **Air Tindi,** from communities around Great Slave Lake, tel. (403) 920-4177; **Buffalo,** from Hay River, tel. (403) 873-6112; **Great Bear Aviation,** from communities along the Mackenzie River, tel. (403) 873-3626 or (800) 661-0719; **Northwestern,** from Fort Smith, tel. (403) 872-2216; **North-Wright Air,** from communities along the Mackenzie River, tel. (403) 920-4287; and **Ptarmigan Airways,** from communities around Great Slave Lake and the Arctic coast, tel. (403) 873-4461.

Bus
Frontier Coachlines, 328 Old Airport Rd., tel. (403) 873-4892, offers bus service five times weekly from Hay River to Yellowknife ($64.50 one way), with connections from there to Greyhound's Canadian services.

Getting Around
Flag charge for a cab is $2.50, then it's $1.30 for every kilometer. To the campground is $9, to the airport $11; call **City Cab** at (403) 873-4444. Rental-car agencies include: **Avis,** tel. 873-5648; **Rent-A-Relic,** tel. 873-3400; and **Yellowknife Motors,** tel. 873-4414. Rates start at $30 per day and $174 per week for a small car, plus 20 cents per kilometer. **The Sports Traders,** 5 Old Airport Rd., tel. 893-9030, rents bikes for $5 per hour and $20 per 24 hours. **Overlander Sports,** 5103 51st St., tel. 873-2474, rents canoes and kayaks—great for getting around nearby waterways—for $30 per day and $180 per week. It's closed Sunday.

Tours
Raven Tours, tel. (403) 873-4776, runs a three-hour City of Gold Tour that takes in all the sights of New Town, Old Town, Latham Island, and a sled-dog kennel; $30 per person. The tour departs daily at 1:15 p.m. from the visitors center. They also offer guided hikes to Cameron River Falls ($40 per person) and flightseeing (from $50 per person).

SERVICES AND INFORMATION

Services
The **post office** is located at 4902 50th Street. **Arctic Laundromat,** 4310 Franklin Ave., is open daily 8:30 a.m.-9 p.m. **Photo Works,** in the Centre Square Mall, tel. (403) 873-2389, develops film in one hour and has a limited range of camera supplies.

    Stanton Yellowknife Hospital is located on Old Airport Rd. at Range Lake Rd., tel. 920-4111. For the **RCMP** call 920-8311.

Books And Bookstores
Yellowknife Public Library is located on the second floor of Centre Square Mall at 5022 49th St., tel. (403) 873-5980. Although small, it has newspapers from throughout Canada and lots of literature on the north. It's open year-round, Mon.-Thurs. 10 a.m.-9 p.m., Fri.-Sat. 10 a.m.-6 p.m. **Yellowknife Book Cellar,** in the Panda Mall, tel. 920-2220, has a wide selection of northern and Canadian literature. The north's biggest publisher, **Outcrop,** at 5022 51st St., tel. 920-4652, has back issues of *Up Here* for sale and catalogues of all books they publish.

Tourist Information
The **Northern Frontier Visitors Centre** overlooks Frame Lake at 4807 49th St., tel. (403) 873-4262. It is stocked with brochures on everything you'll need to know about Yellowknife, historic photographs, and interesting displays. It's open in summer, daily 8 a.m.-8 p.m., the rest of the year, weekdays only. For more information on Yellowknife and the surrounding communities write to: Northern Frontier Visitor's Association, P.O. Box 1107, Yellowknife, NT X1A 2N8; tel. 873-3131 or (800) 661-0788.

Yellowknife's modern skyline as seen from Old Town

COMMUNITIES IN THE VICINITY OF YELLOWKNIFE

Within a 250-km radius of Yellowknife are five communities accessible only by air, or in the case of Reliance and Lutselk'e, by boat. Each receives few casual visitors, and if you plan to stay overnight, you should reserve accommodations before arriving. **Air Tindi,** tel. (403) 920-4177, flies to each of the communities.

Lutselk'e

Formerly known as **Snowdrift,** this community of 260 Chipewyan Dene is located on a peninsula extending into the East Arm of Great Slave Lake. The Hudson's Bay Company established a post here in 1925, which quickly attracted Chipewyan families from the surrounding area. Nearby you'll find some excellent fishing and sheer cliffs that drop into the lake. **Snowdrift Co-op Motel,** General Delivery, Lutselk'e, NT X0E 1A0, tel. (403) 370-3511, has three rooms, each with shared bath; $115 per person.

Reliance

This Chipewyan Dene community of 150 is located on a peninsula jutting into McLeod Bay at the far end of the East Arm. Yellowknife is 250 km to the west. The remains of a stone house built by George Beck, an early barrenlands explorer, are located in town.

Lac La Martre

This community of 400 Dogrib Dene is located on the southeast shore of a lake of the same name 160 km northwest of Yellowknife. A North West Company trading post was established on the lake in 1793. Today, the community functions much as it did then, relying on the area's abundant fish and mammals to provide a subsistence lifestyle. **Meni Khon Hotel,** General Delivery, Lac La Martre, NT X0E 1P0, tel. (403) 573-3161, has a few rooms in town and a lodge on the northeast shore of the lake.

Rae Lakes

This community had until recently been used as an outpost for hunting by the Dogrib Dene. It is located on the shore of a lake that is part of a chain between Great Slave and Great Bear Lakes. Permanent facilities and new housing have kept the population around 200. **Gameti Motel,** General Delivery, Rae Lakes, NT X0E 1R0, tel. (403) 997-3031, has eight rooms with private bath and the staff can organize fishing trips; rooms start at $100 per person.

Snare Lake

Until recently this community was, like Rae Lakes to the west, an outpost for hunters of the Dogrib Dene. The community of 100 is located east of Rae Lakes. No accommodations are available.

RIVERS OF MYTH,
MOUNTAINS OF MYSTERY

Tucked into the southwest corner of the territories—between the Mackenzie River to the north and east and the Yukon Territory and British Columbia to the south and west—is a wild, uninhabited, roadless land of jagged peaks, thundering rivers, a waterfall twice the height of Niagara, and pristine lakes so full of fish that you'll need to bait your hook behind a tree. Not only is it one of North America's most remote mountain regions, it is one of the least understood. Scientists are only recently beginning to unravel the mysteries of the strikingly varied landforms within **Nahanni National Park,** a UNESCO World Heritage Site. The region's history is equally mysterious. A little-known band of

Indians once lived here, high in the mountains, who were feared by the Slavey Dene who lived along the Liard and Mackenzie rivers. Legends of lost gold mines, tropical valleys, and headless bodies have been luring adventurers to the area for over 100 years. The first white men to travel up the **South Nahanni River** were fur trappers and missionaries. Those who managed to return brought back stories that helped create the region's mythical allure. Today, visitors from around the world come to paddle down the South Nahanni (Canada's finest wilderness river), climb in the Cirque of the Unclimbables, or just fly into this spectacular part of the world. But with names on the map like Headless Creek, Deadmen Valley, Hell's Gate, Funeral Range, Devils Kitchen, Broken Skull River, and Death Canyon, you'd better tell someone where you're going.

Nahanni National Park is visited by fewer than 1,500 people each year. Roads have replaced rivers as transportation routes through much of the region, but communities built around fur-trading posts still remain. The **Mackenzie Hwy.,** which begins in northern Alberta, ends 427 km west of Hay River in **Fort Simpson,** the main jumping-off point for wilderness trips into the Nahanni and beyond. For more information on the region write to Nahanni-ram Tourism Association, P.O. Box 177, Fort Simpson, NT X0E 0N0; tel. (403) 695-3182 or (800) 661-0788.

Saamba Deh Falls Territorial Park
From the Yellowknife junction, the Mackenzie Hwy. continues west through a typical northern boreal forest, along the way crossing many small creeks. Approximately 136 km from this junction, the road crosses **Trout River,** which flows alongside Saamba Deh Falls Territorial Park. The falls are directly downstream from the road bridge, and are easily accessible from the day-use area. Here, the river is forced through a narrow gorge, exploding into the deep pond below. Worthwhile is the one-km hike upstream from the day-use area to **Coral Falls,** named for the abundant marine fossils found in

ALBERT FAILLE

Each break-up from 1916 to 1961, Albert Faille left Fort Simpson by scow in a feverish, determined quest for the elusive Nahanni gold. Some said it was sheer lunacy, others said a waste of time. But his relentless obsession and exploits against insurmountable odds created the Faille legend, which has become synonymous with the Nahanni.

Of Swiss descent, Faille was born in Minnesota and first ventured into Nahanni Country in 1927. He was one of the earliest men to tackle the river alone, and at the time, the first to winter there in seven years. He built a cabin at the mouth of the Flat River, but it was at Murder Creek, upstream from the cabin, that Faille believed his fortune in gold lay. At times he'd be given up for dead, and rumors and tales would begin to unfold—but then he would turn up at Fort Simpson for supplies. He spent most winters in a small cabin that still stands today, overlooking the Mackenzie River in Fort Simpson. He died there in 1974. His scows still lie out front, ready for break-up and another attempt for the elusive key to finding gold. His final trip is documented by a 1961 National Film Board production that can be seen in the Fort Simpson and Blackstone visitor centers.

the surrounding limestone banks. Most common are crinoids and brachiopods that are around 400 million years old (Late Devonian period). The trail is well defined at first, then climbs steeply, making getting down to the river level in one piece rather interesting. The alternative is to scramble down along the river as soon as the trail begins climbing. The **visitors center**, tel. (403) 770-4141, has a small fossil display and free coffee. Across the parking lot is a TV room where the friendly staff can put on videos pertaining to the region's natural and human history; it's open mid-May to mid-September, daily 8 a.m.-8 p.m. The park also has a small campground with showers, bug-proof kitchen shelters, and well-maintained sites for $10 a night.

From here, the Mackenzie Hwy. continues in a northwesterly direction to a junction with the Liard Hwy. (which heads south to Fort Liard and into British Columbia). Past the junction, it crosses the Liard River by ferry and, after 94 km, ends in Fort Simpson.

Trout Lake

This small community was established in the late 1960s as a permanent base for the Slavey Dene who had hunted, trapped, and fished in the area for thousands of years. It is located in a heavily wooded area where the Island River drains into Trout Lake, approximately 100 km east of Fort Liard. The town's only link to the outside world is by charter flight from Fort Liard or Fort Simpson or by a winter road from the Mackenzie Hwy., just east of Saamba Deh Falls Territorial Park. With a name like Trout Lake, it's not surprising that the fishing is excellent, especially for lake trout, pickerel, and whitefish. The best spot is at the lake's northern end, where the Moose River flows into the lake. The main problem with coming here to fish is that you reach your daily limit too quickly. The local Dene band runs a fishing lodge on the lake. The lodge costs $60 per person per day, with use of kitchen facilities, or $160 per person including meals and guided fishing. Boat rentals are also available. For more information call (403) 695-9800. **Deh Cho Air**, tel. 770-4103, in Fort Liard, flies to Trout Lake and also offers day-trips to the lake for $150 per person.

Jean Marie River

The Slavey Dene people of this small community (population 70) still hunt, trap, and fish for a living in the old way but are best known for their moose-hair tufting and porcupine-quill work which can be purchased in Fort Simpson and Yellowknife. Located at the confluence of the Jean Marie and Mackenzie rivers with no summer road access, the people of the community travel downstream to Fort Simpson to trade and buy supplies. No visitor services are available, but those en route down the Mackenzie are always welcome to drop in. Fort Simpson is 68 km downstream, along a section of river dotted with islands.

FORT SIMPSON

Best known as one of the jumping-off points for Nahanni National Park, the town of Fort Simpson (population 1,000) is located at the confluence of two major rivers—the Liard and Mackenzie—and at the western terminus of the Mackenzie Highway. Throughout summer the town is a hive of activity, a constant buzz of floatplanes taking off to remote fly-in fishing lakes, groups of Gore-Tex-clad adventurers from around the world checking their equipment before heading off for an adventure of a lifetime down the South Nahanni River, and paddlers stopping in on their way to the Arctic Ocean. The town provides a good base for exploring the region—whether by car, plane, boat, or on foot. Wildlife is abundant, and the lakes and rivers teem with fish.

History

It wasn't until 1815, after Alexander Mackenzie had paddled by on his way to the Arctic Ocean, that a permanent settlement was established at this strategic location. Originally known as "Fort of the Forks," it was built by North West Company in 1804 but was renamed Fort Simpson in 1821. As well as being an important fur-trading post, it was a stopping point for barges plying the Mackenzie River loaded with supplies, fuel, and furs. Missions were established in 1858 and 1894 and the area's potential for agriculture began to be realized. The government operated an experimental farm here for years, but it was closed in 1969 when a highway linking Fort Simpson to the outside was completed and importing food overland became practical. During the 1960s the town became a base for oil exploration along the Mackenzie Valley and an administrative center for the territorial government.

Around Town

At one time the town's main street was Mackenzie Dr., along the riverfront. But when the highway was completed, many buildings were moved closer to it. Now most town services are along 100th Street. At the south end of Mackenzie Dr. is an area known as "The Flat," where many people lived until severe flooding in 1963

forced relocation of homes. The large tepee and other structures here, known as the **Papal Grounds,** were built for a visit by Pope John Paul II on 20 September, 1987. Walking north from here along Mackenzie Dr., a sternwheeler on the riverbank soon comes into view. Built in 1920, this boat was one of many that plied the Mackenzie River. Also here is a small monument noting the importance of the river in the town's history. Across the road is the site of the Hudson's Bay Company post; the only original building remaining is the company's outhouse. Continuing farther along the river you pass the site of an Anglican church, the RCMP, an early hotel, the Power Corporation building, and the cabin of Nahanni legend Albert Faille. Faille wintered here between his gold-seeking trips. Peering through the windows and marveling at the wooden scows laying in the yard will give you some insight into the life of this amazing man, particularly if you've watched the National Film Board documentary about him shown at the visitors center (see "Services and Information," below). Faille is buried behind the post office on 100th Street.

Nahanni Mountain Lodge

Ted Grant, owner of Simpson Air, has built a rustic lodge at one of his favorite fly-in fishing spots. Nahanni Mountain Lodge is on Little Doctor Lake, 90 km west of Fort Simpson. Besides reeling in fighting northern pike here, you can go swimming, hiking, canoeing, or just kick back on the sandy beach surrounded by some of the world's wildest mountain scenery. The lodge sleeps eight and has a stove, fridge, and wood heaters. Canoes, paddles, and a small motorboat are also supplied. The short 20-minute flight (which leaves from the floatplane base on Mackenzie Dr.) is spectacular—Little Doctor Lake marks a sudden terrain change, with the mountains of the Nahanni Range rising steeply behind it. This is only a taste of the spectacular country farther west. With a little wheeling and dealing, you might be able to arrange a detour flight into Nahanni National Park. Three days at the lake, including use of all facilities, costs $650 per person for up to three people, $500 per person for 4-8. For more information contact Simpson Air, P.O. Box 260, Fort Simpson, NT X0E 0N0; (403) tel. 695-2505.

Recreation And Events

Little Doctor is not the only lake with great fishing. **McGill Lake** and **Mustard Lake** are two more of the many fly-in spots with trophy-size northern pike, pickerel, lake trout, and arctic grayling. If you've never gotten hooked on fishing, perhaps golf sounds better. Down by the entrance to town on Antoine Dr. is the local golf course. It can boast only a few holes, and has no clubhouse or rentals, but the local golfing population is proud of it.

The big event in Fort Simpson is the annual **Deh Cho Daze,** the third weekend of August. It's a summer festival with a talent show, native games, and plenty of northern food.

Accommodations And Food

Rooms in both of Fort Simpson's hotels are little more than basic. **Maroda Motel,** P.O. Box 248, Fort Simpson, NT X0E 0N0, tel. (403) 695-2602, charges $95 s, $110 d; **Nahanni Inn,** P.O. Box 248, tel. 695-2201, has a coffee shop (open daily at 8 a.m.) and dining room, $105 s, $115 d. Both are within walking distance of everything. Along the road to the Papal Grounds is **Fort Simpson Campground.** The sites—$5 a night —provide ample privacy, and a large supply of firewood is available. Anyone heading into the Nahanni with a river outfitter may pitch a tent at the airstrip compound for free; ask permission first.

Transportation

The main airport is 12 km south of town ($15 in a cab, tel. 403-695-2777). Two airlines fly to Fort Simpson, both from Yellowknife (all connections from the south are through the territorial capital). **Buffalo Airways,** tel. 874-3333, a connector airline for Air Canada, flies from Yellowknife, Mon.-Fri. at 10:40 a.m. **Ptarmigan,** tel. 873-4461, departs daily except Sunday. The one-way fare from Edmonton is $457, $731 for a 14-day APEX round trip. The floatplane base and airstrip used by **Simpson Air** are in town.

Save a moose, honk your horn.

BOB RACE

Services And Information

Groceries and basic camping supplies are available from **Northern,** but you should stock up in Hay River. On 97th Ave. is a **bank** (C.I.B.C.), on 100th St. are a **post office, liquor store** (with a ration system in effect), and **gas station.**

At the south entrance to town is an excellent **visitors center,** tel. (403) 695-3182. Inside is a re-creation of the original Hudson's Bay Company post and some interesting historical displays. Don't miss the 1961 National Film Board documentary on Nahanni legend Albert Faille which is shown, along with others, in the theater; open May 15-Sept. 15, daily 8 a.m.-8 p.m. Diagonally opposite the visitors center is the **Tourist Service Centre** with coin showers, a car wash, and a laundromat. You could also use the laundry facilities in the apartment block on 101st Avenue. Also opposite the visitors center is the town's only bar.

LIARD HIGHWAY

Although this highway, which follows the Liard River Valley from Fort Simpson to Fort Nelson (British Columbia), was officially completed in 1984, it wasn't marked on most maps until the late '80s and didn't really become an all-weather gravel highway (read passable) until the early '90s.

From the Mackenzie Hwy., southeast of Fort Simpson, to Fort Nelson is 394 km of relatively straight road through a boreal forest of spruce, aspen, and poplar. Wildlife along this route is abundant; chances are you'll see moose and black bears, especially at dawn and dusk. Save a moose, honk your horn. The only services are at Fort Liard.

Lindberg Landing

Although the highway parallels the Liard River, access to the water is limited. One of the first landings is 100 km south of the Mackenzie Hwy. at the home of Ed and Sue Lindberg, who provide accommodation and have an amazingly diverse vegetable garden. Ed Lindberg's father, Ole, arrived from Sweden in the mid-1920s and was the first permanent settler along the river. The service offered by the Lindbergs is excellent for those beginning or ending a journey down the South Nahanni River. **Blackstone Aviation** will pick you up at the landing and drop you upriver, allowing you to float back to Lindberg Landing farm and finish your trip with a bed, beer, and shower. Reservations for rooms are essential; no walk-ins. Dinner, bed, and breakfast is $60 per person. A housekeeping room, which sleeps four, is $60. For bookings write to P.O. Box 28, Fort Simpson, NT X0E 0N0. From within the territories call 1311 and ask the operator to connect you to Pointed Mountain Channel Mobile JR3-6644. From the north, Lindberg Landing is marked by a small sign in a tree. If you pass Blackstone Territorial Park you missed it.

Blackstone Territorial Park

Just south of the Lindberg's homestead, where the Blackstone River drains into the Liard River, a small territorial park has been established at a site known as **Blackstone Landing.** A visitors center overlooks the river and from here a short trail leads along the river to an abandoned cabin. The campground has flush toilets, showers, and two bug-proof, woodstove-equipped kitchen shelters hidden among the trees. Sites cost $10 a night. Black bears are common so keep your food securely stored. The visitors center has interesting displays on the area's history, a good selection of videos, and information on Nahanni National Park (although registering for a trip into the park must be done in Fort Simpson); open mid-May to mid-September, daily 9 a.m.-9 p.m.

From the park, Fort Liard is 114 km farther south. The highway crosses many small creeks, passes the winter road to **Nahanni Butte,** and provides views of the Liard Range to the west. Approximately 68 km south of Blackstone Territorial Park is a winter road that was cut through the muskeg to the now-abandoned Paramount Mine, on the opposite side of the Liard River. It is a pleasant one-km hike (15 minutes each way) down to the river.

Nahanni Butte

Named for the steeply sided butte across the South Nahanni River, this small Slavey Dene community of under 100 is located across the Liard River from the highway. Although you can drive to it in winter, the rest of the year it is accessible only by plane or boat. The town is fairly modern. It was established by the government to house a group of once-nomadic natives who, at times, traded with the Tahltan and Tlingit of the Pacific coast. For many years Nahanni National Park headquarters was here and a small office still operates in summer for "checking-out" after a river trip. Most paddlers stop by anyway as the town is in a picturesque setting and holds an interesting log church and log school. Except for a small general store, no services are available. **Blackstone Aviation,** tel. (403) 695-2111 or call the operator on 1311 and ask for Arrowhead YJ3-9704, flies from Lindberg or Blackstone landings to Nahanni Butte for $180 round trip.

FORT LIARD

Best known as the "Tropics of the North," this town of 400 is set among a lush forest of poplar and birch on the banks of the Liard River. The southern location, warm climate, and rich soil mean that residents are able to grow a variety of vegetables. Log homes and green gardens make the six-km detour from the Liard Hwy. worthwhile.

The North West Company established a post in 1807 where the Petitot River drains into the Liard, but abandoned it after many of the residents were massacred by natives. In 1821, after the company merged with the Hudson's Bay Company, the post reopened, but trade was continually disrupted by warring native tribes. Until the 1960s most of the Dene inhabitants spent winter away from Fort Liard, and it wasn't until the highway opened to Fort Nelson that modern development began. Traditional lifestyles are still important to residents, nearly all of whom spend time trapping, hunting, fishing, and making clothing and crafts.

Birchbark Baskets

The women of Fort Liard are famous for these baskets, made for storing food, collecting berries, carrying supplies, or even boiling water. Birch is abundant in the area and has a remarkably pliable nature, ideal for bending and sewing. The bark contains a natural wax making it not only rot resistant, but waterproof. Baskets are still made in the long, tedious process handed down from generation to generation. They are sewn together with specially prepared roots and decorated with porcupine quills. If you are unable to afford a soapstone carving from Cape Dorset, these baskets are a good second choice for a northern souvenir. They are available from the small gift store on Fort Liard's main street, or in Fort Simpson and Hay River.

Practicalities

The small but well-maintained **Hay Lake Campground** has pit toilets, firewood, and bug-proof kitchen shelters. It's located along the Fort Liard access road; sites are $8 a night. The small motel in town has basic rooms, each with a kitchenette, for $90 s, $120 d; tel. (403) 770-4441. Also in town is a small restaurant, gift store, and, back on the highway, a gas station open 7 a.m.-11 p.m.

Deh Cho Air, General Delivery, Fort Liard, NT X0G 0A0, tel. 770-4103, flies from Fort Liard into Nahanni National Park, and to Trout Lake for legendary fishing.

NAHANNI NATIONAL PARK

Through this rugged land of mountains flows one of the most spectacular, wildest, and purest stretches of whitewater in the world—the **South Nahanni River.** Protecting a 300-km stretch of this remote river is 4,766-square-km Nahanni National Park, which boasts some of the world's most breathtaking, undeveloped mountain scenery. The park holds North America's deepest river canyons and a waterfall twice the height of Niagara. It's home to legends of deadly Indian tribes and hapless prospectors whose bodies turned headless. The roadless park is a vast wilderness inhabited only by bears, mountain goats, Dall's sheep, caribou, moose, and wolves, and is accessible only by air or water.

The best way to really experience the park is on a one-to-three-week canoe or raft trip down the river, offered by four outfitters. However you decide to visit the park, whether with an outfitter, on your own carefully prepared expedition, or on a flightseeing trip, it will be an adventure that will remain with you for the rest of your life.

Of Myths And Legends

Slavey Dene, who lived on the lowlands along the Mackenzie and Liard rivers, feared a mysterious group of Indians living high in the Mackenzie Mountains. The mountain people, who became known as the Nahanni (meaning "the people who live far away"), would travel down the South Nahanni River each spring in boats up to 20 meters long. The boats were constructed of moose hide stretched over a spruce frame. Upon arrival at the trading post, the Indians would dismantle the boats, trading furs and the moose hides before returning on foot to the mountains.

Around 1900 a Nahanni Indian arrived at the trading post with a chunk of quartz bearing gold. That got some people's attention. In 1905 Willie and Frank McLeod began prospecting tributaries of the Flat River in search of an elusive mother lode. Three years later their headless bodies were discovered at the mouth of what is now known as Headless Creek; for many years thereafter, the entire valley was called Deadmen Valley. Very quickly, stories became rampant of gold mines, murder, lush tropical valleys, and a tribe of Indians dominated by a white woman. These stories did nothing but lure other prospecting adventurers to the valley—Jorgenson, Shebbach, Field, Faille, Sibbeston, Kraus, and Patterson. Many died mysteriously: Jorgenson's skeleton was found outside his cabin, his precious rifle gone; Shebbach died of starvation at the mouth of Caribou Creek; the body of Phil Powers was discovered in his burned out cabin; Angus Hall just plain disappeared.

The Land

The **Mackenzie Mountains** rise abruptly from the lowlands west of the Mackenzie River. The **South Nahanni River** starts high in these mountains, northwest of the park along the NWT/Yukon border. Flowing in a roughly southeasterly direction for 540 km, it drains into the Liard River, a major tributary of the Mackenzie River. The South Nahanni, cut deeply into the mountains, is known as an "antecedent," that is, it preceded the mountains. It once meandered through a wide-open plain. As uplift in the earth's surface occurred, the river cut down through the rising rock strata and created the deep, meandering canyons present today.

NAHANNI NATIONAL PARK

RAM PLATEAU

DEATH CANYON

DRY CANYON CREEK

DEADMEN VALLEY

PRAIRIE CREEK

HEADLESS CREEK

KRAUS HOTSPRINGS

JACKFISH RIVER

TO NAHANNI BUTTE, LIARD RIVER, AND LINDBERG AND BLACKSTONE LANDINGS

TLOGOTSHO PLATEAU

SHEAF CREEK

MEILLEUR RIVER

THE GATE

FUNERAL RANGE

WRIGLEY CREEK

MARY RIVER

CATHEDRAL CREEK

CLEARWATER CREEK

FIGURE 8 RAPIDS

SUNBLOOD MOUNTAIN

VIRGINIA FALLS

MARENGO CREEK

RIVER

FLAT RIVER

NORTHWEST TERRITORIES

YUKON

FLOOD CREEK

SOUTH NAHANNI

CARIBOU RIVER

MACKENZIE MOUNTAINS

RABBITKETTLE LAKE

RABBITKETTLE HOTSPRINGS

RABBITKETTLE RIVER

© MOON PUBLICATIONS, INC.

15 mi

15 km

Tufa Mounds

One of the most remarkable geological formations in the park occurs at **Rabbitkettle Hotsprings,** a seven-km hike from Rabbitkettle Lake. Two flat-topped mounds, the larger 27 meters high and 60 meters wide, are formed completely of tufa. Tufa, a rocklike substance, is formed when dissolved minerals, in this case mainly calcium carbonate, rise to the earth's surface as a thermal spring, radiating outward and forming a series of terraces known as rimstone dams. These tufa mounds are about 10,000 years old and are the largest in Canada. The delicate surface, sculptured into intricate patterns, is easily damaged, therefore hikers heading here must be accompanied by a warden, who is stationed at Rabbitkettle Lake.

Virginia Falls

From their highest point, these falls on the South Nahanni River drop 92 meters. Water from the South Nahanni River cascading over the escarpment is separated on one side by a great pinnacle of rock. The smaller side of the falls is 55 meters. A 1.3-km portage on the south side of the river follows the path previously taken by the river. The falls have migrated upstream through gradual erosion, creating Fourth Canyon.

Fourth, Third, Second, And First Canyons

These four canyons, immediately downstream of Virginia Falls, form one of the most extensive canyon systems north of the 60th Parallel. The canyon walls are up to 1,200 meters high and 19 km long. At **The Gate,** a sharp turn through the Third Canyon, the river flows through a narrow gap where the canyon walls rise 460 meters. Between Second and First canyons is a wide floodplain where **Prairie Creek** drains into the South Nahanni River. From this area, **Tlogotsho Plateau** dominates the southern skyline. **First Canyon** has the highest walls, almost vertical and towering 1,000 meters above the river; not a place for the claustrophobic. Through the canyons are four sets of rapids including **Figure Eight Rapids,** best known for producing waves up to 1.5 meters high.

Flat River

Running the Flat River is for experienced whitewater enthusiasts. It is a 125-km run from the start at **Seaplane Lake,** just outside the park boundary, to the river's confluence with the South Nahanni River between Fourth and Third canyons. Along its course, the Flat River spews through a series of chutes and ledges known as Cascade-of-the-thirteen-steps rapids (class VI) and passes a number of 15-meter limestone hoodoos. It was along the banks of this river that most of the prospecting in the area took place. At the rivermouth is a pile of logs, the remains of a cabin built by Albert Faille. Also at this site is a cabin built by Fred Sibbeston, who wintered here in 1944 with his wife, mother, and five children.

Kraus Hotsprings

These hot springs, just downstream of First Canyon, are named for Gus and Mary Kraus, who lived here on and off between 1940 and 1971. Bubbling up through fine mud, the hot springs remain at a constant temperature of 35° C year-round. Sulphuric acid is formed when hydrogen sulphide in the water comes into contact with oxygen in the air. The acid erodes any tufa that forms, and, more importantly for those planning a relaxing soak, it produces a strong rotten-egg smell. Many exotic plants thrive here, a legacy of the Krauses' garden.

Running The South Nahanni With An Outfitter

For most people, whether experienced canoeists or never-evers, the advantages of a trip down the South Nahanni River with a licensed outfitter far outweigh the disadvantages. Four companies, all based in Fort Simpson, have licenses to operate guided river trips. Each offers trips of varying lengths—three weeks from Moose Ponds, two weeks from Rabbitkettle Lake, or 8-12 days from Virginia Falls. Itineraries are worked out so that no more than four to seven hours per day are spent on the river, leaving plenty of time for hiking, exploring, and viewing wildlife. Craft used are either rafts, 5.5-meter canoes, or longer voyageur-type canoes. The small canoes hold two people and are generally for those with some previous paddling experience. Inflatable rafts are great if you want to lay back and relax as you float down the river under a guide's supervision. Only Nahanni River Adventures offers trips in the voyageur canoes, which are eight meters long and seat seven, including a guide. They are an excellent compromise, offering the stability of a raft, but with the feeling of canoeing, you can paddle as much, or as little, as you like.

Prices between operators vary little and are generally $2000-3500. Some offer a small discount for those with their own tent, others charge more for those without. Check whether the price includes GST (seven percent). Most importantly, talk to each outfitter (they all love "their" river, so getting them to talk is no problem). Guided trips operate late June to early September and many dates fill up fast.

Outfitters include: **Nahanni River Adventures,** P.O. Box 4869, Whitehorse, Yukon Y1A 4N6, tel. (403) 668-3180; **Nahanni Wilderness Adventures,** Box 4, Site 6, R.R. 1, Didsbury, Alberta T0M 0W0, tel. (403) 637-3843; **Whitewolf Adventure Expeditions,** 41-1355 Citadel Dr., Port Coquitlam, BC V3C 5X6, tel. (800) 661-6659; **Black Feather,** 1960 Scott St., Ottawa, Ontario K1Z 8L8, tel. (613) 722-9717.

Your Own Whitewater Expedition

Experienced whitewater enthusiasts planning their own trip down the Nahanni have three main components to organize: transportation into the park, transportation down the river, and supplies.

Entering the park: To prevent the cost of a second air charter at the end of your trip it is best to pull out along the Liard River at Blackstone or Lindberg landings, a full day's paddle from the park boundary. **Blackstone Aviation,** P.O. Box 117, Fort Simpson, NT X0E 0N0; tel. (403) 695-2111, is the only charter operator who is based at the pull-out point, meaning that you can start and finish the trip at the same place. Blackstone flies a Cessna 185 on floats, capable of carrying two passengers, a canoe or kayak, and up to 200 kilograms of gear. Charter rates are $560 to Virginia Falls, Rabbitkettle Lake $900, and Moose Ponds $1350. Air mileage from Fort Simpson is longer and therefore more expensive but the town has canoe rentals, restaurants, motels, groceries, and an airport with connections to the outside world. **Simpson Air,** P.O. Box 260, Fort Simpson, NT X0E 0N0; tel. 695-2505, also has a Cessna 185 on floats; charter rates from Fort Simpson are: Virginia Falls $882, Rabbitkettle Lake $1164, and Moose Ponds $1680. Maximum gear load is

100 kilograms plus a canoe or kayak. For larger groups, they fly a Twin Otter that can haul six people, three canoes, and 320 kilograms of gear to the same points for $2279, $3007, and $4340 respectively. Simpson Air is used by all the outfitters and is always flying into the park, so you may be able to organize an inexpensive pick-up at Nahanni Butte or Blackstone Landing. Otherwise a van back to town with **Fort Simpson Taxi,** tel. 695-2777, will run $250. Moose Ponds is closer to Watson Lake (Yukon) than any NWT community, therefore chartering a plane from Watson Lake will cost less. But then you'll have the inconvenience of getting back there after your float trip.

Down the River: The river can easily be divided into four sections. From Moose Ponds to Rabbitkettle Lake takes three to five days and includes a 60 km stretch of rapids. From Rabbitkettle Lake to Virginia Falls is a two-to-three-day float down one of the river's easier stretches. After a short but steep portage around the falls there is a three-to-four-day paddle through spectacular canyon scenery with many sets of rapids to an area known as "The Splits." Here the river flows into a broad floodplain, passing the community of Nahanni Butte and draining into the Liard River. Allow two days to get to Blackstone Landing from The Splits. The entire trip from Moose Ponds can be done in under two weeks, but make sure to allow extra days for hiking, exploring, or just relaxing.

Most people choose canoes for the trip, although kayaks and inflatable rafts are also feasible. Whatever craft you decide to use will need a spray deck, and all gear should be securely waterproofed. **Simpson Air,** in Fort Simpson, has two-person canoes for rent; $125 per week includes paddles and life jackets. **Nahanni River Adventures** and **Nahanni Wilderness Adventures** also rent canoes ($27-30 per day) and rafts ($150 per day). All rentals should be organized well before the summer season begins.

Supplies: Charter operators have very generous load limits, allowing you to take plenty of food. But no amount of food can substitute for good prior planning; a crate of oranges picked up in British Columbia's Okanagan Valley or vegetables from Paradise Gardens, near Hay River, all help to make the trip more enjoyable— and oranges float if they finish overboard. Fort

Simpson has a small grocery store, but don't count on finding your favorite brand of anything, especially at your favorite price. Stock up on plenty of bug repellent, bring lots of film, and if you bring a video camera, don't forget extra batteries—you'll be hundreds of miles from the nearest power source.

Hiking

Renowned for its river running, the park also has some fantastic hiking opportunities. Apart from the portage route around Virginia Falls, the park has no developed trails. **The Cirque of the Unclimbables,** near the Yukon border, is a spectacular arc of sheer-walled rock rising nearly 1,000 meters. It is a mecca for rock climbers from around the world but is in a nearly inaccessible part of the **Logan Mountains.** Most climbers access the region by helicopter from Watson Lake. From the South Nahanni River, a three-day hike up **Britnal Creek** is an alternative. **Rabbitkettle Hotsprings** is a seven-km hike from Rabbitkettle Lake, a staging area where floatplanes drop river runners off. Most guided trips allow time for a hike to these amazing tufa mounds. All hikers heading to the hot springs must be accompanied by a park warden based at the lake.

The eight-km hike to the summit of **Sunblood Mountain** from Virginia Falls is one of the park's most popular hikes. Breathtaking views of the surrounding mountainscape and the river below are afforded from the top. **Marengo Falls,** four km from Virginia Falls, is another popular destination. Farther downstream the **Tlogotsho Plateau** is reached by an 18-km trek up Sheaf Creek; the **Ram Plateau** is accessible along Deadmen Valley; and six km up **Dry Canyon Creek** is a much smaller tundra-like plateau.

Camping

Campsites along the river should always be chosen on alluvial fans or sandbars occurring at the mouth of tributaries. Primitive campsites are located at Rabbitkettle Lake, Virginia Falls, and Kraus Hotsprings.

Virginia Falls is a good base if you don't plan on a trip down the river. **Blackstone Aviation,** tel. (403) 695-2111, can carry three passengers and gear (without canoe) to the falls for $560 each way. **Deh Cho Air** offers the same overnight package for $300 per person round trip, but you'll need six people to get this rate. All campers should register at park headquarters in Fort Simpson.

More Information

A lot has been written about the Nahanni, both the natural and human history. One well-known book is *The Dangerous River* (1990) written by R.M. Patterson. Patterson is one of the river's legendary figures, and spent many years in Nahanni Country with Albert Faille. Another storyteller and writer, Dick Turner, homesteaded for many years beside the Lindbergs on the Liard River. He is best known for his book *Nahanni* (1975), describing his life trapping and hunting in the Mackenzie Mountains. *Nahanni: River of Gold, River of Dreams* is a contemporary look at the river through a series of yarns told by one of the river's most experienced guides, "Nahanni" Neil Hartling of Nahanni River Adventures. *National Geographic* published an article about the river in September 1981.

The outfitters on the river are experts in their own right and can answer many of your questions long before you arrive. For specific information on the park write to Superintendent, Nahanni National Park, Postal Bag 300, Fort Simpson, NT X0E 0N0; tel. (403) 695-3151. **Park Headquarters,** once located in Dick Turner's old cabin at Nahanni Butte, is now in Fort Simpson Visitors Centre. Register for trips, watch a documentary, read a book, or wander around the displays. It's open May 15 Sept. 15, daily 8 a.m.-8 p.m. The same service on a smaller scale is offered at Blackstone Territorial Park. Each of the air charter companies based at Fort Simpson, Lindberg Landing, and Fort Liard can tailor flights to suit your need. By waiting around until the plane is full, or by booking in advance, you have more of a chance of keeping the cost down. **Blackstone Aviation,** tel. 695-2111, offers one-hour flights into the southern end of the park for $300 ($75 per person) or a half-day trip including time on the ground at Virginia Falls for $560 ($140 per person). From Fort Simpson, **Simpson Air** offers half-day trips including time at Virginia Falls for $750 (seats four) or on busy days in a Twin Otter, which seats 14 for $2500. **Deh Cho Air,** tel. 770-4103, in Fort Liard has half-day charters including time at the falls for $900 ($150 per person for six). In each case, inquire about discounts for cash.

MACKENZIE RIVER VALLEY

Between the treeless barrenlands and the jagged peaks of the Mackenzie Mountains flows one of the world's mightiest rivers—the Mackenzie. The river begins at Great Slave Lake and flows in a northwesterly direction 1,800 km northwest to the Arctic Ocean, draining one-fifth of Canada in the process. In places it is three km across. The lowlands of the wide valley flanking the river are covered in a boreal forest of black spruce, tamarack, and paper birch, with an understory of moss and lichens, high bush, cranberry, and blueberry. East of the river is 31,400-square-km **Great Bear Lake,** eighth-largest lake in the world.

For thousands of years the North Slavey Dene lived along the Deh Cho (meaning "big river"), hunting, fishing, and trapping. In 1789 Alexander Mackenzie became the first European to travel the river, which now bears his name. After his reports of rich fur resources reached the outside, the North West Company established fur-trading posts along the river. The Dene, who were originally nomadic, settled at the trading posts, forming small communities. In addition to these native settlements, communities along the river today include old fur-trading posts and the modern oil and government towns of **Norman Wells** and **Inuvik,** respectively. North of Fort Simpson and south of the Arctic Circle are four riverside communities, **Wrigley, Fort Norman, Norman Wells,** and **Fort Good Hope.** The only community on Great Bear Lake is **Deline** (formerly Fort Franklin), a base for fishing trips. Just above the Arctic Circle, east of the Mackenzie River, is **Colville Lake,** famous for its world-class artists. The only road into the region begins at Fort Simpson and extends north to Wrigley. In winter this road continues to Norman Wells along the frozen river and ends at Fort Good Hope. In summer, the only highway is the Mackenzie River, along which tugs and barges carry freight to and from Hay River. Ambitious hikers in the area can attempt the challenging 372-km **Canol Heritage Trail,** which begins across the river from Norman Wells and heads deep into the rugged Mackenzie Mountains. For information on the Mackenzie River and its communities write to Sahtu Tourism Association, P.O. Box 115, Norman Wells, NT X0E 0V0; tel. (403) 587-2054 or (800) 661-0788.

Traveling The Mackenzie River
Paddlers in canoes and kayaks set out along the river every summer with the Arctic Ocean in their sights. The entire trip, from Fort Providence to Tuktoyaktuk, is 1,800 km but can be broken up into shorter sections. Generally the river has no rapids and is more of a paddle than a float, but strong winds and sudden storms can create high waves that are a real danger. Advance planning is required as communities are generally at least 200 km apart. The prime canoeing season on the river is late June-August. This leaves little time for a long trip, but the days are generally sunny with up to 24 hours of daylight. Bugs can be a problem, more so on the land than while paddling; avoiding marshy camping areas will help, as will a bug jacket and repellent with plenty of DEET. The RCMP should be informed of your plans and approximate arrival times. Boats along the river will generally keep an eye out for paddlers and pull alongside for a chat. Communities along the river all have grocery stores but prices are high. Wherever you decide to end the trip (Inuvik is a popular destination) you must organize with an airline to get the canoe back to civilization or be prepared to sell it in the north.

If you're really adventurous, the **Rat River Route** may be to your liking. This entails pulling out of the Mackenzie River north of Arctic Red River, portaging 75 km up the Rat River to MacDougall Pass, paddling the Bell River to the Porcupine River, and then into the Yukon River into Alaska.

Once a year the *Norweta,* a small cruise boat, sails from Yellowknife to Inuvik on a ten-day (one way) journey, staying in Inuvik for a week and then returning to Yellowknife the following week. Cost of the all-inclusive trip is $3795 per person one way for a cabin with two berths or $5195 single occupancy. For more information write to Whitlock Family, NWT Marine Group, 5414 52nd St., Yellowknife, NT X1A 3K1; tel. (403) 873-2489.

Wrigley

In 1994 a road was completed to the town of Wrigley, 225 km northwest of Fort Simpson. It is the first section of an all-weather road planned to extend to Inuvik eventually. A ferry crosses the Mackenzie River at **Camsell Bend,** 84 km out of Fort Simpson, from where the road passes through thick boreal forest to Wrigley.

Most of the community's 160 residents are Slavey Dene who live a semitraditional lifestyle, having settled in the area since the North West Company's Fort Alexander opened at the mouth of Willow Lake River in 1817. Over the next 150 years, the community moved several times. The present community of Wrigley sits at the site of an airstrip built during WW II. Opposite Wrigley is **Roche qui-Trempe-à-L'eau,** meaning "the rock that plunges into the water." It's an isolated hill that has been eroded away by the river on one side, creating a sheer cliff that drops 400 meters into the water below. Peregrine falcons are occasionally seen swooping down on cliff swallows that nest here.

Petanea Co-op Hotel, General Delivery, Wrigley, NT X0E 1E0, tel. (403) 581-3102, has five rooms with shared bath for $110 per person per day, $160 with three meals. Ask here about boat rentals. The hotel also has a small coffee shop and a dining room that opens in the evening. Camping anywhere along the river is accepted.

NORMAN WELLS

Norman Wells (population 600), an oil town on the Mackenzie River, has a fascinating history and is a good staging area for trips into the surrounding mountains, along the many rivers, or to world-class fly-in fishing lodges. The town is best known by adventurers for the **Canol Heritage Trail,** a wilderness trek following a route punched through the Mackenzie and Selwyn mountains to transport oil to Alaska.

Unlike other settlements along the Mackenzie River, Norman Wells did not originate as a trading post but owes its existence to oil. Oil seeps along the riverbank were known to the Dene who named the area "Le Gohlini," which translates to "where the oil is." And Alexander Mackenzie reported oil in the area in 1789 on his historic voyage to the Arctic Ocean. But it wasn't until 1919 that the first well, "Discovery," was

CATHY CARLSON

Look for peregrine falcons at Roche qui-Trempe-à L'eau

drilled, and it was 1932 before it became productive. Increased mining activity in the western Arctic and a change from woodburning riverboats to those using petroleum-based fuel meant that demand for oil quickly grew. Soon more wells were drilled to supply the town's busy refinery.

Canol Project

The large U.S. military force present in Alaska during WW II needed oil to fuel aircraft and ships, in place for expected Japanese attacks. The strategically located Norman Wells oil fields were chosen as a source of crude oil—with little regard for the engineering feat needed to build a pipeline over the Mackenzie Mountains. To this day, it remains one of the largest projects ever undertaken in northern Canada. Over $300 million was spent between 1942 and 1945, employing 30,000 people who laid 2,650 km of four- and six-inch pipeline, 1,600 km of telephone lines, and built a road over some of North America's most isolated and impenetrable mountain ranges. Conditions were terrible; makeshift camps housed thousands of men, temperatures dipped to 40 below, and the isolation took its toll. Through the impossible terrain thousands of tons of equipment was hauled, pump stations were installed, and camps set up. Then, less than a year after completion, the pipeline was very quietly abandoned for less expensive oil sources elsewhere. In 1947 the pipeline was dismantled and sold. Today, the roadbed remains, strewn with structures, trucks, and equipment used in the project's construction.

Norman Wells Today

Despite the ill-fated Canol Project, oil production at Norman Wells oil fields has continued to increase. Today the field is tapped by 160 wells producing 10 million barrels a year. Crude oil is piped to Canada's oil-rich province, Alberta, via the Norman Wells–Zama pipeline. Six manmade islands in the middle of the Mackenzie River, directly offshore from town, allow oil extraction to continue throughout break-up and freeze-up of the river. Norman Wells also serves as a fire-fighting base, transportation hub, and regional government center.

The **Norman Wells Historical Centre,** tel. 587-2415, tells the story of the Canol Project through historical displays, photographs, artifacts recovered from along the road, and an excellent propaganda movie, commissioned to help finance the project. The center is officially open in summer, daily 10 a.m.-10 p.m., but chances are you'll have to go to the Sahtu Tourism Association Office, in the NorthwesTel Building, to organize a tour. That office is located halfway to town from the airport. Next door is an interesting church. Actually, the church is fairly normal but the congregation is unique. Roman Catholics meet on one side, Protestants on the other. The center of town, a 20-minute walk from the airport, is a semicircle of semipermanent buildings around a dusty parking lot. Also in town you'll find a bank, motels, restaurants, Northern, and a post office. Farther down the road is a small refinery and, overlooking the river, a gazebo from where the islands can be seen.

Accommodations And Food

Yamouri Inn, P.O. Box 268, Norman Wells, NT X0E 0V0, tel. (403) 587-2744, is located in the center of town and has a bar and restaurant; $95 s, $115 d. Across the parking lot is **Rayuka**

Inn, P.O. Box 308, tel. 587-2354, which is slightly more expensive. Closer to the airport is **Mackenzie Valley Hotel,** Bag Service 1250, tel. 587-2511, $100 s, $115 d. The town has no developed campgrounds; pitching your tent beside the Mackenzie River is an accepted practice (but don't leave valuables in it). The cheapest place to eat is the coffee shop or dimly lit cocktail lounge in the Yamouri Inn.

Transportation

Norman Wells has an impressive three-story airport—complete with an observation deck and revolving baggage claim—not bad for a town of 600 people. It is a one-km walk into town. **Canadian North,** tel. (403) 587-2361 or (800) 665-1177, has daily flights from Yellowknife to Norman Wells, continuing north to Inuvik. One way to Norman Wells is $295, $325 for a 14 day APEX round trip. **North-Wright Air,** tel. 587-2333 or (800) 661-0702, flies from Norman Wells to all Mackenzie River communities, including Inuvik.

Information

The **Sahtu Tourism Association** is based in the NorthwesTel Building along the road to the airport. The office provides information on the town, outlying communities, and the Canol Heritage Trail. It's open year-round, Mon.-Fri. 9 a.m.-5 p.m.; tel. (403) 587-2054.

Canol Heritage Trail

Considered by many to be one of the world's great wilderness hikes, the Canol is by no means typical. It follows the Canol Road (see "Canol Project," above) from Mile Zero (**Canol Camp**) on the west bank of the Mackenzie River across from Norman Wells, to Mile 230 on the Yukon border—a distance of 372 km (distances on the trail are in miles, a legacy of imperial measurement). To hike the entire trail takes three to four weeks. Following the road causes little problem, but the logistics of getting to the beginning of the trail, arranging food drops, crossing rivers, and returning to Norman Wells require much planning. Every year a few hikers attempt the entire length of the trail, while many others opt for a shorter section. The trail has been done on horseback, motorcycle, mountain bike, and all-terrain vehicle, but walking is the most popular and reliable.

The most popular jumping-off point is Norman Wells, from where you can charter a plane or helicopter and be dropped as far along the trail as desired. From the Yukon side you can drive from Ross River to Mile 208. Many hikers organize food drops with charter operators in Norman Wells to help ease the load.

All bridges along the route have been washed out, making many river crossings necessary. The most difficult of these is the **Twitya River** at Mile 131. This fast-flowing, cold (3-4° C) river is approximately 50 meters wide and up to five meters deep. Inner tubes purchased in Norman Wells (ask at ESSO Resources) are a popular way of floating gear across, but check that they inflate before hitting the trail. General consensus is that the crossing is easier upstream of the old bridge. With two or more persons a length of rope can be strung across the river for ferrying packs across.

Along the length of the trail are many Quonset huts used during construction of the road. Many are uninhabitable but others have bunk beds and cookstoves.

The best source of information and current trail conditions is the Sahtu Tourism Association, P.O. Box 115, Norman Wells, NT X0E 0V0; tel. (403) 587-2054.

OTHER COMMUNITIES

Fort Norman

The Slavey Dene name for this small community (population 300) is Tullt'a, meaning "where the two rivers meet." Its strategic location where the **Great Bear River** joins the Mackenzie River has made it a transportation hub since the days of Sir John Franklin. Upstream five km are the **Smoking Hills,** where an exposed seam of coal burns permanently. The first trading post was built here in 1810. An Anglican church, built of squared logs and dating to the 1860s, sits on the riverbank, beside the Hudson's Bay Company post. Many houses have colorful tepees in their yards, which are used for drying and smoking fish. The tepees provide a stark contrast to the modern school and the Norman Wells–Zama pipeline, which passes through the outskirts of the community. The Great Bear River is navigable for its 128 km distance into Great Bear Lake with the exception of one set of rapids

which can easily be portaged. The river's clear, aqua-colored waters provide excellent fishing for arctic grayling. Archie Lennie of **Northland Adventure Tours,** General Delivery, Fort Norman, NT X0E 0K0; tel. 588-3341, runs various tours on the river in a jet boat—either fishing, sightseeing, or up to Fort Franklin. **Fort Norman Lodge** (General Delivery, tel. 588-4311) has rooms with single and double beds, all with shared bathroom and kitchen. Meals can also be arranged. Rates are $99 s or d per night. **North-Wright Air,** tel. 587-2333, flies daily to Fort Norman from Norman Wells; $83.46 one way.

Deline

Formerly known as Fort Franklin, this community of 550 is located on Keith Arm of **Great Bear Lake,** at the outlet where the Great Bear River begins flowing west to the Mackenzie River. A North West Company trading post opened here in 1810 but closed soon after. It was reopened by the Hudson's Bay Company in 1825 as a winter home and supply depot for Sir John Franklin, who led several expeditions to the Arctic in search of the Northwest Passage. Then it was abandoned again. With the discovery of pitchblende ore at Port Radium in the 1920s, traffic on the lake and river increased and a small community grew. Today the Slavey Dene of Deline live a traditional lifestyle, trapping, fishing, and making crafts, including moccasins for which they are well known. The tepee-shaped church is worth a visit, and the hike along the shore of Great Bear Lake offers rewarding vistas and passes a number of historic sites (ask at the hotel). **Great Bear Lake Hotel and Restaurant,** General Delivery, Deline, NT X0E 0G0, tel. (403) 589-3705, is a modern but basic accommodation in the middle of town. Rooms have private bathrooms and kitchenettes; $120 per person. Also here are a coffee shop and restaurant. Groceries and crafts are available at **Northern. North-Wright Air,** tel. 587-2333, flies daily from Norman Wells to Deline; $125.19 one way.

Where The Big One Won't Get Away

Great Bear Lake is one of the world's best freshwater fishing lakes, and has the records to prove it. This lake holds world records for *all* line classes of lake trout; the overall world record, caught in 1991, weighed in at a whopping 66.5 pounds. It also holds world records for most classes of arctic grayling, including the overall record. Around the lake are a number of small fishing lodges offering all-inclusive packages. You can get a scheduled flight to Deline—the only community along the lake—then a charter flight out to the lodges. For details contact the Sahtu Tourism Association or call (800) 661-0788.

Fort Good Hope

Overlooking the Mackenzie River and flanked by boreal forest, this Slavey Dene community of 550 is located on the east bank of the Mackenzie River, just south of the Arctic Circle and approximately 193 km downstream of Norman Wells. A trading post established here in 1805 by the North West Company attracted not only the Slavey Dene but Inuit, who lived in the Mackenzie Delta. During the 1860s, Father Emile Petitot, a well-known northern missionary, constructed **Our Lady of Good Hope Church,** which has been declared a National Historic Site. The church's interior is decorated in ornate panels and friezes painted by Petitot, depicting aspects of his travels and life in the north.

One of the highlights of a trip to Fort Good Hope is visiting **The Ramparts,** where 200-meter-high cliffs force the Mackenzie River through a 500-meter-wide canyon. Although the cliffs continue for many kilometers, the most spectacular section is upstream of town and can be reached on foot or by boat. Arrange boat rentals and tours through **Ramparts Hotel,** General Delivery, Fort Good Hope, NT X0E 0H0; tel. (403) 598-2500. This hotel overlooks the

river and has a restaurant with a simple menu, at northern prices; expect to pay $15-25 for a main meal. Rooms are $110 per person. Ask here about river tours. **North-Wright Air,** tel. 587-2333, flies daily from Norman Wells to Fort Good Hope, $109.14 one way.

Colville Lake

This community of 50 North Slavey Dene, located just north of the Arctic Circle on the southeast shore of Colville Lake, was established in 1962 when a Roman Catholic mission was built. It is the territories' only community built entirely from logs. The largest building is the church, which supports a bell weighing 454 kilograms. The mission was built by Father Bern Will Brown, who has now left the church and is one of the north's most respected artists. His paintings, which depict the lifestyle of northerners, are in demand across North America. Brown is also the host at **Colville Lake Lodge,** which combines excellent fishing for lake trout, arctic grayling, northern pike, whitefish, and inconnu, with a small museum highlighting life in the north. The lodge also has an art gallery, boat and canoe rentals, and common kitchen facilities. It is located in the town of Colville Lake. For more information write to Bern Will Brown, Colville Lake via Norman Wells, NT X0E 0V0. By phone, contact the mobile operator in Whitehorse (Yukon) and ask to be connected to 2M4486 on the Chick Lake "Y.R." Channel. **North-Wright Air,** tel. 587-2333, flies daily to Colville Lake from Norman Wells, $155.05 one way.

BOB RACE

WESTERN ARCTIC

The far northwestern corner of the territories, where the mighty Mackenzie River drains into the Arctic Ocean, is linked to the outside world by the Dempster Hwy., the continent's northernmost public road. The region, entirely above the Arctic Circle, encompasses the Mackenzie River Valley and the vast barrens that flank the Arctic Ocean. To the north is Banks Island.

The **Mackenzie Delta**, a 90-km-long and 60-km-wide twisted maze of channels, is one of the world's greatest waterfowl nesting grounds and is home to muskrats, beavers, and marten, the mainstay of an early fur-trading economy. In the vicinity of the delta live red foxes, lynx, wolves, black bears, and moose. Large numbers of both woodland and barrenground caribou migrate through the region in early spring and fall; the Porcupine herd, named for the Porcupine River, migrates as far as Alaska. Arctic foxes inhabit the Arctic coast, while the king of the land, the grizzly bear, lives on the tundra. **Banks Island** has the world's largest population of musk oxen, protected by a new national park. Beluga whales spend summer in the shallow waters around the delta and can be viewed from the air or in a boat. Hundreds of thousands of birds migrate to the delta each spring; among them swans, cranes, hawks, bald eagles, and peregrine falcons.

At the end of the Dempster Hwy. is the region's largest community, **Inuvik**, a planned government town. **Aklavik**, west of Inuvik on a low area of land in the middle of the delta, was officially moved to Inuvik but its residents stayed. **Tuktoyaktuk** is a "must see" for those who want to dip their toes in the Arctic Ocean. To the east is **Paulatuk**, a traditional Inuvialuit community known for its excellent arctic char fishing, as well as its proximity to the home range of the Bluenose caribou herd. The community of **Sachs Harbour**, on Banks Island, is a good base for exploring **Aulavik National Park.**

For more information write to Western Arctic Tourism, P.O. Box 2600, Inuvik, NT X0E 0T0; tel. (403) 979-4321 or (800) 661-0788.

Driving The Dempster Highway

This 741-km highway, which begins east of Dawson City in the Yukon, is the only road leading into the western Arctic. It ends at Inuvik, but from November to late March you can drive on a winter road across the frozen Mackenzie Delta all the way to Tuktoyaktuk on the Arctic Ocean.

Finished in 1978 after nearly 20 years of work, the highway stretches through some of North America's most inhospitable terrain. It was named after RCMP Inspector W.J.D. Dempster, who was sent to look for the "lost patrol" —a team of Mounties who disappeared near Fort McPherson during the winter of 1910-11. (He found them—dead.) Driving the Dempster Hwy. should not be taken lightly. Services are few and far between, and the gravel road has a reputation for shredding tires. Always carry spare gas and tires, have plenty of water, and be prepared to drive slowly. Many large mammals are seen from the highway but the most impressive sight is the **Porcupine caribou herd,** which migrates through the area each spring and fall.

The **Western Arctic Visitors Centre** in Dawson City (in the B.Y.N. building on Front St.) is a good place to head before commencing the long drive north. It's open June-Sept., daily 9 a.m.-9 p.m.

The Dempster Hwy. crosses the **Arctic Circle** at Km 403, then climbs into the Richardson Mountains. The Continental Divide, at Km 471, marks the Yukon/NWT border. West of the divide, water flows to the Pacific Ocean; eastside waters end up in the Arctic Ocean. The highway then descends to the **Peel River,** crossed by ferry from mid-June to October, and by an ice bridge most of the rest of the year. No crossings are possible during freeze-up and break-up.

Fort McPherson

After crossing the Peel River the highway soon comes to Fort McPherson, a Gwich'in Dene community on the river's east bank. The tribe lives at the eastern edge of their territory and has strong links to the Yukon and Alaska. A Hudson's Bay Company post was established here in 1840, and in 1852 a nearby Dene village was moved to Fort McPherson, away from the annual flooding that occurred at lower elevations. An RCMP post here became an important center for annual patrols throughout the western Arctic. It was from here, on 21 December 1910, that a patrol led by Inspector Fitzgerald left for Dawson City. The four members perished on the return trip, just one day short of Fort McPherson. An account of their journey is found in Dick North's *Lost Patrol*. The patrol is buried on the banks of the Peel River and a monument stands in their memory. Well worth a visit is **Fort McPherson Tent and Canvas,** a thriving local business producing high-quality backpacks, tote bags, and tents; open Mon.-Fri. 9:30 a.m.-5 p.m.

Tetlit Service Co-op, tel. (403) 952-2417, has the only rooms in town; $100 s, $125 d. **Nutuiluie Territorial Campground** is located 10 km south of town, with sites for $10. A **visitor center** is also located here.

Arctic Red River

One hour's drive northeast of Fort McPherson is another ferry crossing, this time over the Mackenzie River (mid-June to October, 9 a.m.-midnight). Here, at the confluence of the Mackenzie and Arctic Red rivers, a small mission was established in 1868, followed soon after by a Hudson's Bay Company post. For hundreds of years it has been a popular fishing spot for Dene and, today, traditional fishing camps still operate on the river; look for fish being prepared and dried by the ferry landings. The most recognizable landmark in town is a red-roofed mission church built in 1931. It stands on a small rise overlooking the river. The town has few services and may or may not have gas, so top up in Fort McPherson for the 180 km run to Inuvik. To visit the community, which is off the main ferry route, you must tell the ferry operators, who will happily make the detour for you.

caribou

South of Arctic Red River is the **Peel River Preserve.** High in the Mackenzie Mountains, this habitat is home to Dall's sheep, moose, lynx, woodland caribou, and grizzly bears. It is accessible only by traveling up either the Arctic Red or Peel rivers.

INUVIK

You must see Inuvik with your own eyes to believe it, and then you may still doubt what you see: brightly painted houses on stilts, a monstrous church shaped like an igloo, metal tunnels snaking through town, and a main street where businesses have names such as Eskimo Inn, 60 Below Construction, and Polar TV. It's obviously a planned community, transformed from some architect's drafting board into full-blown reality high above the Arctic Circle. All aspects have been scientifically planned, right down to the foundations—all structures sit on piles of rock, ensuring stability in the permafrost and preventing heat from turning the ground into sludge.

walrus

History

In 1954 the Canadian government decided to build an administrative center for the western Arctic. The traditional center was Aklavik, located in the middle of the Mackenzie Delta. But since Aklavik had continual problems with erosion and flooding, and offered little room for expansion, a new site was decided upon. The location chosen was a large, level area alongside the East Channel of the Mackenzie River, 200 km north of the Arctic Circle and just below the treeline. Inuvik, meaning "place of the people" in Invialuktun, was the first planned Canadian town above the Arctic Circle. By the summer of 1961, most of the major construction had been completed.

Today Inuvik serves not only as a government headquarters, but also as a transportation hub and oil-and-gas exploration base. The Canadian Armed Forces Station, which closed in 1986, has been converted to the Aurora Cam-

INUVIK

MARINE BYPASS RD.

NOT TO SCALE

NAVY RD.

WOLVERINE RD.

CENTENNIAL ST.

INUIT RD.

BONNET PLUME RD.

KUGMALLIT RD.

KINGMINGYA RD.

INUIT RD.

MUNICIPAL AIRSTRIP

INGAMO HALL ■

MACKENZIE RD.

MARINE BYPASS RD.

FRANKLIN RD.

HAPPY VALLEY CAMPGROUND

ROBERSTON'S B & B ●

LOUCHEUX RD.

BREYNAT ST.

TWIN LAKES

HAPPY VALLEY

LIBRARY

TO GO'S ■

INUVIK SKI CLUB ●

NORTHERN IMAGES ●

TRAPPER PUB ●

ESKIMO INN ●

NORTHERN ●

FRANKLIN RD.

LAUNDROMAT ●

IGLOO CHURCH ■

ARCTIC TOUR CO. ● & BOREAL BOOKS

WESTERN ARCTIC NATURE TOUHS ■

DISTRIBUTOR ST.

MACKENZIE HOTEL ●

VISITORS CENTRE ■

RESEARCH CENTRE ■

BOMPAS RD.

WATER ST.

POST OFFICE ■

TO GOLF COURSE, CHUK PARK, AIRPORT, AND DEMPSTER HWY.

DOCK ●

BOOT LAKE RD.

MACKENZIE RD.

FINTO MOTOR INN ●

SPRUCE HILL DR.

HOSPITAL ■

DUCK LAKE

DUCK LAKE ST.

MACKENZIE RIVER (EAST CHANNEL)

BOOT LAKE

© MOON PUBLICATIONS, INC.

pus of Arctic College. The town's population of 3,000 consists of an equal mix of Dene/Métis, Inuit, and nonnative people. The nonnative population rises and falls with the fortunes of the oil and gas industries. Current proposals to tap the vast reserves of natural gas under the Mackenzie Delta would push the town's economy out of the doldrums and bring increased wealth to the region.

Things To See And Do

It is very easy to spend a day walking around town, checking out the unique considerations involved in living at a latitude of 68° N. *Utilidors,* for example, snake around town, linking businesses, residential houses, and passing right through the middle of the schoolyard. These conduits contain water, heat, and sewerage pipelines, and are raised above the ground to prevent problems associated with permafrost. Inuvik's most famous landmark is **Our Lady of Victory Church,** commonly known as the **igloo church** for its distinctive shape. The church, located on Mackenzie Rd. near the visitors center, is not always open; ask at the rectory for permission to enter. The interior is decorated with a series of paintings by Inuvialuit artist Mona Thrasher, depicting various religious scenes. Opposite is the **Inuvik Research Centre,** one of three support facilities for scientific projects throughout the Arctic. It's open year-round, Mon.-Fri. 9 a.m.-5 p.m. Each Wednesday at 3 p.m., informal talks are given about current projects. West along Mackenzie Rd. is **Ingamo**

Hall, a three-story structure built with over 1,000 logs. This far north, trees are not large enough for construction, so the logs, cut from white spruce, were transported by barge down the Mackenzie River. The best views of the delta are, naturally, from the air, but the next best thing is to climb the 20-meter observation tower in **Chuk Park,** six km south of downtown.

Tours

It seems that everyone who visits Inuvik takes at least one tour, whether it be around town, on the delta, or to an outlying community. **Arctic Tour Co.,** 181 Mackenzie Rd., tel. (403) 979-4100 or (800) 661-0721, offers a town tour that lasts about two hours, taking in all the sights and making a quick trip onto the tundra; $20 per person.

Western Arctic Nature Tours, beside the igloo church on Mackenzie Rd., tel. 979-3300, offers an extensive variety of flightseeing tours using the municipal airstrip at the west end of Mackenzie Rd., while **Arctic Tour Co.** air tours leave from Inuvik Airport; both companies provide ground transportation to their respective bases. Tours to Tuktoyaktuk and Aklavik start at $100. Western Arctic Nature Tours also offers trips to remote **Herschel Island** located in the Beaufort Sea. The island was a major whaling station during the early 1900s but today only ruins remain. This trip is especially good for birdwatchers—over 70 avian species have been recorded on the island. The flight to the island passes **Iuvavik National Park** in the northern

igloo church

Yukon, providing opportunities to see musk oxen, caribou, and grizzly bears. A two-hour stay on the island costs $250 per person, including the 90-minute (each way) flight. Overnight stays begin at $375 per person.

Boat tours are another good way to experience the vastness of the delta. Both the air-tour companies mentioned above act as agents for local boat-trip outfitters; expect to pay $30-35 for a two-hour cruise to a bush camp where tea and bannock will be served. Evening tours on the river including a traditional northern meal cost $50-65. Also offered are fishing trips (from $120), naturalist tours (from $125), or a boat trip to Aklavik or Tuktoyaktuk returning by plane (from $135).

Recreation
The town has no set hiking trails, but in summer you can hike along the tracks used by cross-country skiers in winter. Two trails—four and six km—begin from the ski club on Loucheux Rd., opposite the elementary school. They may be muddy. The treeline passes invitingly close to town to the east. Look for trails leading in that direction out by Marine Bypass Rd. and Long Lake.

On the east side of the road, just before the town turnoff, is the world's northernmost 18-hole golf course (see "Holman" in the "Arctic Coast" section for *the* world's northernmost course). **Lunar Links** has no swank clubhouse, no driving range, no putting green (in fact not much green at all), and has been carved out of an old excavation site. You'll need a scorecard from the visitors center to find your way around.

Drinking And Dancing
Inuvik's most famous nightspot is **The Zoo,** in the Mackenzie Hotel, where a colorful mixture of oil field workers, German backpackers, drunken Aussies, fur-coated southerners, pin-striped businessmen, and locals who've been kicked out of every other place in town converge to listen to the latest band that lost its way somewhere near Whitehorse and wound up in Inuvik. There's no cover charge and things usually end around 2 a.m. Next door is the more mellow **Brass Rail Lounge,** where the bar is covered in roofing materials—a legacy of the owner's profession before becoming involved in the hotel business. If the bar's quiet, the owner will join you in sam-

pling his specially imported German liqueur, kept behind the bar for when outsiders drop by. **Sly Fox** in the Eskimo Inn is a locals' hangout, as is **Trapper Pub** across the road, where local musicians jam on Saturday afternoons at 4 p.m., hoping one day to play at The Zoo.

Festivals And Events
After a month of darkness, the first day that the sun rises above the horizon is celebrated with the **Sunlight Festival** (5-6 January). Although the sun actually rises at about 1:30 p.m. on the 6th there's a parade the day before, as well as ice-skating and an exciting fireworks display at Twin Lakes. This event was picked up by international media networks a few years back, bringing unexpected attention to the town. **Summer Solstice** in June also provides a cause for celebration, although as the sun doesn't set for a month, the actual date of the festival is of little importance. Celebrations on the weekend closest to the solstice include traditional music and dancing. **The Great Northern Arts Festival,** the third weekend of July, features demonstrations, displays, and sales of northern art. And on the second weekend of October, street dances, parades, northern games, and traditional foods highlight **Delta Daze.**

Accommodations
Each of Inuvik's three motels has a coffee shop, restaurant, and basic rooms with private baths starting at $115 s, $125 d. **Mackenzie Hotel,** 185 Mackenzie Rd., P.O. Box 1618, Inuvik, NT X0E 0T0, tel. (403) 979-2861, is the nicest and is in town. Also in town is **Eskimo Inn,** 133 Mackenzie Rd., P.O. Box 1740, tel. 979-2801. On the way to the airport is **Finto Motor Inn,** 288 Mackenzie Rd., P.O. Box 1925, tel. 979-2647, which has a good view of the delta.

A few families run bed and breakfasts, which are usually only slightly cheaper than the motels but provide a good way to meet the locals. **Robertson's B&B,** 41 Mackenzie Rd., P.O. Box 2356, tel. 979-3111, is close to downtown and its large outdoor deck offers a great view of the delta; $80 s, $90 d. Others are **Gardiner Guesthouse,** 22 Kingmingya Rd., P.O. Box 1937, tel. 979-4408, and **Outlook B&B,** 78 Boot Lake Rd., P.O. Box 2318, tel. 979-3789.

Happy Valley Campground is located on a bluff overlooking the delta. It has a number of private, unserviced sites and a gravel parking area for RVs and trailers who need power. Facilities include flush toilets, showers, and firewood; sites are $12 a night. Outside of town toward the airport is **Chuk Park;** it's quiet but has limited facilities.

Food

If you don't mind your wallet taking a battering, the thing to do this far north is sample the local fare. The least expensive way to do this is at **To Go's,** 69 Mackenzie Rd., tel. (403) 979-3030, which has a few tables and a take-out menu. Caribou burgers ($4.50) are the same price as regular hamburgers, while musk ox burgers ($5.50) are cheaper than mushroom burgers. Pizza starts at $10; extras such as musk ox are $2, and the Northern Pizza—with the works—is $17. You can also buy caribou steaks ($7.25 per pound) and musk ox steaks ($8.25 per pound) for cooking on a campfire. It's open daily till 3 a.m. The coffee shop in the **Mackenzie Hotel** is the most popular breakfast hangout, but it can get smoky. The **Green Briar Dining Room,** tel. 979-3536, also in the Mackenzie Hotel, serves a good selection of northern cuisine (starting at $13.95 for a caribou burger); open from 5 p.m. The **Peppermill Restaurant,** tel. 979-2999, in the Finto Motor Inn, offers much of the same; try caribou steaks smothered in blueberry sauce (made from locally picked blueberries), $16.50. The town's only supermarket is located at 160 Mackenzie Road. Prices aren't as high as you might expect.

Getting There

Inuvik Airport is small but always busy, thanks to its status as the hub of air transport in the western Arctic. A cab to the airport, 12 km south of town, is $23 for one or two, $27 for three, and $32 for four. **Canadian North,** tel. (403) 979-2952 or (800) 665-1177, flies into Inuvik at least once daily from Yellowknife; $401 one way, $441 for a 14-day APEX round trip. Sit on the left side of the plane for views of the Mackenzie Mountains. From Edmonton, the least expensive high-season fare is $681 round trip. **NWT Air,** tel. 979-2341 or (800) 661-0789, flies the same routes. **North-Wright Air,** tel. 587-2333, flies from Norman Wells to Inuvik. **Alkan Air,** tel. 668-6616, based in Whitehorse (Yukon), flies to Inuvik via Old Crow. **Aklak Air,** tel. 979-

3777 or (800) 661-0713, flies from Inuvik to all western Arctic communities. **Arctic Wings,** tel. 979-2220, has scheduled flights to Aklavik and Tuktoyaktuk from the municipal airstrip, located within walking distance of town. All other companies use Inuvik Airport.

Arctic Tour Co., tel. 979-4100 or (800) 661-0721, operates scheduled bus service to Inuvik from where Greyhound leaves off in Dawson City (Yukon). The bus departs Gold City Tours in Dawson City on Monday and Friday at 8 a.m.; $198 one way, $350 round trip. To bus it one way and return by air is $369. Reservations are essential.

Touch the Arctic Adventure Tours, tel. (800) 661-0894, offers a variety of air tours to Inuvik starting at $1063 for three days out of Edmonton.

Getting Around

For a taxi call (403) 979-2525 or 979-2121. The cabs don't have meters; fares are set: $4.50 anywhere around town, $23-32 to the airport, and $260 to Tuktoyaktuk on the winter road. Car rentals are available from **Avis,** tel. 979-4571. **Northern Recreation,** 60 Franklin Rd. behind the laundromat, tel. 979-2098, rents mountain bikes for $20 per day and canoes with paddles and life jackets for $25 per day.

Services

The **post office** is at 187 Mackenzie Rd., opposite the visitors center. **Sweet Scent Laundry** is located on the corner of Mackenzie Rd. and Tununuk Place; you need tokens from the coffee shop in front. **Northern Images,** upstairs at 115 Mackenzie Rd., has a fantastic collection of paintings and sculptures from throughout the territories. The **hospital** is located at the east end of town opposite the Finto Inn, tel. (403) 979-2955. For the **RCMP** call 979-2935. The local newspaper is the *Inuvik Drum,* published each Thursday (50 cents).

Information

The **library,** tel. 979-2749, located in the center of town, has a fairly extensive collection of northern books and literature; open Monday and Friday 2-5 p.m. and Tues.-Thurs. 10 a.m.-9 p.m. **Boreal Books,** 181 Mackenzie Rd., tel. 979-3748, has a large selection of northern material, both new and used, as well as relevant topographical maps and marine charts.

The **visitor center** is located at the top end of town; open in summer, daily 9 a.m.-8 p.m. For road and ferry information call 979-2678 or (800) 661-0752. For the local weather forecast call 979-4183.

THE MAD TRAPPER OF RAT RIVER

For seven long weeks, ravaged by brutal winter temperatures, hunger, and exhaustion, a man whose identity remains a mystery to this day led Mounties on an astonishing chase through the Arctic. No one quite knows what instigated the murderous events of the winter of 1932, nor from where the mad, mysterious trapper came. Natives knew him as "the man who steals gold from men's teeth"; they were afraid of him and rumors surfaced that he was a notorious Chicago gangster.

In 1931 a man going by the name Albert Johnson arrived in Fort McPherson. He first raised a few eyebrows by purchasing unusually large amounts of ammunition and supplies with a fistful of notes. Then he left for the Rat River region to build a small cabin that doubled as an impregnable fortress—evidence that from the start he anticipated trouble. Answering complaints of a strange white man interfering with traplines, Constable King went to question Johnson. Instead of answers, King was met by a bullet.

A seven-man posse, carrying 20 pounds of dynamite, came from Aklavik to bring the gunman in. For 15 hours Johnson withstood the mounted siege, finally forcing the posse to retreat. Johnson fled, heading west. In temperatures that dipped below -40° C, and with meager supplies, four Mounties took up the chase. Four times Johnson repelled them with gunfire, killing a Mountie in the process. It became obvious to the Mounties that, against incredible physical hardships, Johnson was attempting to cross the mountains to Alaska. His cunning kept him alive for seven weeks, long enough for "Wop" May, a famed bush pilot, to be summoned. Surrounded by 17 men and with Wop May circling overhead in a plane loaded with bombs, Johnson never had a chance. His death ended the north's most notorious manhunt but was the beginning of the mystery—just who was the Mad Trapper of Rat River?

AKLAVIK

Theoretically, this community in the middle of the Mackenzie Delta was abandoned over 20 years ago. But don't tell that to the 700 Dene and Inuit who call Aklavik home. The Hudson's Bay Company post, established here in 1918, became the trading and transportation center of the muskrat-rich Mackenzie Delta. River erosion and surface instability seriously threatened the physical existence of the town so the federal government decided to relocate it to the East Channel, 58 km west. The planned town of Inuvik serves the purpose of the government well. But for many delta old-timers, living in a town that sprang from the muskeg isn't their cup of tea. In fact, since Inuvik was established, this ramshackle community, cut off from the outside world, has reported steady population increases.

Wooden sidewalks, a legacy of Aklavik's one-time importance, link the Hudson's Bay Company post and a mission church (now a small museum) to newer structures, built before the big move east was announced. Many large houses still stand, testimony to the fortunes made by prosperous traders in days gone by. Trails lead in all directions from town, inviting the curious to explore this small delta island. The most popular attraction is the grave of Albert Johnson, (see the Special Topic "The Mad Trapper of Rat River"), who sparked the north's most famous manhunt.

Tours And Transportation

Most people arrive in Aklavik as part of a tour from Inuvik, either through **Western Arctic Nature Tours**, tel. (403) 979-3300, or **Arctic Tours Co.**, tel. 979-4100. On clear days, the 20-minute flight is awe inspiring. Both companies offer flights to Aklavik with a one-hour town tour ($85-100), but a better way to experience the delta is by boat. To boat one way then fly the other is $115-135. Tours that combine Aklavik and Tuktoyaktuk begin at $169.

If you would like to spend more time in town, scheduled flights leave daily from the airport (Aklak Air, tel. 979-3777) and the municipal airstrip (Arctic Wings, tel. 979-2220) in Inuvik. Usually the tour operators can arrange cheaper flights and advise on accommodation in the small hotel in Aklavik. Between December and

March a winter road is constructed between Inuvik and Aklavik.

TUKTOYAKTUK

Most travelers, not satisfied with driving to the end of the road, hop aboard a small plane in Inuvik for the flight along the Mackenzie Delta to Tuktoyaktuk, a small community perched precariously on an exposed gravel strip on the Beaufort Sea. Although it would be a harsh and unforgiving place to live, a visit to "Tuk," as it is sensibly known, is a delightful eye-opener. The community is spread out around **Tuktoyaktuk Harbour** and has spilled over to the gravel beach, where meter-high waves whipped up by cold Arctic winds roll in off the Beaufort Sea and thunder up against the shore. The most dominant features of the landscape—apart from the modern military D.E.W. (Distant Early Warning) satellite dishes—are pingos, massive mounds of ice forced upward by the action of permafrost. The mounds look like mini-volcanoes protruding from the otherwise flat environs. The ice is camouflaged by a natural covering of tundra growth, making them all the more mysterious. Some 1,400 pingos dot the coastal plain around Tuk, one of the world's densest concentrations of these geological wonders peculiar to the north. **Ibyuk,** visible from town, is the world's largest pingo. It's 30 meters tall and has a circumference of 1.5 km.

History

This area was traditionally the home of Karngmalit, or Mackenzie Inuit, who lived along the coast in small family camps hunting whales. Earlier this century, an epidemic of influenza wiped out over half of their people. As Herschel Island lost importance as a base for whaling in the Beaufort Sea, the Hudson's Bay Company opened a post at the safe harbor of Tuk in 1937. Reindeer herding was attempted in the late 1930s, with animals brought over from Scandinavia. Today a large herd of these mammals— the same species as the indigenous caribou but a little smaller—live in the area. A D.E.W. Line station was constructed in 1955. Although the residents har-

vest seals and whales, most wage earners are land-based, involved in government, transportation, and tourism. The town is also a base for oil and gas exploration in the Beaufort Sea.

Around Town

Most visitors see Tuk from the inside of a transporter van driven by accommodating locals who never tire of the same hackneyed questions about living at the end of the earth. The bus stops at *Our Lady of Lourdes,* once part of a fleet of vessels which plied the Arctic delivering supplies to isolated communities. Here also are two mission churches built in the late 1930s. A stop is also made at the Arctic Ocean, where you are encouraged to dip your toes in the water or go for a swim if you really want to impress the folks back home. (Tuk is actually on the Beaufort Sea, an arm of the Arctic Ocean, but who's telling). For a few extra bucks you are given some time to explore on your own. This will give you a chance to walk along the beach, climb a nearby pingo, and check out the well-equipped ocean port.

Practicalities

Tuk is the most popular flightseeing destination from Inuvik and a variety of trips are offered by the two tour operators in Inuvik. Trips start at $100, which includes the return flight (worth the price alone) and a tour of the town. The flight into Tuk is breathtaking—the pilots fly at low altitudes for the best possible views. For those who wish to spend longer in Tuk (there are enough things to do to hold your interest for at least one day), both companies offer extended tours. For tour details contact **Western Arctic Nature Tours,** tel. (403) 979-3300, or **Arctic Tour Co.,** tel. 979-4100. Overnight trips, airfare and tour only, will cost from $135. Before you flash your cash, check with both operators for the best deal. **Aklak Air** has scheduled flights from Inuvik twice daily for $112 one way; tel. 979-3377.

Hotel Tuk Inn, P.O. Box 193, Tuktoyaktuk, NT X0E 1C0, tel. 977-2381, and **Pingo Park Lodge,** P.O. Box 6000, tel. 977-2155, are of an acceptable northern standard. Prices start at $115 s, $140 d, and both have dining facilities. Camping is ac-

deer

ceptable; down on the beach is a favorite place to pitch tents, but check the weather forecast (tel. 979-4183) before putting too much faith in your trusty canvas companion. **Northern,** for groceries, and a **post office** are by the public dock. Crafts are available in a small store next to *Our Lady of Lourdes.*

PAULATUK

The western Arctic's smallest community, Paulatuk, has a population of 110 Inuvialuit Inuit who live a traditional lifestyle hunting, trapping, and fishing. A Roman Catholic mission and trading post, established in 1935, attracted Inuvialuit families from camps along the Arctic coast. Their descendants continue living off the abundant natural resources still available today. The community is located on a sandy strip of land between the Beaufort Sea and an inland lake along a rugged stretch of coastline, 400 km east of Inuvik. To the northeast are the **Smoking Hills,** seams of coal, rich with sulphide, that were ignited centuries ago and still burn today, filling the immediate area with distinctively shaped clouds of smoke.

The Hornaday and other rivers whose headwaters are north of Great Bear Lake drain into the ocean near Paulatuk, providing unparalleled opportunities for extended whitewater trips (experienced paddlers only). **Parry Peninsula,** to the west of Paulatuk, is a major staging area for the **Bluenose caribou herd,** which migrates across the north. The coastal cliffs of **Cape Parry Bird Sanctuary** are a nesting site for rare murres. In spring local outfitters will take you far out onto the pack ice of **Amundsen Gulf** in search of polar bears.

Practicalities
The only accommodation in town is **Paulatuk Hotel,** General Delivery, Paulatuk, NT X0E 1N0, tel. (403) 580-3027, with eight rooms with shared bath and a small restaurant; $110 per person. You can camp along the beach, but ask at the hamlet office before pitching your tent. **Kopatkok Arctic Sightseeing** leads fishing and day tours around the area. Contact David Ruben at General Delivery or call 580-3222. The only scheduled flights to Paulatuk are on **Aklak Air,** tel. 979-3777, leaving Inuvik on Tues-

day and Friday ($262.50 one way). Check with Inuvik tour operators for cheaper deals.

BANKS ISLAND

Banks Island is one of the best places in the western Arctic for viewing wildlife, including foxes, polar bears, wolves, and the world's largest concentration of musk oxen. The island is separated from the mainland by **Amundsen Gulf** and from Victoria Island by **Prince of Wales Strait,** and is the most westerly island in the Canadian Arctic archipelago. Through the barren, low rolling hills that characterize this island flow a number of major rivers including the **Thomsen,** the northernmost navigable river in Canada. On northern Banks Island is **Aulavik National Park,** recently established in the Thomsen River area. To get to the park you need to charter a plane in Inuvik.

Sachs Harbour (Ikaahuk)
The only permanent settlement on Banks Island is Sachs Harbour, located at the foot of a low bluff along the southwest coast, 520 km northeast of Inuvik. An abundance of white foxes had attracted Thule people to the island for centuries, and early Arctic explorers such as Beechley and McLure had charted the island. But it wasn't until the late 1920s that three delta Inuit families settled permanently in what is now known as Sachs Harbour. The island has always been regarded as one of the finest trapping areas in the Canadian Arctic, and the people who lived here were able to afford luxuries such as washing machines and holidays to Aklavik. The town of 200 remains relatively self-sufficient. The first weekend of May is the **White Fox Jamboree,** a three-day festival of traditional northern games, food, and dance.

Practicalities
Arctic Tour Co., tel. (403) 979-4100, and **Western Arctic Nature Tours,** tel. 979-3300, offer naturalist trips to Banks Island, starting at $970 for three days. Cost includes return airfare from Inuvik, tours onto the tundra in search of wildlife, tent accommodations, and all meals. It may be cheaper to organize your own tour through **Banks Island Tundra Tours,** General Delivery, Sachs Harbour, NT X0E 0Z0. Two local

families offer accommodations: **Lena Wolki B&B,** General Delivery, tel. 690-3451, has rooms for $175 per person including meals; Margaret Carpenter also has rooms. Camping along the beach should be okay, but check first with the hamlet office. The town has no restau-rants, only a small co-op grocery store (closed Sunday). **Aklak Air,** tel. 979-3777, has a twice-weekly scheduled flight to Sachs Harbour from Inuvik; $330.50 one way. This is the flight used by Arctic Tour Co., so inquire here about cheap-er fares.

ARCTIC COAST

Imagine a strip of coastline that stretched from San Diego to Seattle with an offshore island the size of California and a total population that would fit easily into a couple of jumbo jets; with-out traffic lights, power lines, road systems, or McDonald's, and a complete absence of trees. Such is the Arctic coast. For nine months of the year it is a cold, frozen land where it seems no life-forms could possibly exist. Then, during the short Arctic summer, the land comes alive. Its rivers provide what many regard as the ultimate canoe trips, naturalists and photographers are drawn by the abundant wildlife-viewing oppor-tunities, and anglers from around the world ar-rive, hoping to catch the most prized of all north-ern fish, the delicious **arctic char.**

Lowland arctic makes up the bulk of the re-gion, including the Arctic coast mainland and lower Arctic islands such as King William, Prince of Wales, and Victoria (the world's 12th-largest island). It is a land of low rolling hills, scoured by glacial ice during the last ice age, deeply in-cised by meltwater streams, and scattered with shallow lakes. **Boothia Peninsula,** in the east part of the region, is a classic example. This, the northernmost point of mainland on the con-tinent, is a bleak, barren land, rarely penetrated, even by the Inuit.

For centuries, Copper and Netsilik Inuit spent summer traveling the length of the Arctic coast, fishing and hunting seals and caribou. They moved as the seasons dictated, and had no permanent settlements. As the quest for a north-west passage to the Orient heated up, the Hud-son's Bay Company began establishing posts at remote locations throughout the region. These posts attracted the nomadic Inuit, whose lifestyle began to change as a result. The posts formed the basis of today's seven Arctic coast commu-nities. In many, the characteristic red-and-white-trimmed H.B.C. buildings still stand, as do stone churches built by missionaries.

All communities, except Pelly Bay, rely on supplies barged down the Mackenzie River from Hay River once a year. Otherwise the only links to the outside world are by plane. Scheduled flights from Yellowknife serve all communities except **Bathurst Inlet,** where charter flights bring guests into one of the world's premier nat-uralist lodges. For whatever reason you visit this fascinating region it is important to be pre-pared. Each community has a hotel serving meals, but reservations should be made well in advance. Groceries and basic camping sup-plies are available in all communities, but there are no banks.

For more information write to Arctic Coast Tourist Association, P.O. Box 91, Cambridge Bay, NT X0E 0C0, Canada; tel. (403) 983-2224 or (800) 661-0788.

CAMBRIDGE BAY (IKALUKTUTIAK)

Cambridge Bay, located on the southeast coast of 212,688-square-km **Victoria Island,** Can-ada's second-largest island, is a busy admin-istrative center for the Arctic coast region. The Inuit name for the bay is Ikaluktutiak, meaning "fair fishing place." For hundreds of years before European arrival, Copper Inuit gathered here in summer to take advantage of the abundant caribou and seals, and to fish for arctic char. These people fashioned tools and implements from copper, hence the name Copper Inuit. Doc-tor John Rae, who visited the bay in 1851 in search of the Franklin Expedition, was one of many Arctic explorers who stopped to rest in its sheltered waters.

The Hudson's Bay Company established a trading post here in 1921, and bought Roald Amundsen's schooner *Maud* as a supply ship. After being used for many years, the ship fell into disrepair and sank in the bay. It is still visible from the shores of Old Town, resting in the shallow waters of Cambridge Bay. A stone church, built by Anglican missionaries in the 1920s, is a Cambridge Bay landmark.

The landscape surrounding the bay is very barren, but the summit of **Mt. Pelly,** a 1.5-km (each way) hike from town, affords a panoramic view and a chance to spot musk oxen. In town, the **Ikaluktutiak Co-op** operates a fishery that is a major supplier of arctic char to the rest of Canada, and **Central Arctic Meats** processes caribou and musk ox. Both are open to visitors, selling smoked arctic char and musk ox jerky, respectively. **Northern Images** has a variety of arts and crafts for sale, including ivory carvings and traditionally decorated parkas.

The **Arctic Coast Tourist Association,** tel. (403) 983-2224, has a visitor center in town; open in summer, daily 9 a.m.-5 p.m.

Accommodations And Food

Campers can pitch tents along the shoreline, as long as they're out of sight of the community. For those wanting to stay indoors, choices are: **Ikaluktutiak Co-op Hotel,** P.O. Box 38, Cambridge Bay, NT X0E 0C0, tel. (403) 983-2215, $110 per person and $50 per person extra for meals; **Enokhok Inn,** P.O. Box 103, tel. 983-2444, with self-contained units, each with a kitchenette, $125 per person; and the newest accommodation, **Arctic Islands Lodge,** P.O. Box 92, tel. 983-2345, where each room has private bath, and a restaurant and laundry are on the premises, $145 per person. Meals are available in the hotels, groceries from **Northern.**

Tours And Transportation

Touch the Arctic Adventure Tours, tel. (800) 661-0894, offers three- to six-day tours to Cambridge Bay from $746 per person including round-trip airfare from Edmonton, two nights accommodation at Arctic Islands Lodge, and one northern dinner. Airlines serving Cambridge Bay include **Canadian North,** tel. (403) 983-2434 or (800) 665-1177; **NWT Air,** tel. 983-2591 or (800) 661-0789; and **First Air,** tel. 983-2919 or (800) 267-1247. Each has two to six flights per week from Yellowknife; $354 one way, $389 for a 14-day APEX round trip. Most Canadian North flights continue to Resolute and some to Iqaluit. If you are planning to visit Arctic

coast communities east of Cambridge Bay, First Air provides connections.

HOLMAN (ULUQSAQTUUQ)

Apart from Cambridge Bay, the only other community on Victoria Island is Holman (population 300), located on the western side of the island on **Diamond Jenness Peninsula.** The community is located on a gravel beach at the end of horseshoe-shaped Queens Bay and is surrounded by steep bluffs that rise as high as 200 meters. The area is renowned for arctic char and trout fishing and silkscreen printing done by local Copper Inuit. The small museum is also worth visiting for its displays of native artifacts. Holman has a golf course, the most northerly in the world. Playing a round of golf here is really something to tell the boys back at the country club; for the record, the course is at a latitude of 70 degrees 44 minutes North. Each August the course hosts the **Billy Joss Open,** attracting sports celebrities from as far away as the U.S.

Copper Inuit had traditionally wintered on nearby Banks Island and spent summer hunting caribou on Victoria Island. But when a Hudson's Bay Company post that had been on Prince Albert Sound was moved to what is now Holman in 1939, the Inuit began to settle around it. As they moved to the post, they were taught printmaking by a missionary, Rev. Henri Tardl, who had come to the settlement as an oblate missionary. To this day printmaking is a major source of income for the community. Trapping and hunting also contribute.

Practicalities

Holman's only hotel is the **Arctic Char Inn,** General Delivery, Holman, NT X0E 0S0, tel. (403) 396-3501. The town has no established campgrounds, but many locals camp at Okpilik Lake. If you'd like to be closer to town ask at the hamlet office, located at the back of town, for the best place to pitch a tent. Meals are available at the Arctic Char Inn and groceries across the road in **Northern.** Local arts and crafts are available in the museum, a little farther up the road by the **post office.**

The only scheduled flights into Holman are twice weekly from Yellowknife with **First Air,** tel. 396-3063 or (800) 267-1247; $490 one way, $666 for a 14-day APEX round trip.

COPPERMINE (KUGLUKTUK)

South of Holman on the mainland coast is the Inuit community of Coppermine (population 1,000), which sits at the mouth of one of North America's finest wilderness rivers. It is located 600 km north of Yellowknife on **Coronation Gulf,** a vital link in the Northwest Passage.

History

Historians believe that Inuits fished at the mouth of the **Coppermine River** for over 4,000 years before Samuel Hearne arrived there on 14 July 1771. The Hudson's Bay Company had sent Hearne to find the source of the copper that traders were starting to bring in to H.B.C. posts farther east. When Hearne and his Chipewyan Dene guides neared the rivermouth, they encountered a party of Copper Inuit. Relations between the Dene and Copper Inuit had traditionally been tense, and as the result of an argument the Inuits were massacred. Hearne named the site of the tragedy Bloody Falls, now a popular hike from Coppermine. As the great inland caribou herds began to decline in number, Inuit spent more time near the coast hunting sea mammals. In 1927, a Hudson's Bay Company post was established at the rivermouth, followed by an Anglican mission and RCMP outpost in 1932, and a weather station in 1937. Today fishing and hunting play an important role in the local economy, as does oil-and-gas exploration and tourism.

Coppermine River

The Coppermine River makes for one of North America's classic paddling trips, combining tundra wilderness with unparalleled opportunities for viewing moose, wolves, caribou, grizzly bears, and musk oxen. A sense of history prevails—after all, it's the same route north taken by Hearne, Franklin, and Hood. The headwaters of this remote river are below the treeline at a series of joined lakes, 360 km north of Yellowknife. The 325 km float from the headwaters to Coppermine takes around 10 days, but most people allow time for tundra hikes, arctic char fishing,

and relaxing. The river flows primarily through tundra, but the valley is characteristically lushly vegetated, creating prime habitat for larger mammals. Hawks, falcons, and eagles nest in the cliff faces along the route. The only portage is at Bloody Falls, 16 km from the ocean. **Whitewolf Adventure Expeditions,** 41-1355 Citadel Dr., Port Coquitlam, B.C. V3C 5X6, tel. (800) 661-6659, offers 12- and 14-day river expeditions in canoes and rafts; from $3085 out of Yellowknife.

Things To Do Around Town

Although most keen naturalists are drawn to nearby Bathurst Inlet Lodge (see below), the immediate vicinity of Coppermine provides many opportunities for wildlife viewing. The best way to get a feel for the area is by hiking along one of the numerous trails that radiate from town. The trail to **Bloody Falls** is less than 20 km one way but the going can get rough. Chances are you'll want to make numerous stops, both to search out routes through the many swampy sections of the trail, and to admire the colorful tundra vegetation. Rewards are ample, none more so than the final destination where the Coppermine River plunges into a narrow canyon. Most hikers opt to camp here overnight. Other possible hikes include walking along the beach west of town to **Expeditor Cove,** and climbing the rocky ridge above the garbage dump road for a view of town and the ocean. **Aime's Arctic Tours,** P.O. Box 158, Coppermine, NT X0E 0E0, tel. (403) 982-7206, organizes fishing trips to nearby islands and up the Coppermine River for arctic char. Inquire at the **Hunters and Trappers Association Office,** tel. 982-4908, by the recreation center for other outfitters. The year's biggest festival is **Nattik Frolics,** at the end of April, which includes traditional northern sports and other not-so-traditional events such as poker and snowmobile races. A **fishing derby** on the first weekend of September attracts arctic char enthusiasts from throughout the north; call 982-4471 for details.

Practicalities

Coppermine Inn, P.O. Box 282, Coppermine, NT X0E 0E0, tel. (403) 982-3333, is spread out at the west end of town. Guests have a choice of motel rooms or self-contained units. A-frames are $125 per person. Breakfast, lunch, and dinner are $15, $20, and $30, respectively, and should be booked in advance. Nonguests may also eat here but should book meals a day in advance. **Northern,** just up from the dock, sells groceries and souvenirs, and usually has white gas (check supplies before flying in, tel. 982-4171). The town has a **post office, library** and **craft shop,** but no bank.

The airport is located a short walk from town and is served by **First Air,** tel. 982-3208 or (800) 267-1247, from Yellowknife; $285 one way, $388 for a 14-day APEX round trip.

BATHURST INLET

Bathurst Inlet, 210 km east of Coppermine, is the name of an expansive bay, an abandoned Hudson's Bay Company post, and a popular naturalist lodge. The H.B.C. established a trading post on the southwest side of the inlet at the mouth of the **Burnside River** in the 1930s. Various Inuit had inhabited the Bathurst Inlet area for thousands of years, but the post, along with others along the rugged coastline, was the first permanent settlement. In 1964 the H.B.C. moved the post across the inlet and 120 km north to **Bay Chimo.** Four years later the post closed for good. The small Inuit community here, now known as **Umingmaktok,** continues to prosper and is one of the north's more traditional communities. Residents are noted for crafts, which they peddle at Bathurst Inlet Lodge.

Bathurst Inlet Lodge
Glenn Warner, a former Mountie, and his wife Trish, bought the various H.B.C. buildings at the mouth of the Burnside River and in 1969 opened what has evolved into the north's most renowned naturalist lodge. Most of the original buildings remain—as a lounge, dining room, and guest rooms for up to 25 visitors at a time. But it is not the quaint red-and-white-trimmed H.B.C. buildings that attract people from around the world. It is the chance to become immersed in the fascinating natural world of the Arctic, with a soft bed and a hot shower at the end of each day. One of the beauties of the lodge, apart from its magnificent setting, is the diversity of things to see and do in the surrounding area. Wildflower enthusiasts will be enthralled by resident naturalist Page Burt's understanding of the land as she leads hikes onto the tundra.

The *Arctic Queen,* a pontoon boat, cruises the inlet in search of ringed seals and musk oxen grazing on the shore. Birdwatchers will be captivated by the number of sea- and shorebirds who spend summer in the area. Local Inuit families, who have become part owners of the lodge, teach guests their own interpretation of the land's natural history. And there's plenty of time for fishing, photography, hiking, or just soaking up the scenery.

Rates for the lodge include charter flights from Yellowknife, seven nights accommodations at the lodge, all meals, guided day-trips (except flightseeing, $200), and a traditional drum dance on your final night. Essentially, all you have to do is get to Yellowknife. Cost is $2940 out of Yellowknife; $3403 out of Edmonton. The floatplane leaves from Back Bay in Old Town Yellowknife at 3618 McAvoy Road. For more information contact Bathurst Inlet Lodge, P.O. Box 820, Yellowknife, NT X1A 2N6; tel. (403) 873-2595, fax 920-4263.

GJOA HAVEN (URSUQTUQ)

Gjoa Haven is the only settlement on **King William Island,** which is separated from the mainland by the narrow **Simpson Strait.** The island had long been the traditional territory of the Netsilik Inuit, who were expert seal hunters. Early explorers named it King William Land, mistakenly thinking that it was part of the mainland. The island has been the scene of much conjecture ever since the disappearance of Sir John Franklin, one of many explorers sent to find the elusive Northwest Passage. One of the Franklin expedition's main mistakes was underestimating the Netsilik, whose advice could have prevented the tragedy. Roald Amundsen made no such mistakes on his 1903-06 expedition. After spending two winters on King William Island, at a harbor he named after his ship *Gjoa,* learning from the Netsilik, he went on to become the first person to successfully navigate the Northwest Passage. Today the location of what Amundsen called "the finest little harbor in the world" is home to around 700 Inuit who live a traditional lifestyle—hunting, fishing, and making crafts such as wall hangings and soapstone carvings. The well-signposted **North-**

west Passage Historical Park tells the story of the search for the passage and the part Gjoa Haven played in it. The trail is three km long and can be boggy early in the summer. Ask at the hamlet office, tel. (403) 360-7141, just up from Northern, for an interpretive brochure explaining the historical importance of sites along the trail. Apart from the excellent arctic char fishing, Gjoa Haven is a good base for sled dog trips across Rae Strait to Spence Bay. The end of winter is celebrated with the **Qauvarrik Carnival,** which takes place on the still-frozen bay in front of the community. The carnival features events for everyone—an egg toss, blindfolded sled race, harpoon throw, all with small cash prizes. For outsiders, winning the weightlifting competition will cause some problems—first prize is a 44-gallon drum of fuel!

Practicalities

Amundsen Hotel, Kekertak Co-op, General Delivery, Gjoa Haven, NT X0E 1J0, tel. (403) 360-6176, sleeps 18 in six rooms, so if it's busy, you'll be sharing a room; $110 per person plus $60 per person for meals. The small restaurant is open to nonguests, but reservations should be made in advance. For groceries head to **Northern** and for local crafts to the **Kekertak Co-op,** behind the hotel.

The only scheduled air service to Gjoa Haven is with **First Air,** tel. 360-6612 or (800) 267-1247, via Cambridge Bay from Yellowknife; $547 one way, $766 for a 14-day APEX round trip.

TALOYOAK

Formerly known as Spence Bay, this Inuit community of 550 lies in low, rolling hills and is surrounded by fish-filled lakes. It is located on the west side of an isthmus linking the mainland to **Boothia Peninsula.** The tip of this peninsula, 250 km north of Taloyoak at Bellot Strait, is the northernmost point of mainland on the continent. Spence Bay was named by John Ross, a British explorer who wintered in the area in the early 1830s. Taloyoak, its Inuit name, refers to a caribou blind built by early natives to corral and kill caribou. The Netsilik Inuit traveled great distances through the region—hunting, trapping,

and trading. By following Inuit directions, John Ross escaped certain death after becoming icebound. His abandoned vessel, a paddle-steamer, the first such boat to be used for Arctic exploration, was a source of wood and iron to Inuit for many years. It is interesting that Ross was able to accurately pinpoint the North Magnetic Pole to a spot along the southwestern coast of Boothia Peninsula. The pole, which annually moves 25 km north and six km west, has since moved many hundreds of kilometers to a point northwest of Resolute.

It was not until 1947 that a permanent settlement was established at Spence Bay, one of the only safe harbors on the west coast of Boothia Peninsula. Local Netsilik and Inuit artisans are known for their stuffed "packing dolls" of animals such as whales and seals. At the mouth of the harbor stand the distinctive red-and-white Hudson's Bay Company buildings. A short hike leads to a stone caribou blind. It is also possible to travel overland to **Fort Ross,** or 80 km north to **Thom Bay** where the *Victory* was abandoned by Ross in 1929. Inland are lakes where the local Inuit travel each summer to fish.

Practicalities

The **Paleajook Hotel,** General Delivery, Spence Bay, NT X0E 1B0, tel. (403) 561-5803, has rooms with shared facilities for $110 per person. Meals are an extra $50 per person per day. A semi-official camping area is located near an old mission church, west of the post office. Meals are available at the Paleajook Hotel and should be booked in advance. Groceries and limited camping supplies are available at **Northern** or **Paleajook Co-op.** Ask at the Hunters and Trappers Association for locally harvested food such as arctic char, caribou, and muktuk; tel. 561-5066. The community also has a **post office** and **medical center** but no bank.

The small airport, within walking distance of town, is served by **First Air,** tel. 561-5400 or (800) 267-1247, from Yellowknife; $612 one way, $857 for a 14-day APEX round trip. First Air also flies to Spence Bay from Iqaluit twice weekly; the Tuesday flight is a real milk run with seven stops. **Lyall's Taxi and Cartage,** tel. 561-6363, operates a cab service and boat tours.

PELLY BAY (ARVILIQJUAT)

Pelly Bay is a Netsilingmiut Inuit community of 300 located 177 km southeast of Spence Bay. The community is named for Sir Henry Pelly, an early governor of the Hudson's Bay Company. It grew around a Roman Catholic mission established in 1935. The mission's founder, Father Henry, was for many years the only *qallunaaq* (nonnative) to reside here. Today the residents of Pelly Bay continue to fish and hunt as they have for generations. Its location deep in Pelly Bay makes accessibility for barge traffic nearly impossible and gives the town the distinction of having the highest cost of living of any community in the north.

A stone church, built by Father Henry, houses a small museum; located on the road to the dock. In the immediate vicinity of the community are a number of interesting sites. On the top of a nearby hill is a unique cross built out of empty gasoline drums by early missionaries. Also close to town are a number of *inukshuks* and scraps of metal from the fuselage of a U.S. plane. Hikes lead along the rocky shoreline, inland to fishing lakes, and to archaeological remains of Inuit camps. Seals and, occasionally, narwhals are seen in the bay. **Netsilik Tours,** General Delivery, Pelly Bay, NT X0E 1K0, tel. (403) 769-6077, offers a variety of day and overnight tours by boat, dogsled, ATV, or snowmobile from $90 per person per day.

Practicalities

The lack of tourist facilities here is more than made up for by the friendliness of the locals. **Inukshuk Inn,** General Delivery, Pelly Bay, NT X0E 1K0, tel. (403) 769-7211, has six rooms with shared facilities, a TV room, and a small restaurant; $110 per person, meals are $60 per day. Meals in the restaurant are by prior arrangement, whether a guest or not. Groceries are available at **Koomiut Co-op,** next door to the hotel. The town has no bank and alcohol is not allowed. Ask at the Co-op about campsites close to town.

First Air, tel. 769-7302 or (800) 267-1247, flies into Pelly Bay three times weekly from Yellowknife; $659 one way, $923 for a 14-day APEX round trip. Connections are also made through to Iqaluit twice a week. The airstrip is located in town.

KEEWATIN

The Keewatin stretches along the west coast of **Hudson Bay** from north of Churchill, Manitoba to the Melville Peninsula and west to the heart of the barrenlands. Each summer vast herds of caribou migrate across the region to their calving grounds. Wolves, foxes, and grizzlies are scattered throughout the region while musk oxen graze in small herds in **Thelon Game Sanctuary.** Polar bears migrate along the coastal regions and are best viewed at **Wager Bay.** The thousands of lakes and rivers dotting the region are alive with fish; arctic char is dominant, but huge lake trout and whitefish also inhabit all lakes large enough not to freeze to the bottom. Whaling took place throughout the Arctic, but Hudson Bay was affected more than anywhere. All species were hunted to near extinction during this period and today whales exist in only a fraction of their former numbers. The most common sea mammal here is the ringed seal, which spends summer basking on the shoreline or ice floes.

Dorset and Thule cultures inhabited the region for thousands of years before European whalers arrived, but it was the latter that had the most dramatic effect on animal populations. Trading posts, built to support the whaling industry, attracted the Inuit and, in time, communities developed around them. **Rankin Inlet** is the largest of seven communities and the transportation hub of the Keewatin.

For more information write to Travel Keewatin, P.O. Box 328, Rankin Inlet, NT X0C 0G0; tel. (819) 645-2618 or (800) 661-0788. The area code for all Keewatin communities is **819.**

RANKIN INLET
(KANGIQTINQ)

Rankin Inlet is the communication, administrative, and transportation center of Keewatin region. It is located on rocky terrain, west of where the Meliadine River drains into Rankin Inlet, approximately 25 km from Hudson Bay. It wasn't established until 1955 when the North Rankin Nickel Mine opened. A Hudson's Bay Company store, hospital, homes, three churches, and a school were soon added to the mine structures as many Inuit moved to the area seeking a wage. In 1958, the Department of Indian Affairs, appalled at the living conditions of the nomadic Inuit, set up a relocation program, moving them to **Itivia,** one km southeast of Rankin Inlet. Here the government constructed a number of huts, a school, and a store. Due to a depletion of ore, the mine closed in 1962 and the population dipped to 350. Itivia was deemed a failure soon after. An arts and crafts manufacturing program was the turning point in Rankin Inlet's fortunes. Although recovery has been slow, the population has increased to 1,500, and today the streets are the typical northern clutter of weathered buildings joined by a net of electrical wires. The Keewatin's only paved road leads to the airport.

Around Town

The **North Rankin Nickel Mine** is located on a gravel hill overlooking the harbor and town. Although it has been closed for over 30 years, much of the machinery remains, slowly rusting away and leaving a graphic memory of the eastern Arctic's first mine. Across the road from the mine site is a commercial fish-processing plant where arctic char is prepared for shipment south. From the mine site the road continues down to the harbor where there's a dock and a small fleet of fishing boats. On the opposite side of town, near the Matchbox Gallery, a one-km trail leads to Itivia. Little remains of the settlement but from the site there is a good view of the **Barrier Islands.** An important archaeological site is located 10 km north of town on the **Meliadine River.** The area was never particularly good for hunting but had been used for centuries as a seasonal fishing camp. Many stone tent rings, foundations of semi-subterranean houses, and

a number of graves can be found in the area. The road to the site is used by locals going fishing so if you walk you may be able to hitch a ride along the way. Alternatively, **Hudson Bay Tour Company,** tel. (819) 645-2618, will make the run out there with an Inuit guide.

Marble Island

Lying 40 km east of Rankin Inlet is an island where many dramas have been played out over the years. The lineaments are simple; it is a barren island dominated by slabs of cream-colored quartzite protruding from an otherwise featureless terrain. The earliest European traders and explorers probably landed on the island as early as the 1600s. In 1721 Capt. James Knight and his crew were searching for the Northwest Passage when his two ships were wrecked on a shallow bar at the east end of the island. Everyone made it ashore, and a stone house was built to winter in. One by one they perished, waiting for a rescue that never came. During the late 1800s the island was used as a wintering site for whalers. Today it is regarded as a mystical place; Thule camps can be seen along with the remains of Knight's house and the site of an open-air theater, used by the whalers for entertainment. The least expensive way of visiting the island is with **Hudson Bay Tour Company,** tel. (819) 645-2618.

Accommodations And Food

Rankin Inlet's three accommodations are all in

ESKIMO ICE CREAM

Recipes vary from region to region depending on the ingredients available. This version is from the eastern Arctic and, once started, must be completed without interruptions.

Pound an amount of seal fat until soft, then melt over low heat until there is a thick layer of grease on the base of the pot. Grind up dried arctic char roe and berries, stir slowly into the melted fat; make sure the temperature remains low—a guide is to keep the mixture at a temperature that is not too hot to touch. Add salt to taste. If the mixture congeals, water will soften it up. Freeze the mixture, then serve with bread or meat.

the center of town and should be able to organize transportation from the airport if you book a room in advance. **Nanuq Inn,** P.O. Box 175, Rankin Inlet, NT X0C 0A0, tel. (819) 645-2709, has ten rooms with cable TV in each and shared bathrooms. The inn also has a coffee shop, dining room, and lounge; $115 per person. **Keewatin Guest Lodge,** P.O. Box 220, tel. 645-2402, is more like a bed and breakfast, but without the breakfast; $100 per person. The largest in town is **Siniktarvik Hotel,** P.O. Box 190, tel. 645-2807, where each of the 65 rooms has a private bath, and a restaurant and lounge is available for guests. Rates are $136 per person.

Northern has a good range of groceries and a snack bar serving fast food (closes 5 p.m.). Dining in the two hotel restaurants is expensive, but not outrageously so.

Transportation
Rankin Inlet is the transportation hub of the Keewatin. **NWT Air,** tel. (819) 645-3445 or (800) 661-0789, flies in from Yellowknife five times weekly ($476 one way, $438 for a 14-day APEX round trip), and Winnipeg three times weekly ($607 one way, $595 round trip). **First Air,** tel. 645-2961 or (800) 267-1247, flies from Iqaluit to Rankin Inlet via Coral Harbour. For a cab call 645-2411.

Services And Information
The **post office** is located behind the Siniktarvik Hotel; the only bank is a C.I.B.C. in the Kissarvik Co-op. For the **medical center** call (819) 645-2816. A small **visitor center,** tel. 645-5091, is located in the Siniktarvik Hotel where you can also buy crafts. The **Travel Keewatin** office is in the Government Building, west of the old mine site; tel. 645-2618.

WHALE COVE (TIKIRARJUAQ)

Whale Cove's Inuit name means "where many people arrive," a reference to the whalers, trading ships, and Inuit who stopped here. This small community of 200 is located 80 km south of Rankin Inlet, on a peninsula where the Wilson River drains into Hudson Bay. The area was explored in 1613 by Captain Thomas Button, and from the early 1700s onward Hudson's Bay Company traders regularly visited the area. It

wasn't until 1959 that the community was officially established. At this time, the federal government began moving Caribou Inuit to the coast where they adapted their hunting and fishing skills to the abundant coastal resources.

The community has little to offer in the way of tourist facilities but provides a unique opportunity to view traditional Inuit lifestyles, including women scraping caribou skins, and fishermen returning with their daily catches. On one side of the town are large tanks, filled each summer with fuel for the winter. On the other side is a small dock and beach. The beach is lined with freighter canoes, engines, and the ubiquitous snowmobile. Behind town is **Whale's Tail Monument,** built in 1967 to celebrate the community's link to the ocean. A rough trail leads to this viewpoint. Other trails lead inland to a number of lakes, the deeper ones supporting lake trout and whitefish.

Practicalities
The **Issatik Co-op Hotel,** Whale Cove, NT X0C 0J0, tel. (819) 896-9252, is in the center of town and has six rooms, each with a private bathroom; $200 per person per day includes three meals. Ask at the hamlet office next door about camping, tel. 896-9961. A **grocery store** and **post office** are located by the fish plant opposite the waterfront. The only scheduled flights to Whale Cove are with **Calm Air,** tel. 645-2846, from Rankin Inlet; $87 one way, $96 for a 14-day APEX round trip.

ARVIAT

For many centuries Arviat (formerly known as Eskimo Point), 240 km southwest of Rankin Inlet, was a summer camp for Pallirmiut Inuit who came to the coast to hunt seals. They spent the rest of the year inland, but during their time in the area in the late 1600s they made contact with traders from Churchill. A Hudson's Bay Company post was established in 1921, followed by Roman Catholic and Anglican missions. Inuit were attracted to the settlement for food, medicine, and trade goods. During the 1940s and '50s migration patterns of the caribou changed and their numbers declined, causing great hardship for the remaining inland Inuit who were relocated to Arviat by the Canadian Government. Today this community of 1,300 is still largely dependent on hunting, trapping, and fishing for its livelihood.

To the south is **McConnell River Bird Sanctuary,** a 330-square-km area of wetlands and tidal flats that is a breeding ground for 250,000 lesser snow geese and a staging area for one million birds each fall. For boat transfers to the sanctuary or to good fishing areas, call the hamlet office, tel. (819) 857-2841.

Practicalities

Padlei Inns North, P.O. Box 90, Arviat, NT X0C 0E0, tel. (819) 857-2762, has 10 rooms, a lounge, and a laundry; $190 per person includes three meals.

Calm Air, tel. 857-2997, flies daily from Rankin Inlet; $185 one way, $203 for a 14-day APEX round trip.

CHESTERFIELD INLET (IGLULIGAARJUK)

This community of 290 north of Rankin Inlet was an important medical and educational center for the eastern Arctic until the government helped other communities develop their own facilities. Although there was much whaling activity in Hudson Bay in the 1700s, it wasn't until 1912 that the Hudson's Bay Company established a post on the Keewatin Coast, at Chesterfield Inlet. The community, situated on a gravel strip of a land overlooking the inlet, has a number of historic buildings including the impressive three-story **St. Theresa Hospital,** built in 1931.

Kanayuk Sammurtok Outfitting, General Delivery, Chesterfield Inlet, NT X0C 0B0, tel. (819) 645-2618, offers half-day tours of the community, three-day tours up the inlet to archaeological sites, and five-day tours up the coast to Cape Fullerton, the site of the eastern Arctic's first RCMP post (which has been restored to its original condition).

Practicalities

The only tourist services are at **Tangmavik Hotel,** General Delivery, Chesterfield Inlet, NT X0C 0B0, tel. (819) 898-9975; $170 per person includes three meals.

Calm Air, tel. 898-9103, has daily flights from Rankin Inlet; $93 one way or $102 for a 14-day APEX round trip.

BAKER LAKE (QAMANITTUAQ)

Baker Lake (population 1,000), located west of Chesterfield Inlet, is the only inland Inuit community. Rankin Inlet is 260 km to the east and, surprisingly, the geographical center of Canada is located a few kilometers to the northeast. The community is a good jumping-off point for sightseeing in **Thelon Game Sanctuary** or canoeing the various wilderness rivers to the south and west.

The local population is thought to have descended from a group of Inuit of the Thule culture who migrated onto the barrenlands to hunt caribou. Before the Hudson's Bay Company established a post in 1916 on an island in the lake, few whites had ventured into the area. The post moved to the present site in 1936 and the community has been steadily expanding since. Local Inuit are renowned for their art, much of which reflects the importance of the caribou herds. Their artworks can be viewed at the **Jessie Oonark Arts and Crafts Centre.**

DAN HERINGA/NWT ECONOMIC DEVELOPMENT & TOURISM

Inukshuks *were built by the Inuit as a navigation aid on the featureless tundra.*

Accommodations

Snow Goose Inn, P.O. Box 270, Baker Lake, NT X0C 0A0, tel. (819) 793-2200, only has three rooms, but the hosts can organize tours of the community and pick-ups for canoeists; $150 per person includes three meals. The other two accommodations, **Baker Lake Lodge,** P.O. Box 239, tel. 793-2905, and **Iglu Hotel,** P.O. Box 179, tel. 793-2801, are similarly priced. Camping is possible along the lakeshore, but check with the hamlet office before pitching a tent.

Services And Information

Calm Air, tel. (819) 793-2873, has flights daily from Rankin Inlet into Baker Lake; $218 one way, $240 14-day APEX round trip.

Limited groceries and camping supplies are available at **Northern.** The **Akumalik Visitors Centre,** tel. 793-2456, is located in the 1936 Hudson's Bay Company trading post.

Thelon Game Sanctuary

This 67,340-square-km sanctuary was established in 1927 for the sole purpose of wildlife conservation. Its dominant natural feature, the **Thelon River,** begins from 200 km east of Great Slave Lake and is the largest unaltered watershed emptying into Hudson Bay. The river flows through a wide valley, surrounded in barrenlands, yet lined with stands of spruce, protected from the elements by the valley wall. The Beverly caribou herd—numbering 330,000—migrates through the sanctuary. Other mammals present are wolves, musk oxen, moose, wolverines, foxes, lynx, and grizzly bears. Rare raptors, such as the peregrine falcon, nest in the sanctuary along with 10,000 Canada geese.

The Thelon River has been designated as a Canadian Heritage River, not only for its abundant wildlife and natural heritage but for the unique wilderness recreation it offers. Canoeing is by far the most popular activity. Although it is possible to begin a canoe trip from the Upper Thelon or Hanbury rivers, strenuous portages are required to do so. The most popular put-in point is the confluence of these two rivers, from where it is 300 km to Beverly Lake or an extra 100 km of open-water paddling to the community of Baker Lake. Great Canadian Ecoventures (see below) offers guided trips down the section of the Thelon River that flows through the sanctuary. Prices start at $2500 (out of Winnipeg)

for a 16-day expedition. Using this company's facilities and planes but floating down unescorted will save 30-40%.

Great Canadian Ecoventures

This well-established company, based at **Kasba Lake** at the headwaters of the **Kazan River,** offers a variety of options for wilderness adventures. The best feature is the flexibility. For experienced wilderness canoeists, do-it-yourself trips allow a large saving. The Kazan River is the most popular for independent travelers, although the Thelon, Dubawnt, and Elk rivers are all possibilities. Sample prices, including round-trip air charter from Winnipeg to Kasba Lake, one night and three meals at Kasba Lake Lodge, canoes, paddles, maps, and air-charter pick-up, are from $1135 per person for an eight-day paddle or $2305 for a 35-day paddle along the entire length of the Kazan River. Escorted canoe trips start at $2500 for eight days and $3925 for a series of "Dance with the Wildlife" tours, based at known grazing and crossing areas and hosted by experts in various fields of study. For information write to Great Canadian Ecoventures, P.O. Box 25181, Winnipeg, MB R2V 4C8, Canada; tel. (204) 586-4584.

REPULSE BAY (NAUJAT)

Although Repulse Bay was used as a refuge for whaling ships, a permanent settlement wasn't established until 1962. The community is located right on the Arctic Circle, at the south side of an isthmus between the Gulf of Boothia and Hudson Bay. The community sits on sloping land, overlooking Repulse Bay, and with steep coastline cliffs on either side. The bay is good for whalewatching, especially in August when belugas and narwhals can often be seen from the shoreline. Contact the hamlet office, General Delivery, Repulse Bay, NT X0C 0H0; tel. (819) 462-9952, for details of outfitters offering fishing trips or tours up the coast to either **Harbour Island**—the site of an old whaling camp—or a stone house built in 1846 by explorer John Rae.

Practicalities

Naujat Co-op Hotel, General Delivery, tel. (819) 462-4304, has private bathrooms and a TV

polar bear

room; $200 per person includes three meals. **Calm Air,** tel. 645-2846, flies three times weekly from Rankin Inlet into Repulse Bay; $322 one way, $345 for a 14-day APEX round trip.

Wager Bay

Isolated, rugged terrain and a rich food base contribute to make Wager Bay—which penetrates 150 km into the Arctic tundra—prime habitat for a wide variety of land and sea mammals. This abundance of wildlife has led to proposals that the bay and a wide strip around its perimeter be designated a national park. The south shore is one of the Arctic's major polar bear denning sites. Ice floes, which remain in the bay until midsummer, make hunting ringed seals easy for the bears. Seals, in turn, are attracted by healthy populations of arctic char. On the land, caribou graze on the tundra throughout summer, attracting wolves and wolverines. In contrast to other flatter areas of the barrenlands, the landscape surrounding the bay features 500-meter cliffs, prime nesting sites for the rare gyrfalcon, waterfalls cascading down glacially carved rock, and rocky crests, with sweeping panoramas of the bay.

The closest community to Wager Bay is Repulse Bay, 160 air km northeast and much farther by boat, making it too far for Inuit hunters. **Sila Lodge,** 774 Bronx Ave., Winnipeg, MB R2K 4E9, tel. (204) 663-1411 or (800) 663-9832, located on the shoreline, is the only accommodation in the bay. The cost of staying at the lodge is, as you'd expect, very expensive.

Seven nights, including air charter from Baker Lake, boat tours, and all meals, is $3500.

CORAL HARBOUR (SALLIQ)

Coral Harbour (population 500) is the only community on 40,663-square-km **Southampton Island,** a large island of low, rolling hills that rises from the waters of the north end of Hudson Bay. Upon its shores one of the Arctic's most intriguing tragedies occurred in 1902-03 when the last remaining **Sallirmiut Inuit** mysteriously died. The Hudson's Bay Company established a post on **Coats Island** to the south, to serve fleets of whalers. In 1927 it was moved to the head of South Bay on Southampton Island to serve Inuit who had been moved to a newly established Anglican mission. The community today is very traditional, relying heavily on the abundance of sea mammals in the immediate vicinity.

Coral Harbour is the best jumping-off point for trips to the large walrus colonies in the region; the animals gather in the thousands along the coast and on Coats and Depot islands. Other mammals often seen are polar bears and ringed and bearded seals. Also on Southampton Island is the **Harry Gibbons Bird Sanctuary,** a nesting site for various species of geese, including 200,000 lesser snow geese. And within hiking distance of Coral Harbour are the spectacular **Kirchoffer Falls** and various historic and prehistoric sites.

The Mystery Of The Sallirmiut

Arctic historians engage in much speculation as to who the Sallirmiut were and what caused their demise. But it is known that in the winter of 1902-03, after surviving on a bleak and inhospitable spit of land for many hundreds of years, they all died. They may have descended from the Dorset Culture, who disappeared elsewhere in the north around 700 years ago, or from the Thule, who had evolved into the Inuit culture found elsewhere in the Canadian Arctic. Whoever their ancestors, this splinter group settled at **Native Point,** 60 km southeast of the community of Coral Harbour, and remained in near-total isolation, culturally distinct from the rest of the world. They lived a Stone Age existence until that fateful winter earlier this century, building homes from stone, sod, and whalebone, and hunting sea mammals with flint-headed weapons. Their demise was probably caused by contact with a whaling fleet that transmitted a disease such as dysentery or smallpox—killing off the entire Sallirmiut population in one long winter. The following year visitors to the settlement found bodies everywhere, with dogs being the only sign of life.

The site, a two-hour boat trip from Coral Harbour, attracts few visitors. But walking around the 100-odd houses with sun-bleached bones scattering the rocky ground provokes feelings of veneration for a now-extinct culture that, after surviving unbelievable natural hardships, was wiped out by fellow man.

Practicalities

The two lodges at Coral Harbour are **Esungark Hotel,** Katudgevik Co-op, Coral Harbour, NT X0C 0C0, tel. (819) 925-9969, which sleeps 12 in three rooms, $150 per person, and **Leonie's Place,** P.O. Box 29, tel. 925-9751, which has six double rooms, $180 per person. Both rates include three meals. Ask at the hamlet office about camping.

Calm Air, tel. 645-2846, flies three times weekly from Rankin Inlet to Coral Harbour; $322 one way, $354 for a 14-day APEX round trip. Once a week **First Air,** tel. 925-9767 or (800) 267-1247, flies from Rankin Inlet to Coral Harbour and across Foxe Channel to Cape Dorset and Iqaluit on Baffin Island. For details of outfitters contact the hamlet office, tel. 925-8867.

BAFFIN AND BEYOND

Baffin Island, the surrounding administrative region, and the islands of the high Arctic sit atop the continent of North America—a vast, rugged, virtually uninhabitable, and relatively unexplored part of the world that has only recently been viewed as a viable travel destination. Within this area are endless opportunities for adventure travel, whether it's hiking in two of the world's most remote national parks, canoeing a Canadian Heritage River, climbing the towering peaks along the spectacular fiords of North Baffin Island, or making the ultimate trip—to the North Pole. If you're looking for something equally satisfying but less challenging, you can visit the many prehistoric Thule sites, chase the legend of the ill-fated Franklin Expedition, view the abundant sea mammals from the safety of a boat, visit islands that are home to millions of seabirds, learn more about the Inuit culture by visiting the 14 communities, and, yes, you too can visit the North Pole, with a champagne lunch thrown in.

Baffin Island is the world's sixth-largest island (after Australia, New Guinea, New Guinea, Borneo, and Madagascar) at 507,500 square km. Most of the island is lowland arctic, made up of gently rolling hills, rarely rising more than 700 meters above sea level and broken only occasionally by a rocky headland or bluff. The southern end of the island is made up of three distinct peninsulas, two of which are separated by **Frobisher Bay** where **Iqaluit,** largest town in the region, lies. In lower-central Baffin Island, northwest of Iqaluit, is the **Great Plain of the Koukdjuak,** which rose so quickly from the surrounding sea that colonies of seals became landlocked in two large lakes and have evolved into freshwater mammals. The northeastern coast of Baffin Island, from Cumberland Peninsula to Bylot Island, is the mountainous Arctic. Here, glaciated peaks rising over 2,000 meters are incised by steep-sided fiords cutting deeply into the land. **Auyuittuq National Park,** on Cumberland Peninsula, is the most accessible part of this spectacular region and attracts hikers and mountaineers from around the world.

For information on the Baffin region write to: Baffin Tourism Association, P.O. Box 1450, Iqaluit, NT X0A 0H0; tel. (819) 979-6651 or (800) 661-0788. The 300-page *Baffin Handbook* is excellent reading and packed with hints for anyone planning an extended trip through the region. For a copy send $18.50 (includes postage and GST) to P.O. Box 8, Iqaluit, NT X0A 0H0.

IQALUIT

Iqaluit is the government, transportation, and administrative center for all eastern Arctic communities. In 1999, the town—which was known as **Frobisher Bay** until 1987—will become capital of Canada's new territory, Nunavut. The terrain on which the community is built is uninspiring, a glacially scoured landscape of rocky ridges and exposed bedrock. The land is dotted with many lakes, the coastline with many islands. It is located on Koojesse Inlet at the northwest head of **Frobisher Bay** on southern Baffin Island. The Canadian capital, Ottawa (2,080 km south), is closer than the territorial capital, Yellowknife (2,260 km west).

The first recorded contact the local Inuit had with Europeans was in 1576 when Sir Martin Frobisher entered the bay that now bears his name. He was searching for the Northwest Passage. Instead he found ore samples that he mistakenly thought were gold. He returned with 15 ships and had established a camp before the mistake was realized. Although whalers frequented the area in the 18th and 19th centuries, it wasn't until after the construction of the north's largest United States Air Force base in 1942 that the community took hold. The Hudson's Bay Company established a post, and in 1959 the federal government moved its regional headquarters to the townsite. Although many of the 2,000 Inuit who live here earn a wage, Iqaluit is still relatively traditional.

Sights
The best place to begin a visit is **Unikkaarik Visitors Centre,** located on the beach at the southeast end of town. The staff supplies brochures and maps and can set up trips with local outfitters. (You'll need a map; although there are street signs, no one uses them.) Also here is a life-size marble carving of an Inuit drum dancer and a model of the inside of a Thule sod house. Next door, housed in a restored Hudson's Bay Company post, is the **Nunatta Sunagutangit Museum,** housing a collection of prehistoric and historic artifacts. Farther along the beach is a sod house. Behind the visitors center is Arctic Ventures gift shop and, farther up the hill, a lookout and another gift shop. From this gift shop a gravel road leads five km east to **Apex,** a residential part of Iqaluit. Before Apex, a road leads to some historic Hudson's Bay Company buildings.

Most businesses, including the airport, are to the west of the visitors center. A 15-minute walk south from the airport is **Sylvia Grinnell Territorial Park,** 148 hectares of rolling Arctic tundra. Over 160 species of plants have been recorded in the park, and the cliffs there provide excellent views across the bay. A trail leads up Sylvia Grinnell River, but the going is rough.

Qaummaarviit Historic Park
Twelve km west of Iqaluit near Peale Point, a small island (connected to the mainland only at low tide) has been inhabited intermittently for nearly 1,000 years. Thule Inuit, who migrated from Alaska, settled on the island for the abundance of both sea and land mammals in the vicinity. More than 3,000 tools and 20,000 bones have been discovered. Today, a series of boardwalks leads through the sod houses on the south end of the island and through a shallow valley to graves and tent rings.

Outfitters
To get to Qaummaarviit you'll need to use the services of an outfitter. Both **Qairrulik Outfitting,** P.O. Box 863, Iqaluit, NT X0A 0H0, tel. (819) 979-6280, and **North Winds,** P.O. Box 849, tel. 979-0551, offer trips to the island; $90-130 per person includes a bannock meal. You can also charter a boat from either company for fishing, whale-watching, or taking a trip to fossil beds.

Events
Toonik Tyme, a weeklong festival at the end of April, is a celebration of spring with traditional Inuit games, a snowmobile race to Lake Harbour, harpoon throwing, igloo building, and a community feast.

IQALUIT

NOT TO SCALE

FEDERAL RD.

AIRPORT

AIRPORT INN

NAVIGATOR INN

FROBISHER INN

DISCOVERY LODGE

ASTRO HILL COMPLEX

HOSPITAL

APEX RD.

TO APEX

BAYSHORE INN

NORTHERN

ARCTIC VENTURES

LOOKOUT

VISITORS CENTRE
MUSEUM

TO SYLVIA GRINNELL T. P.

KOOJESSE INLET

© MOON PUBLICATIONS, INC.

Accommodations

Iqaluit has five hotels, a couple of B&Bs, and a campground. **Airport Inn,** P.O. Box 148, tel. (819) 979-4336, is basic but each room has a kitchenette; $115 s, $130 d. Other choices are: **Bayshore Inn,** P.O. Box 1240, tel. 979-6733, with good views but simple rooms, $125 s, $130 d; **Frobisher Inn,** P.O. Box 610, tel. 979-2222, which has a good restaurant, $131 s, $140 d; **Discovery Lodge,** P.O. Box 387, tel. 979-4433, the pick of the bunch, $141 s or d; and **Navigator Inn,** P.O. Box 158, tel. 979-6201, across the road from the Discovery, $145 s, $150 d.

The bed and breakfasts are in Apex, five km east of town. They are **By-the-sea B&B,** P.O. Box 341, tel. 979-0219, and **Kamotiq Inn,** P.O. Box 54, tel. 979-5937. Both are $75 s, $95 d including breakfast and transportation from the airport.

Camping is available at **Sylvia Grinnell Territorial Park,** a 15-minute walk ($5 taxi ride) from the airport. The park's facilities include tent platforms, foul-weather shelters, pit toilets, and fire rings.

Food

Coffee shops are located in **Northern** and the **Navigator Inn,** while a small bakery is located in the Astro Hill Complex. For something more substantial, the **Navigator Inn** is a favorite, especially on Friday nights for pizza. The rest of the week, arctic char and caribou are served and there's a good salad bar. For dessert, fresh fruit is flown in and delicious chocolate crepes, made in-house, are served. All other hotels have licensed dining with local specialties such as Cumberland Sound scallops, seal, and shrimp served in season. The **Kamotiq Inn** has two dining areas—an igloo-shaped dome and an enclosed patio, complete with umbrellas. They offer a buffet lunch as well as regular lunch and dinner menus that include the only Mexican food in town.

Transportation

The distinctive yellow terminal, a short walk from downtown Iqaluit, is a northern landmark. The airport is always busy and handles 10,000 take-offs and landings per year. **Canadian North,**

Travel by dog team is a unique way to visit the sights around Iqaluit.

WOLFGANG WEBER/NWT ECONOMIC DEVELOPMENT & TOURISM

tel. (819) 979-6470 or (800) 665-1177, and **First Air,** tel. 979-5396 or (800) 267-1247, fly from Yellowknife to Iqaluit via Resolute ($770 one way, $709 for a 14-day APEX round trip) and to Montreal ($715 one way, $820 round trip). **NWT Air,** tel. 979-6905 or (800) 661-0789, also flies from Yellowknife, but via Rankin Inlet; $755 one way, $740 round trip. First Air also links Iqaluit to communities in the Keewatin, along the Arctic coast and to Nuuk, in Greenland.

Air Baffin, tel. 979-4018, has scheduled flights to all communities on South Baffin Island. They also have flightseeing from $90 per person for a 30-minute tour.

Services And Information

Iqaluit has a post office, banks, one-hour photo developing, a hospital, and an indoor pool. The **Unikkaarvik Visitors Centre,** tel. (819) 979-4636, has all the information you'll need for touring through the Baffin region; open year-round, Mon.-Fri. 10 a.m.-noon and 1-7 p.m., Sat.-Sun. noon-7 p.m. The local newspaper, *Nunatsiaq News,* tel. 979-5357, comes out weekly and is available by subscription; C$30 per year, C$45 from the United States.

LAKE HARBOUR (KIMMIRUT)

This community, on the south coast of **Meta Incognita Peninsula** 120 km south of Iqaluit, overlooks a picturesque harbor. The peninsula is separated from the mainland of northern Que-

bec by Hudson Strait. From the low peaks of this peninsula flows **Soper River,** one of the world's great wilderness canoeing rivers. Jutting westward are the low-lying wetlands of **Foxe Peninsula.** In spring the nearby floe edge is a good place for viewing sea mammals.

The anchorage of Lake Harbour was the most important on South Baffin Island for whaling ships. The Hudson's Bay Company opened a post in 1911, and during WW II a radio station was set up. Although most of the population moved to Iqaluit in the 1960s, the local Inuit population of 350 remains steady, hunting, fishing, and carving local soapstone, distinguished by its apple green color.

A limestone outcrop, immediately to the east, has good views. A variety of geological formations and flora can be found close to town. To the northwest is a chain of lakes including **Shoogle Lake,** which has a 60-meter waterfall at its far end. Many of the lakes offer excellent fishing for landlocked arctic char. **Akavak Outfitting,** General Delivery, Lake Harbour, NT X0A 0N0, takes boat trips to 3,500-year-old archaeological sites at McKellar Bay and Cape Tanfield. They also rent canoes and other gear for trips down the Soper River.

Practicalities

Kimik Co-op Hotel, P.O. Box 69, tel. (819) 939-2093, has 12 rooms with private bathrooms; $185 per person includes three meals. Although the community has no established campgrounds, the beach is only a short walk from the airport and, with advance bookings, you can eat at the hotel. White gas and groceries are available at the co-op.

First Air, tel. (800) 267-1247, serves Lake Harbour three times weekly from Iqaluit; $119 one way, $157 for a 14-day APEX round trip.

Katannilik Territorial Park

The watershed of the **Soper River** is protected by this 1,500-square-km park that spans Meta Incognita Peninsula from Frobisher Bay to the community of Lake Harbour near Hudson Strait. The Soper River has carved out a deep valley near **Mt. Joy** (610 meters) and becomes wider and shallower as it flows through low-lying wetlands to the south. To the east the peninsula is nearly devoid of vegetation but the river valley is carpeted in colorful wildflowers and is lined with willow bushes. The most common mammals are arctic foxes and arctic hares. A herd of 3,000 caribou grazes throughout the area. Ermines and lemmings are also present. Just upstream from **Fleming Hill** is one of the world's few deposits of high-quality lapis lazuli. Four km north of Lake Harbour is **Soper Lake.** At the southern outlet are reversing falls where water drains out of the lake at low tide and pours back in again at high tide. At the north end of the lake is **Soper Falls.**

The easiest way to explore the park is on foot from Lake Harbour. Two designated landing strips can be accessed by Twin Otter or helicopter from Iqaluit from where you can hike to Lake Harbour. The third, and most challenging option, is to charter a boat in Iqaluit and be dropped at the northeast corner of the park. The hike from here to Lake Harbour would be 120 km. Park information and trail maps are available at Unikkaarvik Visitors Centre in Iqaluit or from the park at P.O. Box 1000, Iqaluit, NT X0A 0H0; tel. (819) 979-4636. **Country Walkers,** P.O. Box 180, Waterbury, VT 05676-0180, U.S.A., tel. (802) 244-1387, offers seven-day, fully guided hiking trips for all abilities into the park from mid-July to August; $2600 from Iqaluit.

lake trout

BOB RACE

CAPE DORSET (KINGAIT)

For a community recognized around the world for fine arts and crafts, the cluster of weathered houses on a small island off the southwest coast of Baffin Island bears little resemblance to an art colony. Cape Dorset is named for the remains of an ancient people who flourished in the area between 1000 B.C. and A.D. 1000. The cape is actually an island, attached to the Foxe Peninsula of southwest Baffin Island only at low tide. The Hudson's Bay Company established a trading post at the cape in 1913, and in 1953 a nursing station was built to help avert diseases that ravaged other communities. Also in this year James Houston, an award-winning writer, and his wife arrived. They spent 10 years working with the local Inuit, encouraging the development of soapstone carving and printmaking. They also initiated the formation of the **West Baffin Eskimo Co-operative,** which has since gained international recognition for the artists it represents. Today the industry is worth $4 million annually with 75% of the local residents earning all or part of their income from the production of art.

Called soapstone, but really a form of serpentine, the soft rock used for carving is generally a mottled dark green. It is found 130 km east of Cape Dorset at **Korak Inlet,** and many artists spend summer at this site. If you walk around the streets of Cape Dorset you'll see artists at work, but to buy work head to the co-op overlooking the bay, tel. (819) 897-8944. Also of interest are numerous Thule sites, including two within walking distance of the airport. **Mallikjuak Island** can be reached on foot at low tide and has some high peaks offering good views and more archaeological sites.

Practicalities

Kingnait Inn, General Delivery, Cape Dorset, NT X0A 0C0, tel. (819) 897-8863, has 17 rooms with private bathrooms; $200 per person including three meals. No designated camping areas exist, but anywhere out of sight of the community should be all right. Nonguests may eat at the hotel with advance reservations. The hotel also has takeaway service.

The airstrip, within walking distance of the hotel, is served by **First Air,** tel. (800) 267-1247, three times weekly from Iqaluit; $240 one way, $336 for a 14-day APEX round trip. These flights continue to Rankin Inlet.

BELCHER ISLANDS

Chances are, these islands will never make the cover of *Islands* magazine, nor will they ever be on the main tourist trail. But for those who seek them out, the enchanting lifestyle of local Ungava Inuit and the absolute isolation the islands afford will be unforgettable.

The islands are spread over 5,000 square km of southern Hudson Bay—low, barren, and windswept, with only one settlement, that of **Sanikiluaq** on Flaherty Island. Although geographically and culturally removed from the rest of the Northwest Territories, the islands are nevertheless politically a part, administered from Iqaluit 1,024 km to the north.

Inuit migrated to the islands from northern Quebec 200 years ago, but with no airstrip, surrounded by shallow waters, and a four-day kayak trip from the mainland, they remained almost forgotten.

The lack of land mammals meant that the Inuit had no source of furs for clothing. But living near one of the densest wildfowl nesting areas in Hudson Bay, the Inuit became one of the few peoples in the world to use feathered bird skins for clothing. Their tradition of making such clothing remains, although today they supplement their wardrobe with modern down-filled garb. The islanders are also known for their carvings of bird figures from dark green argillite.

Practicalities
Amaulik Hotel, Mitiq Co-op, Sanikiluaq, NT X0A 0W0, tel. (819) 266-8821, has accommodations for 18 in seven rooms with shared bath; $175 per person includes three meals. The campground, on a gravel beach north of the harbor, can become windy. Access to the islands is by **Air Tindi,** tel. (514) 636-9445, from Great Whale River (marked on some maps as Kuujjuarapik) and La Grande in Quebec.

HALL BEACH (SANIRAJAK)

Although part of the mainland, the flat, lowland region of Melville Peninsula, separated from Baffin Island by the narrow Fury and Hecla Strait, is part of the Baffin region. On its northeastern coastline are the communities of **Hall Beach** and **Igloolik,** good bases for fishing trips or exploring Thule historic sites.

Thule Inuit have hunted and fished on the peninsula for 7,000 years. A D.E.W. Line station, constructed in 1955, attracted Inuit who stayed and became dependent on a wage economy. A few years ago, when news reached the Inuit that the 20-meter radar screens were to be dismantled, they asked that the screens remain—they served as ideal landmarks on the otherwise featureless tundra. Their request was granted.

Hall Beach certainly isn't the place to come for scenery but there is good arctic char fishing and viewing of sea mammals such as walrus and seals. Numerous archaeological sites are located in the area, including the Uglit Islands four km offshore, where you'll find broken-down sod houses and grave sites. Between town and the airstrip are the remains of a whale, estimated to be 500 years old. **Siqjariaqjuk Outfitting,** General Delivery, Hall Beach, NT X0A 0K0, can organize dogsled, snowmobile, and boat trips. Ask about a crashed Lancaster Bomber from WW II, 60 km from the community.

Practicalities
Hall Beach Hotel, General Delivery, tel. (819) 928-8952, has five rooms, each with three beds; $170 per person with three meals. Ask here or at the hamlet office about camping.

Canadian North, tel. 928-8845 or (800) 665-1177, and **First Air,** tel. (800) 267-1247, fly twice weekly from Iqaluit to Hall Beach; $407 one way, $448 for a 14-day APEX round trip.

IGLOOLIK (IGLULIK)

North of Hall Beach is Igloolik, large by Arctic standards, with the usual clutter of buildings. It is surrounded by low-lying topography and is a small island, separated from the mainland by Hector Strait. Archaeological sites on the island provide records of nearly unbroken habitation since 2000 B.C. Captain William Parry spent the winter of 1822-23 on the island; a grave of one of his English sailors who died in the spring is located just outside town. Before the Hudson's Bay Company established a post in 1939, the Inuit had traveled to Pond Inlet and Repulse Bay to trade. Of the various Thule and Dorset sites, those at Ungalujat Point, 18 km from Igloolik, including a ceremonial house, are the most interesting. In town, the **Igloolik Research Centre,** tel. (819) 934-8836, a large, mushroom-shaped building, is a government facility for scientific research and also functions as a weather and seismic station. They also have a general Arctic reference section and small library.

Practicalities

Tujormivik Hotel, General Delivery, Igloolik, NT X0A 0L0, tel. (819) 934-8814, is $175 per person per day including three meals, usually local game or pastas in the evening. Ask here about outfitters for fishing and wildlife viewing. There is no set area for camping; ask at the hamlet office, tel. 934-8830.

First Air, tel. (800) 267-1247, flies from Iqaluit to Igloolik four times weekly; $407 one way, or $428 for a 14-day APEX round trip.

PANGNIRTUNG (PANNIQTUUQ)

This community sits in a spectacular setting, flanked by sheer cliffs rising nearly 1,000 meters out of Pangnirtung Fiord. Most visitors come here on their way to somewhere even more awesome, **Auyuittuq National Park** (see below).

The fiord was a base for whalers as early as 1840 but it wasn't until 1921, a decade after the decline of the whaling industry, that the Hudson's Bay Company established a trading post. Through the years a community has grown with Inuit from other areas moving here. Today, with a population of 1,100, "Pang," as it's best known, is Baffin Island's second-largest community.

Although the national park to the north is the main drawcard, the picturesque community itself is worth exploring. The **Ukama Trail** follows a well-worn path from behind the arena along the west bank of Duval River, passing numerous waterfalls; six km (2.5 hours) one way. Another trail, to the top of **Mt. Duval** (670 meters), begins near the campground and is seven km (3-3.5 hours) each way. The views from the summit are spectacular, but the hike is strenuous.

Kekerten Historic Park

For nearly a century, hundreds of whaling ships plied the waters of the Baffin region. Instead of returning to their European or American ports, many overwintered here at the end of the short summer season. This historic park, on a small island south of Pangnirtung, is one of two shore-based whaling stations in the eastern Arctic. The site has been partially restored; interpretive signs explain the importance of the artifacts and foundations that remain. The *Easonian,* a ship used to hunt beluga whales, burned in 1922 and is visible at low tide. From May to mid-June, access to the island is by snowmobile, after mid-July by boat. **Leopa Akpalialuk Outfitting,** P.O. Box 305, Pangnirtung, NT X0A 0R0, tel. (819) 473-8988, offers a 12-hour trip including lunch for $420 for two people. The price drops to $85 per person for a group of six.

Accommodations And Food

Auyuittuq Lodge, General Delivery, tel. (819) 473-8955, is located on a slight rise overlooking an old whaling station and the fiord. Their 50 rooms with shared bath and laundry cost $120 per person; $65 extra for three meals. The rate includes airport transfers. **Pisuktinu Tungavik Territorial Campground** is located east of town over the Duval River, a 20-minute walk from the airport. The campground is free but has only pit toilets (ask at Auyuittuq Lodge for showers). In bad weather the Anglican Church, behind Northern, opens its doors to campers. Groceries and white gas are available at **Northern.**

The dining room in Auyuittuq Lodge was renovated in the mid-'80s. Fixed-price dinners cost $30 per person, with arctic char served in season. Mealtimes are 7-9 a.m., noon-1 p.m., and 6-7 p.m.; reservations required. Near the airport is a snack bar.

Services And Information

The **airport** is located behind the main community and within walking distance of all services. **First Air,** tel. (800) 267-1247, has six flights weekly from Iqaluit; $197 one way, $226 for a

14-day APEX round trip. Connections can also be made from Yellowknife ($989 round trip) and Montreal ($904 round trip).

Angmarlik Visitors Centre has information on the community, relics from whaling days, a library, and Inuit elders on hand to interpret the area's natural history. The staff here can also organize outfitters and trips to a char-fishing camp 20 km from Pangnirtung; open in summer, daily 9 a.m.-9 p.m.; tel. 473-8737.

AUYUITTUQ NATIONAL PARK

Auyuittuq, meaning "The Land that Never Melts," is a 21,000-square-km wilderness of vast icefields, glacial lakes, some of the world's highest cliffs, and one long valley paralleled by peaks nearly 3,000 meters high. The most popular trip within this totally undeveloped park is the hiking over **Akshayak Pass** (also called Pangnirtung Pass).

The Land

The park is part of a spine of mountains along the **Cumberland Peninsula,** which was formed by the same forces of Continental Drift that separated Baffin Island from Greenland. Draped over these mountains is **Penny Ice Cap,** a sheet of ice up to 300 meters thick that covers 6,000 square km. This icefield is drained on all sides by glaciers, slow-moving rivers of ice that have sculpted many of the park's features, including a 97-km-long valley that cuts across Cumberland Peninsula. The highest elevation of the valley occurs midway along its length at Akshayak Pass (500 meters). From the pass, the **Weasel River** flows south to Summit Lake and South Pangnirtung Fiord, and the **Owl River** flows north into Davis Strait. Along the southern half of the valley are Mounts Asgard, Thor, and Overlord, steep granite peaks that attract climbers from around the world.

Flora And Fauna

Plantlife in the pass is best observed around summer solstice when the ground is carpeted by masses of purple **willow herbs, arctic poppies,** and **arctic willow.** This sparse vegetation supports very few species of animals. The **lemming** is the most common mammal, although their numbers differ dramatically from season to season. Also common are the large **arctic hare** and the small **arctic fox.** Although the **polar bear** is essentially a seal hunter, it occasionally wanders inland to feed on berries. **Caribou,** rare in the pass but occasionally seen in the northwest corner of the park, are hunted by **wolves.** Birds most commonly seen are **ptarmigan, ravens,** and **snowy owls.** The **red-throated loon** is also common during the short nesting season. **Cape Searle,** adjacent to the park, is the breeding ground for 10,000 **northern fulmars.**

Practicalities

A trip to Auyuittuq requires advance planning, preparation, and, for those attempting the pass, experience in the wilderness. Hikers must ford swiftly flowing streams and negotiate ankle-wrenching slopes of glacial moraine. No services are available, and the barren land offers no trees to block the wind or provide firewood. Most trips begin with a boat or snowmobile trip (Pangnirtung Fiord is choked with ice until mid-July) from Pangnirtung to **Overlord Warden Station** ($205 for two, $25 per extra person) where a campground is set among huge boulders. Many hikers travel only as far as Summit Lake, returning to Overlord the same way. This section of the trail is the most inspiring and also crosses the **Arctic Circle,** which is flanked by the towering peaks of Mt. Odin to the west and Mt. Thor to the east. The second half of the valley is broader and less impressive, its terrain is more rugged, and it is traveled by fewer people. If you plan to hike the entire pass, you will have to prearrange a pick-up at Broughton Island. Travel is by snowmobile or dogsled in early summer and by boat after mid-August. Although the most popular time of year for hiking is July and August, late June is good for the 24 hours of daylight.

Park information centers are located in Pangnirtung, tel. (819) 473-8828, and Broughton Island, tel. 927-8834. For further information on the park write to Auyuittuq National Park, P.O. Box 353, Pangnirtung, NT X0A 0R0. Each center has topographical maps of the park ($9 each) and fishing licenses ($3).

BROUGHTON ISLAND (QIKIQTARJUAQ)

On an island of the same name, this community of 500 Inuit adjoins an area rich with seals, whales, and polar bears. The community is located off the east coast of Baffin Island on a raised beach flanked by glaciated hills. It is a five- to six-hour trip from the terminus of the Akshayak Pass hiking trail in Auyuittuq National Park, and it is for that reason that many people spend time here. The community came into being when Inuit families were moved to the site to help construct a D.E.W. Line station in 1956. **Pikaluvak Outfitting,** General Delivery, Broughton Island, NT X0A 0B0, tel. (819) 927-8316, has a 10-meter boat for drop-offs and pick-ups in Auyuittuq ($220 one way for two), or for viewing the abundant icebergs, sea mammals, and colonies of seabirds along the Baffin Island coast.

Practicalities

If you're planning a trip with Pikaluvak Outfitting, ask about their Quonset hut (no running water or electricity) for $35 per night. **Tulugak Co-op Hotel,** General Delivery, tel. (819) 927-8833, has rooms with private baths and is close to the airport; $185 per person includes three meals. The campground has running water, tent platforms, and is one km from the community. **Northern** sells groceries and white gas.

First Air, tel. (800) 267-1247, flies six times weekly from Iqaluit to Broughton Island with some flights stopping at Pangnirtung; $277 one way, $388 for a 14-day APEX round trip.

CLYDE RIVER (KANGIQLUGAAPIK)

This remote community is located on a floodplain, surrounded by mountainous scenery. It's near the mouth of Clyde Inlet, a fiord that slices southwest into the mountainous east coast of Baffin Island. Most of the 500 residents of Clyde River live a traditional lifestyle, fishing and hunting. The site has never been a traditional hunting ground but Inuit families moved here in the 1950s when the Hudson's Bay Company opened a post to take advantage of high seal prices.

Sawtooth Mountain, 25 km from the community, is a good vantage point for viewing the surrounding peaks and bays. Unfortunately, to reach most other sights in the area will require the services of an outfitter. **Qullikkut,** P.O. Box 27, Clyde River, NT X0A 0E0, offers a variety of fishing and sightseeing trips. Rates are $275 per person per day by dog team and $300 per person by boat. At Cape Hewitt, 35 km from town, are tent rings from the Thule culture; at Cape Christian is an abandoned U.S. Coast Guard Station; and farther down the coast is **Isobella Bay,** breeding ground for many of the world's remaining bowhead whales. These slow, copepod-eating whales were decimated by whalers in the 1800s and their numbers have never recovered.

Practicalities

Qammaq Hotel, General Delivery, tel. (819) 924-6222, charges $190 per person including three meals. Camping is $100 per week, which includes use of bathroom facilities. Meals are available at the hotel, groceries from **Northern.**

First Air, tel. (800) 267-1247, flies from Iqaluit; $402 one way, $553 for a 14-day APEX round trip.

POND INLET (MITTIMATALIK)

In late spring and early summer the waterways around Pond Inlet host the highest concentrations of sea mammals in the eastern Arctic. Narwhal, beluga, and bowhead whales, polar bears, seals, and walruses can all be viewed from the floe edge or a boat. Across the channel from the community is **Bylot Island Bird Sanctuary.** In summer 50 species of birds nest here, including tens of thousands of murres and kittiwakes and a major part of the world's snow goose population. Also on the island are hoodoos, archaeological sites, and glaciated peaks rising to 2,000 meters.

The first Europeans in the area, Robert Bylot and William Baffin, came in 1616, but the local Inuit, who have strong links to the Greenland Thule, hunted in the area well before then. The first permanent settlement on the southern shore of Eclipse Sound was an RCMP post established in 1921. The community has grown to 800, mostly Inuit, living in a brightly colored clump of civilization overlooking Bylot Island.

Mt. Herodier (765 meters) is a 15-km (one way) hike from town with only one difficult stream crossing. If the weather cooperates, kayaking is a great way to explore Eclipse Sound. Eclipse Sound Outfitting, P.O. Box 60, Pond Inlet, NT X0A 0S0, tel. (819) 899-8817, rents kayaks for $45 per day. The company can also organize snowmobile trips to the floe edge (best time for wildlife viewing is early July), dogsled trips around the sound, and boat trips to historic sites and over to Bylot Island. The rate is $300 per person per day, which includes all meals and overnight accommodations.

Practicalities

Saunig Hotel, General Delivery, tel. (819) 899-8928, has 15 rooms, each with two single beds and a private bathroom; $215 per person per day includes three meals. The hotel has a gift shop selling carvings and can set up tours onto the sound. Salmon Creek, two km west of town, has a campground with tent platforms. You can also pitch your tent on the beach just west of town. Meals are available with advance reser-

Although the Inuit have been strongly influenced by white settlers, many retain a traditional lifestyle.

vations at the hotel; groceries are available from **Northern.**

First Air, tel. (800) 267-1247, flies from Iqaluit each evening to Pond Inlet; $529 one way, $727 for a 14-day APEX round trip. **Field Guides,** P.O. Box 160723, Austin, Texas 78716-0723, U.S.A., tel. (512) 327-4953, offers a 10-day tour that incorporates all the best wildlife-viewing spots on Eclipse Sound and Bylot Island; $2650 from Pond Inlet.

ARCTIC BAY AND VICINITY

The northern reaches of Baffin Island are made up of two peninsulas, **Borden** and **Brodeur.** These desolate plateaus of land are divided by **Admiralty Inlet,** the world's longest fiord and also one of the deepest. No one knows just how deep it is, but at one point its depth is so great that, combined with upwellings of water, currents, and tides, an expanse of water remains ice-free year-round. This phenomenon, which has intrigued scientists for decades, is known as a polynya. The only inhabited area is on Borden Peninsula.

Arctic Bay (Ikpiarjuk)

Arctic Bay is surrounded on three sides by hills and on the fourth by **Admiralty Inlet.** The only road in the Baffin region connects the community of 500 to **Nanisivik,** to the east. The area has been occupied by nomadic Inuit hunters for nearly 5,000 years. The first permanent settlement was a Hudson's Bay Company post established in 1924. Remains of prehistoric cultures can be found around the area, including **Uluksan Point,** a low-lying area to the west of the community. To the east is a distinctive cairn, erected by the crew of a government steamer who wintered here in 1910-11.

Lancaster Sound

Between the northern tip of Baffin Island and the rugged southern coast of Devon Island is Lancaster Sound, the eastern entrance to the **Northwest Passage.** Each year tens of thousands of sea mammals migrate through this corridor, in turn attracting seabirds and polar bears. Each spring they must wait at the floe edge that spans the sound, until the ice has broken up and they are free to travel through to the islands of the high Arctic. This spectacle of mammals and birds is the destination of a high Arctic expedition offered by **Niglasuk Co.**, Arctic Bay, NT X0A 0A0, tel. (819) 439-9949. Four seven-night trips are undertaken each June, with a base camp established on the shoreline closest to the floe edge and daily trips made to view the wildlife. The cost is $3500 per person from Arctic Bay. This tour books up months in advance.

Prince Leopold Island is a flat-topped, barren island of 85 square km rising 300 meters from the waters northeast of Somerset Island. In summer it supports four species of seabirds who nest in the hundreds of thousands on the island's narrow ledges. The island has been designated a migratory bird sanctuary.

Nanisivik

The infrastructure at Nanisivik, 21 km east of Arctic Bay, has been in place since 1974. It serves the 300 workers who mine the silver, lead, and zinc deposits on the shore of Strathcona Sound. To protect against the high winds that howl through camp, all buildings have curved walls. Once extracted, ore is stored on the beach for summer shipment to European markets. No tours of the mine are offered, nor are there any tourist services.

The **Midnight Sun Marathon,** which takes place on the weekend closest to 1 July, is the world's northernmost. The race, which attracts marathoners from around the world, is run between Nanisivik and Arctic Bay; the most grueling event is 84 km. For information call the mine at (819) 436-7502 or (416) 869-0772 in Toronto.

Practicalities

Enokseot Hotel, P.O. Box 69, Arctic Bay, NT X0A 0A0, tel. (819) 439-8811, charges $120 per person per night, with meals an extra $60 per person. The campground is at **Victor Bay,** five km from the community ($10 in a taxi). These accommodations are handy if you'd like to visit Lancaster Sound without forking out for a seven-day trip. If that's the case Niglasuk Co. can arrange travel to the floe edge ($400 per person per day). Food is available, cafeteria-style, at the hotel, and groceries from **Northern.**

The airport is at Nanisivik, 21 km from Arctic Bay. Taxis meet all flights. **Canadian North,** tel. 436-7493 or (800) 665-1177, and **First Air,**

tel. (800) 267-1247, fly twice weekly from Iqaluit; $519 one way, $727 for a 14-day APEX round trip. From Yellowknife both airlines fly to Nanisivik via Resolute.

RESOLUTE: GATEWAY TO THE HIGH ARCTIC (QAUSUITTUQ)

Although small, the community of Resolute is an important jumping-off point for expeditions to the high Arctic. It also holds an important scientific research station and a number of excellent outfitters. The community is located on Resolute Bay on the south coast of **Cornwallis Island,** a low-lying island on the north side of the Northwest Passage.

William Parry was the first white man to report seeing the island, and in the 1850s the island was the center of much activity during the search for the lost Franklin Expedition. In fact, the town was named after the HMS *Resolute,* one of the vessels involved in the search. An airfield established in 1947 as a weather station soon became the hub of air transportation in the high Arctic.

Since the late 1950s, Resolute has been operations base for the Polar Continental Shelf Project, a program of Arctic research. The research center and a weather station at the airport are open for tours. Near the dock is a small aquarium stocked with local specimens. The surrounding hills, once under the sea, are full of fossils, and five km west of the airport are Thule tent rings.

A Controversial Move

In 1953 Inuit families from Inukjuak, Quebec and Pond Inlet were relocated to Cornwallis Island and Southern Ellesmere Island; more followed in 1955. At the time, the Dept. of Northern Affairs and National Resources claimed the island was a land of plentiful resources and the move was for the good of the Inuit. More recently it has been revealed that they had been moved to help reinforce Canada's right to sovereignty in the islands of the high Arctic. The full story is only just beginning to be revealed but apparently, after the families were separated into two groups, they were left in a totally alien environment, with scant regard for their needs and feelings. With only a U.S. Forces garbage dump as a food source they were lucky to survive. For 35 years little was known about their plight and it wasn't until 1988 that they received their first government support and the promise of repatriation. After a two-year inquiry by the Royal Commission into Aboriginal Peoples, a report released in July 1994 concluded that "the relocation plan was an ill-conceived solution that was inhumane and damaging in its design and effects," and that "there was a significant lack of care and skill in various aspects of the project, including a severe shortage of clothing and bedding during the first winter, causing hardship and suffering." It also recommended that the Canadian government apologize and provide compensation.

High Arctic International Explorer Services

This company is the leader in high Arctic outfitting and is based in Resolute. Although they offer day-trips and accommodations, they are best known for their long expeditions, including to Polar Bear Pass, Otto Fiord on Ellesmere Island, and Qaanaaq in northern Greenland. In Resolute they offer accommodations for 10 people in six rooms; $130 per person includes three meals and transfers. For more information write to P.O. Box 200, Resolute, NT X0A 0V0; tel. (819) 252-3875.

Other Practicalities

The other, much larger, accommodation in Resolute is **Narwhal Arctic Services,** P.O. Box 88, tel. (819) 252-3968, near the airport, which sleeps 70 in 66 rooms. Meals are served cafeteria-style and the demands of government workers keep the standard of food high. Camping is available at **Resolute Lake,** one km from the airport, and at Mecham River, a further five km. **Northern** and the **post office** are by the airport and the accommodations and other services are in the Inuit village, eight km away. The road has regular traffic, and commuting between the two is relatively easy.

Resolute is a long way from anywhere; in fact London is closer than many U.S. cities. **Canadian North,** tel. 252-3880 or (800) 665-1177, and **First Air,** tel. (800) 267-1247, have flights from Yellowknife; $495 one way, $485 for a 14-day APEX round trip; and Iqaluit, $618 one way, $594 for a 14-day APEX round trip.

From Montreal the fare is $996 one way, $1016 for a 14-day APEX round trip. **Kenn Borek Air,** tel. 252-3849, and **Bradley Air Services,** tel. 252-3981, have aircraft for charter with Kenn Borek Air offering scheduled flights from Resolute to Grise Fiord ($219 one way), Nanisivik ($225 one way), and Pond Inlet ($328 one way).

Devon And Beechley Islands

Devon Island, to the north of Baffin Island across **Lancaster Sound,** is a smaller version of its southerly neighbor. The eastern part of this 350-km long island is lowland arctic, while in the west, cliffs drop 1,000 meters into the ocean below. West of Cape Sparbo are the **Truelove Lowlands,** lake-strewn meadows that have been the scene of much Arctic research and are currently the site of a summer camp of the Arctic Institute of North America, based in Calgary.

Off the island's southwest coast is **Beechley Island,** where the Franklin Expedition wintered while searching for the Northwest Passage. Beechley is only an island at high tide; at low tide a sandbar joins it to Devon Island. It was here, on one of the many gravel beaches on the north side of the island, that graves and artifacts were found, giving clues to the fate of one of the Arctic's most famous sagas. Access is by snowmobile, boat, or chartered Twin Otter from Resolute, 100 km away.

The Parry Islands

To the west of Resolute are **Little Cornwallis Island** and the uninhabited islands of **Bathurst** and **Melville,** collectively known as the Parry Islands. Little Cornwallis Island is home to the **Polaris Mine,** northernmost metal mine in the world. It is a modern, year-round operation producing lead and zinc for European markets. The self-contained operation employs 200 and even boasts an indoor pool.

Polar Bear Pass, on Bathurst Island, is an ecological reserve with high concentrations of land mammals and birds. Generally it is visited only by Inuit hunting parties and scientific expeditions. High Arctic International Explorer Services, based in Resolute, offers seven-day camping expeditions to the pass late June to mid-July; $2809 per person.

The **magnetic north pole,** which is continually changing positions in a wobbly, circular motion, currently lies in the general area of **Cameron Island,** to the north of Bathurst Island. It was first located in 1831 when James Ross found his compass dipping downward on King William Island, just off the Arctic coast. The pole moves due to magnetic distortions caused by convection deep below the earth's crust. On the southwest coast of Cameron Island is **Bent Horn A-02,** an oil well operated by Panarctic Oils, a company that has been at the forefront of high Arctic oil exploration since 1968. Oil produced here is so light that it can be used directly in diesel engines on site; the rest is shipped to Montreal.

ELLESMERE ISLAND

Ellesmere Island sits at the top of the North American continent, a wild, rugged landscape of steep-sided fiords and glaciers. At 212,688 square km, it's the 10th-largest island in the world. It extends 800 km from its southern coast and the picturesque community of **Grise Fiord** to above the 83rd Parallel, and east to within 30 km of Greenland. **Axel Heiberg Island,** to the west of Ellesmere and separated by narrow **Eureka Sound,** has peaks over 1,000 meters. On the east coast of Axel Heiberg Island, across from **Eureka** (a high Arctic weather station), are the **Geodetic Hills.** In the hills is a fossilized forest, the remains of thick forests that grew in a lush valley here, 40 million years ago.

High Arctic International Explorer Services, based in Resolute, offers expeditions to **Otto Fiord,** an alternative to visiting **Ellesmere Island National Park.** Here, a 3.5-hour flight north of Resolute, a camp is set up on the shore of the fiord; cost is $3968 per person for seven nights from Resolute.

Grise Fiord (Aujuitittuq)
Overlooking Jones Sound and backed by the spectacular ice-capped peaks of southern Ellesmere Island, this small Inuit community of 130 has reached near-mythical status as North America's northernmost community. Here, at a latitude of 76° N, the sun dips below the horizon for 3.5 months each year and

the sound is only ice-free in August.

Otto Sverdrup coined the name Grise—which means "pig" in Norwegian—when he wintered here in 1899-90. The community was born in 1953, when Inuit from Port Harrison and Pond Inlet were brought here as part of a relocation program. Today the Inuit live a traditional lifestyle, hunting, trapping, and fishing. Although Resolute, 383 km southwest, is the major hub of the high Arctic, Grise Fiord is used as a staging point for trips into the interior of Ellesmere Island and to Greenland, accessible by dogsled and snowmobile for six months of the year.

Grise Fiord Inuit Co-op, General Delivery, Grise Fiord, NT X0A 0J0, tel. (819) 980-9913, can organize outfitters for all seasons, has a recently refitted lodge ($185 per person including three meals), and sells groceries.

Kenn Borek Air, tel. 980-9913, or 252-3489 in Resolute, flies between Grise Fiord and Resolute twice weekly; $219 one way, $438 round trip.

Ellesmere Island National Park
This 37,775-square-km park is literally at the top of the world. It extends from a vast icefield in the central part of Ellesmere Island to the northern coastline where the Grant Land Mountains drop dramatically into the Arctic Ocean. **Mt. Barbeau** (2,629 meters) is the highest peak in North America east of the Rockies. **Lake Hazen,** in the center of the park, is the most popular destination for backpackers. It is 80 km long and the largest lake north of the Arctic Circle. The lake is a thermal oasis, attracting diverse species of birds and mammals during the short summer season. The park receives less than 10 cm of precipitation annually, making it one of the driest areas in the world. But where wind has deposited soil, pockets of lush vegetation manage to survive, and brightly colored arctic flowers soak up the sun's rays. The most common mammals here are foxes and hares, although Peary caribou, musk oxen, and wolves are also present. The park also provides suitable nesting habitat for 30 species of birds. The best place for viewing all wildlife is the Lake Hazen area.

The main access point is park headquarters at Tanquary Fiord, a five-hour flight in a chartered Twin Otter from

TO THE TOP OF THE WORLD

On 6 April 1909, an expedition led by American explorer Robert Peary—including four other men, five sledges, and 38 dogs—became the first to reach the geographic North Pole.

Every year audacious adventurers attempt to reach the pole under their own steam, with dogs, and on snowmobiles. But relative to the South Pole or the summit of Mt. Everest, the North Pole receives few visitors. From the most popular staging area, Ward Hunt Island, it's 772 km to the pole. Most expeditions spend at least two years in preparation, including a few months under Arctic conditions, and budget upward of $1 million. For less adventurous adventurers it's possible to get there on an organized trip in a couple of days, have a champagne lunch, and return to a warm bed at night. From Resolute, **High Arctic International Explorer Services** offers seven-day trips on four dates in April. The tour cost, including dogsledding in Greenland and a stop at the north magnetic pole, is $9887. A cheaper option, without the trimmings, would be to get a group of six people together and charter a Twin Otter from **Bradley Air Service** in Resolute. The flight, with an overnight stop in Eureka, costs $24,000. **Quark Expeditions,** tel. (800) 356-5699, often charters a Russian icebreaker—complete with all the facilities of a top hotel and an onboard helicopter—for the long trip north; $15,000 per person.

Resolute. Both Resolute charter companies fly to the park but it is very expensive. An alternative is through **Canada North Outfitting,** 87 Mill Ave., Almonte, Ontario K0A 10A, tel. (613) 256-4057, which coordinates air charters, bringing together travelers to the park. Depending on numbers, the cost from Resolute would be $1430-3070 per person round trip. You will need to be totally self-sufficient and prepared for all climatic conditions. From Tanquary Fiord the hike to Lake Hazen is 130 km, including one glacier crossing. For more information write to Superintendent, Ellesmere Island National Park, P.O. Box 353, Pangnirtung, NT X0A 0R0; or call (819) 473-8828.

Ward Hunt Island

North of the national park at the mouth of Markham Fiord is four-km long Ward Hunt Island. At 83° 5 minutes N, it's the northernmost point of land in North America. Therefore it is the main staging point for land-based expeditions to the North Pole, 772 km farther north.

Alert

The high Arctic weather station of Alert, 170 km west of Ward Hunt Island, is the continent's northernmost occupied site and has been since 1950. The average high temperature in July is only 6.5° C. Temperatures in winter are not as harsh as you might expect, rarely dropping below –40° C. But the base is in total darkness for four months of the year.

BOB RACE

BOOKLIST

GEOGRAPHY AND TRAVEL

Kane, Alan. *Scrambles in the Canadian Rockies.* Calgary: Rocky Mountain Books, 1992. Routes detailed in this guide lead to summits, without the use of ropes or mountaineering equipment.

Kariel, Herbert G. *Alpine Huts in the Canadian Rockies, Selkirks, and Purcells.* Canmore: Alpine Club of Canada, 1986. Covers the history of all huts in the Rockies, with current access routes and status and descriptions of nearby peaks to climb.

Kunelius, Rick, and Dave Biederman. *Ski Trails in the Canadian Rockies.* Banff: Summerthought, 1981. Detailed guide to cross-country skiing in all national parks of the Canadian Rockies.

MacDonald, Janice E. *Canoeing Alberta.* Edmonton: Lone Pine Publishing, 1985. Comprehensive guide to all navigable rivers in the province.

Patterson, Bruce. *The Wild West.* Canmore: Altitude Publishing, 1993. From the Calgary Exhibition and Stampede to the working ranches of Alberta's foothills, this book covers all aspects of life in the West.

Patton, Brian, and Bart Robinson. *The Canadian Rockies Trail Guide.* Banff: Summerthought, 1992. This regularly updated guide, first published in 1971, covers all hiking trails in the mountain national parks.

Savage, Brian. *Ski Alberta.* Edmonton: Lone Pine Publishing, 1985. Comprehensive guide to cross-country ski trails across the province. Downhill ski areas are also detailed.

FLORA AND FAUNA

Alberta Forestry, Lands, and Wildlife. *Alberta Wildlife Viewing Guide.* Edmonton: Lone Pine Publishing, 1990. Describes where to see particular species of animals, with color photos, small maps of certain areas, and best viewing seasons.

The Atlas of Breeding Birds of Alberta. Edmonton: Federation of Alberta Naturalists, 1992. Comprehensive study of all birds that breed in the province with easy-to-read distribution maps, details on nesting and other behavioral patterns, and color plates.

Buffalo. Edmonton: University of Alberta Press, 1992. A series of essays by noted historians and experts in the field of the American bison, addressing their disappearance from the prairies, buffalo jumps, and current problems in Wood Buffalo National Park.

Gray, David R. *The Muskoxen of Polar Bear Pass.* Markham: Fitzhenry & Whiteside, 1987. A detailed yet entertaining look at the lives of one of North America's least understood mammals.

Herreo, Stephen. *Bear Attacks: Their Causes and Avoidances.* New York: Nick Lyons Books, 1985. Through a series of gruesome stories, this book catalogues man's stormy relationship with bruins, provides hints on avoiding attacks, and tells what to do in case you're attacked.

Lauriault, Jean. *Identification Guide to the Trees of Canada.* Markham: Fitzhenry & Whiteside, 1989. Makes tree identification easy through drawings of leaves, and maps detail distribution of species.

Nelson, Joseph S. *The Fishes of Alberta.* Calgary: University of Calgary Press, 1992. Describes 59 species of fish and provides maps of their distribution. Also looks at fish management and fishing in the province.

Scotter, George W. *Birds of the Canadian Rockies.* Saskatoon: Western Producer Prairie Books, 1990. Description of most recorded species including habitat and habits. Color photos.

Scotter, George W. *Wildflowers of the Canadian Rockies.* Edmonton: Hurtig Publishers Ltd., 1986. Color plates of all flowers found in the mountain national parks. Chapters are divided by flower colors, making identification in the field easy.

Smith, Hugh C. *Alberta Mammals: An Atlas and a Guide.* Edmonton: Provincial Museum Of Alberta, 1993. Writing from a database accumulated by the author over 23 years as curator of mammalogy at the Provincial Museum, this book describes range, identifying characteristics, and habitat of each species, accompanied by full-page maps of their distribution.

Vacher, André. *Summer of the Grizzly.* Saskatoon: Western Producer Prairie Books, 1985. True story of a grizzly bear that went on a terrifying rampage near the town of Banff.

Wetlands of Canada. Ottawa: Polyscience Publications, Environment Canada, 1988. Each chapter deals with a region of Canada and its specific areas of wetland.

HISTORY

Alberta in the 20th Century. Edmonton: United Western Communications Ltd., 1991. Each volume of this series covers a decade in the history of Alberta through a comprehensive essay.

Fryer, Harold. *Ghost Towns of Alberta.* Langley, B.C.: Stagecoach Publishing, 1976. Alberta's ghost towns are unlike those found in the western states of the United States.

Many towns have slipped into oblivion and this guide looks at more of these than you'd ever dreamed existed.

Hamilton, Jacques. *Our Alberta Heritage.* Calgary: Calgary Power Ltd., 1977. Available in one hardbound copy or as five softcover editions, each covering a different aspect of the province's history.

Jones, David. *Empire of Dust.* Edmonton: University of Alberta, 1987. Complete history of Alderston and the surrounding prairie; a sorry story of drought and the destruction it brings.

MacGregor, James. *A History of Alberta.* Edmonton: Hurtig Publishers, 1981. Complete history of Alberta from a wild frontier to world leader.

Marty, Sid. *Men for the Mountains.* New York: Vanguard Press, 1979. Written by a park warden, this book tells the story of those who lived in the Canadian Rockies and the risks and adventures involved.

Newman, Peter C. *Company of Adventurers.* Markham: Penguin Books Canada, 1985. The story of the Hudson's Bay Company and its impact on Canada.

Sandford, R.W. *The Canadian Alps: The History of Mountaineering in Canada.* Canmore: Altitude Publishing, 1990. Complete human history of the Canadian Rockies from the earliest explorers to first ascents of major peaks.

Schäffer, Mary T.S. *A Hunter of Peace.* Banff: Whyte Museum of the Canadian Rockies, 1980. This book was first published in 1911 by G.P. Putnam & Sons, New York, under the name *Old Indian Trails of the Canadian Rockies.* Tales recount the exploration of the Rockies during the turn of the century with many of the author's photographs appearing throughout.

Smith, Cyndi. *Off the Beaten Track.* Jasper: Coyote Books, 1989. Accounts of women adventurers and mountaineers and their impact on the early history of western Canada.

Touche, Rodney. *Brown Cows, Sacred Cows.* Hanna: Gorman, 1990. The story of the development of Lake Louise ski area as told by a former general manager.

Woodman, David C. *Unravelling the Franklin Mystery.* Montreal: McGill-Queen's University Press, 1991. Many volumes have been written on the ill-fated Franklin Expedition. This one, using Inuit recollections, is among the best.

PALAEONTOLOGY

Grady, Wayne. *The Dinosaur Project.* Toronto: Macfarlane, Walter, & Ross, 1993. Tells the story of palaeontological expeditions to China and the Albertan badlands and how the work has enhanced our knowledge of dinosaurs and their movements between Asia and North America. Accounts of actual field trips are given as well as easy to read backgrounds on each area.

Gross, Renie. *Dinosaur Country.* Saskatoon: Western Producer Prairie Books, 1985. Describes Alberta's earliest inhabitants, their habitat, why they disappeared, and the history of dinosaur hunting in the province.

Russell, D.A. *An Odyssey in Time: The Dinosaurs of North America.* Toronto: University of Toronto Press, 1989. Complete details of all known dinosaurs on the North American continent.

Spalding, David A.E. *Dinosaur Hunters.* Toronto: Key Porter Books, 1993. Tells the story of the men and women who have devoted their lives to the study of dinosaurs.

POLITICS AND GOVERNMENT

Bone, Robert. *The Geography of the Canadian North.* Toronto: Oxford University Press, 1992. An in-depth look at the role

Canada's north has played and will play in the management of world resources, and the impact of self-government upon the region.

Wood, David G. *The Lougheed Legacy.* Toronto: Key Porter Books, 1985. Tells the story of Peter Lougheed's 14-year reign as premier of Alberta.

Watkins, Ernest. *The Golden Province.* Calgary: Sandstone Publishing, 1980. A political history of Alberta from 1905, focusing on the Social Credit Party.

PERIODICALS

The Canadian Alpine Journal. Canmore, Alberta. Annual magazine of the Alpine Club of Canada with articles from its members and climbers from around the world.

Canadian Geographic. Ottawa: Royal Canadian Geographical Society. Bimonthly publication pertaining to Canada's natural and human histories and resources.

Equinox. Markham, Ontario. This bimonthly publication looks at Canada's natural world and man's relationship with it.

Explore. Calgary. Bimonthly publication of adventure travel throughout Canada.

Up Here. Yellowknife: Outcrop Ltd. Bimonthly magazine of life in Canada's north.

FREE CATALOGUES

Alberta Accommodation and Visitor's Guide. Alberta Hotel Association. Lists all hotel, motel, and other lodging in the province. Available at all tourist information centers or by calling (800) 661-8888.

Alberta Campground Guide. Alberta Hotel Association. Lists all campgrounds in the province. Available at all tourist information centers or by calling (800) 661-8888.

Tour Book: Western Canada and Alaska.
Booklet available to members of the
Canadian or American automobile
associations.

LITERATURE

Mowat, Farley. *Never Cry Wolf.* Toronto:
McClelland and Stewart, 1990. This story
of living with Arctic wolves on the Keewatin
barrenlands is an international bestseller
and has been made into a feature film.

Turner, Dick. *Nahanni.* Surrey B.C.: Hancock
House, 1975. One of the north's most celebrated authors recounts stories of early life in
the north and particularly on the South
Nahanni River.

REFERENCE

The Atlas of Alberta. Edmonton: Interwest
Publications Ltd., 1984. Historical, resource,
city, and town maps of Alberta.

Daffern, Tony. *Avalanche Safety for Skiers &
Climbers.* Calgary: Rocky Mountain Books,
1992. Covers all aspects of avalanches
including their causes, practical information
on how to avoid them, and a section on
rescue techniques and first aid.

Gray, D.M. and D.H. Male. *Handbook of
Snow.* Toronto: Pergamon Press, 1991.
Comprehensive guide on everything you ever
wanted to know about snow but didn't ask
because no one else would have known
either.

*Guide to Manuscripts: The Fonds and
Collections of the Archives, Whyte Museum
of the Canadian Rockies.* Banff: Whyte
Museum of the Canadian Rockies, 1988.
This book makes finding items in the Whyte
Museum easy through alphabetical lists of
all parts of the collection.

Hare, F.K., and M.K. Thomas. *Climate
Canada.* Toronto: John Wiley & Sons, 1974.
One of the most extensive works on
Canada's climate ever written. Includes a
chapter on how the climate is changing.

Karamitsanis, Aphrodite. *Place Names of
Alberta.* Calgary: University of Alberta Press,
1991. An ongoing toponomy project. Volume
1 alphabetically lists all geographic features
of the mountains and foothills with explana-
tions of each name's origin. Volume 2 does
the same for southern Alberta's geographical
features.

Patterson, W.S. *The Physics of Glaciers.*
Toronto: Pergamon Press, 1969. A highly
technical look at all aspects of glaciation, why
glaciers form, how they flow, and their effect
on the environment.

INDEX

Page numbers in **boldface** indicate primary reference. *Italicized* page numbers indicate information found in captions, charts, illustrations, maps, or special topics.

ABOUT THE AUTHORS

Australians Nadina Purdon and Andrew Hempstead had traveled to four continents each before teaming up to spend a summer exploring the Alaskan wilderness and a winter skiing the legendary slopes of British Columbia's Red Mountain. Their first taste of travel writing was the following summer, updating sections of the fourth edition of Moon's *Alaska-Yukon Handbook.* After another two years on the road—exploring the Fijian Archipelago, skiing across the United States from one coast to the other, pulling flat beer in an English pub, and updating the second edition of *British Columbia Handbook,* they headed east to write this book.

Nadina Purdon

After dragging themselves away from what they regard as one of the most beautiful regions on earth they have headed down under to work on Moon Publications' upcoming *Australia Handbook.* When not on the road Nadina enjoys windsurfing and hanging out at the local beach, while Andrew goes surfing, fishing, and golfing.

Andrew Hempstead

MOON HANDBOOKS—THE IDEAL TRAVELING COMPANIONS

Moon Handbooks provide travelers with all the background and practical information he or she will need on the road. Every Handbook begins with in-depth essays on the land, the people, their history, arts, politics, and social concerns—an entire bookshelf of introductory information squeezed into a one-volume encyclopedia. The Handbooks provide accurate, up-to-date coverage of all the practicalities: language, currency, transportation, accommodations, food and entertainment, and services, to name a few. Moon Handbooks are ideal traveling companions: informative, entertaining, and highly practical.

To locate the bookstore nearest you that carries Moon Travel Handbooks or to order directly from Moon Publications, call: (800) 345-5473, Monday-Friday, 9 a.m.-5 p.m. PST.

THE PACIFIC/ASIA SERIES

BALI HANDBOOK   by Bill Dalton
Detailed travel information on the most famous island in the world. 428 pages.   **$12.95**

BANGKOK HANDBOOK   by Michael Buckley
Your tour guide through this exotic and dynamic city reveals the affordable and accessible possibilities. Thai phrasebook. 222 pages.   **$13.95**

BLUEPRINT FOR PARADISE: How to Live on a Tropic Island   by Ross Norgrove
This one-of-a-kind guide has everything you need to know about moving to and living comfortably on a tropical island. 212 pages.   **$14.95**

FIJI ISLANDS HANDBOOK   by David Stanley
The first and still the best source of information on travel around this 322-island archipelago. Fijian glossary. 198 pages.   **$11.95**

INDONESIA HANDBOOK   by Bill Dalton
This one-volume encyclopedia explores island by island the many facets of this sprawling, kaleidoscopic island nation. Extensive Indonesian vocabulary. 1,200 pages.   **$25.00**

JAPAN HANDBOOK   by J.D. Bisignani
In this comprehensive new edition, award-winning travel writer J.D. Bisignani offers to inveterate travelers, newcomers, and businesspeople alike a thoroughgoing presentation of Japan's many facets. 950 pages.   **$22.50**

MICRONESIA HANDBOOK: Guide to the Caroline, Gilbert, Mariana, and Marshall Islands
by David Stanley
Micronesia Handbook guides you on a real Pacific adventure all your own. 345 pages.   **$11.95**

NEW ZEALAND HANDBOOK   by Jane King
Introduces you to the people, places, history, and culture of this extraordinary land. 571 pages.
$18.95

OUTBACK AUSTRALIA HANDBOOK   by Marael Johnson
Australia is an endlessly fascinating, vast land, and *Outback Australia Handbook* explores the cities and towns, sheep stations, and wilderness areas of the Northern Territory, Western Australia, and South Australia. Full of travel tips and cultural information for adventuring, relaxing, or just getting away from it all. 355 pages.   **$15.95**

PHILIPPINES HANDBOOK   by Peter Harper and Evelyn Peplow
Crammed with detailed information, *Philippines Handbook* equips the escapist, hedonist, or business traveler with thorough coverage of the Philippines's colorful history, landscapes, and culture. 600 pages.   **$17.95**

SOUTHEAST ASIA HANDBOOK   by Carl Parkes
Helps the enlightened traveler discover the real Southeast Asia. 873 pages.   **$21.95**

SOUTH KOREA HANDBOOK   by Robert Nilsen
Whether you're visiting on business or searching for adventure, *South Korea Handbook* is an invaluable companion. Korean glossary with useful notes on speaking and reading the language. 548 pages.   **$14.95**

SOUTH PACIFIC HANDBOOK   by David Stanley
The original comprehensive guide to the 16 territories in the South Pacific. 740 pages.   **$19.95**

TAHITI-POLYNESIA HANDBOOK   by David Stanley
All five French-Polynesian archipelagoes are covered in this comprehensive guide by Oceania's best-known travel writer. 235 pages.   **$11.95**

THAILAND HANDBOOK   by Carl Parkes
Presents the richest source of information on travel in Thailand. 568 pages.   **$16.95**

THE HAWAIIAN SERIES

BIG ISLAND OF HAWAII HANDBOOK   by J.D. Bisignani
An entertaining yet informative text packed with insider tips on accommodations, dining, sports and outdoor activities, natural attractions, and must-see sights. 350 pages.   **$13.95**

HAWAII HANDBOOK   by J.D. Bisignani
Winner of the 1989 Hawaii Visitors Bureau's Best Guide Award and the Grand Award for Excellence in Travel Journalism, this guide takes you beyond the glitz and high-priced hype and leads you to a genuine Hawaiian experience. Covers all 8 Hawaiian Islands. 1,000 pages.   **$19.95**

KAUAI HANDBOOK   by J.D. Bisignani
Kauai is the island Hawaiians visit to get away from it all. 274 pages.   **$13.95**

MAUI HANDBOOK   by J.D. Bisignani
"No fool-'round" advice on accommodations, eateries, and recreation, plus a comprehensive introduction to island ways, geography, and history. Hawaiian and pidgin glossaries. 393 pages. **$14.95**

HONOLULU~WAIKIKI HANDBOOK: The Island of Oahu   by J.D. Bisignani
A handy guide to Honolulu, renowned surfing beaches, and Oahu's countless other diversions. Hawaiian and pidgin glossaries. 354 pages.   **$14.95**

THE AMERICAS SERIES

ALASKA-YUKON HANDBOOK by Deke Castleman and Don Pitcher
Get the inside story, with plenty of well-seasoned advice to help you cover more miles on less money. 460 pages. **$14.95**

ALBERTA AND THE NORTHWEST TERRITORIES HANDBOOK : Including Banff, Jasper, and the Canadian Rockies by Andrew Hempstead and Nadina Purdon
Explore the rich history, rustic towns, and rugged wilderness of the pristine Canadian countryside. 466 pages. **$17.95**

ARIZONA TRAVELER'S HANDBOOK by Bill Weir
This meticulously researched guide contains everything necessary to make Arizona accessible and enjoyable. 445 pages. **$16.95**

ATLANTIC CANADA HANDBOOK: New Brunswick, Nova Scotia, Labrador, Prince Edward Island, and Newfoundland by Mark Morris and Nan Drosdick
Canada's eastern seaboard provinces boast a varied European heritage manifested in local cuisine, crafts, and architecture. 450 pages. **$17.95**

BAJA HANDBOOK: Mexico's Western Peninsula including Cabo San Lucas by Joe Cummings
A comprehensive guide with all the travel information and background on the land, history, and culture of this untamed thousand-mile-long peninsula. 362 pages. **$15.95**

BELIZE HANDBOOK by Chicki Mallan
Complete with detailed maps, practical information, and an overview of the area's flamboyant history, culture, and geographical features, *Belize Handbook* is the only comprehensive guide of its kind to this spectacular region. 263 pages. **$14.95**

BRITISH COLUMBIA HANDBOOK by Jane King
With an emphasis on outdoor adventures, this guide covers mainland British Columbia, Vancouver Island, the Queen Charlotte Islands, and the Canadian Rockies. 381 pages.
$15.95

CANCUN HANDBOOK by Chicki Mallan
Covers the city's luxury scene as well as more modest attractions, plus many side trips to unspoiled beaches and Mayan ruins. Spanish glossary. 257 pages. **$13.95**

CENTRAL MEXICO HANDBOOK: Mexico City, Guadalajara, and Other Colonial Cities by Chicki Mallan
Retrace the footsteps of Cortés from the coast of Veracruz to the heart of Mexico City to discover archaeological and cultural wonders. 391 pages. **$15.95**

CATALINA ISLAND HANDBOOK: A Guide to California's Channel Islands
by Chicki Mallan
A complete guide to these remarkable islands, from the windy solitude of the Channel Islands National Marine Sanctuary to bustling Avalon. 245 pages. **$10.95**

COLORADO HANDBOOK by Stephen Metzger
Essential details to the all-season possibilities in Colorado fill this guide. Practical travel tips combine with recreation—skiing, nightlife, and wilderness exploration—plus entertaining essays. 416 pages. **$17.95**

COSTA RICA HANDBOOK by Christopher P. Baker
Experience the many wonders of the natural world as you explore this remarkable land. Spanish-English glossary. 574 pages. **$17.95**

GEORGIA HANDBOOK by Kap Stann
Discover the Old South of mint juleps and magnolia blossoms, and enjoy Georgia's legendary hospitality. Includes detailed information on the upcoming 1996 Summer Olympic Games. 350 pages. **$16.95**

IDAHO HANDBOOK by Bill Loftus
A year-round guide to everything in this outdoor wonderland, from whitewater adventures to rural hideaways. 282 pages. **$14.95**

JAMAICA HANDBOOK by Karl Luntta
From the sun and surf of Montego Bay and Ocho Rios to the cool slopes of the Blue Mountains, author Karl Luntta offers island-seekers a perceptive, personal view of Jamaica. 230 pages. **$14.95**

MONTANA HANDBOOK by W.C. McRae and Judy Jewell
The wild West is yours with this extensive guide to the Treasure State, complete with travel practicalities, history, and lively essays on Montana life. 427 pages. **$15.95**

NEVADA HANDBOOK by Deke Castleman
Nevada Handbook puts the Silver State into perspective and makes it manageable and affordable. 450 pages. **$16.95**

NEW MEXICO HANDBOOK by Stephen Metzger
A close-up and complete look at every aspect of this wondrous state. 375 pages. **$14.95**

NORTHERN CALIFORNIA HANDBOOK by Kim Weir
An outstanding companion for imaginative travel in the territory north of the Tehachapis. 765 pages. **$19.95**

NORTHERN MEXICO HANDBOOK: The Sea of Cortez to the Gulf of Mexico
by Joe Cummings
Directs travelers from the barrier islands of Sonora to the majestic cloud forests of the Sierra Madre Oriental to traditional villages and hidden waterfalls in San Luis Potosí. 500 pages. **$16.95**

OREGON HANDBOOK by Stuart Warren and Ted Long Ishikawa
Brimming with travel practicalities and insiders' views on Oregon's history, culture, arts, and activities. 461 pages. **$16.95**

PACIFIC MEXICO HANDBOOK by Bruce Whipperman
Explore 2,000 miles of gorgeous beaches, quiet resort towns, and famous archaeological sites along Mexico's Pacific coast. Spanish-English glossary. 428 pages. **$15.95**

TEXAS HANDBOOK   by Joe Cummings
Seasoned travel writer Joe Cummings brings an insider's perspective to his home state.
483 pages.   **$13.95**

UTAH HANDBOOK   by Bill Weir
Weir gives you all the carefully researched facts and background to make your visit a success.
445 pages.   **$16.95**

WASHINGTON HANDBOOK   by Archie Satterfield and Dianne J. Boulerice Lyons
Covers sights, shopping, services, transportation, and outdoor recreation, with complete
listings for restaurants and accommodations. 419 pages.   **$15.95**

WYOMING HANDBOOK   by Don Pitcher
All you need to know to open the doors to this wide and wild state. 495 pages.   **$14.95**

YUCATAN HANDBOOK   by Chicki Mallan
All the information you'll need to guide you into every corner of this exotic land. Mayan and
Spanish glossaries. 391 pages.   **$15.95**

THE INTERNATIONAL SERIES

EGYPT HANDBOOK   by Kathy Hansen
An invaluable resource for intelligent travel in Egypt. Arabic glossary. 522 pages.   **$18.95**

MOSCOW-ST. PETERSBURG HANDBOOK   by Masha Nordbye
Provides the visitor with an extensive introduction to the history, culture, and people of these
two great cities, as well as practical information on where to stay, eat, and shop. 260 pages.
$13.95

NEPAL HANDBOOK   by Kerry Moran
Whether you're planning a week in Kathmandu or months out on the trail, *Nepal Handbook* will
take you into the heart of this Himalayan jewel. 378 pages.   **$12.95**

NEPALI AAMA   by Broughton Coburn
A delightful photo-journey into the life of a Gurung tribeswoman of Central Nepal. Having lived
with Aama (translated, "mother") for two years, first as an outsider and later as an adopted
member of the family, Coburn presents an intimate glimpse into a culture alive with humor,
folklore, religion, and ancient rituals. 165 pages.   **$13.95**

STAYING HEALTHY IN ASIA, AFRICA, AND LATIN AMERICA
by Dirk G. Schroeder, Sc D, MPH
Don't leave home without it! Besides providing a complete overview of the health problems that
exist in these areas, this book will help you determine which immunizations you'll need
beforehand, what medications to take with you, and how to recognize and treat infections and
diseases. Includes extensively illustrated first-aid information and precautions for heat, cold,
and high altitude. 200 pages.   **$10.95**

TIBET HANDBOOK: A PILGRIMAGE GUIDE   by Victor Chan
This remarkable book is both a comprehensive trekking guide to mountain paths and plateau
trails, and a pilgrimage guide that draws on Tibetan literature and religious history. 1104 pages.
$30.00

IMPORTANT ORDERING INFORMATION

FOR FASTER SERVICE: Call to locate the bookstore nearest you that carries Moon Travel Handbooks or order directly from Moon Publications:

(800) 345-5473 • Monday-Friday • 9 a.m.-5 p.m. PST • fax (916) 345-6751

PRICES: All prices are subject to change. We always ship the most current edition. We will let you know if there is a price increase on the book you ordered.

SHIPPING & HANDLING OPTIONS: 1) Domestic UPS or USPS first class (allow 10 working days for delivery): $3.50 for the first item, 50 cents for each additional item.

Exceptions:
- **Moonbelt** shipping is $1.50 for one, 50 cents for each additional belt.
- Add $2.00 for same-day handling.
- UPS 2nd Day Air or Printed Airmail requires a special quote.
- International Surface Bookrate (8-12 weeks delivery):
  $3.00 for the first item, $1.00 for each additional item. Note: Moon Publications cannot guarantee international surface bookrate shipping.

FOREIGN ORDERS: All orders that originate outside the U.S.A. must be paid for with either an International Money Order or a check in U.S. currency drawn on a major U.S. bank based in the U.S.A.

TELEPHONE ORDERS: We accept Visa or MasterCard payments. Minimum order is US$15.00. Call in your order: (800) 345-5473, 9 a.m.-5 p.m. Pacific Standard Time.

MOONBELTS

Made of heavy-duty Cordura nylon, the Moonbelt offers maximum protection for your money and important papers. This all-weather pouch slips under your shirt or waistband, rendering it virtually undetectable and inaccessible to pickpockets. One-inch-wide nylon webbing, heavy-duty zipper, one-inch quick-release buckle. Accommodates traveler's checks, passport, cash, photos. Size 5 x 9 inches. Black.   **$8.95**

New travel handbooks may be available that are not on this list. To find out more about current or upcoming titles, call us toll-free at (800) 345-5473.

ORDER FORM

Be sure to call (800) 345-5473 for current prices and editions or for the name of the bookstore nearest you that carries Moon Travel Handbooks • 9 a.m.–5 p.m. PST
(See important ordering information on preceding page)

Name: _____Date: _____

Street: _____

City: _____Daytime Phone: _____

State or Country: _____Zip Code: _____

QUANTITY	TITLE	PRICE

Taxable Total_____

Sales Tax (7.25%) for California Residents_____

Shipping & Handling_____

TOTAL_____

Ship: ☐ UPS (no PO Boxes)   ☐ 1st class   ☐ International surface mail

Ship to: ☐ address above   ☐ other _____

_____

_____

Make checks payable to: **MOON PUBLICATIONS, INC**. P.O. Box 3040, Chico, CA 95927-3040 U.S.A. We accept Visa and MasterCard. **To Order**: Call in your Visa or MasterCard number, or send a written order with your Visa or MasterCard number and expiration date clearly written.

Card Number: ☐ **Visa**   ☐ **MasterCard**

☐ ☐ ☐ ☐   ☐ ☐ ☐ ☐   ☐ ☐ ☐ ☐   ☐ ☐ ☐ ☐

Exact Name on Card: _____

expiration date: _____

signature_____

WHERE TO BUY THIS BOOK

BOOKSTORES AND LIBRARIES:
Moon Publications Handbooks are sold worldwide. Please contact our sales manager for a list of wholesalers and distributors in your area that stock our travel handbooks.

TRAVELERS:
We would like to have Moon Publications Handbooks available throughout the world. Please ask your bookstore to contact us for ordering information. If your bookstore will not order our guides, please contact us for a free newsletter and catalog.

MOON PUBLICATIONS, INC.
P.O. BOX 3040
CHICO, CA 95927-3040 U.S.A.
TEL: (800) 345-5473
FAX: (916) 345-6751
e-mail: **travel@moon.com**

TRAVEL MATTERS

Travel Matters is Moon Publications' quarterly newsletter. It provides today's traveler with timely, informative travel news and articles.

You'll find resourceful coverage on:

- **Money**—What does it cost? Is it worth it?
- **Low impact travel**—tread lightly travel tips
- **Special interest travel**—cultural tours, environmental excursions, outdoor recreation, adventure treks, and more
- **Travel styles**—families, seniors, disabled travelers, package and theme tours
- **Consumer reviews**—books, language aids, travel gadgets, products, and services
- **Facts and opinions**—reader's letters and Moon Handbook author news
- **Moon Handbook booklist**—the latest titles and editions, and where and how to purchase them

To receive a free copy of *Travel Matters*, write Moon Publications Inc., P.O. Box 3040, Chico, CA 95927-3040, or call toll-free (800) 345-5473, Monday–Friday, 9 a.m. – 5 p.m. Pacific Standard Time.

THE METRIC SYSTEM

1 inch = 2.54 centimeters (cm)
1 foot = .304 meters (m)
1 mile = 1.6093 kilometers (km)
1 km = .6124 miles
1 fathom = 1.8288 m
1 chain = 20.1168 m
1 furlong = 201.168 m
1 acre = .4047 hectares
1 sq km = 100 hectares
1 sq mile = 2.59 square km
1 ounce = 28.35 grams
1 pound = .4536 kilograms
1 short ton = .90718 metric ton
1 short ton = 2000 pounds
1 long ton = 1.016 metric tons
1 long ton = 2240 pounds
1 metric ton = 1000 kilograms
1 quart = .94635 liters
1 US gallon = 3.7854 liters
1 Imperial gallon = 4.5459 liters
1 nautical mile = 1.852 km

To compute celsius temperatures, subtract 32 from Fahrenheit and divide by 1.8. To go the other way, multiply celsius by 1.8 and add 32.

Fahrenheit   Celsius

230° — 110°
220°
210° — 100° Water Boils
200°
190° — 90°
180°
170° — 80°
160°
150° — 70°
140° — 60°
130°
120° — 50°
110°
100° — 40°
90°
80° — 30°
70°
60° — 20°
50°
40° — 10°
30°
20° — 0° Water Freezes
10°
0° — -10°
-10° — -20°
-20° — -30°
-30°
-40° — -40°

inch 0   1   2   3   4

cm 0 1 2 3 4 5 6 7 8 9 10